MARIANA MESA:

SEVEN PREHISTORIC SETTLEMENTS

IN WEST-CENTRAL NEW MEXICO

PAPERS OF THE PEABODY MUSEUM OF ARCHAEOLOGY AND ETHNOLOGY
HARVARD UNIVERSITY
VOLUME 72

Frontispiece. Camp area and Mariana Mesa, looking southeast.

MARIANA MESA:
SEVEN PREHISTORIC SETTLEMENTS IN WEST-CENTRAL NEW MEXICO

Charles R. McGimsey III

A Report of the Upper Gila Expedition

PEABODY MUSEUM OF ARCHAEOLOGY AND ETHNOLOGY
HARVARD UNIVERSITY, CAMBRIDGE, MASSACHUSETTS

1980

To
J.O. Brew, Watson Smith, and Mary McGimsey, who, in their own ways, have helped make possible this report

*A current list of all publications available
can be obtained by writing to the
Publications Department, Peabody Museum, Harvard University
11 Divinity Avenue, Cambridge, Massachusetts 02138*

© 1980 BY THE PRESIDENT AND FELLOWS OF HARVARD COLLEGE
ISBN 0-87365-198-7
LIBRARY OF CONGRESS CATALOG CARD NUMBER 79-57109
PRINTED IN THE UNITED STATES OF AMERICA

Contents

Foreword J. O. Brew xvii

Acknowledgments xix

Environmental Setting 1

Field and Analytic Procedures 4

Mariana Mesa, A.D. 850–1300 11

A Methodological Approach to the Past: The Descriptive Type 17

PREFATORY NOTE 17

ARCHAEOLOGICAL DATA 19
   Selection 20
   Description 24
   Classification 26
   The Unit 26, The Type 27, The Pattern 31
   Time-Space and Other Typological Sets 32
   The Descriptive Type 33

Site 616 37

DESCRIPTION 37

HISTORY OF THE SITE 37

TRADE RELATIONS AND FINAL ABANDONMENT 38

DATING CONSIDERATIONS 42

ARCHITECTURE 43

   The Rooms 43
   Construction 45
   Walls 45, Floors 46, Doorways 46, Firepits, Ventilators, and Deflectors 47, Passthroughs 48, Enclosures 48, Cists and Niches 48, Mealing Bins 48, Roofs 49

POTTERY-MAKING AT SITE 616 49
   Construction 49
   Plain and Slipped Pottery 50, Corrugated Pottery 50
   Decoration 51
   White-slipped Pottery 51, Red-slipped Pottery 51, Corrugated Pottery 52
   Discussion 52
   Artisan Types 54

STONE ARTIFACTS 55
   Tools Fashioned by Pecking 56
   Tools Fashioned by Pecking and Grinding 56
   Tools Fashioned by Chipping 57
   Tools Fashioned by Chipping and Grinding 57

BONE ARTIFACTS 57

MINOR CRAFTS 58

OTHER CONTEXTS AND ACTIVITIES 58
   The Household 58
   Technological Specialization 59

LIVING AND EXCAVATION UNITS 60
   Area A 60
   Room A1 60
   Firepit 60, Mealing Bin 60, Comment 62, Artifacts 62

Room A2 62
Artifacts 62

Room A3 62
Firepit 63, Mealing Bin 63, Artifacts 63

Area B 63

Room B1 63
Mealing Bins 64, Ventilator 65, Doorway 65, Comment 65, Artifacts 65

Room B2 66
Firepit 67, Doorway 67, Comment 67, Artifacts 67

Room B3 67
Doorways 67, Comment 68, Artifacts 69

Room B5 69
Firepit 69, Doorway 69, Comment 69, Artifacts 69

Room B7 69
Firepit 70, Doorways 70, Comment 70, Artifacts 70

Area C 70

Room C1 71
Cist 71, Doorway 71, Comment 71, Artifacts 71

Room C2 71
Mealing Bins 71, Doorway 73, Human Skeleton 73, Comment 74, Artifacts 74

Room C3 74
Doorway 74, Comment 74, Artifacts 74

Room C4 76
Doorway 76, Comment 76, Artifacts 76

Room C5 78
Firepit 78, Mealing Bin 78, Enclosures 78, Deflector 78, Doorways 79, Comment 79, Artifacts 79

Room C6 80
Cist 80, Passthroughs 80, Doorways 80, Comment 80, Artifacts 80

Room C7 80
Artifacts 81

Room C8 81
Artifacts 81

Room C9 81
Mealing Bins 81, Doorways 82, Passthroughs 82, Artifacts 82

Room C10 82
Firepit 83, Ventilator 83, Passthrough 83, Deflector 83, Doorway 83, Comment 83, Artifacts 83

Area D 85

Room D1 85
Firepit 86, Comment 86, Artifacts 86

Room D2 86
Mealing Bins 86, Comment 87, Artifacts 87

Room D3 88
Firepit 88, Comment 88, Artifacts 88

Room D5 88
Mealing Bin 88, Firepit 88, Ventilator 88, Ladder Socket 90, Cists 90, Comment 90, Artifacts 91

Area E 91

Room E1 91
Firepit 91, Ventilator 91, Deflector 91, Ladder Sockets 93, Comment 93, Artifacts 93

Room E2 93
Mealing Bin 93, Firepit 93, Ventilator 93, Ladder Sockets (?) 94, Deflector (?) 94, Cists 94, Comment 95, Artifacts 95

Area F 95

Room F1 95
Doorways 97, Comment 97, Artifacts 97

Room F2 97
Firepit 97, Ventilator 97, Deflector 97, Mealing Bin 97, Doorways 98, Comment 98, Artifacts 98

Kiva 98
Firepit 100, Deflector 100, Ventilator 100, Ladder Sockets 101, Foot Drum 101, Wall Niche 101, Postholes 101, Roof 101, Artifacts 101

Walk-in Well 101

Rooms Associated with the Well 102

Burials 102
Skeleton 1 102, Skeleton 3 104, Skeleton 5 104, Comment 104, Artifacts in Walk-in Well 104, Artifacts in Mealing Room 104, Artifacts in Small Room 104

SUBSISTENCE MATERIALS 104

POTTERY — DESCRIPTIVE TYPOLOGY 105

White-slipped Pottery 106
Material 106, Vessel Shapes and Areas Slipped and Painted 107, Comment 107, Surface Finish 108, Decoration 110

Red-slipped Pottery 116
Material 116, Vessel Shapes, Areas Painted, and Colors Combined 118, Surface Finish 118, Decoration 118

Plain and Corrugated Pottery 120
Material 120, Vessel Shapes 120, Construction and Surface Finish 121, Decorative Effects 121

POTTERY — PROBLEM TYPES 121

Regional Time-Space Types 121
White-slipped Pottery 124, Red-slipped Pottery 126, Other Types 127, Usefulness of Diagnostic Features 127, Whole and Restorable Vessels 128

Artisan Types 128

OTHER OBJECTS OF CLAY 130

Sherd Scrapers 130

Pipes 130

Toy Vessels 130

Figurines 130

STONE ARTIFACTS 131

Manos 131
Material 131, Shape 131, Finger Grips 132, Associated Metate Type 133, Size 133, Methods of Using Manos 133

Metates 136
Fine-grained Metates of Sandstone 137, Fine-grained Metate of Calcareous Tuff 137, Medium-fine-grained Metates of Calcareous Tuff 137, Medium-grained Metates of Calcareous Tuff 137, Medium-grained Metate of Vesicular Basalt 137, Medium-coarse-grained Metates of Vesicular Basalt 137, Coarse-grained Metates of Vesicular Basalt 137, Comment 137

Roughly-shaped Mortars 139

Pestle 140

Bowls 140

Shaftsmoothers 140

Polishing Pebbles 141

Pecking Stones 142

Axes 143
Three-quarter-grooved 143, Notched 145

Pick 145

Hammers 145
Round-ended 145, Elongated Flat-ended 147, Equilateral Flat-ended 147, Irregular Flat-ended 148, Hammer with Off-center Haft 148

File (?) 148

Hoe (?) 148

Points and Blades 148

Snub-nosed Scraper 148

Unretouched Flakes 149

Chips 150

Cores 150

Choppers (?) 150

Pot Cover (?) 151

Pot Supports 151

Worked Sandstone Slabs 151

Scoria Cylinders and Cones 151

Scoria Object 152

Jet Buttons 153

Figurines 153

Disc Beads 153

Pendants 154

Mosaic Fragments (?) 155

Stone Balls 156

Hematite Cylinders 157

Shaped Objects 157

Quartz Crystals 157

Naturally Shaped Stone Objects 157
Concretions 157, Weathered Stones 158, Other 158

BONE ARTIFACTS 159

Awls 159
Head of Bone Unworked except by Original Splitting 159, Head of Bone Intact 159, Head Wholly Removed 159, Splinter Awls 159, Skewer Awls 160, Eyed Awl 160, Fragments 160, General Comment on Awls 160

Scrapers 160
End Scrapers 160, Side Scrapers 160

Rings 161

Tubes 161

Pierced Phalanges 162

Weaving or Matting Tools (?) 162

Hairpin (?) 163

viii

Pendants 163
Carved Pendants 163, Dewclaw Pendants 163, Bison Mandible Pendant 163, Figurine Pendants 163

Fragments of Worked Bone 163

ANTLER ARTIFACTS 163
Flaker (?) 163
Rubbing Tools 163

SHELL ARTIFACTS 163
Bracelets 163
Pendants 164
Cut Shell 164, Whole Shell 164, Tinkler Pendants (?) 165

Disc Beads 165
Figurines 165
Frogs 165, Bats (?) 165

Conical and Cylindrical Objects 165
Worked Fragments 166
Unworked Fragments 166

OTHER ORGANIC ARTIFACTS 166
Basketry 166
Mat Impression 166
Cotton Cloth 166
Fur Cloth (?) 167
Netting 167
Wooden Ceremonial (?) Stick 167
Painted Wood Fragment 167

RAW MATERIALS 167
Hematite 167
Limonite 168
Malachite and Azurite 168
Clay 168
Vessel Clay 168, Slip Clay (?) 168

Turquoise 168
Iron Pyrite 168
Calcitic Limestone 168
Diatomaceous Earth 168
Pine Resin (?) 168

HUMAN SKELETAL REMAINS FROM SITE 616 169
Skeleton 1 169
Skeleton 2 169
Skeleton 3 169
Skeleton 4 169
Skeleton 5 169
Skeleton 6 170
Incomplete Skeletal Remains 170

Site 143 171

DATING CONSIDERATIONS 173
ARCHITECTURE 173
Ceremonial Feature 173
Central Area 173, Ramp 174, Stairway 174

Room 1 175
Room 2 175
Cists below Rooms 1 and 2 176

SUBSISTENCE MATERIALS 176
POTTERY 176
White-slipped Pottery 176
Red-slipped Pottery 176
Plain and Corrugated Pottery 176

OTHER OBJECTS OF CLAY 177
Figurines 177
Sherd Discs 177

STONE ARTIFACTS 178
Manos 178
Shaftsmoothers 178
Chipped Shaftscraper 178
Polishing Stones 178
Pecking Stones 178
Points and Knives 178
Gravers 178
Side Scrapers 178
Unretouched Flakes 179
Chips 179

Core 179
Choppers 179
Flat Stone 179

BONE ARTIFACTS 179
Awls 179
Splinter Awls 179
End Scrapers 179
Rings and Tubes 179
Worked Fragments 179

ANTLER ARTIFACT 179

SHELL ARTIFACTS 179

RAW MATERIALS 180

HUMAN SKELETAL REMAINS 180

Site 481 181

HISTORY 181

DATING CONSIDERATIONS 186

ARCHITECTURE 188
Masonry Types 188

LIVING AND EXCAVATION UNITS 188
Room 1 190
Artifacts 190
Room 2 190
Artifacts 190
Room 3 191
Artifacts 191
Room 4 191
Artifacts 191
Room 5 191
Artifacts 191
Room 6 191
Artifacts 192
Room 7 192
Artifacts 192
Room 8 192
Artifacts 193

Room 9 193
Artifacts 193
Room 10 193
Artifacts 193
Room 11 193
Room 12 193
Artifacts 193
Room 13 193
Artifacts 193
Rooms 14 and 15 193
Room 16 193
Artifacts 194
Room 17 194
Artifacts 194
Room 18 194
Artifacts 194
Room 19 194
Artifacts 194
Room 20 195
Artifact 195
Room 21 195
Room 22 195
Artifacts 195
Room 23 195
Artifacts 195
Room 24 195
Artifacts 195
Room 25 195
Artifacts 196
Room 26 196
Artifact 196
Room 27 196
Artifacts 196
Room 28 196
Artifacts 196
Room 29 196
Artifacts 196
Room 30 196
Artifacts 196
Room 31 197
Artifacts 197

Room 32 197
Artifacts 197

Room 33 197
Artifacts 197

Room 34 197
Artifacts 197

Kiva 197
Firepit 198, Deflector 198, Ventilator 198, Ladder 199, Roof 199, Niches 199, Artifacts 200

Pithouse 1 200
Artifacts 201

Pithouse 2 201
Artifacts 202

SUBSISTENCE MATERIALS 202

POTTERY — DESCRIPTIVE TYPOLOGY 202

White-slipped Pottery 202
Material 202, Vessel Shapes and Areas Slipped and Painted 202, Surface Finish 203, Decoration 203

Red-slipped Pottery 204
Material 204, Vessel Shapes and Areas Slipped and Painted 204, Surface Finish 205, Decoration 205

Plain and Corrugated Pottery 205
Material 205, Vessel Shapes 205, Construction and Surface Finish 205, Decorative Effect 205

POTTERY — PROBLEM TYPES 205

Regional Time-Space Types 205
White-slipped Pottery 205, Red-slipped Pottery 211

Artisan Types 211
White-slipped Pottery 211

Intrasite Distribution Types 213
White-slipped Pottery 213

Whole and Restorable Vessels 216

OTHER OBJECTS OF CLAY 216

Sherd Discs 216

Sherd Pendants 217

Pipe 217

Toy Vessels 217

Figurines 217

STONE ARTIFACTS 217

Manos 217
Material 217, Shape 218, Finger Grips 219, Associated Metate Type 219, Size 220

Metates 220
Trough Metates 220, Slab Metates 220, Basin Metate 220

Mortars 220

Pestle 221

Bowl 221

Polishing Pebbles 221

Rubbing Stones 221

Pecking Stones 221

Axes 221

Whetstone 221

Hammers 222

Points 222

Side Scrapers 222

End Scraper 222

Unretouched Flakes 222

Chips 222

Cores 223

Scoria Cylinders 223

Disc Bead 223

Pendants 223

Ornament (?) 223

Disc 223

Grooved Objects 223

Quartz Crystal 223

Concretion 223

BONE ARTIFACTS 223

Awls 223
Head of Bone Intact 223, Head of Bone Unworked except by Original Splitting 224, Head Wholly Removed 224, Splinter Awls 224, Skewer Awls 224, Awls of Unidentified Form 224

Weaving or Matting Tools (?) 224

Ring 224

Tubes 224

Pierced Phalanges 225

Figurine 225

xi

Disc Bead 225
Serrated Tool 225

ANTLER FLAKER 225

SHELL ARTIFACTS 225
Bracelets 225
Pendants of Whole Shells 225
Unworked Fragments 225

RAW MATERIALS 225
Hematite 225
Limonite 225
Malachite 225
Kaolin 225
Turquoise 225
Other 226

HUMAN SKELETAL REMAINS 226

Site 494 227

DESCRIPTION AND HISTORY 227

DATING CONSIDERATIONS 229

LIVING AND EXCAVATION UNITS 230
Room A1 230
Artifacts 230
Room A2 230
Artifacts 230
Room A3 230
Artifacts 230
Room A4 230
Artifacts 230
Kiva A 231
Artifacts 232
Room B1 232
Artifacts 232
Room B2 233
Artifacts 233
Room B3 233
Room B4 233
Artifacts 233

Room B5 233
Artifacts 234
Room B6 234
Artifacts 234
Room B7 234
Artifacts 234
Room B8 234
Artifacts 235
Kiva B 235
Artifacts 235

SUBSISTENCE MATERIALS 236

POTTERY — DESCRIPTIVE TYPOLOGY 236
White-slipped Pottery 236
Material 236, Vessel Shapes and Areas Slipped and Painted 236, Surface Finish 236, Decoration 236

Red-slipped Pottery 237
Material 237, Vessel Shapes, Areas Painted, and Colors Combined 237, Surface Finish 237, Decoration 237

Plain and Corrugated Pottery 237
Material 237, Vessel Shapes 238, Construction and Surface Finish 238, Decorative Effect 238

POTTERY — PROBLEM TYPES 239
Regional Time-Space Types 239
White-slipped Pottery 239, Red-slipped Pottery 239

Whole and Partially Restorable Vessels 239

Intrasite Distribution Types 241
White-slipped Pottery 241

Comment 241

OTHER OBJECTS OF CLAY 243
Figurine 243
Worked Sherds 243

STONE ARTIFACTS 243
Manos 243
Material 243, Shape 244, Finger Grips 244, Associated Metate Type 244, Size 244

Metates 245
Mortar 245
Polishing Pebbles 245
Rubbing Stones 245

Pecking Stones 245
Axes 245
Hammers 245
Whetstones 245
Points 245
Unretouched Flakes 246
Chips 246
Core 246
Scoria Cylinders 246
Hematite Cylinder 246
Shaped Stone Object 246

BONE ARTIFACTS 246
Awls 246
Tubes 246
Pierced Phalange 246

ANTLER FLAKER 246

SHELL ARTIFACTS 246

RAW MATERIALS 246

HUMAN SKELETAL REMAINS 246
Skeleton 1 246
Skeleton 2 247
Incomplete Skeletal Remains 247

Site 601 249

DATING CONSIDERATIONS 250

LIVING AND EXCAVATION UNITS 250
Room 1 250
Artifacts 250
Room 2 250
Artifacts 250
Room 3 250
Artifacts 250
Room 4 250
Artifacts 251
Other Rooms 251
Artifacts 251
Circular Depression 251

POTTERY — DESCRIPTIVE TYPOLOGY 251
White-slipped Pottery 251
Material 251, Vessel Shapes and Areas Slipped and Painted 251, Surface Finish 251, Decoration 252
Plain and Corrugated Pottery 252
Material 252, Vessel Shape 252, Construction and Surface Finish 252, Decorative Effect 254

POTTERY — PROBLEM TYPES 255
Regional Time-Space Types 255
White-slipped Pottery 255, Red-slipped Pottery 255, Plain and Corrugated Pottery 255

OTHER OBJECTS OF CLAY 255
Figurine 255
Sherd Discs 255

STONE ARTIFACTS 255
Manos 255
Metates 256
Polishing Pebble 256
Pecking Stone 256
Hammer 256
Points and Knives 256
Flake and Chips 256
Scoria Object 256
Bead 256

RAW MATERIALS 256

SUBSISTENCE MATERIALS 256

Site 188 259

THE HOUSE 259

DATING CONSIDERATIONS 259

LIVING AND EXCAVATION UNITS 259
Room 1 259
Room 2 260

SUBSISTENCE MATERIALS 260

POTTERY — DESCRIPTIVE TYPOLOGY 260
White-slipped Pottery 260

Material 261, Vessel Shapes and Areas Slipped and Painted 261, Surface Finish 261, Decoration 262

Plain and Corrugated Pottery 262

Material 262, Vessel Shape 262, Construction and Surface Finish 262, Decorative Effect 263

POTTERY — PROBLEM TYPES 264

Regional Time-Space Types 264

White-slipped Pottery 264, Plain and Corrugated Pottery 264

STONE ARTIFACTS 264

Manos 264

Metates 265

Pecking Stones 265

Point 265

Scrapers and Unretouched Flakes 265

Chips 265

Pendant 265

Flat Sandstone Slabs 265

BONE ARTIFACTS 265

Awls 265

SHELL ARTIFACTS 265

ORGANIC ARTIFACTS AND RAW MATERIALS 265

Matting (?) 265

Hematite 265

Site 486 267

DATING CONSIDERATIONS 268

LIVING AND EXCAVATION UNITS 268

Unit 1 268
Artifacts 268

Unit 2 268
Artifact 268

Unit 3 268
Artifacts 268

Unit 4 268

Unit 5 269

SUBSISTENCE MATERIALS 269

POTTERY — DESCRIPTIVE TYPOLOGY 269

White-slipped Pottery 269

Material 269, Vessel Shapes and Areas Slipped and Painted 270, Surface Finish 271, Decoration 271

Red-slipped Pottery 272

Plain and Corrugated Pottery 272

Material 272, Vessel Shape 272, Construction and Surface Finish 273, Decorative Effect 274, Comment 274

POTTERY — PROBLEM TYPES 274

Regional Time-Space Types 274

White-slipped Pottery 274, Plain and Corrugated Pottery 275

STONE ARTIFACTS 275

Manos 275

Convex Surface 275, One-hand Manos 275

Grinding Slab 276

Rubbing Stones 276

Polishing Pebbles 276

Pecking Stones 276

Points and Knives 277

Secondary Chipping on All Major Faces 277, Secondary Chipping on Major Edges Only 277

Flakes 277

Cores and Unidentified Fragments 277

Chopper 277

Chipped Slab 277

Minerals 277

ANTLER FLAKER (?) 277

Sandstone Hill Pueblo 286

Appendix A 287

POTTERY DESCRIPTION FOR ALL SITES 287

Paste 287

Construction 288

Decoration 289

Vessel Shapes and Sizes 289

Other Aspects 290

Whole Vessels versus Sherds 290

Pottery Modes and Attributes for All Sites 290

Paste: All Pottery 290, Slip: White- and Red-slipped Pottery 291, Paint: White- and Red-slipped Pottery 292, Vessel Shapes: All Pottery 292, Areas Slipped and Painted: White Pottery 292, Areas Slipped and Painted: Red Pottery 292, Surface Finish: White- and Red-slipped Pottery 292, Decoration: White- and Red-slipped Pottery 292, Construction: Plain and Corrugated Pottery 292, Surface Finish: Plain and Corrugated Pottery 292, Decorative Effect: Plain and Corrugated Pottery 293, Comment 293

Appendix B 294

TREE-RING SPECIMENS 294

Appendix C 295

CORN 295

References 296

FIGURES

Frontispiece. Camp area and Mariana Mesa, looking southeast
1. Panoramic views of Mariana Mesa area from Trechado Peak 2
2. The field camp, looking northwest 5
3. Measuring-in artifacts with grid and plumb bob 7
4. Tripod for photographing large artifacts in the field 8
5. Map of the Mariana Mesa area 12
6. Skeletal remains from various sites 15
7. Plan of Site 616 36
8. Panoramic view of Site 616, looking southwest from the dike 39
9. Plan of Trechado Spring Site 40
10. Site 616. Sketch of a typical section of adobe brick wall 45
11. Site 616. Detail of west wall of Room F2, showing adobe bricks 47
12. Site 616. Plan of Area A 61
13. Site 616. Room A1, looking east 62
14. Site 616. Plan of Room B1 64
15. Site 616. Room B1, looking south 65
16. Site 616. Plan of Room B2 66
17. Site 616. Room B2, looking south, showing pot supports in firepit 67
18. Site 616. Plan of Rooms B3, B5, and B7 68
19. Site 616. Showing sandstone masonry in Area C 70
20. Site 616. Plan of Rooms C1, C3, C6, and C9 72
21. Site 616. Room C1, looking west, showing masonry typical of Area C 73
22. Site 616. Plan of Rooms C2, C5, and C10 75
23. Site 616. Room C2, showing mealing bins 76
24. Site 616. Plan of Rooms C4 and C8 77
25. Site 616. Room C5, showing mealing bin, with duck pot, awl, and sherd scoop 78
26. Site 616. Room C5, looking south, showing enclosures with cists and curved deflector wall 79
27. Site 616. Room C8, looking north, showing upright sandstone slabs and postholes subdividing the room 81
28. Site 616. Room C9, looking east, showing area of destroyed mealing bins 82
29. Site 616. Room C10, looking north over ventilator shaft in south end of room 83
30. Site 616. Plan of Area D 84
31. Site 616. Room D1, looking north 85
32. Site 616. Room D2, looking south 87
33. Site 616. Plan of Room D5 89
34. Site 616. Room D5, looking south, showing ventilator shaft and firepit 90
35. Site 616. Plan of Rooms E1 and E2 92
36. Site 616. Room E2, looking south 94
37. Site 616. Room E2, showing cists and hip recess in south wall 95
38. Site 616. Plan of Rooms F1 and F2 96
39. Site 616. Room F2, looking west 97

40. Site 616. Plan of kiva 99
41. Site 616. East half of kiva, looking south 100
42. Site 616. Plan of walk-in well and associated rooms 103
43. Pottery rim and vessel forms from Site 616 108
44. Pottery vessels from Site 616 109
45. Decorative modes on black-on-white pottery from Site 616 111
46. Decorative modes on black-on-white pottery from Sites 481, 616 112
47. Decorative modes on black-on-white pottery from Site 616 113
48. Decorative modes on black-on-white pottery from Site 616 116
49. Pottery vessels found in Room D1, Site 616 117
50. Black-on-red sherds from Site 616 119
51. Profiles of mano shapes from Site 616 131
52. Under surfaces of manos from Site 616 136
53. Roughly shaped mortars from Site 616 139
54. Shaftsmoothers from Site 616 141
55. Axes and pick from Site 616 143
56. Hammers from Site 616 146
57. Objects of chipped stone from Site 616 149
58. Objects of volcanic scoria from Site 616 152
59. Carved and drilled stone objects from Site 616 154
60. Miscellaneous objects of stone, shell, and clay from Site 616 156
61. Bone awls with head of bone unworked, except by original splitting, from Site 616 158
62. Bone awls from Site 616 159
63. Bone scrapers from Site 616 161
64. Small bone objects from Site 616 162
65. Objects of shell from Site 616 164
66. Plan of Site 143 172
67. Site 143. Traxcavator excavating circular depression 174
68. Site 143. Stairs leading from central area, across Room 2 to Room 1 175
69. Site 481. Plan of the pueblo 182
70. Site 481. View looking north before excavation 183
71. Site 481. Sketches illustrating sequence of room construction 184
72. Site 481. Masonry types in various rooms 189
73. Site 481. Remodeled firepit in plaza east of Pithouse 2 192
74. Site 481. View of Room 13, looking northwest 193
75. Site 481. Remodeled late-style rectangular firepits built within Room 25 195
76. Site 481. Plan of kiva 198
77. Site 481. View of south half of kiva 199
78. Site 481. Detailed view of kiva firepit, deflector, and mouth of ventilator 200
79. Site 481. View of northwest corner of kiva 200
80. Site 481. View of Pithouse 1, looking northeast 201
81. Typical black-on-white sherds from Site 481 203
82. Typical black-on-red sherds from Site 481 204
83. Pottery rim and vessel forms from Site 481 210
84. Pottery vessels from site 481 212
85. Plan of Site 494 228
86. Site 494, Area A. General view, looking south 231
87. Site 494, Area A. View looking north over Rooms 1 and 3 231
88. Site 494, Area A. View of kiva, looking south 232
89. Site 494, Area B. Rooms 4 and 6, looking northwest 232
90. Site 494, Area B. View looking east over Rooms 3 and 6 233
91. Site 494, Area B. View looking northwest over Rooms 4 and 6 234
92. Site 494, Area B. View of kiva, looking southwest 235
93. Typical black-on-white sherds from Site 494 237
94. Pottery-rim and vessel forms from Site 494, Areas A and B 238
95. Pottery vessels from Site 494, Areas A and B 240
96. Plan of Site 601 248
97. Typical sherds from Site 601 253
98. Site 601. Neck-corrugated vessel from the floor of Room 2 255
99. Pottery-rim and vessel forms from Site 601 257
100. Plan of Site 188 258
101. Typical sherds from Site 188 262
102. Pottery-rim and vessel forms from Site 188 263
103. Plan of Site 486 266
104. Site 486. View of Unit 2, looking south 269
105. Site 486. Exterior firepit in Unit 4 270
106. Pottery-rim and vessel forms from Site 486 271
107. Typical sherds from Site 486 272
108. Manos from various sites 278
109. Metates, bowls, mortars, and rubbing stone from various sites 279
110. Mortars, grooved tool, and pestle from various sites 280
111. Axes from various sites 281
112. Hammers from various sites 282
113. Points from various sites 283
114. Bone and antler objects from various sites 284
115. Clay objects from various sites 285

TABLES

1. Distribution by descriptive types of black-on-white sherds from Site 616   114, 115
2. Distribution by descriptive types of black-on-red sherds from Site 616   122, 123
3. Distribution by descriptive types of plain and corrugated sherds from Site 616   124
4. Distribution by regional time-space types of whole and restorable pottery vessels from Site 616   129
5. Classification by dimensions of manos from Site 616   133
6. Distribution by descriptive types of manos from Site 616   135
7. Classification by dimensions of metates from Site 616   137
8. Distribution by types and provenience of slab metates from Site 616   138
9. Size and provenience of disc beads from Site 616   155
10. Distribution by descriptive types of all pottery sherds from Site 143   177
11. Dimensions of rooms in Site 481   190
12. Distribution by descriptive types of black-on-white sherds from Site 481   206, 207
13. Distribution by descriptive types of black-on-red sherds from Site 481   208
14. Distribution by descriptive types of plain and corrugated sherds from Site 481   209
15. Distribution by descriptive types of manos from Site 481   218
16. Dimensions of rooms in Site 494   230
17. Distribution by descriptive types of all pottery sherds from Site 494, Areas A and B   242
18. Distribution by descriptive types of manos from Site 494, Areas A and B   244
19. Distribution by descriptive types of all pottery sherds from Site 601   254
20. Distribution by descriptive types of all pottery sherds from Site 188   264
21. Distribution by descriptive types of all pottery sherds from Site 486   273

FOREWORD

The genesis of a scientific expedition is often far from clear. Ideas circulate in a desultory fashion for some time. People say that something of the kind would be a good thing to do. Graduate students get wind of it and, with an eye to thesis possibilities, begin offering themselves for positions on the staff. Travel agencies send brochures. Senior professors worry about who's going to pay for all this. The "Administration" wants to know who has authorized it, and on what authority. And, suddenly, somehow it all comes together, is funded and scheduled, often without anyone being really sure how, or perhaps even why. This was not the case with the Upper Gila Expedition of the Peabody Museum. We know how it started.

Sometime in the late 1930s, it must have been early in August, Donald Scott, the Director of the Museum, and I were seated, watching the sunset, on the steps of a hardware and farm machinery shop in Springerville, Arizona. We were discussing what we would do next, after the Awatovi job in the Hopi country was finished. We had been visiting Emil Haury's camp at Forestdale, on the Mogollon Rim, and our minds were still full of the questions and problems of the transitional region between the Plateau and the Gila-Salt Basin.

One of us pointed out, and I think it was Scott, that we were at that moment on the edge of a large area about which virtually nothing was known archaeologically. During the first decade of the century, Walter Hough had excavated pithouses at Luna, New Mexico. Later, Paul H. Nesbit of Beloit College had dug the Starkweather ruin in the Tularosa drainage; and the Peabody Museum had in its storage a few pots Sam Lothrop had picked up from local collectors in the Pie Town-Quemado region. The territory we were contemplating was a crude rectangle of some 15,000 square miles, bounded at the corners by St. Johns, Arizona on the northwest, Magdalena, New Mexico on the northeast, Silver City, New Mexico on the southeast, and Clifton, Arizona on the southwest. Around it were regions about which much more was known: the Zuni-Acoma area to the north, the central Rio Grande to the east, the Mimbres to the south, and the Pinedale-Show Low area to the west. To an archaeologist a gap of that magnitude is a major challenge so, then and there, we decided to tackle it.

The extensive testing and partial excavation at Awatovi ended in 1939. Then came World War II, and it was not until 1947 that we were able to implement the decision we had made that evening in Springerville. By then I had succeeded Scott as head of the Museum and Edward Bridge Danson, former Director and until recently President of the Museum of Northern Arizona, and an active member of the Advisory Council of the National Park Service, was a graduate student at Harvard. He and I began a rapid survey of the area which lasted through three summers, the third by Danson alone, after digging had begun north of Quemado. The survey recorded 638 sites (Danson 1957).

Since so much of the survey occurred in the Gila River drainage, the entire project was designated the Upper Gila Expedition of the Peabody Museum. This has produced a geographic anomaly since the sites excavated by McGimsey and described by him in this report all lie within the drainage pattern of the Little Colorado River. The ephemeral streams that drain the region, when they flow at all, flow northwesterly in the general direction of the extinct volcanic crater which contains Zuni Salt Lake. The sites are within a small area a few miles north of Quemado, in Catron County, New Mexico on the way to Adams Diggings, Fence Lake, and Atarque.

Dr. McGimsey has presented the history of the expedition with such clarity, accuracy, and care that it is unnecessary to say more about it here than that excavation began in 1949 and extended through 1954, with a hiatus in 1952 when there was no party in the field. The field director was Watson Smith, except for the summer of 1950, when McGimsey served in that capacity.

J. O. Brew, *Director*
Upper Gila Expedition

Acknowledgments

The Peabody Museum Upper Gila Expedition was developed by Donald Scott and J.O. Brew of the Peabody Museum, Harvard University, and the work was under the overall direction of Brew from its inception. This report is a record of excavations carried out during three seasons (1949 through 1951) under that program. The general area centers on Mariana Mesa, a topographic feature that extends north some 15 miles from the town of Quemado in Catron County, west-central New Mexico.

The list of people who have been directly associated with the work of the Upper Gila Expedition in the vicinity of Mariana Mesa is a long one. In fact, aside from J.O. Brew and Watson Smith, who acted as directors or advisers throughout, I am the only person directly connected with each of the field seasons discussed herein. The expedition personnel in 1949 comprised Jo Brew and Wat Smith, who was field director, and Raymond H. Thompson and me as their assistants. Evelyn N. Brew and Molly K. Thompson jointly shared the task of cataloguing. The student workers included Robert G. Baker, Thomas Davis, Jr., Gordon K. DeVoto, James E. Hannum, Arthur H. Rohn, Jr., Malcolm D. Shepherd, Howard W. Stoudt, Jr., and Perkins Wilson. Throughout the 1949 season Edward B. Danson, who was conducting the survey division of the expedition, was present in camp and available for consultation. We are indebted to his assistant, Harold E. Malde, for many photographs and the field maps of the sites excavated during this season. During both the 1949 and 1950 seasons the expedition was extremely fortunate in having as its cook, Lindsay C. Thompson (Lin also cooked for one section of the expedition during the 1951 season). All who have partaken of his sumptuous repasts (and indeed that probably includes a large number of Southwestern archaeologists, for Lin cooked at both Alkali Ridge and Awatovi) will recognize how fortunate we were in this respect.

In 1950 I served as field director of the expedition with the able assistance of Robert G. Baker. Mary E. McGimsey, assisted by Hester Davis and Agnes Bierman, assumed the task of cataloguing the many specimens obtained. The field crew, aside from those just named (for all hands labored with shovel and trowel), included Thomas Davis, Jr., Hal Eberhardt, Conrad ("Bud") Johnson, James Johnson, Irving Kaufman, Donald Kennedy, Arthur H. Rohn, Jr., and Charles E. Rozaire. We are indebted to Conrad Johnson and Irving Kaufman for the field maps made during this season.

In 1951 only a small crew remained in the Mariana Mesa area to conduct mopping-up operations. The major portion of the expedition moved to the general area of Largo Creek, south of Quemado. The Mariana Mesa division was again under my direction with the help of Robert Ravicz, Charles Conger, and Mary E. McGimsey, who, in addition to her duties as cataloguer and excavator, now assumed those of cook. During the last few weeks of the season, Dionysio Jiron and Frank Montoya of Quemado assisted in the excavation.

The expedition as a whole must express its appreciation to the entire town of Quemado, which not only supplied the expedition with the necessities of life but also accepted it as part of their community. Particular appreciation must be expressed to James R. Hogg and his family. We camped and excavated on their land through the three seasons, and their frequent assistance and many kindnesses have afforded us some of our warmest memories. The expedition is also indebted to Frank A. Hubbell, who with understanding and forbearance permitted us to make numerous excavations in the midst of his grazing land. At one time or another, Clayton Cox, James Livermore, and E.E. Engle of Quemado stored expedition material, and they, as well as the Stoudt brothers and the Thomas Davis family of Quemado, the Becker family of Springerville, and Clair Gurley of Gallup provided friendly and professional help on occasions too numerous to mention. George Adams of Quemado, by making a Traxcavator available to the expedition, made feasible the excavation of Site 143; and appreciation must be expressed to Cecil Wren of Quemado, who provided a small tractor for backfilling at a time when it was sorely needed.

The work was supported in part by grants from the Wenner-Gren Foundation for Anthropological Research and by the Clark Fund of Harvard University.

In analyzing the material, I have been able to call freely on the knowledge of many specialists, and it is only through their efforts that many segments of this report have achieved any significance. Paul C. Mangelsdorf of the Botanical Museum, Harvard University, analyzed the charred corn; C. Earle Smith and Robert Dressler of the Botany Department, Harvard University, analyzed the other vegetal remains; Barbara Lawrence of the Museum of Comparative Zoology, Harvard University, assisted in identifying the animal bones; Charles E. Stearns, Davis Stuart, and Donald Zeigler assisted in problems of geological identification and interpretation; while William J. Clench, Ruth Turner, and Robert E. Greengo identified the shells. Terah L. Smiley and the Laboratory of Tree-Ring Research at the University of Arizona analyzed the dendrochronological specimens.

Regarding the period of field and laboratory research, particular mention must be made of Jo Brew and Wat Smith. All the work accomplished by the several seasons of the Upper Gila Expedition is primarily the result of the unceasing efforts of these two men. I am particularly indebted to them not only for their work with the expedition as a whole but also for their constant personal advice, encouragement, and stimulation. In these latter respects, I must also acknowledge a debt to Stephen Williams, Gordon R. Willey, John W. Roberts, and Philip Phillips.

In 1970 I returned to Cambridge, where Steve Williams, then Director of the Peabody Museum, made the Museum's resources available to me; and perhaps of even greater benefit in its way was Phil Phillips's generosity in placing at my disposal his study in Bolton. Here I was able to work virtually undisturbed for an entire month — a boon indeed.

Then, in the summer of 1976, Douglas Schwartz made available the resources of the School of American Research in Santa Fe. It was there that the nearly final review of the manuscript was done, and this assistance — with the stimulating surroundings, both personal and institutional — is gratefully acknowledged.

Many other individuals have made important contributions. Karen S. Young prepared most of the site plans and maps, assisted by Carolyn F. Shakel. Sue Ruiz, Marcia H. Smith, and Carol Gifford did the final typing. Raymond H. Thompson, an early participant in the Upper Gila work, again entered the picture during the 1970s (in his capacity as Head of the Department of Anthropology, University of Arizona) by providing Wat Smith and others with office space and facilities for essential typing and editorial work.

Hester Davis, an Upper Gila crew member in 1950 and (in the southern branch) in 1951, in her official capacity as Arkansas State Archaeologist, periodically assumed many of my own official responsibilities during the 1970s, thus making it possible for me to prepare the manuscript for publication.

During the 1970s also, Wat Smith worked extensively with me in bringing the manuscript through its final stages to publication. Without his untiring help and stimulation, the manuscript might never have reached the printer. His contributions during this period, like those he made during the formative and active stages of the field research, cannot be measured in any ordinary terms. He led me down the initial paths of anthropological research, and then, by generous application of his time and knowledge, made it possible for us together to review the original manuscript and prepare it for publication. Moreover, he reviewed the literature, provided the updated evaluations of the chronological placement of sites, and made many other essential contributions too numerous to itemize in detail.

I also feel deeply indebted to Jo Brew; and I confess to being more keenly aware in 1977 of the extent of that debt than I was 25 years ago. Without Jo the Upper Gila project and this report, as well as others deriving from its excavations, would not have materialized. In a very vital sense, that says it all. Without Jo, and others like him who make research possible, none of the rest of us can perform.

Mary E. McGimsey has been an active and essential element in every aspect of the research. She was part of the initial planning team, and a crew member in the field research; for two of the three field seasons and all of the subsequent laboratory work, she directed and participated in the processing and recording, and she is responsible for some of the field and nearly all of the laboratory photography. Her contributions to the initial manuscript ranged from routine typing to intellectual stimulation, and her subsequent participation has been continuous and equally varied. In short, though her name appears in this manuscript but seldom, I would like to acknowledge her contributions as an active colleague in all aspects of the research and to this report.

Charles R. McGimsey III
Arkansas Archeological Survey
University of Arkansas Museum
Fayetteville, Arkansas, 1977

Environmental Setting

Although sporadic expeditions have passed through or near Quemado and Zuni Salt Lake since Coronado's time, few descriptions have appeared concerning the nature of the region itself.

Mariana Mesa is on the southern edge of what Fenneman (1931, pp. 317–319) has described as the Colorado Plateau. Topographically, the region is basically level and consists of denuded Cretaceous sedimentary deposits covered with alluvium and dotted with lava-capped remnants or mesas. These mesas are often quite extensive. Evidence of Tertiary and Quaternary volcanic activity can be found throughout the area and is indicated not only by the flat lava-topped mesas but also by volcanic dikes and plugs (Dane and Bachman 1965).

Mariana Mesa is more or less typical of the region. Flat-topped with a thin lava cap, it is approximately 15 miles long from north to south and seven miles across at its widest point. The north edge rises abruptly from the 7,000-foot (2,100 m) general level of the region to a maximum level of 7,800 feet (2,350 m). The southern portion of the mesa slopes down gradually and the mesa disappears as a unit just north of U.S. highway 60 and east of Quemado. Its borders are very irregular, having been encroached upon to a greater or lesser extent by the headward expansion of ephemeral streams and the general process of erosion. The seven sites discussed herein are at an elevation of between 7,200 feet (2,195 m) and 7,400 feet (2,255 m), and are located on slopes or low ridges extending from or adjacent to the base of the northern end of Mariana Mesa.

The region of Mariana Mesa is centrally located with respect to the drainage pattern of the Southwest. Stream flow in almost every direction is away from this general area (fig. 5), and a walk of a hundred miles in almost any direction would bring one to the headwaters or large tributaries of nearly every major river system draining the Southwest between the Rio Grande and the Colorado River. Twenty-five miles to the east the Rio Salado and other tributaries of the Rio Grande can be reached; at an equivalent distance to the south rises the Tularosa River, a headwater of the Gila River; 75 miles to the southwest are the headwaters of the Salt River, while within 100 miles to the north are the Navajo and Chaco rivers, which drain into the San Juan. The region itself technically falls within the Little Colorado River drainage, although it is doubtful that much runoff from Mariana Mesa ever reaches the Little Colorado River. Nonetheless, the drainage pattern of the ephemeral streams of the area extends westward from just east of Mariana Mesa, passing both to the north and to the south of the mesa; and after joining Largo Creek near Nations Draw, some 20 miles to the west, the system continues on to become the Carrizo Wash, which eventually unites with the Little Colorado River just below St. Johns, Arizona. The region of Mariana Mesa, in short, forms the extreme southeast corner of the Little Colorado drainage.

Precise rainfall data for the immediate area are not available, but the average annual rainfall is between 10 and 15 inches, with variation of generally less than 20 percent (Cory 1935). The region as a whole is in the upper portion of the Upper Sonoran vegetation and life zone, although occasional scattered sections extend up into the Transition Zone (Bailey 1913).

From the point of view of primitive economy the region may well have been moderately attractive. While there are no permanent streams and only occasional springs, there is enough rain to produce good grass and extensive juniper and nut pine forests. The area falls within the precipitation and elevation limits discussed by Hack (1942, pp. 22–25) as permitting the growth of corn, and we know from the archaeological remains that corn, beans, and other crops were known to the Indian inhabitants. More than likely, the primary agricultural technique was floodwater farming (Hack 1942, pp. 26–31; Bryan 1929, pp. 444–456; Bryan 1941, pp. 219–242) on the banks of arroyos, on flood plains of the larger ephemeral streams, the bottoms of small arroyos, and perhaps trinchera fields, although no direct evidence was found for any of these methods. There are no extensive dune deposits nor are there any permanent streams, so the other

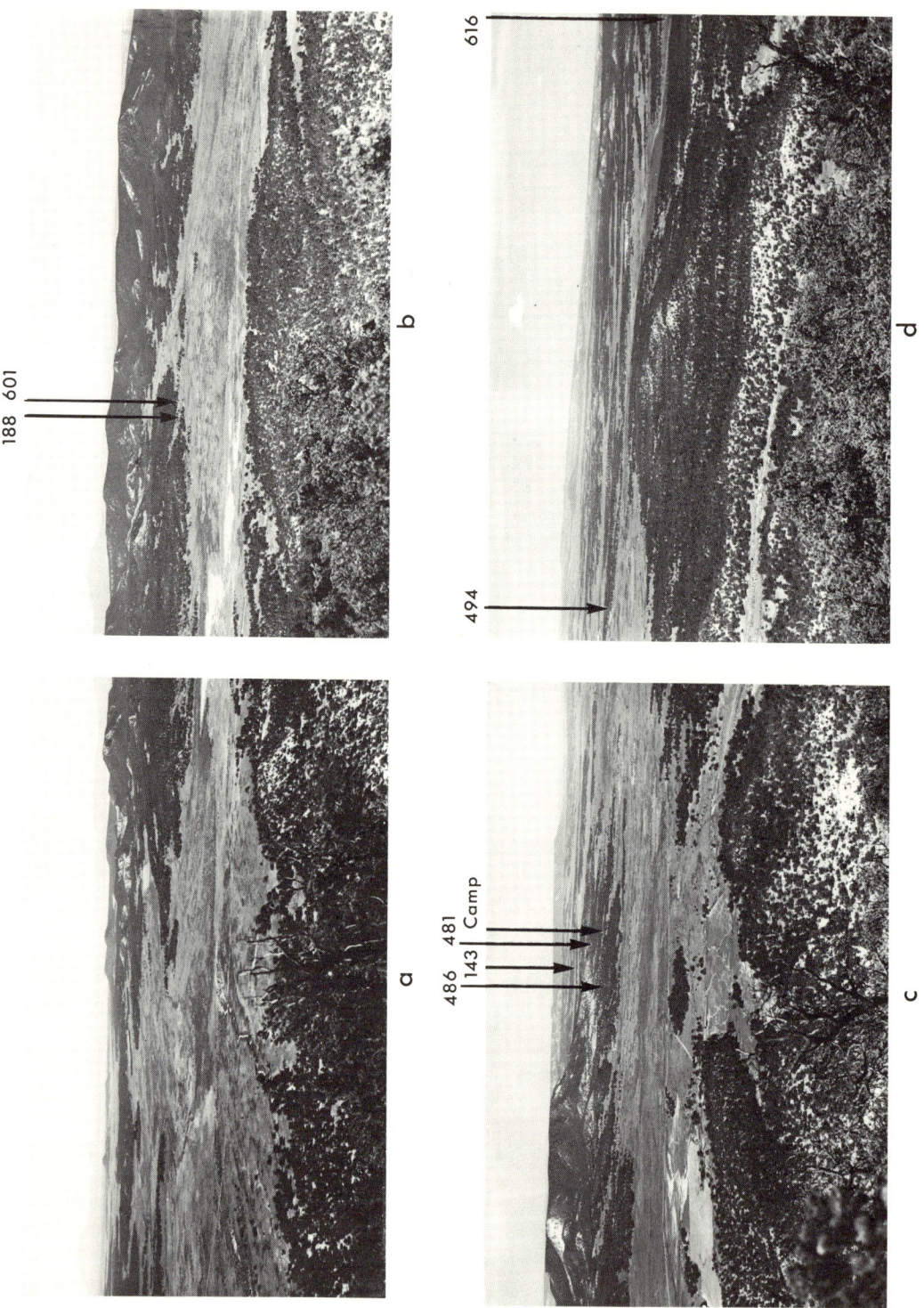

Figure 1. Panoramic views of Mariana Mesa area from Trechado Peak, showing locations of most of the sites discussed. Compass bearings are approximately: a. south; b. southwest; c. west; d. northwest.

methods of primitive agriculture discussed by Hack (1942, pp. 32-37) doubtless were of little importance.

Although, statistically speaking, the variation from the mean annual rainfall is lower in this area than for much of the Southwest or for the country as a whole, this cannot be interpreted as indicating a stable or dependable environment for primitive agriculture. One or two years of rainfall within the lower limits of the variation might not seriously deplete any agricultural surplus, but any less rainfall over a longer period could cause serious hardship as evidenced by the period of drought around 1950. One other important factor is that individual rainstorms are generally localized, and this pattern of local storms may well shift from year to year. This factor alone would probably necessitate some mobility on the part of primitive agriculturalists.

The region had an ample quantity of other resources to offer its prehistoric inhabitants. Detailed observations were not made in the field, but it seems that typical Upper Sonoran fauna (see V. Bailey 1931, p. 4; F.M. Bailey 1928, p. 7, pl. 2, for complete listing) is present in the area today and doubtless was even more numerous in the past. For the artisan, petrified wood was scattered over the mesa sides in quantities which, while by no means approaching that found in the Petrified Forest, would have been more than adequate for the needs of the prehistoric population. In addition, nodules of obsidian could be obtained from the lava in the area, and there were frequent deposits of quartzite cobbles and other stone suitable for working. For larger artifacts and building materials, lava of varying grades from vesicular to dense basalt is everywhere at hand, and sandstone outcrops are frequent in the area. Clay deposits can be found in the Cretaceous sediments; and although none have been tested, they would presumably be satisfactory for the manufacture of pottery. All in all, the region provided a more than adequate economic base for its prehistoric inhabitants.

Field and Analytic Procedures

In 1946 the Peabody Museum of Harvard University began the organization of a long-term program of archaeological survey and excavation in west-central New Mexico and east-central Arizona, under the direction of J.O. Brew, assisted by Edward B. Danson, then a graduate student at Harvard. The area is contained in a quadrangle cornered by St. Johns, Arizona, on the northwest, Clifton, Arizona, on the southwest, and Magdalena and Silver City, New Mexico, on the northeast and southeast respectively. It includes almost 15,000 square miles. The program was designated the Peabody Museum Upper Gila Expedition, since by far the major portion of the area included in the initial program is drained by the upper reaches of the Gila River. For the purposes of this report, however, this sobriquet is something of a misnomer, because all the sites discussed herein fall not into the region of the upper Gila, but in an area whose drainage pattern, such as it is, belongs more properly to that of the Little Colorado River.

In the summer of 1947 the first party was placed in the field. During that summer the entire region outlined above was rapidly surveyed by Brew and Danson, and 110 sites were recorded. On the basis of this initial survey it was decided to concentrate subsequent work in the more northerly section of the outlined area. The following summer two groups were in the field: one, again composed of Brew and Danson, intensified the survey of a portion of the northern section, while the second, of which I was a member, excavated Bat Cave under the direction of Herbert W. Dick. The Bat Cave excavation was a joint operation with the Department of Anthropology of the University of New Mexico. During that summer the major part of the proposed excavation of Bat Cave was completed, although a brief supplementary investigation was made by Dick two years later (Dick 1965). The survey division of the expedition recorded and made collections from 366 additional sites, concentrating on all valleys found in a band about 25 miles wide from north to south, and stretching from Springerville, Arizona, to Magdalena, New Mexico (Danson 1950, 1957).

In the summer of 1949 a base camp was established 13 miles north of the village of Quemado, New Mexico, just east of State Route 117 (Smith 1950). Since the expedition program called for the continued use of this camp for several years, it was practical to set up relatively permanent though movable structures in the form of wooden tent floors and frames, together with a wood-framed and roofed kitchen and mess hall. In the second season a shower stall was added. The camp was situated on the edge of the valley floor at the northern foot of Mariana Mesa,* in an area of low scrub juniper and, at least during the first season, grass. During the second and third summers (1950 and 1951), as a result of the general drought conditions then prevalent throughout this part of the Southwest, the piñon and juniper began to die and much of the grassland became dry, dusty, and vegetationless, so that the area lost its verdant appearance and, in occasional small sections, assumed the aspect of a dust bowl. Although the drought reached almost disastrous proportions for the local inhabitants, it caused the archaeologists little inconvenience other than the occasional liberal flavoring of their food by "dust devils."

From this camp, excavation was begun with student workers under Watson Smith as field director. The objective was the investigation of sites which would span the entire prehistory of the Mariana Mesa area, and, with this end in view, three sites were selected for the 1949 season. Site 486,** one of the relatively rare early sites made up of individual architectural units, proved to be badly eroded and little material remained. After excavating the single preserved but

---

*On New Mexico Map No. 64, Grazing Service and Range Surveys, 1938, this mesa is labeled Sorano Mesa; and on the applicable U.S.G.S. maps it is spelled Mariano. The expedition, however, did not encounter either of those designations in the field, and the local appellation, Mariana Mesa, has been adopted herein.

**The site numbers are those designated by the survey division of the Upper Gila Expedition. Sites were numbered sequentially in the order found (Danson 1957, p. 6).

Figure 2. The field camp, looking northwest.

largely sterile habitation area, the crew, under the direction of Raymond H. Thompson, was shifted to Site 494, selected as typical of the small contiguous-room units. Fortunately it proved to be better preserved. It consisted of two multiple-room surface units: Unit A of four surface rooms and an associated subterranean structure, and Unit B with eight surface rooms and an associated subterranean structure. Thompson's crew spent the remainder of the season excavating completely the two units of this site. I directed the work at Site 481, which appeared to be a later pueblo of 10 to 12 contiguous surface rooms with an associated kiva. It was planned to excavate this site entirely as a basis for sampling other similar sites in the region. As is so often the case, the surface appraisal of its size greatly underestimated its actual proportions. By the end of the season 34 surface rooms had been excavated or trenched. While this number included all surface rooms, there were indications of subsurface dwellings.

During this season the survey division under Danson made an intensive reconnaissance of the area adjacent to the base camp taking in approximately 75 square miles, within which 157 aditional sites were located. These, with five sites encountered in subsequent seasons by other members of the expedition, brought the total number of sites recorded by the survey to 638 (Danson 1957, p. 6).

The Upper Gila Expedition returned to the Quemado area the following summer under my direction with a somewhat larger crew of student workers. During this season, parts of four additional sites were excavated and partial excavation of the features underlying Site 481 was carried forward. Preliminary analysis of the material from Sites 494 and 481 had suggested that the occupation of these sites covered most of the middle time range of the prehistoric occupation of the Mariana Mesa region. Consequently the primary goal of the 1950 field season was to obtain data relative to the earliest and latest periods of intensive occupation. The most recently occupied permanent sites in the area consisted of large contiguous-room pueblos generally constructed in the form of a hollow square. The entire crew spent the first half of the 1950 season excavating a portion of one such ruin, Site 616. A total of 22 surface rooms out of an estimated 500 were completely excavated, as were three contemporaneously occupied pithouses, a D-shaped kiva, and a combination walk-in well and potter's clay pit — all of the latter being located in the plaza of the site. (I had occasion to visit this extremely important site again in 1967. In the intervening period almost every room had been thoroughly and systematically looted: a staggering loss, for archaeologists could have come closer to doing an ethnographic-type material-culture study of this site than at any other in the Southwest that I know of.)

During the latter half of the season, the crew was split into three groups; two began work in sites representing the earlier occupation of the area while the third continued work in the late sites. During this part of the season, Sites 143, 601, and 188 were partially excavated. Site 188 proved to be a small two-room jacal unit. Site 601 was a small U-shaped unit, of which a part of one wing was apparently of jacal construction while the remainder of the unit was of lava-cobble masonry. Both of these sites were felt to represent the earlier occupation of the area, with Site 188 being the earlier of the two. Prior to excavation, it had been thought that a great kiva existed at Site 616. When this proved to be what has now been interpreted as a walk-in well, excavation was begun at an approximately contemporary site, Site 143, which, to judge from the large circular depression clearly visible, also appeared to have a great kiva. This large circular structure was the only unit excavated at Site 143. (The 1967 visit indicated that this entire site also had been systematically looted.) During the closing days of the 1950 season a semisubterranean pithouse below Rooms 9 and 10 was trenched at Site 481.

Preliminary examination of the evidence suggested that these seven sites overlapped or nearly overlapped in time, and together were representative of all but the earliest occupation of the area; however, a number of gaps and problems were still evident. As a result, in 1951, while the main body of the expedition shifted its base camp south of Quemado and began excavating a number of sites around Largo Creek (reported in Smith 1973), three members and I remained at Mariana Mesa and conducted small excavations in five of the seven sites, omitting only Site 486 and Site 494. During the latter half of the 1951 season, this group began excavation of Site 638 on top of Cerro Colorado, which with its adjacent sites appears to represent the earliest known occupation of the general area. In 1953 and 1954 (no party went to the field in 1952) the entire expedition returned to Site 638 and spent these seasons excavating that and immediately adjacent sites (Bullard 1962).

This report is not concerned with regional summaries or intepretations of broad scope, but rather concentrates on elucidating certain details of the prehistoric context of one small area of west-central New Mexico, while presenting the basic data from the archaeological excavations in such a manner that their utility to problems other than these considered here can be of maximum benefit to other investigators.

A discussion of field and laboratory procedures employed is not in itself productive of archaeological data. On the other hand, the methods utilized in data collection provide a part of the scientific context essential to any evaluation of that data.

Trenches had to be dug prior to systematic excavation at only three sites. At the remainder, surface features were sufficient to determine approximate structure outlines. At Site 188, exploratory trenches were required in order to locate the houses. At Site 616, a large masonry and adobe pueblo, room outlines were not particularly evident on the surface, and trenches were laid out extending from outside the pueblo across the room bounds and into the plaza. Exploratory trenches were also needed to locate the two kivas at Site 494. The initial trenches at Sites 188 and 616 were laid out in two-meter squares. (The metric system was employed consistently by the Upper Gila Expedition.)

The excavation of a room or small unit was generally undertaken by a single individual who handled that unit from start to finish. A trench 50 centimeters deep was begun in the center of the room and extended toward one wall. Once the wall had been encountered, the trench was continued around the inside, thus outlining the interior of the room. The remaining center "island" of fill was then removed with greater rapidity. Upon completion of this 50-centimeter level, the second level was begun by putting down a pit in one corner to locate the floor. As a rule, the floor area was most clearly defined and recognizable in room corners. When the floor was encountered, the remainder of the fill was removed in 50-centimeter levels to a depth of approximately 15 centimeters above the floor. In general, the 50-centimeter levels were dug with pick and shovel, trowel work being reserved for the final 15 centimeters and special features.

The soil was almost never screened, and consequently some artifacts undoubtedly were lost. However, additional information that might have been gained was not felt to be worth the time required to recover it.

Material encountered in each level was catalogued together, being sorted in the field simply into general categories of stone, bone, sherds, and so forth. Artifacts found directly in contact with the floor were left in place insofar as possible, until after the room had been photographed. Their positions were then measured, and they were catalogued individually.

Following the removal of the fill of a room and the completion of room notes, test holes were generally put down in the four corners of the room until sterile soil was reached. In this manner it could be determined whether trash areas or architectural features underlay the room; the relationship of the wall bases to each other and to the room floor could be checked, and the nature of the wall bases observed. At Site 616 and Site 481 some walls and other architectural features were torn down and notes taken thereon. Perhaps not enough of this consciously directed destruction was undertaken, for this is often the only way in which certain valuable information can be garnered. Of course, at times circumstances dictate that there be no destruction, e.g., the excavation of ruins in a National Monument, or at the request of an owner that the ruins be left intact. It is possible, however, that where no conscious destruction takes place and rooms are simply backfilled, in instances where preservation is unnecessary, much valuable data may be lost.

During the first season all records were maintained by the field director and his assistants. During the final two seasons the student excavators prepared field notes of all units that they excavated. Detailed descriptions and at least two scale drawings were made for every room or unit — a blowup showing floor dimensions and walls, and a detailed floor plan showing floor features, artifact locations, and wall abutments. Cross sections were also drawn whenever needed. In general, measurements were made along perpendiculars from the room walls and from corner stakes. Depths were recorded from designated corner stakes, which were later shot in for absolute depth when the entire site was surveyed. To assist in recording rooms whose floors were covered by a wealth of material (one room contained over 70 individually catalogued objects on or near the floor), a 2-by-3-meter frame laced with string into 10-centimeter squares was constructed. This grid was laid across the top of the room walls, and with the aid of a plumb bob artifacts were quickly and accurately located and plotted on graph paper (fig. 3).

Except in the first season all artifacts were briefly described and located in detail according to a standard form, as they were found. This form was stamped directly on paper bags or on tags to be tied on muslin bags, and a duplicate form stamped on a 3-by-5 inch card was placed inside. Both bags and tags were prenumbered so that the field-worker was able to use these numbers to refer to the artifact in his field notebook discussions; these same numbers were utilized

Figure 3. Measuring-in artifacts with grid and plumb bob, at Site 616, Room C5, looking north. (R. G. Baker and H. A. Davis at work.)

in the field catalogue and in this report — a system that greatly facilitated both field notation and laboratory analysis, for there was never any confusion about the specific artifact being referred to by the field-worker or laboratory analyst.

When the artifacts were brought to camp, the provenience information was recorded on catalogue cards; the artifacts were described in detail and drawn. A photographic tripod was rigged (fig. 4), and all large artifacts were photographed. This combined descriptive and photographic record had to suffice for the large stone artifacts, as they were too bulky for shipment and were left in the field. The rest of the materials, including all sherds, were shipped to the Peabody Museum and were available for further analysis.

For large stone tools, architectural features, and contextual associations, the observations made in the field on the basis of the problem orientations and information then felt to be pertinent had to suffice, despite their occasional shortcomings resulting from insufficient or misdirected observation. For the remainder of the artifacts, other than sherds, problem analysis was begun, using the field descriptions as a base, with further observations being made whenever they proved to be necessary.

The sherd material, because of the sheer size of the sample, had to be handled in much the same manner as the artifacts left in the field. The material was initially observed in the laboratory, but by and large

Figure 4. Tripod for photographing large artifacts in the field. (C. R. McGimsey III at work.)

these initial observations had to serve. Although, on occasion, limited samples were restudied or the entire collection checked for attributes with restricted occurrence, it was recognized from the first that an attribute with general distribution would require an appearance of extreme significance, before a second handling of the complete collection consisting of thousands of sherds would be undertaken. The result was an initial and careful analysis of the problems to be investigated, in an attempt to determine in advance what attributes and characteristics of the pottery would be pertinent to each problem, and in how much detail they should be observed. Inevitably, these decisions were modified slightly as analysis proceeded and, occasionally, they were countermanded by practical factors. In any scientific analysis the value of an observation must constantly be weighed against the time and expense required to make it.

With the rather broadly defined orientation of the present study, it rapidly became apparent that sorting pottery into the regional time-space types (e.g., Colton and Hargrave 1937; Hawley 1936; Colton 1953; Colton 1962–1965; Wheat, Gifford, and Wasley 1958; Smith 1962; Breternitz 1966; Hargrave 1974), noting variant or new types of the same order, and calculating percentages for these groups would not be adequate for the questions being asked here or potentially of concern to others.

These published types were largely designed to emphasize characteristics that appeared to be diagnostic of a given site or area at a certain period of time. They generally have proven to be acceptable tools for establishing relative chronologies as well as suggesting patterns of communication. In an area previously unworked, the initial types of this kind are apt to reflect accurately the action types* of the sites excavated. As other sites are excavated in the same general region, these same types often are used not only as the basis for classification of the new material (perhaps desirable for comparative purposes, though a comparison of individual modes is often more informative), but also as the sole means of describing the new material. This procedure, while resulting in the creation of nice, neat, regional blocks of type distributions, does not always reflect reality and certainly does not forward the cause of archaeological problem solution. Are the artifact norms from these other sites actually identical to those already described? Given the variability of culture and cultural material it seems unlikely. Yet, if no other description of the material is provided, intersite variations are easily ignored or glossed over, and other workers are unaware of their presence or at least of their particularities. Nor do such types provide the kind of broad and overt problem base that is needed to facilitate the investigation of a wide variety of problems. At best they represent a partial truth, for while they illustrate the existence of a very real and important uniformity over a temporal and geographic span, they generally fail to delineate the specific nature of this uniformity, and tend to obscure equally important variations. In view of the differences in overt and covert problem orientation, it perhaps is not surprising that the establishment of specific typological boundaries satisfactory to any large number of investigators is rarely achieved.

In order to surmount the shortcomings of the published types (here designated regional time-space types) without losing their valuable features, and to make the basic data available for typological grouping relevant to a variety of problems, the technique of descriptive types was developed and utilized for all the ceramic data discussed herein (and for the manos at Site 616). The creation and uses of descriptive types are fully discussed on pages 17–35.

The nonceramic artifacts are grouped and presented in categories designed to emphasize the general character (material, form, or use) of the included objects. If the descriptions of individual units included within typological groups are presented in sufficient detail to permit study of the individual units, and to permit the recombination of the individual units into other typological groups pertinent to differ-

---

*For a discussion of "idea" and "action" types see pages 29–30 herein.

ent problems, it matters little whether the organization adopted for presentation is along the lines of "stone," "shell," or of "household utility tools," "food procurement tools," and so forth. (Of course, it is possible that a particular organization adopted might necessitate or reflect an orientation on the part of the investigator describing the material, which could cause him to overlook important features.) In the present report the material has been initially divided for presentation into such categories as "stone," "bone," and "shell," for it was felt that this, rather than some more imaginative or functionally oriented scheme, was most likely to facilitate ready reference.

The terminology employed conforms whenever possible with Woodbury (1954) for the stone artifacts and with Kidder (1932, pp. 195–304) for artifacts of other materials. Unless explicitly stated to the contrary, the terms conform to the definitions established by these two authors. Variations of the Mariana Mesa material within these definitions are brought out.

Related to, but separate from, the question of the details to be observed, is that of the number of observations to be presented in a report. The polar extremes are to present all data felt to be significant, and conversely, to present the conclusions alone, including only whatever data happen to be essential to the discussion. There are disadvantages to both extremes although they are of a completely different nature. Presentation of the conclusions alone forces the reader to assume, without possibility of proof, that the author's groups and interpretations are correct. More important is the fact that it inhibits the use of the material for any problem other than those based upon the specific interpretations made by the author. On the other hand, presentation of all the data used in the analysis, or considered potentially significant, necessitates a wealth of photographs and drawings as well as a tremendous amount of descriptive writing (though, of course, a sufficiently myopic problem orientation might obviate this necessity). Complete presentation is often shunned, both because of the time involved in preparing it and because of the cost of publishing it.

Presumably, an ideal procedure would involve: the presentation of all features necessary to enable the reader to visualize the material, those attributes significant to the problems under consideration, other features whose significance the author was aware of, and any that he felt might prove to be of value, even though that value had not as yet been demonstrated. Unfortunately the practical factors of limited research funds and high publication costs inhibit the attainment of any such ideal presentation. Given limited funds, is it more important to publish the undocumented or partially documented conclusions of several expeditions, or the complete observations and results of only one? Perhaps, as has been suggested (Kidder 1932, pp. 8–10), the answer lies in doing less excavation and more complete publication of what is done (Taylor 1948). In any event, some adequate compromise between practical and ideal presentations must be sought.

Generally, conclusions alone are inadequate even if the analysis has been unusually complete. If only limited conclusions are attempted and the basic data are not presented, it becomes difficult to justify the field expenditure or destruction of the basic resource, because only a limited amount of the potential return will have been realized. In point of fact, the problems now being undertaken by archaeologists can be pursued only by presentation and comparison of detailed data, which must be published or in some manner made available to other investigators. The lumping of all corrugated pottery under a single descriptive head or the general statement that "manos were present in great abundance" will no longer suffice, if in fact it ever did.

The two errors of omission most frequently encountered in the presentation of data are failure to record positional or contextual information about individual or even groups of artifacts — although there are some notable exceptions to this (DiPeso 1951, 1953; Smith 1952) — and presentation of the material in such a manner or in groups so large that significant variations among included items are completely obscured. Occasionally information supplementary to these limitations is on deposit at a museum or other place of storage (a common situation in the case of sherd counts, for example), and the data can ideally be obtained by inquiry and search, but just as often this is not possible or practical. Often the data are no longer extant or are not readily available, and the only other but frequently unfeasible solution is for the inquirer to journey to the source in person. Nonetheless, if the analysis of the material has been reasonably complete or the results not particularly controversial, the slight additional information or substantiation of results to be gained by publication of all observable detail is not worth the extra cost. Obviously, little is to be gained by publishing pages of data solely to prove a point already sufficiently demonstrated elsewhere and generally accepted. Each case must be judged on its own merits.

The use of microfilm or microfiche is often recommended for the publication of large masses of data in an extremely condensed form. These procedures are suitable, however, only if the total mass is so great as to preclude its feasible publication more extensively. Comparatively few readers have easily available the means of enlarging the images, with the result that in most cases the data will go unread (though this restriction may well be changing).

In this report the presentation of descriptive data is relatively complete regarding those factors whose significance was known or suspected. This presentation is designed primarily for reference rather than for general reading, and an attempt has been made to design a method of giving detailed information as concisely as possible. The numerically represented pottery tables are not particularly conducive to immediate interpretation, but despite their obvious drawbacks and inconveniences they do possess the advantage of maximum brevity. Thus this form of presentation makes it possible to describe in considerable detail the observations upon which the problem types and summaries are based, as well as certain other data, which, if occasionally hidden behind systems of symbols, are at least more readily available than they would be if the reader were required to send or come to the Peabody Museum to obtain it. That portion of the data relevant to the problems investigated in this report is summarized in the discussion of those problems; so the general reader should not find it necessary to refer extensively to the detailed description of artifacts or the tabular presentation of the numerically presented descriptive pottery types.

Mariana Mesa,
A.D. 850–1300

Of the seven sites reported here, Site 486, a small group of individual structures, was the earliest occupied (A.D. 850–900). Site 188, a small contiguous-walled jacal unit, was occupied about A.D. 1075, while Site 601, a small U-shaped unit of contiguous rooms, may have been inhabited slightly later (probably around A.D. 1100). Site 494 had two small units of contiguous rooms separated slightly in time, but each with an associated subterranean structure. The units at this site seem to have been occupied around A.D. 1125. Site 481, though including at least one earlier pithouse, was primarily a moderate-sized site of contiguous surface rooms (at first, two separate but contemporaneous groups of rooms which, at the end, were amalgamated into a single unit). The main occupation of Site 481 probably covered a span from the late 1000s to the mid 1200s. Site 616, a large site of approximately 500 contiguous surface rooms, was constructed in a hollow square. Contemporaneous pithouses, a kiva, and a walk-in well were contained within the square. Occupied from about A.D. 1100 to 1300, this site and perhaps the Trechado Spring site (fig. 9), which also was built in a hollow square with an interior walk-in well, evidently were the last ones occupied in the area. At Site 143, which was probably contemporaneous with both Site 481 and most of Site 616, only a single late (approximately A.D. 1200) ceremonial structure was excavated.

By A.D. 950 the population of west-central New Mexico occupied scattered settlements varying in size from units of no more than one or two families, to occasional communities consisting of several dozen individual houses without apparent arrangement over a limited area. The Upper Gila Expedition Survey (Danson 1957) showed that the favored location for these small communities was higher up the drainage system than was later the case. Generally the houses were constructed on low ridges or other elevated areas overlooking valley land.

It would be interesting to know the extent of individual and group identification with aggregates larger than the individual community. The groups certainly were relatively self-sufficient though well aware of their neighbors. There is no indication of any aggressive activity at this time.

Never in the period of the history of Mariana Mesa with which we are concerned do there appear to have been any major communication barriers. The inhabitants partook of the cultural heritage of their neighbors on all sides. The white-slipped pottery and the general house forms were northern in their association; the plain and corrugated pottery appears to have basically southern affiliations; and the later red-slipped wares were western. Nevertheless, it generally seems that these groups were more closely identified, and perhaps felt themselves to be more closely identified, with the people inhabiting the region to the north and west of Mariana Mesa. Possibly their ancestors first entered the area by following the drainage of the Little Colorado to its uppermost reaches, there to remain and develop in anything but cultural isolation.

Extensive, or at least extended, trade relationships are indicated even in the scanty data from Site 486. Here, a few aberrant sherds suggest trade in pottery vessels; and shell certainly reached the Mesa by trade. In fact, shell was traded in, though never in large quantities, throughout the period under review. Diorite may have been obtained from the granite mountain ranges of central and southern Arizona, and the lignite used in the "buttons" at Site 616 may have come either in the form of raw material or as finished products from the present-day Hopi, Marsh Pass, or other regions with outcrops of coal layers in the Mesa Verde sandstone. These items indicate the nature of the goods traded, but, other than the general sparseness of their occurrence, they provide little data relative to the volume of such trade. Our best indication of this comes from the red-slipped pottery at Site 616. If most of this pottery was traded in, as seems likely, then the extent of trade and its importance was much greater, at least in the later sites, than the other data would lead one to suspect. In other words, the inhabitants of those later sites depended on intergroup trade to provide "essential" items basically utilitarian in nature. In all probability the establishment and maintenance of dependable commercial relation-

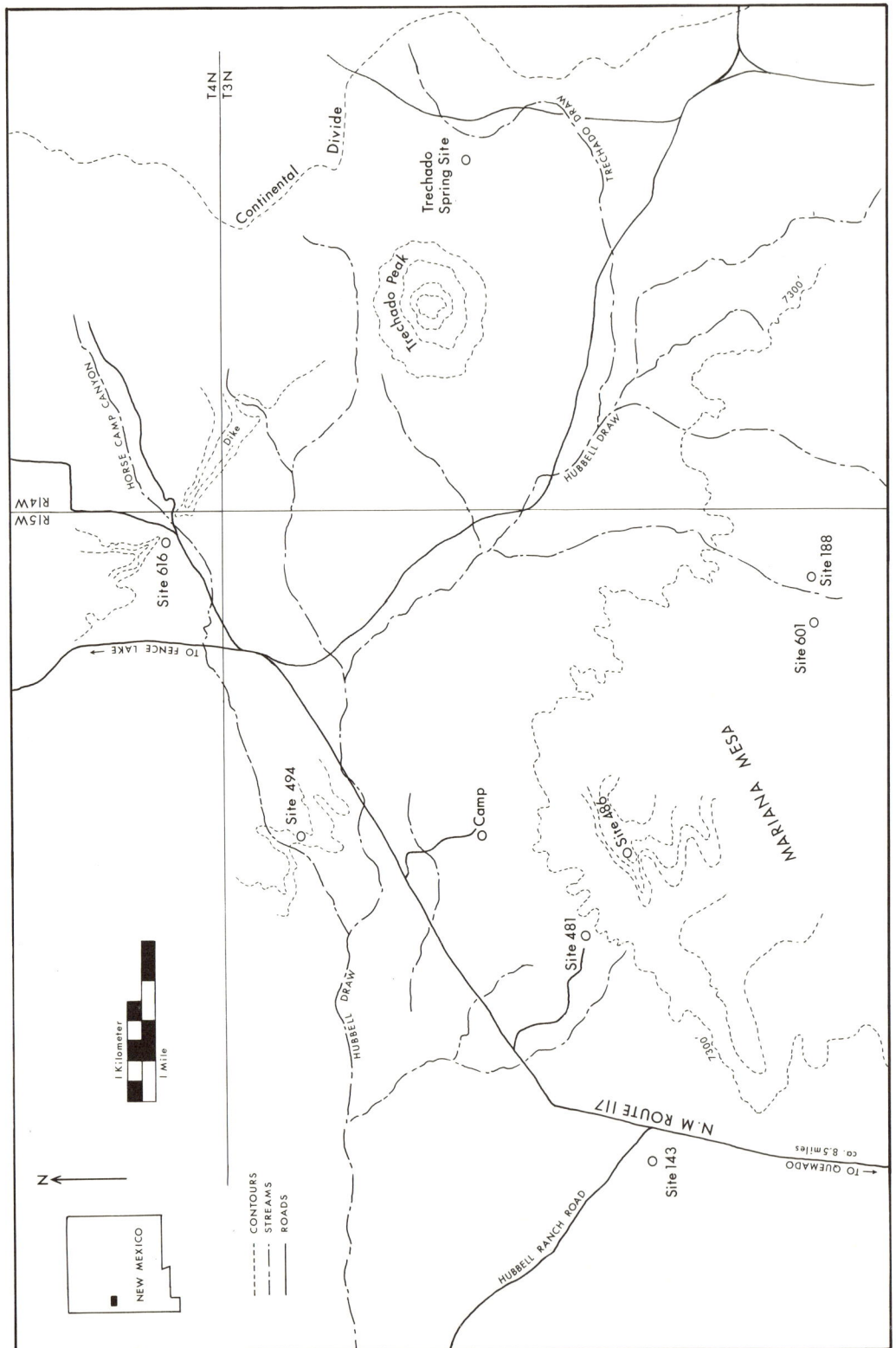

Figure 5. Map of the Mariana Mesa area.

ships with other groups at varying distances from Mariana Mesa were not considered a luxury by the inhabitants, but were an absolute necessity if normal material standards of daily living were to be maintained. Another factor suggesting the extent of intergroup communication over broad areas of the Southwest is the spread and adoption of styles of pottery decoration. The abstraction and crystallization of these transitory traits as regional time-space pottery types have enabled archaeologists working in the area to place sites relative to others over a wide area, within amazingly fine temporal limits.

At Site 486 and the earliest structures at Site 481, each family presumably occupied a single house independent of its neighbors. At Site 486 the ground was cleared and the floor area excavated slightly. The walls had a lava-cobble masonry base and possibly a form of jacal upper structure, but we have little evidence of the latter. At Site 188 the preparation of the floor area was similar, but here the walls were of jacal with only a line of lava cobbles placed at the base rather than any real cobble masonry. However, at this site we see the first evidence for contiguous-room construction, a design feature that became universally adopted in the area subsequent to this period. At Site 188 the two contiguous rooms possibly belonged to the same family, but at other, later, sites the increased size of these contiguous-roomed structures indicates that different, though perhaps related, family groups constructed their houses immediately adjacent to one another (Dean 1969, pp. 139–143, 148–150, 191). The occupants of Pithouse 1 and the other pithouses at Site 481, as well as the first arrivals at Site 494, continued to adhere to an earlier tradition of somewhat deeper floor excavation. At Site 481 the walls of the early subterranean rooms were still of wood and adobe, but the first occupants of Site 494 had made the transition to lava-cobble masonry. Unless the walls of Site 601 were extensively robbed of stone, at least some of the rooms of this pueblo were of combined masonry and jacal construction. At least two rooms at this site, which could represent temporary storage areas, were entirely of jacal with a row of cobbles at the base, resembling those at Site 188, while the last rooms built appear to have had walls entirely of lava-cobble masonry. In no case did the builders excavate the floor area of rooms at Site 601.

The period during which these early sites were occupied reflects the final stages of a widespread architectural transition from excavated pithouses with jacal walls to surface rooms with masonry walls. This transition was not an orderly one. In the long view we can say that the floors were excavated less and less while wall construction changed progressively from jacal, to combined jacal and cobble masonry, later to lava-cobble masonry, and finally to sandstone (or at Site 616, adobe) extending to full height. In house design there was a progression from scattered individual units to units of contiguous rooms, and finally to the amalgamation of these independent multiple-room units into a single large structure. As is evident from the descriptions that follow, each pueblo responded to these trends in an individual manner.

With the construction of the final surface rooms of Site 494 and the first surface rooms of Site 481 and Site 616, the region entered a new period of architectural development, primarily involving variations in stone size and materials for constructing the walls and the care with which this material was placed. As seen at Site 481 the masonry styles progressed from walls of lava cobbles, set in no discernible courses through somewhat irregularly coursed lava masonry and similarly treated sandstone blocks, to a well-coursed regular sandstone-block style. Throughout the sequence many of the walls at both Site 494 and Site 481 had a single basal layer of larger lava boulders. An interesting feature of the double-faced wall construction at these sites is that the interior face was consistently constructed of smaller cobbles than those used for the exterior.

Wall styles changed. A new style always appeared on the exterior face of the double wall. On a later wall that style would appear on the inside face, being replaced on the outside face of that wall by a subsequent style. At Site 616 the inhabitants first constructed walls resembling those at Site 494 and Site 481, but this group soon shifted to adobe bricks and used this material almost exclusively until the introduction of well-coursed sandstone-block masonry for the construction of outside walls and, in rare instances, interior walls.

The compass orientation of the room walls at all the later sites (Sites 494, 481, 143, and 616) was approximately the same. They were not oriented north–south but rather on lines roughly 30° west of north, and 30° north of east.

At Site 486 and the early rooms at Site 481, outdoor firepits may have been used almost exclusively, but later were returned to their earlier position in or near the center of the room floors. The outside firepits were generally circular and lined with sandstone slabs. At Site 481 these exterior firepits had a subsidiary ashpit in the center of the firepit. This pit was covered with a sandstone slab and probably served to store coals overnight. At Hawikuh, there were some firepits with circular ashpits in their bottoms (Smith, Woodbury, and Woodbury 1966, p. 56). At first the interior firepits, unlike the exterior ones, consisted of simple rectangular pits excavated into the floors of rooms, but later these also were slab-lined. With the exception of the southern firepit in Room 6, none of the interior firepits at Site 481 had the auxiliary hole in the floor. This was a feature primarily associated with outdoor firepits. At Site 616 one interior firepit was also so equipped (Room D1). Site 481 and 486 had one octagonal firepit each.

At Sites 494 and 481 were the first indications of permanent mealing bins, a feature found in all areas of Site 616. At Site 616 about half of the rooms with firepits also had a single mealing bin. At this site there were also special rooms set aside for grinding, which contained from three to five bins.

Only the later sites had kivas clearly in association. If Sites 188 and 486 were temporary farming communities, this might explain the absence of kivas there. However, Site 601 appears to have been permanently occupied and, except for the circular depression of dubious significance, there are no indications that a kiva was present.

The white-slipped pottery appeared to have been made locally, for it displayed certain local variations of the regional time-space pottery traditions of form, finish, and decoration. Throughout the early part of the period with which we are concerned, the white-slipped pottery of Mariana Mesa was better polished than contemporary pottery made elsewhere. Similarly, the tendency noted in other areas, for the exterior of bowls to be unslipped and for the slip of all vessels to be very thinly applied (e.g., the Escavada-Gallup-Chaco Black-on-white pottery sequence to the north), which became more prominent around Mariana Mesa at Sites 188 and 601, never really got a foothold at Site 616 at that time or subsequently. In later times the tendency for white-slipped pottery to be made in the form of jars almost to the exclusion of other forms is notable.

Except for three sherds found on the surface of Site 486, black-on-red pottery did not appear in the area until the time Site 494 was occupied. It was relatively rare at both Site 494 and Site 481 but was quite popular at Site 616. At all sites the bowl was by far the dominant form of this pottery, with only a few jars and occasional ladles being found. The forms, the diversity of decorative handling, and other factors suggested that this type of pottery may largely have been traded into the area, probably from sites to the west and northwest.

Wide clapboard-corrugated pottery was found only at Sites 486 and 188, but the narrow clapboard-corrugated types were found at all sites. The indented-corrugated style first appeared at Site 188, but here and at Site 601 the indentations were large and occurred only on pottery with wide bands. Vessels with fine corrugations over their entirety first occurred at Site 494, when wide-band, corrugated pottery disappeared entirely. Apparently indented-corrugated pottery reached Mariana Mesa a little later than the Red Mesa area to the north reported by Gladwin (1945, pp. 59–65), that is, if it is assumed that the white-slipped decorative tradition — the main basis for the local dating — developed contemporaneously in the two areas. Corrugated pottery of material mode keys (I) — dense gray paste with angular opaque inclusions — and (J) — gray paste with coarse sand inclusions — appeared to be much more prominent in the early sites (although the samples were small) and vessels of these materials almost disappeared in the later sites. There was a high correlation between these materials and vessels with wide-band corrugation and large indentations.

In all sites about two-thirds of the plainware vessels were well finished, while the other one-third were rough, gritty, and generally not so well made. Plainware decreased rapidly in popularity. It had been the preferred ware in the early sites but was almost absent at Site 616. At Sites 486, 188, and 601 plainware was almost exclusively in the form of jars, with the bowl form quite rare. At Site 494 and all sites occupied subsequently, there was a sharp reduction in the actual and proportional quantity of plainware, and a direct reversal occurred. The bowl was now nearly the sole form constructed, with plainware jars almost nonexistent. This shift correlated with the introduction of indented-corrugated jars, which replaced the plain jars almost entirely and rather abruptly. Most plain and corrugated bowls were intentionally smudged on the interior; and this feature on vessels of all sites excavated around Mariana Mesa seems to be established here comparatively early.

The most drastic break in the ceramic continuity at Mariana Mesa occurred between the occupation of Site 601 and that of Site 494. It was at this latter site that red-slipped pottery and indented-corrugated pottery were introduced and the manufacture of plain jars was almost discontinued. Despite this, it seems unlikely that any great span of time separated the two sites.

The changes noted in stone artifacts in the 350 year history of Mariana Mesa under consideration were not numerous. Manos at first were short and used on trough metates. The transition from this style of grinding to the large manos and slab metates first occurred at Site 188. Slab metates became more numerous at Site 601 and thereafter were the principal type employed. The introduction of the longer manos came shortly after slab metates first appeared. Manos with a cross section other than rectangular did not appear in any number until the occupation of Site 616, when metates began to be consistently placed in bins.

Metates may have been considered unusually important over and above their strict utilitarian nature. For one thing, usable metates were almost never left

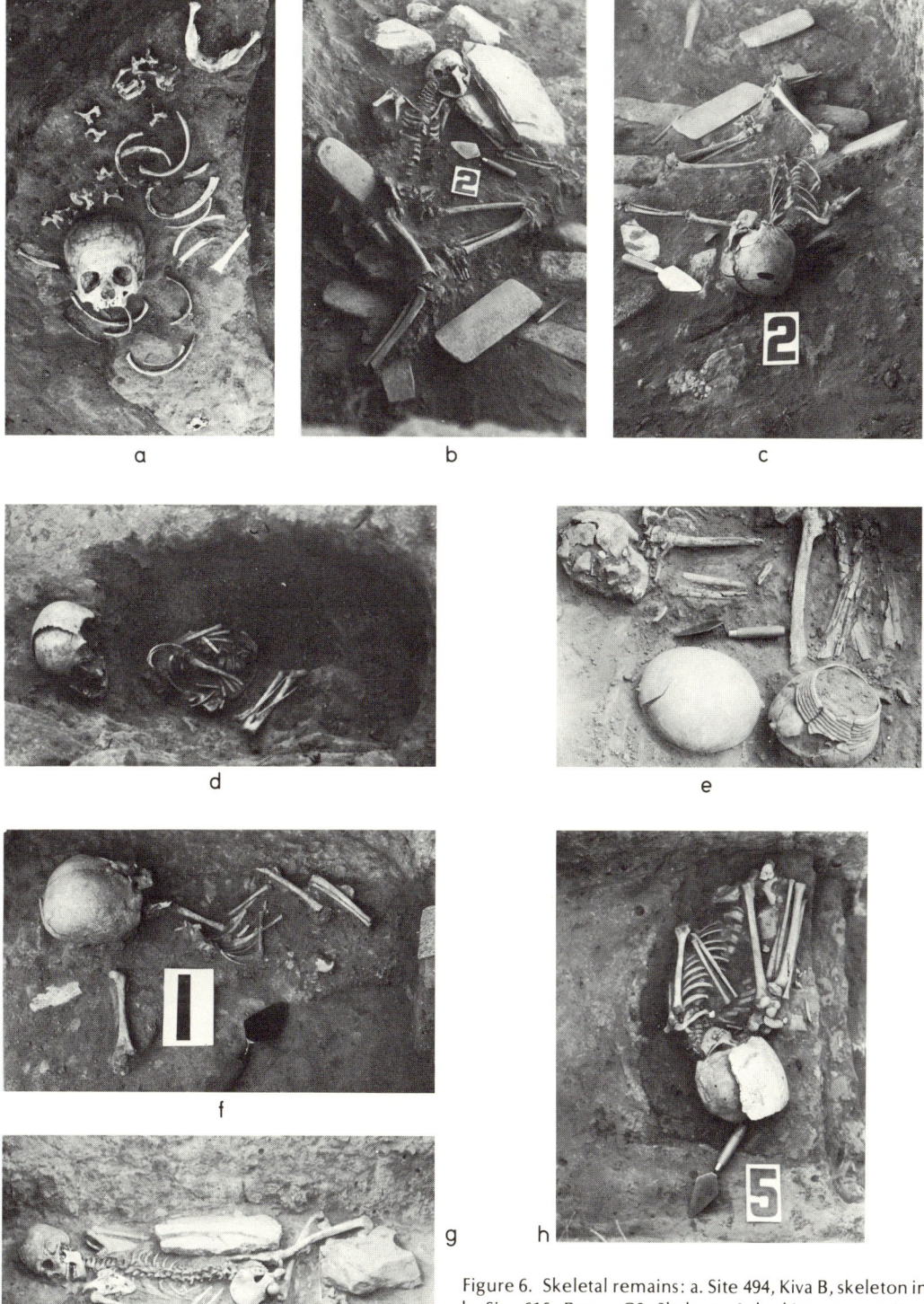

Figure 6. Skeletal remains: a. Site 494, Kiva B, skeleton in fill; b. Site 616, Room C2, Skeleton 2, looking east; c. Site 616, Room C2, Skeleton 2, looking west; d. Site 494, Room B6, burial against west wall; e. burial south of Site 143; f. Site 616, walk-in well, Skeleton 1; g. Site 616, Room E1, Skeleton 4; h. Site 616, walk-in well, Skeleton 5 in east wall of mealing room.

behind when a site was abandoned. At some sites, both at Mariana Mesa and elsewhere in the Southwest, no metates at all, other than small fragments, have been found, even though a reasonable quantity of other major categories of stone implements remained. Secondly, at Site 616 the mealing bins alone appear to have been deliberately destroyed, and in Rooms D2 and C9, for example, it appears that a definite attempt was made to carry away the metates, although a great quantity of nearly every other type of material was left behind — despite the fact that much of this other material represented a considerably greater investment of time in its manufacture, and was more readily transportable than the metates.

On axes at Site 616 the ratio of poll height to total height appears to have remained constant, which does not seem to be the case at the other sites; and the action type of an axe at these sites evidently differed from that at Site 616. The contours of the earlier axes were slightly different, the most notable variation being the upsloping groove on axes from Sites 494 and 481 — that is, the groove at the handle end was farther from the cutting edge than the groove at the opposite end of the axe.

No temporal change was observable in bone artifacts. With rare exceptions (e.g., the serrated scraper at Site 481) the bone tools from all sites fell well within the range of tools from Site 616. The few exceptions probably reflected little more than the incompleteness of the Site 616 sample. Changes in frequency of tools or variations in tool design could not be determined because of the small sample size from most sites. Similarly, the absence of certain types of bone artifacts from the earlier sites is not significant. However, proportionately, bone tools appeared as frequently at the earlier sites as at the later ones.

Few deliberate burials were located but they were representative of nearly the entire time span. The earliest was that south of Site 143, later in date was the one from Site 494, while those at Site 616 represented the latest part of the period. All the deliberate burials had been placed on their side in a flexed position and, with the exception of one of those south of the camp, all had been placed with the head to the north or northwest. Generally, pottery was in immediate association. Both corrugated and black-on-white vessels, but not redwares, were found with burials. (Could this be a further indication that redwares were traded in and were foreign?) It is considered unlikely that the adolescent skeleton in Room C2 of Site 616 and the young adult skeleton found in Room E1 of Site 616 represent deliberate burials, primarily because of the circumstances in which the bodies were found, but also because these two differed from the pattern of burial for the area.

Throughout the history of Mariana Mesa there had been a tendency for the sites to become larger, and for individual house groups to become both larger and more closely associated. It is a widespread condition discernible over a considerable area in the Southwest, and doubtless was completely independent of any factors related to possible danger of attack.

With the exception of Site 616, all sites excavated apparently were carefully stripped of usable artifacts after abandonment. The architectural layouts of Site 616 and Trechado Spring (fig. 9) were such that they could have been defensive in nature and possibly were so planned. Pressure from outside groups may have been responsible for the period of rapid population increase at Site 616, an increase which perhaps caused the shift of populations of both Sites 143 and 481 to Site 616. Perhaps the introduction of sandstone-block masonry, the presence of a large-stone-exterior-face-with-small-stone-interior-face double wall in Room C10 (p. 45) — almost the only occurrence of this feature at Site 616 — the elongated rooms (Rooms C5 and C10), and the presence of a few firepits with a central auxiliary hole reflected the addition of a group from Site 481; for at that site these features all had been frequent just prior to abandonment but were otherwise absent at Site 616.

The abandonment of Site 616 may well have been under duress, as a result of pressure from either alien groups or other related groups forced to become more than normally mobile and aggressive because of a gradually deteriorating agricultural situation. The latter possibility is considered the more likely one, at least for this particular part of the Mariana Mesa area, and is more fully discussed on pages 38–42. In any event, shortly after the departure of the inhabitants from Site 616, the entire region apparently became virtually deserted.

A Methodological Approach to the Past: The Descriptive Type

PREFATORY NOTE

Depending upon one's perspective, 20 years can be a long or a short period of time. Since in my case it is four-fifths of my professional life, a review of the original report of the Mariana Mesa excavations, in the form of my doctoral dissertation, more than 20 years after it had been written, has been, to say the least, an interesting and in some ways an educational experience.

Except for certain descriptive sections, I completed my dissertation at Harvard in late 1954, though it was not officially submitted until the fall of 1957 when I returned from three years' field research in Panama. In 1970, through the courtesy of Philip Phillips, who made his studio in Bolton, Massachusetts, available to me for a month, I renewed my acquaintance with it. Unfortunately for my dissertation, however, the bulk of that time was occupied in completing an entirely different manuscript, later published as *Public Archeology* (1972).

That brief revisit, however, was a revealing one, and much of what I felt then I still feel even after another brief period of reacquaintance (made possible by Douglas Schwartz and the School of American Research in Sante Fe in 1976). As a result, this report is being published essentially as it was originally written in 1954, except for some clarification, occasional elaboration (e.g., the sections on dating and additional problem types), and seemingly endless corrections.

The facts have not changed and there is, therefore, no reason to revise the basic data, that is, the site or artifact descriptions, which, in reality, form the bulk of the report. Nor do the intrasite interpretations need to be revised. Regional comparisons, which were minimal to begin with, might well bear some rethinking, but I am ill-prepared to do this. I believe those who have maintained their familiarity with the Southwest, which I have not, can relate, with relative ease, the facts presented in this volume without benefit of advice from one who now must be considered an outsider. As a measure of change and the advancement of knowledge over the past 25 years, this report therefore might make an interesting document for reviewers.

Review of this introductory chapter has been even more interesting for a variety of reasons. For one thing, it serves to throw certain shadows on the essentialness of any one individual's contributions to a profession. In a sense, however, it also reveals the reverse, the necessity for strong statements by individuals which, for whatever combination of reasons, serve to help redirect a profession — and without which change could be inordinately slow.

It seems to me that the present report, both in a negative and in a very minor positive way, is illustrative of these points. The ideas expressed in this chapter were not newly created by me, though at the time of writing I thought that the particular combination of some of them had not been expressed in detail before. Yet, without anyone else's having read my dissertation, most of these ideas and their combinations are more or less commonplace now. In short, with respect to most of my crystallization or "innovative contributions," I was serving simply as one among many voices of my time — a sobering thought.

I have observed the phenomenon of individuals crystallizing current thinking (though on much more general and important levels) on at least two other occasions. I entered the field of anthropology in the fall of 1947. A year later Taylor's *A Study of Archeology* (1948) was published and within the next two years became the topic of considerable discussion, with its author being regarded as the originator of a whole new trend in archaeological thinking. Frankly, for some time I could not understand what the discussions were all about. Taylor had simply said what all my professors had been saying in all my courses in archaeology. So, what was new? It was not until I had had an opportunity to do fairly extensive reading in graduate school, and thus to develop a bit of historical perspective, that I began to realize what had happened.

Not that the ideas Taylor was presenting were so new or innovative in the context of the time. Most persons, or at least many, in the field were thinking and acting in much the same way. Taylor's contribution, and it was a useful one, is appropriate especially to archaeology, for it can be appreciated only in a temporal context. It presented, in a crystallized version, much of the then current thought; and was remarkable (and remarked upon) primarily because, as a total statement, it was in some contrast to the general tenor of much, but not all, thought of a generation earlier.

The so-called new archaeology is another case in point. In detail there seems little that is startlingly new about it, to me or to most of my peers or even to many of those of earlier generations. Yet the writings of Binford and others do constitute a pulling together of many individual ideas in a way that has served to focus the profession's attention on them. They have created healthy discussion and to some degree a redirection of, or at least a new emphasis on, certain areas by a larger segment of the profession.

No such major recrystallization was being attempted here. In a minor way, I was trying to call for (or more accurately, make more readily achievable by demonstrating a methodology) the investigation of all aspects of culture through the establishment of a more flexible descriptive base for the typological concept. The main ideas had already been voiced by Brew, Taylor, and others, and were subsequently reemphasized and somewhat redirected by Binford and the "new archaeologists."

Similarly, the essential role of problem formulation, now called research design, which then still seemed to need emphasis, happily has, to a considerable degree, taken its proper place in normal archaeological field and laboratory procedures.

I am not certain of the extent to which the presumed need for first resolving time-space problems, as a logical prerequisite to resolving *all* other problems, has been overcome, largely because it is not specifically discussed in much of the current literature. Nevertheless, the current emphasis on non-time-space problems seems to provide, if anything, an even more impressive break from earlier approaches.

The other side of the coin seems to be the unfortunate fact that a number of ideas discussed herein, though not necessarily new even when I presented them at the time of writing the dissertation, apparently still need to be emphasized, some 25 years later.

One such idea, though it certainly has seen progress in archaeological practice, is the continuing need for developing archaeological analogy (with resulting hypotheses and testing) based on solid ethnographic data, in order to improve upon the essential correlations between human behavior and artifact forms, distributions, and associations. This area of concern and its application to all phases of human endeavor, past and present, provides one of the core elements for the future development of archaeology as a scientific discipline.

Perhaps most disappointing to me is the apparent necessity of continuing to point out the shortcomings of the single-problem typological method for the basic description and presentation of complicated archaeological data. Brew admirably expressed the problem in 1948, yet even now, 30 years later, it has not been adequately addressed. The progress made in this area seems to have come about almost accidentally through experimentation with computerization of data. I still believe, 25 years after writing it, that the "descriptive type" approach proposed here offers a particularly fruitful way of meeting the problem. In this connection, it should be noted that while most of the report stands as written in 1951 to 1954, the analyses represented by the artisan and intrasite distribution types, which perhaps serve to illustrate further the application of the descriptive type concept, were done in the 1970s. These analyses, however, simply follow up leads that had been noted in 1954, but had not been developed then because of limited time. Interestingly, because of the descriptive type method of presenting the basic data, it was possible to carry out this additional and more detailed analysis without further reference to the potsherds themselves.

Perhaps it is necessary to comment that the descriptive type, properly employed, represents in no sense a return to an emphasis on purely descriptive archaeology. Far from it. Instead it provides a mechanism whereby archaeology can handle description in such a manner that it becomes possible to concentrate on the resolution of a wide range of various problems that are determined to be crucial to the profession. Effective utilization of the descriptive type requires that problems be thought through in advance of the field and the laboratory research, and thus be incorporated in a research design. Only by doing this, will the necessary descriptive attributes be observed in adequate detail and embodied in the final descriptive types. These attributes will then be available for combination and recombination into different specific problem-oriented typological sets, as may be appropriate for diverse problems like culture history, recognition and interpretation of socially interacting groups, and the analysis of functional activities.

I feel that the remainder of this chapter — basically unchanged except for minor editorial clarification of what I wrote nearly 25 years ago — also has a certain interest for what it can tell us, both positively and negatively, about the progress of our profession. Perhaps others will agree.

I also hope that it will serve to introduce and bring into more widespread use the concept of the descriptive type as a basic analytical tool.

ARCHAEOLOGICAL DATA

Most sciences gain their individuality through the nature of the problems and data with which they primarily concern themselves, and join the community of science through the utilization of the resultant information for the establishment of general principles. The science of archaeology is delineated by its investigation and determination of those cultural aspects of human history which, for whatever reason, did not receive or have not received adequate written or oral documentation. It is firmly united with anthropology and the social sciences through the utilization of the data derived from this study for the formulation of general postulates and principles relevant to the study of culture. Whether by so doing an archaeologist is transmuted into an anthropologist or social scientist is a terminological consideration of minor significance. The important point is the basic orientation of the individual investigator and of his reports toward these more general theoretical considerations.

It is commonly recognized that the cultural remains available to archaeology are limited and that, as a result, archaeology is unable to reconstruct completely the undocumented past. This, quite naturally, limits the areas of culture theory to which the results of archaeology can pertain. Such data-imposed restrictions are disheartening, however, only if the inclusion of archaeology, ethnology, and social anthropology under the rubric "cultural anthropology" is taken to mean that all must provide information of an identical nature. When it is recognized that each provides a certain portion of the total data required for the attainment of the communally defined goals, it becomes easier to outline the general area of archaeology's contribution as this is affected by the nature of its data. For the purpose of determining the interpretative potential of archaeology, the discussion of the total data of cultural anthropology can be categorized into the nonmaterial and the material aspects of culture, and the static and the dynamic aspects of that material.

The division between nonmaterial and material culture is, in a sense, a somewhat arbitrary and unempirical one. The distinction generally appears to be drawn on the basis of facility of perception by more than one person and relative degree of permanence. That is, those phenomena which either cannot be experienced by more than one person (e.g, ideas and concepts as such) or do not maintain a relatively stable and continuously observable form (e.g., interpersonal behavior) are generally designated as "nonmaterial." Relative to archaeology, the nonmaterial aspect of culture can be defined as that portion of culture which exists in the minds of the cultural participants and is exemplified by their behavior toward one another or toward the nonhuman environment. This definition closely conforms to the one generally adopted by cultural anthropologists for application to ethnographic situations although, in point of fact, a specific exemplification of mother-in-law avoidance, for instance, is as material a phenomenon as an exemplification of an axe. Be that as it may, the important point in this discussion is that archaeological data can yield information pertaining to nonmaterial culture only where the ideas and behavior patterns have modified the surviving nonhuman environment, and only insofar as the relationship between the material form and the "nonmaterial" behavior or ideas affecting that form have been adequately conceptualized and documented. A surprisingly large number of human actions affect in one way or another the nonhuman material contexts in which they occur, and presumably a large portion of this influence has a patterned relationship with the initiating action, so that the field of archaeological interpretation is not necessarily so restricted in this regard as it seems at first. Unfortunately the existence and extent of the patterned relationships between behavioral actions and those material forms generally available to archaeologists have seldom been subjects of major research. Even observers of living cultures upon whom the initial theoretical formulations must in large part depend have neglected this area. Until more work has been done along these lines, the areas of culture open to archaeological investigations will continue to be unduly restricted.

Material culture consists of the relatively permanent concrete manifestations affected by or resulting from the ideas and behavior of individuals or groups of individuals. The amount and variety of material culture preserved is the basic determinant of the possible extent and nature of archaeological reconstruction and interpretation. The nature of, and conditions attendant upon, this preservation have been dealt with repeatedly and need not be discussed here. Perhaps we should note that the preserved material permits extensive inferences as to the probable ephemeral existence of units and aspects of material culture other than those preserved, so that the potential scope of archaeological interpretation extends considerably beyond the actual physical remains.

Archaeological data (from the point of view of most anthropological problems) are, by their very nature, relatively static, a situation almost unique in the social sciences. They are also no longer subject to continuing manipulation and modification by their cultural creators — a feature that often complicates the work of other social scientists, necessitating recordings and photographs when they are dealing with problems related to static data. Archaeological data, at least ideally, move or are moved only through the action of natural agencies or by the archaeologist himself.

The units of preserved material culture and the static spatial relationships of these units are the two basic aspects of archaeological data. That is, they are the only two aspects available to the immediate sense awareness of the analyst. While only the units themselves and the spatial relationships of units are directly observable, the principles necessary to infer certain time relationships from the nature of the material units and their spatial relations are well advanced both in archaeology and in other sciences (e.g., stratigraphy, dendrochronology, and Carbon 14 analysis). Consequently, archaeological interpretations have become increasingly possible in problem areas where knowledge of temporal relations is essential.

Archaeology shares with all historically oriented sciences the inability to observe directly any dynamic relationship and is further restricted in that, except for historical archaeology, it cannot avail itself of any recorded observations of these relationships (though fortunately, there are often records of *presumably* analogous ones). However, it does not follow that archaeological data are completely without value to a study of cultural dynamics. The nature of many dynamic relationships is validly and often more efficiently inferred through an analysis of their concomitant static relationships. Nonetheless, while dynamics form a part of the direct *observations* of a science of contemporary matters, they can form only an inferred and comparatively small portion of the *results* of archaeological analysis. While this is true, it must be emphasized that the relative degree of validity existing between archaeological interpretations and contemporary observations, or inferences drawn from either concerning cultural dynamics, is not absolute, but depends upon many factors. Recorded observations of a process are generally more reliable than inferences relative to that process derived from observation of its static elements; but this is not always so, particularly when the inferences are made by an observer with a more complete control of the relevant data. For example, detailed and perceptive accounts by scientifically trained observers of nineteenth-century Polynesian cultures often attributed to those cultures material and nonmaterial traits and characteristics which were sometimes refuted by archaeological and historical reconstruction.

Most if not all interpretations of archaeological materials depend, for their inspiration, on the similarity of the data to particulars or processes observed by or known to the investigator, or reconstructed on the basis of theories developed by related sciences. Insofar as such interpretations are derived from solidly based generalizations, they can be used in the analysis of other problems. But great caution must be exercised that they not be used as a means for "proving" the initial generalizations. The incipient circularity is obvious. On the other hand, such analysis may serve as an extra check on an initial generalization by demonstrating that it (the initial generalization) appears to remain valid in an additional context; i.e., correct or incorrect, the generalization maintains contextual congruity. Similarly, when several diverse theories suggest interpretations of the data in a corroborative manner, the probability of the validity of the reconstruction, and of the theories, is enhanced. Worldwide ethnological studies provided just such checks on the general theories proposed by early anthropologists based on the few cultural contexts then known to them; and often failure of the original theories to maintain effective congruity in newly observed cultures caused those theories to be drastically revised or even abandoned. Archaeological studies provide a similar check on anthropological theories that profess to be effective over time as well as space.

In sum, the broadest principles of anthropology must eventually be applicable over space, time, and varying culture contexts. Essentially the unique contributions of archaeology to anthropological knowledge lie in the realm of extending the temporal dimension. Thus, together with ethnology and social anthropology, archaeology establishes an ever widening range of cultural content and context, against which general principles may be checked and from which they can be formulated. (In addition — although this is not the place to discuss the point — perhaps a case also can be made for the philosophical and psychological value of knowledge *per se* concerning what has gone before.) Obviously the areas of culture theory to which archaeology can contribute are directly proportional to the scope and precision of the cultural context that it is able to reconstruct. Thus, reconstruction of synchronic and diachronic contexts must be the archaeologist's *modus operandi* but should never constitute his ultimate goal.

The methodological assumptions and concepts essential to an accurate and efficient reconstruction of this broad cultural context involve an understanding of the basic analytical techniques of selection, description, and subsequent manipulation of data as they pertain to archaeology.

Selection

The human mind is totally incapable of perceiving all of nature through immediate sense awareness, and in fact does not completely perceive more than a small portion of what it is capable of apprehending. The mind is and must be constantly selective. In general an observer tends to perceive only those aspects of those units that have or are thought to have pertinence to himself or his problems. Thus only a small segment of what the eye perceives obtrudes upon the mind of the observer in a meaningful way.

A conchologist upon seeing a shell may perceive certain features (that is, abstract them from the total features of the object) and in this manner identify the shell as a freshwater specimen, while a scientist trained in another field, attempting to describe "completely" that same shell, might record several pages of data and yet never "see" the particular features that served to categorize it so neatly and promptly for the conchologist. The conchologist knew what features to look for in relation to his formulation of the problem. It is a truism that we see only what we look for.

The material of archaeology is scanty and we are obligated to utilize it to the fullest. Only by so doing will archaeology be able to make anything approaching its potential contribution to science as a whole. Paradoxically, this cannot be accomplished by consciously or unconsciously attempting everything. The problem areas must be outlined in detail, the particular problems to be investigated chosen, and, in the light of this, the material scientifically observed and analyzed so that the resultant interpretations will justify the time, money, and energy expended in obtaining them.

At times "problem-oriented research" has seemed in danger of typifying by implication and connotation a particular research approach which we can approve or disapprove, carry out or ignore. This implication is unfortunate in view of the fact that problem orientation and scientific analytical research are almost synonymous.

It is even less feasible to describe a unit completely than it is to observe it completely. When the selection of factors to be described is unconscious or poorly organized, it is likely to be, in a sense, inefficient (that is, while the mind is conditioned in its perception by its background, these selective responses are apt to be inappropriately applied). Intelligent selection of factors to be observed and described can be only in terms of their actual or hypothesized significance to a particular problem, whether it be a problem of earning a living, driving a car, or establishing the contemporaneity of two archaeological sites. No "fact" or observation has inherent significance; its significance is wholly determined by its relationship to a problem or problems.

When defined in these terms it is unlikely that many would actually deny the inevitable "problem orientation" of all research. When objections to problem orientation are raised, the speaker generally is rejecting, justifiably, the narrow channeling of observations in the field and during analysis along lines of limited interest or preconceived theoretical assumptions. This situation might better be termed misdirected problem orientation. Problem orientation should never act as a blinder. The competent field and laboratory investigator is always receptive to new and unexpected data concerning both problem and observation. Indeed, it is rarely possible to predict completely what factors will be significant to a problem before observation and analysis. The worker must always search for additional significant factors as analysis proceeds, for that is often the first and only time that they become apparent. This might even entail restructuring the problem as it was initially stated. On the other hand, disdain for limited receptivity, or disapproval of narrowly defined problem orientation and analysis, can never provide tenable ground for neglecting the careful definition and delineation of the problem that the researcher himself is investigating. (This delineation is, in itself, a problem.) Some basis, conscious or unconscious, for the selection of features to be observed and described is inevitable. Only insofar as this is recognized and selection consciously directed will observation and analysis avoid being haphazard, inefficient, and incomplete.

Anyone observing a culture in action is speedily made aware of the need for selective description because of the obvious impossiblity, despite the desirability, of even approximating a description of the total flux of culture; but the archaeologist in the field is perhaps less aware of this limitation. Relatively speaking, so little data are available to the archaeologist that it is easy to assume that observation of all significant features is a practical possibility. This situation has perhaps encouraged a tendency to systematize and stabilize observations into set patterns, without regard to the specific problems that these observations are intended to solve. The assumption is often made that one system, if properly designed, will be adequate for all problems. Debate generally has revolved around the nature and makeup of such a system rather than the nature and validity of the assumptions and problems underlying its construction and use. This tendency, I believe, remains with us despite exhortations against it (e.g., Brew 1946, pp. 50-58). We continue, in our reports, to present our observed data via a single typological scheme.*

*It has now (1977) become popular to subdivide types into varieties and varieties into subvarieties, and so on *ad infinitum* (e.g., Wheat, Gifford, and Wasley 1958). While the type-variety concept does have value in that it provides for finer subdivisions of analytical control, it nonetheless remains

Anyone who, with some particular problem in mind, has had occasion to check the reports of even the most competent and astute observers has quickly realized that all significant features were not and indeed could not have been recorded. Unless the report has undertaken the analysis of the particular problem in the same form in which the reader conceives it, the necessary data may have been stated in insufficient detail, and, more than likely, were not even recorded in the field notes.

While detailed problem analysis has often been neglected, at least as a basis for establishing initial observations and descriptions, we occasionally find an overemphasis on problem orientation of a more general nature. One of the most generally accepted criteria in archaeology for determining which features should be observed has been that of their "historical significance." Such a problem orientation is at once too broad and too specific. Almost every characteristic of every cultural unit no doubt has significance for some aspect of historical reconstruction, if we were but aware of it, so that little guidance in the determination of characteristics to be observed is provided by this concept. In practice, however, "historical significance" usually refers to those observations pertinent to the problem area of broad-scale temporal ordering and/or cultural relationships of sites. There is no question that this constitutes a valid problem area; on the other hand, it is by no means the only problem area with which archaeology must concern itself.

It was overemphasis on such "historical" problems (and the occasional implication that they were the only proper ones) that probably instigated Taylor's searching review of American archaeology as practiced up to 1946. The overall program of archaeological endeavor that Taylor outlines is quite complete. But in practice, at least as recommended in *A Study of Archeology* (1948), he appears to overstress the importance of the identification of classificatory groups that were significant to the cultural participants who created the material. While this may have been simply overemphasis for effect, it unfortunately leaves the impression that he disregards the important information to be gained from the study of units and types that have been conceptualized by the investigator for their known or hypothesized ability to help answer certain questions. For example, he says that an archaeologist "should try to make his systematic creations [and his typologies are just that] conform to those of the former culture." (Taylor 1948, p. 130).

Whether intended or not, such a statement implies that typological discriminations recognized by the cultural participants are the only categories properly significant to archaeology and anthropology, and further, that the archaeologist can recognize or determine the classificatory standards of the cultural participants when, in fact, they can be inferred only with greater or lesser assurance.

Phillips, Ford, and Griffin (1951, pp. 63-64), in discussing this particular subdivision of the problem (i.e., "historical" vs. "cultural"), correctly point out that many noncultural or "empirical" types are, for the moment at least, simply working types and that as knowledge increases they can and will be redefined to more closely approximate cultural types. On the other hand, it does not follow, as they seem to imply, that the development of cultural types is the ultimate goal of all analysis, or that noncultural types are *ipso facto* working types. The discernment of types that reflect divisions recognized by the people who made or used the materials is eminently desirable and, in fact, essential to many of the most important problems of archaeology, but such types cannot be the sole or the ultimate typological goal. Other types that also approach "perfection" (defined in relation to their ability to answer questions), and are not therefore properly designated "working types," will have little or no resemblance to any type recognized by the cultural participants, because the problems to which they apply are such that it would have been unlikely or even impossible for the cultural participants to formulate or be aware of them. For example, who among us today can predict the durability of contemporary artifact styles sufficiently to abstract and conceptualize as a type that particular range or complex of artifacts that will be the chronological hallmark of United States civilization during the 1950s, 1960s, or 1970s? Yet, few would deny that the determination of chronological relationships (which necessitates chronological or time-space types) is an important problem area of archaeology.

It is interesting to speculate about the factors that may have been operative in determining the emphasis of archaeology toward broad-scale, time-space systematics. No doubt, there is a historical basis for a time-space problem orientation among archaeologists, a tendency probably encouraged by the fact that early interpretations of cultural context and process had been based on insufficient data. As the errors from this early cultural approach became increasingly evident, *any* such interpretations came to be regarded as hypothetical and unempirical. On the other hand, a minimum of detailed data often permits fairly reliable chronological interpretations of a general nature. That is, the immediate results of surface survey or

---

simply a refinement of the initial typological categorization. If the initial typological divisions were not appropriate to the study of a particular problem, no amount of additional subdividing will help.

small test excavations can often be phrased in terms of the relations between cultures and time periods. Furthermore, the time intervals generally obtained in this manner are usually assumed to be commensurate with major geographical units (e.g., culture areas) and major ethnic groups (e.g., tribes), so that coordination of the results is readily feasible. The danger, of course, is that inferences based on limited data will be phrased in such a way that they will appear to apply to more features of the culture than the nature of the data analyzed actually warrants.

Perhaps another reason for the early direction taken toward time-space analysis and the emphasis on chronology is related to the nature of the temporal factor itself. The absolute spans of time and those particularly pertinent to archaeological problems (i.e., days, seasons, years) are universal. Therefore, any indications of temporal context, however obtained, are immediately applicable to a wide variety of problems and diverse cultural contexts. The initial emphasis on chronicle also may be related in part to the linguistic and cultural orientation of the investigators. That is, until a worker operating within the framework of an Indo-European language is able temporally to correlate the material being investigated with the present or with some familiar temporal period, any description of it seems incomplete and discussion difficult. The determination of exact functional or contextual relations, while logically of equal significance to the final description and elucidation of the past, nevertheless is somewhat less urgent from this linguistic point of view. One suspects that the initial archaeological emphases might have been different had the first two generations of archaeologists been largely Navajo.

For a long time there was a certain confusion about the relation and integration of these various approaches to problem areas within archaeology (as distinct from possible historical explanations of how or why differential emphasis may have arisen). For example, there is still a feeling that the investigation of time-space systematics, as it is generally practiced, is solidly grounded in fact and basically empirical in nature (e.g., note the selection of the terms "empirical" and "cultural" types for use in opposition by Phillips, Ford, and Griffin 1951, p. 63) while, on the other hand, investigation of so-called functional problems is regarded as entirely interpretative in nature, with at best a tenuous relationship to empirical data (the sort of thing which, while fun on Sunday, is best ignored during the working week). But archaeological time relations can no more be observed than can use or function; all are inferred from the data. Since all interpretations in archaeology arise from the same basic data and are derived by similar techniques, any contention that one particular problem orientation has a more empirical basis than any other cannot be validated.

It is still true, however, that the premises and assumptions utilized in the interpretation of the basic data for problems of time-space systematics have been thought through in greater detail and have been tested in a wider range of circumstances. Consequently, their validity, as well as the cause and extent of variation, is understood with greater clarity and accuracy. Quite possibly, this presently unbalanced situation cannot be corrected completely, but the extent to which such a supposition is valid has only begun to be tested.

The impression that functional interpretations are less empirical may also arise from the fact that they often deal with aspects of nonmaterial culture, but this alone does not necessarily make them more ethereal, hypothetical, or abstract. A surge of anger or the custom of headhunting is as concrete a phenomenon as is the temporal relationship of two objects (Kroeber 1949, p. 184), and each is equally amenable (or rather neither is amenable) to direct observation by the archaeologist. It is true that in archaeology reconstructions of such nonmaterial aspects of culture are occasionally on a higher level of inference (that is, a longer chain of inference is necessary to attain the result), but this does not establish an *a priori* basis for regarding such results as less reliable. The reliability of any result must be judged solely on the basis of the probable validity and applicability of the premises and assumptions and of the data to which they are applied. Other things being equal, a longer chain of inference invokes decreased reliability, but an answer obtained through the use of three well-documented hypotheses is more likely to be correct than one reached by means of a single guess or dubious association.

In sum, one problem area is neither necessarily nor absolutely more empirical or on a lower level of abstraction than the other. The difference in reliability of results is largely traceable to the fact that, at present, the assumptions necessary to time-space systematics have been more extensively formulated and these formulations have been subjected to greater documentation and analysis than have those of others. Only further research can determine to what extent this present disparity in the reliability of assumptions and explicit principles must continue.

In a similar manner the opinion is frequently expressed that the analysis and determination of time-space coordinates are prerequisites to the study of the functional interrelationships of cultural units. Like so many generalizations this expresses only a partial truth and, if taken literally, is, in fact, in error. The problem areas of time-space systematics and contextual or processual reconstruction are not successive as wholes. It is possible to investigate either problem area without reference to the other, and generalizations on a reasonably high level can be formulated by this independent analysis. For example, it might be possible to reconstruct the entire process of grinding corn by observing mealing bins, manos, and so on, without knowing when this equipment was utilized. It would be equally possible to determine the period of their use while knowing nothing about the nature or method of this use and the processes involved. However, for either group of interpretations to obtain its greatest significance both must be used in conjunction. (It is this combined approach that Taylor recommended.) Neither area is logically esssential to the other but any attempt to proceed far along a single line of inquiry, without reference to both, can ultimately result only in erroneous or at best incomplete analysis. As a matter of fact, the separation of the two for consideration of any units larger than actual physical aggregates (e.g., individual artifacts or assemblages such as a mealing bin, whose cohesiveness as a unit can perhaps be safely assumed) is impossible except as a temporary theoretical abstraction. The discussion of larger cultural aggregates necessitates at the very least the assumption or implicaiton of contemporaneity of the included units; likewise any significant temporal ordering of units larger than individual artifacts involves ultimately the implication or assumption that clusters of units so ordered reflect or represent pertinent cultural aggregates.

On an even higher level of analysis, archaeology can formulate certain generalizations regarding man and culture with little or no reference to the findings of ethnology and physical anthropology; however, generalizations, to be meaningful and valid, must soon be coordinated with the findings of all branches of anthropology. The same relationship exists on increasingly higher levels among various disciplines and the branches of science.

Ideally it is essential that the basic data be selected and presented so that they are amenable to study and classification relative to all problem areas with which the science as a whole is concerned. Practically, however, this is impossible. The only feasible technique by which any one problem can be solved is that of carefully selecting, describing, and classifying the factors pertinent to that problem while ignoring, at least temporarily, the others. The important point is that, insofar as possible, no problem orientation should cause the analyst to select and present his data in such a manner that they cannot also be applied to the solution of other equally important problems. A historian can observe, interpret, and report on his basic documents in any way he desires regarding any particular problem but, unless he then proceeds to shred the documents, they are available to others unsullied and unbiased by any classificatory and interpretative manipulation on his part.

When an archaeologist observes, describes, and presents his data, some part of the basic information normally is destroyed just as it is during excavation. Published descriptions generally must be presented according to some taxonomic scheme, and when this scheme is based upon features pertinent to only one or a limited number of problems, then characteristics, patterns, and relationships important to other classifications and problems may be irreparably obscured. Placing the total collection on permanent deposit may make possible subsequent reexamination, but sometimes only sample collections can be preserved in museums, and even they must be arranged according to some particular (and subjective) typological classification; thus, effective restudy for the solution of other problems is difficult if not impossible. Any selection of the data to be presented must be partial, of course, just as no excavation technique can effect complete recovery, but attention must be directed to theories and methods that will facilitate recognition and presentation of those characteristics and relations having the greatest significance for the widest variety of problems. During the initial selection, description, and presentation of basic data, archaeology can ill afford a narrowly defined problem orientation.

Description

Carefully selected, accurate description is the foundation of all interpretation and one of the first tasks to confront the archaeologist both in the field and in the laboratory. Determining the factors to be described or ignored is therefore one of the most important facets of analysis.

The characteristics and relationships selected for description can be placed in one of three categories concerning the purpose for which the selection is made. The first category includes those features enabling the reader to visualize the object or situation. Many characteristics, while of little consequence for problem solution, should nonetheless be recorded to facilitate the formation of a correct image in the mind of the reader. The second category involves those features that are significant for the problems under investigation at the time. These two determinants are of primary importance for the problems examined in any one report, but when that report, and that report alone, involves a particular set of basic data, the author is under an additional obligation to describe and present, insofar as practicable, the characteristics and relations required for problems other than those considered in his own study — including those features he feels *might* prove to be of value even though that value has not yet been demonstrated. These features, extraneous to the problems under immediate consideration, yet significant for other problems an author is aware of, form the third category. In this respect it seems that Brew (1946, p. 51) has overstated his case when he observes that it is folly to attempt to "describe our material according to the needs and interests of posterity, which we cannot possibly know." Granted one cannot know the precise requirements of the future and that attempts in this direction should not become the rationale for a haphazard recording of a welter of unassorted detail (doubtless this is what Brew feared), nevertheless, an inability to predict precisely the needs of others or of the future provides small excuse for failure to make some attempt to provide for them. In addition, an author may know of other problems and their requisite observations, but decide (for any number of valid reasons) not to analyze his data with respect to those questions.

Selection and description of features in this third category obviously cannot be complete for all problems. Not only is this logically impossible, but such practical factors as time, finances, and the knowledge and procedures available to the investigator serve to limit the amount of description. Thus it is essential that the described features in this category be carefully and thoughtfully selected. In the first two categories a report should be judged for both accuracy and completeness; in the third category accuracy alone should form the main basis for critical judgment, though an assessment of the completeness is also appropriate. While it is legitimate to question an author's choice of problem(s), once it is granted that his choice is valid, he can hardly be criticized for not expending a great deal of effort describing features not specifically related to the problems with which he is concerned. On the other hand, the report can be criticized for not making a sufficient attempt to present the salient features in this third category, or for presenting new data in a manner which needlessly negates the utility of the basic data for problems other than those investigated.

We should note that when units are described for the purpose of solving more than one problem, there can be no "primary" or "secondary" features in their general description. There can be and are features that are of primary or secondary importance for one particular problem, and the same features may even maintain this relationship for several problems, but this must be demonstrated in every case and cannot be assumed. A feature that is primary for the consideration of one problem may well be secondary for another or of no significance whatsoever (e.g., while clay is perhaps primary to the technological analysis of a sherd by the ceramist, design is often primary to the problem of the dating of that sherd by the archaeologist). Naturally, one or another feature may more readily lend itself to the initial sorting of material into groups, but the order in which sorting criteria are applied is of no theoretical importance.

Few if any publications describe every artifact recovered individually, and with material like pottery any such attempt generally is impossible. Most publications resort to a technique that might be labeled "typological description," that is, individual units are described only as exemplifications or members of a particular "type." What is "described" is an idealized unit rather than any observable unit itself. In fact this technique is so prevalent that the basic distinctions between the concepts of description, typology, and classification are at times disregarded and the terms used as synonyms.

Description involves the presentation of some or "all" of the characteristics and relations of a single unit or, via typological descriptions, groups of units. Typology refers to the conceptual amalgamation of individual units into groups or types based on their relative identity with respect to one or more characteristics. These diagnostic characteristics normally are selected for and determined by their relevance to a particular problem or group of problems. Classification is the arrangement or ordering of the units or the types that constitute the data according to a definite scheme or hypothesis.

Typological description is a legitimate and in fact essential technique, but all too often initial description of archaeological field data is presented in terms of typological groups having a single or unnecessarily narrow base, while the specific problem orientation and classification scheme are frequently not even stated. As a result, the data are unalterably biased in a manner unknowable to the reader (and perhaps unknown to the writer), and only partially presented, with no basis for determining which elements of the description are diagnostic.

It must be remembered that it is appropriate to describe individual units *solely* as members of a typological group only if there are no differences between included individual units that are significant to the solution of any problem to which the units may be applied. Once a number of objects have been described only as members of a type it is no longer possible to reorient those member units with respect to nondiagnostic attributes based on the typological description alone; it is necessary physically to manipulate the material itself or else restudy complete descriptions of the individual units. Any such reclassification normally is impossible for the reader of a report, who all too often is not even provided with the classificatory basis for, or explanation of, the initial assignment of the units to the particular groups. Almost never are the diagnostic criteria (upon which units were assigned to types) set out in a report. Thus, the reader is not even in a position to judge the degree or nature of the similarity of the included units. When initial description is by typological groups, the basis for classification must be clearly stated. That is, the reader should be presented with the problems that the typology is designed to solve, the diagnostic criteria for assigning units to those typological categories, and, preferably, a discussion of the reasons for choosing those criteria.

Classification

Although the terms classification and typology are sometimes employed as if they were completely interchangeable, classification is actually the broader term and includes typology as one of its forms.

Typology involves the establishment of a theoretical basis for categorizing units of nature into groups for particular purposes. Since typology is a means of ordering data, it is thereby a classification device, but classification includes not only ordering data into groups but also placing them into sequences or other arrangements according to some hypothesis for the solution of a particular problem.

The question to which the analysis is directed will determine which attributes will be considered diagnostic and how the various attributes will be subdivided (e.g., clay type and tempering material might be diagnostic to a problem concerned with the sources of raw materials — the clays and tempering materials being broken down into subdivisions determined by the local geology — while degree of polish or vessel form would be nondiagnostic features for this particular typological classification). Once diagnostic traits are identified, units can be recognized and individual units considered together despite their individual differences. The resultant types and patterns thereby become available for whatever analysis the typology was designed to forward.

There can be no single typological basis or classificatory system according to which all data can be grouped and ordered satisfactorily for all problems. The consequences of this fact enormously complicate the presentation of thorough scientific description of the basic data. During analysis the basic data must be utilized to define any number of units, and these units must then be combined and recombined into types and ordered (classified) into various sets for the solution of the specific problems to which a particular set might pertain.

In the initial description and presentation of basic field data, the function of archaeology is to recognize and present descriptive units that will enable and facilitate the conceptual amalgamation of those basic descriptive units into type sets in such a way that the basic data can be applied to the greatest number of problems. The primary concepts involved in this task are those of the unit, the type, and the pattern.

THE UNIT

All of nature is in essence a continuum, that is, it is a continuously integrated whole. Therefore, the recognition and abstraction of any segment as a unit (e.g., a projectile point, a site, or a phase) is more or less arbitrary. Yet, it is valid and often profitable to conceive of nature as consisting of many integrated units each of which has the property of temporal and spatial existence, a specific and organized content, and a contextual position including both those units it directly affects and those directly affecting it.

Any one such unit can be thought of in terms of its smaller constituent units, and these "subunits," with their interrelations in space and time, are inherent aspects of the larger unit. Nature thus depicted becomes a complex of units variously related as wholes to parts and as joint parts within one whole.

The recognition and abstraction of any particular unit as such depends partly on its cohesiveness and partly on the cultural (including scientific) indoctrination and problem orientation of the individual observer.

The perception of a unit is never based on the nature of the entire unit and it is impossible, or at least impractical, to verbalize even for descriptive purposes all the characteristics perceived. The aspects described may be features of the nature or content of a unit itself (or subunit, e.g., an appendage), or characteristics of the unit or subunit (e.g., color), or even certain aspects of its contextual associations. Thus, for a unit to be recognizable and intelligible to a group of investigators it is essential that the characteristics by which it is isolated (the diagnostic features) be made explicit. For a unit that has a sharply defined limit of material cohesiveness, such as an axe or a house, there is generally little debate as to whether two investigators are perceiving the same total unit (though they may not be perceiving the same attributes of that unit). We can be less certain that this is the case when the unit under consideration is an archaeological phase or even a site. The verbal symbols employed by all should refer to the same attributes of the units in question. Otherwise, communication between investigators is not only difficult but actually confusing and misleading. This becomes particularly evident when units are conceptually combined with other "similar" ones to form a type.

The unitary character of certain archaeological remains (pots, rooms) is almost self-evident and there can be little doubt that the archaeologist is recognizing and abstracting units that have characteristics and limits reasonably identical with those perceived by the original users (whether or not the archaeologist and the maker have selected the same attributes as essential to the description and conceptualization of the objects making up the unit). Cultural units whose content and limits are more diffuse are more difficult and often impossible for the archaeologist to recognize. What group of rooms or structures was felt to constitute a unit (e.g., one family's property) by the occupants? What geographical area (if any) was regarded by the people occupying a particular site as their territory? Units such as these are difficult for any nonparticipant in the culture to perceive for usually they have no readily apparent material cohesiveness, and, unless the investigator is able to infer the attributes that were or are being used by the cultural participants in their identification of these units, he will be unable to determine the nature or even the existence of the latter with any accuracy.

Any unit (or any type) can be approached from three points of view, each pertinent to a different set of problems: (1) A unit — a cat, an axe — can be analyzed as an entity unto itself, the problems concerned revolving around the nature and constitution of that unit independent of its particular context. It is possible to conduct a detailed analysis of a cat as an integrated, independent object without ever knowing or needing to know that that particular cat lived in an apartment or that cats as a type (and therefore, including by definition the particular cat being analyzed) are descended from a certain ancestral form; (2) A unit (or a type) can be viewed as representing an end result of the action of many other units or types, with that unit's consequent reaction. The cat can be looked upon not as an entity independent of relative time, space, and contextual relations but rather as a result of those relationships. It is the cat that it is "because" of its heredity, or because it lived in an apartment, had had little sun but good food, was hit by a car and broke its leg; (3) A unit can be viewed as potentially capable of initiating certain reactions in other units should those other units come into its effective context. The cat can be analyzed from the point of view of its rat-catching potential or its soothing effect on the jangled nerves of its owner. To put it another way, there is the nature of the unit itself, the nature and result of the impingement of other units upon the initial unit, and the nature of the initial unit's impingement or effect upon other units.

THE TYPE

Conceptualization of objects or situations differs from simple recognition, for through conceptualization an image can be brought to mind for consideration when the object or situation itself is not a part of the immediate present or externally apprehended context. The essential or minimal criterion of effective conceptualization is the ability to recognize a manifestation or example of the concept when it occurs. To "possess" the concept "dragon" one must be able to recognize one, should it ever be encountered. This example draws attention to the fact that abstraction and idealization permit a mental picture of an object even though an example of it has *never* been perceived — something made possible by the recognition of the separate elements making up its component parts, in this case the concepts "lizard," "wings," "fire," and so on.

Without conceptualization "types" could not exist, for a type is not a unit or material entity with an independent existence like that of a particular rock, pottery vessel, or social configuration. A type is a concept that embraces two or more units based on the essential identity of one or more of their characteristics with reference to a particular problem. It is an individual mental construct with a nucleus of standard features: an ideal, a norm, and individual exemplifications.

A type becomes a scientific concept only when expression and communication of this ideal and norm permit others to recognize the exemplifications. Since any unit illustrating a type (when viewed in totality) is unique — even in the age of machine production — obviously any assumption that two or more units are "identical" cannot be based on their total features but rather only on certain features; that is, any amalgamation of units into a single typological class must ignore certain characteristics of those units as at least temporarily insignificant or irrelevant. The characteristics to be selected from the many observable or inferable ones (a distinction between the two forms should be maintained) and the degree of their similarity ("identical" is no more than a specifically limited range of variation around a central norm) can be determined only by reference to the problem(s) that the formulation is designed to help solve. This "partial" descriptive nature of a type is the basis of its utility but also constitutes its greatest limitation. Only by consciously or unconsciously ignoring the greater portion of a unit and concentrating on certain of its characteristics is it possible to gain effective understanding of these characteristics and of the unit to which they belong. At the same time we must consciously and constantly guard against ignoring characteristics of the unit that are pertinent to the problem, and avoid drawing conclusions so broad that, by their nature, they will extend beyond the observed aspects of the units studied. A particular type may be adequate for the solution of more than one problem, but because of the detailed selection of particular features inherent in the formulation of a type, this is unlikely to be the case unless the type was established with those several problems specifically in mind. Multiple problem applicability of a type can never be an *a priori* assumption.

Much archaeological practice appears to restrict use of the term "type" to those categories of material established on the basis of the material's possession of certain characteristics that evidently have a restricted temporal and/or spatial occurrence. Some (e.g., Krieger 1949) would add to these requirements that of recognition by the original workers. A type pertinent to the problems of temporal and spatial ordering may or may not have been perceived as a discrete category by the cultural participants, but for *that particular problem* it is not important one way or the other whether it was or not. Types recognized by the makers undoubtedly had the property of temporal and spatial duration; so that if the nature of this temporal and spatial duration can be discovered, perhaps such a type will serve for both problems. On the other hand, the time-space cohesion of a cultural type might well extend over too long or too short a period or area for the specific problem of time-space correlation under consideration.

As defined herein, "type" designates a logical category and although such a category includes the restricted form of type discussed by Krieger and others, it is obviously broader in scope. It is essential to clear thinking that the characteristics of any one particular problem type be rigorously defined as Krieger (1944, 1949), for example, has attempted to do, but it would seem advisable that the general term "type" be left free to designate a broad category of classification rather than be restricted to any one specific problem orientation. Perhaps, as suggested in this report, modifying words can be used to indicate the nature and purpose of individual types or typological series. To some extent this has already been done — for example: "horizon style" for types based on decorative features widespread in geographic area but of relatively limited duration, and "tradition" to designate the relative identity of certain artifact characteristics over a long period of time but within a more or less stable and/or restricted geographic area. ("Tradition" is also used to refer to a "historical pattern" of decorative development.) It might clarify discussions if other kinds of types were delineated. As there are many characteristics and problems on which typological groups can be based, it is possible to categorize various types themselves according to the features and/or problems that are prominent in their establishment. There are, as Steward (1954) notes, "types of types."

Because attention in the literature has been concentrated on the identification of individual types and (occasionally) on their definition rather than on the processes of selection, description, and conceptualization that are basic to the formulation of all types, a number of misunderstandings concerning the nature and utility of typological categories have developed.

The "lumpers-splitters" controversy seems to arise from a misconception about the problem orientation of any typological analysis and the apparent impression that a useful scheme can be formulated *in abstracto* without reference to any problem. The situation occurs most often when an investigator is faced with a great mass of material that he feels he must describe. The question of the detail in which it should be described comes up immediately, and unfortunately is sometimes answered in a rather arbitrary or cavalier fashion, or else the material is described in just enough detail to distinguish it from any other material known to the investigator. The "lumpers-splitters" debate can never be resolved so long as it is concerned with the features that should or should not be described. First of all, we must ask what *problems* are to be investigated. Only after that has been decided can the pertinence or significance of particular characteristics be determined. There can be no ultimate decision concerning "lumping" or "splitting." The descriptions made and the typological groups formed for the solution of any problem must be as detailed or as general as that specific problem or group of problems may demand.

Closely related to this are several misconceptions revolving primarily around the fallacy of the single ideal type or, more precisely, the single classificatory series. Although the nonexistence of a single "ideal" type useful in all situations has been adequately demonstrated (e.g., Brew 1946, pp. 51–52; Krieger 1944, pp. 284–286) and accepted in theory by the vast majority of workers, awareness of all the ramifications of this is not always demonstrated. As discussed above, the material presented in a report usually must be described in terms of a limited typological series (a process to be differentiated from a single classification of the data before presentation). There is no error or danger in this technique *per se;* indeed, short of describing every artifact individually, it is ultimately unavoidable. The danger lies rather in the assumptions implicit in the formulation and utilization of these types.

Perhaps the greatest source of confusion lies simply in the failure of most authors to present the nature of, or basis for, establishing the typological series, with the correlated tendency on the part of the author, or more often the reader, to apply the resultant types to a wide variety of problems for which they are not appropriate (as no restrictions are apparent in their initial formulation and presentation). For example,

Colton has written, "A *pottery type* can be defined as a group of pottery vessels which are alike in every important characteristic except form, for the vessels may have a variety of shapes and still belong to the same type." (1953, p. 51). Until we know how "importance" is determined, such a definition provides little guidance. Obviously a pottery type so defined is not designed to solve any problems where shape is a diagnostic feature. By failing to associate the type with any specific problem, the idea of an ideal type is fostered even though the existence of an ideal type may be specifically denied. Unfortunately this back-door approach to the ideal type is equally conducive to inaccuracies and confusion.

The difficulties inherent in using a single classificatory scheme and the failure to define its basis are particularly evident in ceramics, chiefly because the greater quantity and complexity of this material generally necessitates its presentation and often its analysis according to the types established under a single classificatory scheme. Failure to bear in mind the problem orientation(s) and consequent diagnostic criteria by which this classification and its included types were established can result only in endless confusion and incorrect interpretation.

Possibly all of the units conforming to the diagnostic criteria established for Kiatuthlanna Black-on-white, for example, will occur in, or will have been made by, individuals who spoke the same language, and were descended from common ancestors, who intercommunicated and thus probably had a common cultural background and context; that is, they were part of a cohesive historical and social unit. Furthermore, the typological criteria selected by the archaeologist as diagnostic of Kiatuthlanna Black-on-white may also have been recognized by the cultural participants as diagnostic of a certain type, or at least as diagnostic of a norm actually in use for a specific period within a limited geographic area, whether recognized as such or not. From every observation of present-day cultures, however, it seems extremely unlikely that the set of criteria utilized to establish Kiatuthlanna Black-on-white could conceivably cover all of these possibilities. Yet at one time or another assumptions leading to most of them apparently have been made by archaeologists. As with the "lumpers-splitters" controversy, discussion or consideration of types all too often originates on a level that precludes the possibility of any satisfactory answer. Until the particular problem orientation has been defined, the appropriate diagnostic criteria of, for example, Kiatuthlanna Black-on-white or Pueblo II cannot be established; for it is impossible to decide whether a group of sherds does or does not fall within the range of Kiatuthlanna Black-on-white or whether a site is or is not Pueblo II without some problem orientation that establishes the diagnostic criteria for delineating the typological units and for developing the classificatory scheme of the material.

Concurrent with and related to this unrestricted multiple utilization of pseudo-ideal types is the occasional tendency to justify the recognition of a particular typological category on the basis of some cohesiveness supposedly inherent in the material. The result is the apparent implication that there is only one niche or type into which each unit can properly be placed. This suggestion derives largely from biological systematics that on superficial examination appear to have an inherent basis. But we should note that whereas students of biology or evolution, because of the nature of biologic reproduction, do have one definite basis for *ordering* their units irrespective of any problem — since the mode of reproduction provides an inherent biological or genetic justification for arranging units in a particular sequence — there is no inherent feature demanding that the biologist group such units into particular types. We cannot state at the present time that there is or is not an inherent basis for bounding the largest biological categories, for the ultimate implication of any such statement involves the question of a single or multiple creation, a debate far beyond the scope of this paper. As yet there is no known factor inherent in biological material that determines the establishment of any specific typological bounds. For example, "species" as a category of biological unit is established on the basis of a *defined degree* of structural similarity and *presumed* ultimate genetic relationship; other equally valid typologic groups of biologic material have been based on similarity of environmental location, utilization, and so on.

Idea and Action Types

Is typology inherent in the material? Since the characteristics chosen to define a type have been abstracted from the data, it is evident that, in a sense, the type is "inherent" in that data. That is, the individual units provide the exemplifications and characteristics from which the ideal type was abstracted. More often, however, the question is whether the makers of these objects did in fact formulate typological concepts so as to produce objects that permit the archaeologist to recognize the existence and nature of those very same formulations.

Before this question can be discussed in detail, it is necessary to differentiate between an "idea" and an "action" type. An idea type of an object or situation is an inferred average, a summarization of all the ideas individually held, consciously or unconsciously, by the members of a community who direct their individual efforts toward a particular goal. It can be exemplified only in the minds of the individuals of that community. In short, the idea type is more nearly subject to analysis by cultural anthropologists and others who can obtain from individuals the necessary data to formulate an idea type. It can never be obtained through archaeological materials. An action type is a conceptualization of the norm of the physical exemplifications resulting from the individual idea types as these are manifested by and through the actions of individuals and/or groups. The particular exemplifications of an action type will approximate the parent idea type to a varying degree, depending upon a wide variety of circumstances (e.g., the skill of the individual workers in visually expressing their ideas), and thus the action type abstracted from these physical examples can only approximate the initiating idea type. The one may almost duplicate the other, or the variation may be so great as to make it difficult to recognize the relationship. The principles necessary for accurately or even approximately predicting the one from the other have not to my knowledge been developed as yet.

The action type may or may not have been recognized as such (i.e., distinct from the initiating idea type) by the cultural participants, but, whether or not this was the case, the archaeologist can often recognize it. While such an action type perceived by the archaeologist may duplicate or closely approximate a norm actually in existence when the units were in use, there can be no assurance that this norm was recognized by the users. Any such estimate is further complicated by the fact that the primary characteristics utilized in the definition of any type by the users of those units not only varied with their function and that of the particular objects, but also was at least partially dependent upon factors of linguistic and mechanical habit patterns that usually are unknowable to the archaeologist. Fortunately, whether an action type was consciously conceptualized as a type by the cultural participants — or the degree to which it resembled the initiating idea type — is relatively or totally unimportant for many problems in anthropology and archaeology. In most cases it is more important to determine whether the type recognized by the archaeologist approximates a norm and range of variation actually existing at the time the units were used. A basic assumption, of course, is that the possible variation among units of any item of culture is so great that any group of intercommunicating individuals will tend to concentrate their efforts within a certain range of variation, and that their activity and its results will therefore cluster more or less closely around a norm. Whether or not an observer (archaeological or ethnological) can infer the nature of this action type will depend on the knowledge available to, and the ability of, the observer, the completeness of his sample, the sharpness of the boundaries (i.e., lack of intergradation with other norms), and the degree of cohesiveness or small range of variation around that norm. In the search for action types the nature of the problem requires that recognition of criteria should not be restricted to those of sheer descriptive similarity or "identity." Characteristics of inferred and observed contextual and patterned associational correlations must also be considered.

Abstractive versus Descriptive Types

There has been occasional debate as to whether a type can be formulated legitimately from a single example. Obviously a type cannot consist of a single unit, since by definition it refers to the conceptual identity of two or more units. On the other hand, a type can be tentatively formulated on the characteristics of only one unit. In so doing it is necessary to assume what must ultimately be demonstrated, namely, that the unit described is representative of other existing but presently unavailable units, and that the basis for the typological formulation has significance for some problem. The difficulty lies in making the assumption that a single more or less fortuitously obtained and observed specimen is truly representative of any significant norm.

Rouse (1939, pp. 11-12), in discussing the problem, distinguishes between "types" as abstractions and "types" as simply descriptions of a particular aggregate of material ("...the term 'type' seems to have been applied to at least two different concepts, a group of artifacts or as an abstract kind of artifact which symbolizes the groups." Rouse 1939, p. 11). Here he refers to a confusion between typology and description. Rouse's type as an abstraction includes the ideal and perhaps the normative aspects of a type, as the term is used here. On the other hand, his type as a descriptive category, while quite commonly found in archaeological literature, is the confusing result of not making explicit the basis for a typological formulation. The units included in the latter form are doubtless exemplifications of a type, in that they were grouped according to their identity with regard to certain of their characteristics; however, the published description of these exemplifications fails to single out those characteristics, so that the ideal and normative aspects of the type are unknown to the reader. All that is presented is a more or less heterogeneous group description of the material itself.

The confusion between the description of the ideal aspect of a type and the description of a group of exemplifications of a type is most often encountered in the two methods of approaching a typological formulation. For example, it is possible to design or formulate an ideal type mentally with a range of possible or permissible variations (a formulation that may be modified as the material is handled), and then to sort through the material in an attempt to recognize and segregate exemplifications of this type. The second technique is to decide, regarding a particular problem or problems, what features should be observed before or, on occasion, during analysis and then to recognize and describe the material, unit by unit with respect to these features. Later, the units may be grouped according to their similarity in all or certain of their described attributes, and the results of this grouping may then be formulated as a type, with the usual characteristics of an ideal (the possession of those attributes used in the establishment of the group), a norm (the range of variation represented by the artifacts described, whose limits were defined when the group was established), and particular exemplifications (the specific artifacts included). Once a typological group has been established by either method, it then becomes possible to describe the units as a group according to both diagnostic and nondiagnostic attributes — a procedure that was earlier designated "typological description." This *general description* of a specific group of exemplifications of a type is sometimes improperly called a "type," and, while mainly a terminological matter, use of the same term for such different entities has led to much confusion in the past. A typological formulation *describes* material only incidentally; its primary function is to establish the basis for associating units into a group, and the diagnostic characteristics used for this purpose must be explicit. Of course, in discussing a group exemplifying a type other features can be presented, but those features extraneous to the concept of the type may well not occur in another group of exemplifications of the same type. For that matter, the extent of the range and variation of particular diagnostic attributes may vary among different groups within the limited definition of a particular type. For example, one of the diagnostic attributes of Type A may be a color range of red through orange; one group of exemplifications of that type may all be orange, a second group all red, and the third a mixture.

The Mode

From a typological group we can abstract factors which — though not originally used for establishing the type — still appear to be constant for the group (and perhaps for other groups as well). This was Rouse's procedure in selecting attributes to be designated as modes; that is, he chose attributes characteristic of previously formulated types. Presumably his modes included attributes used in the original formulation of the typological groups as well as those recognized and abstracted later, for some of his modes must have formed, at least implicitly, the basis for the initial establishment of the groups. It is literally impossible to place separate units together in a group without some reason for doing so. These conscious or unconscious factors of identity (even if they are nothing more significant than "all those sherds within reach") become the expressed or unexpressed basis for the type. But if the diagnostic criteria are not overtly set out and the reason for their selection and delimitation not clearly stated, the odds are tremendous that the type will be misused.

We should realize that some types, as established, emphasize one aspect or another. A type formulated by the first method described above (formulation of the type in advance) is generally defined with limits sufficiently broad to include a number of specific groups of exemplifications, a fact that stresses the ideal aspect of the type. A type formulated through the second technique (initial description, based on criteria selected for being pertinent to one or more problems, followed by description of specific typological groups) is formulated from or with reference to a particular group of exemplifications and problems, and the range of variation allowable under its definition is not likely to be so broad (though, of course, it may be). Thus its identification with a particular group of exemplifications is emphasized.

The mode is a valid and extremely useful concept, for it permits the investigator to concentrate on a single kind of attribute, thus facilitating the study of that attribute and the analysis of problems for which that attribute is significant, while all other attributes can be temporarily ignored. To define it in more precise terms, a mode is a type that has as its diagnostic feature a single kind of attribute. A mode can be based on an observable or an inferable characteristic. The distinction between Rouse's "modes" (types based on a single attribute) and "types" (types formulated with a number of diagnostic attributes — Rouse makes a further distinction by restricting diagnostic features of types to observable attributes, which he feels increases their "descriptive" flavor) is logically a difference of degree rather than of kind, and both concepts are distinct from the description of a typological group. Despite the fact that a mode is generally abstracted from a particular group, when Rouse speaks of tracing the distribution of modes in space, he is (as he realizes) referring to the abstract ideal aspect of the mode.

THE PATTERN

Basically a pattern, like a type, is a concept and does not itself have material existence but rather consists of an ideal, a norm, and specific exemplifications. True, in everyday speech a single organization or layout of entities (or even the stabilized form of a single unit) is spoken of as a pattern (e.g., a clothing pattern) in much the same sense that a single unit is identified as "being" a particular type. A pattern, when reduced to its essential characteristics, is a particular relationship that is recognized to occur repeatedly in space and/or in time between entities (that is, between units or types or even stimulus-response situtations). This *repetitive relationship* is then abstracted from the observed or inferred data and conceptualized as a pattern.

As Spaulding (1953, pp. 305 ff.) suggests, this repetitive relationship can be "recognized" via a computer and the degree of repetition (or clustering, in the case of a type) can be expressed in statistical terms. Nevertheless, the units or features expressed quantitatively and set into the machine have to be initially abstracted by the anthropologist as possibly pertinent to his problem, and the interpretation of the extent and nature of the cultural significance, if any, of any resultant clustering again must be determined by the anthropologist. Computerized statistical techniques simply provide another, and often the only practical, means of recognizing and quantifying the existence and degree of correlation between units or attributes already abstracted from the data as possibly significant for the problem under investigation. Ford correctly points out (1954, pp. 390-391) that the mere fact that a clustering or patterning of traits has statistical significance does not in itself impute cultural significance (factors other than human ones tamper with the laws of pure chance) or the existence of cultural types and patterns. However, the demonstration that a statistically significant correlation exists between units or factors whose interrelationship has been previously unrecognized is certainly suggestive and effectively points up a line of investigation worth checking. Similarly, it provides a mathematical test and expression of conclusions reached by more subjective techniques.

Patterning is essential to the recognition of both units and types. The existence and perception of a unit are made possible by the fact that its subunits have maintained (or, for the purpose of the problem being investigated, can be considered to have maintained) a stable and thus, in a sense, patterned relationship over a period of time. This quality of relative stability has been defined by Whitehead (1925, p. 121) as that of "endurance." A unit without this quality relative to a problem is perhaps better termed an event. Viewed statically the subunits of a unit are ordered, organized, or arranged rather than patterned; however, the subunits of a unit viewed dynamically can be considered to have a patterned (i.e., repetitious) relationship. A single unit (but not an event) also can have a patterned (i.e., recurring) relationship with other units or types. Similarly, types can be formulated from the organization or existence of a group of characteristics or processes repeated in, or connected with, a number of units, or because a number of units have a repeated association with one another or some other type or situation.

Basically the relationship itself is primary in a pattern, but the elements having the relationship are also significant, for both affect the nature of the pattern and the inferences that can be drawn from it. There are different kinds of patterns, as well as various kinds of types, and it is generally advisable to distinguish between these variations. In every case the characteristics and entities employed in the pattern and the purpose for which it is to be used, should be made explicit. By so doing, misinterpretations of the nature of the relationship (like the operational implication that potsherds "breed" in the interpretation of types and patterns of pottery-making in the southwestern United States, as pointed out by Brew 1946, pp. 56 ff.) can largely be avoided.

Archaeology is vitally concerned with the recognition of patterns, for their establishment permits inference of total patterns from partial patterns or even from partial elements of those patterns. Furthermore, based on the nature of this patterning and its context, inferences often can be made about the cause and effect of the pattern. The data of archaeology alone among the social sciences provide the basis for checking hypotheses relating to patterns of cause and effect over extended periods of time. However, archaeology is unable to *observe* either dynamic patterns or the patterns of relationship of a single unit to others. These must be inferred. Archaeology can only observe the *organization* of the *elements* of a single unit or of the units of a process, and *patterns* existing between *types* abstracted from them. In archaeology, typology is as essential to the recognition of patterns as patterning is to the recognition of types.

Time-Space and Other Typological Sets

Normally it is necessary to formulate a typological set for each problem being investigated.

The typological set referred to in this report as regional time-space types comprises the "classic" ceramic types of the Southwest and elsewhere. Over and over this typological set has unquestionably demonstrated its utility in elucidating problems concerning the temporal and spatial placement (and therefore probably a cultural relationship) of ceramic materials and other contextually related objects. But when this set also is utilized as the single basis for the description and presentation of basic ceramic data great harm is done, in that the ability of the initial observer and of others to utilize the data for other problems is unduly restricted.

For example, it is often possible to distinguish within a coherent assemblage of pottery certain specimens that vary in one or a few attributes or modes, slightly but consistently, from other specimens within the same assemblage in such a way as to suggest the probability that the separate groups were made by different potters, all working within the same school or tradition, but exhibiting individual idiosyncrasies.

Such distinctions are often archaeologically useful, and they have been observed and recorded in this study under the rubric of "Artisan Types," as further discussed on pages 54–55, 128–130.

Such a typological set could not have been established from data presented solely in the typological description of the ceramics as time-space types. Nor could recognition and establishment of the intrasite distribution set have been possible (see pp. 213 ff., 241 ff.).

A more basic method of descriptive presentation is necessary if this multiple problem formulation of different typological sets is to become possible. The approach suggested here is the establishment of the descriptive type as the basic method for the *presentation* of basic archaeological data (see pp. 33–35).

The actual information derived from the particular artisan types or intrasite distribution types established in this report is of minor importance. Recognizing the need of the initial investigator and of others to be able to manipulate the basic data into different typological sets, each designed for a specific problem, *is* vital.

The Descriptive Type

The task of describing, analyzing, and presenting to the reader the data from a collection of 50,000 potsherds or even 50 projectile points can raise formidable methodological problems. As noted, it is literally impossible to observe and describe all or even all archaeologically pertinent attributes of those objects. A selection must be made based upon the nature of the problem or problems to which the data derived from these objects are to be applied; that is, what attributes are pertinent to the questions being asked? Where the problems are few and the number of pertinent observations limited, it is generally possible to make a straightforward descriptive presentation of the observations. As the number of problems and pertinent observations increases, the problem of presenting the basic data becomes increasingly complex.

The simplest technique of presentation is that of describing individually every object with respect to all features pertinent to every problem under consideration. While this is perhaps the best procedure, a large quantity of objects, combined with the need for a large number of observations, often necessitates the adoption of some more practical method. The technique most frequently chosen has been termed "typological description," that is, the objects considered identical regarding a certain problem are taken to constitute a group or "type," and the individual objects are then presented solely as members of this type rather than described individually. This technique facilitates the presentation of material and the analysis of that particular problem. However, no one set of observations is satisfactory for every problem. Thus, there are a number of limitations inherent in the technique. For example, the reader is unable to resort contained units according to features not considered diagnostic to the type definition. When a type has been defined in such a way that *all* diagnostic traits need not be present in every unit (and this is common in typological descriptions in the literature) the reader will be unable to determine the extent of agreement between the included individual units and the established type. Further, he will generally be completely unaware of the nature and certainty of the distribution of nondiagnostic traits. In short, this technique of presentation is appropriate only insofar as we can validly assume that none of the variations between units included within a type are signficiant to any of the problems to be considered. This assumption is open to serious question whenever a typological grouping composed of complex objects is applied to various problems — unless all of these problems were considered in the establishment of that type.

The technique of typological description as it is normally employed is ill-suited to the basic description of complex objects that are pertinent to a variety of problems. An extension of this technique is required. In brief, the criteria diagnostic of or pertinent to *all* problems to be studied must be determined and the data abstracted and handled in such a manner that units having particular attributes relevant to specific problems can be combined and recombined into different types as demanded by the analysis of the various problems. For this purpose the only units that can be included within the same basic descriptive category are those with attributes identical within limits applicable to every problem under consideration.

This basic category, here termed a "descriptive type," is an aggregate of units whose characteristics are considered identical with respect to *all* problems to which the units undergoing analysis are felt to be applicable. In practice, attributes relevant to each problem should be delineated, and the material sorted and described relating to these problems as well as to any others that become apparent as analysis proceeds. Because of the multiple diagnostic characteristics involved in their establishment, the number of exemplifications of each descriptive type is often small, and normally the descriptive types themselves are not directly applicable to the solution of any of the several problems. Rather, these types form the basic categories from which specifically oriented problem types are formed. In essence, the descriptive type constitutes the lowest common denominator of practical description, providing a serviceable alternative between the description of every artifact and the presentation of the total sample according to only a single-problem typological description.

Normally several of these descriptive types will need to be amalgamated in order to form a type applicable to a specific problem. For example, two problems to be analyzed via a study of pottery sherds might involve the observation of five different paste attributes, three different temper attributes, two attributes of construction techniques, and ten different design attributes. If the material were to be handled only once for these two problems (assuming the sample size is too great to permit separate sortings), no two sherds differing in any of these 20 attributes could be described together as units within a single descriptive type. Yet problem "A" might have no reference to design. Therefore all those units differing only in design could be placed together when forming problem types for the analysis of this problem. Alternatively, problem "B" might pertain solely to design. Thus, for the analysis of this problem, design modes alone would be diagnostic and problem types would be established that might very well contain units having various combinations of paste, temper, and/or construction modes. We can readily see that had either series of problem types been used as the sole means of presenting the basic data, the other set of problem types could not have been formulated either by the reader or by the original analyst (except by resorting the sherds themselves).

Use of the descriptive type does not make it possible to present all the available data and, in most instances, some readers probably will feel that certain other information should have been abstracted and duly recorded. Yet the descriptive type does facilitate presentation of the basic data undisturbed by amalgamation into groups that submerge variations of individual units thought to be significant; and thus the basic data that are recorded remain flexible. They can be combined and recombined by both reader and author into a number of types, based on various factors, for a number of problems. Furthermore, the precise correlation of individual attributes and study of the spatial distribution and other associations of these attributes are made possible.

If only a portion of the total sample is appropriate to a particular problem, only those descriptive types containing the applicable diagnostic criteria need be abstracted from the total sample and combined into suitable types. Examples of this selective utilization of the basic descriptive types in a variety of problems will be reviewed in the various site descriptions in this report.

In addition to facilitating the presentation of considerable detail and the ready ordering of this material into different sets of problem types, there is another major advantage to be gained from using descriptive types. They reduce confusion regarding the appropriate utilization of derived sets of problem types. If notation is made of the descriptive types included within each problem type, evaluation of that type for application to a different problem or another area is greatly facilitated, for it is possible to determine easily the total range and proportionate representation of the diagnostic and nondiagnostic characteristics observed and included within the type. Furthermore, the frequently noted disparity between the material included in and the conclusions drawn from a single problem type by different observers can be lessened, or at least the basis for their difference understood more readily.

The concept of the descriptive type can be applied to any group of materials. However, its use is particularly effective in handling a large sample about which many interrelated observations must be made (e.g., ceramics). With groups composed of a small number of artifacts and/or about which few observations are necessary, other methods of handling the basic data are often more effective.

The recording of a wealth of data, of course, does not in itself involve or require complete or even partial objectivity. Attributes utilized in descriptive types should be delineated with specific problems in mind, and these problems will determine the permissible range of variation of the attributes observed. Neither the descriptive types nor the even more restricted problem types should be lifted out of the context of the particular problem(s) for which they were formulated, without first determining if it is appropriate to do so on the basis of the total characteristics of the units contained and those pertinent to the new problems. Descriptive types and their included examples are readily amenable to ordering and reordering, but only in relation to the various attributes utilized in their formulation and description. Even descriptive types must be carefully reviewed for applicability before being used as the basic building blocks for the construction of typological sets in analyzing other problems than those for which they were designed.

In this report the attributes abstracted for use in descriptive types have been assigned numerical and place (row) values for easy notation on the tables. For example, number "1" in row "A" of the pottery tables refers to a particular material that is defined in full in appendix A. Thus, in table 1, the notation "1113" under White-slipped Pottery denotes a descriptive type composed (in brief) of sherds with the following characteristics: gray paste, white slip, and black mineral paint; from necked jars with the exterior slipped and painted; slipped surfaces — even, smooth, and lustrous; polishing marks rarely evident; the slip polished before the application of the paint; and with a basic design of rectilinear bands and rectangular units of varied internal makeup. If any sherd differed in *any one* of these attributes, it was placed in a separate descriptive type.

There are terminological or mnemonic difficulties in using descriptive types. Separate titles for every descriptive type would be unwieldly to present and too numerous to remember in toto. Number, letter, or other symbolic designations, while concise, have been criticized as being even harder to recall and difficult to associate with individual observations or particular descriptive types. We must remember, however, that these descriptive types are working categories designed solely for the persons actually analyzing, re-analyzing, or utilizing the basic data. They are not intended as types to be bandied back and forth by research workers over a cup of coffee. Thus, the mnemonic objections, to my view, are meaningless.

Far more important is the fact that this approach to the basic information yields computer-ready data. In time, and that time is not yet at hand, the pages of our publications may not need to be burdened with voluminous basic data. The researcher who needs this information can punch a console on his desk and receive the information he needs from a national or regional data bank. Until that time, utilization of numerically represented descriptive types will afford today's researcher that same capability for reworking the basic data, either manually or perhaps by feeding them into his own computer, without his needing to have the material itself actually available (unless, of course, he insists on asking questions that require information not considered or recorded at the time the material was initially described).

The artifacts in this report are described via all three basic methods. The concept of the descriptive type is utilized to handle the volume of observed detail required by the complex and widely applied ceramic data, and is also used in describing the manos. Other materials of less complexity or more limited problem applicability (e.g., the bone awls) involve simple typological description, though even here data on individual catalog numbers are given in order that possibly significant variations of individual artifacts within the typological norms can be brought to the reader's attention and he can then correlate them with other attributes or with distributional criteria. Finally, when practical and desirable, objects have been described individually.

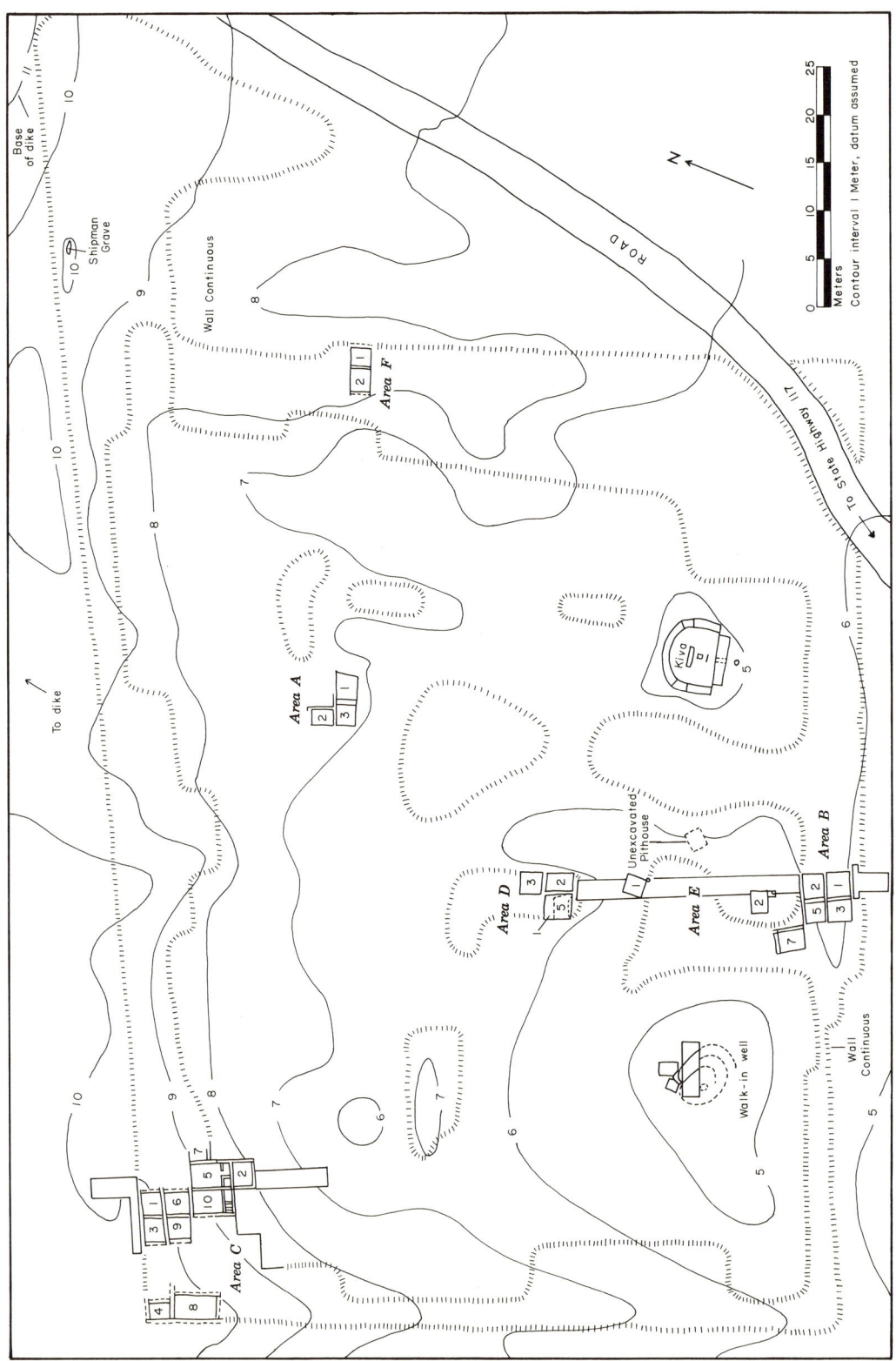

Figure 7. Plan of Site 616.

Site 616

DESCRIPTION

Trechado Peak is a volcanic plug rising several hundred meters above the valley floor, 3 miles east-northeast of the north point of Mariana Mesa. Radiating from this somewhat circular extrusion is a series of volcanic dikes forming knife-backed ridges that in some cases extend for a distance of several miles. One such dike extends approximately northwest from Trechado Peak. At a point 2.5 miles from Trechado Peak, a small stream — part of the drainage system flowing west around the north point of Mariana Mesa — has cut through the dike so that the Continental Divide swings some 4 miles east at this point. Site 616 (figs. 7, 8) is located at the foot of the southwestern slope of the dike on the northern bank of this ephemeral stream.

The floor of the valley of this small stream is covered with grass and low scrub but trees are rare. However, on the slopes of the ridges above, piñon and juniper occur in profusion. The dike itself, with sides too steep and soilless for much vegetation to get a foothold, towers over the northeast corner of the pueblo like a giant tumbledown wall of irregular volcanic cobbles.

A person standing on this dike enjoys an excellent view of the territory and of Site 616 itself (fig. 8). The pueblo, as it appeared just prior to its abandonment, must have been an impressive sight. A large, irregularly rectangular plaza (200 by 250 m) was entirely enclosed by multiple rows of rooms, except in two places where room groups were united by short, single, sandstone walls. Along most of the north, south, and east edges of the plaza this border was 1 to 4 rooms thick, but along the eastern edge, and particularly in the southeast corner, rooms were 4 to 6 deep. These and all other rooms at the site were a single story high. Although there were internal doorways, entrance to most rooms was apparently gained primarily from the roof. Two single rows of rooms projected into the plaza from the southern border and there were, in addition, seven isolated room clusters within the plaza. These clusters consisted of 3 to 12 rooms each. The plaza also contained a number of single rooms either wholly or partly subterranean, one and perhaps two subterranean kivas, and, in the southwestern corner, a large excavation entered by a ramp that apparently provided the pueblo with an internal water supply and, perhaps incidentally, a source of clay.

There may have been as many as 500 to 600 rooms in the pueblo and, to judge from the rooms excavated, a large proportion of these were in use at the time the pueblo was abandoned. The large population working on the flat roofs of the rooms, carrying on their activities in the plaza and tending their fields, which probably were located on the flat floor of the valley bordering the stream, must have presented the viewer with a picture of bustle and activity.

At an early point in the historic settlement of the region a lumbering establishment, "Horse Camp Mill," was located in the immediate vicinity of the pueblo, which by this time consisted solely of low mounds, a few shallow depressions, and the ubiquitous potsherds. A gravestone on the north corner of the site, dating from this period, marks the burial place of Al Shipman, one of the workers at the mill. Local tradition records that his demise was a case of mistaken identity which followed a post-party discussion among some of the employees. Apparently he was an innocent bystander who chose an inopportune moment to come between two of the more active participants, at least one of whom had a gun. Accordingly, Site 616 is variously known locally as the Horse Camp Mill Site and the Shipman Site.

HISTORY OF THE SITE

All features excavated at Site 616 apparently were occupied contemporaneously or very nearly so. In this sense the site had little time depth. On the other hand, there is no reason to believe that all features at the site were built within a brief period of time.

Architecturally, the earliest known section of the site appeared to be Area A. The small lava-cobble masonry used in constructing this cluster of rooms was strikingly similar to that of the last rooms built at Site

494 and some of the earlier rooms at Site 481. If we are correct in assuming that there was a general sequence of architectural development throughout the region of Mariana Mesa, it would follow that the construction of Area A was roughly contemporaneous with that of the similarly constructed sections of these neighboring sites. No pottery or other artifacts of the earlier period were found to substantiate this hypothesis, but it is not surprising since at least part, if not all, of Area A appeared to have been occupied until the time the pueblo was abandoned, and the associated artifacts were, therefore, representative of the later period. Refuse areas that might have yielded material from different periods in the history of the pueblo were not located.

From one or two units of several contiguous rooms, this community, like others in the Mariana Mesa area, grew to include a considerable number of such groups of rooms. At one point during its occupation there may have been as many as ten or more clusters of rooms. Probably the construction of the subterranean rooms was initated during this early period. Each room cluster, presumably occupied by a closely knit social unit, may have had a pithouse associated with it in an arrangement similar to that found at Site 494. An insufficient number of surface and subterranean rooms were excavated to determine with assurance whether or not this was the case. Although unquestionably Room D5 and possibly room E1 were no longer in use at the time the pueblo was abandoned, material found on the floor of Room E2, including a Tularosa Black-on-white jar, was identical to that found in the surface rooms. The pithouses were not remnants of a preceding period of occupation but were contemporaneous with the surface rooms, and at least some continued in use up to the time of abandonment.

The architects of Area D, another of the independent room clusters, did not utilize the lava-cobble masonry that previously had been standard. The construction technique used by then, and the one that remained dominant throughout the construction of most of the rest of the pueblo, was that of adobe walls supported by a basal section of lava or sandstone cobbles. This technique was unique among the sites investigated in the vicinity of Mariana Mesa and thus was difficult to relate to the general picture of architectural evolution in the area. Presumably this innovation occurred at some time after the final abandonment of Site 494, but in all likelihood it was contemporary with the late period and perhaps even the middle period of the occupation of Site 481. The rooms of Area D — and probably the unit whose eastern segment was Area B — were begun at this time. Some rooms in Area C may date from the same general period.

Most of the construction began as small room clusters. Some of these grew and perhaps were amalgamated with one another, while other groups remained independent and fairly stable. By this time the village had attained considerable size and the community plan probably resembled that of Site 143 or a small edition of present-day Zuni, New Mexico, with room groups of varying size scattered rather helter-skelter over a small area, but with most of the walls of the different units oriented in the same general direction.

Apparently, population increases were primarily responsible for the pueblo's growth rather than a pattern of room abandonment and new construction over a long period by a relatively stable group. Some time after the introduction of adobe-wall construction, the rate of immigration to this village accelerated rapidly. Instead of the occasional addition of single, or at most several, rooms or the beginning of a small new unit, the village now entered upon a period of rapid expansion in which whole rows of rooms, perhaps even several contiguous rows, were built simultaneously. Generally, two or more parallel east-west walls were constructed extending over a considerable distance, and then north-south walls were built dividing these areas into rooms. Most of Area C and Area F and some of Area B was built in this manner. Sandstone-block masonry for exterior walls was introduced during this period of construction and eventually was used for some interior walls as well. This construction resulted in the amalgamation of a number of the original, small, separate room clusters and, finally, in the formation of a completely closed rectangle of rooms surrounding a central plaza. It seems unlikely that this ultimate form was the result of completely haphazard accretion.

TRADE RELATIONS AND FINAL ABANDONMENT

To judge from the ceramics and the few other indications that have survived, the occupants of the pueblo traded primarily with groups to the north and west. Quite probably, the sites serving as the direct sources of supply for most of the imported ceramics and certain other materials were located in a sector between present-day Zuni, New Mexico, and Show Low, Arizona, at a distance of 25 to 75 miles. Most of the red-slipped ware, which apparently was traded in, derived from this general area. Shells possibly reached Mariana Mesa from sources to the southwest, while turquoise and jet may have come from the north and west. The occupants were undoubtedly aware of and in contact with groups to the south and east, but their basic orientation at this time seems to have been to the northwest. It is perhaps significant that such an orientation followed the major drainage pattern — although the primary cause was probably historic rather than synchronic — for this apparently was the direction of the inhabitants' closest historic affiliations as well as their contemporary trade associations.

The same picture of population instability and ultimate concentration in large sites, followed by complete abandonment of entire areas, is found throughout a large section of the Southwest at about this same time, and has been attributed to a number of causes: disease, drought, arroyo-cutting, enemy peoples, and internecine warfare, to name a few. More extensive excavation at Site 616 probably would have provided considerable data on this point; unfortunately, this is no longer possible as the site has been ravaged by pothunters.

With the exception of Site 616 all the sites excavated in the area of Mariana Mesa had been virtually stripped of artifacts and, in some instances, even of building materials, presumably by the inhabitants at the time of abandonment. Room floors were left barren, and the excavator gets an impression that the inhabitants carefully removed and took with them all of the more valuable materials, and that following abandonment the sites may have been visited by others for the purpose of salvaging anything useful which remained.

The situation at Site 616 is in startling contrast. Here, anyone viewing an excavated room can easily imagine the occupants as having simply stepped outside to see what some ruckus was about, but expecting to return momentarily. Artifacts are in disarray, but it would appear that frequently almost all preservable accoutrements of a room in active use are present. For example, Room B1 contained more than 60 artifacts, a total that does not include beads, stone chips, or the seven pottery vessels. This abundance leads me to conclude that the abandonment of the pueblo was neither gradual nor carefully planned, and that the final exodus was probably made under duress.

Surely more material — much of it readily portable and quite valuable in that it represented a considerable investment of time and skill — would have been removed had there been any reasonable opportunity to do so. For the same reason, it seems that the entire region must have become virtually deserted at this time. Some of the rooms, with a large number of artifacts and whole vessels littering the floor, apparently stood intact until natural decay and the weather brought about their collapse. (In this connection it is interesting to note that very few sherds found on floors could not be assigned to restorable vessels.) In other rooms the roof burned and collapsed at the time of or shortly after the site's abandonment, but even the resulting debris would not have been sufficient to

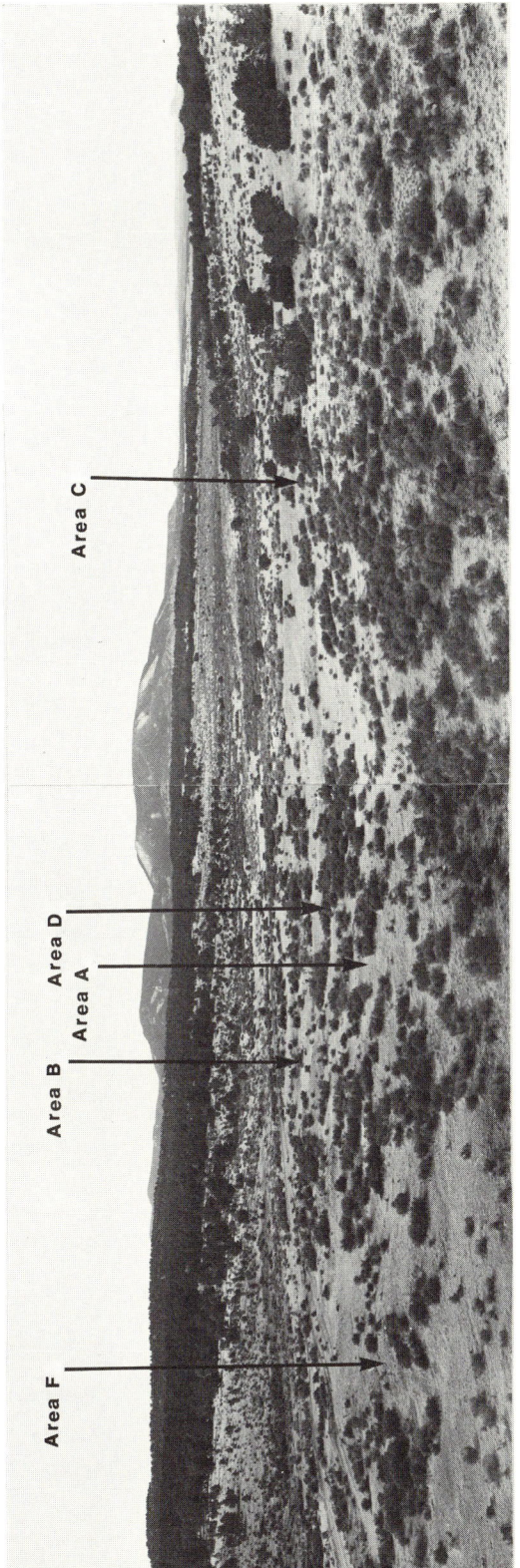

Figure 8. Panoramic view of Site 616, looking southwest from the dike.

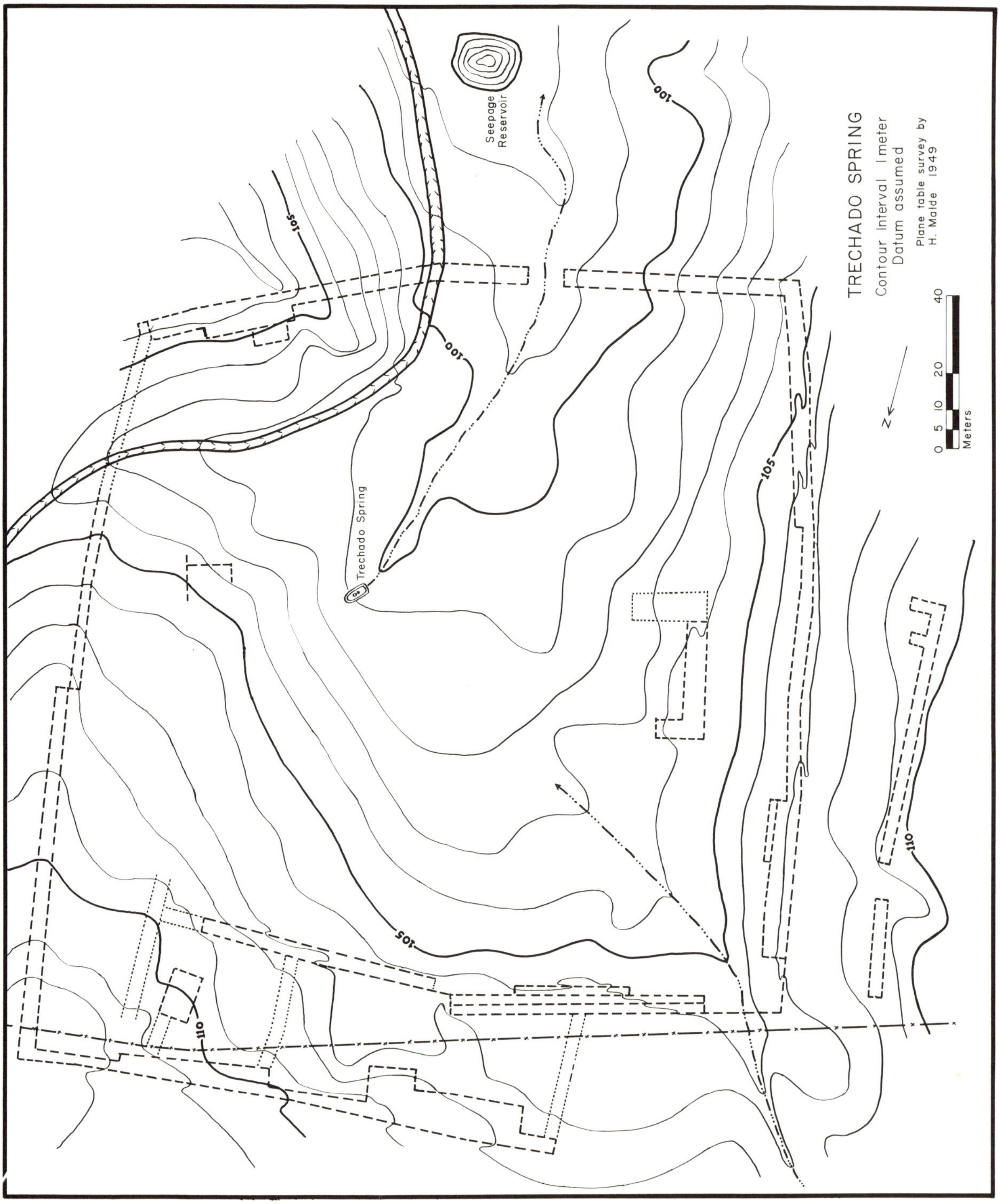

40 • Mariana Mesa

Figure 9. Plan of Trechado Spring Site.

prevent any groups still living in the area from rummaging through the remains and removing whatever was usable. Unless visiting was prevented by superstition or fear, the only plausible answer is that no villages in the region continued to be occupied for any extended period following the exodus from Site 616. Occasional hunting parties and/or nomadic groups could and may have passed through, but it would not have been practical for them to do more than casual looting — extensive perhaps, but hardly intensive.

While there is reason to believe that the final departure from the pueblo was a hasty one, it is more difficult to determine, on the basis of the information presently available, whether the pueblo was deserted because of or immediately after a hostile attack. The single most persuasive support for this hypothesis was the skeleton of a young girl found sprawled in the roof debris of Room C2. Her right arm had been broken off at the midpoint of the humerus and she had been struck on the head with consierable force by an axe-like implement. The evidence indicates that immediately after her death the roof, where her body lay, burned and collapsed, carrying the body with it to the floor of the room. No attempt was made to bury the body. Her death certainly appeared to have been a violent one, and had the pueblo been occupied afterwards, it seems likely that some more formal burial would have been provided. Another example was the skeleton of a young adult male found stretched out on the floor of Room E2. There was no positive evidence that he died violently but the apparent circumstances surrounding his death and the subsequent lack of attention to his body may also indicate that his demise was associated with an attack on and subsequent abandonment of the pueblo.

The relative abundance of fragments of human skeletal material scattered throughout the site also suggested an absence of formal burial at the end of the site's history. Perhaps this occurred at other sites as well, but most reports do not provide such data. Some features in the rooms, the mealing bins in particular, apparently were deliberately destroyed. In Room C9 and Room D2 the metates and other materials from the bins had been removed no farther than the adjacent floor area or the roof of the room, as if plans for the removal of these artifacts had been hastily abandoned and they had simply been left where they lay. The main section of Area C and a portion of Area B seemed to have been burned at that time.

Even if we assume an attack was the cause of abandonment, we are left to speculate on the causes of such an occurrence as well as the identity of the attacking group. In a number of large sites in this general area of the Southwest, e.g., the Mesa Top Site at Cebolleta Mesa (Ruppé 1957) and Casa Malpais near Springerville (Danson and Malde 1950), the location and structural features indicated that defense was undoubtedly a primary consideration. In every instance these sites were large and were among the last ones to be occupied in their respective areas. Many other areas, with fewer signs of active hostility, provide plausible evidence for this inference. Mariana Mesa is a case in point. Here, as elsewhere, there was a possibly unrelated historic tendency for the face-to-face social unit to become larger, but until the final period of occupation this happened gradually, and sites exhibited no defensive characteristics beyond those inherent in any normal dwelling. At Site 616 there seemed to be a relatively sudden influx of people, and subsequently the site design made defense at least easy and practical. If the need for defense decided the choice of a site during this final period, it is likely that Site 616 and Trechado Spring (fig. 9) were chosen as gathering points because of their potentially dependable internal water supply.

The Trechado Spring Site, located several miles north and east of Mariana Mesa, is large and not unlike Site 616 in that its layout included a completely enclosed plaza containing a walk-in well. This well is in use today. Of course, other factors may have determined the choice of the site, before an internal water supply was sought.

If mutual security was a motive for establishing larger, readily defended sites, the question arises: Protection from whom? There are two possibilities: nomadic bands not related historically or socially to the occupants of the pueblos — the so-called enemy people — or, alternatively, related groups from other pueblos — that is, internecine warfare.

The first hypothesis assumes that wandering bands entered the region harassing hunting parties from the pueblos, making sporadic attacks on the villages themselves, burning crops, and in general making life extremely difficult for the more sedentary inhabitants. A few years of such activity might well cause a people to band together for defense and possibly to abandon an area altogether, even when no pueblos have been successfully attacked and destroyed. A large or concentrated sedentary group, dependent upon agriculture as well as hunting and gathering to provide for its needs, could be reduced to desperate straits after a few years of intensive or even intermittent harassment, during which crops were burned or stolen and the movement of hunting parties severely restricted. On the other hand, the lineal and cultural descendants of these sedentary peoples later demonstrated extraordinary staying power in the face of incursions by European groups which encroached upon their territory and threatened their way of life. Are we to assume that the ancestors of the historic Pueblo groups were so conditioned culturally and psychologically that, when similarly threatened during the precontact period, they simply abandoned their homes and a vast territory to the new arrivals?

The second hypothesis involves internecine warfare, which was not the dominant motif for the historic Pueblos that it was for some other American Indian groups (e.g., the Iroquois, or the historic Plains tribes). Nor is there any evidence that warfare was prominent throughout most of Pueblo history. Only during one specific period (ca. A.D. 1300) are there strong indications that war and defense were important. If this strife was internecine in character, we must adequately explain this momentary lapse from an earlier and later cultural outlook. An extended period of drought, a lower water table, and consequent arroyo cutting might have combined to provide such a reason. Crop failures and decreased agricultural production would eventually be reflected in increased population mobility; witness the situation in the "dust bowl" during the 1930s. The population of the "poorer" areas, singly or in groups, would move to other regions.

If the agricultural situation deteriorated, some areas of concentrated population would have had to be abandoned; for the decay of the agricultural system through natural forces would be hastened by the increased agricultural load in the more favored areas, resulting from the unusual population concentrations within a limited region. This hypothesis would account satisfactorily for the abandonment of sites and entire areas where there are no, or only limited, indications of forceful external pressure.

If the second hypothesis is sound, Site 616 and Trechado Spring would represent the final gathering points of the inhabitants of the Mariana Mesa area. At Site 616 an attack by another group, whether successful or not, may have provided the *coup de grace* to a gradually worsening agricultural situation and forced the inhabitants to a decision, one perhaps already pending. They picked up what they could salvage, perhaps fearing a subsequent attack, and departed from the area, soon to be followed by their erstwhile neighbors.

As yet there is no conclusive evidence for or against either hypothesis, although in the light of the present data internecine warfare brought about by natural factors would appear more likely. In fact, both hypotheses remain possible, and both may have been operative in varying degrees.

DATING CONSIDERATIONS

Site 616 must have been occupied over a considerable period from late Pueblo II through almost all of Pueblo III, judging from the ceramic complex, which is summarized in terms of the painted types below.

While the eight tree-ring dates provide no evidence for an early beginning, they are consistent with a termination during the late 1200s, as shown in the table at the top of the next page.

As Bannister, Hannah, and Robinson observed: "It is possible to date the Kiva at A.D. 1243, with both reused and repair timbers present. The other dates extend the occupation at least into the 1280s."

Architectural evidence indicates that Area A represents the earliest occupation. Masonry in that section closely resembled that in the late rooms at Site 494 and the earlier rooms of Site 481. Area D and parts of Areas B and C apparently came later (perhaps the middle period of Site 481), and Area C was the latest of all.

All evidence is generally consistent, and the inference of a first occupation around A.D. 1100 or 1150 or a little later, with final abandonment at about A.D. 1300, seems acceptable.

CERAMIC COMPLEX

Type	Quantity	Dates Breternitz	Carlson
Reserve Black-on-white (5 variants)	409	A.D. 940–1100+	
Wingate-Puerco Black-on-red*	914	1050–1200	1050–1200
Wingate Polychrome	38	1030–1200	1100–1200
Tularosa Black-on-white	5572	1150–1300	
St. Johns Polychrome	1121	1175–1300	1175–1300
Heshotauthla Polychrome	447	1275–1400	1300–1375
Pinedale Polychrome	147	1275–1350	1275–1325
Springerville Polychrome	94	1200–1325	1250–1300
Other types	7	(all late)	

Wingate Black-on-red was combined with the former Puerco Black-on-red at the Second Southwestern Ceramic Conference, 1959, with Puerco being regarded as a late variant of Wingate, perhaps as late as 1250.

TREE-RING DATES

Provenience	Dates (Bannister, Hannah, and Robinson 1970, p. 16)
Room 3, Area C	A.D. 1203 p – 1247 v*
	1195 p – 1282 v
	1231 p – 1285 v
Room 5, Area C	1190 p – 1286 vv
Kiva	1166 p – 1236 c
	1142 p – 1243 c
	1159 p – 1243 r
	1189 p – 1263 c

*See symbol code, appendix B (p. 294).

ARCHITECTURE

The pueblo did not obtain its final form as the result of a single preconceived architectural design. During the initial period of construction, when only one or two rooms were built at a time, the main problem for the builders was the relationship of new rooms to the rooms already in use or, if a new unit was begun, its placement relative to the units already there. Insufficient excavation was done at Site 616 to determine the standards that may have affected architectural design, or the relationship, if any, between particular clusters of rooms and individual subterranean rooms.

It seems clear, in view of the results, that during the final period of construction the family units (if such were the building groups) which added elements did so within the limits of a scheme broadly conceived and generally accepted by those responsible for new construction. It would be interesting to know whether this scheme was overtly expressed and which, if any, groups within the pueblo decided its formulation and execution. Overt or not, the direct result of this program was a completely enclosed plaza containing a walk-in well, one or two kivas, pithouses, and clusters of surface rooms. The outside walls of the exterior rooms of the pueblo formed a straight line so that the overall exterior outline of the pueblo was rectangular. The only major deviation was an armlike extension of rooms to the east of the northeast corner. The exterior wall of the pueblo was generally of large sandstone-block construction, at least in Areas C and F, though in some sections, perhaps where the walls of older units were incorporated (e.g., Area B), the exterior wall was of adobe. At the two points where room units were not contiguous, the walls of the adjacent units were united by a single wall of standstone. No rooms or room groups were constructed outside the exterior wall. Any expansion which took place following the completion of the exterior wall was completely internal, unless the extension at the northeast corner is an exception.

The Rooms (figs. 10–39)

The surface rooms designed and built by the inhabitants of Site 616 were of three, or perhaps four, general types. The simplest of them lacked floor features. These may have been storerooms and, perhaps, sleeping quarters: Rooms A2, B3, C1, C3, C4, C6, C8, and F1. If they served as storerooms, there was little indication of the materials kept there. Seeds were found in the fill of Rooms C3 and F1 and on the floors of Rooms B3 and C8. Only Room B3, with its large quantity of seeds and the pile of sandstone slabs, actually resembled a storeroom. There was some miscellaneous equipment — axes, manos, awls, pecking stones, etc. — on the floors of Rooms A2, C3, and C6. In contrast, the items found on the floors of Rooms C1, C4, and C8 were not directly utilitarian, that is, beads, quartz crystals, or unusually shaped stones. Other than a bone awl, nothing was found on the floor of Room F1.

The dimensions (in meters) and the areas (in square meters) of these rooms are below.

SIMPLEST SURFACE ROOMS

Room No.	SE – NW	SW – NE	Area
A2	2.75	1.90	5.25
A2	2.75	1.90	5.25
B3	2.60	2.40	6.25
C1	2.10	2.30	4.80
C3	2.20	2.30	5.00
C4	1.50	1.85	3.60
C6	2.55	2.20	5.60
C8	2.15	3.95	8.50
F1	2.35	2.30	5.40

The second room design was that of a general-purpose unit or living room, which probably served as the focal point of a family's activities. Half of the rooms excavated were of this design, including Rooms A1, A3, B2, B7, C5, C10, D1, D3, F2, and perhaps Rooms B5, D5, E1, and E2. Each of these rooms had a firepit and six were also equipped with a single mealing bin.

The firepit was always located to one side of the center of the room. If it was placed just to the north or south of the center line, it was centrally located with respect to the east and west walls; if it was to the east or west of center, it was centrally located with respect to the north and south walls. Although most firepits were adjacent to the center line of the room, one (Room D5) was against a wall. Beyond this the exact location of the firepit, the orientation of its long axis, and its location relative to other room features, or the shape of the room itself were apparently matters of personal preference. The southern half of the room was the most frequent choice for the firepit (seven rooms), with the eastern half next (four rooms).

The accepted procedure was to place one long side of the single mealing bin against the wall of these "living" rooms, with the upper end of the metate 40 to 50 cm from the corner, providing cramped but presumably adequate quarters for the person grinding. On occasion, the wall behind the bin had been hollowed out slightly at hip level, perhaps to allow for "expansion" on the part of the user of the bin. In every case the mealing bin was in the half of the room opposite the firepit, but no further regularity was apparent. Three of the single mealing bins were placed against the north wall (in Rooms A1 and A3 the grinder faced the east, in Room D5 the west), and three were against the west wall (in Rooms C5 and F2 the grinder faced the south, in Room E2 the north).

The dimensions and the areas (in meters and square meters respectively) of these rooms are below.

GENERAL PURPOSE UNITS

Room No.	SE – NW	SW – NE	Area
A1	2.70	3.15	8.50
A3	2.35	2.70	6.35
B2	2.20	2.50	5.50
B5	2.30	2.40	5.50
B7	2.90	2.20	6.40
C5	4.80	2.85	13.60
C10	4.80	2.60	12.50
D1	2.45	2.65	6.50
D3	2.45	2.45	6.00
D5	1.60	2.25	3.60
E1	2.10	2.10	4.40
E2	2.25	1.90	4.25
F2	2.45	3.10	7.60

The third room design was more specialized, namely that of mealing rooms or, perhaps more accurately, grinding rooms, which were equipped with three to five mealing bins each. Five such rooms were excavated, including Rooms B1, C2, C9, D2, and the mealing room associated with the walk-in well. No two rooms were exactly alike. Rooms B1 and C2 each contained three contiguous bins extending from the south wall in Room B1 (the grinder faced east), and the west wall in Room C2 (the grinder faced north). The room affiliated with the walk-in well had four bins. Three of these were contiguous in a north–south line beginning next to, but not touching, the north wall (the grinder faced east). The fourth bin was single (the grinder faced south), placed between the row of bins and the east wall. All bins in this room were unusual, in that no part of any of them touched a wall of the room. Rooms C9 and D2 each contained five bins, four of them contiguous in a line from the east and north walls respectively. In Room C9 the single bin was also against the east wall, and a person using it faced those using the other bins. The fifth bin in Room D2 was rather unusual. Situated against the north wall between the row of bins and the west wall, it was oriented at a 45° angle to the other bins and to the room walls. Unlike all other bins at the site, only two sides of the bin (the rear and right) were slab-lined and the bin was not set into the floor. That is, the floor slab of the bin was level with, rather than below, the level of the room floor. The "metate" was a circular slab of sandstone set at an angle to the floor on an adobe wedge. It showed almost no signs of abrasion. If this apparent "mealing bin" was actually so used, it must have been for a rather special kind of grinding.

The only seeds found in direct association with these bins were cactus and chenopodium.

The dimensions and the areas (again, in meters and square meters) of these rooms are below.

GRINDING ROOMS

Room No.	SE – NW	SW – NE	Area
B1	2.50	2.55	6.35
C2	2.25	2.30	5.20
C9	2.40	2.30	5.50
D2	2.55	1.95	5.00
Well Room	2.30	1.60	3.70

Possibly there was a fourth kind of specialized room — a craft or work room.

Room B1, because of its contents, and the grinding room adjoining the walk-in well, because of its location, could be identified as craft rooms for the manufacture of pottery or other objects; hence the bins in these rooms may have been utilized primarily, if not entirely, for this work rather than for grinding foodstuffs.

The average size of the storage rooms and of the mealing rooms was quite similar (5.55 square meters and 5.51 square meters respectively), though individual variation for storage rooms in particular was fairly marked (e.g., 3.6 to 8.5 square meters).

Apparently there were three separate patterns for the living rooms. The pithouses were smallest (4.08 square meters on the average), while the surface living rooms averaged 6.54 square meters. The two living rooms in Area C were quite different, and were more than twice as large, averaging 13.05 square meters. This size corresponded closely to the pattern of the large sandstone-walled rooms at Site 481, and may be another indication of an affiliation between the inhabitants of that site and the builders of Area C at Site 616, as discussed on pages 47 ff.

Construction

WALLS (figs. 10, 11, 19, 21)

Construction was nearly always begun by digging a shallow trench 5 to 20 cm deep to outline the room to be built and to form a footing trench for the masonry. The wall bases consisted of two to five irregular courses of cobbles set in a liberal amount of adobe. In Area A, the entire walls consisted of this type of masonry; even when *this* style of masonry was later abandoned, however, the cobble-and-adobe wall base was frequently retained. In some of the later adobe walls, sandstone and lava cobbles were used in constructing the wall base, and, in a few instances, even for walls built of sandstone blocks. The wall base filled the trench and often extended 5 to 10 cm above the original ground level. To some extent the builders attempted to keep the tops of these basal sections level. That is, in each room the trenches were dug to a relatively constant depth of 15 to 20 cm below the natural contours of the ground, while the basal wall section was built up to provide a level surface on which was begun the construction of the more regularly coursed masonry (either adobe or sandstone blocks).

All of the walls excavated, except those in Area A, were of one of two basic materials: sandstone blocks or adobe bricks.

The builders took advantage of natural cleavage planes in selecting and forming sandstone blocks, but the exposed faces of the blocks and occasionally other parts were generally shaped by pecking. The sizes of these blocks varied considerably but the general range was on the order of 15 by 25 by 10 cm or, toward the other end of the scale, 8 by 10 by 3 cm. The last two dimensions given are respectively the length and height of the exposed face of the block. The sandstone walls were double, but, unlike the double sandstone walls of Site 481 (p. 16), only rarely (e.g., the west wall of Room C10) was there any significant variation in the sizes of the stones used on opposite sides of the same wall. In the best examples of sandstone-block masonry the blocks were fairly uniform in size and laid in regular courses. Others were less well done and the west wall of Room C8 evidently had been in danger of collapsing. A few sandstone-block walls were chinked with sherds or occasionally with thin sandstone spalls.

The adobe walls were constructed of adobe bricks

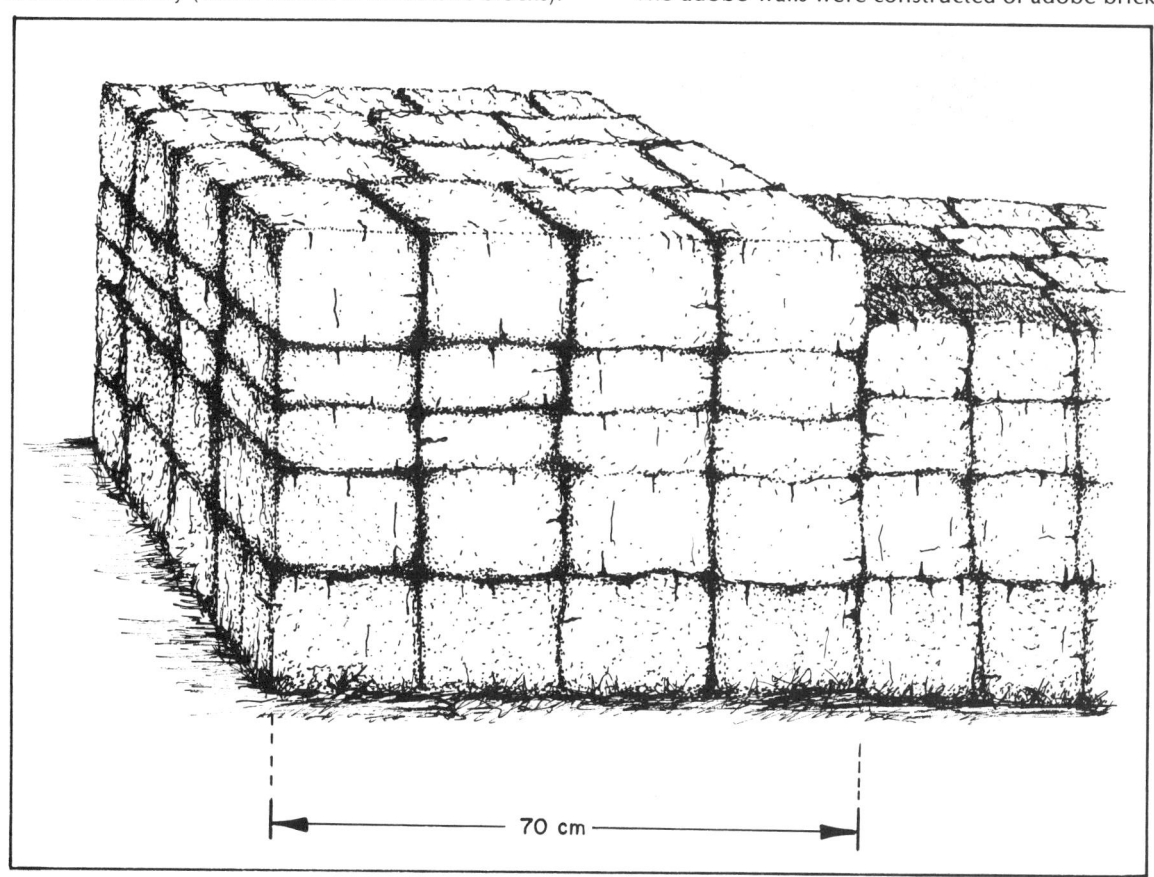

Figure 10. Site 616. Sketch of a typical section of adobe brick wall.

laid in fairly regular courses (figs. 10, 11). A few walls were 2 bricks thick and one was 4, but most were 3 bricks thick. The bricks apparently were sun-baked (not fired) and hand-formed rather than molded. They were rectangular with straight sides. On the whole, the size varied considerably, with the dimensions of the bricks ranging from 15 to 20 cm in length and 5 to 15 cm in height. They generally were 8 to 10 cm in width, though the extreme range was from 6 to 14 cm.

The adobe walls seemed to have been built in units some 70 cm in length (whether the wall was 2, 3, or 4 bricks thick). The horizontal courses of bricks tended to be level and of uniform height through the entire unit, from face to face extending the length of the unit, and the vertical divisions were continuous (i.e., there were no bonds between outer and inner courses). In each vertical set of courses (e.g., the inner or outer and perhaps medial face[s] the bricks, placed one over another, tended to be of the same length so that there were continuous vertical divisions between bricks from top to bottom for that (inner, outer, or medial) set. In other words the visible (or any other) face of a wall showed horizontal and vertical divisions extending the length and height of the unit. The horizontal divisions were common for all sets of courses for that unit, but the vertical divisions were never common between sets (except at the end of the unit), thus providing the only bonding present.

Adobe mortar was used between the bricks. In the east wall of Room C5 two sandstone blocks had been used to effect a bond between two adobe wall units.

There has been some debate about the utilization of adobe bricks in the Southwest prior to the arrival of the Spanish, but the question is basically one involving the definition of a "brick." Although no example has been reported of bricks made in prepared molds, there are several instances of individually hand-molded bricks from late Anasazi sites, as distinguished from the turtle-backs from some Basket Maker III and Pueblo I sites. (Brief discussions of the subject appear in Judd 1916, p. 245, and Smith 1952, p. 9.)

Nearly all of the adobe walls excavated at Site 616 were later torn down, two with extreme care, the others as an adjunct to backfilling the site. The results of this deliberate dismantlement, as well as the recovery of a number of individual loose bricks (notably on the floor of the cist in Room D5), left no doubt in the minds of the excavators that at Site 616 bricks were made and utilized in the construction of the walls. Unfortunately, sun-dried bricks laid in adobe mortar which have aged for several centuries do not separate readily one from another. Cleavage was often good but never perfect and the situation was complicated by the existence of weather cracks. Moreover, photographs of the attempts to separate them reveal less than actual inspection of the walls themselves.

The interior surfaces of many, and probably all, walls were covered with a coat of light tan, sandy adobe plaster, which did not survive well. There were no observed cases of extensive replastering but the sample was not a large one.

FLOORS

At the time the wall trench was dug and the basal portion of the wall built, the floor area was leveled off. This seems to have been accomplished both by excavation and by filling, and the floor-leveling process exposed the basal sections of some walls, at times extending even below the wall base, while the filling caused the bases of other walls to be as much as 40 cm below floor level. The floors were reasonably level in most rooms, though on occasion the absolute depth of different sections of a room floor varied by as much as 20 cm. Generally this change in level was not particularly noticeable. The floors were plastered and sometimes replastered with a hard, tan, adobelike material slightly different in composition from that found on the walls. In many of the rooms the junction between walls and floor was a smooth curve rather than a sharp angle.

DOORWAYS

All but three of the 16 doorways found had been deliberately sealed by the occupants of the rooms. Open doorways connected Room C3 with Room C9, Room C2 with Room C5, and Room C4 with an unexcavated room to the east.

It is interesting to note that only in Area C—which, with its careful sandstone masonry and large rooms, appeared to be one of the latest additions to the pueblo, perhaps through ingress of a related group— were open doorways found. Despite the hypothesis that Area C and Site 481 may have had close ties, open doorways, while present, were not a common feature of late rooms at Site 481.

Only the two sealed doorways in the south wall of Room B3 were in an outside wall, although there may have been others at one time. The doorways ranged in width from 36 to 53 cm, with 46 cm the average. The sills of two were at floor level, the remainder were 10 to 30 cm above the floor. The sill of the doorway connecting Room C2 with Room C5 was 60 cm above the floor of Room C2, but here there was a step 35 cm high, the riser of which was a sandstone metate placed on edge. Generally the sills were edged with sandstone slabs and frequently a single sandstone slab formed the entire sill. The doorways were sealed with adobe and rock, the latter either lava or sandstone occasionally placed in irregular courses. In a few

Figure 11. Site 616. Detail of west wall of Room F2, showing adobe bricks.

instances (e.g., Room C10), the doors were sealed with a cored wall, faced on both sides with stone and the center filled with rubble. These were the only examples of cored masonry at Site 616. Both sides of the sealed doorways were finished equally well.

FIREPITS, VENTILATORS, AND DEFLECTORS

Thirteen rooms and the kiva contained firepits. All were rectangular and the one in Room E1 was nearly square. They were constructed by making a rectangular excavation in the floor of the room. In the pithouses (Rooms E1 and E2) no slabs were used. In the surface rooms, a single sandstone slab or occasionally two slabs were set up along each side (only two sides were slab-lined in the firepit in Room B5). Generally the tops of the slabs were secured in place by adobe, and adobe was used to round off the corners and joints between the slabs. The floor of the firepit was of burned adobe in Rooms B5, C10, D1, D3, F2, and the kiva, while in the other rooms sandstone slabs had been set into the firepit floors. The square firepit in Room E1 was 26 cm square and 26 cm deep. The rectangular firepits were 42 to 56 cm long and 30 to 34 cm wide, except for three that were respectively 38, 40, and 45 cm wide. In depth most ranged from 14 to 26 cm below room floor, two were 34 cm deep, and one was 50 cm deep. Three firepits contained subsidiary circular holes in the center of their floors (pp. 78, 83, 86). In Room C5 the hole was 20 cm in diameter and 23 cm deep and was not covered with a sandstone slab. In Rooms C10 and D1 the holes were bell-shaped with mouth diameters of 10 cm, maximum diameters of 17 cm, and depths of 28 and 22 cm, respectively; they were covered with sandstone slabs. These subsidiary pits may have served as depositories for keeping coals overnight. Similar features were found at Hawikuh, near Zuni (Smith, Woodbury, and Woodbury 1966, p. 56), at Sandstone Hill Pueblo (Barnett 1974, p. 11), and in Rooms 6 and 25 at Site 481 (pp. 192, 195). The trench in the northern half of the floor of the kiva firepit may have had a similar function.

The kiva, the pithouses, and Room C10 each had a ventilating shaft in connection with the firepit. In the pithouses this consisted of a chimneylike, oval shaft just outside the eastern part of the south wall, extending downward from ground level to meet a slitlike aperture that penetrated the wall at floor level. Since this slit generally extended higher than the desired height of the final opening, the upper portion of the front of the slit was closed by an adobe and sandstone plug, leaving a basal opening approximately 25 cm square. In Rooms E1 and E2 this ventilator opening was flush with the south wall of the rooms, and a deflector slab had been set into the floor between the opening and the firepit. In Room D5 a somewhat more ingenious architectural design was employed. The ventilator shaft and opening were set into a recess at the east end of the south wall, while the firepit was built adjacent to the center of this wall. In this manner the need for a deflector was obviated, and the already restricted floor was not cluttered by adding one. In the kiva a trench was dug through the bench and into the south wall, where it likewise met a vertical shaft extending down from the surface. The trench through the bench was probably roofed with stone slabs such as covered the rest of the bench, for no impressions of a small-timber roof were found. No sandstone slabs were found *in situ*, however. A sandstone-slab deflector was set into the floor between the ventilator opening and the firepit.

Room C10 was somewhat unusual in design, with two south walls 90 cm apart. The area between them showed no evidence of a floor or of use. A stone-walled tunnel at the level of the room floor joined the walls and connected with small rectangular holes in each of them, thus providing ventilation to the rooms from outside. No indication of the nature of the roof of this tunnel was found, though probably there had been one. The need for a double wall with connecting tunnel — when certainly a single hole in the main south wall of the room would adequately satisfy the same physical requirements — is cause for speculation. In order to protect the firepit (which was centrally located in the room) from a direct draft, a low curved ridge 25 cm high was constructed beginning on the west side of the ventilator opening. This ridge ran north for 70 cm and then curved eastward for 80 cm, thus breaking the flow of air. A similar deflector arrangement was found in the adjacent Room C5, though here protection was necessary because of an open doorway rather than a ventilating system as such.

PASSTHROUGHS

Small square holes (ranging from 15 by 15 cm to 30 by 30 cm), extending through the walls from one room to another, may have served as ventilators and/or passthroughs. In Room C9 an open hole at floor level connected this room with an unexcavated room to the south, and in this same room there was a sealed opening 50 cm above the floor in the wall between Rooms C9 and C6. A similar waist-high opening connected Room C6 and Room C10. A floor-level connection existed between Room F2 and the unexcavated room to the west, while in Room B1 there was a rectangular hole just above floor level in the south wall. This latter hole, in an outside wall of the pueblo, was probably designed primarily for ventilation. It had been sealed. On the other hand, the two holes found in Room C6 may have served as passthroughs at one time, though both had been sealed before the pueblo was abandoned. They were similar in size to the others but were located 50 cm above floor level. The sills of these holes were of adobe and the sides were lined with sandstone slabs. Generally, the roof was formed of a sandstone slab. In the hole connecting Room C6 with Room C10 four small poles, 2 to 3 cm in diameter, bridged the distance between the tops of the sandstone slabs lining the walls. In Room F2 a sandstone slab deflector had been set into the floor, to protect the firepit from the draft passing through the ventilating hole in the west wall.

ENCLOSURES

The southern half of Room C5 was divided into two closetlike enclosures by the ventilator tunnel. The walls setting off these enclosures were built directly on the floor rather than set into a trench. Both enclosures contained depressions or cists in the floor. The circular floor cist in the western enclosure, located against the east wall, was 40 cm in diameter and 40 cm deep. The cist in the eastern enclosure, located almost in the doorway, was oval (35 by 40 cm) and 15 cm deep. Both were semihemispherical in cross section. The sides and bottom were smooth but unplastered.

CISTS AND NICHES

In addition to the two cists described above, a number of other rooms contained cists or niches of one form or another. In the floor in the southeast corner of Room C1 there was a cist 30 cm on each side and 29 cm deep, with a small irregular extension to the northwest. It was roughly finished and unplastered. A roughly rectangular excavation, which may have served as a cist, was located against the center of the west wall of Room C6. This cist was 75 cm long, extended 40 cm into the room, and was 40 cm deep. The base of the west wall, which over the rest of its length was only 24 cm below the floor, was extended down 40 cm to form the west wall of the cist. All four walls of the cist were plastered. In the subterranean Room D5 a large semihemispherical cist with flat floor and arched walls and roof had been excavated into the east end of the north wall just to the rear of the mealing bin. This large cist, excavated beyond the north wall, was approximately 90 cm in diameter and 76 cm high. It had two small auxiliary cists, one in its floor and the other in its east wall. It is described more fully in connection with room D5 (pp. 90–91).

A small niche 6 cm in diameter, 13 cm deep, and 30 cm above the floor, in the center of the east wall of Room D5, also may have been affiliated with the grinding process. A small niche 10 cm in diameter and 15 cm deep was located in the south wall midway between the firepit and the ventilation shaft and 25 cm above the floor. Room E2 also contained a large wall niche 70 cm deep, 40 cm wide, and 40 cm high, located in the west end of the north wall where a person using the mealing bin would face it. The floor of the niche was 18 cm higher than the room floor. In front of the niche there was a small steplike shelf about the same level as the niche floor, a little wider than the niche and extending into the room 20 to 25 cm. The niche was set off from the shelf by a rounded ridge 12 cm high. Through the shelf at its west end was a bell-shaped cist with mouth diameter of 10 cm, maximum diameter of 14 by 17 cm, and depth of 25 cm. At the juncture of the west and south walls of Room E2 and 23 cm above the floor a small niche with mouth diameter of 15 cm and depth of 13 cm extended into the west wall. It too may have been affiliated with the mealing bin.

The excavated portion of the kiva revealed one small niche with an oval entrance (23 cm long by 19 cm high) and 18 cm deep, located in the east wall midway between the wall of the south bench and the northeast pilaster and 50 cm above the kiva floor.

MEALING BINS

The initial step in the construction of the mealing bins was an excavation into the room floor. The excavation was, in top view, rectangular but the sloping base for the metate remained unexcavated. The dimensions of the bins were quite consistent throughout the site. Most ranged between 50 and 60 cm in length, though the bins in Room E2 and those in Room D2 were 70 cm long. All were between 40 and 50 cm wide. The depth of the floor of the mealing bins below room floor ranged from 10 to 20 cm. All bins except that in Room E2 (and Room D5?) were lined with sandstone slabs as were the bin floors. In several (Rooms B1, C9, D2, F2) the room wall served as one side, but in most of the bins adjacent to room walls a slab was set in place, flush against the wall. These slabs and the metate itself were secured in position with adobe. There was usually a strip of adobe 5 to 7 cm wide on either side of the metate and slightly lower than its surface. In Room F2 fragments of several manos had been set into this adobe border. In several of the bins a sherd had been set into the adobe at the lower left corner of the metate, serving as a scoop. In the eastern bin in Room C2 this scoop was formed by a flat wooden slat. The upper ends of the metates were generally 10 cm higher than the room floors, and 5 to 10 cm lower than the tops of the back-wall slabs.

The angle at which the metates were set varied widely. Those that could be measured are listed below.

METATE ANGLES

Room A1 — single bin — 31.5°
Room A3 — single bin — 28.0°
Room B1 — south bin — 28.0°
Room B1 — north bin — 28.0°
Room C2 — west bin — 31.0°
Room C2 — center bin — 18.0°
Room C2 — east bin — 28.0°
Room C9 — single bin — 26.0°
Room C9 — west bin — 40.0°
Room D2 — north bin — 19.0°
Room D2 — single bin — 27.0°
Room E2 — single bin — 23.0°

When metates found *in situ* were removed from their bins, we observed that on the underside there was often an irregular area 10 to 15 cm across with a moldy white appearance caused by material resembling flour in color and consistency. Pepper (1920, p. 378) notes the ceremonial use of finely powdered white sandstone. This powdery substance on the underside of the metates at Site 616 may represent a similar practice.

Not all metates were set into bins. Many were found loose on room floors or among the debris from the roof. They probably were placed on the floor or roof wherever and whenever needed, supported at the proper angle by loose cobbles.

ROOFS

Despite the frequent occurrence of charred beams, there was little solid evidence concerning roof construction. Impressions observed in burned roof adobe suggest that large beams 8 to 10 cm in diameter were laid parallel across the tops of the walls. The interstices were filled with smaller poles 2 to 3 cm in diameter laid parallel to the larger beams. Some grass and a thick layer of adobe were placed over these beams.

Two of the pithouses (Rooms D5 and E2) were probably roofed in a manner similar to that of the surface rooms, but room E1 was too shallow for this exact method. Apparently the upper half of the walls was of pole-and-adobe construction, but there was no indication of the nature of the roof.

The kiva may have been roofed by crib-work construction using the pilasters and the corners of the bench for supports, but there was little direct evidence for it, other than the sections of a number of large logs 10 to 15 cm in diameter in the fill and on the floor.

It is doubtful that any attempt was made to roof the walk-in well. The attached mealing room may have been roofed but the nature of this roof is not known.

POTTERY-MAKING AT SITE 616

Construction

Pottery clay, probably obtained locally, was blended with a variety of tempering materials. Clay used in making white-slipped or red-slipped vessels was generally mixed with an angular opaque material, which in all probability consisted of finely fragmented sherds. Occasionally, small quantities of quartz sand and other materials were noted, but these may have been natural impurities in the clay rather than intentional additions.

Clay for the construction of most of the corrugated pottery may have been obtained from a different source, for the color of the final product was generally a dark brown rather than a gray. However, color variation observed in a few sherds suggested that this difference owed its origin to variation in firing rather than to use of a different clay. Whatever the case with regard to the clay, quartz sand rather than crushed sherds served as tempering material for the corrugated pottery, and this paste ranged from slightly vitreous to dull and powdery. Both the amount and size of the temper as well as its constituents of sand, rock, and mica varied, but not drastically or according to any discernible pattern. The variations within this norm were so gradual that no division was evident, nor was there a patterned correlation of any such variation with other factors internal or external to the pottery.

A small group of corrugated vessels was made from a different clay (paste modes keys [I] and [J], p. 120), which was more dense, became gray when fired, and had a shattering rather than a crumbling consistency. It was tempered with quartz sand and, apparently, crushed sherds.

In general, the noncorrugated pottery was well finished and coiling marks or fractures were rarely visible. The evidence suggested that the pottery was built up by coiling, though we do not know whether it was in the form of closed rings or continuous spiral. To judge from the corrugated ware, the favored technique was that of continuous spiral. Occasional coil fractures were evident on basal parts, leaving little reason to believe that large basal portions of vessels other than miniature ones were formed by modeling.

Pottery of all types was at least sometimes formed with the aid of a *puki*. The few *pukis* recovered consisted of basal sherds of vessels that had been broken.

Ladle handles were generally made by rolling a flat slab of clay into a hollow cylinder. This tube was often reinforced by a fillet of clay in the center of the end attached to the ladle bowl while the other end was closed. Open U-shaped ladle handles were also used.

PLAIN AND SLIPPED POTTERY

The vessel walls were quite uniform in thickness but occasionally the base was slightly thicker. The insides of jars showed bands of fine parallel ridges generally running around the circumference of the vessel as if the interior finishing had been accomplished by moving a handful of material, perhaps grass, back and forth while turning the vessel slowly with the other hand. Jar exteriors and the interiors and exteriors of bowls were finished by polishing with a small, hard polishing pebble. The polished surfaces in almost every instance were smooth, even, and lustrous, but the polishing marks were not readily apparent. On white-slipped vessels the polishing generally was done after the vessel was slipped but before it was painted; however, on the red-slipped vessels there was considerable variation. The interiors and handles of ladles were well finished, but often, except for the slip, little attention was given to the outside of the ladle bowls.

The slip was applied to all surfaces of bowls and ladles, and the entire exteriors of jars. Generally on jars the slip extended down the interior surface of the neck. In other words, every portion of the vessel normally visible was slipped. Occasionally smeared streaks of slip material appeared on the interiors of white-slipped jars, apparently from the unwiped hand of the potter. One black-on-white jar had a smear as if a rag soaked in slip material had been pressed against the inside surface. This is meager evidence but it suggests that the slip may have been applied by means of a rag dipped into slip material and then wiped over the vessel.

CORRUGATED POTTERY

In every case but one, corrugated vessels were built by continuous counterclockwise coiling. No coils were obliterated and generally on indented vessels the first 8 to 12 basal coils were not modified. The number of unmodified basal coils ranged from 4 on one vessel to 20 on each of four vessels (three of which were medium-sized jars from Room C10). The beginning of indentation did not correlate with the upper edge of the *puki* in which the base was formed; in fact, in four cases the indenting began with the very first coil. There was no noticeable change in the indenting technique over any one vessel except that in six instances the indentations on the base were rather wavy. The indenting of all vessels but one was handled in such a manner that vertical fingerprints (observable on 95 percent of the vessels) were left with a more or less marked "Z" slant to the indentations. Experiments indicated that these indentations were formed by placing the edge of the left thumb against the coil so that it pointed upward, and then applying pressure downward. Actually the "Z" slant in nearly an upright triangle on some vessels suggested that the pressure was more backward than downward, and the wavy bases showed than an occasional potter tended more toward the use of the tip rather than the edge of the left thumb. At any rate, the method of forming the indentations was remarkably uniform throughout the site. The only exception was on one vessel apparently indented with the right thumb pointing downward. Here, unlike all other vessels where the thumb flattened the entire width of the coil, the thumb only extended over and flattened the top half of the coil, so that the lower edge was left as a high unindented ridge. The final rim coil was not indented on one-third of the vessels, and two coils were left plain on one-quarter of the vessels. On nearly all others three coils were left plain. In one instance the unindented rim section was 4 coils wide, and in two instances the indenting continued through the final coil though the top of this last coil was evened off. Fingernail marks could be seen only occasionally and never on more than a small group of sherds from any one room.

After the vessel was completed, the general practice was to brush lightly over the exterior with a polishing stone or some similar hard tool, which served to smooth down any rough points and flatten the edges of the coils and tops of indentations. Occasionally the polishing was only spotty and only where it was needed, especially on small vessels. Only rarely was it heavy enough to begin to spread or displace the clay and in no case did it obliterate or even badly smear coils or indentations. This smoothing was less frequent in the vessels made of the gray clay, but nearly all of these appear to have been wiped with some sort of soft material. Quite possibly this wiped effect was the result of the heel of the hand being rubbed over the surface during manufacturing. Perhaps the movements of potters using this gray clay were slightly different from those of potters using other types of clay.

On nearly all vessels there were two or three coils

per centimeter, though on several very small vessels there were as many as four. The coils on vessels of material mode keys (I) and (J) tended to be slightly broader (averaging two coils per centimeter), and the indentations were more widely spaced.

The interiors of most corrugated vessels were smooth and even and appeared to have been worked over with a rather broad instrument (approximately 0.5 cm in width). Lustrous streaks were only occasionally evident. Two vessels seemed to have been smoothed with the fingers or some other soft object, for the surfaces, while even, were slightly gritty. The interior surfaces were usually rather matte or slightly lustrous, but there was often more variation on a single vessel than between different vessels. The clay in the matte areas was often minutely roughed up as if the interior had been polished or smoothed when the clay was rather dry. The more lustrous areas were generally near the rim. The basal portion of the interiors of bowls had been polished by parallel strokes going back and forth across the area. The sides of the bowl interiors were polished by a series of long (10 to 15 cm) strokes all parallel to the rim. Apparently a section was polished in this manner, then the vessel rotated and an adjacent section done until the entire interior had been covered.

The thickness of the vessel walls was remarkably uniform both within and between vessels. All fell within the range of 6 to 8 mm and on an individual vessel the variation was generally less than a millimeter. The bases of the corrugated vessels from Site 616 were never recessed nor were the basal coils thicker than the others, but in a number of vessels the basal section had been thickened (up to 11 mm) by adding clay to the inside surface.

All bowls were smudged on the interior but only two jars were so treated.

Decoration

WHITE-SLIPPED POTTERY (figs. 44e-k, m, p-t; 45-48; 49h-l)

In general the painting on the black-on-white pottery was carefully executed. Large areas of color were first outlined and then filled in. The edges of painted elements were usually sharp, but fairly often the paint was watery or runny so that the edges became fuzzy. Jars were painted from a circular line just below the neck to an area about halfway between the center of the base and the widest portion of the vessel. The lower edge of the design was generally circular but occasionally polygonal. Often there were simple line decorations on jar necks. On bowls and ladles the interior was painted in a band with the decoration beginning at a line just below the rim. The center was generally unpainted with a circular or occasionally polygonal area left undecorated; but on rare occasions a small decorative element was placed in this central area and in a few instances the rims were ticked. Some ladles were decorated with adjacent but unconnected triangular units usually filled with the checkerboard pattern of decorative mode (h). The upper surface of ladle handles was often decorated with simple, usually linear elements and not infrequently this design extended to the sides or encircled the handle.

During analysis of the black-on-white sherds we observed in at least 24 instances that the interior of basal sherds of jars had a large, irregular blotch or black stain 5 to 10 cm in diameter, which seemed to be the residue of a small pool of black paint that had been used or wiped up. The obvious explanation is that the paint supply was kept conveniently at hand by placing it inside the vessel being decorated. This would have inhibited free movement of the vessel and, if such was the case, the brushes used must have attained considerable length (i.e., greater than the height of the jar), for the small diameter of the jar mouth all but prohibits passage of the hand to dip the brush. These stains were never seen on other than basal sherds, and on several occasions these dried pools of paint occurred on sherds from restorable vessels found on the floors of the rooms; so the secondary use of sherds as paint palettes does not provide the answer, at least in every instance. On two occasions we noted large pools of slip material on basal sherds and on a number of others streaks of slip were evident on the interior, indicating that the potters had not wiped their hands before placing them inside the vessel.

RED-SLIPPED POTTERY (figs. 44a-d, n, o; 49a-g; 50)

The variation in skill exhibited on the black-on-red vessels was considerable. Most designs were well conceived and well laid out but the execution ranged from neat and precise to extremely sloppy. The glaze-paint designs in particular looked inferior to the others. In part this was simply a reflection of the medium, but not entirely so; for lines (even thick ones), frequently crossed at the corners, were of extremely unequal widths, or were not parallel. Some black paint was very watery and soaked into the vessel while other paint, sometimes on the same vessel, was thick and remained on the surface.

All black-paint design layouts on the interiors of bowls and the exteriors of most jars were in the form of wide bands. On rare vessels these bands were subdivided into repetitive panels; more often the design was broken up into what might be termed pseudopanels. At first glance there appeared to be separate panels, but closer inspection showed that they interlocked at one small point. Most of the designs were in a running interlocking style. On a few jars, particularly those decorated with motif (A), there was no lower bordering circle. The bottom of the design was irregular, consisting of the bottoms of the scrolls. The exterior white designs on bowls were generally bands of simple linear elements not enclosed within bordering lines. We noted on a number of vessels that where a panel or design element was repeated around the circumference of a bowl, one panel or a single element differed from the others.

CORRUGATED POTTERY

The indentations were doubtless regarded by the potters as decorative elements, but they have been described in the section on construction (pp. 50–51). There were a few instances of pattern-indented corrugated vessels, in which the most popular type consisted of alternating bands, several coils wide, of indented and unindented areas (fig. 49m). On a few, indentations were made over a limited area of each coil, resulting in a zigzag pattern of indentation. Sometimes these patterns took the form of diamonds or of vertical chevrons.

Discussion

If the inhabitants of Site 616 (or any other site) had been asked about the types of pottery made or used in the pueblo, it is unlikely that they would have mentioned descriptive or typological factors resembling those delineated and readily used by archaeologists in their analysis of temporal and geographical aggregates. The people would probably have differentiated vessels on the basis of their function — that is, in terms of the jobs they were intended to perform.

Probably their discussion would then have shifted to features found on vessels obtained from outside sources (as opposed to those locally made), and, in addition, to the differences found in the products stemming from these sources, as well as to variations in the work of individual potters.

The breakdown of the ceramic products employed at Site 616 into corrugated ware, white-slipped ware, and red-slipped ware is obvious. (The plainware vessels were sufficiently rare to constitute a novelty rather than a type relevant to the following discussion.) There is reason to believe that to the inhabitants these divisions had more significance than that of simple descriptive variation.

The dichotomy between corrugated and painted pottery is particularly apparent to viewers living in any age. However, it is evident that the inhabitants looked upon the corrugated pottery as a separate functional category, not one based solely upon techniques of decorative manipulation. Only two basic forms were used in the construction of corrugated pottery. The most common shape was the open-necked jar. As a group these were the largest vessels in use at the pueblo. The second form was the bowl. These — like the white-slipped pottery — had straight sides and tended to be smaller than those with a red slip. However, unlike the bowls of the two painted wares, each of which had a limited size range, the corrugated bowls ranged in size from miniatures to that of the average red-slipped bowl.

Corrugated bowls and jars apparently were utilized primarily, if not entirely, for cooking. The larger jars may have served on occasion for bulk storage. It is quite likely that the corrugations and indentations, while decorative, also served to convey heat more rapidly. At any rate, most corrugated vessels were used extensively in association with a fire, for they were encrusted with varying quantities of a sootlike substance, which worked into the many interstices, occasionally nearly filling them. A high percentage of the corrugated ware was found on the floor of the rooms, also indicating that as a group they were closely associated with the hearth rather than with work areas on the roof tops. Small corrugated bowls that seem too small for use over the fire apparently served as storage containers, for one contained a quantity of hematite. Probably most miniature vessels were designed for some purpose other than as toys to entertain the children.

The differences between the red- and the white-slipped pottery were particularly evident in the forms utilized. The bowl, generally large and with an insloping rim, was the primary form for red-slipped pottery. Red-slipped small-mouth jars and ladles, though not unknown, were infrequent. The red-slipped jars tended to be smaller and more nearly globular than the white-slipped jars, and the indented fingerholds found in some of the latter never occurred in the former. Ladles were also smaller. In contrast, large oval-shaped jars were the principal form of the white-slipped pottery. A few bowls were found, but these were smaller than those with red slips and, like the corrugated bowls, had straight rims.

Within each of the two categories of slipped pottery (white and red) there was a greater interchange of finishing techniques, design elements, and decorative techniques than was shared between the two categories, though certainly the dichotomization was by no means complete. In other words, artisans involved with one category of pottery displayed a tendency to associate certain designs and techniques with a particular slip, in contrast to the designs and techniques employed on the other slips. Another indication that these pottery divisions were very real ones to the inhabitants is the fact that every household unit containing a number of vessels had a few of each category. Apparently a red-slipped jar was not a substitute for a white-slipped jar, nor could a white-slipped bowl replace a red-slipped bowl in all of its functional aspects. Whether to use red-slipped pottery or white-slipped pottery was not simply a matter of taste or personal choice. Vessels of both types seemed to be necessary for the successful upkeep and operation of the household.

The living units excavated at Site 616 give us a good idea of the range and variety of pottery vessels to be found in a typical living unit. While we may not be able to recognize the hand of an individual potter, we can at least assume that vessels exhibiting widely divergent techniques and skills were made by different potters. By this criterion vessels found within any individual room at Site 616 could not conceivably have been made by a single potter.

When a family wanted to add to its supply of pottery vessels, one member of the family unit would not gather up the necessary materials from where they were stored in a corner of the room, repair to the roof with them, and proceed to construct the vessel or vessels required. It is extremely unlikely that even divergent abilities possessed by different members of the same family could account for the variety of techniques and decorative concepts.

The inevitable conclusion seems to be that at a large pueblo such as Site 616 there was a certain degree of labor specialization. There were indications that this specialization extended to crafts other than pottery. By extension, this question of labor specialization leads directly to that of trade, for trade can be looked upon simply as labor specialization within wider geographical and social limits. But only rarely is the positive identification of trade materials, pottery or others, readily accomplished. If the geology of the area is known, then technological studies may permit us to recognize the source of materials foreign to the site under consideration. Such studies are also the only reliable source of information on firing techniques employed in the construction of pottery.

If a particular raw material, method of construction, or decorative style is uncommon at a site, is this proof of foreign derivation? And if so, was the raw material or the entire vessel brought to the site, and by whom? Obviously neither technological nor stylistic analysis, alone or together, can completely answer these questions. In this instance, geological knowledge of the area in question is scanty and circumstances prevented extensive technological studies. So, for an analysis of pottery, trade, and labor specialization we must depend primarily upon data obtained by other means.

A number of principles served as guides in the evaluation and interpretation of the data:

1. Pottery made at a single site can be expected to be reasonably consistent in the composition and proportions of the basic materials. Materials or their use that are atypical with respect to the norms for the site are suspect. Of course, factors other than the importation of pottery could cause this variation. For example, at Site 616 variation between the slipped wares (in which sherd temper was prominent) and the corrugated pottery (where quartz sand was used almost exclusively) may have had a functional correlation, in that the latter evidently was used to a large extent for culinary purposes. Technological analysis is essential to any thorough investigation of this subject, for the results of macroscopic observation alone have proved unreliable.

2. Pottery made locally would be constructed and fired by more or less standard techniques. Any pottery with a technique quite different from that employed in the construction of similar pottery most probably was made by an artisan reared or at least instructed by a group other than the local one.

3. Local styles of decoration and construction will conform to a historical tradition and a pattern of geographical distribution. If an entire pottery sample at a site does not conform to pottery found at adjacent sites, then probably the entire population of that site had recently moved into the area. It is improbable that a group, at least in the southwestern United States, would import all of its pottery (or its potters). Even if it did so, this practice could be expected to have continued over a long period of time, so that historically the sample would conform to the same degree as did pottery made locally.

4. If the village is of considerable size there will be one or more local variations or interpretations within the general tradition. Conversely, the less stylistic variability exhibited, the more likely is the pottery to have been made at a single site and by a limited number of potters. Occasionally pottery styles might become so standardized over an entire area that it would be virtually impossible to distinguish pottery from different sites. In these instances the rate of intercommunication and pattern of social control would have been much more rigid than was the case with the relatively independent autonomous pueblos in the Southwest. Unfortunately, the limited size and nature of the pottery samples obtained by the archaeologist are often such that it is extremely difficult to abstract local patterns. Usually only the more general regional traditions and patterns can be recognized.

5. The variability of local styles and their deviation from broader areal and temporal patterns are correlated with a number of factors: the psychological orientation of the potters and their village toward variation, the extent of their communicative isolation from other groups, and, in a broader sense, the nature of the medium. All these factors will affect the nature and degree of local variation, which also correlates in

some measure with the number of individuals in the village who engage in the manufacture of pottery; but the resulting degree of variability differs from group to group, probably through the interplay of the other factors mentioned above.

6. This ratio of variability between style variation and number of potters, while not constant between groups, is probably relatively constant for the activities of a single group within any one medium. In other words, the resident potter would not hew closely to common construction standards and decorative styles when making one group of pottery and then proceed to exhibit extensive individual variation in the construction and decoration of a second group. Here again other considerations such as those of function or use enter the picture. Ceremonial or practical factors could severely limit the variation allowable in the construction and decoration of a certain group of pottery, whereas the variability of other pottery made by the group would be subject only to the more general limitations discussed above.

7. Individual variation is most likely to be exhibited in the execution of particular design elements and in slight variations in technique rather than in style. If few potters were active at a site (or the archaeological sample is small), it is generally impossible to recognize individual handiwork.

Bunzel (1929, pp. 56, 62–63) — who originated or at least inspired most of these principles — also observed that pottery made for sale tends to be more repetitive than that made for home consumption. It is difficult to assess the value of this principle in relation to the prehistoric situation. For one thing "sale" to Bunzel meant disposal to a completely alien group (the tourist) whose importance to the potter is primarily economic. In this situation the personal status of the potter as a craftsman is more often derived from the potter's own group. This may or may not have been true in prehistoric times, where sale was only to members of one's own village or to groups from which one expected or desired materials of high quality in return. Bunzel notes that this decorative repetition on products for sale comes from necessity rather than choice. Perhaps (although this may be simply romanticism) in the pre-Spanish period there was generally a greater emphasis on craftsmanship in the true sense and less pressure to mass-produce pottery for sale.

To return to the pottery in use at Site 616, apparently all or nearly all of the white-slipped pottery was made by the potters living at the pueblo. Macroscopic examination revealed no major differences in the basic materials utilized. The potters mainly followed the decorative styles of the regional time-space types of Tularosa Black-on-white and Reserve Black-on-white.

Their interpretation of these more general styles had fairly narrow limits, although there may have been as many as three local stylistic variations. It may be significant that decorative motif (IV), considered most typical of the general Tularosa type, was the only one found almost equally in all three local variations.

The impression given by the white-slipped pottery is that the potters were part of a closely knit communication unit, and one that did not encourage extensive experimentation or extreme variation in the practice of the ceramic art. It is most likely that this degree of conformance would exist within a single pueblo or a localized, inward-directed communication unit, rather than represent the work of a number of potters scattered over a wide area.

Artisan Types

Despite the general uniformity of the white-slipped pottery, we can abstract three stylistic trends. The individuals using the pottery probably were aware of the distinctions discussed below, whether or not they utilized them as a basis for designating types significant to them. These distinctions may represent slight variations in the work of three individual groups of potters operating within the pueblo, and therefore they have been designated "artisan types."

The first and most aberrant of these local stylistic types (Artisan Type A) had a thin (or, rarely, watery) flat, white slip, strongly emphasized decorative modes (j) and (k) and, to a lesser but still major extent, decorative modes (e) and (h). Decorative modes (a)-(d) were relatively rare. Though it constituted only 25 percent of the sherds of the type, nearly all of the slipped pottery with a matte finish is included in the type as defined. This pottery conformed more closely to Reserve Black-on-white than to Tularosa Black-on-white in certain features of slip and decoration. However, it differed from Reserve Black-on-white vessels described in other areas in certain other characteristics (jars dominant, bowls and ladles slipped on all surfaces, and so on). Even more significantly, it differed from Reserve pottery as described elsewhere in a manner conforming to the localized black-on-white standards found at Site 616. The potters responsible for this group perhaps had moved to the village from another area shortly before; but although their product was distinct they appear to have been intimately connected with the same specific pottery-making ideas and ideals that directed the other potters residing at the pueblo.

The second type (Artisan Type B) had a flat, white slip thickly applied. While infrequently utilizing nearly all decorative modes, it used primarily decorative motif (I) (85 percent). Within this motif it strongly emphasized decorative mode (c) (68 percent). Only on sherds of decorative mode (b) does one find the poor surface finish of surface finish type 2. Most of these came from the fill of Room D5, again suggesting that this may have been the work of a single potter or small group of somewhat careless potters (by Site 616 standards).

The third local stylistic type (Artisan Type C) utilized a thick, creamy slip and also exhibited a decided tendency to emphasize decorative motif (I), but particularly decorative modes (a) and (c). All the sherds in this sample were well finished.

The rarity of glaze paint on white-slipped pottery suggests that it was a new medium unpopular with the potters of the pueblo. It may first have been introduced to the local potters on red-slipped ware that was traded in, and perhaps a number of local artisans had begun to experiment with it on their white-slipped products. The general association of glaze paint with the thin, flat, white slip and decorative modes (b), (h), and (j) suggests that the potters responsible for local Artisan Type A were also chiefly involved with this pottery.

Most of the corrugated pottery conformed closely to a single material type: brown paste with sand inclusions — paste mode key (H). The construction techniques were consistent for all vessels made of this material. Like the white-slipped pottery the decoration of this portion of the corrugated pottery — although exhibiting considerable variation on individual vessels — was all patterned closely after a limited number of styles. Apparently a number of artisans were actively making this pottery but the only reason to believe that any was made elsewhere than at Site 616 is the unusual indenting technique of the right thumb pointing down, employed in the construction of a single vessel. The difficulty of safely transporting the large and relatively fragile jars, if nothing else, would tend to discourage any widespread trading of this pottery.

Possibly the gray-paste, corrugated pottery was made elsewhere. Upon macroscopic examination the clay and to some extent the inclusions appeared to differ from those of paste mode key (H), from which the major portion of the corrugated pottery was constructed. The coils were slightly larger and less flat, and the indentations were more widely spaced. One of the two variations in construction or indenting technique occurred on a vessel of gray paste. These deviations in technique are striking, especially considering the uniformity of the rest of the corrugated pottery. Taken together with the apparently different materials employed and its relative rarity, it seems reasonable to suggest that this pottery may not have been native to the site.

The red-slipped pottery, on the other hand, is much more difficult to interpret. Despite the recovery of 100 restorable red-slipped vessels, we could abstract very few patterns relative to the materials used, construction techniques employed, and decorative styles favored, or to recognize any extensive correlation between these factors — in marked contrast to the rest of the pottery. Only one material type has been presented — gray to tan-orange paste with angular opaque inclusions — paste mode key (F) — not because it was felt that only one major type was utilized but because without technological analysis it proved impossible to determine the cause of the considerable variations or to recognize any patterns in them. The construction techniques were not much more varied than with the white-slipped pottery, but it probably is significant that on the red-slipped pottery none of these variations were found in consistent association with other factors. The variation in vessel decoration also may indicate that the red-slipped pottery had slightly different functions from those of the white-slipped pottery, but there is no reason to believe that the nature of this difference required or permitted extensive fluidity of expression. The variability of the red-slipped pottery was distinctly out of character for the potters of Site 616, and the pottery as a group did not conform to the principles set forth earlier for locally constructed pottery. For these reasons it is felt that a considerable portion, though possibly not all, of the red-slipped pottery was made elsewhere and reached Site 616 through trade. This factor, as well as, or rather than, the possible difference in function of the red ware, might account for the emphasis in red-slipped pottery on the more readily transportable bowl form at Site 616.

STONE ARTIFACTS

In general, stone tools were carefully made and well finished. The artisans seem to have taken considerable pride in their work, and axes, hammers, metates, manos and other tools were finished with a degree of care far beyond that required for the effective use of the tools. On the other hand, the tools apparently were regarded as strictly utilitarian, and little time was spent in adding unnecessary embellishments. If any such decorative or symbolic additions were used, they must have been of a perishable nature.

Since excavation was conducted entirely within living units rather than refuse areas, few data were obtained about the occupants' concept of what constituted a "worn-out" artifact. There was no apparent attempt to use as construction materials only those artifacts that were no longer serviceable; in fact the few manos and metates utilized in construction appear to conform in every way with those still used for grinding. Similarly, there is no indication of any attempt to select older, worn-out axes for use as pounding tools, for some axes in near mint condition appear to have been used as hammers. On occasion these were subsequently resharpened so that they again served as axes. The people apparently were inclined to select the tool nearest at hand for their immediate purpose, rather than consciously to select "old" tools for purely secondary purposes, even when such use destroyed or seriously impaired the ability of a carefully and laboriously constructed tool to function in the manner for which it was originally designed.

Tools Fashioned by Pecking (figs. 51–56, 58)

Manos, metates, stone bowls, pot supports, all hammers except the elongated flat-ended type, and all objects of volcanic scoria were formed solely by pecking the stone into the desired shape. The pecking stones and perhaps some of the axes and hammers may have been employed for this work, but since these tools were not so numerous as might be expected — considering the large number of artifacts fashioned in whole or in part by pecking — the irregular lava cobbles readily available from the dike probably were utilized whenever a pecking stone was needed. The supply of these cobbles was so abundant and so convenient that quite possibly they were picked up, used, and promptly discarded.

The manos appear to have been constructed according to four action types. Three of these types, differentiated on the basis of the degree of coarseness (resulting from the material employed — sandstone, calcareous tuff, and vesicular basalt), were fashioned according to a single standard of size approximately 11.6 cm wide, 30 cm long, and from 1 to 6.8 cm thick. The width of these tools was quite uniform and obviously correlated with the maximum width comfortably and securely gripped by the hand. Those having widths below 10 cm were generally on manos used so extensively that their edges had been partially worn away. The median length, in turn, was 1 cm less than the median width of the metates. The fourth mano type was 10 cm shorter than the first three. Manos of this type generally were of basalt. No metates were found of this width, so some other factor must have been operative in determining the desirable length. These manos may not have been associated with metates and, although their use was doubtless similar, their function may have been entirely different. A new mano of any type generally was under 5 cm in thickness but considerable variation was exhibited. Finger grips were known but occurred rarely. Manos with finger grips may even have been heirlooms, and there is a suggestion that finger grips were associated more often with the shorter manos, an older style.

At least three material types of metates were recognized by the inhabitants, but regardless of material or other factors (e.g., whether or not the metate was to be placed in a bin) all were constructed in accordance with a single size type. The mean lengths for each of the different materials ranged from 38.8 to 44.3 cm, the width from 28.9 to 31.8 cm, and the thickness from 6.1 to 8.5 cm. However, the actual limits of this size type must have been fairly broadly defined, for individual specimens ranged from 35 to 52 cm in length and from 24 to 41 cm in width. A new metate was approximately 10 cm thick. The sides and ends of the metates, like those of the manos, were carefully finished but the undersides of the metates were less well done.

The three stone bowls recovered were roughly finished and of approximately the same size. They did not appear to have been used as mortars.

The round-ended hammers were natural oval cobbles carefully selected for overall shape and size. They were unmodified except for a centrally located hafting groove pecked around the short circumference. They showed battering on both ends and would have served admirably as pecking tools whenever more force was required than could comfortably be attained by a hand-held pecking stone, or when a more restricted area of contact was desired than that provided by a flat-ended hammer.

The equilateral flat-ended hammers basically resembled the modern maul. They were well finished and, in contrast to the elongated flat-ended hammers, were shaped solely by pecking.

A group of objects of volcanic scoria including irregular flat-ended hammers and scoria cylinders and cones could have been ground to shape, but the irregular surfaces suggest that their final shape was obtained by pecking. These objects seem to fall into three groups but it is not at all clear how any of them were used. The so-called hammers were approximately the same height as the scoria cylinders but had twice as large a diameter; all had hafting grooves, whereas only a single cylinder had even the rudiments of a central groove. The final category consisted of a single specimen resembling a short thick mano. This tool could have served as an abrader.

Tools Fashioned by Pecking and Grinding

Most tools of dense igneous stone were fashioned by pecking and subsequent grinding, that is, the axes, the shaftsmoothers, the elongated flat-ended hammers, the hammer with the off-center haft, and the pick.

The mortars may not belong in this category, as they were fashioned from any hard flat stone, apparently with no particular standards for the overall form. The stone was mainly shaped by rough chipping and subsequent pecking. The bowl area was doubtless pecked out, but whether the surface of the concavity was then ground during its manufacture or solely through use is a matter of conjecture.

The axes were apparently made in accordance with a single, fairly rigidly defined idea type. Although there were some variations in actual size (height ranged from 10.6 to 16.2 cm) the contours and proportions of the specimens were nearly uniform. Their mean height was 13.3 cm, width 4.9 cm, and length 6.7 cm. The hafting groove was the only part of the axe not finished by grinding. Its location on axes in mint condition maintained a constant relationship to the ends of the artifact, which can be expressed as a ratio of poll height to overall height of 1:3.4.

All surfaces of shaftsmoothers were finished by grinding. These artifacts showed more diversity in detail than any other general category of stone tool. The idea type which directed the construction of these artifacts appears to have been subject to considerable individual modification. A hunter's arrows are directly related to success on the hunt and, correlated with this, to the status of the individual. As a result, the manufacture of these implements may have been subject to more individual interpretation than were artifacts not so directly related, actually or apparently, to individual success and status (e.g., a mano or even an axe).

Although arrived at by two different routes, the elongated flat-ended hammers generally conformed to a single pattern. Half of them apparently were initially designed as such. The other half were axes subsequently modified according to the idea type for hammers. Basically, the bit of the axe was shortened so that the groove became centrally located and the end of the bit was squared and flattened. The outstanding difference between the two subgroups is that the original hammers were full-grooved whereas those that were initially axes were three-quarter-grooved. The hafting of only one reworked axe had been modified to a full groove, probably when the transition was made from an axe to a hammer. It is significant that even one changeover was made. At this pueblo, hammers were full-grooved, axes three-quarter-grooved; but this correlation was perhaps considered desirable rather than imperative, either functionally or sociologically. Possibly the artifacts of this reworked type served as general all-purpose hammers while the other hammer forms had — at least primarily — more restricted functions.

Tools Fashioned by Chipping (fig. 57)

Chipped stone tools appear not to have been used in any quantity by the inhabitants of Site 616. The paucity of small chipped stone tools in our sample is puzzling, for we found no other artifacts that could have replaced these. If there was considerable technological specialization at the village — which seems possible — the reason for this scarcity may be simply that we did not excavate the right section of the pueblo. It may be significant that the area between the kiva and the walk-in well, including Rooms B1, B2, D1, D5, E1, and E2, contained most of the unworked animal bone at the site as well as most of the chips and flakes recovered.

The projectile points and blades exhibited some variations in form and material. If abandonment of the pueblo was wholly or partly the result of an attack, it is possible that some of the former were not indigenous to the pueblo itself but derived from the group attacking the village.

Most of the chips were of petrified wood, but only a single object that was definitely an artifact was made of this material. Hence, it is possible that the chips themselves represented the end product rather than being a by-product of the manufacturing process, a process consisting of little more than detaching chips from an unprepared core by percussion. Certainly some, termed herein "unretouched flakes" (see pp. 149–150) showed evidence on one or more of their naturally sharp edges of having been used as cutting implements.

Tools Fashioned by Chipping and Grinding

Artifacts treated in this manner were, without exception, of materials which have very poor concoidal fracture. The chipping was effected by heavy blows that detached flakes one or more centimeters in size. These generally served to rough out the general shape of the artifact. The finishing touches were then done by grinding. This was the case with the pot covers, door slabs, ventilator slabs, and similar objects. Generally these were of sandstone, and grinding was done only when it was necessary to remove some imperfection in the natural tabular fracture. If there were no imperfections, the grinding was generally omitted — that is, the chipped edges were not ground smooth. The manufacture of the hoe was simply a more refined version of this same general process. One side of this tool was ground down to a sharp edge, which appeared to have been deliberately nicked or chipped slightly, resulting in a serrated cutting edge.

BONE ARTIFACTS (figs. 61–64)

With few exceptions, artifacts of bone were constructed by simple modification of the natural bone through cutting, or grinding, or a combination of the two processes. The types entitled "Head of bone intact," "Head of bone unworked except by original splitting," "Head wholly removed," and "Splinter awls" were generally made from deer or pronghorn metapodials. These bones were usually split and the medial portion was ground down to a point, presumably on a sharpening stone, though none were recovered. It is not at all unlikely that the inhabitants subdivided this group of awls along other lines perhaps related to the duties performed, but whether these divisions are reflected in the overall length of the awl, the bone utilized, the angle of taper of the points, or some other factor, is not known.

The skewer awls and the eyed awls, on the other hand, were probably recognized by the inhabitants as individual categories. These tools were formed from the shafts of long bones extensively ground down. In the skewer awls no trace of the original surface of the bone remained. These awls may have been tools or hair ornaments, or perhaps straight pins or skewers to secure cloth and skins. The eyed awls were made from well-ground sections of the shafts of long bones. A hole was cut and ground into the wide or butt end. These awls may have been used to sew or weave textiles from grass or other fiber.

The matting or weaving tools were not unlike the eyed awls in general appearance but were made from well-polished rib sections with one end ground to a dull, gradually tapered point.

The side scrapers were made from the pelvic sections of a deer, the larger extremities of which were cut and ground away while the central section, naturally rather sharp, was made sharper by grinding. The end scrapers were formed by cutting off the proximal end of the humerus of a pronghorn. The proximal end of the shaft was ground on a flat surface to an angle of 30° or 40°. Subsequently the upper portion of this same end was ground on a convex surface at a lower angle, exposing a long U-shaped section of the central hole. One of these specimens — the only stone or bone tool recognizably decorated — had fine lines in a rectilinear pattern.

MINOR CRAFTS

While many other crafts must have been practiced, the particular evidence concerning them is infrequent. Specific comments about the materials recovered at Site 616 are included in the discussion of particular artifact categories.

OTHER CONTEXTS AND ACTIVITIES

The Household

It is rarely possible to determine with assurance that a particular set of rooms was considered the property of an individual family unit. However, the high-standing walls that reveal some aspects of the ventilation pattern, the differing form and function of the various rooms, and the relative abundance of artifacts enable us to speculate on this matter at Site 616.

The so-called living rooms containing a firepit and often a single mealing bin probably formed the essential focal point of a family's activities. A single family, especially an extended family, might conceivably require more than one living room, but it is unlikely that any family unit could function adequately without ready access to at least one such room. In most instances at Site 616 a room without floor features, other than an occasional cist, adjoined this living room. These two units in conjunction probably formed the basic "apartment" during the final period of the pueblo's occupancy. A mealing room was added to some but not all household units. At other earlier sites a living room alone provided the main requirements of a family's dwelling.

In this report the identification of rooms with particular household units depends primarily upon proximity and an association of rooms of appropriate function. The apartments may have tended toward a linear arrangement extending from the outer to the inner wall of the pueblo. The ventilation pattern is of minimum assistance for, at the time with which we are concerned, there was a tendency to seal doorways between rooms. Apparently the occupants had come to prefer the roof entry even when wall entry would have been more convenient. A sealed doorway did not necessarily indicate that one or the other of the two rooms was no longer used. In some cases there can be little doubt that both rooms (for example, Rooms B1 and B2) remained in use despite the existence of a sealed doorway in their common wall. Also, the seal generally was carefully finished on both sides.

From the information available, it is suggested that the following rooms belonged to separate household units: Room A1, a single living room; Rooms A2 and A3, a living room and a storeroom which probably were closely associated with Room A1 but may have been abandoned some time earlier, while Room A1 apparently continued in use; Rooms B1 and B2, a mealing room and a living room; Rooms B3 and B5, a storeroom and a living room; Room B7, a living room; Rooms C2 and C5, a mealing room and a living room with an open door connecting them; Rooms C1, C6, and C10, two storerooms and a living room; Rooms C3 and C9, a storeroom and a mealing room connected by an open door (there are indications — namely the sealed doors and passthroughs — that this apartment was closely connected with or was a part of the immediately preceding one); Rooms D1 and D2, a living room and a mealing room; Room D3, a living room, perhaps abandoned; Rooms F1 and F2, a storeroom and a living room; and the individual pithouses E1 and E2. The few open doorways and the limited amount of excavation combine to make some of these suggested associations tentative at best, and in many instances it is evident that there were other rooms of an apartment that we did not clear. For these reasons the discussion below, of the artifacts associated with a typical household, must be regarded as no more than suggestive.

Insofar as could be judged from the present sample the average well-equipped household contained approximately 30 pottery vessels (one apartment — Rooms C2 and C5 — contained over 60 vessels) consisting of about eight slipped jars (range: 3 to 19), eight slipped bowls (range: 7 to 18), two ladles (range: 0 to 3), two corrugated bowls (range: 1 to 16), five corrugated jars (range: 0 to 10), and a number of eccentric and miniature vessels. The different households varied considerably and the suggested norms must be considered somewhat intuitive since the ranges given in some instances are drawn from households in which not all rooms were excavated. The limited sample may well be the cause of the extensive variation, as there was a tendency for different vessel forms to be associated with one or another type of room within the household. Slipped jars tended to be located in mealing rooms (18 jars in four rooms) and to a less extent in storage rooms (17 jars in seven rooms). The corrugated jars and the slipped bowls were fairly evenly distributed throughout the household though fewer were found in the storage rooms. Corrugated bowls were also rather common but, unlike the slipped bowls, were somewhat more likely to be encountered in the storage rooms than elsewhere. Ladles and seed jars were most often found in living rooms, while unusual forms and miniatures were generally in both living rooms and storage rooms. This latter association is interesting in view of the number of unusually shaped stones, quartz crystals, and similar objects also found in the storage rooms. Except for Room B3 there is little direct evidence of material actually stored in those rooms bare of features, and the appellation "storage room" may be ill chosen. They may have functioned instead as sleeping rooms and thus as storage areas for personal items rather than bulk supplies of food or other reserves.

In addition to pottery, each household was equipped with pieces of limonite, malachite, and generally hematite, a number of axes (2 to 7), awls (1 to 6), and at least one hammer, though Rooms B1 and B2 contained five. Every household had at least one metate and five or six manos; those with attached mealing rooms had as many as 12 metates and 30 manos. On the average there were three manos for every metate, although occasionally this ratio rose to seven manos for every metate.

Apparently every household did its own grinding but each mealing room may well have served a number of households, probably those containing members of an extended family or similar cohesive social unit. Room C9 — which once opened into the room (a living room?) to the south by way of a door as well as by a ventilator or passthrough — at one time also had a passthrough into Room C6. Room C6, in turn, was apparently associated with Room C10, a second living room. Thus both families could have conveniently utilized the facilities of Room C9, and as long as the passthroughs were open it would have been possible to deliver ground meal to the respective households without awkwardly clambering to the roof and then down a second ladder. These mealing rooms and the roofs above them were perhaps social centers which drew people engaged in other crafts as well.

Some other units excavated, in addition to the kiva, may have been affiliated with more aesthetic aspects of the community's life than day-to-day living. Possibly all of the semisubterranean and subterranean rooms maintained some of their earlier ceremonial significance despite the seemingly mundane appurtenances found in Room E2. In this capacity they could have served small clan groups or an extended family, while the larger kivas were reserved for activities affecting larger aggregates or the community as a whole. Only one such large kiva was excavated, but there were surface indications of at least one other (just south of Area C) at the village. Similarly, certain atypical features of Rooms A1 and C10 suggest — but with very meager evidence — a limited ceremonial affiliation, perhaps connected with clan activities. The presence of a slab floor in Room A1, a feature found elsewhere in the village only in the kiva, plus the apparent age of this room, is cause for speculation — as is the case with the false wall and ventilator shaft in Room C10. Our lack of knowledge of specific kiva features, including those to be expected in a clan meeting room, make any such identification difficult.

Technological Specialization

The evidence for technological specialization in ceramics at Site 616 has been presented in detail in the discussion of pottery-making. Briefly, the ceramic data suggest that nearly all of the white-slipped pottery, most of the corrugated pottery, and a small amount of the red-slipped pottery was actually made at Site 616. There are strong indications that not every woman was her own potter. The stylistic variation found within a single room, and even more so in a single household, was entirely too great to be attributed to any one artisan or even several closely related potters. Pottery clay was found in only three of the 13 households excavated. Three local styles of white-slipped decoration were recognized, indicating that there may have been three groups of artisans responsible for the manufacture and distribution of this pottery throughout the pueblo. An attempt was made to localize the origin of these three styles within the pueblo, but was unsuccessful because of insufficient excavation.

In a number of respects the unit made up of Rooms B1 and B2 differed from the other households. It contained a few jars, many awls and hammers, and an unusually large quantity of hematite, other minerals, and clay. Moreover, the metates and most of the manos were fine-grained sandstone rather than a graded series of grinding surfaces, and the metates in the bins were all set at approximately the same angle, whereas those in other sets of bins were at different angles. Hence the family occupying this unit may have engaged in some specialized craft or activity, perhaps concerned with pottery-making. It is noteworthy that the manos associated with the mealing room at the walk-in well, a room that may have been used for working clay, were nearly all of sandstone also.

Other clues suggest that there was some craft specialization at Site 616 and that artisans practicing similar crafts tended to reside near one another. The most significant nonceramic indication is related to the importation and manufacture of shell artifacts. Almost all of the unworked shell, and to a lesser extent the worked shell, was found in Areas C and D. The latter area contained more fossil shell, while bead manufacture seems to have been restricted to Area C. Conversely, stone chips indicative of stoneworking and the practice of certain other crafts were concentrated primarily in Areas B and D and the walk-in well. This distribution corresponds with and may be related to the occurrence of unworked animal bone. There is also negative evidence for specialization in that the present sample, though representing approximately 13 households, contained no tools at all in certain categories (e.g., stone drills, bone-working tools, and so on). If every household equipped itself with tools for nearly every trade it would seem likely that one or more examples of the stone and bone implements utilized in these crafts would have been found. On the other hand, if only a limited number of artisans used certain specialized craft tools, the absence of certain types from the recovered sample is readily understandable.

LIVING AND EXCAVATION UNITS

Area A

Area A was an L-shaped three-room unit, one of seven clusters or islands of rooms situated within the enclosed plaza of Site 616. Three of these small three- or four-room clusters, including Area A, were located in the northeast corner of the plaza. The general architecture suggested that Area A was one of the first built at the site, but it apparently was still occupied at the time the site was abandoned (fig. 12).

A single continuous wall formed the north walls of Rooms A1 and A3. It was constructed of small angular lava cobbles laid in irregular courses (five courses remain). The east wall of Room A1, the west wall of Room A3, and the three walls of Room A2 were similarly built. Whether or not this cobble masonry simply formed the base for an adobe upper portion could not be determined, but no known adobe wall had a cobble base that extended above floor level as these walls did (40–50 cm). Probably the cobble masonry continued throughout the walls, the only such walls to be found at Site 616. The wall separating Rooms A1 and A3 was constructed of adobe with a single course of lava cobbles at the base. The south walls of Rooms A1 and A3 appeared to be completely out of context with respect to the general technique in the construction of the rest of Area A. We assume that this south wall of medium sandstone blocks laid in regular courses was built much later, replacing the original wall during a period of renovation. Perhaps the interior adobe wall dated from the same time. All the walls had an average thickness of 25 to 30 cm. The pattern of wall abutments indicates that Rooms A1 and A3 were built as a unit and that Room A2 was added later.

Room A1 (figs. 12, 13)

The 30 to 40 centimeters of fill was hard packed and almost devoid of artifacts. A stone slab (52 by 47 by 2 cm) came from the northeast corner of the room just above the floor. The edges had been shaped by chipping but it was otherwise unworked. This slab and those from Rooms A2 and A3 may have formed doors or hatch covers.

The floor was laid with large sandstone slabs neatly fitted together and the interstices filled with adobe plaster. Only Rooms A1, A3, and the kiva were so treated. Several slabs were missing from the southeast corner. A mano, #2033 (1721), formed a part of the floor in the southwest corner.

FIREPIT

Both the sides and bottom of the firepit were lined with fitted sandstone slabs. A sandstone pot support was found in the fill of the firepit while a second was on the floor of the firepit against its north wall.

MEALING BIN

The walls of the mealing bin consisted of single sandstone slabs. The metate itself was missing, though its shape was clearly outlined in the adobe. A rectangular

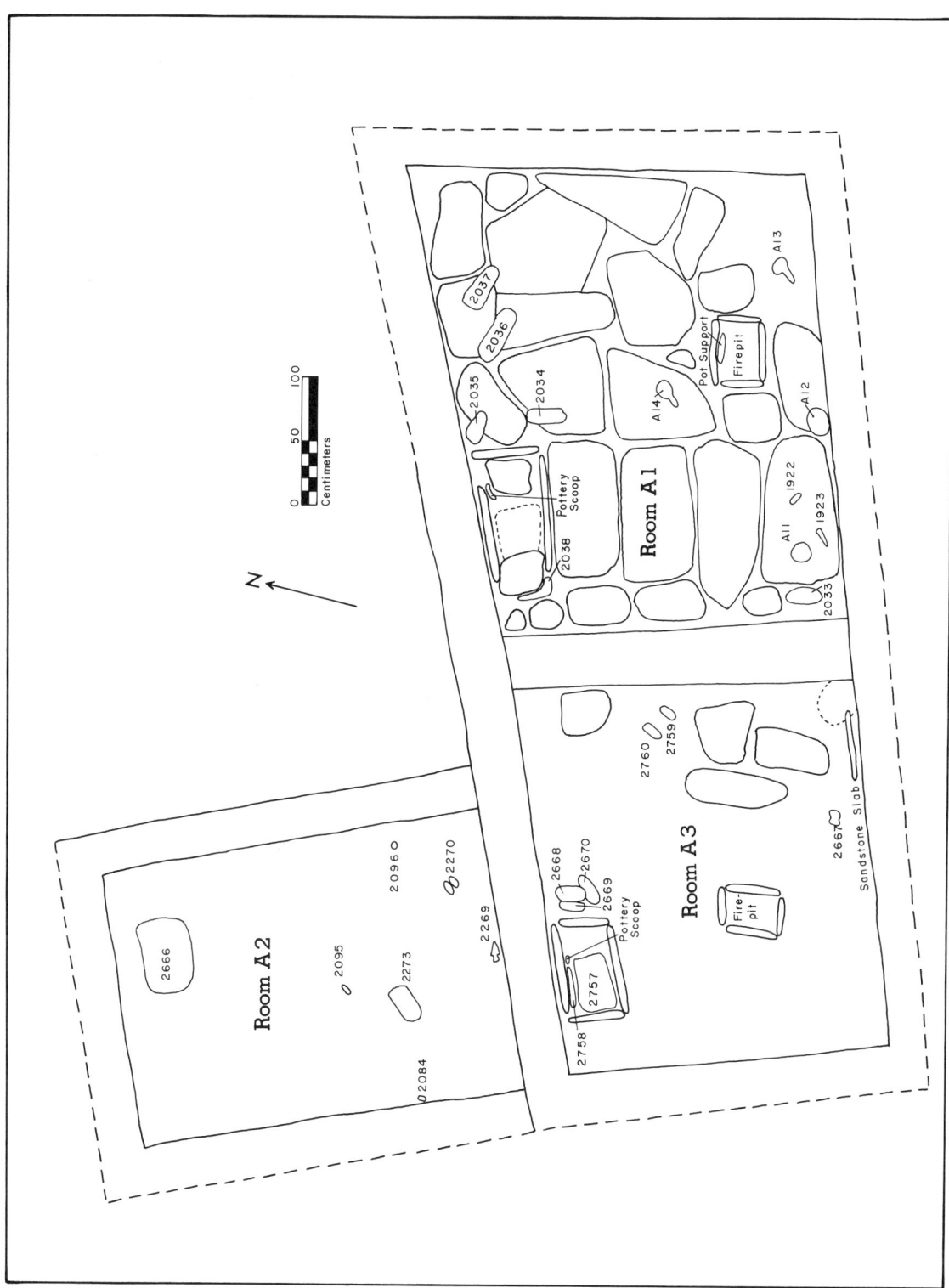

Figure 12. Site 616. Plan of Area A.

Figure 13. Site 616. Room A1, looking east.

sandstone slab was set into the adobe at the foot of the metate, and a Tularosa Black-on-white ladle sherd was set into the adobe at the left-hand corner of the foot of the metate, to serve as a scoop.

COMMENT

Only the missing metate suggested that this room was abandoned prior to the exodus from the entire pueblo. Perhaps it was removed at the time the occupants departed. The careful paving of the floor of the room was interesting and puzzling. Only the kiva and perhaps Room A3 had been similarly treated. Does this indicate that Room A1 also had a religious or ceremonial function, perhaps in connection with a particular clan's activities? It may also be significant that on the basis of its architecture this room appeared to be one of the oldest at the site. There is suggestive evidence that the oldest rooms at Site 481 had some clan significance.

ARTIFACTS

In this and in subsequent sections, a numeral preceded by the symbol # indicates the field catalogue number of the specimen referred to. A numeral preceded by a capital letter (e.g., A12) refers to the field catalogue designation of a whole or restorable pottery vessel. A numeral in parentheses indicates the descriptive-type classification of the specimen, as discussed on pages 105–106, and as listed in tables 1–3, 6, 12–15, 17–21.

Field catalogue numbers are listed only for specimens found on floors, as an aid to their identification as shown on the associated floor plans.

Fill

Stone: Polishing pebble
Bone: Awl, head split but unworked; awl, skewer
Shell: Unworked fragments

Floor

#1921, scoria cylinder; #1923, awl, head split but unworked; #2033, mano (1721), set into floor; #2034, mano (1931); #2035, mano (1721); #2036, mano (1221); #2037, mano (1721); #2038, mano (1221)

Pottery vessels: A11, St. Johns Polychrome bowl; A12, St. Johns Polychrome bowl (fig. 44o); A13, Tularosa Black-on-white ladle (fig. 44s); A14, Reserve Black-on-white ladle (fig. 44t)

Firepit

2 pot supports

Room A2 (fig. 12)

A rectangular sandstone slab (57 by 27 by 2 cm) which may have been resting on the floor was found leaning against the center of the south wall overlying an axe (#2269).

No definite floor level could be recognized in this room, but a level approximately 30 cm below surface was arbitrarily identified as such, because just below it was a layer of fine red sand. Perhaps this sand had originally served as a base for a flagstone flooring that was subsequently removed. The room may have fallen into general disuse.

The lack of floor features suggests that this was a storage room, but the lack of a definable floor level was puzzling, unless the floor was once paved.

ARTIFACTS

Fill

Stone: Mano fragment
Pottery vessel: Heshotauthla Polychrome bowl

Floor

#2084, shell figurine of frog (fig. 65d); #2095, worked bone fragment; #2096, cut shell pendant; #2269, axe; #2270, hammer, irregular flat-ended (fig. 56b); #2273, mortar, roughly shaped; #2666, metate, fine sandstone

Room A3 (fig. 12)

A sandstone slab (60 by 30 by 2 cm) was found leaning against the east end of the south wall.

The exact level of the original floor was difficult to locate over most of this room, but the presence of a few sandstone slabs in the eastern part indicated that at one time this floor was paved with flagstones, as was that of Room A1.

FIREPIT

Four sandstone slabs made up the sides of the firepit, and its bottom was paved with several small pieces of sandstone. The firepit was filled with ash, but no pot supports were in association.

MEALING BIN

The mealing bin was also lined with four sandstone slabs as was the flat area at the foot of the metate, which was of medium-coarse vesicular basalt (#2757). A pottery scoop (Puerco Black-on-red bowl sherd) was located at the left side of the foot of the metate, and the metate itself was somewhat farther from the left wall of the bin than from the right wall. This wider bordering area was partially paved with an old mano (#2758).

Although the metate was still in the mealing bin, the condition of the floor and the general scarcity of artifacts suggest that this room was abandoned or at least not in active use while the site was still being occupied.

ARTIFACTS

Fill

Stone: Mano
Pottery vessel: Pinedale Black-on-red jar

Floor

#2667, hammer, equilateral flat-ended; #2668, mano (1631); #2669, mano (2422); #2670, mano (2122); #2757, metate, medium-coarse vesicular basalt, set in mealing bin; #2758, mano (1421), set in mealing bin; #2759, mano (1421), set in floor; #2760, mano (2221), set in floor

Area B

Area B consisted of five rooms excavated in the west-central portion against the south wall of the pueblo, which at this point comprised a double or triple row of rooms. Rooms B2, B5, and B7 appeared to have been living rooms equipped with a firepit but no other major floor features; Room B1 with its set of three mealing bins was doubtless primarily a work area, while Room B3 was a storeroom.

From a study of wall abutments and styles of wall construction, it would appear that the inner row of east-west rooms extending west from Room B5 was constructed first; and since the south wall of this row continued as the south wall of Room B2, the latter room may have been built at the same time, although there was a break in the north wall between the two rooms. All the walls of this section were constructed of adobe resting on a footing made up of small lava cobbles and adobe. Rooms B1 and B3 were added later, at a time when the occupants were beginning to experiment with different methods of wall construction, for the east wall of Room B1 was solid adobe without a footing of lava cobbles. The wall separating the two rooms was also without a lava-cobble footing and, while basically of adobe, contained numerous lava cobbles and sandstone slabs. This wall, unlike most at the site, was not set into a trench but was begun directly on floor level. Room B7 may have been constructed somewhat later, since its north wall was adobe with sandstone blocks laid in courses. Considering that the north, east, and west walls of Room B7 must all have been built simultaneously, they exhibited amazing diversity of styles. The west wall had the standard adobe-and-lava-base construction, the east wall was solid adobe, and the north wall, which abutted the other two, was adobe with sandstone blocks laid in courses, the only such wall excavated in Area B. Perhaps these walls were remodeled.

Room B1 (figs. 14, 15)

The top few centimeters of fill was of material that had washed in from the surrounding area, but below that and extending to or almost to the floor the fill was primarily of material from the roof. This roof fall consisted of charcoal, adobe, and soil of various colors. Mixed with it were adobe and occasional cobbles derived from the walls. In some areas, particularly in the southern section of the room, a stratum of soft, sandy, multicolored soil separated the roof fall from the floor, suggesting that considerable time elapsed between the abandonment of the room and the collapse of the roof. There were almost no artifacts in the fill above the roof fall; most of them were mixed with the lower portions of the roof material just above floor level. These artifacts may have been on the roof when it collapsed. Because of the proximity of much of the roof material and associated artifacts to the floor itself, it is quite possible that some artifacts listed as being on the floor were originally on the roof, and in a few instances the reverse may be true.

The floor was of the natural adobelike soil, hard-packed, and stained black from use, with a maximum difference of 15 cm between the levels of the highest and lowest areas. No subfloor strata were evident but the floor may have been "resurfaced," for the top of a pecking stone was barely visible sticking through the surface of the latest floor. The articulated bones from the paw of an animal about the size of a small dog were found on the floor east of the central of the three mealing bins.

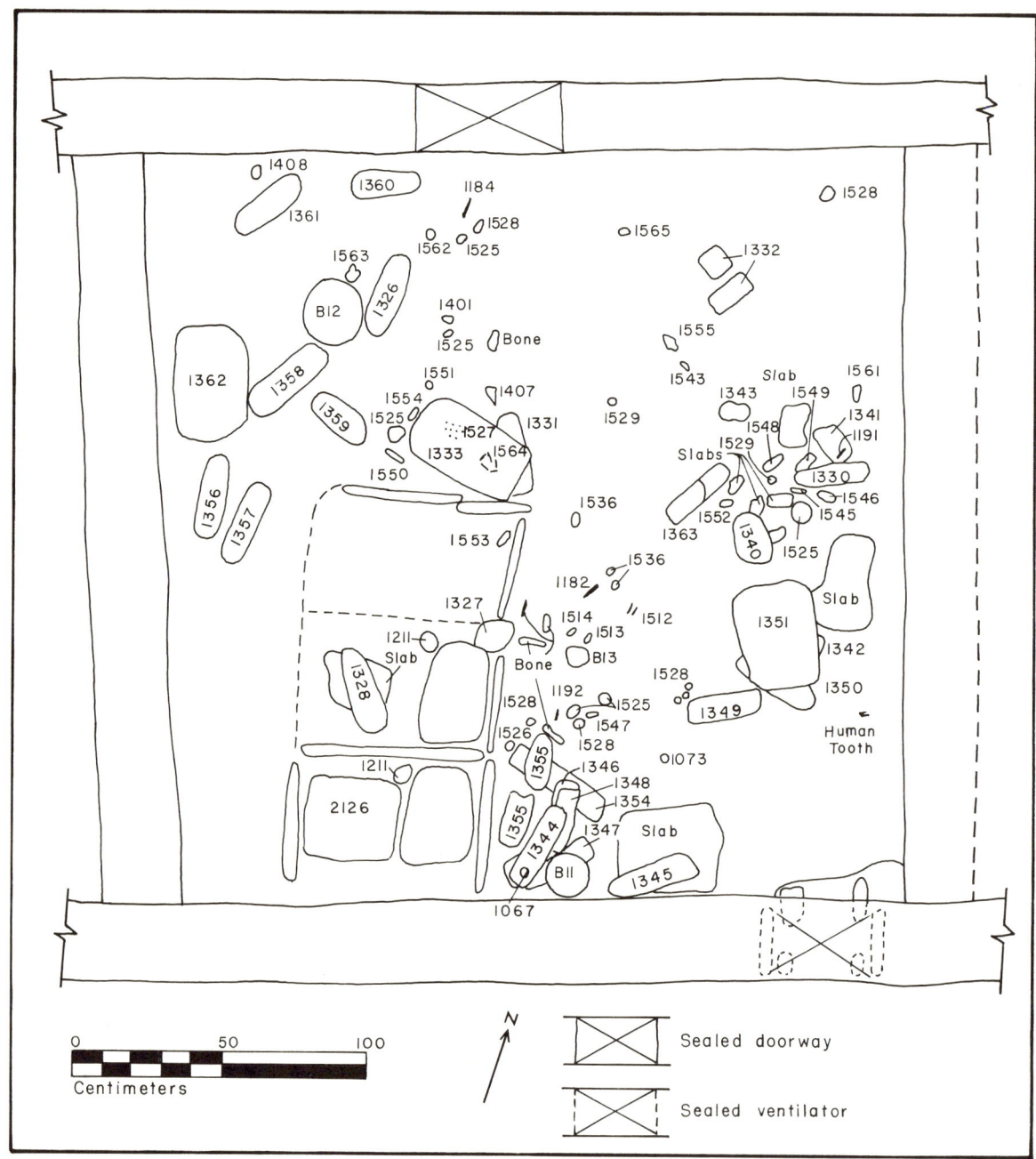

Figure 14. Site 616. Plan of Room B1.

MEALING BINS

A set of three contiguous slab-lined mealing bins near the southwesterly corner of the room had been partially destroyed when found. Only the southern bin remained in its original condition. From the other two bins the metates, the back slabs, the dividing slab, and, in the north bin, the floor slab had been removed or knocked down. The sandstone slabs were found lying in the area between the bins and the west wall, and three metates, any two of which could readily have fitted in the bins, were lying on the floor of the room. All the metates were of fine-grained sandstone. Each bin had had a sherd scoop set into the adobe at the left side of the foot of the metate. Separate pieces of a single Tularosa Black-on-white ladle had served as scoops in the south and center bins.

Figure 15. Site 616. Room B1, looking south.

VENTILATOR

At the east end of the south wall, set 12 cm above the floor, there once had been a ventilator hole 20 cm square, which was lined with sandstone slabs. These slabs and the sill projected approximately 10 cm into the corner of the room. The ventilator had been sealed with adobe and small rocks.

DOORWAY

The center of the north wall had a sealed doorway, which was originally 52 cm wide with a sill 40 cm above the floor. The north wall of Room B1 had subsequently been plastered so that visually no trace of the door remained.

COMMENT

It seems evident that this was a workroom, though what crafts were practiced here is less readily ascertained. The presence of balls of clay, a large quantity of hematite and other minerals, two mortars, and eight polishing pebbles strongly suggested pottery making. However, all of these, except perhaps the clay, could have been used along with the bone awls for other purposes, for example, working and decorating skins.

It is interesting that the metates found in this room, including the one remaining in the bin, were all of fine-grained sandstone. If, as seems likely, the two metates missing from the bins were among those found in the room, then the metates in this set of bins were not graduated as to coarseness. Seven manos were piled on the floor on the east side of the bins; the 15 others were scattered around the room. Most of these manos were also of sandstone. The emphasis on fine-grain sandstone grinding implements suggests that the function of this set of bins was more specialized than, or at least different from, that of the graded sets found in Rooms C2 and D2.

ARTIFACTS

Fill

Stone: 35 chips; hammer, elongated, flat-ended (fig. 56e); hammer, round-ended; metate; 2 unworked sandstone slabs
Bone: Awl, head split but unworked; awls, 2 fragments; carved pendant (fig. 64f); tube
Antler: Rubbing tool
Other: Clay (11 oz); limonite (1 oz)
Pottery vessels: Heshotauthla Polychrome bowl; 2 Puerco Black-on-red jars (fig. 44n); Wingate Black-on-red bowl

Floor

#1067, malachite (3¼ oz); #1073, 2 beads, red stone; #1154, polishing pebble; #1183, carved bone pendant; #1184, awl, head split but unworked (fig. 61e); #1191, quartz crystal; #1192, pierced phalange; #1326, mano (2021); #1327, mano (1821); #1328, mano (1221) #1330, mano (1821); #1331, mano (1321); #1332, mano (1321); #1333, metate, fine sandstone; #1340, roughly shaped mortar (fig. 53c); #1341, roughly shaped mortar (fig. 53b); #1342, axe; #1343, hammer, elongated, flat-ended (fig. 56i); #1344, mano (1931); #1345, mano (3421); #1346, mano (1421); #1347, mano (1821); #1348, mano (1821); #1349, mano (1121); #1350, mano (1021) (fig. 108e); #1351, metate, fine sandstone; #1354, mano (1721); #1355, mano (1721); #1356, mano (2221); #1357, mano (2221); #1358, mano (1931); #1359, mano (1321); #1360, mano (3221); #1361, mano (1821); #1362, metate, slab, medium vesicular basalt (fig. 109g); #1363, mano (1821); #1401, chip; #1407, awl, splinter (fig. 62b); #1408, pendant, stone; #1512, 2 bone tubes; #1513, unretouched flake; #1525, clay (1 lb); #1526, diatomaceous earth (½ oz); #1527, 18 beads, (15 black stone, 3 shell); #1528, hematite (1 lb, 10 oz); #1529, malachite and azurite (3 oz); #1536, 3 unretouched flakes; #1543, pierced phalange; #1545, hematite (2 lbs); #1546, shaft-smoother; #1547, polishing pebble; #1548, scoria cylinder (fig. 58d); #1549, scoria cylinder; #1550, bone tube (fig. 64l); #1551, polishing pebble; #1552, polishing pebble; #1553, polishing pebble; #1554, pierced phalange; #1555, stone point (fig. 57b); #1561, incised felsite pebble (fig. 59a); #1562, polishing pebble; #1563, polishing pebble; #1564,

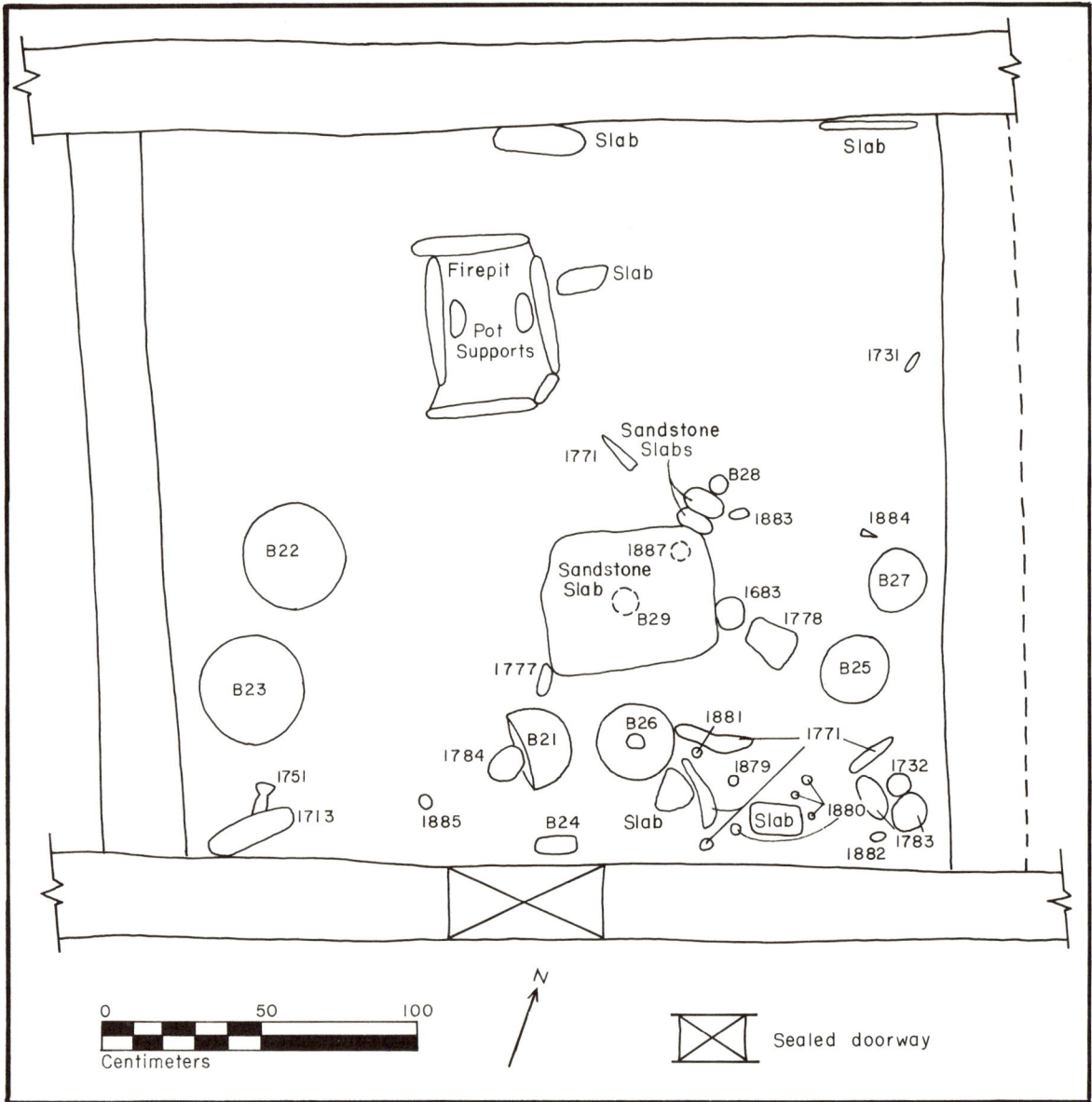

Figure 16. Site 616. Plan of Room B2.

awl, head of bone intact (fig. 62g); #1565, unusual, naturally shaped stone object; #2126, metate, fine sandstone, set in mealing bin

Pottery vessels: B11, St. Johns Polychrome bowl; B12, Springerville Polychrome bowl; B13, plain-ware seed jar

Room B2 (figs. 16, 17)

The upper portion of the fill was of hard adobe, but just above the floor there was a layer of softer sandy material. Charred roof beams and most of the artifacts in the fill were in and just above this softer layer. Some of the roof fragments rested directly on the floor and small pieces were found inside the bowls that were on the floor.

The floor was even and fairly level except for the northeastern section where it sloped sharply upward to the corner. It was covered with a layer of adobe plaster. Two rectangular sandstone slabs were leaning against the north wall. Other smaller sandstone slabs and a larger door slab were in the southeast quarter of the room along with most of the artifacts.

Figure 17. Site 616. Room B2, looking south, showing pot supports in firepit.

FIREPIT

The firepit, a rather irregular rectangle, was lined with sandstone slabs. The floor was of baked clay. It was excavated to a depth of 15 cm below the floor of the room and when found contained a deposit of ash 8 cm deep. Two pot supports were standing upright in the firepit, nearly touching the centers of its long sides. They were set into the ash but did not reach the firepit floor.

DOORWAY

There was a sealed doorway near the center of the south wall.

COMMENT

Apparently the roof partly burned and collapsed at the time this room was abandoned or shortly thereafter. Considerable wind-blown material then sifted into the room before adobe from the disintegrating walls effectively sealed the deposit. It is quite possible that some of the material found on the floor, including a dozen or more small irregular sandstone slabs, the large (64 by 48 cm) rectangular door slab, and some of the other material in the southeast corner slid to the floor from the roof as the roof collapsed. Some fine clean sand was found in one of the corrugated bowls on the floor (B27).

ARTIFACTS

Fill

> Stone: Axe; 7 chips; hammer, elongated, flat-ended; 5 manos and 1 mano fragment (1021, 1121, 1821, 2021, 2221, 2821); pendant
> Other: Turquoise, unworked fragment

> Pottery vessels: 2 St. Johns Polychrome bowls; Tularosa Black-on-white bowl

Floor

> #1683, mano fragment (1231); #1713, mano (1721); #1731, scoria cylinder; #1732, shaftsmoother (fig. 54d); #1751, hammer, round-ended; #1771, animal bone, unworked; #1777, mano fragment (1131); #1778, mano (1231); #1783, 2 pecking stones; #1784, clay (1 lb, 7 oz); #1879, polishing pebble; #1880, 4 chips; #1881, hematite (1½ oz); #1882, polishing stone; #1883, limonite (5 oz); #1884, skewer; #1885, chip; #1887, hematite (1 oz); worked sandstone slab

> Pottery vessels: B21, B22, B23, Hesotauthla Polychrome bowls; B24, Querino Polychrome legged vessel; B25, Pinedale Polychrome bowl; B26, Tularosa Black-on-white jar; B27, B28, corrugated bowls; B29, plainware miniature bowl

Firepit

> 2 pot supports

Room B3 (fig. 18)

There were only occasional traces of charcoal and fragments of roof adobe in the fill, and artifacts were rare. There were many sandstone blocks from the east wall and a few other stones strewn through the fill. A few fragments of a human skeleton were widely scattered.

The floor, of compact, light brown, adobelike soil with a scattering of charcoal over it, was fairly level except in the southwest corner where it sloped upward into the corner.

DOORWAYS

All doorways in the walls of Room B3 had been sealed with adobe and lava cobbles. The doorway in the north wall had a sandstone sill 30 cm above the floor. The adobe sill of the doorway in the eastern part of the south wall was only 20 cm above the floor. In fact the remaining "doorway" may have been a ventilator, for it extended to the floor and was comparatively small. An area some 35 cm square had been sealed with adobe and some small cobbles (one of which was a mano fragment). The condition of the wall above 35 cm was poor and it could not be determined whether the opening had originally extended higher, thus forming a narrow doorway. A solid adobe seal was not normal practice for a doorway, so this was probably a floor-level ventilator hole approximately 35 cm square.

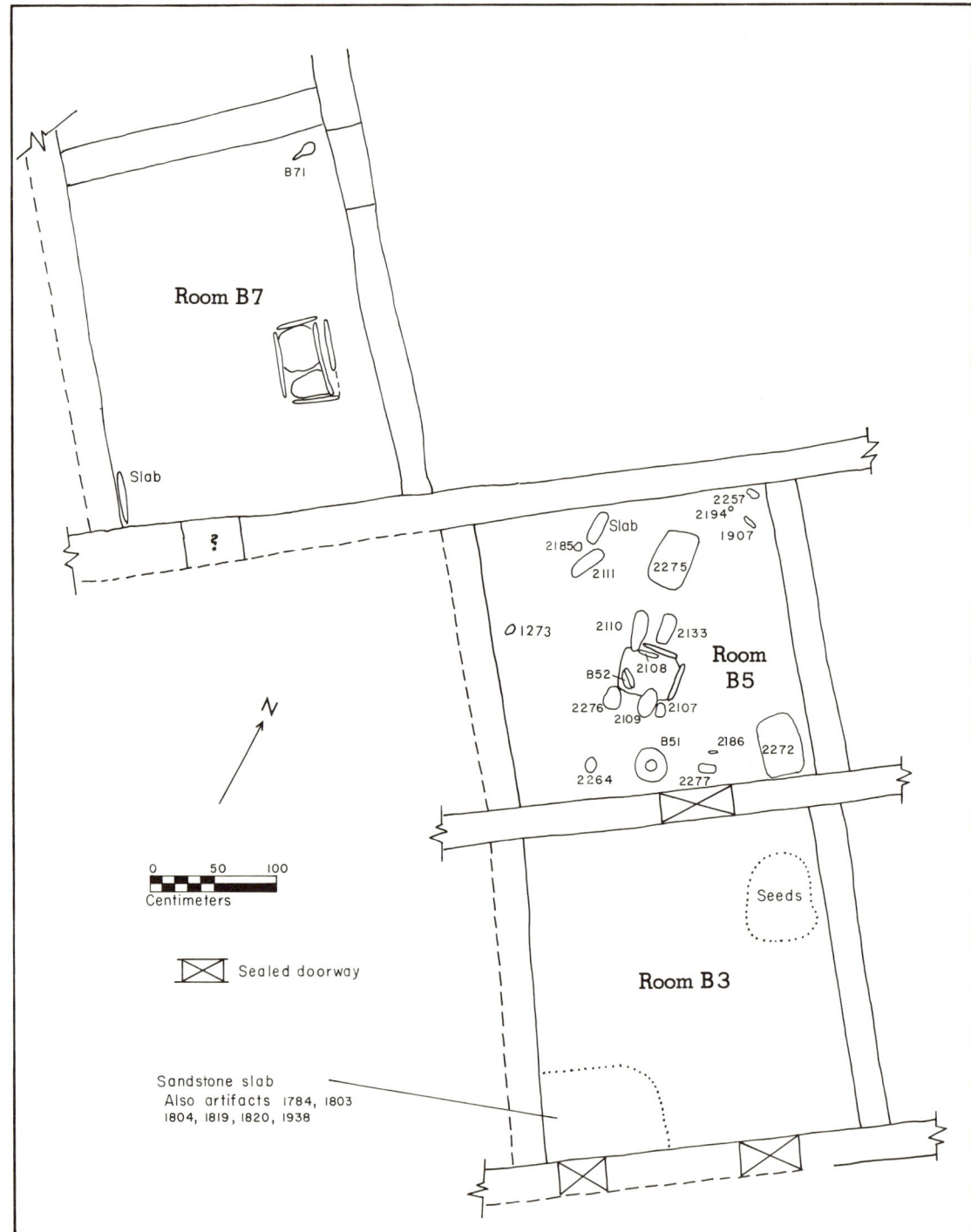

Figure 18. Site 616. Plan of Rooms B3, B5, and B7.

COMMENT

The absence of floor features and the paucity of artifacts indicate that this was a storeroom. The question of what was stored can be at least partially answered. In the northeast corner was approximately a half-bushel of seeds of the general Chenopodium-Amaranth-Cactus group. They were in a compact pile though there had been some scattering by rodents.

No trace of a container was found, but there may have been a perishable container such as a basket. In the southwest corner was a pile of irregular, unshaped slabs of tabular sandstone, the largest of which was 50 by 35 cm. Mixed with these slabs were six artifacts — one mano, three mano fragments, and two axes. One of the axes had served as a hammer and probably had been used to chip and shape the edges of the slabs, while the manos may have been employed to smooth down any surface irregularities.

ARTIFACTS

Fill

Stone: Chip; 2 mano fragments
Bone: Pierced phalange
Shell: Bead

Floor

#1748, mano fragment (3321); #1803, mano fragment (2221); #1804, mano (1831); #1819, mano fragment (1321); #1820, axe; #1938, axe

Structural

Mano fragment (2231), one of a number of rocks used in construction of south wall

Room B5 (fig. 18)

The fill was relatively homogeneous with very little evidence of charcoal or roof material. There were a few sherds, miscellaneous bones, mano fragments (from the walls?), and other small stones present. The only whole artifact was a slighty damaged small triangular point of obsidian (#1892, fig. 57c). The lack of roof material suggests that the roof of this room remained in position for some time after the abandonment of the pueblo.

The floor was fairly irregular and sloped up slightly to the east, particularly in the northeast corner. It was plastered with gray clay that sloped up and joined the wall plaster so that the junction of floor and wall was a smooth curve.

FIREPIT

The firepit had been excavated 18 cm into the floor. Two sides were lined with upright sandstone slabs but the other two sides sloped down in a smooth curve to the bottom of the pit. Ash to a depth of 5 cm filled the firepit. A mano that was in the pit rested on top of this ash. An adobe pot support was in immediate association, and one or more of the manos lying around the firepit may also have been utilized to brace vessels placed over the fire.

DOORWAY

The one doorway, which once had given access to Room B3 or perhaps to the outside before Room B3 was built, had been sealed with adobe and lava cobbles. The sill was 27 cm above the floor.

COMMENT

This room apparently had the normal accoutrements of a general living room: central firepit with its pot supports, portable grinding implements, two axes (one with a badly chipped blade), a jar, a few items of personal adornment, and smaller tools.

ARTIFACTS

Fill

Stone: 3 mano fragments (1131, 1631, 1731); point (fig. 57c)

Floor

#1907, hairpin (fig. 64b); #2107, axe; #2108, mano (1721); #2109, mano (2112); #2110, mano (1121); #2111, mano (1021); #2133, mano (1121); #2173, awl, splinter, embedded in floor plaster (fig. 62c); #2185, polishing pebble; #2186, awl, fragment; #2194, pierced phalange (fig. 64i); #2257, mano (1831); #2264, 8 chips; #2272, metate, fine sandstone; #2275, metate, fine sandstone; #2276, pot support; #2277, axe; #2276, clay (5 lbs)

Pottery vessels: B51, Tularosa Black-on-white jar; B52, corrugated bowl

Room B7

The fill of this room contained a number of sandstone and lava blocks presumably from the north wall. These blocks, and those in the section of the wall that remained standing, generally had one fairly flat face which formed the face of the wall. This characteristic, foreshadowing the walls of neatly coursed, well-shaped sandstone blocks, is one reason for regarding Room B7 as the last of the excavated rooms in Area B to be constructed. There was almost no evidence of roof fall in the fill.

The floor, which was fairly level throughout, had been plastered with a layer of hard, light tan clay 1 to 3 cm thick. This floor plaster sloped up to the walls except on the north, so that the junction of floor and wall was a smooth curve. The walls were also plastered but the plaster was slightly different from that on the floor for it was a lighter yellow-tan, and more sandy. The floor was stained by flecks of charcoal and dirt, and one Tularosa Black-on-white ladle was found (B71).

A broken flat sandstone slab (52 by 45 by 2.5 cm) was leaning against the south end of the west wall and a number of small sandstone slabs lay on the floor near the firepit. A small amount of trash underlay the floor, another indication that this room may have been built a little later than the others in the area.

FIREPIT

The firepit had been remodeled twice. The original firepit measured 60 by 40 cm and was 30 cm deep. It was slab-lined and apparently had had a floor of baked adobe. The first remodeling made the firepit smaller. The original east wall slabs were left in place but a new wall slab was placed parallel to and 10 cm inside the original slabs. The narrow space between the slabs was filled with adobe and plastered over. The top of one of the original wall slabs remained visible through the floor plaster. The pit was deepened slightly at this time and the bottom lined with sandstone slabs. The final remodeling consisted simply of placing coarse, compacted sand in a layer 2 to 6 cm thick over the bottom of the firepit. There were 20 cm of yellow-gray and gray compacted ash present in the final version of the firepit.

DOORWAYS

There were possibly two doorways in the walls of this room as indicated by what appeared to be sandstone doorsills set into the wall at a height of approximately 20 cm. One was at the west end of the south wall, the other at the north end of the east wall. In neither case were the walls in sufficiently good condition for any cleavage to be determined. If doorways had existed they must have been sealed with adobe.

COMMENT

The lack of artifacts suggests that this room was abandoned prior to the general exodus from the pueblo but, if so, the very "cleanliness" of the room and fill shows that it was not used as a depository for refuse as were so many abandoned rooms at other sites. Either the room simply happened not to contain many artifacts when the occupants departed, or perhaps later visitors to the room may have had the time and inclination to remove most of the material.

ARTIFACTS

Fill

  Stone: 4 chips; mano
  Bone: Tube; 2 worked fragments

Floor

  B71, Tularosa Black-on-white ladle

Figure 19. Site 616. Showing the excellent exterior sandstone masonry in Area C.

Firepit

  Pot support

Area C

Area C consisted of a section of the northwest corner of the pueblo. Ten rooms were excavated in this area, nine of them completely.

In general, the north-south walls in Area C abutted the east-west walls and the latter were continuous through several rooms. One exception was the southeast corner of Room C8, another was the southwest corner of Room C2. It seems that the row of rooms containing Rooms C6 and C9 was the earliest to be built. All of these walls were basically of adobe. They were set in a trench and the basal two or three courses were of mixed sandstone and lava cobbles. Of the rooms excavated Rooms C5 and C2 probably were built next, for the technique of wall construction was similar, though here there was a tendency to use only sandstone cobbles in the basal courses. Room C10 and the outer row of rooms including Rooms C1, C3, C4, and C8 were the last to be built. Here the "outside" walls, and the internal dividing wall in Room C10, were of sandstone-block construction. The blocks were shaped and the walls of these last rooms were very well constructed (fig. 21). An exception was the west wall of Room C8, which had begun to collapse inward during the time the room was occupied. The internal dividing walls separating these rooms were of adobe and sandstone courses in Room C1, and solid adobe in the west wall of Room C3 and the east wall of Room C4. The north, east, and south walls of Room C8 were similar to those in Rooms C5 and C2; this room may thus have been one of the earliest with sandstone-block construction for the outside wall. In every case, except the internal divider in Room C5, the walls extended below the room floors, some only 10 cm and one nearly 40 cm, but the average was approximately 25 cm.

Room C1 (figs. 20, 21)

There were a great many sandstone slabs throughout the fill, doubtless derived from the walls. Just above the floor there was evidence of roof fall, a number of artifacts (awls, chips, manos, bowls, ladles, polishing pebbles, and beads), and no less than 25 restorable vessels.

The floor was quite even and had been coated with a thin adobe plaster. A small quantity of what appeared to be charred green corn was in a pile against the west wall.

CIST

A small, unlined, basically rectangular cist, with an irregularly shaped small extension to the northwest, had been excavated into the floor in the very southeast corner of the room. The rectangular portion of the cist was approximately 30 cm on a side and 29 cm deep.

DOORWAY

A doorway sealed with sandstone blocks was located in the center of the south wall, its sill 10 cm above the level of the floor.

COMMENT

The number and variety of pottery vessels (five corrugated bowls, nine polychrome bowls, six black-on-white jars, two ladles, a seed jar, a duck pot, and a miniature jar) as well as nine polishing pebbles, which apparently had been on the roof of this room, suggested that the roof area was serving as a work area for one or more potters or perhaps as a display area for several potters and/or traders. The floor artifacts were rather strange, consisting almost entirely of unusual, naturally shaped stones, concretions, quartz crystals, and the like — probably medicinal or ceremonial objects, or merely curiosities. The beads on the floor were found in an incomplete sequence of 18 black beads alternating with one turquoise bead.

ARTIFACTS

Fill

> Stone: Axe; ball (fig. 60d); 128 beads (75 red stone, 36 black stone, 17 turquoise); 8 chips; concretion; 6 manos and mano fragments (1121, 1131, 1821, 1921, 2231, 3421) (#2001, fig. 108n); metate fragments; 2 pendants; 9 polishing pebbles; 2 quartz crystals; 2 scoria cylinders (#1515, fig. 58c); hematite cylinder
>
> Bone: Awl, skewer, partial; figurine (fig. 64g); awl, split but unworked (fig. 61g)
>
> Shell: 103 beads; pendant, cut shell; pendant, tinkler; unworked fragments
>
> Other: Clay (5 oz); limonite (1¼ oz); malachite (14¾ oz)
>
> Pottery vessels: 5 corrugated bowls; 5 Heshotauthla Polychrome bowls; Pinedale Polychrome bowl; Puerco Black-on-red miniature pitcher; St. Johns Polychrome ladle; 3 St. Johns Polychrome bowls; Tularosa Black-on-white ladle; Tularosa Black-on-white miniature seed jar; 6 Tularosa Black-on-white jars; Wingate Black-on-red seed jar; Reserve Black-on-white miniature pitcher (fig. 44e)

Trench north of room
> Unretouched flake

Floor

> #1532, concretion; #1648, malachite (¼ oz); #1649, #1650, 2 unusual, naturally shaped stone objects; #1651, unretouched flake; #1652, hematite cylinder; #1653, awl, head split but unworked (fig. 61h); #1659, 80 beads (75 black stone, 5 turquoise — fig. 59g); #1660, quartz crystal
>
> Pottery vessel: C11, Reserve Black-on-white duck figurine (fig. 44j)

Room C2 (fig. 22)

Charred beams and adobe from the roof were resting on or above the floor. Intermingled with and resting on this roof material were a number of artifacts (an axe, 14 manos, 5 metates, awls, pendants, bowls, jars) and a fully articulated human skeleton. This material and the body apparently were on the roof when it burned and collapsed at the time the pueblo was abandoned.

The floor was fairly even and plastered, and its plaster curved up to join the wall plaster.

MEALING BINS (figs. 22, 23)

The walls of the three contiguous mealing bins were upright tabular sandstone slabs set into the floor. The

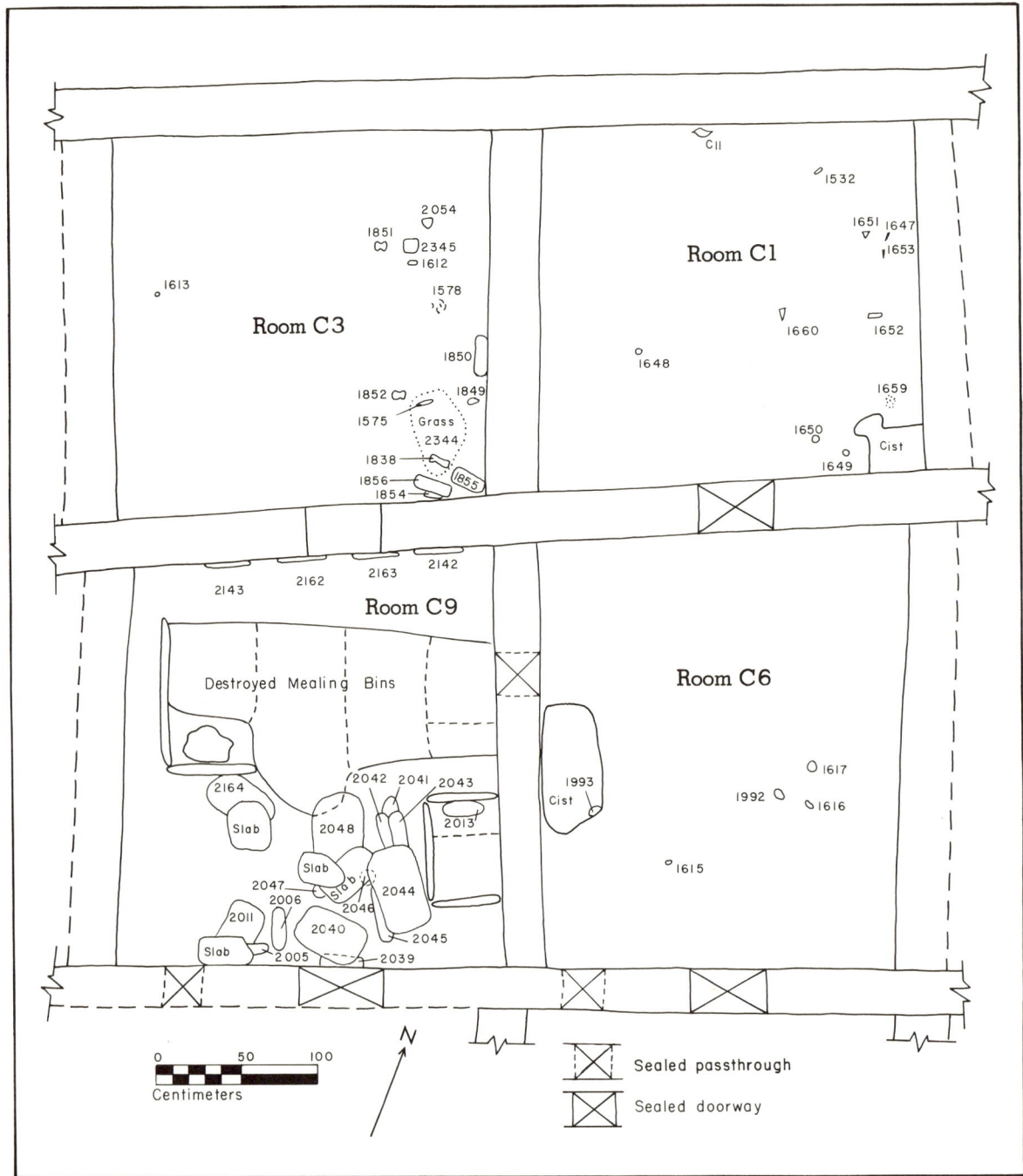

Figure 20. Site 616. Plan of Rooms C1, C3, C6, and C9.

western bin contained a fine-grained sandstone metate (#1691). The bottom of this bin was floored with a sandstone slab and in the eastern quarter with a wood slat. The slat may have served partly as a scoop surface though it was flat and on the right side, whereas most sherd scoops were to the left of the foot of the metate. The metate from the central bin had been removed but a metate (#1417) of medium-grained calcareous tuff, and of an appropriate size to fit the bin, was lying on the floor nearby. The eastern bin contained a coarse-grained metate of vesicular basalt (#1690). All three metates had been set into adobe, the

Figure 21. Site 616. Room C1, looking west, showing masonry typical of Area C.

surface of which was just below the level of the working surface of the metate. There were no pottery or other scoops, except for the wooden slat, to aid in the removal of the ground materials. The floors of the eastern and central bins were 16 cm below the level of the room floor, but the western bin floor was only 8 cm below the room floor. Nevertheless, the metate in the western bin was set at the steepest angle, which was 31° from the horizontal. The central metate had been set at an angle of 18° (as determined from the adobe border), and the coarse-grained metate at an angle of 28°.

Three manos were on the floor on the same side of the bins as a person grinding; one rested on the basalt metate, and a number of others were scattered over the floor beyond the bins. All three mano materials and various shapes (rectangular, wedge, and triangular) were represented. Two of the specimens were mano blanks. A few charred cactus seeds were found on the floor of the western bin and on the adjacent room floor to the north, and restorable vessels were in the central and eastern bins.

DOORWAY

An open doorway in the north wall led into Room C5. This doorway had a sandstone sill with a steplike projection of the same width and height extending from the doorway into both Rooms C2 and C5. This step projected 30 cm into Room C2 and its surface was 35 cm above the floor level. In Room C2 the riser of the step was faced with a metate (#2756).

HUMAN SKELETON

The skeleton was that of a young girl probably in her teens (fig. 6b, c). At the time of her death she appeared to have been wearing a necklace consisting of small black stone beads, a few shell beads, and two turquoise beads. Her right arm had been broken off 9 cm below the shoulder (there was no indication of bone healing) and the lower portion of this arm was not found. In addition, an elongated oval hole (the size and shape of the cross section of the bit of a typical axe) in the top of her skull strongly suggested that she met a sudden and violent end. Apparently her body was simply left sprawled across the roof until the almost immediate collapse of the roof provided burial of a sort.

COMMENT

There is little question that the roof of this room burned and collapsed to the floor, carrying with it the body and the artifacts on the roof. There were many charred beams and fragments. The upper surface of the wood slat in the western mealing bin also was charred. The floor artifacts, the charred slat, and the absence of any loose sandy fill between roof fall and floor indicate that the room had been in use until the roof collapsed. The fact that the skeleton remained articulated, despite having fallen with the roof to the floor of the room, is good evidence that the burning and collapse occurred immediately following the death of the individual.

It is interesting that there were approximately the same number of manos and metates on the roof as there were in the bins and on the floor of the room.

ARTIFACTS

Fill

> Stone: Axe, three-quarter-grooved; 14 manos (e.g., fig. 108d, l); 3 mano fragments; 5 metates; 2 pendants; pot support, fragment
> Bone: Awl, head of bone intact; awl, skewer; tube (fig. 64m); pierced phalange; worked fragment
> Shell: 2 pendants of cut shell
> Other: Jet button; limonite (7 oz)
> Pottery vessels: Corrugated bowl; 6 corrugated jars; Heshotauthla Polychrome bowl; plainware toy bowl; Puerco Black-on-red jar; Reserve Black-on-red pitcher (fig. 44q); 4 St. Johns Polychrome bowls; 10 Reserve Black-on-white jars; Reserve Black-on-white ladle (fig. 44r)
> Skeleton 2: 219 beads, (190 black stone, 2 turquoise, 27 shell)

Floor

> #1170, 4 tubes; #1416, mano (1821); #1417, metate, medium calcareous tuff; #1418, mano (2221); #1420, mano (1221); #1421, mano (1021); #1422, mano (1821); #1423, mano (1221); #1424, mano (3721); #1426, pecking stone; #1457, mano (1221); #1463, mano (1421); #1464, mano fragment (1731); #1465, mano (2831); #1466, mano (1021); #1502, axe; #1503, axe; #1505, 15 whole shell pendants (fig. 65f, g); #1509, awl, eyed; #1690, metate, coarse vesicular basalt, set in east mealing bin; #1691, metate, fine sandstone, set in west mealing bin

> Pottery vessels: C21, Puerco Black-on-red miniature jar; C22, Springerville Polychrome bowl; C23, corrugated bowl; C26, Puerco Black-on-red miniature jar (fig. 44b)

Structural

> #2756, metate, fine sandstone, used as a door riser

Room C3 (fig. 20)

The fill contained numerous sandstone blocks from the walls as well as considerable melted adobe. On the floor, and as much as 50 cm above it, there was evidence of roof fall comprising charred and rotting beams, charcoal fragments, adobe, and various artifacts.

The floor was fairly level but the surface was rough and uneven. There were no floor features.

DOORWAY

An open doorway in the south wall led into Room C9. The sandstone sill was 20 cm above the level of the floor.

COMMENT

The roof of this room apparently burned and collapsed at the time of abandonment or immediately thereafter. Most of the artifacts associated with the roof and on the floor were concentrated in the eastern half of the room. Perhaps the eastern half of the roof gave way first, and all material tended to slide toward this side when the roof fell. In this case, some or all of the artifacts found on the floor may have been initially on the roof. In any event, the scarcity of material on the floor suggests that this room was utilized primarily for storage or perhaps for sleeping.

It is fortunate that this room burned as it did, for the conflagration effectively preserved a considerable amount of material (cloth, basketry, a "shock" of grass, wood) which ordinarily would not have survived. No artifacts of bone were recorded.

ARTIFACTS

Fill

> Stone: 4 axes; 41 beads (5 black stone, 36 red stone); 2 hematite cylinders (fig. 60m, o); 8 polishing pebbles; 6 manos; 4 mano fragments; 3 metates; metate fragment; shaped object
> Shell: 110 beads; bracelet fragment; 2 conical objects; pendant of cut shell (fig. 65e)
> Other: Basket fragments (?); cotton cloth; fur cloth; hematite (5½ oz); limonite (8¼ oz); grooved hematite cube (fig. 60r); netting
> Pottery vessels: 6 corrugated jars; St. Johns Polychrome bowl; 4 Tularosa Black-on-white jars

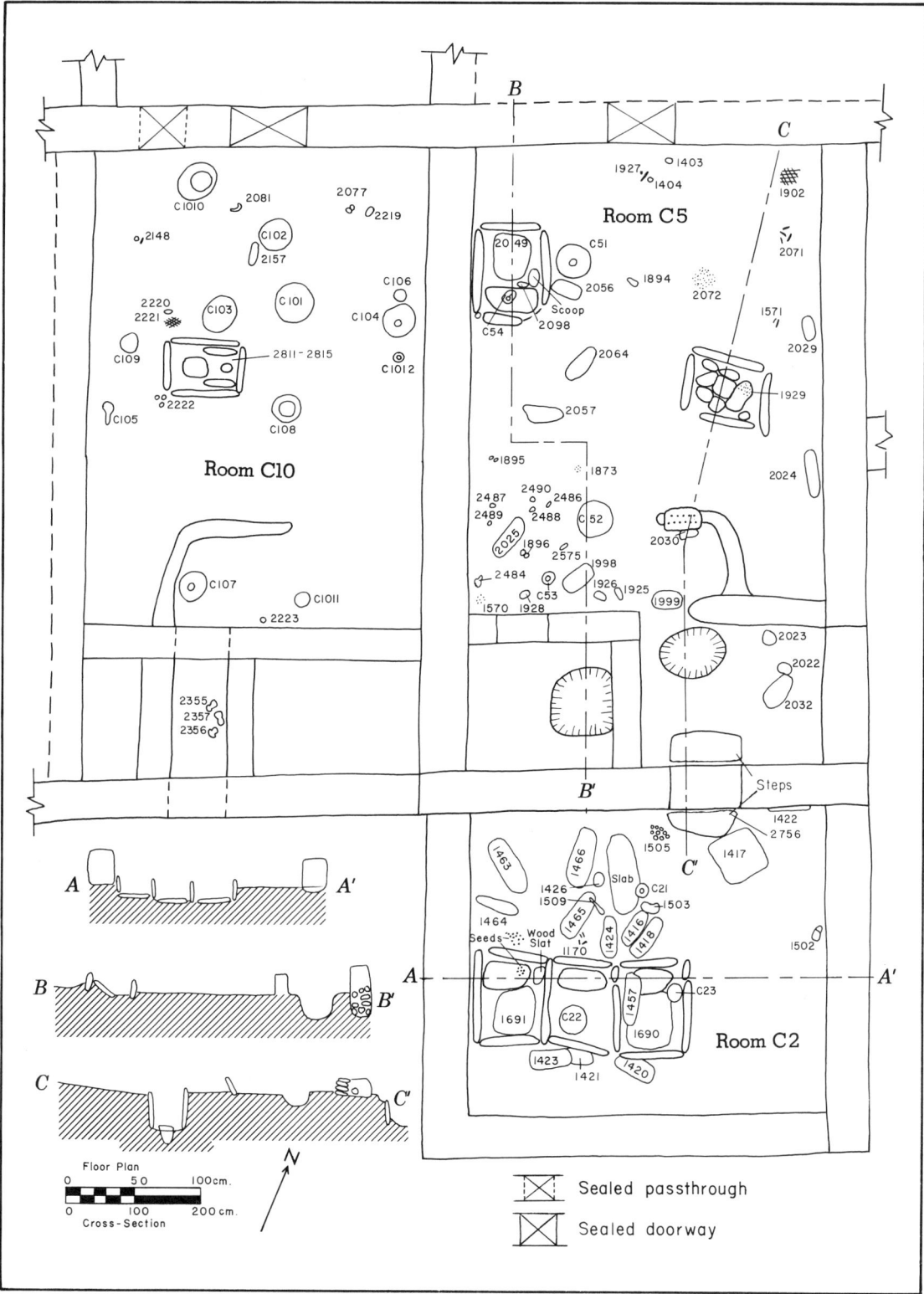

Figure 22. Site 616. Plan of Rooms C2, C5, and C10.

Figure 23. Site 616. Room C2, showing mealing bins.

Floor

#1575, monocot fiber, yucca or agave; #1578, 5 shell bracelet fragments; #1612, concretion; #1613, 55 beads (52 black stone, 3 turquoise); #1838, wood object; #1849, scoria cylinder; #1850, mano (2821); #1851, hammer, round-ended (fig. 56g); #1852, axe; #1854, mano fragment (2221); #1855, mano (1721); #1856, mano (1421) (fig. 108h); #2054, basket fragment; #2344, grass, probably Muhlenbergia; #2345, basket fragment

Room C4 (fig. 24)

Sandstone blocks were scattered throughout the fill though they were more numerous in the upper levels. Approximately 50 cm above the floor there was some charcoal and adobe that may indicate the level of roof fall. At this same level there were scattered human rib and vertebra fragments; below it the fill was slightly more loose and sandy.

The floor was comparatively even and had been coated with a layer of adobe plaster 5 cm thick. There were no floor features.

DOORWAY

In the adobe east wall of the room was an open doorway, with plastered adobe sides and a sandstone sill, 36 cm above the floor.

COMMENT

The roof of this room may have remained in place for some time after the abandonment of the pueblo, allowing considerable windblown and other casual fill to accumulate before giving way. No large charred fragments of beams were found, so the roof probably did not burn.

ARTIFACTS

Fill

Stone: 8 manos (fig. 108k); 2 metates; metate fragment, the back face having had secondary use as a mortar

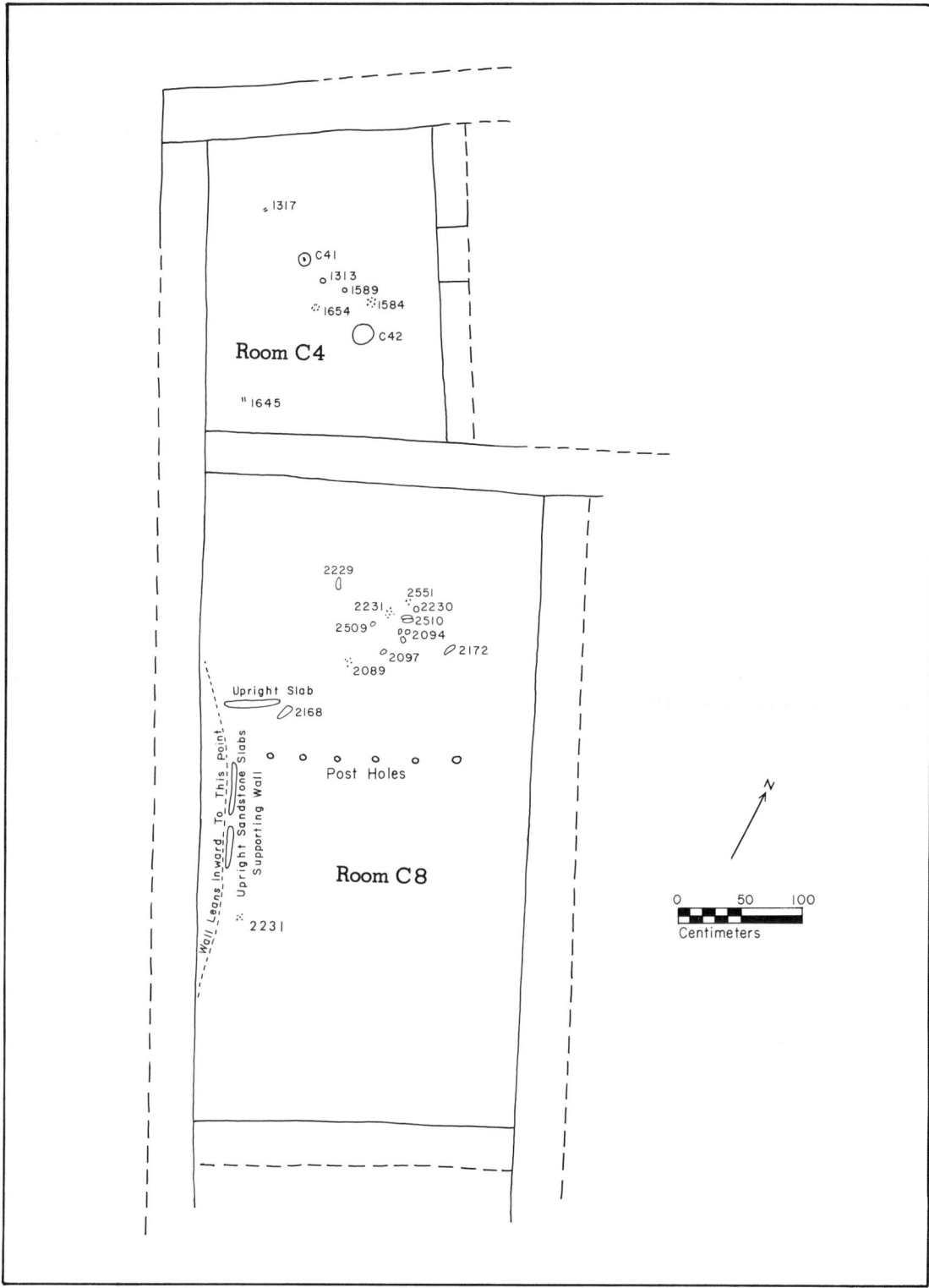

Figure 24. Site 616. Plan of Rooms C4 and C8.

Bone: 2 awls, head split but unworked
Shell: Worked fragments
Pottery vessels: Klageto Polychrome jar; Reserve Black-on-white doughnut-shaped pitcher (fig. 44g); Reserve Black-on-white jar; 2 Tularosa Black-on-white jars

Floor

#1313, quartz crystal; #1317, hematite (1 lb, 7 oz); #1584, 19 beads (18 black stone, 1 turquoise); #1589, limonite (1 oz); #1645, 2 red stone beads; #1654, worked shell fragments

Pottery vessels: C41, Puerco Black-on-red miniature jar; C42, corrugated bowl

Room C5 (figs. 22, 25, 26)

The fill contained a considerable quantity of burned material and numerous artifacts. No levels of definite roof fall could be determined but the burned material extended from just below ground surface to the floor.

The floor was plastered and fairly level though the northern third sloped up slightly. An earlier floor level was found approximately 6 cm lower.

FIREPIT

Each wall of the firepit was lined with a single large sandstone slab while several smaller slabs lined the floor. In the center of the firepit floor a roughly circular hole, 20 cm in diameter and 23 cm deep, was covered by a loose sandstone slab. Both the firepit and the hole were filled with white ash. Similar ash holes were found in Room C10 of Site 616 (p. 83), Rooms 6 and 25 at Site 481 (pp. 192, 195-196), at Hawikuh (Smith, Woodbury, and Woodbury 1966, p. 56), and at Sandstone Hill (Barnett 1974, p. 11). Mixed with the ash in the firepit were several fragments of unworked shell, two shell beads, a small quartz crystal, and seven deer dewclaws. Three of the dewclaws had been biconically drilled in two places; another had a single biconically drilled hole.

MEALING BIN (fig. 25)

The four walls of the mealing bin were also slab-lined and a slab formed its floor. Half of the bowl section of a Reserve Black-on-white ladle had been set into the adobe at the left-hand side of the foot of the metate to serve as a scoop. A small, handled, Reserve Black-on-white "duck" pot (vessel C54, figs. 22, 44h) and an awl (#2098, fig. 62d) lay on the floor of the bin.

ENCLOSURES

Room C5 was unique in having two closetlike enclosures or walled-off areas within the room, or perhaps

Figure 25. Site 616. Room C5, showing mealing bin, with duck pot, awl, and sherd scoop.

it would be more correct to say two small subsidiary rooms (fig. 26). In each enclosure a hole had been excavated into the floor. The hole in the enclosure in the southwest corner of the room was approximately 40 cm in diameter and 40 cm deep and located against the center of the east wall of the enclosure. In the second enclosure, which led to the open door into Room C2, the hole was nearly as large but only half as deep and would appear to have been somewhat inconveniently located with respect to the traffic pattern. Both holes were simply excavated into the subsoil. They were roughly finished with sloping sides and not plastered or stone-lined.

A Showlow Polychrome bowl (C52) was found on the floor. This was a rare type at Site 616. (See Carlson 1970, pp. 73-77, fig. 39.)

DEFLECTOR (fig. 26)

Extending in an arc north and then west of the north wall of the southeastern enclosure was a rounded ridge of adobe approximately 10 cm wide and 15 cm high. Supported by the northern wing of this arc was an upright sandstone slab which, in conjunction with the ridge, served to deflect from the firepit the breeze

Figure 26. Site 616. Room C5, looking south, showing enclosures with cists and curved deflector wall.

entering the room through the doorway from Room C2 and that of the southeastern enclosure.

DOORWAYS

The doorway from the southeastern enclosure into Room C2 is described in the discussion of that room (p. 73). The sandstone sill of this doorway was 20 cm above the floor of Room C5.

The doorways into the enclosures from the central portion of the room were narrower than the normal room doorway, for they measured only 35 cm in width. The one into the southeastern enclosure was at floor level, but that into the southwestern enclosure had a sandstone sill 15 cm above floor level.

A doorway sealed with well-coursed sandstone slabs was located in the center of the north wall of the room.

COMMENT

The history of the construction of this room is rather complex. Originally, the wall setting off the southeastern enclosure may have extended across the entire room, forming the room's south wall. This wall and all the major room walls extended below the level of the floor. At some later time the south extension was added and perhaps at the same time the north and east walls of the southwest enclosure were constructed. These last two walls were built on the surface of the floor rather than set into a trench.

The purpose of this extension, providing as it did for the two enclosures, is not known. The enclosures contained nothing except a few mano fragments.

ARTIFACTS

Fill

Stone: 35 beads (5 black stone, 15 red stone, 15 turquoise); hammer, equilateral flat-ended (fig. 56c); 2 manos; 5 mano fragments; 2 metates; 3 pendants; scoria cylinder

Shell: 574 beads; pendant of cut shell; unworked fragments

Other: Jet button; hematite (1 oz); limonite (1 oz); malachite (½ oz); mat impression

Pottery vessels: Corrugated bowl; 6 corrugated jars; 5 Heshotauthla Polychrome bowls; Pinedale Polychrome bowl; Pinedale Polychrome seed jar; Puerco Black-on-red jar; Reserve

80 • Mariana Mesa

Black-on-white miniature ladle; Reserve Black-on-white shoe-shaped vessel; 5 St. Johns Polychrome bowls; St. Johns Polychrome jar; Tularosa Black-on-white ladle; 4 Tularosa Black-on-white jars

Floor

#1403, unusual, naturally shaped stone object; #1404, concretion; #1570, 74 beads (31 red stone, 3 turquoise, 40 shell), and 2 stone pendants; #1571, 2 shell beads; #1873, 14 shell beads; #1894, scoria cylinder; #1895, mosaic fragments (?), 2 of turquoise; #1896, stone figurine of frog (fig. 59b); #1902, basket fragment; #1925, scoria cylinder; #1926, scoria cylinder; #1927, awl, skewer; #1928, jet button; #1998, mano fragment (1831); #1999, mano (2221) (fig. 108r); #2022, pecking stone; #2023, mano fragment (1231); #2024, mano (1221); #2025, mano (1121); #2029, pot support; #2030, axe; #2032, mano fragment (1321); #2049, metate, medium calcareous tuff, set in mealing bin (fig. 109f); #2056, mano (1921); #2057, mano fragment (1521); #2064, mano (1121); #2071, awl, skewer, fragments; #2072, 129 beads, shell; #2098, awl, head of bone intact (fig. 62d); #2484, concretion; #2486, quartz crystal; #2487, shaped bone object; #2488, unretouched flake; #2489, stone ball; #2490, iron pyrites crystal; #2575, concretion

Pottery vessels: C51, Puerco Black-on-red jar (fig. 44a); C52, Showlow Polychrome bowl; C53, Reserve Black-on-white miniature jar (fig. 44p); C54, Reserve Black-on-white "duck" pot (fig. 44h)

Firepit

#1929, quartz crystal, 7 dewclaw pendants, and 2 shell beads

Room C6 (fig. 20)

The fill consisted of adobe, a few stones, and very few artifacts. A layer of loose sandy soil over the floor as well as the absence of charcoal or other definite signs of roof fall suggested that the roof of this room remained standing for some time after the room was abandoned.

The floor was quite even and covered with a thin layer of plaster, which did not slope up to the walls.

CIST

There was an excavated area in the floor extending 75 cm along the center of the west wall. The sandstone-and-lava base of the west wall, which elsewhere extended only 24 cm below floor level, extended downward 40 cm in the area of the excavation, and here the wall base was plastered as were the three earthen walls of the cist. The excavation did not appear to be an abandoned mealing bin. A mano fragment (#1993) was set into the wall at the southeast corner of the cist.

PASSTHROUGHS

Through the west end of the south wall, 105 cm above floor level, a hole 29 cm square extended into Room C10. The sill was of adobe, the sides were of sandstone slabs, and four small (2 to 3 cm in diameter) poles formed the roof. It had been sealed. Through the north end of the west wall there was a similar hole (also sealed) into Room C9. It was 50 cm above the floor level and only 15 cm square. When open these may have served primarily to pass materials from one room to the other rather than to ventilate.

DOORWAYS

There were doorways sealed with sandstone blocks in the center of the north and south walls of this room. The sills of both were at floor level.

COMMENT

It is possible that this room had been abandoned prior to the time the pueblo itself was deserted, for, unlike most rooms excavated in Area C, it showed little evidence of having been used up to the moment of abandonment.

ARTIFACTS

Fill

Stone: Awl; 2 manos; polishing pebble; worked sandstone slab
Shell: Unworked fragments
Pottery vessels: Pinedale Black-on-red bowl; Puerco Black-on-red bowl; 3 St. Johns Polychrome bowls; Tularosa Black-on-white miniature jar

Floor

#1615, stone ball; #1616, unretouched flake; #1617, pecking stone; #1992, axe, three-quarter-grooved (fig. 55e)

Structural

#1993, mano fragment (1221), set into wall at corner of floor cist

Room C7

A trench was put down in this room, located immediately west of Rooms C2 and C5, but it became necessary to stop work before the south or the east walls or

Figure 27. Site 616. Room C8, looking north, showing upright sandstone slabs and postholes subdividing the room.

the floor were reached. In fact, this trench may not have been within the confines of a room at all.

ARTIFACTS

Fill

Stone: Axe; 55 beads (52 black stone, 1 red stone, 2 turquoise); bowl (fig. 109l); hammer, round-ended (fig. 56f); metate (fig. 109i)
Bone: Awl fragment
Shell: 132 beads; pendant, tinkler
Pottery vessels: 2 St. Johns Polychrome bowls; Tularosa Black-on-white jar

Room C8 (figs. 24, 27)

The fill in this room consisted largely of adobe and of sandstone blocks from the walls. This material extended to the floor with no intervening stratum of loose sandy material. Most of the artifacts in the fill came from a level just above the floor.

The floor was not very level or even, and sloped upward over the northern half of the room. It was covered by a layer of plaster approximately 5 cm thick, but in the south half of the room the plaster was thinner and the floor was not well finished.

The west wall was not well built and had begun to sag inward. To bolster the sagging wall, two sandstone slabs were set into the floor and against the wall in such a manner that the slabs served as props. Between these slabs and the wall an adobe support was constructed.

Apparently a jacal or perhaps simply a woven partition extended east-west across the center of the room, as was indicated by six postholes. The presence of this partition might be related to the weakened wall and consequently unstable roof, but the upright supports were not very large.

The roof did not seem to have been burned but the absence of any loose sandy fill near the floor, and the location of most of the artifacts in the fill at a level just above the floor, suggested that the roof fell very shortly after the room was abandoned. The weakened wall doubtless was a factor. The few artifacts on the floor, like those in Room C1, were mostly of a nonutilitarian nature.

Unlike most rooms at the site, this room was built on top of fill which extended to a depth of 85 cm below the floor.

ARTIFACTS

Fill

Stone: 46 beads (20 black stone, 26 red stone); mano; metate (fig. 109h); roughly shaped mortar; pecking stone; 7 polishing pebbles
Bone: Awl, head of bone intact; 2 awls, skewer fragments; awl, fragment; worked fragment; pierced phalange
Other: Clay (13 oz); malachite (5 oz)
Pottery vessels: Corrugated bowl; corrugated jar; Klageto Black-on-yellow jar; Puerco Black-on-red miniature jar (fig. 44d); St. Johns Polychrome bowl

Floor

#2089, 255 beads (75 black stone, 75 red stone, 5 turquoise, 100 shell); #2094, 2 conical shell objects (fig. 60g, h) and 1 andesite cylinder; #2097, quartz crystal; #2168, mano (1821); #2171, bone tube; #2229, bone figurine (fig. 64a); #2230, stone ball; #2231, 45 turquoise chips (mosaic fragments?); #2509, worked shell; #2510, 2 hematite cylinders (fig. 60p, q); #2551, 4 beads of translucent stone (fig. 59d)

Room C9 (figs. 20, 28)

The evidence indicated that the south portion of the roof of this room had partially burned and collapsed. The northern section may have remained in place so that for a while a lean-to effect was achieved. At any rate, a number of artifacts and some charred roof material were found on or just above the floor in the south half of the room. In the northern half, roof material was less abundant and the fill just above the floor in this area was loose and sandy, suggesting wind-blown drift.

The floor was even and fairly level and the floor plaster did not join the wall plaster in a smooth curve.

MEALING BINS

This room originally contained five mealing bins. Four extended in a line from the east wall of the room

Figure 28. Site 616. Room C9, looking east, showing area of destroyed mealing bins.

almost to the west wall and were arranged so that the person using the bin faced to the south. The fifth bin was against the east wall. A person using this bin would face the north. All these bins had been partly destroyed, and some almost completely. However, five metates and numerous sandstone slabs were found scattered helter-skelter over the floor of the room. It is very unlikely that this room was used following the destruction of these bins. Although two coarse-grained metates were among those that had presumably derived from the roof, all the metates found on the floor were fine-, medium-fine-, or medium-grained.

Apparently all five mealing bins originally had slab-lined walls with slab floors. The bin floors were approximately 20 cm below the room floor. It could not be determined whether scoops were set into the bins.

It is difficult to avoid the interpretation that the mealing bins in this room were deliberately, although somewhat hastily and haphazardly, destroyed. Whether the motivation was simple maliciousness or an intent (not carried out) to remove the material would be difficult to determine.

The south wall behind the single bin had been slightly hollowed out, apparently to allow more hip room for the person using the bin.

Four manos were set into the face of the north wall at floor level, perhaps to provide foot stops for the individuals as they used each of the four bins.

DOORWAYS

An open doorway with a sandstone sill 30 cm above floor level gave access to Room C3. A second doorway in the center of the south wall, with sill at floor level, had been sealed with adobe and courses of sandstone blocks.

PASSTHROUGHS

Near the west end of the south wall at floor level there had been a rectangular hole 30 cm square extending into a room to the south, which was not excavated. This passthrough, like the south doorway, had been sealed with sandstone blocks, which were not flush with the wall face, so that a slight niche remained. There is little doubt that a room existed south of room C9, though perhaps it had not been constructed at the time the passthrough was built. A second passthrough, which had been sealed, was located in the west wall 50 cm above the floor.

ARTIFACTS

Fill

   Stone: 3 axes; about 1,010 beads (500 black stone, 500 red stone, 10 turquoise); 5 chips; 9 manos (e.g., fig. 108f, m); 3 mano fragments; 4 metates; metate fragment; 2 pecking stones; 10 pendants; shaped worked object; 3 unworked turquoise fragments; worked sandstone slab
   Bone: Bison mandible pendant; worked fragment
   Shell: 200 beads, bracelet (fig. 65i); worked fragments; unworked fragments
   Other: Fur cloth fragments; painted wood fragments; malachite (½ oz); pine resin; clay pipe fragment
   Pottery vessels: 2 corrugated jars; 3 Heshotauthla Polychrome bowls; 2 Reserve Black-on-white "duck" vessels (fig. 44i, k); 2 Tularosa Black-on-white jars (fig. 44f)

Floor

   #2005, mano (1521); #2006, mano (1821); #2011, metate, medium-fine calcareous tuff; #2013, mano fragment (1221); #2039, mano (1421); #2040, metate, fine sandstone; #2041, mano (1421); #2042, mano (1521); #2043, mano (1421); #2044, metate, fine sandstone; #2045, mano (3221); #2046, mano (2231); #2047, mano (1821); #2048, metate, medium calcareous tuff; #2164, metate, fine sandstone

Structural

   #2142, mano (3821); #2143, mano (1821); #2162, mano (1821); #2163, mano (1221). All were set into the face of the north wall at the base.

Room C10 (figs. 22, 29)

The 30 cm of fill directly above the floor of this room contained charred beams and other indications of roof fall as well as nearly all artifacts found in the fill. The upper 70 cm of fill contained few sherds or other

Figure 29. Site 616. Room C10, looking north over ventilator shaft in south end of room.

artifacts and only rare charcoal, but did include adobe and occasional stones from the walls.

The floor was fairly level and was covered with a thin layer of adobe plaster, which sloped up the walls and joined the wall plaster in a smooth curve.

FIREPIT

A slab-walled firepit was located in the center of the west half of the room. The floor of the firepit was adobe though one small sandstone slab was set in the floor. In the center of the eastern end of the firepit floor there was an uncovered hole. It was 30 cm deep, with a diameter of 10 cm at the top and 15 cm at the bottom. Both this hole and the firepit itself were full of ash when found, like similar holes in firepits in Room C5 at Site 616 (p. 78), at Site 481 (pp. 192, 196), at the ancient Zuni peublo of Hawikuh (Smith, Woodbury, and Woodbury 1966, p. 56), and at Sandstone Hill Pueblo (Barnett 1974, p. 11). Two sandstone pot supports were in position next to the long sides of the firepit. Mixed with the ash were approximately 1,000 red and black stone beads, 300 shell beads, 40 small pendants (34 of turquoise, 6 of black stone), and a shell frog figurine (fig. 65a).

VENTILATOR

The room had two south walls. They were connected by a rectangular ventilator tunnel with sandstone-block walls and a pole-and-thatch roof. The floor of the ventilator tunnel was plastered and was 7 cm lower than the floor of the room. The areas between the two south walls to either side of the ventilator shaft, when found, were filled with loose, almost sterile soil. There was no indication of floor at any point in these two areas, nor did the walls facing into the areas appear to have been plastered. Apparently the area between the two walls was completely sealed off except for the ventilating shaft which passed through it.

PASSTHROUGH

A sealed passthrough, 29 cm square and 15 cm above the floor, connected room C10 with Room C6.

DEFLECTOR

A deflector ridge of sandstone-block-and-adobe construction extended north into the room for a distance of 70 cm from the west edge of the ventilator, and then curved east for a distance of 80 cm. This ridge was 25 cm high, 15 cm wide at its base, and 8 cm wide at the top. It effectively shielded the firepit from the ventilator.

DOORWAY

A doorway sealed with well-chinked layers of sandstone block was in the center of the north wall, its sill 25 cm above floor level.

COMMENT

This room contained an unusually large number of whole vessels but few of the appurtenances of the potter's trade were present. The numerous beads and other ornaments suggested that this specialty was particularly associated with the occupants. Could it be that the thorough mixture of these ornaments with the ashes of the firepit was an attempt at concealment that succeeded for hundreds of years?

The unique and rather elaborate ventilator design is also cause for speculation, though one hesitates to suggest clan or religious associations with only the slender evidence presently available.

ARTIFACTS

Fill

  Stone: Mano; 4 mano fragments; shaped object
  Bone: 14 dewclaw pendants

Floor

  #2077, hammer, off-center haft; #2081, shell bracelet fragment; #2148, 2 chips; #2157, mano (1121); #2219, shaftsmoother (fig. 54c); #2220, stone pendant (fig. 60s); #2221, fur cloth; #2222, worked shell fragment; #2223, worked shell fragments; #2355, axe; #2356, hammer, elongated, flat-ended; #2357, axe

  Pottery vessels: C102, St. Johns Polychrome bowl; C103, Heshotauthla Polychrome bowl; C104, Tularosa Black-on-white jar; C105, Tularosa Black-on-white ladle; C106, Tularosa Black-on-white miniature bowl; C107, Tularosa Black-on-white seed jar; C108, corrugated jar; C109, corrugated bowl; C1010, corrugated jar; C1011, corrugated bowl; C1012, corrugated miniature jar

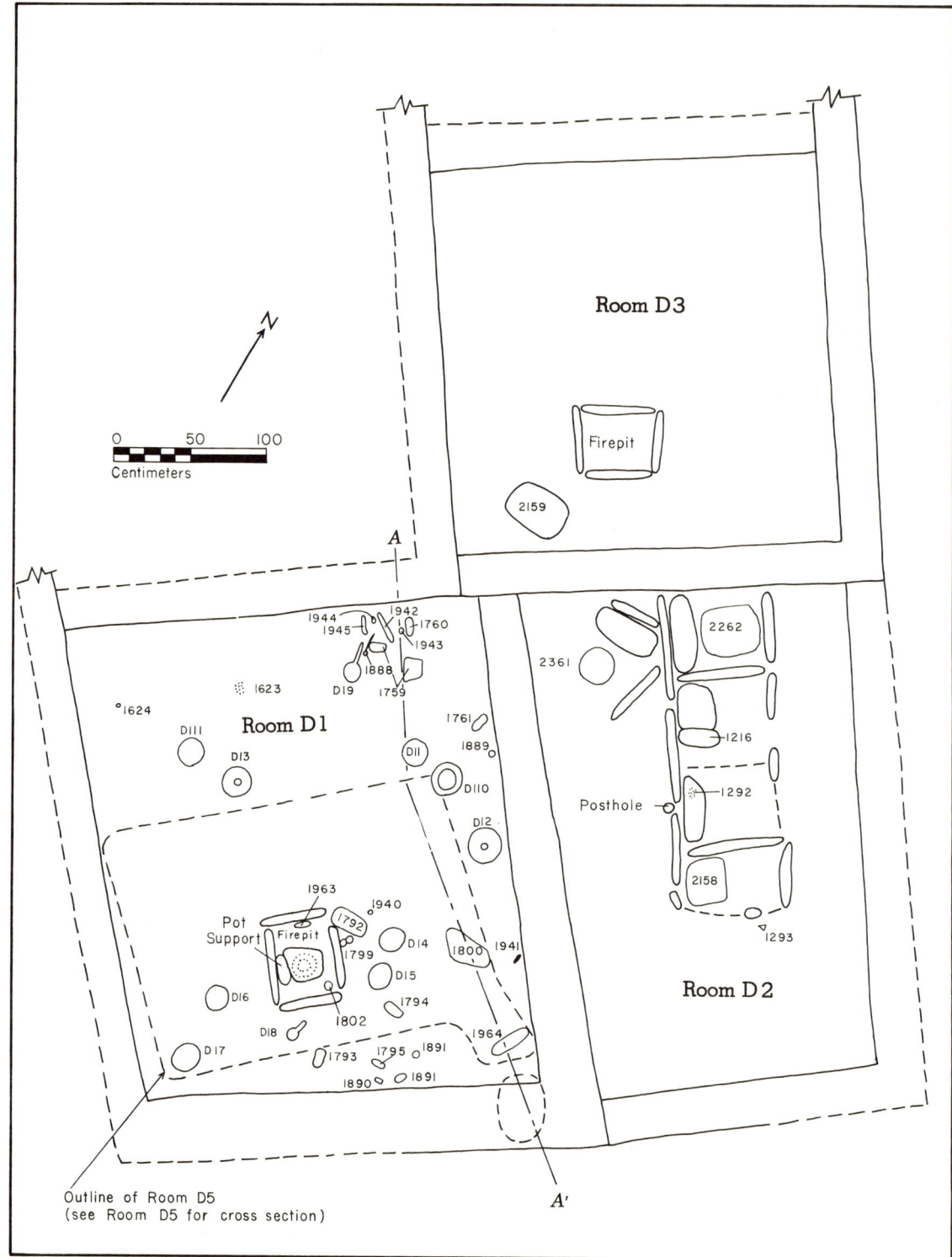

Figure 30. Site 616. Plan of Area D. The line A—A' indicates the profile of Room D5, as shown in figure 33.

Figure 31. Site 616. Room D1, looking north. The depressed southern portion was caused by compression of fill of Room D5 below and reflooring of north half of room.

Firepit

#2812, about 1,300 beads (500 black stone, 500 red stone, 300 shell); 40 small pendants, 34 turquoise, 6 black stone; #2813, shell figurine of frog (fig. 65a)

Area D (fig. 30)

Area D was another L-shaped island of rooms situated within the plaza of the pueblo. Unlike Area A the rooms here were two abreast and the cluster may have contained as many as 16 rooms, but only three of the southernmost surface rooms and an underlying pithouse were excavated.

Apparently this unit grew southward, but probably all three excavated surface rooms and at least the two rooms immediately to the north were built at about the same time, perhaps marking the influx of a group from a formerly outlying community. At the time of this construction, or very shortly before, the pithouse (Room D5) was deliberately backfilled and Room D1 built over the same area. Room D1 was constructed so soon afterward that the fill of Room D5 had not completely settled, and the section of floor immediately overlying Room D5 sank 5 to 10 cm. Room D2 was the last of the excavated rooms in this cluster to be built.

All the walls of this unit were of adobe with a base of two to four irregular courses of lava cobbles from the dike. These walls were set into shallow trenches which generally extended no more than 10 cm below the level of the floor.

Room D1 (figs. 30, 31)

Roof adobe was found on or near the floor of this room over most of its area. The fairly shallow fill was hard-packed adobelike soil, with artifacts scattered throughout.

The floor was in poor condition and, except for a slight color change, difficult to distinguish from the hard-packed fill. The floor over most of the south half of the room was slightly sunken, owing to the settling of the material in the backfilled pithouse below (Room D5), which is further discussed in connection with that room (p. 88). Oddly enough, the north half of the room floor beyond the depressed area had been replastered at one time, the new level being as much as 12 cm higher than the original floor. In fact, altogether there was a difference of 25 cm between sections of the floor in the northern and southern ends of the room. The east, west, and south walls were of adobe construction and had been built as a unit.

FIREPIT

In the center of the south half of the room there was a sandstone slab-walled firepit, 33 cm deep. It may have been located here because the underlying fill could easily be excavated. A sandstone slab centrally located on the floor of the firepit covered an empty bell-shaped cist. The diameter of this cist varied from 10 cm at its mouth to 18 cm near the base, which was 22 cm below the firepit floor. The cist was completely empty although the firepit above was nearly full of ashes when found. An adobe pot support stood in this ash against the west wall, and a mano (#1963) in the firepit probably also served as a pot support. A hand-molded, unfired, miniature bowl was also found in the firepit.

COMMENT

There was no indication that the roof of this room, or that of any room excavated in Area D, had burned. However, the presence of considerable roof adobe right on the floor in this room and the concentration of artifacts immediately above the floor in Room D2 suggested that in both instances the roofs collapsed shortly after the rooms were abandoned.

ARTIFACTS

Fill

>Stone: 2 axes (fig. 55a); 5 chips; 2 manos; 3 mano fragments; metate
>Bone: Awl, head split but unworked (fig. 61k); fossil shell, figurine of bat (fig. 65b); unworked fossil shell
>Other: Limonite (¼ oz)
>Pottery vessels: Reserve Black-on-white pitcher (fig. 49j); St. Johns Polychrome bowl (fig. 49d); Tularosa Black-on-white jar (fig. 49l); Tularosa Black-on-white toy ladle

Floor

>#1623, mosaic fragments; #1624, malachite (¼ oz); #1759, mano fragment (1731); #1760, axe; #1761, axe; #1791, core, petrified wood; #1792, mano (1221); #1793, hammer, elongated, flat-ended; #1794, axe; #1795, axe; #1799, axe, three-quarter-grooved (fig. 55b); #1800, roughly shaped mortar; #1888, awl, head split but unworked (fig. 61j); #1889, pecking stone; #1890, shaftsmoother (fig. 54b); #1891, pecking stone; #1940, stone ball (fig. 60c); #1941, quartz crystal; #1942, awl, head split but unworked (fig. 61b); #1943, chip; #1944, chip; #1945, bone end scraper (fig. 63c); #1963, mano (1121); #1964, mano (1121)

>Pottery vessels: D11, St. Johns Polychrome bowl (fig. 49c); D12, Pinedale Black-on-red jar (fig. 49e); D13, Puerco Black-on-red jar (fig. 49g); D14, Heshotauthla Polychrome bowl (fig. 49f); D15, St. Johns Polychrome bowl (fig. 49a); D16, Pinedale Polychrome bowl (fig. 49b); D17, Tularosa Black-on-white bowl (fig. 49k); D18, Tularosa Black-on-white ladle (fig. 49i); D19, Tularosa Black-on-white ladle (fig. 49h); D110, corrugated jar (fig. 49m); D111, Tularosa Fillet-rim bowl (fig. 49n)

Firepit

>#1802, hand-molded, unfired toy bowl; #1963, mano (1121); adobe pot support

Room D2 (fig. 32)

No charred beams and few indications of roof adobe were encountered in the fill of this room. Probably the present shallowness of the fill contributed to the disappearance of recognizable pieces of roof adobe. A few artifacts were distributed throughout the fill but the major portion of the artifacts in the fill came from a single stratum, which extended over most of the room at a level of 3 to 15 cm above the floor. Except for four mano fragments and one metate, all manos and metates found in the fill came from this stratum.

The floor was in rather poor condition when found, but it was quite even and had been coated with adobe plaster.

MEALING BINS

Four of the five mealing bins were contiguous slab-wall structures extending in a line south into the room from the north wall. All had sandstone-slab floors and all were without scoops of any kind. The floor slab in the southern bin was a used metate (#2158). Many of the wall slabs were out of place or missing and only one metate was *in situ*, a fine-grained sandstone specimen in the north bin.

The fifth bin was rather curious. It was placed at a 45° angle to the room and to the other bins in the area between the north bin and the west wall. Two sides (to the right, and away from the user) had sandstone-slab walls; the other two sides were open. It had a floor slab. The grinding stone, if such it was, was set in adobe in a manner similar to a metate. However, the stone utilized was a thin, roughly shaped, irregular circular sandstone slab, approximately 28 cm in diame-

Figure 32. Site 616. Room D2, looking south. The unusual mealing bin is in the lower right corner.

ter, set at an angle of 27°. It showed only slight evidence of abrasion.

COMMENT

The floor of this room had been stripped of nearly all artifacts. We have reason to believe, however, that many of the objects removed from the floor were taken no farther than the roof of the room. The stratum of artifacts found immediately above the floor apparently contained the debris from the fallen roof. This group of artifacts consisted largely of manos and metates. The location and makeup of this stratum and the fact that the number of metates in it corresponded exactly to the number missing from the bins — plus the fact that these three metates, coupled with the one remaining *in situ*, would provide a graded series (two fine sandstone, one medium calcareous tuff, and one coarse vesicular basalt) — certainly suggest that this material was on the roof of the room and that it had come originally from the floor. Cactus seeds recovered from the floor of the south-central bin were doubtless at least one of the items ground on this set of bins.

There was no evidence that this room burned, but the proximity of the artifact stratum to the floor would indicate that the roof collapsed shortly after the room ceased to be used — unless we assume that the room was abandoned and sealed.

ARTIFACTS

Fill

Stone: Tapered chalcedony cylinder (fig. 60e); 2 shaftsmoothers (#1290, fig. 54a); axe; core; 2 bat figurines (#1160, fig. 59c); 15 manos (fig. 108j, o); 6 mano fragments; 4 metates (#1218, fig. 109a); andesite cylinder (fig. 60i); pecking stone; quartz crystal; 3 shaped objects; snub-nosed scraper

Shell: 2 bracelet fragments; unworked fragments

Other: Malachite (¼ oz)

Pottery vessels: Heshotauthla Polychrome bowl; Puerco Black-on-red *puki* (reworked bowl); Puerco Black-on-red seed jar; Tularosa Black-on-white ladle; 3 Tularosa Black-on-white jars; Tularosa Black-on-white seed jar

Floor

#1213, metate, medium-fine calcareous tuff (fig. 109e); #1216, mano (1631); #1293, point; #2158, metate of fine sandstone, used as floor of north mealing bin; #2262, #2361, metates of fine sandstone, set in north and single mealing bins respectively (fig. 109b, j)

Room D3 (fig. 30)

The fill of this room consisted of soil and melted adobe. There were no charred beams or other indications of roof fall and very few artifacts. A few fragments of human bones were present.

The floor was even and plastered but in rather poor condition when found. The floor plaster sloped up to join the room walls and the firepit wall slabs.

FIREPIT

The firepit was located in the south-central portion of the room. A single sandstone slab formed each wall of the firepit. The corners and the floor were of adobe. The firepit, which extended 23 cm below floor level, contained 19 cm of compact white ash.

COMMENT

The nearly sterile nature of both the fill and the floor contrasted sharply with most rooms excavated in Site 616. This room may have been abandoned at some time prior to the general exodus from the site.

ARTIFACTS

Fill

Stone: Ball; core; mano fragment; metate (fig. 109a); scoria cylinder
Bone: Incised end scraper (fig. 63d)
Other: Jet button; azurite (3 oz)
Pottery vessels: 2 corrugated jars; Pinedale Polychrome seed jar; Wingate Black-on-red seed jar; miniature bowl, partially fired

Floor

#2159, metate, fine sandstone

Room D5 (figs. 33, 34)

The fill of Room D5 was unique; it was soft. Though all other rooms could be cleared only after considerable effort and with the aid of a pick, Room D5 could have been cleared with bare hands. The fill consisted of uncompacted sandy soil with frequent, short, very thin lenses of gray-white ash. There were numerous sherds including fragments of 15 restorable vessels, but no great quantity of other material. In the central portion of the room, 25 cm above the floor, was a fetal skeleton (Skeleton 6). The level in which the skeleton was found was sandy, but ash lenses occurred both above and below it. The tiny bones directly overlay a small fragment of a mano (descriptive type 1931). A pecking stone (#1935), a chunk of limonite weighing 0.25 oz, and several black-on-white sherds were in immediate association. In the same level, but 20 to 50 cm away from the skeleton, were two more pecking stones, two broken clay animal figurines, a bone tube (#1932, fig. 64k), and a 5-oz piece of hematite. Nearly all sherds from restorable vessels came from the stratum in which the skeleton was found. These artifacts may or may not have been intentionally associated with the skeleton, but artifacts of any kind were rare throughout the rest of the fill.

The floor and the walls consisted of well-smoothed, even, natural adobelike soil. Both walls and floor were in excellent condition. There was no indication of wall or floor plaster but there was plaster in association with the mealing bin.

MEALING BIN

Against the north wall a rectangular depression in the room floor extended approximately 10 cm below floor level. From the location and dimensions of this area it seems that a mealing bin had been located here at the time the room was in use. The metate and any other appurtenances had been removed before the room was backfilled. This bin was probably similar to the one found intact in Room E2.

FIREPIT

The firepit was located against the center of the south wall and consisted of a simple rectangular excavation 14 cm deep. The walls and floor were well formed and smooth. Occupying the center of the back wall, an unexcavated adobe projection 20 cm wide and 24 cm high extended 8 cm into the firepit. This projection may have served as one of a pair of pot supports or it may have had some other function.

VENTILATOR

From the southeast corner of the room a rectangular alcove extended to the south. A narrower oval extension had been made to the south of this rectangular one, and a wall of sandstone blocks and adobe had been erected between them, with a small opening at the bottom. The small, oval, chimney-like extension thus formed a ventilating shaft. This ventilating arrangement and the location of the firepit combined to form an ingenious architectural design, obviating the need for a deflector, which would have crowded the already limited floor space.

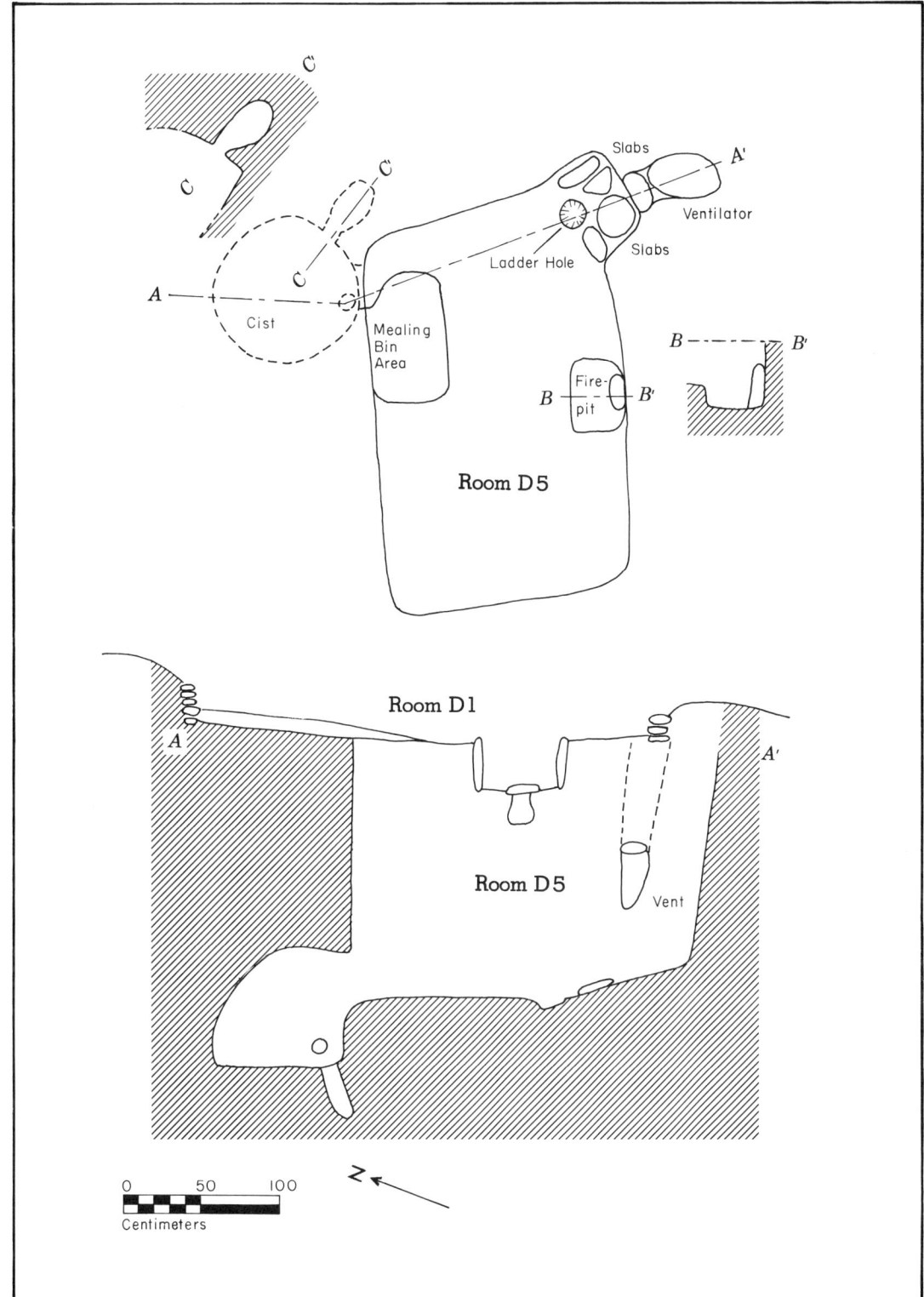

Figure 33. Site 616. Plan and profile of Room D5.

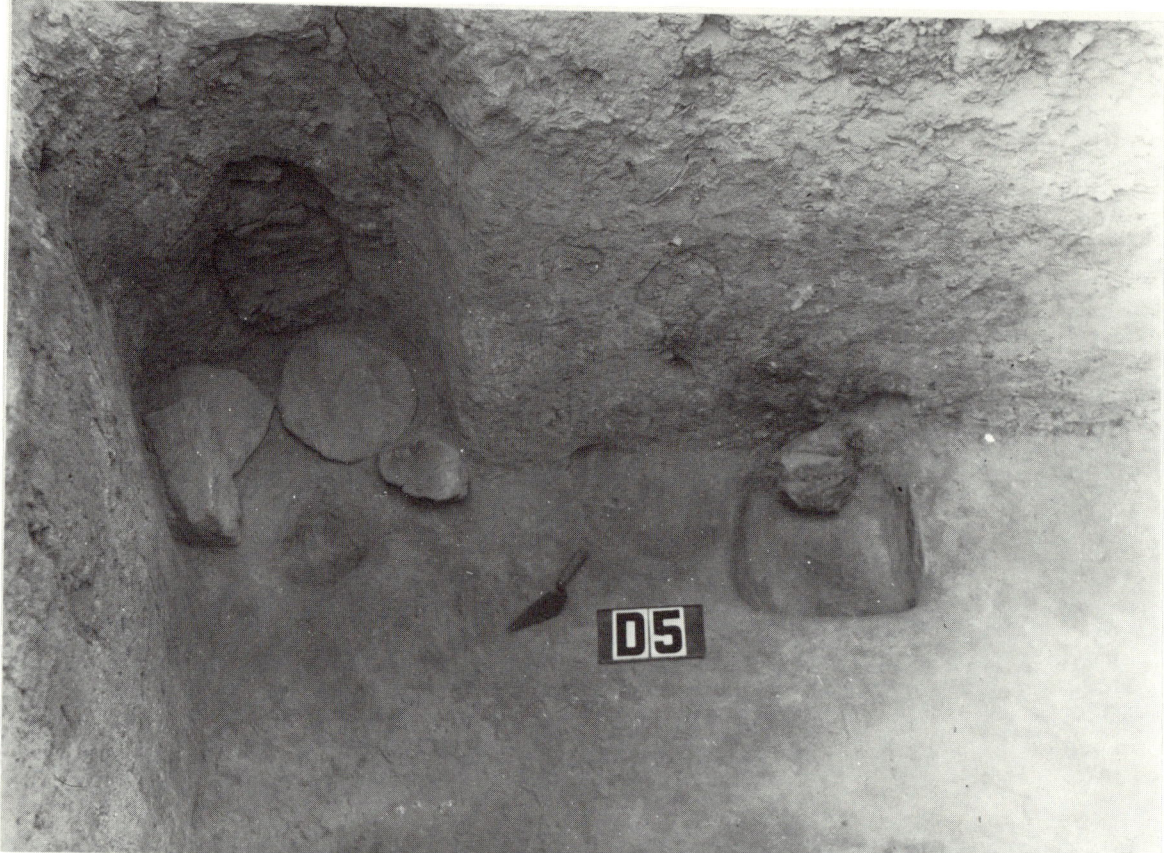

Figure 34. Site 616. Room D5, looking south, showing inset ventilator shaft and firepit with built-in pot support.

LADDER SOCKET

The rectangular alcove provided a recess in which a single-pole ladder might have been placed. This was suggested by the presence of a circular hole, 15 cm in diameter and 10 cm deep, which could have served as the socket, located in front of the center of the opening into the ventilator shaft. The slope of the base of the hole suggested that the ladder angled up to an entrance near the center of the east edge of the roof.

CISTS

Opening off a small circular hole (26 to 28 cm in diameter) — at floor level, at the east end of the former mealing bin along the north wall — a large cist had been excavated from the soil outside and north of the room. The flat floor of the cist was circular and 45 cm lower than the room floor. The walls and roof of the cist were domed. There were two small subsidiary cists extending from the main one. The first, 12 cm in diameter, extended at a slight southerly angle 35 cm below the cist floor, from a point just below the main cist opening. The second extended southeast, 40 cm into the east wall of the main cist. The opening of this cist, which was located 10 cm above the floor of the main cist, was 10 cm in diameter. However, just beyond the opening, the cist expanded to the sides and downward so that its major portion was 20 cm in diameter. The walls and floor of the main cist were thinly coated with a dull black carbonlike substance. Seven rectangular adobe bricks, a little larger but of somewhat the same proportions as the bricks of today, lay on the floor of the cist. The cist had not been deliberately filled but some of the material from the room fill had drifted into it, partly filling it. When cleared the cist was large enough to hold two people.

There were two other small wall cists, one in the center of the east wall, the other halfway between the ventilator alcove and the firepit. The first was 6 cm in diameter, 13 cm deep, and located 30 cm above the floor. The other, 10 cm in diameter and 15 cm deep, was 25 cm above the floor.

COMMENT

This building was stripped and deliberately filled not long before the building of Room D1. The thin levels of ash suggested that the fill consisted at least partially of refuse, but there was no indication that water had stood in the hole at any time, suggesting that the fill probably took place within a relatively brief period. No effort had been made to fill in the cist. It contained only the material that slipped in inevitably as the main excavation was filled. The fetal skeleton referred to above, with objects in possible association, was placed in the excavation during this filling process. The adobe bricks on the floor of the cist and a few sandstone slabs in the ventilator alcove were the only objects left in the room when filling began.

ARTIFACTS

Fill

Stone: 16 chips; hammer, irregular, flat-ended; 5 mano fragments; 3 pecking stones
Bone: Awl, skewer; pierced phalange; ring (fig. 64c); tube (fig. 64k)
Other: 2 clay animal figurines; clay elbow pipe (fig. 60k); hematite (5 oz); limonite (¼ oz); sherd scraper
Pottery vessels: Corrugated bowl; 4 corrugated jars; 2 Heshotauthla Polychrome bowls; 3 Puerco Black-on-red ladles; Springerville Polychrome bowl; 4 St. Johns Polychrome bowls

Fill of cist

Bone: Pierced phalange (fig. 64h)

Area E

The prefix "E" was applied to two subterranean pithouses, Rooms E1 and E2, encountered while digging the trench across the plaza between Areas B and D, and does not designate a clearly defined area within the site.

Room E1 (fig. 35)

The fill of Room E1 was very hard, but below 50 cm the cleavage between the fill and the room walls and floor was marked. Ash was mixed with the soil in the ventilator shaft and a layer of ash, charcoal, and charred beam fragments extended over most of the room from a level approximately 40 cm above floor to the floor itself, becoming more heavily concentrated just above the floor. Artifacts were comparatively rare. One awl and all of the stone artifacts except the chips and flakes were found in the upper 50 cm of fill; and, considering the nature of the walls at this level, some or all of this material must have washed in from adjacent areas.

The room had been excavated into native soil and this soil, well smoothed, formed the walls and floor. There was no indication of plaster on the walls or floor, nor was any associated with the firepit. Unlike the other subterranean rooms, this room was only semisubterranean. The floor was 117 cm below the present ground surface. At a height of 95 cm above the floor the walls changed from native soil to wood and adobe construction. A few postholes which sloped slightly inward could be detected, set back approximately 10 cm from the wall line, but the evidence was too scant for any dependable reconstruction of this upper portion of the wall.

Lying face down on the floor with his right side against the north wall was the skeleton of a young adult male (Skeleton 4, fig. 6g). His knees were flexed to his right, while his head was turned to his left (facing south). His right arm paralleled his right side and was palm down. The upper left arm paralleled the left side but its lower part crossed under the stomach and pelvis with palm up, so that the left hand appeared to be clutching the front portion of the right side of the pelvic girdle. Feet and ankles overlay one another and could have been tied, though of course there was no definite indication that this was the case. A small projectile point was found lying between the tibia and fibula of the right leg midway between the knee and ankle. The occipital region of the skull showed slight evidence of having been battered, but this could have occurred at the time the roof collapsed. A sandstone slab (from the roof?) immediately overlay the central portion of the legs, while another overlay the right side of the body from the pelvis to the central portion of the rib cage. Other than the small projectile point (and the slabs) there were no artifacts in association and no other artifacts on the floor.

FIREPIT

The firepit was an irregularly circular or rounded rectangular affair located in the center of the eastern portion of the room. Its sides were perpendicular and it had a flat bottom 8 cm below the general floor surface. No sandstone slabs were used in its construction and it contained very little ash when found.

VENTILATOR

In a small alcove in the southeast corner of the room a circular ventilating shaft 30 cm in diameter had been excavated, and a wall of sandstone blocks and adobe had been constructed separating all but the lower portion of this shaft from the room proper.

DEFLECTOR

Unlike those in Room D5, the ventilator opening and the firepit of Room E1 were in a direct line, and a deflector was necessary. The deflector slab was not found but a narrow slot in the floor, 35 cm long and located 15 cm south of the firepit, doubtless accom-

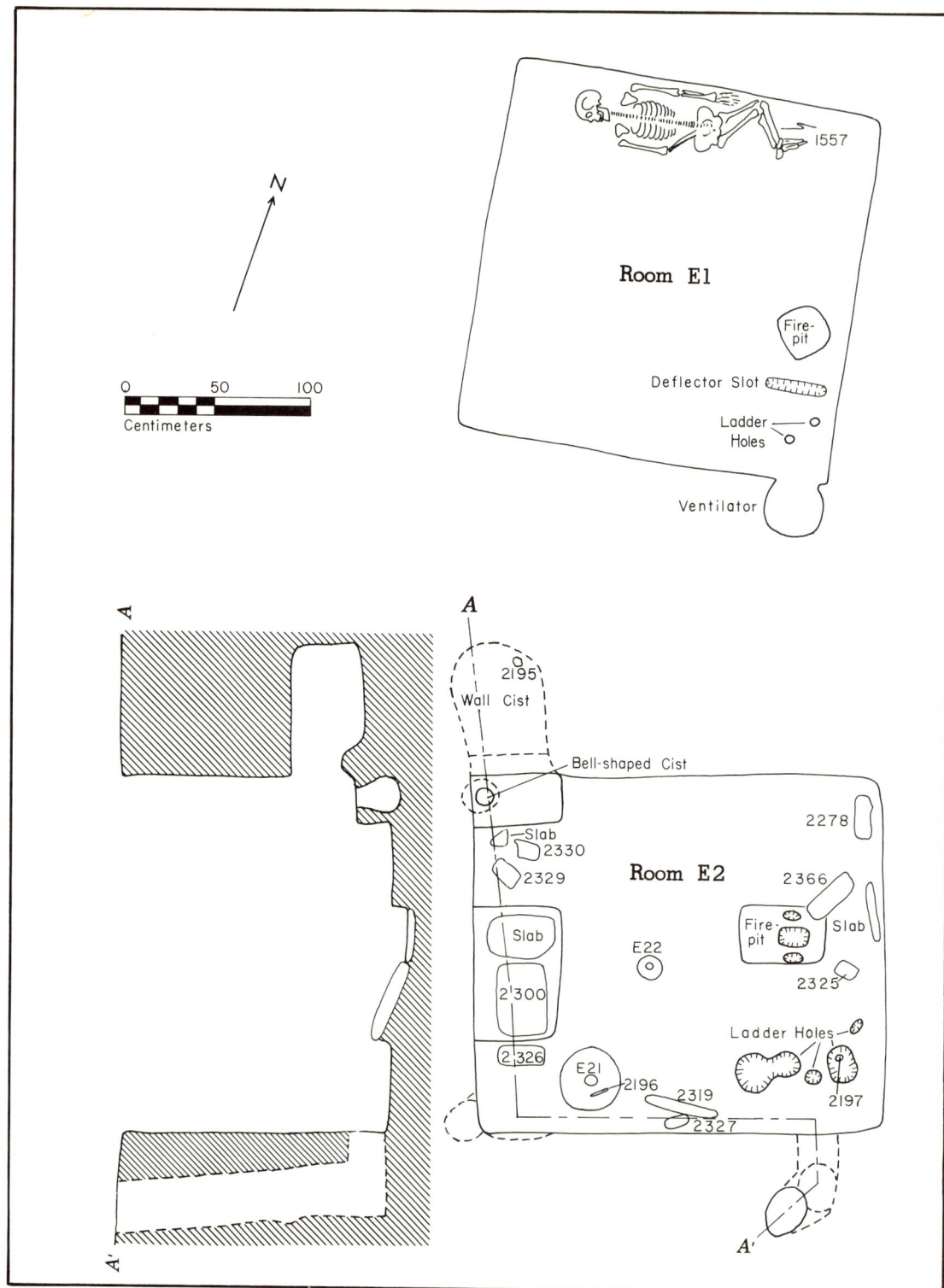

Figure 35. Site 616. Plan of Rooms E1 and E2.

modated a sandstone slab which had served such a purpose.

LADDER SOCKETS

Between the deflector slot and the ventilator opening there were two shallow circular holes. Both were 5 cm deep, with diameters of 11 cm and 8 cm respectively. If one or the other of these holes served as the socket for a single-pole ladder, the roof entrance may well have been located in the center of the east side of the roof directly above the firepit. However, if the two holes served as sockets for a double-pole ladder, as was evidently the case in the kiva, the entrance was probably near the center of the roof.

COMMENT

This room differed from the other two subterranean rooms at Site 616 in that it was only partly subterranean. It was also simpler in design and execution than the other two, and had a different compass orientation.

It was difficult to determine whether this room was in use up to the time the pueblo was abandoned. The room (and its roof) had been stripped of nearly all useful artifacts. The roof burned and fell to the floor before wind-blown or other debris had accumulated, and the room thus did not appear to have been backfilled by the inhabitants. The skeleton lying on the floor did not represent a normal burial. The man may have died at some time during the occupation of the pueblo under circumstances that caused others to strip the room before or after his actual death and then to burn the room after he died. On the other hand, the room may have been stripped at some time immediately before the general exodus from the pueblo, and the man may have hidden or may have been dumped alive or dead into the room at the time of departure, after which the roof burned. If an attack caused the abandonment of the pueblo he may have been killed in the encounter, or may have been a prisoner. Possibly the room was stripped and deserted either right before the pueblo was abandoned or at that time, but the fact that even the deflector slab was removed suggested an unhurried abandonment of the room itself.

ARTIFACTS

Fill

  Stone: 17 chips; hammer, elongated, flat-ended (#1063, fig. 56d); mano fragment; 3 scoria cylinders (#1302, fig. 58e); 2 unretouched flakes
  Bone: Awl, head of bone intact (#1953, fig. 62f); awl, head split but unworked; worked fragment
  Antler: Rubbing tool
  Pottery vessels: Heshotauthla Polychrome bowl; Springerville Polychrome bowl

Floor

  #1557, point (in association with Skeleton 4, figs. 6g; 57d)

Room E2 (figs. 35, 36, 37)

The fill of this room was compact sandy soil that undoubtedly had washed in from the surrounding area. The pottery and artifacts were concentrated in the 50 cm of fill directly above the floor. Some ash and other indications of fire were found in a layer approximately one meter above the floor. If this was related to the roof, then it had burned after considerable material had washed into the room.

Like Rooms D5 and E1 this room had been excavated into the native soil and the walls and floor consisted of this soil, well smoothed and unplastered. The floor was 150 cm below the present ground surface, but at the time of occupation the surface may have been sufficiently higher so that no above-ground extension of the wall was necessary. There were no postholes on top of the walls nor was any trace of the method of roofing found.

MEALING BIN

A mealing bin was flush against the west wall of the room, situated so that the person using it would face to the north. There was a space of 50 cm between the top of the metate and the south wall, and in the south wall at the level of the hips of a person using the bin a hip-sized concavity 5 cm deep had been excavated or worn. The floor of the mealing bin was a sandstone slab set 8 cm below room floor level. The metate, resting on a base of native soil, sloped upward from the base an equal distance above the room floor. The bin was unlined. There was no scoop but the areas along the sides of the metate were trough-shaped.

FIREPIT

The firepit was rectangular with straight, vertical, smooth sides of native soil, which curved at the base to join the irregularly flat bottom of the pit at a depth of 16 cm below the room floor. In a north-south line across the center of the east half of the firepit were three depressions. Each was approximately 5 cm deep but the center one was slightly larger in diameter. The ones on the sides may have held the bases of pot supports. The firepit contained very little ash.

VENTILATOR

The ventilator shaft was set into the south wall 35 cm from the southeast corner, and was roughly oval in

Figure 36. Site 616. Room E2, looking south.

cross section, measuring approximately 35 cm north-south and 25 cm east-west. The shaft did not run straight up but sloped slightly to the southwest toward the top. Apparently the upper portion of the shaft was dug down from ground level while the lower section was excavated through the wall of the room. The engineering was slightly awry for the two sections of the shaft missed coming together, with the result that 50 to 60 cm above floor level the shaft made a sharp jog to the west. The lower section of the shaft was divided from the room by a sandstone and adobe wall. The hole at the base of this wall connecting the shaft with the room at floor level was 24 cm square, and had a sandstone-slab lintel.

LADDER SOCKETS (?)

There was an east-west area containing four shallow holes in the room floor approximately midway between the ventilating shaft and the firepit. The western figure-eight-shaped hole was 14 cm deep in its western section and 9 cm deep in the eastern extension. The larger hole, to the east, was 11 cm deep. These, or the two smaller holes, either singly or jointly could have served as the base for a single- or double-pole ladder.

DEFLECTOR (?)

The relative location of the ventilating shaft and the firepit would seem to have made a deflector desirable if not mandatory, but there was no floor slot, no small postholes, or any other indication that a deflector had existed. If a double-pole ladder was employed the space between the lower one or two rungs could have been blocked off. Such an arrangement would have served admirably as a deflector.

CISTS (fig. 37)

A large rectangular cist had been hollowed out of the native soil at the west end of the north wall, 40 cm square and 70 cm deep. There was a raised sill of adobe 12 cm high at the mouth of the cist, which reduced the height of the opening there to 28 cm. The floor of the cist was 18 cm above the room floor. In the northwest corner of the room directly in front of this cist was a rectangular shelf or step of native soil. The top of this step was flat and level with the floor of the cist, though the adobe sill at the mouth of the cist served to separate the two areas. A small round-bottomed, bell-shaped cist had been excavated into this step at the center of its junction with the west wall. The mouth of this cist was 10 cm in diameter but it enlarged to 17 by 14 cm at the back and was 25 cm deep.

At the junction of the south and west walls 23 cm above the floor was a small cist extending into the west wall. It had a circular mouth 15 cm in diameter, and in cross section was roughly hemispherical with a maximum depth of 13 cm. This cist may had some connection with the mealing bin.

COMMENT

The artifacts and particularly the pottery found directly on the floor and in the fill of this room were unquestionably contemporary in design and execution with those found throughout the rest of the pueblo. This fact, as well as the backfilling of Room D5 by the builders of Room D1, eliminates the possibility that the subterranean rooms at Site 616 were simply relics of an earlier occupation of the site. There was no sure way to tell how long these subterranean rooms had been in use, but Room E2 had every appearance of having been occupied up to the time the pueblo as a whole was abandoned.

ARTIFACTS

Fill

Stone: Bead, turquoise; 24 chips; hammer, elongated, flat-ended; hammer, equilateral, flat-ended; hammer, irregular, flat-ended; hammer, round-ended; mano; 6 mano fragments; 2 metates; pestle; 4 polishing pebbles; 2 scoria cones; 2 scoria cylinders (#1950, fig. 58f); 14 unretouched flakes; turqouise, unworked fragment

Bone: Awl, head split but unworked (fig. 61c); 2 awls, head removed (#1953, fig 62a); awl, skewer; awl fragment; pierced phalange; 2 side scrapers (#1823, fig. 63a); 5 tubes; 4 worked fragments

Other: Limonite (½ oz); malachite (½ oz); #1962, clay pipe stem (fig. 60l)

Pottery vessels: Corrugated miniature bowl; 5 corrugated jars; plainware toy bowl

Floor

#2195, sherd scraper; #2196, awl, head split but unworked (fig. 61f); #2197, chopper; #2278, mano (1721); #2300, metate, coarse vesicular basalt, set in mealing bin; #2319, metate, fine sandstone; #2325, mano fragment (1531); #2326, mano (2221); #2327, mano fragment (1321); #2329, mano fragment

Figure 37. Site 616. Room E2, showing cists in northwest corner and hip recess excavated in south wall directly behind mealing bin.

(1321); #2330, mano fragment (1421); #2366, mano (2221)

Pottery vessels: E21, Tularosa Black-on-white jar (fig. 44m); E22, Tularosa Black-on-white jar

Area F

That part of the pueblo along the center section of the easterly exterior wall was designed Area F, but only two rooms were excavated there.

The exterior wall constituted the east wall of Room F1, and had been constructed of neatly shaped sandstone blocks. It was as well built as the best parts of walls in Area C. All other walls of Rooms F1 and F2 were of adobe, with several somewhat irregular courses of sandstone cobbles as a base. The wall bases extended 10 to 20 cm below the level of the room floors, and the interior north–south walls, like those in Area C, abutted the east–west walls. Apparently Rooms F1 and F2 were built at the same time.

Room F1 (fig. 38)

The upper portion of the fill in Room F1 was hard and consisted of adobe, sandstone blocks, and occasional lava cobbles from the walls of the room. The 30 to 50 cm of material directly above the floor was softer and sandy. Most of the artifacts came from this lower level, and in its upper portion there were a few Chenopodium seeds. There was no trace of roof debris.

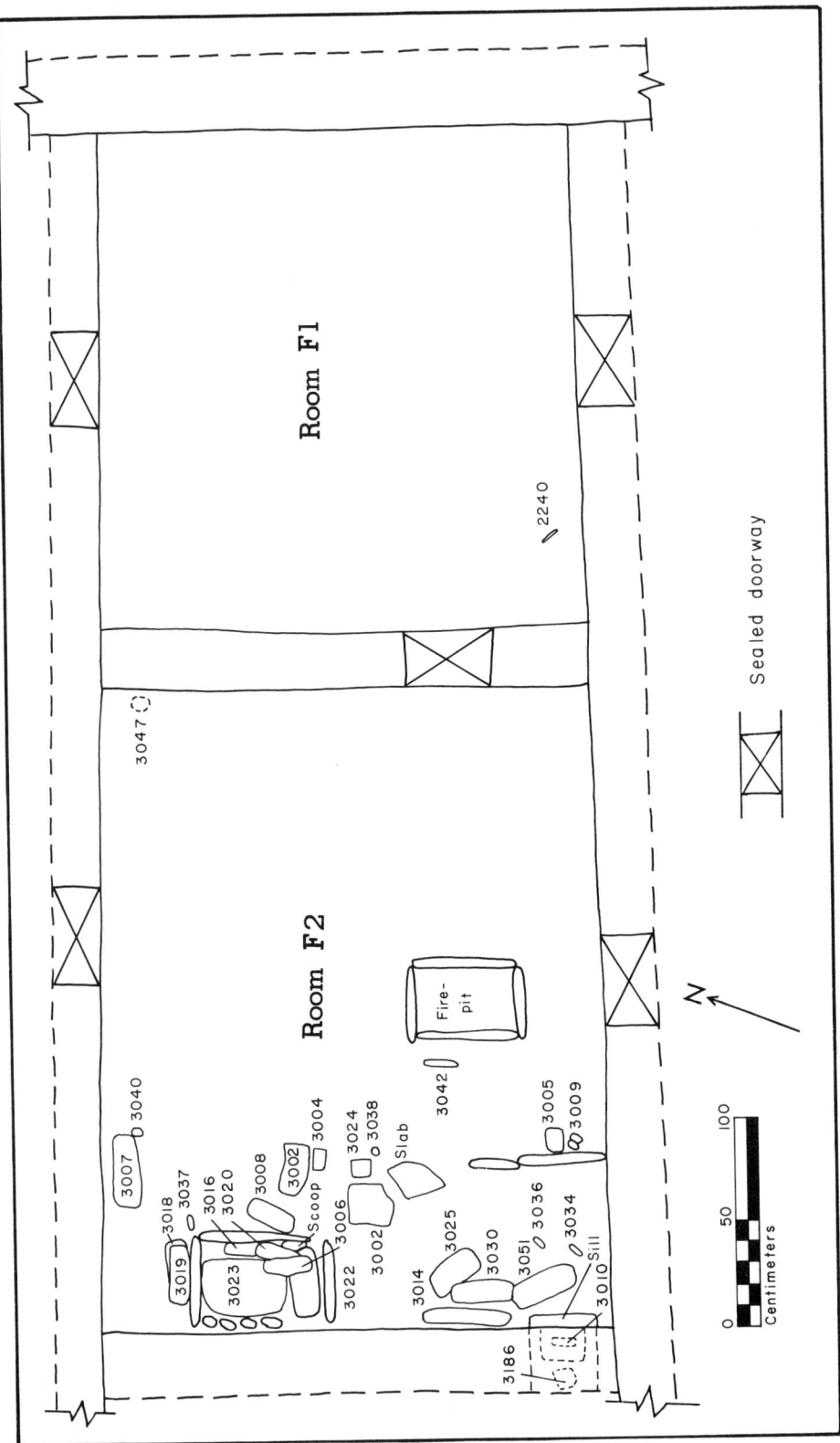

Figure 38. Site 616. Plan of Rooms F1 and F2.

The floor was smooth and even and had a thin plaster coat. There were no floor features.

DOORWAYS

There were sealed doorways in the center of the north and south walls and in the center of the south half of the west wall. Only the east wall, which was the outside wall of the pueblo, had no doorway. The doorways in the west and north walls had been sealed with lava cobbles and adobe, that in the south wall with adobe and sandstone blocks laid in courses. All had been appproximately 40 cm wide, with sills approximately 10 cm above the floor of the room.

COMMENT

Considerable wind-blown material appeared to have been deposited in this room before the walls began to disintegrate. There were few artifacts in the fill or on the floor. Probably this room was still in use up to the time the pueblo was deserted; but it might have been abandoned a little earlier, in which case it apparently did not serve as a depository for refuse.

ARTIFACTS

Fill

Stone: Mano fragment; polishing pebble
Bone: Awl, head split but unworked (#2176, fig. 61d); pierced phalange
Pottery vessel: Tularosa Black-on-white jar

Floor

#2240, awl, skewer

Room F2 (figs. 38, 39)

The fill of Room F2, like that of Room F1, was hard and adobelike in the upper levels but near the floor it became softer and sandier. Roof adobe and beam fragments occurred in this sandy level and for some distance above it. Most of the artifacts came from the lower portion of the fill.

The floor was fairly smooth and even but only thinly plastered.

FIREPIT

The firepit was rectangular with sandstone slab sides. It had been excavated 14 cm into the floor and the slabs projected 7 cm above the floor. The slab on the west side had become tilted inward to about a 30° angle at some time after the initial construction of the firepit, and the triangular space left between the slab and the floor had been filled with adobe.

Figure 39. Site 616. Room F2, looking west.

VENTILATOR

At the base of the west wall, 10 cm from where it joined the south wall, a rectangular ventilating tunnel had been constructed, approximately 30 cm wide and 20 cm high. It opened into the next room to the west, which was not excavated. During the occupancy of Room F2 the adobe sides of this tunnel had worn out or collapsed, so that the sandstone lintel was in danger of falling. To prevent this, the lintel had been propped by an upright mano fragment resting on top of a sandstone block placed in the tunnel. The sandstone slab sill projected into the room.

DEFLECTOR

Two sandstone slabs, set end-to-end, extended from the south wall and perpendicular to it, about halfway between the ventilator and the firepit. These slabs were set 10 cm into the floor and extended 50 cm above it; together they projected 68 cm into the room from the south wall.

MEALING BIN

The mealing bin was set against the south wall and the metate placed so that the person using it would face south. The three sides projecting into the room were formed of sandstone slabs, one of which was a used metate, but, unlike some bins, the side against the wall was without a slab liner. The floor of the bin was 17 cm below the room floor and was paved with a sandstone slab. A flat mano (#3016) had been set into the adobe along the east side of the metate. Between the mano and the bin floor there was a sherd scoop. Several sherds had been set into the adobe along the west side of the metate. A mano of vesicular basalt (#3006) and one of sandstone (#3020) were lying in the bin, while a second sandstone mano (#3018) and one of calcareous tuff (#3019) were neatly stacked on the floor against the north wall of the bin.

98 • Mariana Mesa

DOORWAYS

Doorways sealed with sandstone blocks and adobe were in the north and south walls and another was in the south half of the east wall. The sandstone sills of all were 15 cm above floor level.

COMMENT

This room appeared to have been in use up to the time the pueblo was deserted. The roof, like that of Room F1, did not appear to have been burned but rather to have collapsed gradually some time after the room was abandoned. This was followed by the slow disintegration of the adobe walls.

ARTIFACTS

Fill

   Stone: Chip; blade; scoria object? (fig. 58a); 2 manos; 2 mano fragments; metate; point (fig. 57e); scoria file? (fig. 58b); 2 unretouched flakes
   Other: Limonite (½ oz); malachite (1¾ oz)
   Pottery vessels: 3 corrugated jars; Puerco Black-on-red bowl; St. Johns Polychrome bowl

Floor

   #3002, metate, coarse vesicular basalt, broken; #3004, mano fragment (1931); #3005, mano fragment (2831); #3006, mano (2921); #3007, mano (1221); #3008, mano (1821); #3009, hammer, elongated, flat-ended; #3014, metate, coarse vesicular basalt; #3016, mano (1421); #3018, mano (1121); #3019, mano (3821); #3020, mano (1421), lining mealing bin; #3022, metate, fine sandstone, used as south wall of mealing bin; #3023, metate, medium-coarse vesicular basalt, set in mealing bin; #3024, mano (2921); #3025, mano (1221); #3030, mano (1821); #3034, polishing pebble; #3036, bone, unidentified fragment; #3037, bone, unworked; #3038, concretion (fig. 60j); #3040, weathered stone (fig. 60a); #3042, bone, unworked; #3051, mano (1221); #3186, mano (3822), in ventilating shaft

Structural

   #3010, mano fragment (3821), supporting ventilator tunnel lintel

Below floor

   #3047, shaftsmoother

Kiva (figs. 40, 41)

The upper portion of the fill in the kiva was very hard and nearly sterile. A considerable number of charred beams (approximately 15 cm in diameter), smaller sticks, grass, bark, and adobe with impressions of this material were found on the floor and on the benches, and in the 40 cm of fill above these surfaces. Most of the artifacts found in the fill were in this same level. The western third of the fill in the central portion of the kiva was not cleared.

The main body of the kiva was D-shaped with the flat portion of the D toward the south. A bench 90 to 100 cm above floor level had been constructed in an alcove behind the south or rear wall, extending southward 180 cm but shorter than the rear wall by about 70 cm (i.e., it was inset by 35 cm on each side). A shallower bench at the same height above the floor extended around the arc of the D. It was interrupted by two pilasters of unexcavated soil, each about 2 m from the rear wall and about 180 cm in length. They did not cover the entire width of the bench, but extended to within about 10 cm of its face. The sections of this bench between the pilasters and the south wall were 100 cm deep, while the remainder of the bench was only 70 cm deep.

The presence of metates found at either end of the south bench is of interest. The one located at the west end was stained red (#2795). (The only other metate stained red was the one left in place in the otherwise destroyed set of four linear mealing bins in Room D2.) The mortar found at the entrance to the ventilating tunnel was stained with a green pigment.

The kiva had been excavated into the native soil. The walls of the kiva, the back walls of the benches, and the sides of the pilasters had been covered with a light, buff-colored, slightly sandy plaster applied directly to the native soil. From the way this plaster broke away from the walls, it appeared that the rough sides of the initial excavation had first been smoothed where necessary by the application of adobe. The plaster had then been applied to the smooth wall surfaces that resulted from this patching. The sides of the pilasters facing the center of the kiva were rough and apparently had not been plastered. Some sort of reed matting (some reeds, probably *Gramineae sporabolus* or *sacaton* were found in the fill) or other perishable facing may have been applied to this surface.

The kiva floor was completely paved with sandstone slabs except at the ventilator opening and in an area in the north central section of the floor that appeared to have been torn up. Several sandstone slabs which fitted these areas were found resting elsewhere on the kiva floor, one of them bridging the foot drum. The slabs were very neatly shaped and fitted. The main floor section was paved with large slabs (e.g., 50 by 50 cm, or 30 by 80 cm), but around the firepit, deflector, and other floor features smaller shaped and fitted slabs were used. Areas too small for stones to be practical were floored with an orange adobe that was very

Site 616 • 99

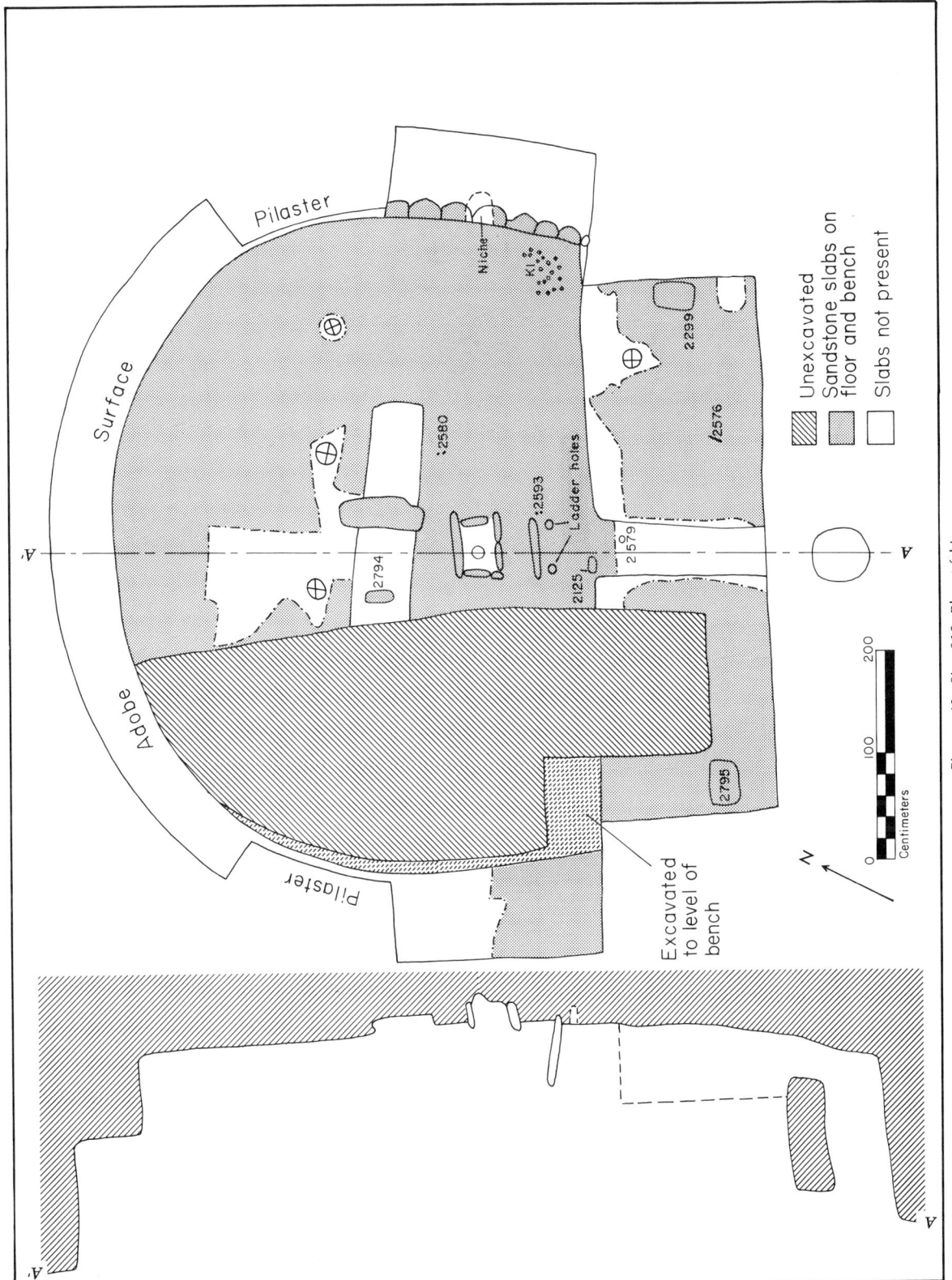

Figure 40. Site 616. Plan of kiva.

Figure 41. Site 616. East half of kiva, looking south.

nearly as hard as the sandstone slabs. The south bench was also completely floored with neatly fitted sandstone slabs, although the slabs along the edge of the bench had fallen away before excavation. The edge of the curved bench between the east pilaster and the south wall was faced with slabs but the rest of the floor of this bench was of hard adobe. The entire south half of the section of the curved bench between the west pilaster and the south wall was floored with sandstone slabs but the north half was covered with hard adobe. Only adobe was used to cover the floor of the northern arc of the bench. The wall-floor junctions were sharply curved but not angular in most instances. However, the floor of the bench around the north arc sloped upward slightly and joined the wall much less sharply than was the case elsewhere.

FIREPIT

The firepit had been remodeled at least three times. The final version was rectangular with sandstone slab walls, and the floor was of baked earth. The southern three-quarters of the floor was 20 cm below the kiva floor. The north quarter of the firepit floor had been excavated 12 cm deeper so that it had a trenchlike appearance. The firepit was approximately half full of ashes when found.

DEFLECTOR

The deflector consisted of a rather irregular but basically rectangular sandstone slab (60 by 80 cm) set into the kiva floor at a point midway between the firepit and the ventilator opening. The deflector slanted toward the firepit at an angle of approximately 10°.

VENTILATOR

A north–south trench had been excavated through the middle of the south bench to the level of the kiva floor. A hole 40 cm in diameter, which was a continuation of this trench, was cut into the south wall for a distance of 50 cm, at which point it met a vertical shaft 60 cm in diameter extending from this level to the surface of the ground. The trench had been roofed with sandstone slabs similar to those forming the floor of the bench. No small supporting poles were found in the area nor were there any grooves indicating their presence, so the slabs alone may have formed the roof. There was a sandstone sill at the mouth of the ventilating tunnel, and the walls and floor of the tunnel were plastered for a distance of 50 to 60 cm from the mouth.

LADDER SOCKETS

Two holes in the floor 50 cm apart were located 10 cm south of the deflector. These holes were 8 cm in diameter and 15 cm deep. Like the deflector they sloped at an angle of 10° from the vertical, and poles placed in them would parallel the deflector slab. They probably were sockets for a two-pole ladder, which led to a roof entrance and smoke hole almost directly above the firepit.

FOOT DRUM

A long, narrow, shallow trench was located in the floor of the kiva just north of the firepit. This trench, which was 50 cm wide and had an east–west length of approximately 3 m, ranged from 9 to 16 cm in depth. The sides and bottom were irregular and unfinished. If a wooden slab had been placed over this trench it could have served as a resonator or foot drum.

WALL NICHE

In the face of the east bench, midway between the pilaster and the south wall and 20 cm below the floor of the bench there was a small wall niche. The mouth of the niche was oval (23 cm wide, 19 cm high) with a slight lip at the bottom of the opening, and it was 18 cm deep. The floor was flat and the sides straight but the back was rounded. There was no indication that there had been any way to close off this niche.

POSTHOLES

Three postholes were found in the section of the kiva floor that was cleared, arranged in a line between the centers of the two pilasters. The westernmost hole (actually nearly central to the kiva as a whole) was 21 cm in diameter and 43 cm deep; the middle of the three recorded holes was 16 cm in diameter and 33 cm deep; the easternmost was 24 cm in diameter at floor level and 50 cm deep, but below floor it expanded to a diameter of 45 cm. All but the top 8 cm of this last hole was filled with a fine white ash. In the top 8 cm there was soil and the remnant of a post 18 cm in diameter. No post was found in the first two holes discussed, and either or both of these holes may have been associated with some earlier model of the kiva.

A fourth posthole was located in the floor of the south bench 70 cm from the east wall and 50 cm from the edge of the bench. This hole was 17 cm in diameter and 46 cm deep. The upper 20 cm was filled with hard-packed earth, probably fill, while the lower portion was tightly packed with fine white ash.

ROOF

The tops of the pilasters and the edges of the kiva were badly eroded, and the charred beams gave little indication of the form of roof present. What indications there were suggested that there had been a basic cribwork of large beams (15 cm in diameter), overlaid with layers of bark, smaller sticks, grass, a second layer of bark, and finally adobe. Several of the large beams had flat surfaces suggesting that the logs had been squared or at least split. A number of large and small irregular sandstone slabs were found among the roof debris. The roof had apparently burned and fallen to the floor.

ARTIFACTS

Fill

Stone: 2 chips; hematite cylinder; hoe (?) fragment (fig. 57f); 3 mano fragments; mano; metate fragment; shaped object; pick, with 3/4 and full grooves (fig. 55d); point (fig. 57a); pot support fragment; unusual, naturally shaped object

Bone: Awl fragment; weaving or matting tool fragment

Other: Slip clay (kaolin?) (2 oz); 3 sherd scrapers

Floor

#2125, roughly shaped mortar (fig. 53d); #2299, metate, medium calcareous tuff; #2576, awl fragment; #2579, azurite (½ oz); #2580, 2 beads, shell; #2593, 2 beads, red stone; #2794, mano (1321); #2795, metate, fine sandstone

Pottery vessel: K1, Tularosa Black-on-white ladle

Walk-in Well (fig. 42)

A large circular depression in the southeast corner of the plaza at first was thought to mark the location of a large kiva. A trench 2 m wide and 6 m long (east-west) was begun in the north-central section of this depression to locate its floor. To our astonishment, excavation in the western end of this trench continued through disturbed soil containing sherds, a few artifacts, and charcoal to a depth of 3 m before sterile soil was reached. Even then no floor level was apparent. The stratum of disturbed soil came to an abrupt end on top of a natural stratum of hard-packed, dense gray clay. In the central and eastern portions of the trench sterile soil in the form of somewhat coarse, tan, sandy soil was reached at a depth ranging from 40 to 190 cm. A section of the top of this latter sterile stratum appeared to have been leveled and utilized as a floor area. This somewhat sloping floor level, which later proved to be a portion of a ramp, was traced as it sloped downward to the north. Here a subterranean room was encountered. This room contained four mealing bins and appeared to open onto the ramp area. A second room, only partially cleared, was found just west of this first room, and it also opened onto the ramp.

This excavation was carried on during the 1950 season. The following year soil-auger test holes, 37 in all, were put down at intervals over the entire area of the depression and beyond. The evidence from the two seasons indicated that the depression marked not a kiva but the location of what had once been a walk-in well.

Despite the excavations and auger test holes it was not possible to reconstruct with complete assurance the exact design of this feature. Most likely a large hole, oval in outline, was excavated into the native soil until the sand-clay aquifer was reached. A ramp approximately 1 m wide apparently began at ground level at the south point of the excavation and sloped downward as it circled the eastern edge of the well, until in the space of a half circuit it reached a depth of nearly 2 m below the surface of the ground. At this point the ramp doubled back on itself, continuing down as it recircled the eastern border of the well until it again reached the southernmost point, where it attained a depth of nearly 3 m and gave access to an excavated area approximately 3 by 5 m in extent. At this depth the rather hard tan soil gave way to a somewhat softer, sandy stratum that was in turn underlain by a stratum of dense gray clay 50 cm thick, a combination forming an excellent aquifer. Even though the Southwest was experiencing drought conditions at the time of our excavations the sandy stratum was quite damp.

This feature not only gave the inhabitants a water supply internal to the pueblo, a priceless possession in times of external stress, but also gave them ready access to a supply of clay. Balls of clay that appeared to be similar (no tests were made) to that obtained from the well were found on the floors of a number of surface rooms.

Rooms Associated with the Well

To the north of the well, at the point where the ramp doubled back on itself, there were two subterranean rooms that appeared to open onto the ramp. The larger of these was completely excavated. Both rooms were rectangular and, like the other subterranean rooms at the site and the well itself, they had been excavated into the naturally hard soil that formed the walls and floor of the rooms. There was no indication that either the walls or the floor had been plastered. The larger room had been excavated to a depth of 110 cm below the present ground surface. The south wall, which separated the room from the ramp, was 40 cm thick and of native soil. A doorway providing access to the ramp occupied the entire west half of this wall. The sill of the doorway was actually a step, for it was 30 cm lower than the floor of the room but 20 cm higher than the level of the ramp. The room contained a row of three contiguous slab-walled mealing bins beginning at the north wall and extending down the north-south centerline of the room. A fourth bin, also slab-walled, was against the center of the east wall of the room. The contiguous bins were placed so that a person using them would face east, while anyone using the single bin would face south. The sandstone floor slabs of the bins were all in place but all of the metates and many of the wall slabs were missing. The single bin, but not the others, had a pottery scoop. This scoop was located on the right rather than the left side of the foot of the metate.

The second room was smaller and oriented at a 45° angle to the first. The east wall, which was of native soil and 40 cm thick, separated the room from the ramp. The doorway, which may have been approximately 75 cm wide, apparently was at the north end of this wall but exact dimensions were difficult to determine, for the southern section had fallen away into the well, and could be seen lying in fragments in the fill of the well just above the clay stratum. The step leading into the larger room continued west beyond the doorway of the large room and curved to the southwest along the outside of the wall of the smaller room, thus serving both rooms. This step was 7 cm higher than the floor of the small room. The doorway in the wall dividing the room from the step and the ramp had a sill 30 cm higher than the room floor. The floor of the room was approximately 140 cm below the present ground surface. There was time to clear only a very small area of this floor along the northeast and southeast walls. No floor features were encountered but probably some were present in the uncleared section of the room.

Burials

Three of the six skeletons found at Site 616 were associated with the walk-in well. (Of the others, only the fetal skeleton in the fill of Room D5 could be considered intentionally buried.)

SKELETON 1 (fig. 6f)

This skeleton of a young child (four to six years) had been placed in a shallow niche in the wall of the ramp at the point where it formed the base of the south wall of the large mealing room. The niche had a flat floor and a back wall that sloped up and out until it met the wall of the ramp. Presumably the niche had been

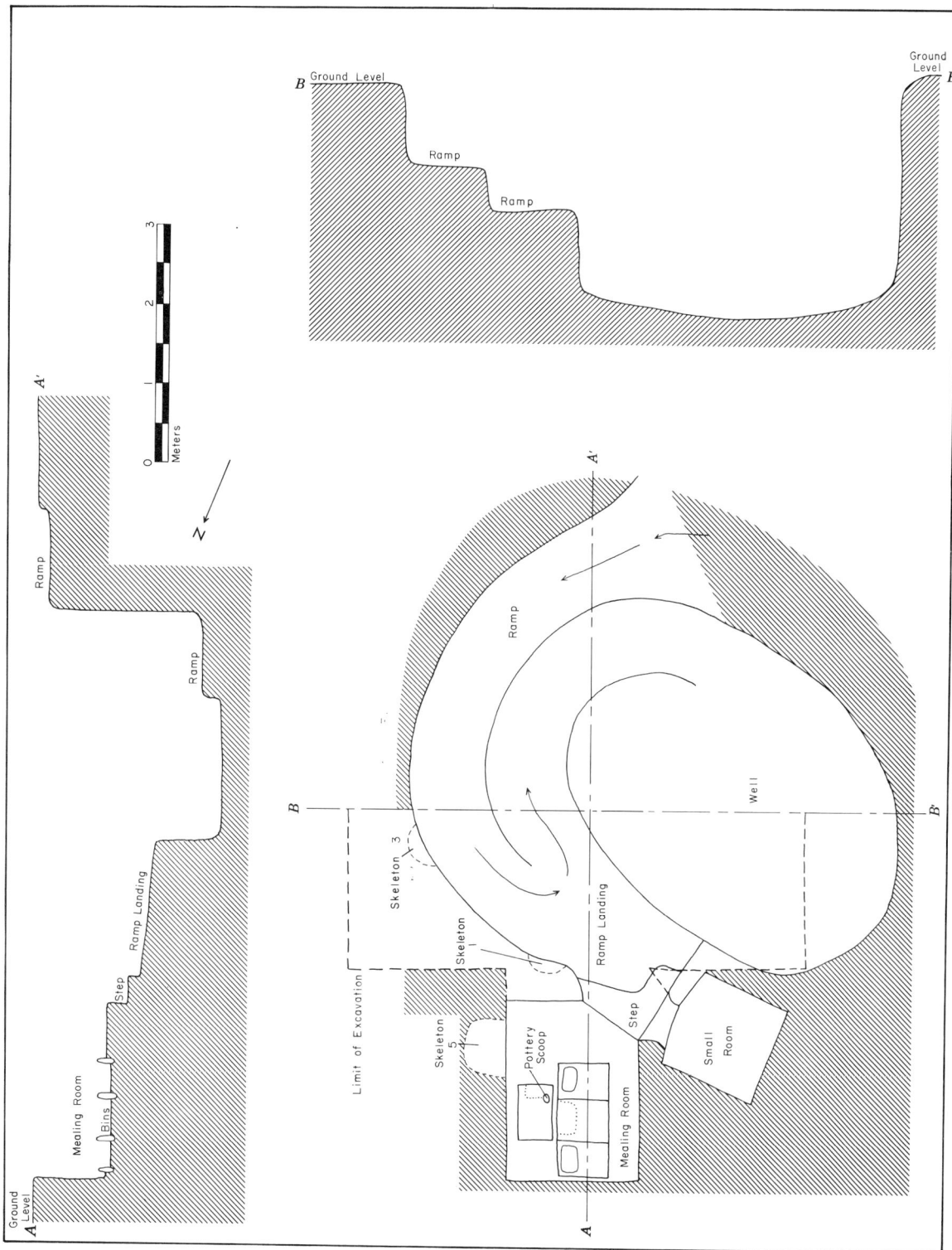

Figure 42. Site 616. Plan and profiles of walk-in well and associated rooms.

sealed over after the burial took place but any such seal had long since been destroyed by natural forces, and erosion had scattered some of the bones before the gradual filling of the entire area had again sealed the niche. The skeleton was tightly flexed and faced the back of the niche with the head to the west. No artifacts were in association.

SKELETON 3

It is difficult to state with assurance the exact circumstances of this burial for it was found shortly after excavation of the wall was begun and long before the various strata were recognized for what they were. In retrospect it seems likely that the body of this infant (approximately one year) had been placed in a niche in the wall of the ramp in much the same manner as Skeleton 1. This niche had been excavated into the wall of the upper section of the ramp at a point approximately 150 cm up the ramp from Skeleton 1. The bones of this skeleton also had become slightly scattered. The body was tightly flexed, facing the back of the niche. The head was to the southeast. A small (13 by 17 cm) rectangular fragment of a worked sandstone slab was found at the top of the skull while a mano fragment, #1352 (descriptive type 1231), was at its feet.

SKELETON 5 (fig. 6h)

A niche 60 cm wide and 60 cm deep had been excavated into the east wall of the large mealing room between the southeast corner and the south end of the single mealing bin. The floor of the niche was approximately 35 cm above the floor of the room. The body of a teen-aged male (?) had been placed in this niche tightly flexed on its side, facing outward. The head was to the north. A large Tularosa Black-on-white jar sherd had been placed over the face. A fragment of worked bone was found near the knees and another near the skull. A polishing stone and an unretouched flake were also in the fill of the niche. This niche had been filled with a dark soil and sealed with adobe and, at the bottom, with two sandstone blocks.

COMMENT

There was no indication that the well was ever roofed in any manner, nor were there any beams or postholes to show whether or how the adjoining rooms were roofed.

Most of the artifacts found within the walls of the rooms came from just above floor, which might be an indication that the rooms at one time had a roof. However, the artifacts found in the well also were largely from the lower portions of the fill. The level of the ramp and the floor of the well could not be established until there had been considerable checking after the initial excavation; so although many of the artifacts may have been resting on the floor, the field notes indicate only that they came from the levels that included the floor. The restorable corrugated and plainware vessels and many of the stone artifacts came from the 250-300 cm level, which extended into the gray clay stratum. The other two vessels and most of the remaining artifacts found in the fill of the well were from the ramp — or just above it — immediately adjacent to the large grinding room. The mortar (#1123) that was found nearly a meter above the gray clay was the only significant artifact high in the fill. The level containing this artifact also had much material that appeared to derive from the east wall of the small room; so the mortar may have washed into the fill of the well from this room at the time or shortly after this wall collapsed.

ARTIFACTS IN WALK-IN WELL

Fill

Stone: 10 chips; chopper; mano; 3 mano fragments; roughly shaped mortar (#1290, fig. 53a); pot cover; scoria cylinder (#1916, fig. 58g); shaftsmoother fragment; unretouched flake

Bone: 2 awl fragments; 2 pierced phalanges (#1319, fig. 64j); 2 tubes

Other: Clay, on the ramp (1 lb); limonite (¼ oz)

Pottery vessels: Corrugated bowl; corrugated jar; plainware miniature bowl; Tularosa Black-on-white bowl; unfired miniature bowl

ARTIFACTS IN MEALING ROOM

Fill

Stone: Axe, notched, fragment (#1376, fig. 55c); 7 chips; 2 choppers; core; 2 manos; 7 mano fragments; roughly shaped mortar (#1811, fig. 110b); pecking stone; 3 polishing pebbles; scoria cylinder

Bone: Awl, head intact (#1876, fig. 62e); awl, skewer; 2 rings (#2594, fig. 64d, e); tube

Antler: Flaker

Other: Calcitic limestone (¼ oz); limonite (¼ oz); malachite (¼ oz)

ARTIFACTS IN SMALL ROOM

Fill

Stone: 3 chips; chopper; mano fragment

Bone: Awl fragment; pierced phalange

SUBSISTENCE MATERIALS

Despite the number of burned rooms and the abundance of other materials, only the scantiest information was available on the dietary habits of the pueblo's occupants.

Nearly two bushels of seeds of the general Chenopodium-Amaranth-Cactus type were recovered, as well as a much smaller quantity of corn (see Appendix C), and, in Room C3, some monocot (yucca or agave) fiber (#1675) and grass seed. Of the 506 animal bones found only 136 could be identified. The unidentifiable bones were almost equally divided between those from the larger and those from the smaller species. Of the identified bones there were 34 pronghorn *(Antilocapra americana)*, 18 mule deer *(Odocoileus hemionus hemionus)*, 8 bison *(Bison bison)*, 45 turkey or other bird (22 from a single skeleton in the fill of Room D5), 21 rabbit or hare, 4 coyote *(Canis latrans)*, 3 dog *(Canis familiaris,* short-snouted), 1 wolf *(Canis lupus)*, 1 bobcat *(Lynx rufus)*, and 1 bighorn sheep *(Ovis canadensis)*. Except for one fragment of deer antler, a portion of a pronghorn pelvis, and several vertebrae, all the deer and pronghorn bones were from the legs and feet, about equally divided between the fore and hind legs. The bison bones were more varied, including a humerus, a metatarsal, a vertebra, a second phalange, an astragalus, a tooth, and two mandibles. The coyotes were represented by two scapulae, a mandible, and a calvarium; the dogs by three humeri, the wolf by a metatarsal, the bobcat by a pelvis, and the bighorn sheep by a calcaneum.

The distribution of these materials was curious. Corn was found only in Area C but there it occurred in every room except Room C8, which contained more animal bones (17) than any other room in Area C. More rooms in Area C burned than elsewhere, which might account in part for this limited distribution, but the smaller and presumably more perishable seeds were more widely distributed (fill of Rooms C3, and F1, and the floor of Rooms B3, C2, C8, and D2). Seed finds were restricted to storerooms (i.e., rooms without floor features) and mealing rooms. Other than the possibility that it was an accident of preservation, no ready explanation for the restricted distribution of the corn presents itself. No bones at all were found in four rooms (Rooms A3, D2, D3, and F1). An average of 54 bones were found in the fill and, rarely, on the floor of each of four rooms (Rooms D1, D5, E1, and E2), the kiva, and the walk-in well. The remainder of the rooms contained from 1 to 21 bones with an average of 8 bones each. These were mostly in the fill, though in six rooms (Rooms B1, B2, C2, C5, C8, and F2) a total of 24 bones was found on floors. A number of bones, all unidentifiable, came from the various trenches. Perhaps the section of the plaza between the kiva and the walk-in well and/or some of the surrounding rooms were utilized more than any other for working on the results of the hunt, as 326 of the 506 bones recovered were from that area. The bones found elsewhere were almost entirely deer or pronghorn, though there were, in addition, a bison bone and several rabbit bones in Area C and a few rabbit and bird bones in Area F.

POTTERY — DESCRIPTIVE TYPOLOGY

The concept, philosophy, and method of formulation of the Descriptive Type have been discussed above (pp. 33–35), and are further explained and defined in appendix A (pp. 290–293).

In this section the application of the analytical procedure developed for designating particular descriptive types at Site 616 (and by analogy at any other site) is discussed and described in the immediately following pages, and the same data are compiled in condensed form in tables 1, 2, and 3. Corresponding discussions and tabular presentations of the descriptive pottery types from other sites appear on subsequent pages and in tables 12–14, 17, 19–21; and analogous arrangements according to the same analytical method as applied to manos are shown in tables 6, 15 and 18.

In all the tables relating to pottery (e.g., table 1) the several descriptive types identified at Site 616 are indicated across the top of the table by sets of four numerals, each set arranged in vertical sequence in successive columns.

The four horizontal rows designated A, B, C, and D indicate the four major categories set forth in the following text, namely Material of Manufacture (row A), Vessel Shapes and Areas Painted (row B), Surface Finish (row C), and Decoration (row D).

The digit appearing in each row in table 1 corresponds to one of the numbered subdivisions listed and defined under one of the four major categories, and is referred to as a "mode."

As an example, let us consider descriptive type 1113 in table 1. Here the uppermost digit (1) in row A identifies the nature of the materials from which the specimens of this descriptive type are constructed, as described in subdivision 1 under A, namely "gray paste." The digit in row B (1) identifies the shape of the vessel and the areas upon it that are painted, as described in subdivision 1 under B, namely a "necked jar." The next lower digit in row C (1) identifies the character of the surface finish, as described in subdivision 1 under C, namely "slipped surface, generally smooth or slick," while the lowest digit in row D (3) identifies the style and details of decoration, as described in subdivision 3 under D (see pp. 110–111).

It thus becomes possible to interpret, define, and localize the specimens of any particular descriptive type by cross-reference between its textual or verbal specifications and its placement on the corresponding table.

Complete descriptive data are presented herewith for the identification of all features of the pottery at Site 616:

White-slipped Pottery

MATERIAL: ROW A

1: Gray paste — mode key (A)
   White slip, thickly applied — modes (b) and (g)
   Black mineral paint — mode (a)
2: Gray paste — mode key (A)
   White slip, thickly applied — modes (b) and (g)
   Black semiglaze paint — mode (b)
3: Gray paste — mode key (A)
   Creamy slip, thickly applied — modes (c) and (g)
   Black mineral paint — mode (a)
4: Gray paste — mode key (A)
   Creamy slip, thickly applied — modes (c) and (g)
   Black semiglaze paint — mode (b)
5: Gray paste — mode key (A)
   White slip, thinly applied — modes (b) and (h)
   Black mineral paint — mode (a)
6: Gray paste — mode key (A)
   White slip, thinly applied — modes (b) and (h)
   Black semiglaze paint — mode (b)
7: Gray paste — mode key (A)
   Thin and/or watery white slip — modes (b) and (i)
   Black mineral paint — mode (a)
8: Gray paste — mode key (A)
   Thin and/or watery white slip — modes (b) and (i)
   Black semiglaze paint — mode (b)
9: Gray paste — mode key (A)
   No slip apparent — mode (a)
   Black mineral paint — mode (a)

Insofar as could be determined by visual inspection and fairly frequent observation with an 11x binocular microscope, there was no major variation in the basic clay, tempering materials, or firing methods used in the construction of the white-slipped pottery. During the initial analysis a number of paste types were recognized, based on slight variations in the nature or proportion of the inclusions, the appearance, fracture, and color of the clay, and so on. As analysis proceeded and these very minor variations proved to have no patterned relationships or discernible significance, the range of permissible variation of most of these factors was gradually increased until only five types remained. Upon completion of the analysis, however, it was found that there were only a dozen or so sherds in four of the types. While these four were descriptively distinct, they were not beyond the possible range of extreme or accidental variation from the single-paste type mentioned above. Consequently, in the pottery tabulations these four were included in material mode key (A), and the nature of the variations and their correlations are brought out briefly below. It is possible, of course, that technical analysis would dispel this visual impression of homogeneity.

Two of the somewhat atypical groups came entirely from Area D and differed primarily in having a very dense shattering paste with either rare opaque angular material and clear sand inclusions or no discernible inclusions whatever. The single sherd in which inclusions were rare was also unusual for the site in lacking a slip. The other two groups were found only in Room C1 and differed in having inclusions of an angular black opaque material and occasional lustrous fragments, resembling mica, either as the only inclusions present or in addition to the more common materials. The few sherds containing only black inclusions also differed in lacking a slip while the others had only a thin watery slip.

The distinction between the flat-white slip and the creamy slip is not an absolute one. There did appear to be a difference in the makeup and consistency of the two slips, but the exact nature and the extent of this difference has not been determined by analysis and thus is difficult to define in exact terms. It was probably the result of a variation in the proportion, or the presence of only one or two of a number of constituent elements, so that the two modes, at least visually, tended to intergrade. In addition to the color distinction emphasized above there were other distinguishing features more difficult to define. The creamy slip had the appearance of solidified heavy cream while the flat-white slip had a harder porcelainlike appearance. If well polished, both became quite lustrous but the creamy slip had a softer, soapy "feel," though as measured on Mohs' scale the hardness of the two was approximately the same. Unlike the flat-white slip, which showed some variation, the creamy slip was always thickly applied and well polished. The observed differences, whatever their bases, do have some pertinence to certain problems. The heavy, creamy slip generally was utilized at a somewhat later period on the black-on-white wares of the Little Colorado; e.g., it was more closely associated with classic Tularosa than the earlier Reserve and Gallup types.

At Site 616 the creamy-white slip was used almost exclusively with decorative motifs I and II. The flat-white slip, taken as a whole, was associated with all decorative modes. The thick white slip, somewhat like the thick creamy slip, was associated principally with decorative mode (c) but was rare only on vessels decorated with modes (j) and (i). In contrast, the thin white slip was used primarily with decorative modes (j) and (i), and while it was also occasionally associated with decorative modes (d) and (e), it was rare elsewhere. The thin watery white slip was found only with decorative modes (b) and (c).

The various slip modes did not exhibit any marked areal clustering and were found on all major pottery forms, though the few examples of thin watery slip occurred only on jars and bowls.

The glaze paint occurred on all the major black-on-white forms though primarily on vessels with a flat-white slip. While a variety of decorative modes was used, nearly all could be considered to fall within the range of those associated with Reserve Black-on-white. It is interesting that the glaze-painted pieces (a technique typical of a subsequent time horizon) were principally associated with vessels decorated along the lines of one of the older decorative traditions. The potter(s) involved many have been "conservative" in decoration while experimental in technique, or the association with the earlier decorative tradition may have been more nearly fortuitous (that is, the potters themselves may not have been aware of this temporal difference in popularity peaks). The use of glaze paint on white-slipped pottery may have been an attempt on the part of local potters to produce on the locally made wares a feature already common on the red-slipped pottery which, it would appear, was primarily imported.

VESSEL SHAPES AND AREAS SLIPPED AND PAINTED: ROW B

1: Necked jar — mode (d)
   Exterior slipped and painted — modes (b) and (d)
2: Neckless (seed) jar — mode (b)
   Exterior slipped and painted — modes (b) and (d)
3: Pitcher — mode (g)
   Exterior slipped and painted — modes (b) and (d)
4: Bowl — mode (a)
   Interior and exterior slipped, interior painted — modes (a), (b), and (c)
5: Bowl — mode (a)
   Painted on interior (no slip) — mode (o)
6: Ladle — mode (h)
   Interior slipped and painted — modes (a) and (c)
7: Ladle — mode (h)
   Interior and exterior slipped, interior painted — modes (a), (b), and (c)
8: Ladle — mode (h)
   Interior and exterior slipped and painted — modes (a), (b), (c), and (d)
9: Other forms (e.g., doughnut, duck, miniature) — mode (i)
   Exteriors slipped and painted — modes (b) and (c)

COMMENT

No more specific breakdown or mathematical expression of these forms was attempted. A clear idea of the range of forms found at Site 616 can be gained through figures 43, 44, and 49. It is likely that there were more pitchers than are indicated by the sherd count. The sherds of jars and pitchers are difficult to separate unless diagnostic features are present. During analysis, sherds were counted as deriving from jars, unless they indisputably came from pitchers. A similar difficulty existed between ladle and bowl sherds. In this case, sherds from vessels with a small diameter were included as ladle sherds even though no distinctive feature such as a handle was present.

There is little doubt that the large-necked jar was the most popular form for black-on-white pottery (80 to 85 percent). Ladles lagged far behind (10 percent). Pitchers, bowls, small-necked jars, and neckless or seed jars were relative rarities. In addition there were a few miniature and aberrant forms such as the so-called duck pots and the doughnut-shaped vessel.

Many of the large jars were equipped with two inset handles placed in opposition at or just below the bottom framing line of the design. These handles have been called "thumb holds" though it seems as likely that the middle fingers were placed in them. This form of handle never occurred on red-slipped jars. A variety of ladle handles was constructed. The majority were hollow tubes varying in cross section from circular to oval to square, often with a half dozen or so clay pellets included inside, giving the handle the effect of a rattle. The circular handles generally had an "ear" or raised nubbin on the upper extremity while the square ones often had two such ears. Small holes were often but not always punched in the handles. A hollow U-shaped handle occurred on an estimated 15 percent of the ladles.

The black-on-white bowls contrasted somewhat with the black-on-red bowls in that the rims of the latter were nearly always markedly incurved while on black-on-white bowls the rims generally were straight or only slightly incurved.

All bowls (except for two sherds from two separate bowls from Room D1 which were unslipped) and all but a few ladles (again from Area D) were slipped on

108 • Mariana Mesa

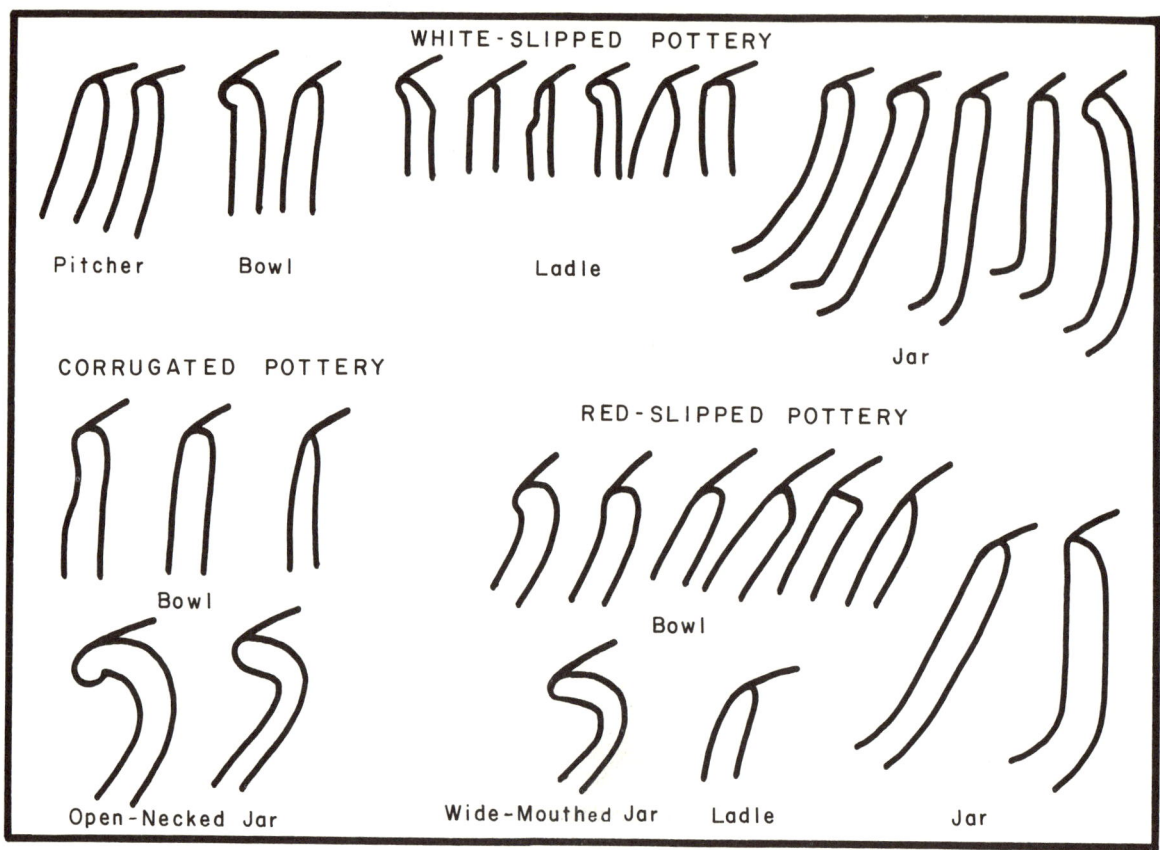

Figure 43. Pottery rim and vessel forms from Site 616.

the exteriors as well as the interiors. The handles of the ladles, the ladle bowl interiors, and rarely the ladle bowl exteriors were painted. Only the interiors of the bowls were painted. In general, the exterior slip on jars continued over the rim and inside the neck. (However, in the tables, only mode [b] is indicated as being present.)

SURFACE FINISH: ROW C

1: Slipped surface generally even, smooth or slick, and lustrous; polishing marks rarely evident; slip polished before application of paint — modes (b), (e), (g), and (i)

2: Slipped surface, undulating but smooth to the touch, high points lustrous; polishing marks generally evident; slip polished before application of paint — modes (a), (f), (g), and (i)

3: Slipped surface even and smooth but matte; polishing marks rarely evident; slip polished before application of paint — modes (b), (e), (g), and (k)

Figure 44. Pottery vessels from Site 616. Miniature and unusual pottery vessels: a. Room C5, floor, Vessel C51, Puerco Black-on-red jar, #2065; b. Room C2, floor, Vessel C26, Puerco Black-on-red miniature jar, #1425; c. Room C1, fill, Puerco Black-on-red miniature pitcher; d. Room C8, fill, Puerco Black-on-red miniature jar, #1913; e. Room C1, fill, Reserve Black-on-white miniature pitcher, #1452; f. Room C9, fill, Tularosa Black-on-white miniature jar, #2173; g. Room C4, fill, Reserve Black-on-white doughnut vessel, #1590; h. Room C5, floor, Vessel C54, Reserve Black-on-white duck figurine, #2099; i. Room C9, fill, Reserve Black-on-white duck figurine, #2002; j. Room C1, floor, Vessel C11, Reserve Black-on-white duck figurine, #1454; k. Room C9, fill, Reserve Black-on-white duck figurine, #2715; l. Room B1, floor, Vessel B13, plainware seed jar, #1209. Miscellaneous restored vessels: m. Room E2, floor, Vessel E21, Tularosa Black-on-white jar, #2373; n. Room B1, fill, Puerco Black-on-red jar, #1091; o. Room A1, floor, Vessel A12, St. Johns Polychrome bowl, #2130; p. Room C5, floor, Vessel C53, Reserve Black-on-white miniature jar, #1705; q. Room C2, fill, Reserve Black-on-white pitcher, #1223; r. Room C2, fill, Reserve Black-on-white ladle, #1205; s. Room A1, floor, Vessel A13, Tularosa Black-on-white ladle, #1806; t. Room A1, floor, Vessel A14, Reserve Black-on-white ladle, #1805.

Site 616 • 109

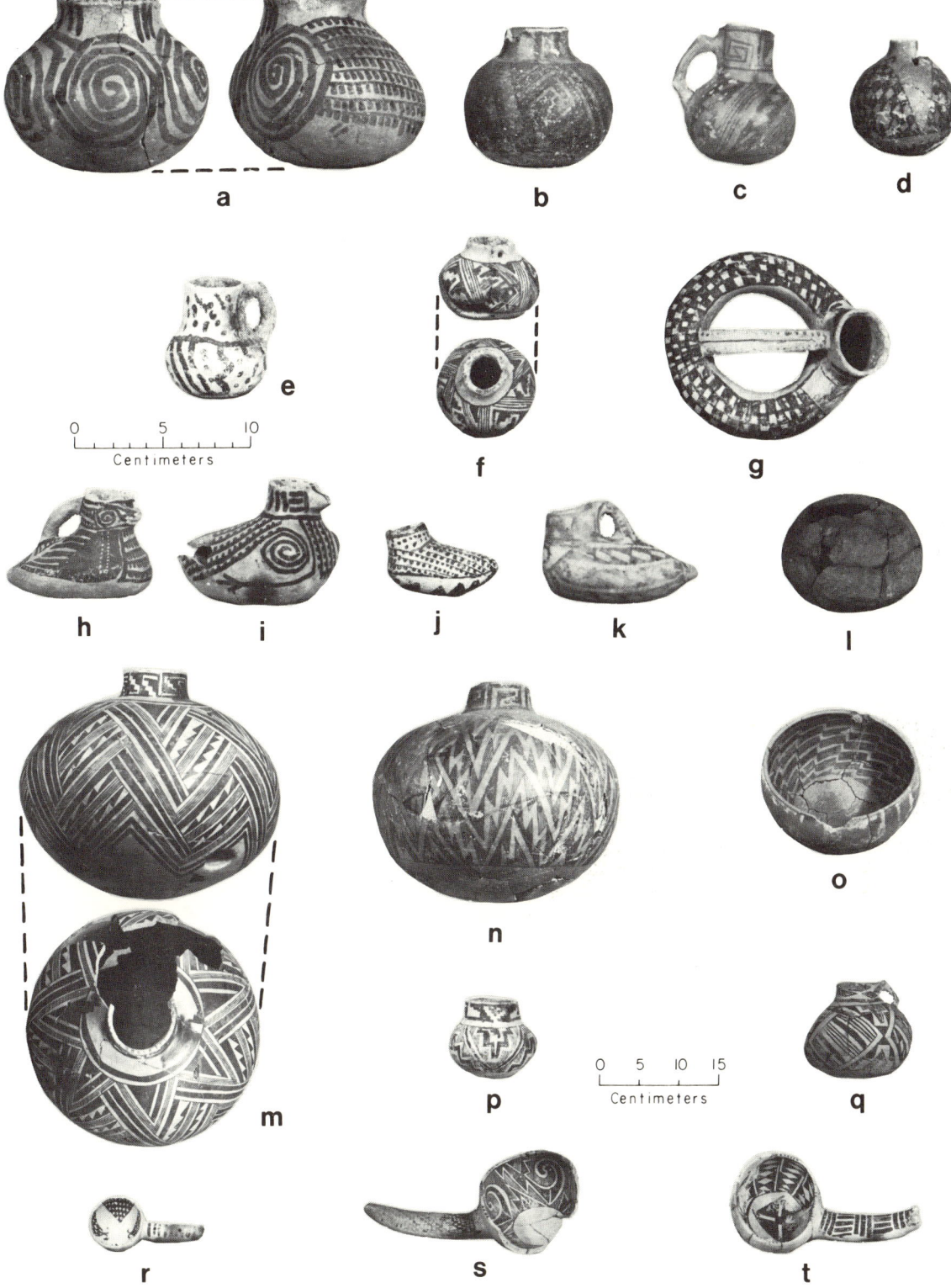

Sherds of Surface Finish Type 2, while descriptively different from those of type 1, did not have as a whole any major associations within Site 616 other than the very fact of their rarity. The distinction has proved of value in other areas, e.g., Chaco Canyon. The well-smoothed matte finish of type 3 is an attribute often associated with the regional time-space type Socorro Black-on-white, but other characteristics of the type were not present (e.g., characteristic paste and temper).

The attention of the reader is called to *A Symmetry Analysis of Upper Gila Area Ceramic Design* by Dorothy K. Washburn (1977). Washburn provides a detailed analysis of the painted pottery from Sites 143, 481, 494, and 616. I differ with Washburn in several interpretations; e.g., she feels, on the basis of decorative factors, that less of the redware is nonlocal. Unfortunately, not enough such detailed decorative analysis has been done on a regional basis for this to be established with certainty. I still feel, on the basis of the total range of ceramic traits, that there is a major difference between the whiteware and redware pottery sample from Site 616. Neither interpretation can be adequately demonstrated on present data, but it is hoped that further studies like those by Washburn will be forthcoming, as they may provide a very provocative and potentially sensitive means for analyzing a very important but complex aspect of prehistoric pottery — the designs themselves.

DECORATION: ROW D

When handling a large number of sherds from a new site or area it is extremely difficult to recognize the more complete aspects of decoration such as the patterns and layouts employed. Unless they are extremely simple and obvious these can generally be ascertained only through study of complete or nearly complete vessels. Since in the initial sorting of the Site 616 pottery all vessels recognized as restorable had been sorted out, these were first studied in an attempt to formulate at least some of the patterns and layout techniques. Even so, it rapidly became apparent that on individual sherds it was rarely possible to recognize with assurance any decorative aspect larger than a motif. Consequently, the whole vessels were again reviewed and the motifs thereon were classified into a number of modes. These modes formed the initial basis for sorting the sherds. Needless to say, not every motif employed was so formulated. Precise boundaries were not established and decisions whether or not to formulate and continue to note newly observed motifs were made during, rather than before, analysis. From practical necessity, these judgments were, at least to a certain extent, subjective.

The following decorative modes take into consideration both the motifs employed and, to a lesser extent, certain characteristics in the manner of execution, such as extremely sloppy handling of the brush, or the design concept, wide spacing, variations in the elements composing the motifs, and so forth. Illustrative examples are shown in figures 45-48.

Motif I: Rectilinear bands and rectangular units of varied internal makeup

1: The main linear elements consist of one or two parallel lines of medium size bordered by a band of four to six parallel lines. The rectangular units show great diversity of makeup although on any one vessel they are usually similar. Most are made up of combinations of straight lines of varying widths, pendent triangles (right, isosceles, or oblique), small solid triangles, half terraces often opposed, negative zigzags, occasionally crosshatched elements, and similar forms. The execution of these designs is generally good and the spacing well organized. The lines are straight and are of fairly even widths throughout their lengths — mode (a).

2: The main linear elements are more or less continuous rectilinear bands of fine parallel lines. Broader lines are common but less frequent than in designs of mode (a) and when present tend to be narrower, i.e., thin to broad rather than broad. The elements making up the rectilinear motifs, while fairly consistent on any one vessel, vary considerably between vessels. The elements employed are usually the same as in mode (a), e.g., lines, solid triangles, half terraces, pendent sawteeth. Taken as a whole, the execution of these designs is less well done than in mode (a). The lines are not so straight or of such constant width. The general spacing of the designs is equally well handled though designs of mode (b) are more widely spaced. The main features of mode (b) that differentiate it from mode (a) are: (1) sloppier execution, (2) less design per unit of area, (3) the use of continuous bands of fine lines, (4) only occasional use of broad lines, and, when present, a tendency for these lines to be less broad than in mode (a). The important point is that on a large number of sherds these variations consistently occur together — mode (b).

3: Despite the differences existing between typical examples of decorative modes (a) and (b) they are by no means mutually exclusive. On some sherds it was almost impossible to make a confident decision as to which mode was represented, and as a consequence during analysis a category including them both was established. For a time, lumping all the material into one group was considered, but the typical examples do show some

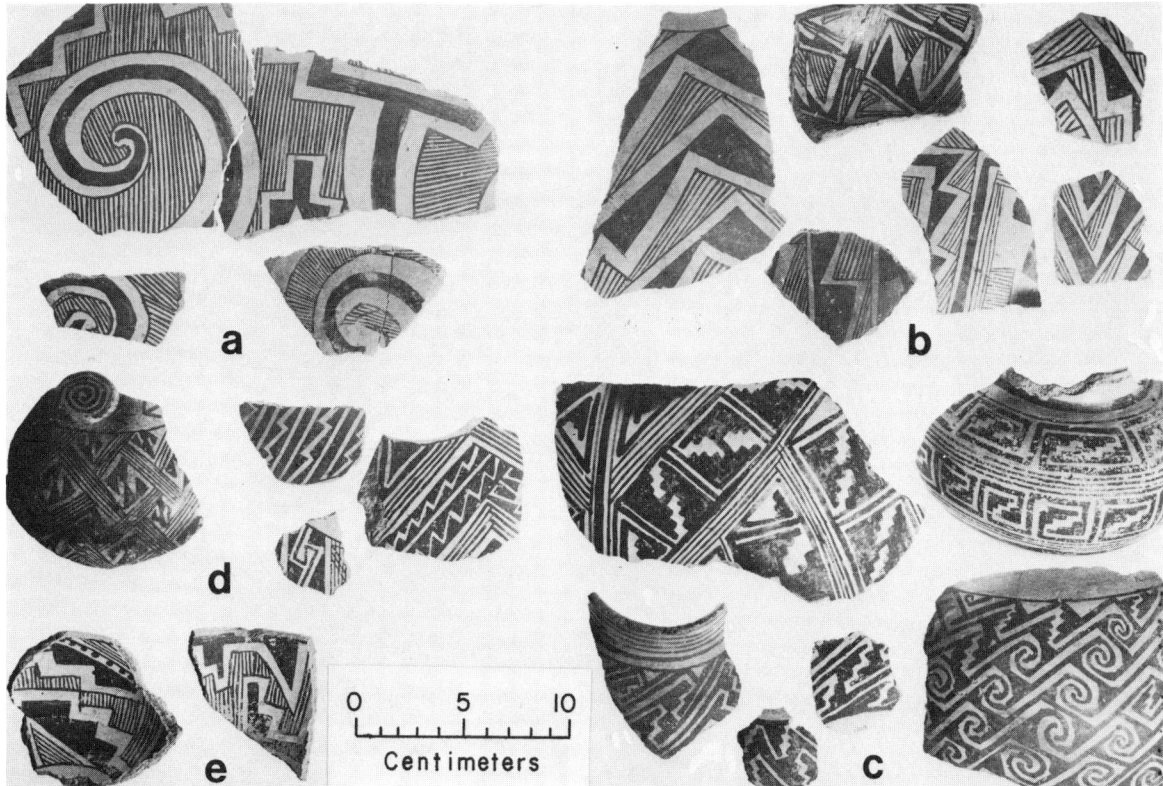

Figure 45. Decorative modes on black-on-white pottery from Site 616: a. decorative mode (d), 4 sherds; b. decorative mode (e), 6 sherds; c. decorative mode (g), 6 sherds; d. decorative mode (f), 4 sherds; e. decorative mode (j), 2 sherds.

significant variation in their distribution and association and appear to represent somewhat different decorative norms and standards of execution, so their separateness has been maintained. There remained, however, the large block of sherds which, while obviously representing the same motif (that is, motif I), could not be satisfactorily segregated into modes (a) or (b). Decorative mode (c) contains these sherds. Despite the internal variation of the material, this mode in conjunction with modes (a) and (b) constitutes a cohesive, decorative motif standing in contrast to the other decorative motifs in use at the site — mode (c).

Motif II: Opposed solid and hatched scrolls

4: While this mode can and occasionally does occur in conjunction with or as a portion of a number of design patterns, it is generally found with a band design where the opposed scrolls form the dominant and largest motif. The execution of this motif is usually careful: the hatching lines are straight, fairly evenly and closely spaced, the distance between them being on the average less than the thickness of the line. Lines bordering the hatched element are the same thickness as the interior lines — mode (d).

Motif III: Lines of opposed pendent sawteeth

5: This decorative mode consists of opposed solid and hatched pendent sawteeth. On most examples the opposed sawteeth interlock, leaving a negative lightning design, on others the tips of the sawteeth touch, resulting in negative squares, diamonds, or parallelograms between the sawteeth. Another point of variation can be found in the spacing of the hatching lines, with the space between the lines varying from less than the width of the lines themselves to almost twice the width of the lines. The bordering lines are almost always the same width as the hatching lines and, similarly, the hatching lines are almost always parallel to the longest line of the triangle (i.e., the hypotenuse if it is a right triangle) — mode (e).

6: In this mode there are lines of opposed solid pendent sawteeth. Like mode (e) these sawteeth either interlock or touch, resulting in either a neg-

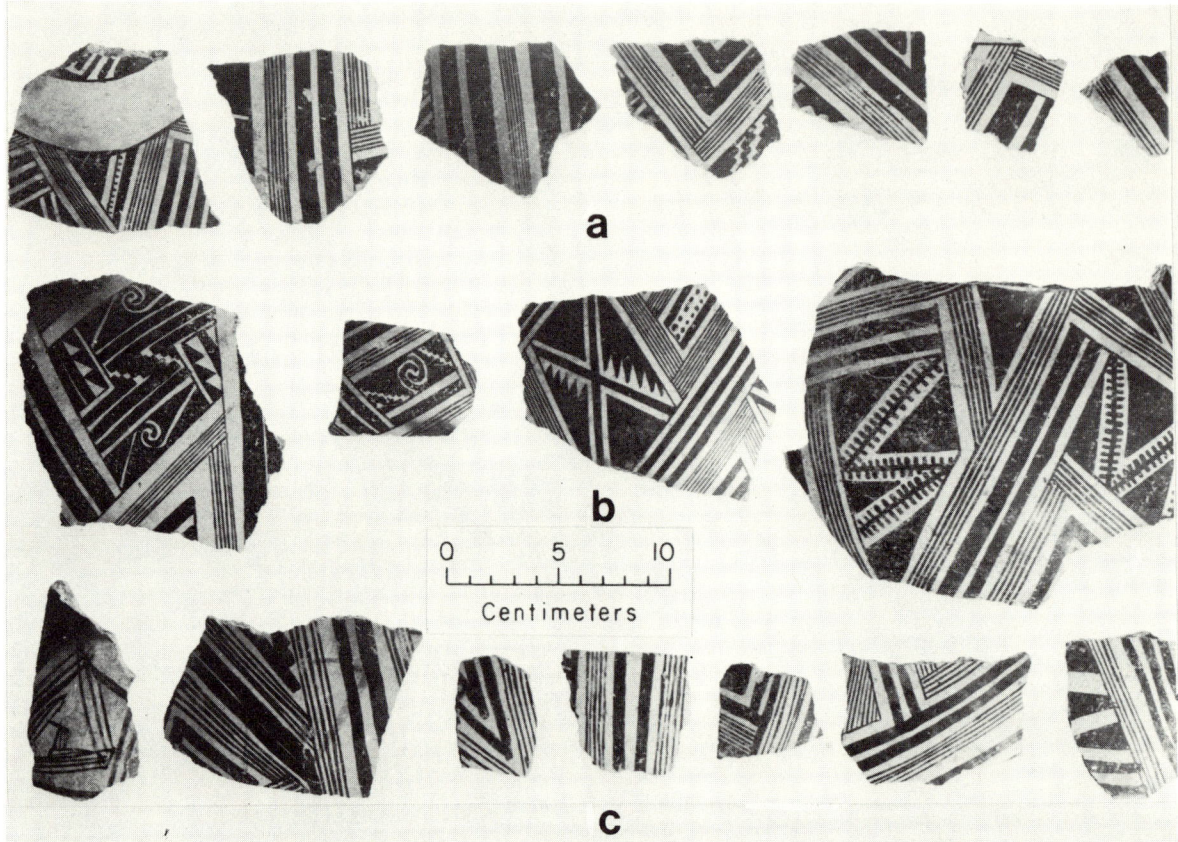

Figure 46. Decorative modes on black-on-white pottery from Sites 481, 616: a. decorative mode (a), 7 sherds; b. decorative elements present on black-on-white vessels decorated with modes (a) to (c), sherd at left is from Site 481, Room 27, and all others are from Site 616; c. decorative mode (b), 7 sherds.

ative diamond parallelogram or a lightning effect. Despite the essential similarity between mode (e) and mode (f), the primary difference being the lack of hatched sawteeth in mode (f), both the use of the two modes and the impression given by them are surprisingly distinct. Mode (f) never forms the overall design of a vessel but rather occurs in bands or short units, serving much the same purpose in the overall design as do the stripes and bands of parallel lines of motif I. Nor do the elements of mode (f) ever reach the size often attained by the individual elements in mode (e). Whereas mode (e) is often the basic or even the sole motif of an entire design, mode (f) is never more than a subsidiary motif and is generally no more than the motif of an individual unit within a design — mode (f).

Motif IV: Interlocking, double-ended keys, scrolls, and half terraces usually occurring in linear chains

7: Despite the variation in the individual elements employed in this mode, the resultant overall effect is quite similar and in fact on a number of specimens several of these diverse elements (e.g., half terraces, triangles with scrolls) are used together in an identical manner as parts of the same design — mode (g).

Motif V: Checkerboard and triangular checkerboard (the latter term refers to the disposition of black and white triangles in a manner analogous to the disposition of black and white squares in the standard checkerboard pattern)

8: Like mode (f) the motif of mode (h) is more generally a subsidiary motif with the exception of its use on small vessels, particularly ladles where it is often the only motif employed — mode (h).

Motif VI: Bands of diagonal hatching

9: The diagonal hatching is almost without exception linear in layout. These bands frequently occur in conjunction with black stripes of medium width. The bordering lines are of the same width as the hatching lines but there is some variation in the width of the band and in the spacing of the hatch-

Figure 47. Decorative modes on black-on-white pottery from Site 616. Upper left column: decorative mode (h), 3 sherds; lower left column: decorative mode (i), 6 sherds; middle column: miscellaneous black-on-white elements, decorative mode (k), 10 sherds; right column: life forms, 6 sherds.

ing lines. On several sherds the hatching is widely spaced in a manner reminiscent of earlier pottery styles, e.g., Gallup Black-on-white (see sherds in upper right corner of figure 48) — mode (i).

Motif VII: Bands of hatching interspersed between stepped solid and hollow triangles

10: This motif generally occurs as a series of repeated units that constitute nearly the entire design. The elements and the size of the units themselves are usually small and the motif is found almost entirely on the smaller vessels, particularly ladles. The bands of parallel lines or hatched areas are of closely spaced fine lines. The execution of this mode, while rarely as sloppy as the worst of mode (b), almost never attains the neatness of execution and layout that is so characteristic of mode (a) and generally of most of the other black-on-white modes — mode (j).

Other Motifs

11: A number of other motifs were recognized, distinctive enough in themselves but occurring on single or rare vessels. Doubtless others were overlooked. The ones observed are listed here and illustrated in figure 47, primarily to show the range of variation in the black-on-white pottery designs found at Site 616. These rare motifs include a variety of life forms (almost the total sample recovered is illustrated in fig. 47d), the negative circle with a central dot, the "screen work" consisting of a narrow-line design superimposed on an area of fine parallel lines, and designs consisting simply of medium-width lines forming a considerable variety of motifs — mode (k).

All decorative modes appeared, at least occasionally, on all black-on-white pottery forms. However, decorative modes (a), (b), and (c) tended to occur more frequently on jars, decorative modes (d) and (g) on bowls and ladles, decorative modes (j) and (h) on ladles. Bowls were more often decorated with eccentric or unusual designs than were jars. Usually the designs on small vessels, rather than being different,

114 • Mariana Mesa

Table 1. Distribution by descriptive types of black-on-white sherds from Site 616

Provenience	Totals	1/1/1/1	1/1/1/2	1/1/1/3	1/1/1/4	1/1/1/5	1/1/1/6	1/1/1/7	1/1/1/11	1/1/2/2	1/1/2/11	1/3/1/11	1/4/1/2	1/4/1/3	1/4/1/4	1/4/1/6	1/4/1/11	1/4/2/2	1/4/2/7	1/6/1/3	1/7/1/2	1/7/1/3	1/7/1/4	1/7/1/5	1/7/1/6	1/7/1/8	1/7/1/9	1/7/2/2	1/8/1/6	1/8/1/7	1/8/1/3	2/1/1/3	2/1/1/4	2/1/1/10	2/1/1/2	2/2/1/2	2/7/1/8	3/1/1/1	3/1/1/2	3/1/1/3	3/1/1/4	3/1/1/5
Totals	5720	119	202	2057	84	108	45	18	6	31	3	5	1	2	4	5	3	7	2	5	47	31	32	30	3	39	8	11	2	7	5	4	4	5	2	4	4	150	110	376	48	3
Rm. A1 Fill	5																																				1					
Rm. A2 Fill	10																																				8				
Rm. B1 Fill	43		27																																				26		
Rm. B2 Fill	44																																						3		
Floor	6																																							2	
Rm. B3 Fill	19															2																									
Floor	1												1																												
Rm. B5 Fill	10	12																																				1				
Rm. B7 Fill	16	9																																							
Floor	9																																								
Rm. C1 Fill	572		363													5	2																					93	70	205	14	
Rm. C2 Fill	590		8			1										1														3												
Floor	8		281															7																								
Rm. C3 Fill	470																																									
Floor	3																																								
Rm. C4 Fill	173		35																																						15	
Rm. C5 Fill	512		219	18			18														17					5	1															
Rm. C6 Fill	292	4	179	16				1													7																					
Rm. C7 Fill	24	9		2																																						
Rm. C8 Fill	101	8	44																		3																					
Rm. C9 Fill	366		129	52	14		1																		12															2		
Rm. C10 Fill	129		78	10																																						
Floor	112		64	5	4																																					
Rm. D1 Fill	38		26	12																																						
Floor	27		21	1																																						
Flr. 2	17		14																																							
Rm. D2 Fill	163	60	4																		4	27	6											4								
Rm. D3 Fill	27	8																																								
Rm. D5 Fill	375		1	4		30														5	13		7			8	7	2										4		167		
Rm. E1 Fill	144	42	26	15	2																		25	2			4		7													
Rm. E2 Fill	99																					7		7			4											43				
Rm. F2 Fill	165																					25	19	20														5	11			
Kiva Fill	528	95	337	30	26	16		3	1												3	4	5																			
Walk- 0-100	381	26	120	1	7																											4									15	
in 100-200	93		33																																						3	3
Well 200-300	67		22																																						3	
Mealing Room	85		53			2									4				1														1									

Quantities do not include whole or restorable vessels.

Table 1. Distribution by descriptive types of black-on-white sherds from Site 616.

Descriptive Types / Provenience	3-1-1-6	3-4-1-6	3-4-1-6	3-4-1-9	3-4-1-11	3-7-1-1	3-7-1-3	3-7-1-4	3-8-1-3	4-7-1-2	5-1-1-3	5-1-1-4	5-1-1-5	5-1-1-6	5-1-1-8	5-1-1-10	5-1-1-11	5-1-2-3	5-1-3-8	5-1-3-10	5-2-1-11	5-3-1-3	5-4-1-1	5-4-2-1	5-4-2-3	5-7-1-1	5-7-1-2	5-7-1-4	5-7-1-8	6-1-1-10	6-6-3-6	7-1-2-3	7-1-3-2	7-1-4-2-3	7-1-4-3-3	7-4-3-3	8-1-3-2	9-1-3-8	9-1-3-9	9-5-3-8	Bases
Totals	1	15	1	1	2	6	6	44	1	6	7	36	41	8	11	59	7	1	17	61	2	6	4	1	2	13	3	15	31	7	3	1	1	1	1	1	1	1	1	2	1665
Rm. A1 Fill	1																																								
Rm. A2 Fill			1																				1																		
Rm. B1 Fill										3																							1								11
Rm. B2 Fill										1																						1									13
Rm. B2 Floor																															3										3
Rm. B3 Fill										2				1		9																									5
Rm. B3 Floor																5																									1
Rm. B5 Fill																											1														
Rm. B7 Floor																																									
Rm. C1 Fill																	20				1									1							1				180
Rm. C1 Floor																	32																								201
Rm. C2 Fill		14									7																														123
Rm. C2 Floor		1			2												7						3	1																	109
Rm. C3 Fill						2																																			238
Rm. C3 Floor																1																									81
Rm. C4 Fill																																									23
Rm. C5 Fill																			17																						170
Rm. C6 Fill																																									41
Rm. C7 Fill																																									31
Rm. C8 Fill																																									2
Rm. C9 Fill																																								2	5
Rm. C10 Fill						4																																			3
Rm. C10 Floor																																									65
Rm. D1 Fill							2																								3										9
Rm. D1 Floor																																									
Flr. 2													41	2																											51
Rm. D2 Fill														5	11	5																									16
Rm. D3 Fill																																									12
Rm. D5 Fill																	6																								12
Rm. E1 Fill																																									
Rm. E2 Fill																19																									
Rm. F2 Fill																				1		6					3														67
Kiva Fill						6		44																																	
Walk-in 0-100												22			4											3		15	8												114
Well 100-200												10			12											4			2												21
Well 200-300															5											6			1	7											33
Meding Room												4																													20

Quantities do not include whole or restorable vessels.

116 • Mariana Mesa

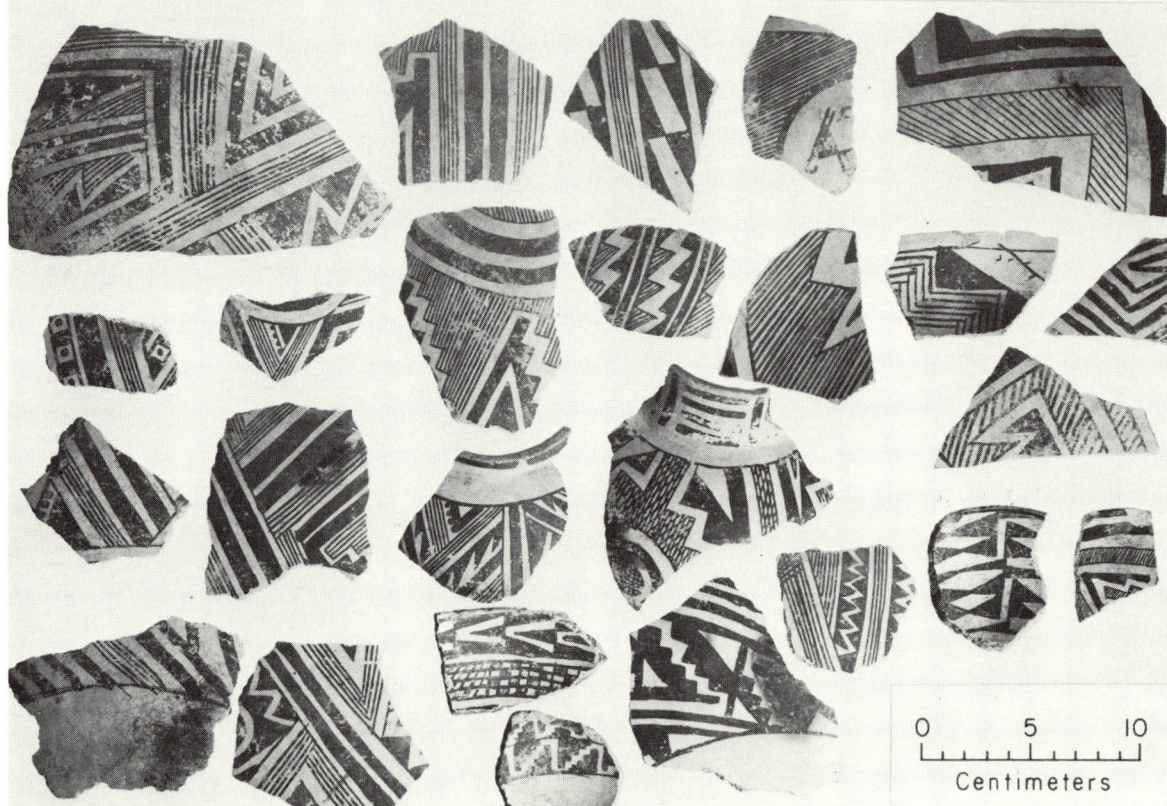

Figure 48. Decorative modes on black-on-white pottery from Site 616. Left section: decorative mode (c), 7 sherds; right section: range of variation and unusual specimens, 18 sherds.

were simply smaller, finer-lined versions of the same decorative modes found on the larger vessels.

Red-slipped Pottery

Greater diversity was evident in the red-slipped pottery at Site 616 than in either of the other major pottery categories: the white-slipped pottery and the corrugated ware. This diversity was evident in almost all aspects, from a wide range of paste color to a great variety of painted color combinations and decorative motifs.

MATERIAL: ROW A

1: Gray to tan to orange paste — mode key (F)
   Orange slip — mode (d)
   Black mineral paint — mode (a)
2: Gray to tan to orange paste — mode key (F)
   Orange slip — mode (d)
   Black glaze paint — mode (b)
3: Gray to tan to orange paste — mode key (F)
   Brick-red powdery slip — mode (e)
   Black mineral paint — mode (a)

4: Gray to tan to orange paste — mode key (F)
   Orange slip — mode (d)
   Black mineral paint, and white paint — modes (a) and (c)
5: Gray to tan to orange paste — mode key (F)
   Orange slip — mode (d)
   Black glaze paint, and white paint — modes (b) and (c)
6: Gray to tan to orange paste — mode key (F)
   Brick-red powdery slip — mode (e)
   Black mineral paint, and white paint — modes (a) and (c)

Despite the great diversity in the appearance of the paste of the redware, extensive observation and analysis failed to reveal any subdivisions with evidence of interpretative significance. For example, during the observation of the 100 restorable vessels recovered, ten subdivisions of paste color were recognized, four of paste appearance, five relating to the presence, location, and extent of a carbon core, two relative to paste texture and fracture, as well as numerous others concerning the slip, crackling, fire-clouding, and so on. These were all recorded on a large chart

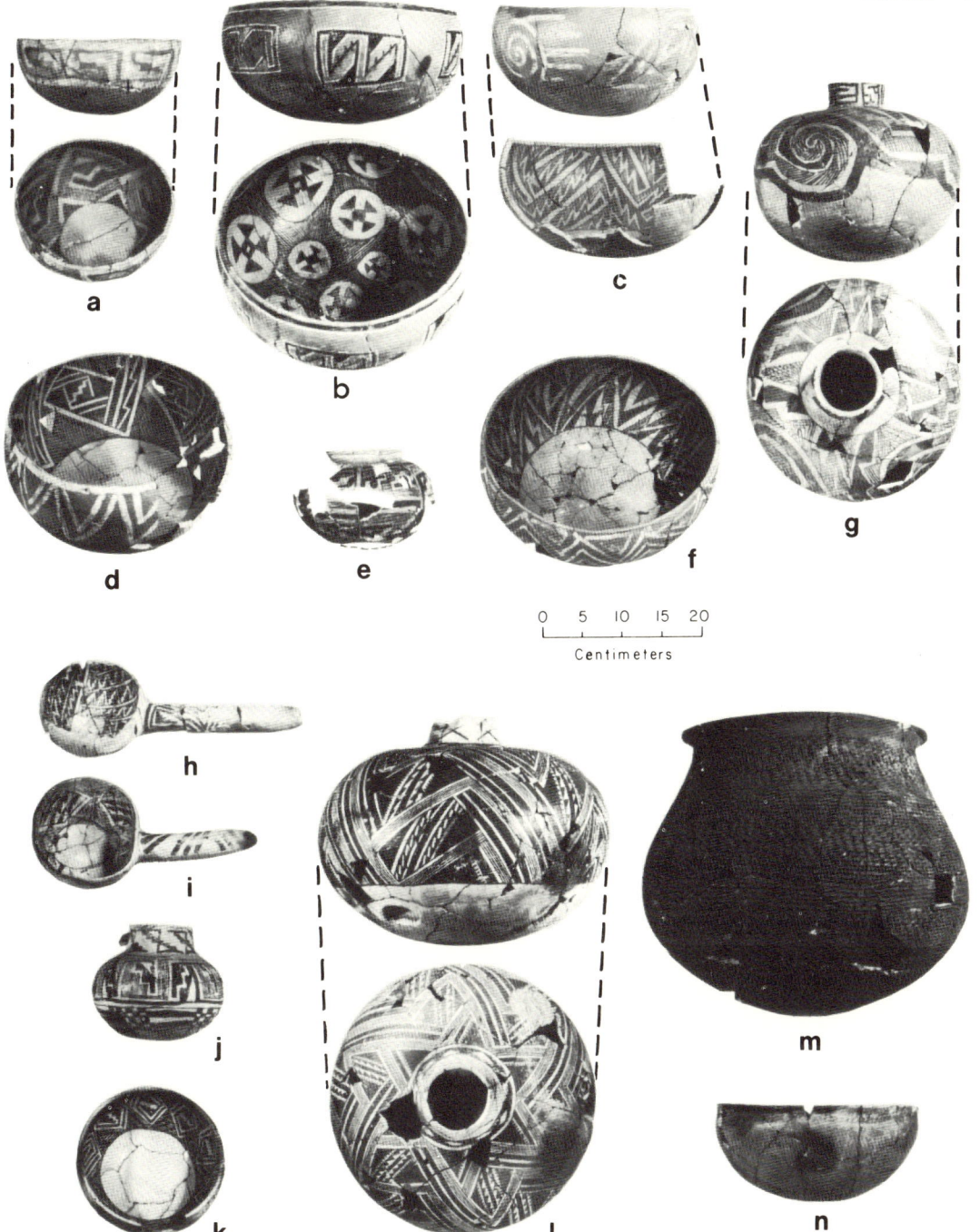

Figure 49. Pottery vessels found in Room D1, Site 616: a. floor, Vessel D15, St. Johns Polychrome bowl, #1758; b. floor, Vessel D16, Pinedale Polychrome bowl, #1754; c. floor, Vessel D11, St. Johns Polychrome bowl, #1762; d. fill, St. Johns Polychrome bowl; e. floor, Vessel D12, Pinedale Black-on-red jar; f. floor, Vessel D14, Heshotauthla Polychrome bowl, #1753; g. floor, Vessel D13, Puerco Black-on-red jar, #1496; h. floor, Vessel D19, Tularosa Black-on-white ladle, #1801; i. floor, Vessel D18, Tularosa Black-on-white ladle, #1756; j. fill, Reserve Black-on-white pitcher; k. floor, Vessel D17, Tularosa Black-on-white bowl, #1755; l. fill, Tularosa Black-on-white jar; m. floor, Vessel D110, corrugated jar, #1763 (1113); n. floor, Vessel D111, Tularosa Fillet-rim bowl, #1492 (1314).

which permitted visual correlation of one mode with any or all of the others and, of course, with nonceramic features as well. This revealed no single or multiple correlation of attributes with one another or in combination with nonceramic features. That some basic differences in material or technique were present seems probable, and failure to discover their pattern of occurrence provides further support for Shepard's (1956) contention that technological analysis is essential to any meaningful study of pottery materials and firing techniques.

The clay contained sufficient vegetal material to cause a dark black color when it was carbonized, which occasionally gave the cross section of sherds a speckled appearance. As the carbon disappeared the clay tended to become gray and light gray to tan. Often the very outside turned to tannish orange, pink, orange, and finally brown. On occasion the angular opaque inclusions could be definitely identified as fragmented sherds. The color-range of paste and slip of this tempering material corresponded to the paste.

Some of the black paint utilized on the red-slipped pottery resembled carbon paint. It was light in color and had a "soaked-in" appearance. However, it occurred directly alongside lines of paint that visually seemed to be basically mineral in composition. Probably this represented mineral paint that had been so watered down that only enough mineral remained to lend color but not substance to the mixture.

With rare exceptions the white paint was permanent. Nonetheless, it generally had a soft chalky aspect and no relief. On a number of vessels, all of which came from Areas B or C, this white paint had a hard finish with a creamy texture and a marked relief. Whether this reflected a difference in the constituent elements or simply in their proportions is not known. This type of white paint was usually associated with black-on-white-on-red decorative modes.

VESSEL SHAPES, AREAS PAINTED, AND COLORS COMBINED: ROW B

1: Bowl — mode (a)
   Interiors black-on-red — mode (a)
2: Bowl — mode (a)
   Interiors black-on-red; exteriors white-on-red — modes (a) and (d)
3: Bowl — mode (a)
   Interiors black-on-red; exteriors black-and-white-on-red — modes (a) and (e)
4: Bowl — mode (a)
   Interiors black-on-red; exteriors black-on-white-on-red, or black-on-white-on-red combined with white-on-red — modes (a), (f), and (g)
5: Bowl — mode (a)
   Interiors black-and-white-on-red or black-on-white-on-red; exteriors white-on-red — modes (b), (c), and (d)
6: Globular small-necked jar — mode (c)
   Exteriors black-on-red — mode (h)
7: Globular small-necked jar — mode (c)
   Exteriors black-and-white-on-red, or black-on-white-on-red — modes (e) and (f)
8: Ladle — mode (d)
   Interiors and/or exteriors black-on-red — modes (a) and (h)
9: Globular neckless (seed) jar, wide-necked globular jars and other forms — modes (c) and (e)
   Exteriors black-on-red — mode (h)

In contrast to the white-slipped bowls, the redware bowls were larger and consistently had slightly incurving rims. The jars also differed somewhat, having a more nearly circular rather than oval outline, and being in general slightly smaller.

A considerable number of red-slipped sherds bore no painted decoration but all appeared to be derived from the basal portions of painted vessels. There was no indication that any plain redware vessels were present.

SURFACE FINISH: ROW C

1: Slipped surfaces smooth and only slightly undulating; lustrous over entire surface, though the streaks of a hard polishing tool are occasionally apparent; the slip was polished before the paint was applied — modes (a), (e), (g), and (i)
2: Slipped surfaces smooth and only slightly undulating; lustrous over entire surface, though the streaks of a hard polishing tool are occasionally apparent; the slip was polished after the paint was applied — modes (a), (e), (h), and (i)

Surface Finish Type 2 occurred twice as often proportionately on jars as it did on bowls.

DECORATION: ROW D

Although the number of design elements employed was perhaps not much greater on the black-on-red vessels than on the black-on-white pottery, the variations in layout and motifs were much more numerous. Similarly, no single motif was dominant on the black-on-red wares analogous to mode (a) on the white-slipped pottery. Whereas the recognition of a small number of motifs permitted the description of almost the entire black-on-white sample, this did not prove possible with the black-on-red pottery. In fact, only three motifs were formally defined and even these did not follow any coherent pattern in design layouts and

Site 616 • 119

Figure 50. Black-on-red sherds from Site 616: a. examples showing the range of variation of designs; b. examples showing the range of variation of designs on sherds and one vessel (C51) all from a single room, C5.

overall patterning. The vast majority of the black-on-red wares bore designs, which, while the elements were readily recognizable, contained motifs that either could not be conceptualized or else occurred on only a small number of vessels. An attempt was made to study the distribution of even these small patterns of repetition; however, no significant distribution or associations could be recognized. The three motifs recognized were as follows:

1: Opposed interlocking solid and hatched scrolls. This mode is basically the same as mode (d) described for the black-on-white pottery. However, there is a much greater range of variation. Most of the examples are curvilinear, but a number of vessels were completed with a rectilinear version of this motif. The hatching lines are thin and of the same width as the bordering lines. They are evenly spaced, with the space between the lines being about as wide as the lines themselves. In general, the execution is good — mode (d).

2: Lines of opposed solid and hatched sawteeth. The utilization of this motif is similar in almost every respect to that of mode (a) on the black-on-white pottery. Usually the lines of pendent sawteeth are zigzag and the sawteeth interlock, resulting in a negative lightning pattern rather than touching at the tips (i.e., negative squares and parallelograms), a variation more common on black-on-white pottery. The hatching lines are thin and evenly spaced, and the execution is generally good — mode (e).

3: Rectilinear, thin and medium-width stripes with bands and areas of close parallel fine lines. While this mode, as defined, is much like modes (a), (b), and (c) on the black-on-white wares, the utilization and dominance of the motif is usually somewhat different. In fact, these aspects might better be called elements, for when the design as a whole can be viewed, they do not form the predominant motif of the vessel. Nevertheless, as seen on sherds, this often forms a characteristic or dominant motif — mode (c).

4: All other motifs and elements — mode (k).

Plain and Corrugated Pottery

The few sherds of plain undecorated pottery found at Site 616 differed in no respect from the corrugated pottery, other than their lack of corrugation. For descriptive purposes the plain and corrugated pottery are readily handled together.

MATERIAL: ROW A (PASTE MODES)

1: Brown paste with sand inclusions — mode key (H)

2: Gray paste with angular opaque inclusions — mode key (I)
3: Gray paste with coarse sand inclusions — mode key (J)

The paste of mode key (J) differed from that of mode key (I) in the proportion, amount, and size of the inclusions. Because of the consistent difference in color, the clay of mode key (H) would appear to be different from that of the other two modes. However, the occasional occurrence on an otherwise typical sherd of mode key (I) of an inner half whose color was nearly identical to that of mode key (H) suggests that this color differentiation may at least partially reflect a rather consistent difference in firing.

The gray pastes of corrugated pottery mode keys (I) and (J) differed from the gray pastes of the painted wares in being more consistently dense, shattering, and angular in appearance. The amount, proportion, and, to a lesser extent, the nature of the inclusions also differed.

VESSEL SHAPES: ROW B

1: Open-mouthed jar — mode (e).
2: Globular neckless (seed) jar — mode (b). This mode was represented by a single small plainware vessel and three sherds derived possibly from a single corrugated jar. The sherds were too small to permit the vessel shape to be reconstructed with confidence, but it would appear to more nearly approximate the seed jar form than any other.
3: Bowl — mode (a).
4: Jar with neck insloping from central inset ridge — mode (f).

The vast majority of the corrugated vessels were open-necked jars. Analysis of the sherds suggested that such jars constituted approximately 90 percent of the total number of vessels, most of the remainder being bowls. However, approximately one quarter of the whole or restored vessels were bowls. This latter proportion, while based on a smaller sample, may be more accurate, for the larger jars would naturally yield a larger number of sherds per vessel, thus skewing any estimate based on a sherd count alone. Jars with insloping necks, neckless seed jars, and miniature vessels of all shapes were rare. The basal portions of the jars with insloping necks were corrugated while the portions above the central ridge were plain. These vessels looked like corrugated bowls to which the upper portions of plainware seed jars had been added as an afterthought.

A possible fifth shape was suggested by a few sherds of descriptive types 1316 and 1318 from Rooms C4, C5, and C9. These sherds appeared to be from straight-sided, flat-bottomed "mugs" 9 to 10 cm in diameter and perhaps 15 cm high. In no instance were there enough sherds for the shape to be positively recognized or for any other attributes to be determined.

CONSTRUCTION AND SURFACE FINISH: ROW C

1: Coiled counterclockwise, indented with left thumb pointing up — mode (a)
   Interior surfaces smooth and even, coils unobliterated on exterior — mode (a)
2: Coiled clockwise, indented with right thumb pointing up — mode (c)
   Interior surfaces smooth and even, coils unobliterated on exterior — mode (a)
3: Coiled counterclockwise, indented with left thumb pointing down — mode (b)
   Interior surfaces smooth and even, coils unobliterated on exterior — mode (a)
4: Presumably coiled, direction unknown — mode (d)
   Exposed surfaces even, smooth, and lustrous —mode (b)
5: Presumably coiled, direction unknown — mode (d)
   Exposed surfaces even, gritty, and matte — mode (c)
6: Molded by hand — mode (e)
   Exposed surfaces undulating and gritty with only the high points lustrous — mode (d)

With the exception of two vessels, the corrugated pottery at Site 616 was constructed of counterclockwise coils that were annealed and indented, with the side of the left thumb pointing upward. One jar of gray paste had been coiled in a clockwise direction and annealed and indented with the right thumb pointing upward. One brownware jar had been annealed and indented with the left thumb pointing downward. Since in this latter instance the thumb did not extend over the entire coil, the lower edge of the coil did not receive any pressure, with the result that the lower edge below the indentations remained as a relatively high, readily observed ridge. There was no indication that the hand was changed when the base was turned over. Fingerprints could be observed macroscopically on most sherds, and a 14x glass would probably reveal them on nearly all of the others; but fingernail marks were extremely rare and never occurred on more than a small number of sherds from any one room or area.

DECORATIVE EFFECTS ON PLAIN AND CORRUGATED POTTERY: ROW D

0: Plain surface without corrugations or other decorative effects — mode (a)
1: Narrow clapboard corrugation — mode (b)
2: Indented corrugation — mode (c)
3: Pattern-indented corrugation — mode (d)
4: Plain and corrugated combined — mode (e)
5: Plain and corrugated combined, interior of vessel smudged — modes (c) and (g)
6: Pattern-indented corrugation, interior of vessel smudged — modes (d) and (g)
7: Indented corrugation, interior of vessel smudged — modes (c) and (g)
8: Narrow clapboard corrugation, interior of vessel smudged — modes (b) and (g)

The majority of the brown-paste bowls and jars and all but a single gray-paste sherd had overall clapboard corrugations and indentations. Three whole jars (E2 [2] and C10 [1]) had narrow clapboard indentations (mode [b]) while two bowls and 11 jars had patterned indentations (mode [d]). The pattern-indented vessels came from all areas of the site though most were from Area C. Fifteen to 20 percent of the brownware sherds were without indentations. Approximately 3 percent were indented only on certain areas so that the indentations formed a pattern (mode [d]).

Since most if not all sherds of descriptive type 1340 probably represented portions of the upper sections of vessels of shape mode (f), the only Site 616 vessels which were truly plainware were a few miniature bowls and the two small seed jars.

Bowls were the only vessel form to be smudged, and all but two of the whole corrugated bowls had been so treated. The smudged surfaces were very smooth and often had an almost metallic sheen. No pattern to their distribution was apparent.

POTTERY — PROBLEM TYPES

Regional Time-Space Types

Most of the pottery from Site 616 can be squeezed into already published descriptions of regional time-space pottery types, although on occasion considerable pressure is required. For comparative purposes, if for no other, it is essential to identify the pottery in terms of those types, but it is at least equally important to point up whether and in what manner the sample from Site 616 deviated from the norms established elsewhere. If these variations are overlooked or ignored, some of the most significant aspects of the pottery analysis are lost. While in many instances the deviation consisted simply of a slight shift from a central tendency previously established, in some cases it involved vessels which, while typical of the published description of a regional time-space type in most respcts, differed from it in one or more criteria normally considered critical in the definition of such types. These latter variations have usually been discussed as variants or varieties, but because these types

Table 2. Distribution by descriptive types of black-on-red sherds from Site 616.

Descriptive Types (A.B.C.D)	1.1.1.2	1.1.1.4	1.1.2.1	1.1.2.3	1.1.2.4	1.1.6.2	1.1.6.4	1.6.2.4	1.8.1.4	1.8.2.4	1.9.1.4	2.1.1.2	2.1.1.3	2.1.1.4	2.6.1.3	2.6.1.4	2.8.1.4	3.1.1.4	3.1.2.4	3.6.1.1	3.6.1.3	3.6.1.4	3.6.2.1	3.6.2.4	4.2.1.2
Totals 2984	15	491	12	3	58	5	329	19	1	11	4	9	1	11	1	71	1	2	53	15	41	5	1	20	24
Rm. A1 Fill 4					2																				
Rm. A2 Fill 10			3				4																		
Rm. A3 Fill 4																									
Rm. B1 Fill 16								3																	
Rm. B2 Fill 7																									
Rm. B2 Floor 8							2																		14
Rm. B3 Fill 26																1									
Rm. B5 Fill 61										5									2					3	
Rm. B7 Fill 38																1			2						
Rm. C1 Fill 294					13			15								6			19						
Rm. C2 Fill 29						5	2																	2	
Rm. C3 Fill 161			8				8	1												15				3	
Rm. C4 Fill 39														4					5						
Rm. C5 Fill 84		9			5		31												2						
Rm. C5 Floor 1																									
Rm. C6 Fill 100		38					3												4					2	
Rm. C7 Fill 92		34					35					3			1			1							
Rm. C8 Fill 111		58			1		15												2					5	
Rm. C9 Fill 319		58	4		7		15		1	6	4			2		4			4		41	5			4
Rm. C10 Fill 156		66			10		14					3													
Rm. D1 Fill 41							10					3													
Rm. D1 Floor 12							7																		
Rm. D1 Flr.2 11							4																		
Rm. D2 Fill 17							8																		
Rm. D3 Fill 23							9																		
Rm. D5 Fill 257	2	53		18			21												8				1		
Rm. E1 Fill 101		54		2			7									2									
Rm. E2 Fill 50							3																		
Rm. F1 Fill 13																									
Rm. F2 Fill 94							42																1		4
Rm. F2 Floor 44							18										1								
Kiva Fill 233		84					48									24			3						
Walk-in Well 0-100 248		37					5		1							19			2						
Walk-in Well 100-200 115							8									8									
Walk-in Well 200-300 54							10									1									
Mealing Room 111																4									5

Quantities do not include whole or restorable vessels.

Table 2. Distribution by descriptive types of black-on-red sherds from Site 616.

Quantities do not include whole or restorable vessels.

Descriptive Types → Provenience ↓	4-2-1-3	4-2-1-4	4-2-2-1	4-2-2-3	4-2-2-4	4-2-3-1	4-3-1-4	4-4-1-4	4-4-2-4	4-5-1-3	4-5-1-4	4-7-1-4	5-2-1-1	5-2-1-2	5-2-1-3	5-2-1-4	5-3-1-3	5-3-1-4	5-4-1-1	5-4-1-4	5-5-1-4	5-7-1-4	6-2-2-4	Bases
Totals	5	643	23	5	217	4	19	31	7	1	7	16	8	18	49	235	14	88	6	25	11	2	38	309
Rm. A1 Fill			1																					2
Rm. A2 Fill																								2
Rm. A3 Fill																								4
Rm. B1 Fill		1			5																			6
Rm. B2 Fill		6																						
Rm. B2 Floor		6	4																					
Rm. B3 Fill					30																			7
Rm. B5 Fill		1			22												1	3					3	25
Rm. B7 Fill		25			75																			83
Rm. C1 Fill		2														1		6						8
Rm. C2 Fill	5	39			39			1							10	58		18					3	16
Rm. C3 Fill		3			4		7		2					3		14		3						
Rm. C4 Fill		10		4												9								
Rm. C5 Fill																					1			
Rm. C5 Floor		27			21		1			1					18	2		9		7	2			
Rm. C6 Fill		6			1													5			2	2		
Rm. C7 Fill		18			2						2				6			1						
Rm. C8 Fill	5	35	10		4		4		1		1					5		12		3				60
Rm. C9 Fill		19												12	15			4	1	7			16	
Rm. C10 Fill												1												
Rm. D1 Fill/Floor Flr. 2																								
Rm. D2 Fill		3																						2
Rm. D3 Fill		16		2	11			5				1				11		9						61
Rm. D5 Fill		7		1	3			13				3	8			46		5		3				
Rm. E1 Fill		37										1						1						
Rm. E2 Fill								12																
Rm. F1 Fill		39														3							4	8
Rm. F2 Fill		22										8				19								9
Rm. F2 Floor		21														21								3
Kiva Fill		132		1			1				1							9		5	5			13
Walk-in 0-100		86														6		1		1	1	7		
Walk-in 100-200		19														22						5		
Walk-in 200-300		75		2							1					9		22						
Mealing Room																								

Table 3. Distribution by descriptive types of plain and corrugated sherds from Site 616.

Provenience	Descriptive Types	Corrugated Pottery															Plain		
	A	1	1	1	1	1	1	1	1	1	2	2	3	3	3	3	A	1	1
	B	1	1	1	2	3	3	3	3	4	1	3	1	1	1	3	B	3	3
	C	1	1	1	1	1	1	1	1	1	1	1	1	1	2	1	C	4	6
	D	1	2	3	7	5	6	7	8	4	2	2	1	2	2	2	D	0	0
Totals		5742	951	4094	158	3	8	14	210	27	50	199	12	1	11	1	3	Totals	29	26	3
Rm. A1	Fill	15	2	6					7											
Rm. A2	Fill	63	3	43	1							16								
Rm. A3	Fill	19	1	12			4					2								
Rm. B1	Fill	39	1	33					4						1					
Rm. B2	Fill	24	3	20								1								
Rm. B2	Floor	14	8	6																
Rm. B3	Fill	20	4	15											1					
Rm. B7	Fill	9		5	3										1					
Rm. B7	Floor	1		1																
Rm. C1	Fill	715	59	593	24				22	3	1	11	1		1				5	5	
Rm. C2	Fill	400	26	357	8				6			3							2	2	
Rm. C3	Fill	526	171	295	12				21	3	10		12				2				
Rm. C4	Fill	35	5	24	1				2	1		2									
Rm. C5	Fill	435	18	364	7			1	3	2	31	9									
Rm. C6	Fill	245	28	194	8				12	3											
Rm. C7	Fill	16	3	9								4							1	1	
Rm. C8	Fill	108	25	75			3		5										2	2	
Rm. C9	Fill	458	170	235	23				22	2		6							1	1	
Rm. C10	Fill	80	7	52	9		2		5		1	4									
Rm. C10	Floor	156	4	140	6				5			1									
Rm. D1	Fill	25	5	17					2			1									
Rm. D1	Floor	4	1	3																	
Rm. D1	Flr. 2	54	4	37	1							9			3				1	1	
Rm. D2	Fill	19	6	9					2			2									
Rm. D2	Floor	5		5																	
Rm. D3	Fill	181	2	170								8					1				
Rm. D5	Fill	383	88	232	12				9	1	2	37			2				5	3	2
Rm. E1	Fill	140	21	99	5	1			7			6			1				1		1
Rm. E2	Fill	446	65	336	18				6	2	4	15									
Rm. F1	Fill	5		5																	
Rm. F2	Fill	30	3	16				4	4			3									
Rm. F2	Floor	1										1									
Kiva	Fill	331	92	209	4				11	3		11			1				2	2	
Walk-in Well	0-100	387	59	260	14				30	6	1	16			1						
Walk-in Well	100-200	157	28	90	5				19			15							1	1	
Walk-in Well	200-300	61	17	39					2	1		2							2	2	
Mealing Room		135	22	88				7	4			14							6	6	

Quantities do not include whole or restorable vessels.

were established by others and because Mariana Mesa is geographically peripheral to most of the areas in which they occurred it was felt that it was inappropriate here to attempt to establish diagnostic criteria for these types on the basis of the present sample.

WHITE-SLIPPED POTTERY

Reserve Black-on-white

Descriptive types: 5113, 5115, 5118, 51110, 5313, 5712, 5718

Total: 158 sherds and 5 vessels

Reference: Martin and Rinaldo 1950, pp. 502–519

There have been numerous published descriptions of Reserve Black-on-white and Tularosa Black-on-white, which have been used as a basis for the discussion and for other references in this volume. They are not individually referred to here, but a comprehensive listing is available in Smith 1971, pp. 263–266; see also Barnett 1974, pp. 40–44, for additional illustrations. Considerations relative to dating appear in Breternitz 1966, p. 90.

The exposed surfaces of vessels from Site 616 were well polished and lustrous. They consistently had a thin, flat white slip through which the paste did not show. In this they differed from those described in the basic literature, for the latter frequently had a slip so thin that the paste was evident through it. A thin watery slip was used very rarely at Site 616 and did not occur in conjunction with other characteristic Reserve features. The form included pitchers, jars (some sherds so labeled may derive from pitchers), and ladles. The latter, unlike those described by Martin and Rinaldo, were slipped on the exterior as well as the interior. All of the black-on-white eccentric vessels (doughnut, shoe, duck, and miniature vessels) were of Reserve Black-on-white. The primary decorative mode on vessels of Reserve Black-on-white at Site 616 were modes (e), (h), (i), and (j). Decorative mode (b) and some sherds of mode (c) fell within the definition of Reserve Black-on-white, but at Site 616 these modes occurred almost entirely in conjunction with vessel forms and features not characteristic of Reserve Black-on-white.

Reserve Black-on-white: Variant A

Descriptive types: 1115, 1715, 1718, 1719
Total: 130 sherds

Martin and Rinaldo 1950, p. 502, note that on a few Reserve Black-on-white sherds the slip was thick enough to be seen in cross section with the naked eye, so that the specimens from Site 616 fell within the limits of their definition. This variant was segregated, however, to emphasize the fact that at Site 616 nearly half of the sample was thickly slipped rather than simply a few sherds otherwise characteristic of Reserve Black-on-white.

Reserve Black-on-white: Variant B

Descriptive types: 9138, 9139, 9538
Total: 4 sherds

The decoration of these sherds was typical of Reserve Black-on-white in execution and motifs employed but no slip was apparent.

Reserve Black-on-white: Variant C

Descriptive Types: 2111, 2112, 21110, 2412, 2718, 4712, 61110
Total: 32 sherds

With respect to general features and decorative style these sherds (with the possible exception of those in descriptive type 2111) were typical of Reserve Black-on-white except that a glaze paint had been utilized.

Reserve Black-on-white: Variant D

Descriptive types: 5138, 51310, 5433
Total: 80 sherds

These sherds differed from typical Reserve Black-on-white in that the slip was very thin and the surface had a matte appearance. Thus they resembled Socorro Black-on-white, but unlike Socorro all surfaces were well finished and the designs were those of Reserve Black-on-white.

Tularosa Black-on-white

Descriptive Types: 1111, 1112, 1113, 1114, 1116, 1117, 11111, 1122, 13111, 1411, 1412, 1413, 1414, 1416, 14111, 1422, 1711, 1712, 1713, 1714, 1716, 1722, 3111, 3112, 3113, 3114, 3115, 3116, 3414, 3416, 34111, 3711, 3713, 3714, 5114, 5116, 51111, 5123, 5411, 5421, 5711, 5714, 7123, 7423
Total: 5,283 sherds and 72 vessels
Reference: Rinaldo and Bluhm 1956, pp. 173–185

There have been numerous descriptions of Reserve Black-on-white and Tularosa Black-on-white, which have been used here as a basis for the discussion and for other references in this volume. They are not individually referred to here, but a comprehensive listing is available in Smith 1971, pp. 263–266; see also Barnett 1974, pp. 49–55, for additional illustrations. Considerations of dating appear in Breternitz 1966, pp. 98–99.

Although this large group of material was classified as Tularosa Black-on-white, only descriptive type 13111 (with a grand total of three examples) fulfilled all the published criteria. Neither Hawley 1936, pp. 46–47, nor Colton and Hargrave 1937, p. 240, mention the jar as a typical Tularosa form. Rinaldo and Bluhm 1956, pp. 180–184, indicate that jars constituted only about 16 percent of the collections sampled by them. However, it is readily apparent that at Site 616 the jar was the principal form of Tularosa pottery, constituting approximately 90 percent of the sample. Ladles and bowls were in the minority. The total count of jar sherds included an unknown proportion of pitcher sherds, but there was no indication that the pitcher was nearly as prominent or characteristic as it has been reported to be elsewhere.

Colton and Hargrave 1937, p. 240, specifically state that Tularosa bowls (and presumably ladles or dippers) were not slipped on the exterior, whereas at Site 616 only one bowl was not slipped on the exterior, and it was not slipped on the interior either. Only two whole ladles were found that had not been slipped on both interior and exterior. Rinaldo and Bluhm 1956, p. 179, state that bowl exteriors were usually slipped. Despite these local differences this group of pottery formed a cohesive unit that fulfilled, in the main, the descriptive requirements of Tularosa Black-on-white.

With a few exceptions this pottery was well finished, lustrous, with polishing marks only occasionally evident. Firing clouds occurred but were not frequent. Decorative motif I was found on 58 percent of the sample. No other motif was particularly prominent and decorative modes (h), (i), and (j) did not occur at all.

Tularosa Black-on-white: Variant A

Descriptive types: 1811, 1812, 1813, 3813
Total: 17 sherds

This small group of ladles was distinctive in that both the exterior and the interior of the bowl sections of the vessels were not only slipped but painted as well.

Aberrant Black-on-white Sherds

Descriptive types: 1613, 3419, 52111, 5433, 6636, 7132, 7433, 8132
Total: 16 sherds

These few sherds did not fall within the range of any published type but none of the variations appeared to have sufficient significance to warrant establishing a new type.

The ladles of descriptive types 1613 and 6636 differed from most of the sample from Site 616 primarily in not being slipped on the exterior of the bowl section. Descriptive type 6636 also had a matte surface.

Descriptive type 3419 was unusual chiefly because its checkerboard design was not generally found on Tularosa vessels, while the seed jar of descriptive type 52111 was an unusual form. The remainder most nearly resembled Reserve Black-on-white: Variant D, but in addition to having a matte appeareance, a thin and/or watery slip was employed and, in descriptive type 8132, glaze paint as well.

RED-SLIPPED POTTERY

Puerco Black-on-red

Descriptive types: 1112, 1114, 1612, 1614, 1624, 1814, 1824, 1914
Total: 775 sherds (maximum: 876; minimum: 370) and 18 vessels. (Descriptive types 1112 and 1114 could be from the bases of either Puerco Black-on-red or St. Johns Polychrome vessels. A somewhat arbitrary 80 percent of these two descriptive types are included here.)

Compiled references to published descriptions of Puerco Black-on-red and Wingate Black-on-red appear in Carlson 1970, pp. 7–17; see also Barnett 1974, pp. 38, 56, for additional illustrations. Dating is considered in Breternitz 1966, pp. 89, 102–103, and Carlson 1970, pp. 9, 15–16. The two types were combined at the Second Southwestern Ceramic Conference in 1959, where Puerco Black-on-red was regarded as a late variant of Wingate Black-on-red, and in the dating analyses in this volume they are considered together. Carlson 1970, p. 9, however, regards Puerco Black-on-red as still a "valid" type.

Although the temper was primarily of opaque angular fragments, the frequency of sand was slightly greater than usual in the other black-on-red types at Site 616. It occurred in almost half of the vessels and two vessels also contained what appeared to be fragments of calcite. The jar form was almost as prominent as the bowl form. A few ladles were also found. The vessels were well polished, though marks of the polishing tool were occasionally quite evident, and not noticeably less well done than vessels of St. Johns Polychrome, which they closely resembled in overall coloring and execution. A few pieces had been polished after the application of the black paint, a technique normally associated, at sites other than Site 616, with St. Johns Polychrome.

Wingate Black-on-red

Descriptive types: 3114, 3124, 3611, 3613, 3614, 3621, 3624
Total: 137 sherds and 2 vessels

The paste of these sherds was like that of Puerco Black-on-red but the slip was a dark brick-red, thickly applied. The slip was never crackled but tended to be powdery and to wear away more readily than the occasionally crackled, orange-red slip of Puerco Black-on-red. The design execution was somewhat careless with the lines wavy and of variable thickness. Contrary to the general rule for black-on-red bowls at Site 616, the two whole vessels had straight rather than incurving rims. Jar sherds made up more than half of the sample and 63 sherds (almost all jar sherds) had been polished prior to the application of the paint. (See comment following Puerco Black-on-red, above.)

Wingate Polychrome

Descriptive type: 6224
Total: 38 sherds

Compiled references to published descriptions of Wingate Polychrome appear in Carlson 1970, pp. 17–27; see also Barnett 1974, p. 56, for additional illustrations. Dating is considered in Breternitz 1966, p. 103, and Carlson 1970, pp. 23–25.

This type appears to consist of Wingate Black-on-red bowls with the addition of a white exterior design similar to that found on St. Johns Polychrome. It is probable that a number of sherds deriving from Wingate Polychrome vessels were counted as Wingate Black-on-red.

St. Johns Polychrome

Descriptive types: 1112, 1114, 1121, 1123, 1124, 4212, 4213, 4214, 4221, 4223, 4224, 4513, 4514
Total: 1,084 sherds (maximum: 1,489; minimum: 983) and 37 vessels. (Descriptive types 1112 and 1114 could be from the bases of St. Johns Polychrome or Puerco Black-on-red vessels. A somewhat arbitrary 20 percent of these descriptive types are included here.)

Compiled references to published descriptions of

St. Johns Polychrome appear in Carlson 1970, pp. 31–41; see also Barnett 1974, pp. 46–48, for additional illustrations. Dating is considered in Breternitz 1966, pp. 93–94, and Carlson 1970, p. 39.

Vessel walls were slightly thicker than reported elsewhere, ranging from 5 to 11 mm. The average vessel wall was 7 mm thick. The slip was thickly applied, often crackled, and generally orange-red. A central carbon streak in the core was rare and occasionally some vessels were overfired. The design execution was average but on some vessels the designs were carelessly proportioned. Over half of the sample had been polished prior to application of the paint. There was considerable diversity in the combination and placement of both the black and the white decoration.

Heshotauthla Polychrome

Descriptive types: 2112, 2113, 2114, 2613, 2614, 2814, 5211, 5212, 5213, 5214, 5514

Total: 541 sherds and 26 vessels

Compiled references to published descriptions of Heshotauthla Polychrome appear in Carlson 1970, pp. 82–83. Dating is considered in Breternitz 1966, p. 77.

There was more variation in wall thickness both within and between vessels of this type than in most of the pottery from Site 616. Vessel walls were from 4 to 9 mm thick and while individual variation was generally less than 2 mm, one vessel was 4 mm thick at the base (with no wear apparent) and 8 mm at the rim. The temper consisted of angular opaque material and occasional quartz. In a few vessels there was some rock temper and what appeared to be calcite fragments. The slip was orange or red-orange and was thickly applied. Bowls were the most popular form but there were a number of jars and one ladle.

Pinedale Polychrome

Descriptive types: 4311, 4314, 4714, 5313, 5314

Total: 141 sherds and 6 vessels

Compiled references to published descriptions of Pinedale Polychrome appear in Carlson 1970, pp. 47–53; see also Barnett 1974, p. 37, for additional illustrations. Dating is considered in Breternitz 1966, p. 88, and Carlson 1970, pp. 51–53.

Basically angular opaque temper was present but a few sherds appeared to have rock temper as well. A carbon streak was found in about half of the vessels and a few had a crackled surface. The slip was orange-red to brick-red and generally thickly applied. The exterior black band was usually continuous with white bordering lines above and below, but occasionally the border was on only one side. On some vessels the exterior design consisted of individual design units bordered by thin white lines.

Springerville Polychrome

Descriptive types: 4414, 4424, 5411, 5414, 5514, 5714

Total: 90 sherds and 4 vessels

Compiled references to published descriptions of Springerville Polychrome appear in Carlson 1970, pp. 41–47. Dating is considered in Breternitz 1966, p. 96, and Carlson 1970, p. 45.

This pottery normally was decorated with a black-on-red interior and a black-on-white-on-red exterior. The black paint was a glaze, dull or with a slight luster, a slight relief, and a tendency to crackle. The white paint was hard, creamy in appearance, and thickly applied so that it had a slight relief. The slip was orange-red, thickly applied. In the sample from Site 616 only angular opaque temper was noted, a carbon streak was very rare, and the vessels were frequently overfired. The vessel walls were 6 to 8 mm thick, the average being 7 mm. Interior bowl designs were confined within a band and were similar to those of Pinedale Polychrome. Exterior decoration consisted of a broad stripe (3 to 5 cm wide) of white paint placed one centimeter or more below the rim, with the addition of black decoration, generally consisting of individual units, placed upon this white stripe. On the rare jars both black-on-red and black-on-white-on-red decoration occurred on the exterior. On a few bowls the interior black decoration was supplemented by occasional white bordering lines.

OTHER TYPES

Pinedale Black-on-red: 3 vessels
Klageto Black-on-yellow: 1 vessel
Klageto Polychrome: 1 vessel
Showlow Polychrome: 1 vessel
Querino Polychrome: 1 vessel

These vessels each conformed reasonably well to the published descriptions and in any event the significance of variations observed on only a single example is difficult to assess. In the case of Klageto Black-on-yellow and Klageto Polychrome no type sherds were available for visual comparison but their similarity to the published descriptions was very close.

USEFULNESS OF DIAGNOSTIC FEATURES

From the foregoing considerations one point seems evident, which may account for some of the difficulties experienced by authors in identifying specific diagnostic features for regional time-space, artisan, or other problem types: individual attributes or even attribute combinations are generally not unique to a specific type; rather it is a varying combination of attributes, or several sets of attributes interdigitated in various ways, which serve to set aside a collection of sherds or vessels that exemplify a specific type in the mind of the analyst. This apparent "fact" emphasizes even more strongly the need for providing the reader with the diagnostic features of specific descriptive types included in each problem type.

WHOLE AND RESTORABLE VESSELS

All whole and restorable vessels recovered from Site 616 are listed according to provenience and regional time-space types in table 4.*

Artisan Types

The white-slipped pottery at Site 616 can be grouped into three somewhat overlapping but nonetheless distinctive sets of attributes. Since very probably all were essentially contemporary, one must look elsewhere for a suggested explanation of these differences.

Although there are differences in the percentages of various vessel forms asociated with each set, the three main vessel forms (jars, bowls, and ladles) were common to all, so if function was the determinant, it is of a more subtle (to the archaeologist) nature than gross use. The hypothesis that the sets represent slight differences in taste — either by those constructing or by those using the vessels does not appear to negate the little evidence available; therefore the term "artisan type" is suggested. (For further discussions see pp. 54–55.)

Descriptive type designations written with a single numeral and three dashes (e.g., 1---, ---5, --2-, or the like) signify that the mode indicated by the numeral is the common denominator of all specimens under

---

*My review of the manuscript in the 1970s revealed one very unfortunate (and embarrassing) omission. I had finished the analysis and nearly all of the writing of the report just before leaving Cambridge for a two-and-one-half-year stint in Panama. Evidently during the process of arranging for this expedition and completing the dissertation, the descriptive types of the whole vessels were either not noted down or were lost. The only record found was of their regional time-space identifications. I located the descriptive type designations of some of them in my original laboratory records, and a major effort was made when I was in Cambridge in 1970 to relocate and redevelop the descriptive types of all of the whole and restored vessels. For a variety of reasons this proved impossible and thus severely reduced my ability to discern artisan types or any other of the many problem types that might have been approached with a whole-vessel sample of the size of that from Site 616. The only positive aspect of this situation was my discovery that after 20 years it was possible (after a refresher course in definitions) to return to those whole vessels that I did review and with considerable ease I was able to develop the descriptive types — with, in the admittedly few instances where I had the earlier records, impressive consistency. The next and truest test would be to see if someone else could also do so on the whole vessels or on the sherds.

consideration and that all other modes in the formula may be variable in this context.

Artisan Type A

Descriptive types: 5113, 5114, 5115, 5116, 5118, 51110, 51111, 5123, 5138, 51310, 52111, 5313, 5411, 5421, 5433, 5711, 5712, 5714, 5718, 7123, 7132, 7433

Total: 331 sherds

Diagnostic features: A thin or watery white slip (5--- and 7---) was universal to vessels of this type.

Over 90 percent of decorative mode (j) (---10) was associated with this slip, as was over 80 percent of decorative mode (h) (---8). Decorative mode (e) (---5) was also relatively popular, especially on jars. In contrast, decorative mode (b) (---2) was almost absent (6 sherds) and decorative modes (a) and (c) (---1, ---3) were rare (20 sherds). Approximately 80 percent of this type was well made and lustrous while the other 20 percent, while well made, had only the high points lustrous; in fact 90 percent of the sherds with only the high points lustrous at Site 616 were associated with this type. Approximately 76 percent of the vessels were jars, 19 percent ladles, and 3 percent bowls. The high proportion of ladles was somewhat in contrast to the other two types. This type also included the only two seed jar sherds and six of the nine pitcher sherds.

The thin, watery slip may be just a sloppy or careless version of this. Four of the six sherds with this slip also had the poorly done surface modes (a), (f), and (g) (--2-).

All in all, this type constituted a technologically distinctive and readily recognizable pattern.

Artisan Type B

Descriptive types: 1111, 1112, 1113, 1114, 1115, 1116, 1117, 11111, 1122, 13111, 1411, 1412, 1413, 1414, 1416, 14111, 1422, 1613, 1711, 1712, 1713, 1714, 1715, 1716, 1718, 1719, 1722, 1811, 1812, 1813

Total: 2,926 sherds

Diagnostic attributes: A white slip thickly applied in association with mineral paint (mode key A) (1---).

Over 90 percent of the vessels were jars, slightly under 8 percent ladles, and only 1 percent bowls, a distribution not unlike that of Type A without the rare forms. Like Type A too, there were a few poorly finished specimens. In contrast, however, slightly over 84 percent of Type B was decorated with decorative modes (a), (b), and (c) (---1, ---2, ---3) while only 13 percent of Type A had these modes. In fact, 68 percent of Type B was decorated with mode (c) (---3). Interestingly, on this type, unlike the other two, there appeared small percentages of every decorative mode other than mode (j) (---10).

Artisan Type C

Descriptive Types: 3111, 3112, 3113, 3114, 3115, 3116,

Site 616 • 129

Table 4. Distribution by regional time-space types of whole and restorable pottery vessels from Site 616.

Vessel type and shape	Totals	A 1 Floor	A 2 Fill	A 3 Fill	B 1 Fill	B 1 Floor	B 2 Fill	B 2 Floor	B 5 Floor	B 7 Floor	C 1 Fill	C 1 Floor	C 2 Fill	C 2 Floor	C 3 Fill	C 4 Fill	C 4 Floor	C 5 Fill	C 5 Floor	C 6 Fill	C 7 Fill	C 8 Fill	C 9 Fill	C 10 Floor	D 1 Floor	D 2 Fill	D 3 Fill	D 5 Fill	E 1 Fill	E 2 Fill	E 2 Floor	F 1 Fill	F 2 Fill	Kiva Floor	M 34	M 35	M 36	M 6	M 33
	240	4	1	1	4	3	3	9	2	1	25	3	26	3	11	5	2	30	4	6	3	5	11	11	4	12	8	5	15	2	7	2	1	5	1	1	1	3	1	1
Reserve B-W, jar	11												10			1																								
Reserve B-W, pitcher	2												1						1																					
Reserve B-W, doughnut vessel	1															1																								
Reserve B-W, duck figurine	4													1				1	1																				1
Reserve B-W, mini jar	1																	1																						
Reserve B-W, mini ladle	1																																						1
Tularosa B-W, jar	28								1		6				4			4				1	2		1		3					2	1		1				
Tularosa B-W, ladle	12	2						1	1		1		1			2		1						1	1	2	1								1				
Tularosa B-W, bowl	2						1																	1		1														
Tularosa B-W, seed jar	2																				1			1			1													
Tularosa B-W, mini jar	4																						3	1		1														
Tularosa B-W, mini bowl	1																							1																
Tularosa B-W, mini seed jar	1										1																													
Puerco B-R, jar	6				2																																			
Puerco B-R, ladle	3												1						1	1								3												
Puerco B-R, bowl	4																					1					1*													
Puerco B-R, seed jar	2																		1							1	1													
Puerco B-R, mini jar	2				1																			1																
Puerco B-R, mini pitcher	1										1																	1												
Pinedale B-R, jar	1		1																																					
Pinedale B-R, bowl	2																																							
Pinedale B-R, seed jar	1																																							
Wingate B-R, bowl	1				1																																			
Wingate B-R, seed jar	2										1												1																
Klageto B-Y, jar	1									1																														
Heshotauthla Poly., bowl	26				1			3			5		1										3	3	2	1	1	2	1			2	1						
Klageto Poly., jar	1																																							1
Pinedale Poly., bowl	4								1		1													1	2	1														
Pinedale Poly., seed jar	2							1							1	1											1													
Querino Poly., legged vessel	1								1																															
Shoulou Poly., bowl	1																													1										
Springerville Poly., bowl	4						1							1														1	1											
St. Johns Poly., jar	2																		1																				1
St. Johns Poly., ladle	1										1																													
St. Johns Poly., bowl	33	2											4		1			5		3						2	1	4											
Brown paste, mode key (H), Corr. jar	38						2						6		6	1		5					2	2		1		2	3		5		3				1		
Brown paste, mode key (H), Corr. bowl	17												1	1		1	1	1				1	1	2		1			1								1		
Brown paste, mode key (H), Corr. mini jar	3								1				1																											
Brown paste, mode key (H), Corr. mini bowl	3							1				1						1																						
Gray paste, mode key (I), Corr. jar	4																																							
Gray paste, mode key (J), Corr. jar	2																											1										1	
Tularosa Fillet Rim, bowl	1																																		1				
Tularosa Fillet Rim, mini bowl	1					1																																		
Brown paste, mode key (H), Plain seed jar	1																																							
Brown paste, mode key (H), Plain mini ladle	1																									1													
Brown paste, mode key (H), Plain mini bowl	1																													1									
Unfired or partially fired, mini bowl	3																																							

*Fragment reworked into a puki?

3414, 3416, 3419, 34111, 3711, 3713, 3714, 3813

Total: 764 sherds

Diagnostic attributes: A creamy slip, thickly applied, in association with mineral paint (3---).

Again, jars were the most popular form (90 percent), ladle popularity approximated Type B, while the popularity of the bowl form approximated Type A.

In addition to the slip, this type was distinctive in its emphasis on decorative modes (a) (---1) (20 percent), (b) (---2) (15 percent), and (d) (---4) (15 percent). Decorative mode (c) (---3) was popular (50 percent) but had not quite the dominance associated with this decorative mode in Type B. The total dominance of modes (a), (b), and (c) on Types B and C set these two types apart from Type A. In this sample at least, all Type C sherds were well finished and lustrous.

OTHER OBJECTS OF CLAY

In addition to the objects discussed below there were several dozen sherds which had been roughly chipped and/or ground to a circular form. No exact count was made of these objects (often termed "silver dollars"). They ranged in diameter from 1.5 to 10 cm with an average of approximately 4 cm. They were made from black-on-white, black-on-red, and corrugated pottery, with black-on-white appearing to predominate. Many of the inset handles from broken jars were apparently saved and their broken edges smoothed so that they could have served as small bowl-like receptacles. Sherds were sometimes used for chinking in the construction of walls and as scoops, set adjacent to the lower left or rarely the lower right (e.g., large room associated with the walk-in well) corner of mealing bins.

Sherd Scrapers: 5 specimens

On four of these scrapers one edge of the sherd had been worn down by abrasion from both sides, giving it a knifelike edge; on the other specimen (Room E2) the abrasion was on one side only. All five specimens were fragmentary, so the total length of the scraping edge could not be determined but in three instances it was at least 7 cm. Four of the fragments were derived from black-on-white jar sherds while the fifth (Room E2) was from a black-on-red bowl. It is difficult to say whether the fact that all five derived from the fill or the floor of subterranean structures has any interpretive significance.

Fill

Room D5 (1); kiva (3)

Floor

Room E2 (1)

Pipes: 3 specimens

Two of the pipes were too fragmentary for the shape to be determined. The third (Room D5, fill, fig. 60k) was an elbow pipe. Its stem was 2.5 cm long, the overall length being 4.5 cm. The stem was of a constant diameter (1.3 cm) and the basal portion was flattened. The diameter of the bowl was 1.3 cm; its depth could not be determined. The fragment from Room C9 was simply a portion of a clay tube and may not represent a pipe stem. However, the hardness of the clay, the lack of inclusions, and the well-finished exterior all made it resemble the other two specimens. In its entirety this stem must have been approximately 1 cm in diameter. The fragment from Room E2 (fig. 60l) was also a pipe stem, circular in cross section and enlarging from a diameter of 0.7 cm at the end to 1.7 cm at the beginning of the bowl. The stem itself was only 2.5 cm in length. The center stem holes on the three specimens ranged from 0.2 to 0.3 cm.

Fill

Room C9 (1); Room D5 (1); Room E2 (1)

Toy Vessels: 4 specimens

Four vessels were so small that they might have served as toys. One (Room E2, fill), a somewhat square bowl with a slightly rounded bottom, unpainted, and roughly finished, was 5 cm in diameter and 2 cm deep. This specimen was about the same size and could have served in the same capacity as the reused inset jar handles. The second specimen (Room D1, fill) was a small unpainted ladle with a bowl diameter of 2 cm and a depth of 1 cm. The two other miniature bowls were unfired. One from the firepit of Room D1 was well shaped and of normal bowl proportions. It had a diameter of 2.5 cm and a depth of 1.5 cm. The remaining specimen (Room C2, fill) appeared to be little more than a smoothed clay ball into which a finger had been pressed and the hole somewhat enlarged; its diameter was 2.8 cm with an overall height of 2.7 cm. These could well have been made by rather than for children, as can be observed today in the modern Hopi towns.

Fill

Room D1 (1); Room C2 (1); Room E2 (1)

Firepit

Room D1 (1)

Figurines: 2 specimens

From the fill of Room D5 came a fragment of clay which appeared to be the barrel-like body (4.2 cm

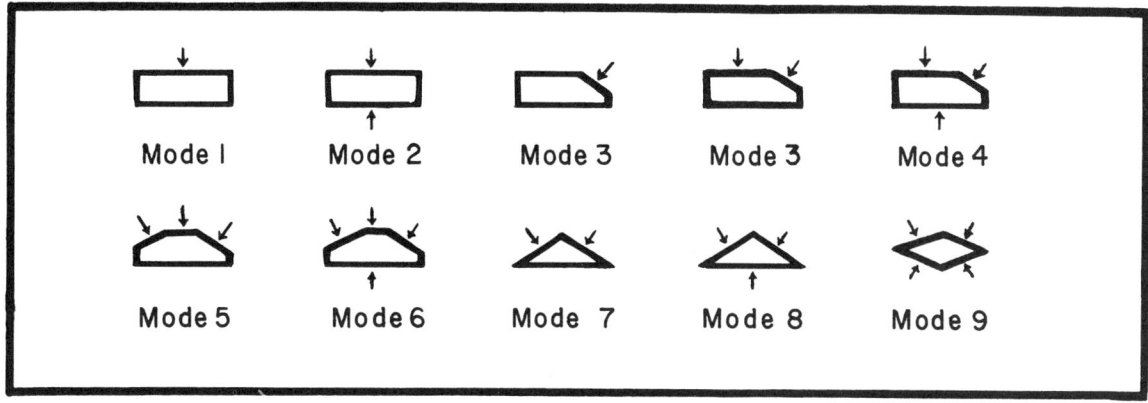

Figure 51. Profiles of mano shapes from Site 616, illustrating the descriptive modes.

long and 2.5 cm thick) of an animal figurine. The tail, legs, and head had been broken off, so identification was impossible. A second specimen from the same area appeared to be half of a body (2.5 cm in diameter) with short, bulbous, tripodlike extensions from the unbroken end, which could represent portions of two legs and the tail or, alternatively, two legs and the head.

Fill

Room D5 (2)

STONE ARTIFACTS

Manos: 273 specimens (fig. 108)

Manos were the largest class of stone implements recovered from Site 616. The quantity of material and the number of pertinent observations resulted in such variation that basic description by typological sets is impractical and descriptive typology is necessary. The various sets of modes are discussed individually while the occurrence of these modes on individual artifacts and their provenience is given in table 6.

MATERIAL: ROW A

Mode 1: Sandstone: 205 specimens

The sandstone utilized was quite hard and fine-grained. No attempt was made to differentiate various grades of coarseness. Approximately 75 percent of the manos at Site 616 were of sandstone and this proportion was relatively constant in all areas of the site.

Mode 2: Vesicular basalt: 50 specimens

Although the metates of vesicular basalt were graded in the field, no variations in the grain of the manos were noted. Insofar as can be determined from the photographs, all were medium-coarse-grained. All of the manos with finger grips and all but one of the manos that appear to have been used on trough metates were of basalt. (No trough metates were found at Site 616.) Forty-one of the specimens were rectangular in cross section.

Mode 3: Calcareous tuff: 18 specimens

This material consisted of hard fragments up to 1 cm in size, cemented with slightly softer material, which erodes or wears more rapidly so that the stone makes an excellent abrader. Half of these manos came from Area C (Room, 1, 2, 9, 10); the rest were scattered over most of the remaining areas of the site. None were found in Area E, the walk-in well, or the kiva. All but four of the 17 that had seen service had been held and used at an angle to the main flat surface.

SHAPE: ROW B

These manos were all rectangular or rounded rectangular in outline, but there was considerable variation in their transverse cross section and the number of surfaces used for grinding (fig. 51).

Mode O: Mano-shaped objects showing no sign of abrasion: 14 specimens

The length and width of these blanks corresponded closely with those of the rest of the manos, although five were the longest specimens recovered. Apparently the inhabitants held no definite notions as to the desirable thickness of new manos (at least within fairly broad limits) for these blanks showed as much variation as the used specimens, ranging from 5.8 cm to 1.6 cm thick. Eight of the 14 specimens came from the four rooms that were equipped with three or more mealing bins. For the site as a whole the ratio of blanks relative to the three materials used was fairly constant, ranging from one blank for every 16 manos of basalt to one blank for every 19 manos of sandstone.

The rectangular cross section was apparently the basic design for all manos, the other cross section shapes developing as the manos were used.

Mode 1: Rectangular in cross section, one face used: 40 specimens

One of the large flat surfaces of manos in this mode was used for fore-and-aft grinding. Pressure must have been exerted fairly evenly or else the mano was reversed frequently, for in almost every instance the used surface remained approximately parallel to the unused surface.

Mode 2: Rectangular in cross section, two faces used: 60 specimens

On manos of this mode both of the broad flat parallel surfaces were utilized for grinding. The surfaces were parallel.

Mode 3: Semiwedge-shape in cross section, one or two faces used: 11 specimens

The manos in this mode (and those of subsequent modes) had been used in a manner similar to those of mode 1 but, in addition, they had been held so that the mano as a whole was at a slight angle to the surface of the metate and thus an additional face was worn. On some specimens the angle of this sloping face to the initial face was very small, on others as much as 30°, but in general it ranged between 10° and 20°. On most, the ridge separating the two used faces was quite evident but on some the line separating the two was rounded, suggesting that the users of these manos had tended to blend the motions that resulted in the two faces, rather than making them separate and distinct actions.

On three of the manos of mode 3 only the angled face was worn, suggesting that both the parallel and angled grinding motions were, or at least could be, distinct rather than necessarily related or sequential movements.

Mode 4: Semiwedge-shape in cross section, three faces used: 19 specimens

The manos in this mode were used in a manner similar to those of mode 2 but, in addition, one long edge of one face had been worn at an angle (i.e., in the manner of mode 3).

Mode 5: Truncated pyramid in cross section, three faces used: 14 specimens

Apparently the cross section of these manos was the result of using at an angle both long edges of the used face of a mano of mode 1. The transition between the three surfaces was quite evident but the line or ridge dividing them was often rounded rather than sharp.

Mode 6: Truncated pyramid in cross section, four faces used: 5 specimens

These manos were like those of mode 5 except that, like manos of mode 2, the second large flat surface had been used for grinding.

Mode 7: Triangular in cross section, two faces used: 50 specimens

In manos of this mode the two used faces, both used at an angle, met, forming the apex of the triangle. Whether these manos were never used in any way but at an angle or whether they simply represent well-worn specimens of mode 5 could not be determined.

Mode 8: Triangular in cross section, three faces used: 41 specimens

The manos in this mode were similar to those of mode 7 except that the larger "basal" surface also had been used for grinding as in mode 6.

Mode 9: Diamond-shape in cross section, four faces used: 21 specimens

Most of these specimens were what might be termed "double mode 3," that is, with parallel initial used surfaces, one edge of each of which (in every case the diametrically opposed edge) had also been used at an angle. However, some appeared to be like a "double mode 7" and were more truly diamond-shaped in cross section. On those specimens where the angle of the two used faces was slight and the separating ridge rounded, the used area approached that of a single convex grinding surface, but in general the delineation of the two faces was well marked.

Although it was not considered as a separate mode during analysis, it was noted that a number of the large grinding surfaces were slightly convex in the short dimension rather than flat. This convexity occurred on 23 manos of sandstone, 13 of basalt, and 3 of calcareous tuff.

FINGER GRIPS: ROW C

Mode 1: Presence of finger grips: 6 specimens

The practice of pecking shallow notches or grooves into the sides of manos was known but occurred only rarely. Two of the six specimens, one from the surface and one from Room C2, had a groove on only one side. All were of basalt, one (from Room B5) had been used on a trough metate, and four of the six appeared to have been constructed (two were broken) in accordance with the small-size type.

Mode 2: Absence of finger grips: 197 specimens

Mode 3: Original presence of finger grips not known: 70 specimens

Fragmentary manos and those that had been used to such an extent that the edges had become a sharp line are included here. Since the overwhelming majority of the other manos were without finger grips, it is probably safe to assume that most of these specimens similarly lacked them.

ASSOCIATED METATE TYPE: ROW D

Mode 1: Flat from end-to-end: 265 specimens

Mode 2: Flat to slightly convex end-to-end on the major portion of the surface, with the grinding surface extending up onto the ends of the mano in a smooth curve: 8 specimens

These modes were delineated to determine the shape of the metate on which the manos were used on the assumption that manos conforming to mode 1 probably had been used only on flat metates while those of mode 2 had seen some service on trough metates. Although eight manos of mode 2 were found, not even a fragment of a trough metate was encountered at Site 616. Perhaps these eight represent "heirlooms."

SIZE

There appears to have been one major action type with regard to the size of manos at Site 616. However, six basalt manos and one of tuff were made in accordance with a second norm some 10 cm shorter than the first (see table 5). All manos of tuff and all but two of basalt conformed closely to one of these two size types. One of the aberrant specimens of basalt was exceptionally small (14 by 7.8 by 2.7 cm, descriptive type 2221, from Room C9, floor); the other was, for a basalt mano, unusually large in all dimensions (41 by 13.5 by 6 cm, descriptive type 2021, from Room B2, fill).

The general shape of this large specimen was that of a mano but it had never been used as such, and may have been made with some other purpose in mind. The vast majority of the sandstone manos clustered closely around the primary norm, but a small number of specimens varied considerably with respect to one or another dimension. Only rarely did an individual specimen show extreme variation in more than one dimension. These sandstone variants, unlike those of basalt or tuff, did not cluster around two norms. One sandstone mano, the smallest, fell into the range of the small type, but the other sandstone manos occurred, apparently randomly, throughout the entire size range. Four of the unusually large sandstone manos were blanks and like the specimen of basalt may have been designed for some other purpose. In fact, only one mano that had definitely been used for grinding was larger (39.2 cm) than 37 cm.

The manos of basalt and tuff were slightly thicker on the average than those of sandstone but, with the latter, thickness may have been largely determined by natural cleavage planes rather than some preconceived norm or idea type.

METHODS OF USING MANOS

There was an obvious correlation and close agreement between the width of the metates and the length of the majority of the manos at Site 616. However, there were no narrow metates such as might be expected in association with the small manos, and in only two instances (Rooms C2 and B5) were metates at the lower end of the width range found in the same room as the short manos.

	Sizes of Manos			
Figures based on 136 complete specimens	Size Type A			Size Type B
	Sandstone 126 manos	Basalt 22 manos	Tuff 11 manos	Basalt: 6 manos Tuff: 1 mano
Length Mean	30.8 cm	30.0 cm	29.2 cm	20.6 cm
Range	21.2-41.5 cm	27.0-33.2 cm	24.5-32.0 cm	20.0-21.5 cm
Standard Deviation	3.3 cm	2.4 cm	2.2 cm	0.6 cm
Width Mean	11.6 cm	11.6 cm	11.8 cm	11.6 cm
Range	7.7-15.4 cm	10.5-12.6 cm	11.0-12.5 cm	11.0-12.2 cm
Standard Deviation	0.9 cm	0.6 cm	0.5 cm	0.5 cm
Thickness Mean	2.8 cm	4.0 cm	3.9 cm	3.7 cm
Range	1.0-5.6 cm	2.7-6.8 cm	3.0-5.3 cm	2.7-5.5 cm
Standard Deviation	0.9 cm	1.2 cm	0.7 cm	0.9 cm

Table 5. Classification by dimensions of manos from Site 616.

There were apparently at least three methods of using manos at Site 616. In the first the rectangular manos were held so that all of one of the large flat faces bore directly on the metate and the two large flat faces remained parallel even after considerable use. Either the motor habits of the users were such that the faces did not wear asymmetrically or, perhaps more likely, the manos were frequently turned end-for-end so that the greater pressure, which probably was exerted on the side nearest the user and under the heel of the hands, was not consistently applied to the same edge. If a mano was frequently reversed, any tendency toward asymmetrical wear would be negated.

In the second method the mano was held so that one long edge was against the metate and the major flat faces were at an angle generally ranging between 10° and 20° to the surface of the metate. When an originally rectangular mano was first utilized in this second manner the angle was considerably less; but as wear developed a larger face (i.e., shape modes 3 and 4) this angle apparently increased, with a 10°-20° angle most often adopted, though on occasion the angle was as much as 30°. The faces exhibiting the greatest angle were rarely the broadest. Sometimes the other edge of the same original major face was also utilized in this manner, in which case manos in the shape of modes 5 and 6 and, ultimately, modes 7 and 8 developed. At first glance modes 3 and 4 and modes 7 and 8 might appear to be minor variations resulting from accident rather than design, but the very consistency of the variations made it appear that they in fact represented discrete entities in the minds of the users. That is, the two short faces of modes 3 and 4 were not looked upon as being the same and perhaps did not have the same utility as the two short faces of modes 7 and 8. Further evidence that a mano of mode 3, for example, was regarded as different from a mano of mode 7 and as being unsuitable for serving in the same capacity is provided by the manos of modes 5 and 6, where, instead of using the short parallel face as the second short face, the user began a second face at an angle. In other words, it was the angle and not the shortness of the face that was important, and it would follow that angled wear resulted from a different function and motor habit than flat or parallel wear.

The manos that were used at an angle were generally but not always used also (first?) in the parallel (that is, flat) position, but three specimens had been used only at an angle. The difference between the flat and angled methods may have been, at least in part, a functional one related to the final stages of grinding or to working with finer material, for 67 percent of the sandstone manos had received some use at an angle as had 13 of the 17 (76 percent) medium-to-fine-grained manos of the calcareous tuff, whereas only 27 percent of the relatively coarse basalt manos had been used in this manner.

The third technique of mano use involved the application of a slight rocking motion during the fore-and-aft grinding movement, so that the large, flat abrading face, instead of being absolutely flat, became convex in the short dimension. This "rocker bottom" feature was present on approximately 25 percent of the basalt manos, 17 percent of the manos of tuff, and 10 percent of the sandstone manos. The functional basis, if any, for this variation in the method of handling the manos is not definitely known. It is probable that the rocking motion would prove to be particularly helpful in the initial crushing of material, a suggestion supported by the more frequent occurrence of this feature on the coarse-grained manos.

It is interesting that there was an almost total absence of what Bartlett (1933, pp. 11-13, fig. 6) has termed "wedge-shaped manos." Actually the major flat faces on six of the 100 manos of shape modes 1 and 2 did taper slightly toward one another, giving the mano a wedgelike appearance such as she describes. This is a much smaller number than one would expect if the motor habits of the users were such that a wedge-shaped cross section would naturally develop through continued use of the mano. At Site 616 the faces resulting from use of the mano at an angle were apparently separate entities. Furthermore, on the six sandstone manos that tapered the average angle was less and the thickness somewhat greater (3.2 cm) than for sandstone manos as a whole, whereas if this feature was the result of long use one would expect the faces to be at a steeper angle and these manos as a whole to be somewhat thinner than the average specimen. It seems likely that the few somewhat wedge-shaped manos present at Site 616 developed, through asymmetrical and atypical wear, from manos used in accordance with the first method described above (the entire original flat face applied to the surface of the metate) rather than through extensive use at an angle to the metate. Perhaps these were simply manos that for some reason were not turned end-to-end during their period of use.

While analyzing the manos of shape modes 3 through 9, it was observed that the ridge dividing the two short faces occasionally ran at a considerable angle rather than parallel to the edges of the mano. Presumably this asymmetrical wear resulted from the continued exertion of a slightly greater pressure against the right or left end of the mano. (Reversing the mano but maintaining the same differential pressure would in this instance tend to increase the asymmetry rather than cancel it out.) Asymmetrical wear

Table 6. Distribution by descriptive types of manos from Site 616.

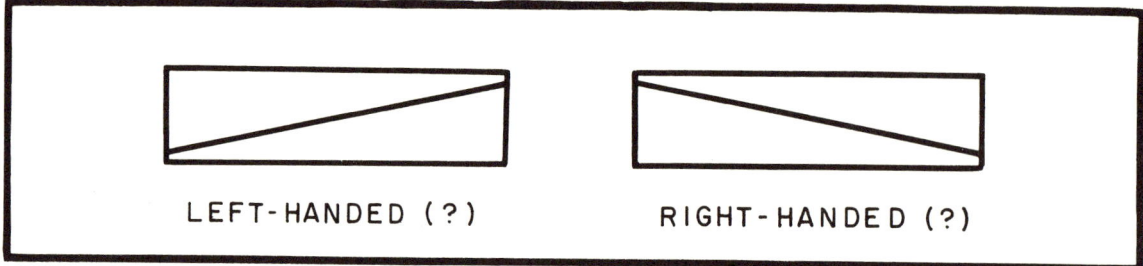

Figure 52. Under surfaces of manos from Site 616, showing asymmetrical ridge, possibly related to handedness.

had already been observed on the metates (see discussion, p. 138) and it had been hypothesized that at least some right-handed persons would tend to exert greater pressure with their right hand. This would cause the end of the face of the mano under the heel of the right hand to wear faster and thus to enlarge somewhat more rapidly. If the greatest wear took place during the downstroke, as the data from the metates indicated (see also Woodbury 1954, p. 69), it would apparently follow that the faces on the manos would wear asymmetrically as shown in figure 52.

Analysis showed that on this basis 68 manos (25 percent) showed evidence of having been used by left-handed people. More than half were from five rooms: B1, C2, C9, D2 and F2, a group that included the two rooms with "left-handed" metates. Only 11 manos or 4 percent (four from Room B1, two from Room A1, and others scattered, including one from Room D2) could be identified, according to this analysis, as having been used by right-handed persons. The other manos were indeterminate in this regard. The implied proportion of left-handed to right-handed people is the reverse of all observations of modern groups and, perhaps even more germane, is directly contrary to the data from the metates (see p. 138). One suspects that the figure should be reversed but no rational basis for doing so was evident. The assumption that the greatest wear took place during the up or return stroke, as Morris suggests (1939, pp. 133-134), would successfully reverse the mano designations, but this still seems to conflict with the data from the metates; for were this the case it would be expected that the *lower* right rather than the *upper* right corner of the metates would show greater wear more frequently (unless, of course, greater pressure was exerted at the upper end of the stroke rather than at the beginning). If we assume that *all* left-handed people were inclined to utilize manos in such a way that asymmetrical wear resulted, while only some right-handed people were so inclined, a ratio is indicated of one in four people being left-handed, which still seems high. Pehaps the basic hypothesis is in error. Individual manos may have been used by several persons, and thus the differential wear could be a result of unrecognized factors.

Manos that to all appearances were still perfectly serviceable were occasionally utilized as building stones, particularly in the construction of mealing bins (see particularly Rooms C9 and F2).

Metates: 65 specimens (fig. 109)

Despite the occurrence of eight manos adapted for use on trough metates, all of the basal grinding tools encountered at Site 616 could be included in Woodbury's category of "flat" metates. All were flat slabs whose cross sections in all three planes generally could be described as roughly rectangular or subrectangular, except one whose edges were round. The grinding face occupied the entire upper surface. The size range fell within fairly narrow limits as indicated in table 7. The mean size and degree of variation did not appear to have a patterned relationship to the different areas within the site and varied only slightly in relation to the material utilized. One sandstone metate (#1218, fig. 109a) not included in the list was somewhat aberrant with respect to size (60 by 40 by 10 cm).

The basalt metates tended to vary in size and outline more than did those of the other two materials, showing a greater tendency toward subrectangular, oval, or irregular shapes. Measurements of thickness are representative rather than consistently minimum, but the recording of the minimum figure would result in only a slight lowering of the mean thickness.

All sandstone metates were described in the field as fine-grained. Variations in the coarseness of sandstone metates have been discerned at other sites in the Southwest, but while minor variations may have been overlooked it is not felt that major differences were present at Site 616. The presence of other material for the coarser-grained metates would eliminate the necessity for any such variation. The provenience of all metates according to materials is shown in table 8.

FINE-GRAINED METATES OF SANDSTONE: 35 specimens

Fill

Room C2 (#1040, #1248, #1283, #1284); Room C3 (#1721, #1722); Room C4 (#1451, #1484); Room C5 (#1687); Room C8 (#1844); Room C9 (#1842, #2031); Room D1 (#1097); Room D2 (#1259, #1262); Room D3 (#1218); Room E2 (#2105)

Floor

Room A2 (#2666); Room B1 (#1333, #1351); Room B5 (#2272, #2275); Room C9 (#2040, #2044, #2164); Room D3 (#2159); Room E2 (#2319); Kiva (#2795)

Mealing Bin

Room B1 (#2126); Room C2 (#1691); Room D2 (#2262, #2361, fig. 50)

Structural

Room C2 (#2756); Room D2 (#2158); Room F2 (#3022)

FINE-GRAINED METATE OF CALCAREOUS TUFF: 1 specimen

Fill

Room B1 (#1207)

MEDIUM-FINE-GRAINED METATES OF CALCAREOUS TUFF: 2 specimens

Fill

Room D2 (#1213)

Floor

Room C9 (#2011)

	Range	Mean	Standard Deviation
Length (cm)			
Sandstone	37-50	44.3	2.9
Basalt	36-52	43.8	4.7
Calcareous Tuff	35-44	38.8	2.6
Width (cm)			
Sandstone	26-36	31.8	2.7
Basalt	26-41	31.1	3.4
Calcareous Tuff	24-34	28.9	2.7
Thickness (cm)			
Sandstone	2.8-10.0	6.1	2.0
Basalt	5.0-10.0	8.5	1.4
Calcareous Tuff	6.0-11.0	8.0	1.8

Table 7. Classification by dimensions of metates from Site 616.

MEDIUM-GRAINED METATES OF CALCAREOUS TUFF: 7 specimens

Fill

Room C2 (#1016); Room C9 (#1839); kiva (#2255)

Floor

Room C2 (#1417); Room C9 (#2048); kiva (#2299)

Mealing Bin

Room C5 (#2049)

MEDIUM-GRAINED METATE OF VESICULAR BASALT: 1 specimen

Floor

Room B1 (#1362)

MEDIUM-COARSE-GRAINED METATES OF VESICULAR BASALT: 5 specimens

Surface

(#1816)

Fill

Room C3 (#1707); Room C8 (#1843)

Mealing Bin

Room A3 (#2727); Room F2 (#3023)

COARSE-GRAINED METATES OF VESICULAR BASALT: 14 specimens

Fill

Room C1 (#1269); Room C3 (#1723); Room C4 (#1680); Room C5 (#1688); Room C7 (#1458); Room C9 (#1846, #2003); Room D2 (#1257); Room E2 (#1827); Room F2 (#3001)

Floor

Room F2 (#3002, #3014)

Mealing Bin

Room C2 (#1690); Room E2 (#2300)

COMMENT

The metates, by definition, were used in connection with a fore-and-aft or reciprocal grinding motion. They doubtless served primarily for grinding vegetal products, particularly maize, to a meal or flour. While there is little archaeological documentation of this, the assumption is rather securely based on their extensive similarity in both shape and position to the artifacts serving in this capacity among the present-day Pueblo Indians. There is some evidence for their use in grinding certain other materials. Both metate #2262 from Room D2 (fig. 109b) and #2795 from the kiva bench were stained red as if used for grinding

Types / Provenience		Fine-grained Sandstone	Fine-grained Calcareous Tuff	Medium-fine Calcareous Tuff	Medium-grained Calcareous Tuff	Medium-grained Vesicular Basalt	Medium-coarse Vesicular Basalt	Coarse-grained Vesicular Basalt
		Col. 1	Col. 2	Col. 3	Col. 4	Col. 5	Col. 6	Col. 7
Rm. A2	Floor	1						
Rm. A3	M B						1	
	Fill		1					
Rm. B1	Floor	2				1		
	M B	1						
Rm. B5	Floor	2						
Rm. C1	Fill							1
	Fill	4			1			
Rm. C2	Floor				1			
	M B	1						1
	Struct	1						
Rm. C3	Fill	2					1	1
Rm. C4	Fill	2						1
Rm. C5	Fill	1						1
	M B					1		
Rm. C7	Fill							1
Rm. C8	Fill	1					1	
Rm. C9	Fill	2			1			2
	Floor	3		1	1			
Rm. D1	Fill	1						
	Fill	2		1				1
Rm. D2	M B	2						
	Struct	1						
Rm. D3	Fill	1						
	Floor	1						
	Fill	1						1
Rm. E2	Floor	1						
	M B							1
	Fill							1
Rm. F2	Floor							2
	M B						1	
	Struct	1						
Kiva	Fill				1			
	Floor	1			1			
Surface							1	
Totals		35	1	2	7	1	5	14

M B: Mealing bin

Table 8. Distribution by types and provenience of slab metates from Site 616.

was a broken specimen and its use as a mortar was probably subsequent to its use as a grinding tool.

In all, 60 metates and five fragmentary specimens were recovered. Ten metates were still set in their mealing bins, and 14 others were on the floor of various rooms. The scarcity of badly worn or fragmentary specimens can doubtless be attributed to the fact that excavation was restricted almost entirely to living units rather than refuse deposits. Three metates, all apparently undamaged and in usable condition, had been used in construction. One had been plastered on end to the north wall of Room C2 below the door into Room C5, forming the rise of the step (#2756, fig. 22); another, also set on end, formed the end of the mealing bin in Room F2 (#3019, figs. 38, 39); while the third served as the horizontal basal stone in a mealing bin in Room D2 (#2262, figs. 30, 32, 109b). Only three metates (#1484, Room C4, fill; #2164, Room C9, floor, fig. 20; #2262, Room D2, floor, fig. 109b) showed even slight abrasion on both of the major flat surfaces, and in no case was the wear of the second surface extensive.

The major variation occurred in the material used and, largely correlated with this, the coarseness of the grinding surface. Three materials with five degrees of coarseness were recognized. While the gradational divisions of relative coarseness were established by appearance rather than by proven effect of actual grinding, there is probably a positive correlation. The division established between medium-coarse and coarse, however, might well prove to have no basis in fact, if the results of grinding could be observed.

The grinding surface on most of the metates was slightly concave longitudinally. The point of greatest concavity was generally at the center or just below (away from the person grinding) the center of the grinding surface.

In addition to the longitudinal concavity we observed, during the initial analysis of the metates in the field, that the grinding surface on most specimens appeared to have a slight torsion. That is, if the four corners of the grinding surface were oriented to an absolutely flat surface, one corner was nearly always lower than the others. On specimens not *in situ* there was no way to tell whether it was the upper right or lower left corner, or conversely, the upper left or the lower right corner that exhibited greater wear. Observation of the ten metates still *in situ* showed that on all ten the upper right corner exhibited the greatest wear. We hypothesized that often right-handed persons might unconsciously exert greater pressure with their right hand as they worked, particularly during the initial portion of the downstroke. Thus, this differential wear could be indicative of the handedness of the users. Thirty-four metates were sufficiently worn

hematite. This use of metate #2262 as well as its secondary use as a small mortar occurred prior to the stone's placement in the mealing bin where it was found, for the red stain and the mortar hole were on the underside of the metate and could not be observed until it had been removed from the bin. From the occurrence of quantities of various other minerals in "mealing rooms" it is possible to infer that these other minerals were ground on metates probably more frequently than the retention of actual stain would indicate. The underside of one other metate (#1680) showed secondary use as a mortar. This metate

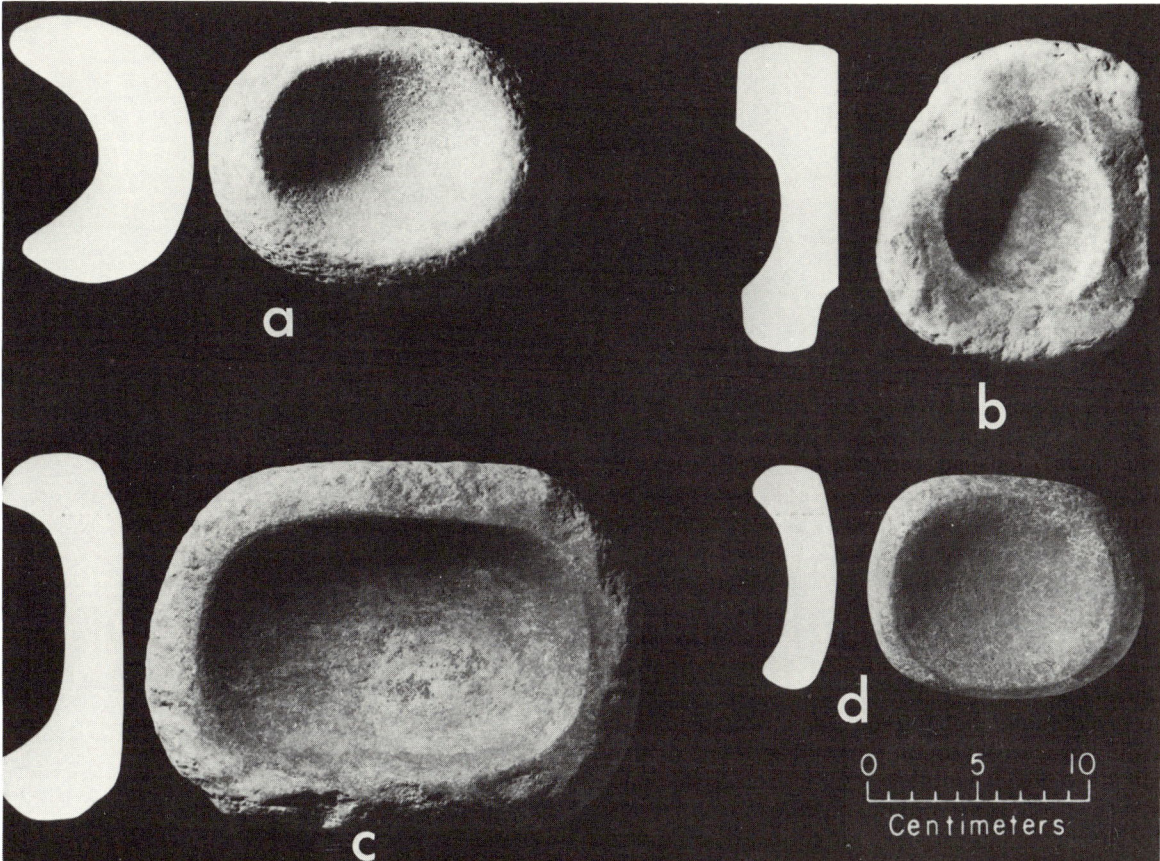

Figure 53. Roughly shaped mortars from Site 616: a. Walk-in well, fill, #1123; b. Room B1, floor, #1341; c. Room B1, floor, #1340; d. Kiva, floor, #2125.

for this torsion to be reliably determined; on two (#1259, #3002) the upper left corner was more worn while on 32 the upper right exhibited greater wear. This suggests that the proportion of left-handed women was 1 to 16 but even if the initial hypothesis is valid these figures must be used with caution, for a variable number of people may have been responsible for the wear of individual metates. The data on this point, derived from the manos, if valid, suggest that at least one in four were left-handed, which seems a bit high (see p. 136).

Roughly-shaped Mortars: 8 specimens

These mortars were stone slabs or boulders roughly shaped by chipping and pecking, with a concavity pecked and/or worn into one surface.

Six were flat, rather thick slabs. Three of these (#1340, #1704, #2273, fig. 53c) had a rectangular outline with rounded corners; one (#1341, fig. 53b) was nearly square with rounded corners; one (#1811) was a circular disc; while another (#1800) was quite irregular in shape, its general outline being that of an elongated oval. The bases were smooth and flat and the sides had been roughly shaped by chipping and pecking, but no attempt was made to remove all irregularities. The seventh specimen, from the walk-in well (#1123, fig. 53a), was an egg-shaped cobble pecked smooth all over. The quartzite mortar from the kiva (#2125, fig. 53d) was also irregular, and, in fact, was a reused one-hand mano, the only such mano encountered at Site 616. The mortar concavity had been pecked into the upper unused surface of the mano. In every case the concavities were regular, smooth, and even. Pecking marks were rarely evident. Six of the eight specimens were of felsite, one of sandstone (#1811), and one of quartzite (#2125). Their measurements are given on page 140.

There is little doubt that mortars were used to grind and mix pigments. Four of the seven specimens with marked concavities contained a trace or a thin deposit of red pigment while a fifth (#2125, fig. 53d) contained

ROUGHLY-SHAPED MORTARS

Cat. No.	Dimensions	Concavity	Provenience
1123	15.4 × 11.8 × 7.4 cm	10.4 × 8.4 × 2.4 cm	Walk-in well, fill
1340	21.5 × 15.5 × 5.0	16.3 × 11.0 × 2.6	Room B1, floor
1341	14.0 × 12.1 × 4.8	7.4 × 7.0 × 1.6	Room B1, floor
1704	22.2 × 17.6 × 4.6	14.2 × 10.0 × 1.0	Room C8, fill
1800	38.0 × 22.0 × 5.0	26.0 × 14.0 × 2.7	Room D1, floor
1811	8.2 × 8.0 × 4.4	4.4 × 4.0 × 0.6	Walk-in well, fill
2125	12.0 × 9.3 × 3.8	9.8 × 8.0 × 1.6	Kiva, floor
2273	20.1 × 13.1 × 4.2	10.4 × 7.0 × 0.8	Room A2, floor

traces of a green pigment. Only the specimens from the walk-in well and Room D1 bore no stains. That the pigments were mixed as well as ground in these mortars is shown by the running stains evident on several of them where the liquid material sloshed over the sides. Of course, other materials could have been ground in these mortars also, but there is no evidence for this.

The mortar found on the floor of the kiva was the only one of quartzite, the only one stained with green pigment, and the only one made on the upper surface of a one-hand mano. Whether this mortar continued to serve as a mano is unknown.

The mortar from Room C8, unlike the others, had a flat rather than a concave working surface, and thus might more nearly fit into Woodbury's palette category (Woodbury 1954, pp. 112-116).

Pestle: 1 specimen

This was a cone-shaped object of quartzite with a flat bottom and rounded tip. It seems likely that this object was utilized in conjunction with the mortars discussed above in much the same manner as a druggist's or chemist's pestle is used to reduce pigments or similar substances to a powder. The pestle was well smoothed all over, with a basal diameter of 2.6 cm and a height of 5.2 cm. It was found in the fill of Room E2.

Bowls: 3 specimens

These specimens were roughly circular, bowl-shaped stones with walls of approximately constant thickness and relatively deep concavities.

Of the three specimens recovered two were of relatively fine-grained basalt, while the third (#2256), a fragment, was of vesicular basalt. All had been roughly shaped both inside and out by pecking. The interiors showed no evidence of abrasion and the inside surfaces were slightly irregular rather than smooth. These specimens did not appear to have served as deep mortars. Their measurements are given below.

Shaftsmoothers: 9 specimens (fig. 54)

There was considerable and not at all consistent variation in these nine artifacts. All were of felsite and the specimens as a group were well finished. All sides were smoothed and often had a polished appearance. The bottoms were consistently flat and generally well finished (where abrasion of the bottom was evident the striations were always parallel to the grooves on the top). Since the tops of all specimens were consistently convex it is unlikely that they were used in pairs. The grooves were always very smooth and slightly lustrous. The average length of the grooves was 4.5 cm, with a general range from 4.2 cm through 4.8 cm, although one specimen (#1732, fig. 54d) was 6 cm long; the width of the grooves, which were semicircular, varied only slightly from 1 cm and the depth was almost constant from end to end, with an average of 0.4 cm and a range from 0.3 to 0.5 cm. With the exception of one specimen (#1890, fig. 54b), which was slightly convex, the grooves were level from end to end. All shaftsmoothers were approximately 3 cm thick; in the other two dimensions they ranged from 7 by 6.5 cm (#1732, fig. 54d) to 5 by 4 cm (#1890, fig. 54b). The others were less nearly square and averaged 4.5 by 7.5 cm in size. Most had only a single groove, but two (#1732, fig. 54d, #3047) had three grooves each, although on #3047 the two outside grooves were on the edges of the specimen, so that only one quarter of the circle was present. On two specimens (#1290 and #1546, fig. 54a) there was a well-marked central ridge running at right angles to the groove. On #1546 the ridge extended on both sides of the groove while on

STONE BOWLS

Cat. No.	Dimensions	Concavity	Provenience
1459	37.0 × 33.0 × 20.0 cm	28.0 × 30.0 × 14.0 cm	Room C7, fill
1460	42.0 × 36.0 × 15.5	37.0 × 30.0 × 10.0	Room C7, fill
2256	(18.0) × (13.0) × 11.0	? × ? × 6.0	Area of kiva, surface

Figure 54. Shaftsmoothers from Site 616: a. Room D2, fill, #1290; b. Room D1, floor, #1890; c. Room C10, floor, #2219; d. Room B2, floor, #1732.

#1290 it was only on one side. The upper surface of #1890 (fig. 54b) while not having a well-delineated ridge, was unusually convex over most of its area with a small, flat, central portion that could have served the same purpose as a ridge. On one specimen (#1546) a second groove had been made on one of the long edges of the artifact, parallel to the short dimension and thus only 2.2 cm long, but in all other respects similar to other grooves.

Surface

(1)

Fill

Room D2 (2); walk-in well (1)

Floor

Room B1 (1); Room B2 (1); Room C10 (1); Room D1 (1)

Below floor

Room F2 (1)

Polishing Pebbles: 47 specimens

These were small, naturally smooth pebbles. The largest dimension ranged from 7.0 to 2.2 cm with a mean of 4.8 cm.

A variety of materials were used without noticeable selectivity. Nineteen were of rhyolite, 11 of a hard greenish shale, 8 of chert, 4 of quartz, and 3 of quartzite. These various materials did not appear to cluster significantly with other observed features or to be located in any particular areas of the site. The pebbles of rhyolite were on the whole slightly larger than the others and, like the ones of shale, were more angular. Those of quartz, quartzite, and chert were very smooth with a natural high polish. Those of quartz tended to be somewhat egg-shaped while the quartzite and chert pebbles were more nearly rectangular.

The polishing facets that distinguished these pebbles as tools were occasionally fairly large and occupied an entire face of the stone (e.g., 4.5 by 2 cm), but more often they were smaller (e.g., 2.4 by 1.1 cm) and were not consistently located on any particular portion of the pebbles. Their location was apparently determined primarily by the presence of an initial natural flatness and/or ease of holding the pebble. On a number of specimens the facets had sharp, well-marked edges. The average tool had three or four polishing facets but the number of distinct facets on a single specimen ranged from one to six. A total of 157 facets occurred on the 47 specimens recovered. On 104 of the facets (distributed over all but six of the pebbles) fine striations could be detected, and microscopic examination might have revealed them on others as well. In every instance some or all of the striations ran parallel to the short dimension of the facet. Four specimens exhibited striations running parallel to the long dimension as well, and seven others bore irregular striations in addition to those parallel to the short dimension.

Three polishing pebbles (from the fill of Rooms C3 and E2, and the floor of Room B5) were stained with red pigment. On four of the larger specimens (from the fill of Rooms C1, C3, C8, and the walk-in well) one end had served as a pecking stone.

Thirty-eight of the polishing pebbles came from six localities: Rooms B1, C1, C3, C8, E2, and the walk-in well. In Rooms B1 and the walk-in well the number of highly polished facets and those bearing obvious striations were equal or nearly so (eight of each in Room B1 and five striated to four polished in the well). Five of the six specimens having only polished facets came from these two areas, while the sixth came from Room B2, which adjoined and was probably related to Room B1. Of the six localities, Room B1 and the walk-in well were the two most likely to have been areas where pottery making was practiced. Perhaps this distribution was in some way related to the potter's craft.

The majority of the polishing pebbles were found in the fill of rooms rather than on the floor, suggesting that the activities with which they were associated were carried out primarily on the roof; but in Rooms B1 and B2, which were probably closely associated with pottery making, the polishing stones occurred on the room floors.

A number of other stones, similar in every respect to the polishing stones except for the absence of observable facets, were encountered in the fill of a number of rooms and in two instances (Rooms B5 and C10) specimens were found on the floor. These stones may have been potential or slightly used polishing stones or they may have been simply shiny pebbles casually brought to the site for any of a multitude of reasons.

Fill

Room A1 (1); Room C1 (9); Room C3 (8); Room C6 (1); Room C8 (7); Room E2 (4); Room F1 (1); walk-in well (3)

Floor

Room B1 (7); Room B2 (2); Room B5 (1); Room F2 (1)

Pecking Stones: 16 specimens

These were natural cobbles or fragments of stone exhibiting signs of battering, whose final shape resulted from use rather than deliberate design.

Ten were of petrified wood, three of quartzite (#1426, #1783, #2022) and one each of fine-grained basalt (#1935), quartz (#2090), and andesite (#1981). Eight were globular in shape with indications of hammering on all surfaces. The other eight, five of petrified wood (#1320, #1903, #2505, #2585, #2591), one of quartzite (#1426), one of quartz (#2090), and one of andesite (#1981), were roughly rectangular in shape and showed battering primarily on the ends or edges. The specimen of andesite was well polished on four sides, broken on one of the long sides, and battered on the remaining short side; it was probably the poll of a broken axe that was subsequently used as a pecking stone. The globular pecking stones averaged 7 cm in diameter, with that of the largest ranging between 10.5 and 8.5 cm, while that of the smallest was 4 cm. The rectangular specimens fell between the limits of the quartzite cobble with dimensions of 17 by 11 by 9 cm and one of the petrified wood specimens with dimensions of 6 by 5 by 3 cm.

These implements were doubtless used for a wide variety of tasks. The occurrence of yellow ochre over the lower half of the basalt specimen from Room D5 suggests that at least one of these tasks was the initial crushing of pigments. It is interesting that very few pecking stones were in immediate association with metates or mealing bins.

The reason for the unusual paucity of pecking stones is not known. Since the excavators were extremely "stone-tool conscious," none were knowingly discarded in the field prior to analysis, and it is unlikely that any large percentage of such stones that had been used were completely overlooked. Either the inhabitants had little use for pecking stones or, perhaps more likely, they were in the habit of picking up a rock when the need arose, and discarding it right afterward. The ready availability of serviceable stone in the immediately adjacent volcanic dike would doubtless have encouraged this practice. Modifications resulting from such casual use would be almost impossible to recognize, and even if observed could usually not be clearly distinguished from the results of the action of natural factors.

Surface

(1)

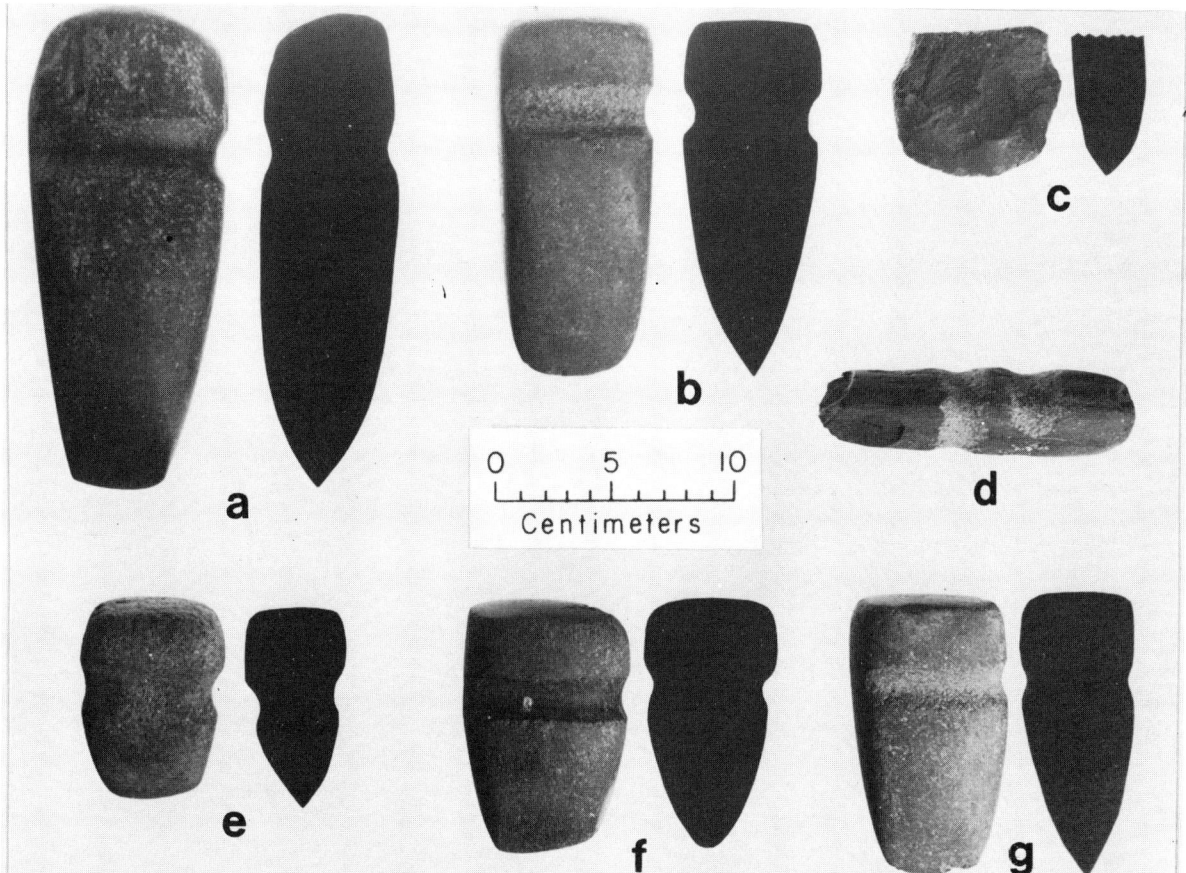

Figure 55. Axes and pick from Site 616. Three-quarter-grooved axes: a. Room D1, fill, #1219; b. Room D1, floor, #1799; e. Room C6, floor, #1992; f. surface, #2296; g. Room C2, fill, #1024. Notched axe: c. Walk-in well, mealing room, fill, fragment, #1376. Pick, with three-quarter groove and full groove: d. Kiva, fill, #2588.

Fill

    Room C8 (1); Room C9 (2); Room D1 (1); Room D2 (1); Room D5 (3); walk-in well (1)

Floor

    Room B2 (1); Room C2 (1); Room C5 (1); Room C6 (1); Room D1 (1)

Below floor

    Room B1 (1)

Axes: 36 specimens

THREE-QUARTER-GROOVED: 35 specimens (fig. 55a, b, e, f, g)

All were of heavy, fine-grained igneous rock. However, there was enough variation in the general composition of the rock to suggest that they did not all derive from a single, limited source. Presumably all specimens were shaped principally by pecking, and except for those abandoned during or shortly after resharpening, all had been well polished, the interior of the groove being the only area that was not always intentionally polished. The groove obtained a sheen incidental to use rather than during manufacture.

Thirty-two of the specimens could be described without question as three-quarter-grooved axes. Three specimens (#1725, #1942, #2017) had grooves completely encircling the axe. In all other respects these three specimens corresponded exactly to the three-quarter-grooved axes, and examination of them suggested that the grooving of the fourth side was done following the initial manufacture of the artifact. The groove was less deep on the fourth side, which maintained the flat surface typical of the ungrooved side of three-quarter-grooved axes and, with the exception of this additional grooving, these specimens can be considered (for descriptive purposes) with the three-quarter-grooved axes.

One other specimen was not three-quarter-grooved (#1581). This was the bit end of a broken three-quarter-grooved axe that had been reground with a half-groove, that is, one face and one end had been regrooved with the apparent intention of continuing to use it as an axe. Whether it was used in this form or the regrooving simply was not completed is unknown, but this axe, like the full-grooved axes, can be considered in all other respects identical to the three-quarter-grooved axes.

All of the axes conformed very closely to a single pattern. They were rectangular with rounded corners in horizontal cross section, with a fair demarcation between planes, that is, while the corners were not angular neither did one face blend gradually into another. The faces were convex with the greatest width occurring just below the groove very close to the balance point of the axe. The ungrooved end was flatter than the faces or the other end and on some specimens was completely flat. The poll was as well shaped and as well polished as the bit, its top either flat or slightly convex. The grooves were well formed, approximately 2 cm wide and 0.25 cm deep. Although these specimens were technically three-quarter-grooved, on fully half of them the grooves tapered toward one another on the fourth side (without actually meeting), rather than ending parallel to one another on the two faces. On all but ten axes the grooves on the two faces were even and parallel; on five the right groove (with the axe held bit down and the ungrooved side toward the viewer) was slightly (0.5 – 0.9 cm) higher; and on the remaining five the left groove was higher. Whether or not this variation indicated differences in hafting is not known. Three of those with the right groove higher and one with the left groove higher were from rooms D1 and D2. The others showed no spatial clustering. Room D2 was also one of the rooms containing left-handed metates and manos.

The average length of the specimens as found gave little indication of the action type or ideal modal shape and dimensions of an "axe" as conceived by the original manufacturers, because many specimens had been resharpened or used for pounding. Therefore, an attempt was made to estimate the original dimensions of the artifacts. It was hypothesized that the groove on an axe was deliberately positioned, the location being determined by the contours and balance of the specimen. In other words, an axe was originally designed so that when hafted it would have the proper "heft." The general contours of the axes from Site 616 suggest that they had originally been manufactured according to a fairly narrowly defined pattern and all were of the same material. Hence it would follow that on new specimens the groove would have an almost constant lineal position relative to the two ends of the axe, that is, the bit and the poll. Ten specimens that appeared to be in mint or near mint condition were selected. (Mint condition was determined by general appearance and minimum curvature of the faces, which would indicate the least amount of resharpening.) Measurement of these specimens revealed that the ratio of poll height (distance from the top of the poll to the center of the groove) to overall height was 1:3.4. Measurement of the poll height of these ten specimens and computation from this measurement of the expected overall height by application of the ratio resulted in a figure which, in every case but one, was within 2 mm of the actual height of the axe. One specimen was 4 mm shorter than the computed height (so may have been resharpened more than had been thought). This consistent result offered strong substantiation of the original hypothesis that the ratio would be almost constant on new specimens. With this ratio as a basis the "original" height of all specimens was computed and used in the measurement list below.

AXES

	Estimated Original Height	Actual Height
Range	10.6 – 16.2 cm	8.1 – 16.2 cm
Mean	13.3	12.0
Size Deviation	1.5	1.8

	Length End-to-end	Width Face-to-face	Length of Cutting Edge
Range	5.9 – 7.7 cm	3.8 – 6.3 cm	3.0 – 5.5 cm
Mean	6.7	4.9	4.2
Size Deviation	0.7	0.7	0.8

Two specimens aberrant in overall size are not included in the list. One (#1581, fig. 55a) was unusually large with dimensions of 19.2 by 8.4 by 6 cm and with a blade length of 3.8 cm. The second was unusually small, 8.4 by 5.8 by 3.6 cm, with a blade length of 3 cm. Both appeared to be in mint condition. Despite their unusual size the poll-groove ratio worked equally well for these specimens. The mean figures in the list could be interpreted as representative of the action type for the site while these last two artifacts probably represent the extreme size deviations from this type.

The particular poll-groove ratio that was so consistent on these axes probably would not apply to axes of widely divergent contours and/or of different materials. As evidence there is the half-grooved axe, which was wedge-shaped, consisting solely of the reused bit end of a regular axe. The half groove on this specimen was located so that the poll-groove ratio was 1:2.8.

Eight specimens had secondary use as hammers (#1036, #1725, #1795, #1938, #2017, #2026, #2296, fig. 55f,

#2357). No discernible logic was involved in the choice of specimens for such use. If the computations of original height were even approximately correct, then apparently almost new axes were used as hammers nearly as often as were those that had been sharpened and resharpened repeatedly. It is possible that they were not permanently so used; that is, they perhaps served briefly for hammering or pecking and then were resharpened so that they again became axes. In only one case had the blade been battered sufficiently for the "cutting" edge to have obtained a breadth of more than 2 or 3 mm, so that it would be a relatively easy matter for the blade to be resharpened. The unusually abrupt inslope of some of the blades suggested that this was the case. None of the reused axes was on the floor of a room containing metates and only two were in the fill of such rooms, so it is not likely that they were used to "resharpen" metates; nor were they associated with sandstone-block masonry. Two specimens (#1119, #2354) had been used for such heavy blows that large chips had been removed from both surfaces and the bit more nearly resembled a crude chopper than a finely finished axe. The poll ends of eight axes also had been slightly battered, suggesting that this end had been used for hammering; four of these were axes with bit ends that had been used for pecking or battering. The ends of six polls were perfectly flat and unusually well polished as if they had been used for rubbing.

Other than those specimens evidently used as hammers, only three axes appeared to be dull, that is, with the blade relatively rounded instead of coming to a rather sharp edge. However, more than two-thirds of the axes were shorter than their estimated original height, presumably as a result of resharpening. Three axes that had been shortened were 4 cm shorter than their estimated original height, six between 2 and 3 cm shorter, eight between 1 and 2 cm shorter, while the remainder were less than a centimeter shorter. Significantly, none were longer than would be estimated through use of the poll-groove ratio. In most cases resharpening was also indicated by an abrupt change in the convexity of the bit face, although on occasion the entire face seemed to have been repecked, so that the curve again became fairly uniform over the height of the bit. In almost every instance the pecking marks of the resharpening process had been obliterated by additional polishing. The striations resulting from this polishing were consistently at right angles to the edge.

Surface

(2)

Fill

Room B2 (1); Room C1 (1); Room C2 (1); Room C3 (4); Room C6 (1); Room C7 (1); Room C9 (3); Room D1 (2); Room D2 (1); trench north of Room B2 (1)

Floor

Room A2 (1); Room B1 (1); Room B3 (2); Room B5 (2); Room C2 (2); Room C3 (1); Room C5 (1); Room C6 (1); Room C10 ventilator tunnel (2); Room D1 (5)

NOTCHED: 1 specimen (fig. 55c)

The bit end of a quartzite axe chipped into shape, oval in cross section and notched on the two ends, was encountered in the fill of the mealing room connected to the walk-in well. This specimen was 7.2 cm long, 3 cm thick, and 6 cm from the blade to the center of the notch at which point the break had occurred. The edge had been sharpened by grinding and the faces of the specimen had been polished for a distance of approximately 1 cm above the edge.

Pick: 1 specimen (fig. 55d)

The head of a pick was recovered from the fill of the kiva. It was of a fine-grained volcanic material and was nearly circular with a diameter of 3.4 cm. The bit had been broken off but the length of the surviving remnant was 13 cm. It had both a full and a three-quarter groove, the latter being above the former. The two grooves were located on either side of the present midpoint of the specimen.

Hammers: 21 specimens (fig. 56)

These were hafted stones whose shapes and visible marks of concussion suggested that they were used to hammer and pound. Although the use of these implements probably varied only a little, the function of the tools included in the various categories delineated below may have been different. With one exception all hammers from Site 616 were centrally hafted. Reused axes whose use and function may have overlapped those of some of the hammers could generally be distinguished from the tools originally designed as hammers, for the axes had insloping faces and a non-central location of the hafting grooves. Those axes that received secondary and perhaps only temporary use as hammers have been discussed under axes (pp. 143–145). However, a number of specimens that apparently were originally designed as axes seemed to have been deliberately and permanently converted to hammers. These latter are included below.

ROUND-ENDED HAMMERS: 5 specimens

These were natural quartzitic cobbles, unshaped (the

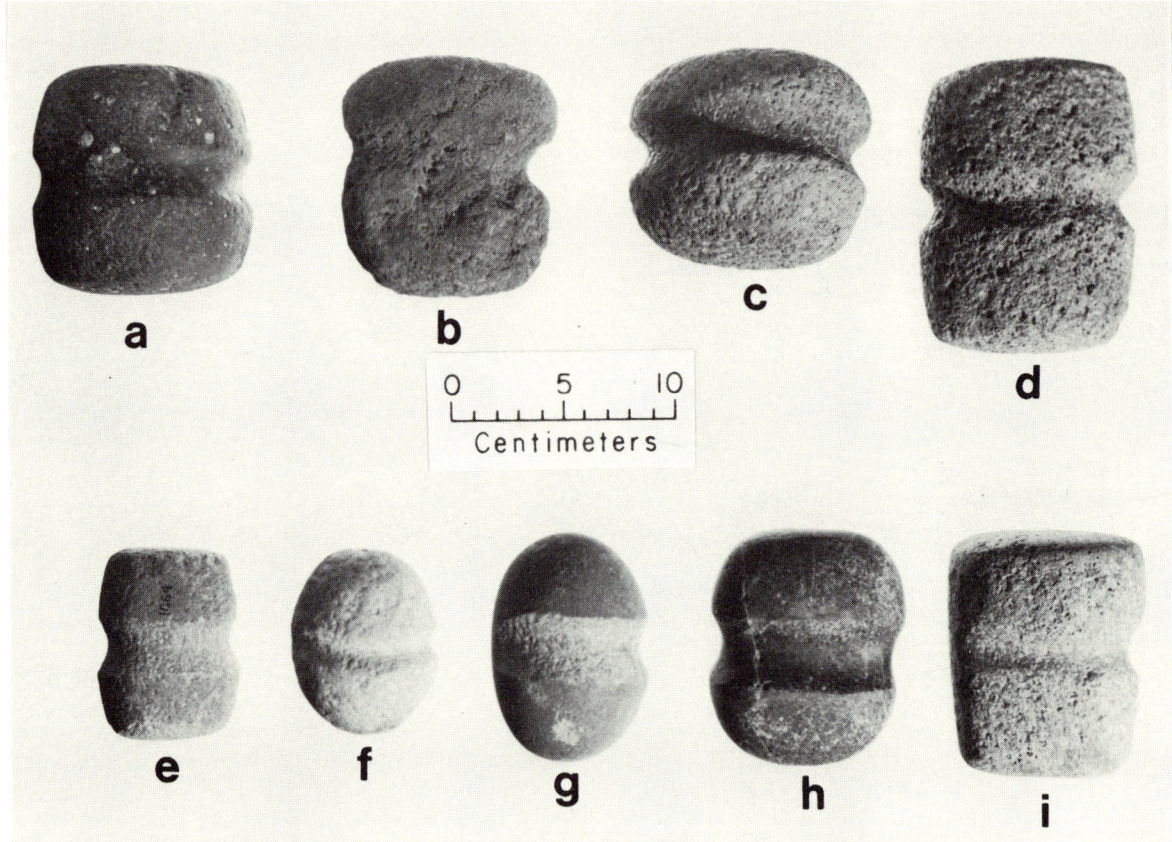

Figure 56. Hammers from Site 616. Round-ended: f. Room C7, fill, #2695; g. Room C3, floor, #1851. Elongated, flat-ended: d. Room E1, fill, #1063; e. Room B1, fill, #1064; h. Room D1, floor, #1793; i. Room B1, floor, #1343. Equilateral, flat-ended: a. Room E2, ventilator, fill, #2104; c. Room C5, fill, #1714. Irregular, flat-ended: b. Room A2, floor, #2270.

faces of #2695, fig. 56f, showed some pecking) except for the centrally located groove that extended in every instance approximately four-fifths of the distance around the short circumference of the hammer. In all dimensions the cross section tended to be an oval or rounded rectangle. The ends were rounded, and in one case (#2695, fig. 56f) almost pointed, rather than flat. The signs of battering were restricted almost entirely to the ends, both ends being utilized on all but one hammer (#1851, fig. 56g). The grooves were pecked into the stone to a depth of about 0.3 cm and had a width ranging from 1.8 to 2.6 cm. The surfaces of the grooves showed almost no evidence of polishing. Dimensions are given below.

The unmodified nature of these implements suggested that either (1) their makers were careless or hurried, (2) their function was such (e.g., perhaps without great ceremonial significance) that carefully finished tools were not considered a necessity, or (3) perhaps most likely, the natural forms available were or came to be considered the ideal type for the particular job at hand, whatever that may have been. It has been suggested that tools similar to at least the smaller of these served as war clubs. They may have been so

ROUND-ENDED HAMMERS

Cat. No.	Length End-to-end	Width Edge-to-edge	Thickness Face-to-face	Provenience
1068	10.3 cm	5.4 cm	4.7 cm	Room B1, fill
1751	10.3	5.5	4.4	Room B2, floor
1851	9.5	6.7	6.1	Room C3, floor
1909	8.0	6.8	6.1	Room E2, fill
2695	7.8	6.6	5.0	Room C7, fill

used but the battering on the ends would suggest that these particular specimens served other purposes as well, perhaps the final dressing of building stones, the shaping of larger stone implements, the "resharpening" of smooth metates, or other tasks requiring a more pointed or restricted area of contact than that offered by the flat-ended hammers, and perhaps more force than that readily or comfortably available through the use of unhafted pecking stones.

ELONGATED FLAT-ENDED HAMMERS: 8 specimens

Four of these specimens appeared to have been originally designed as hammers while the other four were converted axes. Three of the latter were three-quarter-grooved (#1343, #1830, #3009) while the final side of the fourth (#1793, fig. 56h) seemed to have been grooved subsequent to its original manufacture, perhaps at the time of its conversion to a hammer. The four specimens originally designed as hammers had a centrally located full groove. Converted axes tended to be rectangular in horizontal cross section while the regular hammers were more nearly oval or square. The faces of the former bit end of the axes sloped toward one another but the bit end had been worked down, flattened, and smoothed so that the groove became central in location and, except for the insloping faces, the two ends became nearly the same in size, appearance, and shape. There would be no possibility of resharpening these tools so that they could again function as axes. The grooves ranged between 2 and 2.8 cm in width and averaged 0.5 cm in depth. All were of dense basalt except #2356, which was of sandstone. All had been deliberately shaped and all but two (#2356, #1662) had been well smoothed, even polished. Both ends of all but one specimen showed signs of battering but the former bit ends of several of the converted axes showed considerably more use than the poll. One hammer (#1793, the full-grooved converted axe, fig. 56h) bore little evidence of battering at either end. Either this hammer had seen little service or else it served in a somewhat different capacity from the others. Measurements are given below.

It is probable that the elongated flat-ended hammers represented the norm or action type for a general all-purpose hammer, while the other forms served, at least primarily, other more restricted purposes.

EQUILATERAL FLAT-ENDED HAMMERS: 4 specimens

These hammers differed from the others in that their length and width were almost equal to or even slightly greater than their height. They tended to be nearly circular in horizontal cross section, the groove full or nearly so and centrally located. On #2104 (fig. 56a) the groove was within less than 2 cm of meeting (out of a total diameter of 15 cm), whereas on #3109 the groove was within 3 cm of being full. The faces tapered from the groove edge slightly inward to the flat or slightly convex ends, and were smoothed but slightly irregular and not polished. All were of basalt, of which one (2667) was vesicular. Ends were slightly battered. The grooves averaged 2.5 cm in width and 0.5 cm in depth. Measurements are below.

Because of the different length-width-height ratio it seems probable that these tools when hafted had a different "heft" or feel from that of the elongated hammers, and, with their shape, perhaps also a different function. Kidder (1932, p. 55) suggests that similar tools may have been pemmican pounders.

ELONGATED FLAT-ENDED HAMMERS

Cat. No.	Length End-to-end	Width Edge-to-edge	Thickness Face-to-face	Provenience
1063	12.4 cm	8.6 cm	6.8 cm	Room E1, fill
1064	8.1	6.2	4.3	Room B1, fill
1343	10.2	8.2	6.1	Room B1, floor
1662	10.0	9.2	7.8	Room B2, fill
1793	9.9	8.4	5.4	Room D1, floor
1830	8.7	7.6	4.7	Room E2, fill
2356	9.3	8.0	7.9	Room C10, ventilator
3009	9.0	7.9	5.5	Room F2, floor

EQUILATERAL FLAT-ENDED HAMMERS

Cat. No.	Length End-to-end	Width Edge-to-edge	Thickness Face-to-face	Provenience
1714	8.5 cm	10.1 cm	10.0 cm	Room C5, fill
2104	9.2	9.3	9.0	Room E2, fill
2667	8.4	8.9	7.4	Room A3, floor
3109	10.5	10.2	8.0	Surface

IRREGULAR FLAT-ENDED HAMMERS: 3 specimens (fig. 56b)

These specimens were characterized by a lack of careful shaping and by the nature of the material, for all were of volcanic scoria. Their overall contours were much like those of the elongated flat-ended hammers but their faces and ends were very irregular, and since they were of lightweight material they would serve poorly as heavy battering implements. Two were three-quarter-grooved while only the high points of the third (#1974) were grooved. Both ends of the latter were rounded and neither showed much evidence of use, but, on each of the other two, one end was flattened and fairly regular while the other end was more convex and showed more signs of battering. Measurements are below.

It is unlikely that these implements functioned as hammers in the usual sense. Perhaps they served as combined hammers and abraders in some process such as dressing skins. Blows on even soft materials would cause signs of battering to appear on this spongelike material.

HAMMER WITH OFF-CENTER HAFT: 1 specimen

This unique, well-formed and polished specimen (#2077) of fine-grained basalt was three-quarter-grooved, and was found on the floor of the ventilator tunnel of Room C10. The top of the poll and the striking end were rectangular, flat, and parallel. The specimen was rectilinear in horizontal cross section and its faces were parallel, but the edges sloped toward one another so that the top or poll had a diameter of 4 cm, that of the striking end being only 2.5 cm. The width varied from 2.9 cm just below the groove to 2.5 cm at either end, making the striking end approximately square. The total length was 8.3 cm and the center of the groove was located 5.3 cm above the striking end. The groove itself was 1.7 cm wide and 0.2 cm deep.

The off-center location of the haft and the tapering edges of this hammer set it apart and made it in some respects similar in design to the axes. However, the facts that the edges rather than the sides tapered and that the hammering end was square rather than elongated leave little doubt that this was originally designed as a hammer and was not a converted axe. It may have had a specialized function but if so, the nature of this is not known. It was found in immediate association with a shaftsmoother (#2119, fig. 54c). Polishing stones, pottery, and a number of pieces of shell were also on the floor of Room C10.

File (?): 1 specimen (fig. 58b)

This implement of andesite, from the fill of Room F2, conformed more or less to those tentatively designated as files by Kidder (1932, pp. 82-83). It was a naturally flat, thin (1.5 cm) fragment 7.2 cm wide and 8.4 cm long though apparently it was once longer. One of the long sides had been beveled from one side to a sharp edge, which had then been nicked along its entire length.

Hoe (?): 1 specimen (fig. 57f)

This fragment from the kiva fill appeared to have been the notched end of a larger implement, perhaps a hoe. All that remained was the notched butt of a thin (0.7 cm), flat rhyolite slab. The full width was not present (present width 7 cm) and it was broken just beyond the notches (present length 4.8 cm). The faces were flat and very well smoothed as was the end of the butt, but the notches were formed by rough percussion chipping and no attempt was made to obliterate the chipping marks.

Points and Blades: 7 specimens (fig. 57)

These were flakes with bifacial chipping, presumably hafted, and shaped so as to serve adequately for piercing and/or cutting; they can perhaps best be described by reference to figure 57. All but #3062 had secondary chipping on all major faces. That specimen (which is not illustrated) exhibited small irregular "use" chips along its two long sides, perhaps indicating that it served as a knife. One long side was straight but the other was quite curved. Two (#1295, #1892, fig. 57c) were small and triangular. Dimensions are below.

Snub-nosed Scraper: 1 specimen

This fragment from the fill of Room D2 was of obsidian and pyramidal in shape, 2.8 cm long, 1.7 cm wide, and 1 cm thick. One short end had secondary chipping on the convex side only.

IRREGULAR FLAT-ENDED HAMMERS

Cat. No.	Length End-to-end	Width Edge-to-edge	Thickness Face-to-face	Provenience
1829	10.6 cm	6.2 cm	7.9 cm	Room E2, fill
1974	9.5	7.8	7.4	Room D5, fill
2270	9.9	9.3	7.6	Room A2, fill

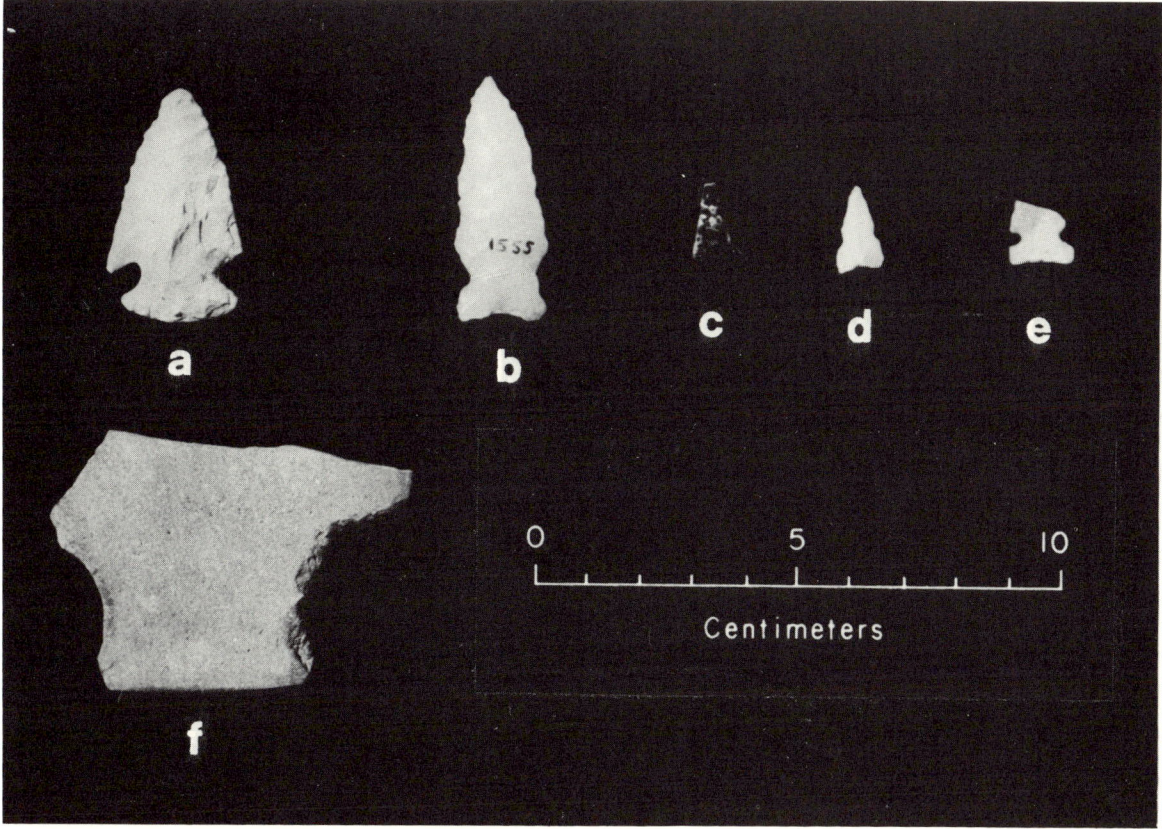

Figure 57. Objects of chipped stone from Site 616. Points: a. Kiva, fill, #2188; b. Room B1, floor, #1555; c. Room B5, fill, #1892; d. Room E1, floor, #1557; e. Room F2, fill, #3068. Hoe fragment (?): f. Kiva, fill, #2577.

Chipped stone was rare at Site 616 with approximately 200 pieces recovered, a total that includes all unmodified chips and utilized flakes, as well as the more uniform and elaborate artifact forms. The scraper was the only specimen, other than the points and blades discussed above, that appeared to have been intentionally formed and finished with secondary chipping.

Unretouched Flakes: 17 specimens

These were flakes without secondary chipping or other intentional shaping but they exhibited along one or, rarely, more than one of their long naturally sharp edges small irregular chips and scars such as result from use as a cutting tool.

Despite the seemingly casual nature of these implements they were quite uniform in size, although there were two shape modes, one rectangular and the other nearly square. Measurements are on page 150.

There were 13 rectangular flakes, including one unusually large specimen (#1867) not included above with dimensions of 4.8 by 2.8 by 0.9 cm, and five square flakes. Three of the square flakes (#1863, #1918, #2774) came from the fill of Room E2. The others came from Room F2 (#3073) and the floor of Room C6 (#1616). All

POINTS AND BLADES

Cat. No.	Material	Length	Width	Thickness	Provenience
1293	Obsidian	2.7 cm	2.4 cm	0.5 cm	Room D2, floor
1555	Chert	4.5	2.1	0.5	Room B1, floor
1557	Chert	1.6	0.9	0.2	Room E1, floor
1892	Obsidian	1.8	0.7	0.2	Room B5, fill
2188	Rhyolite	4.4	2.6	0.8	Kiva, fill
3062	Petrified Wood	5.5	3.1	0.5	Room F2, fill
3068	Rhyolite	(1.2)	1.3	0.2	Room F2, fill

UNRETOUCHED FLAKES

	Size Range of Rectangular Flakes	Size Range of Square Flakes
Length	3.1 – 3.7 cm	3.5 – 4.1 cm
Width	1.2 – 2.2	3.3 – 3.5
Thickness	0.3 – 1.3	0.7 – 2.0

but one of the square specimens were of petrified wood, the exception on being of rhyolite (#1616). All four of the rectangular flakes were of petrified wood. Of the four exceptions, #1867 was of rhyolite and the other three of obsidian (#1651, #2485, #3073). One rectangular flake of petrified wood (#1162) may have had intentional serrations rather than use chips along one edge, but the specimen was too fragmentary for this to be definitely determined.

Fill

Room E1 (2); Room E2 (4); Room F2 (2); walk-in well (1)

Floor

Room B1 (4); Room C1 (1); Room C5 (1); Room C6 (1)

Trench north of Room C1

Fill (1)

Chips: 155 specimens

All except a small handful of the chips recovered were of petrified wood, the exceptions being of rhyolite and andesite. By definition none had been worked or bore evidence of having been used though most possessed naturally sharp edges. In shape and general characteristics they were not noticeably different from the unretouched flakes, although some specimens were larger (up to 8 by 7 by 6 cm) than any that appeared to have been used.

The overwhelming preponderance of chips of petrified wood was curious in that this was almost the only occurrence of that material at the site. Tools of petrified wood were very rare. If these chips represent waste fragments from the manufacture of other tool forms, what has become of the finished implements? If the unretouched flakes and chips are considered a single category, it would be said that approximately 10 percent had been demonstrably utilized, that is, used in such a way or on such material that irregular use flakes were dislodged. Others may have been used without this result; the chips themselves may represent the end product rather than a by-product of a manufacturing process.

The distribution of these chips may be of some significance. The major portion of the chips occurred in or around Area D, the walk-in well, and Room B1 (even those in the fill of Room E2 might have come from the roof of Room B1). These three areas contained three of the four mealing rooms found at the site. Perhaps the roofs of such rooms served as gathering places or focal points for a number of activities for groups of individuals (men and women?); or perhaps this area was the location of an unexcavated workshop of the site's flint knapper(s).

Fill

(Some figures are estimates) Room B1 (35); Room B2 (7); Room B3 (1); Room B7 (4); Room C1 (8); Room C9 (5); Room D5 (16); Room E1 (17); Room E2 (24); Room F2 (1); kiva (2); walk-in well (20)

Floor

Room B1 (1); Room B2 (5); Room B5 (8); Room C10 (2); Room D1 (2)

Cores: 4 specimens

These irregular chunks of stone appeared to have been the source of at least some of the chips described above. None of the striking platforms seemed to have been deliberately prepared. Three, all from Area D (#1215, #1791, #2178), were of petrified wood and one (#1737) was of andesite. Two ranged around 10 by 10 by 7 cm in size while the other two, including the one of andesite, were approximately 5 by 5 by 3 cm.

The distribution of these cores conformed to that of the chips. Chips of andesite as well as the andesite core came from the walk-in well.

Fill

Room D3 (1); walk-in well (1)

Floor

Room D1 (1); Room D2 (1)

Choppers (?): 7 specimens

In no case could it be definitely determined that these objects were actually utilized as tools, and the recorded specimens were representative of a much larger number that were not saved. They consisted of fist-size angular blocks of andesite identical to those distributed profusely over, and derived from, the volcanic dike behind the site. They were of a convenient size and generally had one or more naturally sharp edges. They would have served admirably as choppers or rough scrapers but the modification resulting from such use would not necessarily differ noticeably from that caused by the action of natural forces. These stones occurred fairly frequently in the fill of the rooms excavated, including those where lava cobbles were not utilized for wall construction, and one (#2197) came from the floor of Room E2. Proof of their use is difficult but it seems unlikely that the inhabitants would have completely ignored such readily accessible and serviceable material.

Fill

Room B2 (1); walk-in well (4); trench north of Room C3 (1)

Floor

Room E2 (1)

Pot Cover (?): 1 specimen

This was a piece of tabular sandstone from the walk-in well, 1.5 cm thick, which had been made circular in outline (diameter: 15 cm) by rough chipping. No other modification or mark of use was evident.

Pot Supports: 12 specimens

These were brick-shaped objects of stone or adobe, with a rounded-rectangular cross section and typical size of 27 by 12 by 7 cm. Eleven were of a soft sandstone and one (from Room D1) was of fired adobe. All were smoothly finished and were reddened and smudged from having been placed in a fire. Room D5 had an unexcavated adobe projection extending into the firepit from the edge coterminous with the room wall, which undoubtedly served the same function.

Eight pot supports were in firepits when found. In most instances they were standing on end against one of the long walls of the firepit, either at its midpoint or about one-third of the distance from one end. Where two occurred together they usually were paired against opposite long walls of the firepit. The length of the supports was such that when standing on end in the firepit the upper ends were approximately level with the top of the slabs lining the firepit. Two firepits (Rooms C5, E2), while not having supports in direct association, apparently had them originally, for a pot support was found on the floor of Room C5, and in Room E2 the bottom of the firepit had a pair of slight depressions correctly positioned to receive pot supports. Only three firepits had no sign of this equipment.

Fill

Room C2 (1); kiva (1)

Floor

Room B5 (1); Room C5 (1)

Firepit

Room A1 (2); Room B2 (2); Room B7 (1); Room C10 (2); Room D1 (1)

Worked Sandstone Slabs

Several dozen fragments and about one dozen complete slabs of tabular sandstone 2 to 4 cm thick were encountered in the fill of several of the rooms but no complete count was made. All appeared to have been originally roughly rectangular in outline with rounded corners. The surfaces were naturally flat and smooth, the edges shaped by rough chipping and in rare instances smoothed by pecking. On one or two specimens rough spots on the surfaces had been smoothed by pecking. In size they appeared to have ranged from approximately 52 by 47 by 2 cm to 16 by 12 by 2 cm. The larger specimens could have been door or hatch covers but the smaller specimens must have served in some other capacity. Some may have been from destroyed or not yet built firepits or mealing bin walls; others may have been simply paving stones such as were found on the floor of Room A1, although normally these latter were not intentionally shaped. None had the smooth grease-stained, fire-reddened surfaces characteristic of cooking slabs.

Fill

Room B1 (2); Room C6 (1); Room C9 (1)

Floor

Room B2 (1); ramp of walk-in well, with Skeleton 3 (1)

Scoria Cylinders and Cones: 21 specimens (fig. 58)

These objects of volcanic scoria had an average length of 8.3 cm with a range of 6 to 11.3 cm. Fourteen were nearly circular in cross section with central diameters ranging from 2.8 to 3.9 cm, and diameter variances on individual specimens of 0.3 cm or less. The other seven (#1322, #1548, #1593, #1625, #1916, #1925, #1926) were oval in cross section with central diameters ranging from 3.2 by 2.1 cm on the smallest to 4.2 by 3.5 cm on the largest. The two cone-shaped specimens (#1961, #2191) had diameters ranging from about 3 cm at the "base" to 1.5 cm at the "tip," while the cylinders had their widest diameter at the center with a slight taper toward each end. Two specimens (#1548, #1916, fig. 58d, g) had an oval cross section with a lengthwise torsion of about 45°, so that the greatest diameter at one end was in a plane rotated 45° from that of the greatest diameter at the other end. One circular specimen (#1302, fig. 58e) had a slight groove extending halfway around the center of the artifact. If this specimen (9.9

Figure 58. Objects of volcanic scoria from Site 616. Unidentified object: a. Room F2, fill, #3108. File (?): b. Room F2, fill, #3066. Cylinders: c. Room C1, fill, #1515; f. Room E2, fill, #1950; g. Walk-in-well, fill, #1916. Cylinder with longitudinal torsion: d. Room B1, floor, #1548. Cylinder with central groove: e. Room E1, fill, #1302.

by 3.4 by 3.4 cm) had been wider and broader it doubtless would have been included in the type "Irregular Flat-ended Hammers." The ends of a number of scoria cylinders seemed battered, and it is possible that functionally these and the vesicular basalt hammers formed a single class or type; but descriptively they were two discrete entities, and since there is no solid basis for a functional classification they have been treated separately.

One end of each of seven specimens (#1066, #1302, #1322, #1515, #1533, #1950, #1961, fig. 58c, e, f) appeared to have been somewhat flattened by pounding or grinding, while the sides of three, including the two with longitudinal torsion (#1548, #1877, #1916, fig. 58d, g), showed only slight evidence of rubbing or abrading. Most were roughly finished all over but the surfaces of a few were fairly well smoothed.

The meagre evidence of use as pounders or abraders implies the possibility of some other use for these specimens. Similar implements have been suggested as prayer-plume holders (Smith 1952, pp. 114, 133, 194, 228, 233-234, fig. 31c). In this case not even the cone-shaped specimens would stand alone, but of course they could have been set in a clay base. Present evidence neither supports nor contradicts an interpretation as prayer-plume holders, nor does it suggest any other.

Fill

Room C1 (2); Room C5 (1); Room D3 (1); Room E1 (3); Room F2 (4); walk-in well (2)

Floor

Room A1 (1); Room B1 (2); Room B2 (1); Room C3 (1); Room C5 (3)

Scoria Object: 1 specimen (fig. 58a)

This specimen from the fill of Room F2, with dimensions of 16.9 by 10.9 by 6.2 cm, was shaped very much like a large squat mano but the nature of the material suggested a different function. Perhaps this implement served as an abrader or flesher in treating skins. Although it appeared to be intentionally shaped, it did not show definite signs of wear.

Jet Buttons: 4 specimens

These roughly circular, square, or rectangular objects of jet or lignite may have served as either decorations or buttons. It seems evident that all had the same or similar basic function, but descriptively each was unique. All were biconically drilled from below, the holes joining each other but not penetrating to the upper surface, and on two of them (#1568, #1928) a ridge or buttress had been left on the underside to strengthen this weakened area. In the very corners of the upper surface of one rectangular specimen (#1928), 7.2 by 4.8 by 1.1 cm, conical depressions had been drilled. A turquoise setting was found in one of these, and the other three doubtless had once contained similar turquoise settings, for they still held remnants of what seemed to be pine-resin adhesive. Two rounded rectangular fragments of turquoise (one blue and one green), found on the floor about one meter from the button, may have been two of the missing settings. A little adhesive material observed on the center section of the button may indicate that this surface, or part of it, was once covered with a mosaic. A square button (#1176) 2.2 by 2.2 by 1.8 cm, with rounded corners, had a conical depression drilled into its upper portion that probably had once contained an inset. This specimen was hemispherical in cross section unlike the others, which were subrectangular. The other two buttons were without apparent ornamentation; #1294 was a somewhat irregular rectangle (3.7 by 2 by 1.2 cm), while #1568 was more oval (3.2 by 1.7 cm).

Pepper (1920, plate 1) illustrates a very similar jet button from Pueblo Bonito.

Fill

Room C2 (1); Room C5 (1); Room D3 (1)

Floor

Room C5 (1)

Figurines: 3 specimens

This general category includes three rather disparate objects. Two perhaps had been attached to clothing in much the same fashion as the jet buttons described above; at any rate, their undersides had been similarly drilled. But the third specimen from the fill of Room D2 (#1159, fig. 60b) was without drilled holes, and was almost whalelike in appearance. It was 2.5 cm long by 1.0 cm high by 0.6 cm thick (from side to side) and was made of smoky but translucent quartz. It consisted almost entirely of a rather fishlike head with an upturned nose, a mouth, and cleft chin, it was highest over the eyes, and tapered toward the back of the head. It was well polished although minute striations were evident on top and bottom. The second specimen (#1160, fig. 59c), also from the fill of Room D2, was a batlike representation of calcitic limestone similar to the bat- or birdlike objects of fossil shell. It had outspread wings and measured 3.6 cm from wing tip to wing tip, 2.8 cm from head to tail, and was 1 cm thick. It was well worked by grinding and polishing and the final design details were rendered by incised lines. Small holes were conically drilled from the upper surface in the center of the outer border of each wing. The third specimen (#1896, fig. 59b) was of a well-formed, three-dimensional frog of the same material as the red beads. Its legs and eyes were depicted in relief on the upper surface and the base was flat, though a groove extended completely around the neck. It had a biconically drilled hole in its base that did not penetrate the upper surface. In overall design style this specimen was very similar to the two frogs of Glycymeris shell (fig. 65a, d). Its dimensions were 4.1 cm from head to tail, 3.4 cm wide and 1.3 cm thick.

Fill

Room D2 (2)

Floor

Room C5 (1)

Disc Beads: an estimated 2,876 specimens (table 9)

These beads were made from flat circular fragments of stone, each with a thickness less than its diameter and a very small centrally drilled hole.

In the main, three materials were used for stone beads: turquoise, and two unidentified stones, one buff-red and the other black or gray-black. The red stone was a fine-grained, nonlaminated earthy material with some quartz. It was probably sedimentary in origin but had been subjected to heat. Except for color, the red and the black beads were at first glance very similar in both appearance and texture. Both materials were fine-grained, fairly soft, and readily worn by rubbing. Generally the specimens made from these materials, which constituted the vast majority of all stone beads recovered, were quite small and in most instances the central hole was so small that only the very point of a #10 needle would penetrate it. The beads were almost perfectly circular

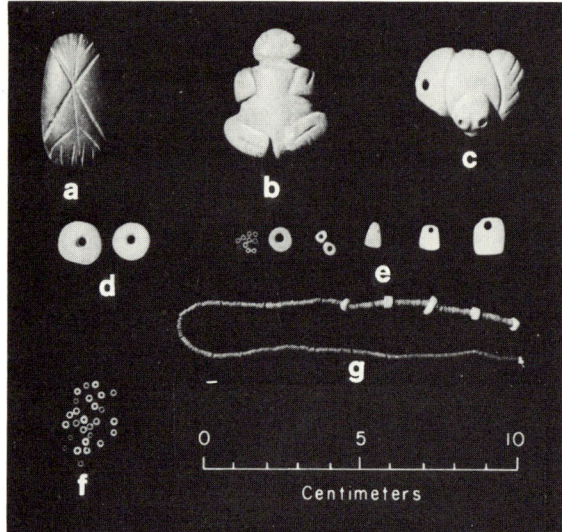

Figure 59. Carved and drilled stone objects from Site 616. Incised felsite pebble: a. Room B1, floor, #1561. Figurine of frog: b. Room C5, floor, #1896. Figurine of bat: c. Room D2, fill, #1160. Beads: d. room C8, floor, #2551. Beads and pendants: e. various rooms. Red and black beads: f. various rooms. Necklace of red, black, and turquoise beads: g. Room C1, floor (in association with Skeleton 2), #1659.

and nearly all were of an almost identical diameter and thickness, with smooth edges and smooth flat surfaces.

Since many beads were found in firepits, it was at first thought that perhaps the red beads were simply those that had come in contact with fire, but a test firing of black beads to 800°C did not turn them red (rather they became gray to white); nor did firing red beads turn them black. Closer examination revealed that the material of the black beads was slightly different in composition from that of the red beads and may have been volcanic in origin.

The turquoise beads were generally larger, thicker, and much less uniform both individually and as a group.

Four beads (#2551, fig. 59d) of an unidentified stone with a cloudy translucent appearance, from the floor of Room C8, were larger than any other stone beads, with diameters between 1.2 and 1.9 cm and thicknesses between 1.2 and 1.4 cm. Their edges and sides were rounded but not evenly finished.

Turquoise pendants (see below) and shell beads were found in many of the same rooms as the stone beads, and in Room C10 there were also black stone pendants and pendants made of dewclaws of deer; the latter were also encountered in the firepit of Room C5.

In three instances beads were found sufficiently undisturbed that partial sequences of beads could be recorded. On the floor of Room C1 there was a string with a repeated sequence of 18 small black beads alternating with one medium turquoise bead (#1659, fig. 59g). There were two partial strings on the floor of Room C8. The first had a sequence of 6 black, 12 red, 6 black, followed by a number of shell beads too broken to count. The second partial string had 6 black, 8 red, 6 black, 6 white, 6 black, 8 red. All of the beads in these last two strings were small. Other similar beads were in association but in no discernible sequences.

Pendants: 63 specimens

This category embraces various small objects with an off-center hole or groove apparently for suspension. They were generally flat, thin, and rectanguloid or, less often, trianguloid. Turquoise was the most popular material, but in the firepit of Room C10 were a half dozen pendants of the same black stone as that from which the beads were made. These and the pendants of turquoise normally were less than 1 cm in their longest dimension and approximately 0.3 cm thick, though a few were slightly larger. Similar in shape but larger was a subrectangular pendant of travertine (2.5 by 1.5 by 0.3 cm) from the floor of Room B1 and a subrectangular pendant of felsite (3 by 1.9 by 0.3 cm) from the fill of Room C1. All had been shaped by grinding and polishing and all had one hole drilled (all biconically except the one of felsite, which was conically drilled) near one apex of the triangular specimens and near the center of one of the short sides of the rectanguloid specimens.

Another form was a plummetlike object 4.8 cm long and oval in cross section (0.85 by 0.7 cm). This pendant (#2220, fig. 60s), from the floor of Room C10, was of a cemented tufaceous material, smooth and polished all over. One end was flat, while the body of the pendant tapered slightly toward the other end, which was rounded. A deep thin groove encircled the pendant 0.2 cm from the flat end.

One turquoise pendant was rectangular but the lower half was at an angle of about 20° to the upper half. It was among the stone and shell beads in direct association with Skeleton 2 in Room C2.

Fill

    Room B2 (1); Room C1 (2); Room C2 (2); Room C5 (3); Room C9 (10); Room C10 (1)

Floor

    Room B1 (1); Room C5 (2); Room C10 (1)

Firepit

    Room C10 (40)

	Small			Medium			Large		
Thickness	approx. 0.06 cm			0.1-0.5 cm			0.5-0.8 cm		
Bead Diameter	approx. 0.2 cm			0.2-1.0 cm			1.0-1.5 cm		
Hole Diameter	less than 0.1 cm			approx. 0.1 cm			0.2-0.3 cm		
Provenience	Red	Black	Turq.	Red	Black	Turq.	Red	Black	Other
Room B1 Floor	2	15							
Room C1 Fill	75	36				15			2 [a]
Room C1 Floor		75				5			
Room C2 Skeleton 2		189	1		1	1			
Room C3 Fill		5		36					
Room C3 Floor		52				3			
Room C4 Floor	18			2		1			
Room C5 Fill	15				5	10			5 [a]
Room C5 Floor	31					3			
Room C7 Fill	1	52	2						
Room C8 Fill	25	20					1		
Room C8 Floor	75	75	5						4 [b]
Room C9 Fill	500*	500*				10			
Room C10 Firepit	500*	500*							
Room E2 Fill						1			
Kiva Floor	2								
Totals	1244	1519	8	38	6	49	1	0	11

* *Estimated.*

a. *Turquoise*
b. *Cloudy translucent stone*

Table 9. Size and provenience of disc beads from Site 616.

Mosaic Fragments (?): several hundred

Two clusters of carefully shaped but undrilled stone fragments were found that may have been parts of mosaics. One group (#2231) from the floor of Room C8 consisted of approximately 45 thin (0.1 cm or less), flat, generally rectangular turquoise chips. The pieces were all quite small (length: 0.3 - 0.5 cm; width: 0.2 cm), but smooth and well shaped, with straight sides. Their small size argued against their being undrilled pendant blanks, while their careful shaping suggested that they were not simply bead blanks. Associated with these turquoise pieces was a well-finished disc of red bead stone. This disc, which was as thin as the turquoise chips, had a diameter of 1.5 cm and a central hole 0.2 cm in diameter.

The second group (#1673), found in a cluster on the floor of Room D1, consisted of several hundred small (0.5 cm or less) fragments of turquoise, malachite, galena, and the red stone from which beads were made. Most were thin (0.1 cm or less) and flat and nearly all were shaped rectangles, squares, or discs, but a few were thicker and irregularly shaped. Some appeared to be reused fragments of broken beads and pen-

156 • Mariana Mesa

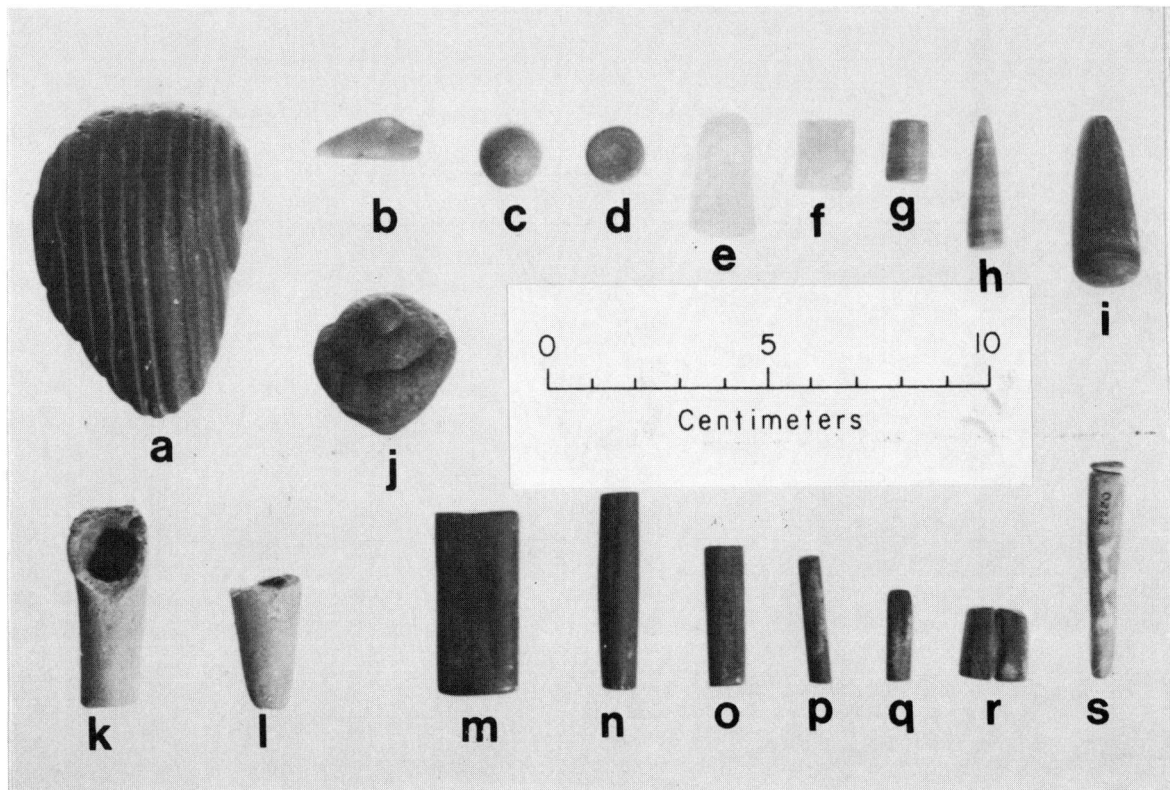

Figure 60. Miscellaneous objects of stone, shell, and clay from Site 616. Unworked laminated stone: a. Room F2, floor, #3040. Figurine (fish?): b. Room D2, fill, #1159. Balls: c. Room D1, floor, #1940; d. Room C1, fill, #1199. Tapered chalcedony cylinder: e. Room D2, fill, #1071. Fluorite cylinder: f. Room C9, fill, #2236. Tapered shell cylinder: g. Room C8, floor, #2094. Conical shell object: h. Room C8, floor, #2094. Tapered andesite cylinder: i. Room D2, fill, #1156. Concretion: j. Room F2, floor, #3038. Clay elbow pipe: k. Room D5, fill, #1869. Clay pipe: l. Room E2, fill, #1962. Hematite cylinders: m. Room C3, fill, #1643; n. Area C, trench, #1171; o. Room C3, fill, #1640; p. Room C8, floor, #2510; q. Room C8, floor, #2510. Grooved hematite cube: r. Room C3, fill, #1644. Stone pendant: s. Room C10, floor, #2220.

dants. The vast majority of this category were of light green turquoise, with some that were more blue in color. In general, the quality of the turquoise appeared to be somewhat better than that found elsewhere at Site 616.

Two thin, shaped, turquoise fragments from Room C5 may also have been bits of mosaic or other originally inlaid fragments. Pieces of what seemed to be a pine-resin adhesive adhered to one surface.

Floor

    Room C5 (2); Room C8 (ca. 45); Room D1 (several hundred)

Stone Balls: 6 specimens

Five stone balls were of azurite, the sixth of an unidentified material (#1615). The surface of the latter was naturally pitted with very small holes; it had the general appearance of sandstone but was harder than most sandstone. Four (e.g., #1940, fig. 60c) were smooth and quite round (diameters: 1.5, 1.5, 1.2, 1.0 cm); another (#2230) was very smooth but had a number of facets, so that its diameter ranged from 1.1 to 1.3 cm. The final specimen (#1199, fig. 60d) was a hemisphere rather than a sphere and thus perhaps should not be described here, but was included because of the similarity in size and material. Its diameter was 1.4 cm and its height 0.8 cm. In the center of its flat base there had been scratched (not drilled) a circular depression (0.1 cm deep and 0.4 cm in diameter).

Fill

    Room C1 (1); Room D3 (1)

Floor

    Room C5 (1); Room C6 (1); Room C8 (1); Room D1 (1)

Hematite Cylinders: 8 specimens (fig. 60m-q)

These cylinders had been ground to shape and were smooth all over, though occasionally facets extending the length of the long dimension were visible. In general they were approximately circular in cross section with diameters ranging from 0.9 to 1.1 cm, but one (#2510, fig. 60p) was smaller with a diameter of 0.6 cm, and one (#1643, fig. 60m) was oval with a diameter varying from 1.1 to 2 cm. In length they varied from 2.5 to 4.3 cm. Both ends were flat and at right angles to the sides on all except #1158, on which one end was flat but at about a 60° angle with the sides, while the other end was rounded.

Fill

Room C1 (1); Room C3 (2); Room D2 (1); kiva (1)

Floor

Room C1 (1); Room C8 (2)

Shaped Objects: 8 specimens (fig. 60)

This residue category contained the worked specimens that could not be logically included in any of the other groups.

A fluorite cylinder (#2236, fig. 60f), not unlike those of hematite, came from the fill of Room C9. It had a diameter comparable to that of the others but was shorter, with a length of only 1.6 cm. It was quite round with flat ends and was well finished and smooth all over, having a cloudy translucent aspect and a greenish color. This may have been a tubular bead blank, for the beginning of a drilled hole appeared in the center of one of the flat ends. A second cylinder (#2100) of aragonite with a reddish, almost translucent, appearance and no trace of a drilled hole, but otherwise similar in shape and dimensions (1.3 cm in diameter, 1.5 cm long) to the one of fluorite, came from the fill of Room C10.

A tapered cylindrical object of chalcedony (#1071, fig. 60e) 2.7 cm high, with a flat base 1.6 cm in diameter tapering to a rounded tip 1 cm in diameter, came from the fill of Room D2. It too was well finished, smooth, and almost translucent. A second somewhat similar tapered cylinder was found in the fill of Room D2. This latter object (#1156, fig. 60i), of andesite, was longer (3.8 cm) and both ends were rounded, but the diameter was nearly the same as that of the chalcedony cylinder (1.6 cm at the thick end to 0.7 cm near the other end). It was well finished but longitudinal facets were evident. An object of cloudy quartz (#2487) very similar to the andesite specimen from Room D2 came from the floor of Room C5. This specimen could be a naturally waterworn pebble but it was smooth and so nearly like the one shown in figure 60i, in overall appearance and dimensions (height: 3.4 cm, diameter tapering from 1.6 cm at one end to 1.2 cm at the other) that it is included here.

In the fill of Room C3 along with the hematite cylinders was a rectangular parallelopiped (1.6 by 1.5 by 1 cm) of hard hematite (#1644, fig. 60r). The four longest edges were somewhat rounded but otherwise the surfaces were quite flat and the edges sharp. Parallel to the long edges and bisecting the two broad faces was a narrow groove that completely encircled the specimen.

On the floor of Room B1 was a thin flat stone of felsite (#1561), oval in outline and basically so in cross section (4.3 by 2.2 by 1.1 cm), although the basal portion of one large side was worn flat and polished. The opposite side was covered with incised lines.

On the floor of the kiva ventilator tunnel, 178 cm from its opening into the kiva, was a multifaceted pebble (#2600) that was very heavy for its size (2.0 by 1.2 by 1.1 cm). It seemed to be made up of malachite inclusions in hematite. The facets completely covered the specimen and all were well polished.

Fill

Room C3 (1); Room C9 (1); Room C10 (1); Room D2 (2)

Floor

Room B1 (1); Room C5 (1); kiva ventilator (1)

Quartz Crystals: 10 specimens

These natural crystals of quartz ranged in height from 2.5 to 4.6 cm and in diameter from 1 to 1.7 cm. Six were unmodified but on the others (#1313, #1534, #1660, #1941) the edges were slightly rounded and the surface on occasion was slightly cloudy. This condition may have been brought about by intentional grinding but could also be the result of natural water-rolling in a stream bed.

Fill

Room C1 (2); Room D2 (1)

Floor

Room B1 (1); Room C1 (1); Room C4 (1); Room C5 (2); Room C8 (1); Room D1 (1)

Naturally Shaped Stone Objects: 14 specimens

No general description of these objects can be made. They may have been saved as curiosities or their presence may have been entirely fortuitous.

CONCRETIONS: 7 specimens

Six concretions of chalcedony of various shapes were

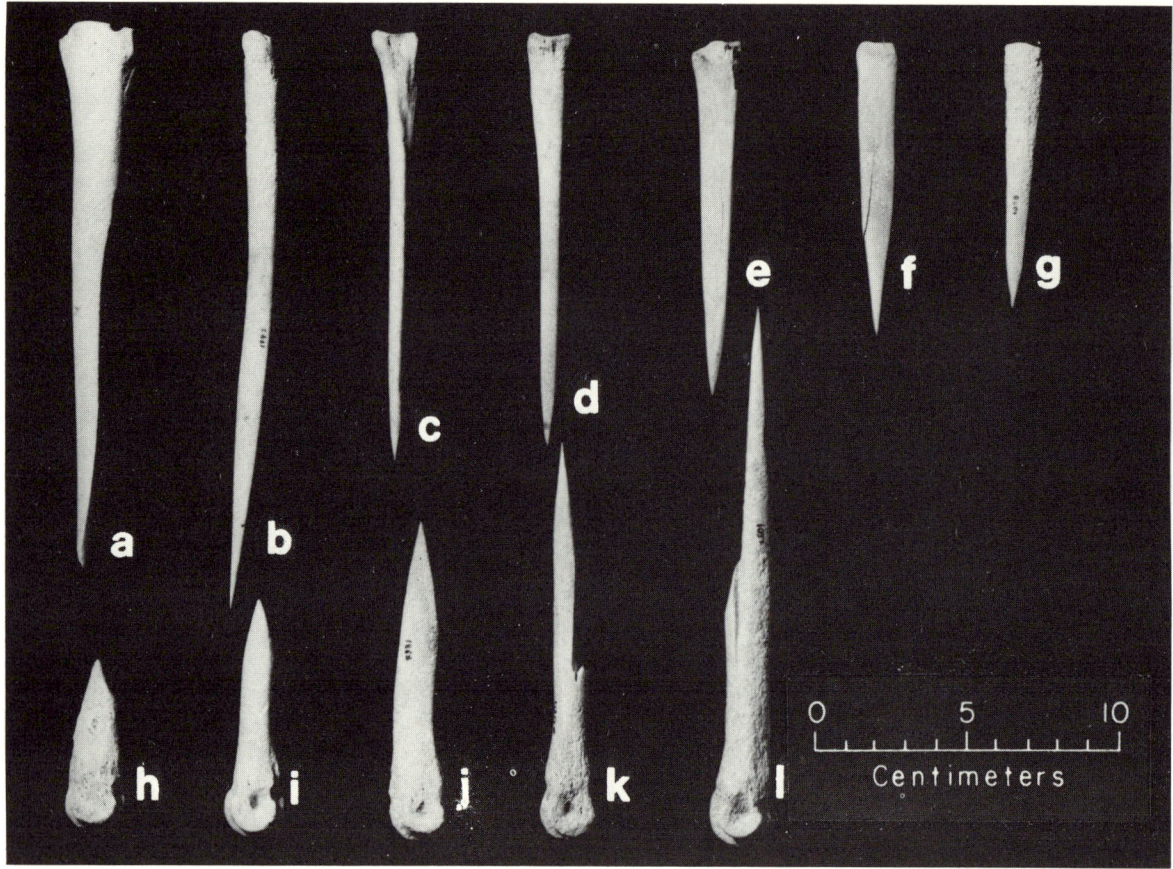

Figure 61. Bone awls with head of bone unworked, except by original splitting, from Site 616: a. Area C, trench, #1050; b. Room D1, floor, #1942; c. Room E2, fill, #1597; d. Room F1, fill, #2176; e. Room B1, floor, #1184; f. Room E2, floor, #2196; g. Room C1, fill, #1058; h. Room C1, floor, #1653; i. Area C, trench, #1053; j. Room D1, floor, #1888; k. Room D1, fill, #1599; l. Area C, trench, #1051.

found. Another (#3038, fig. 60j) of an unidentified material had the appearance of five stacked discs that tapered in size in both directions from the largest central ring.

Fill

Room C1 (1)

Floor

Room C1 (1); Room C3 (1); Room C5 (3); Room F2 (1)

WEATHERED STONES: 2 specimens

A long (6.6 cm) fragment of petrified wood (#1178) rectangular in cross section (1.2 by 1.1 cm) came from the fill of Room C1. It was cloudy in appearance and smooth, perhaps from extensive handling or more likely from being waterworn.

An unidentified laminated stone (#3040, fig. 60a) with alternating hard and soft layers was found on the floor of Room F2. The soft layers had eroded faster than the hard ones, giving it a ridged or corrugated aspect. Viewed from the top it resembled an animal's head in outline. It could have served as a fetish or perhaps simply as a curiosity. Its dimensions were 6.9 by 4.9 by 3.2 cm.

OTHER: 5 specimens

An irregular pebble of quartzite (#1650), 1.1 by 1.1 by 0.9 cm, was found on the floor of Room C1.

A curved cylinder (#2182) of an unidentified soft red stone (not hematite) came from the fill of the kiva. One end was flat and possibly intentionally abraded, the other rounded. Its dimensions were: length 3 cm, diameter 1.4 cm.

An irregularly globular piece of oolitic hematite (#1403) came from the floor of Room C5. The piece was very irregular in shape and pitted but the major portion of its surface was smooth and had a high polish. With its various bulbous projections it could be imagined to represent any number of anthropomorphic beings. Its dimensions were 4 by 3.9 by 3.2 cm.

A fragment of a stalactite (#1565) 2 cm in diameter and 3 cm long was found on the floor of Room B1.

A pebble (#1649), possibly manganese oxide, came from the floor of Room C1. It was brown-black in color, very smooth, shiny, slick to the touch, and heavy for its size. A few small flat planes or facets, which may or may not have been natural, were apparent on the surface.

BONE ARTIFACTS

Awls: 54 specimens

HEAD OF BONE UNWORKED EXCEPT BY ORIGINAL SPLITTING: 21 specimens (fig. 61)

All but one specimen in this group were made from deer or pronghorn metapodials, six from the distal end, 14 from the proximal end. The single aberrant specimen was made from the distal end of a deer or pronghorn tibia. The size range was considerable, with no observable clustering around any particular norm. Lengths ranged from 5.5 to 17.5 cm, the average being 11.5 cm — perhaps mainly the fortuitous result of the original splitting.

Fill

Trench north of Area C (6); Room A1 (1); Room B1 (1); Room C1 (1); Room C4 (2); Room D1 (1); Room E1 (1); Room E2 (1); Room F1 (1)

Floor

Room A1 (1); Room B1 (1); Room C1 (1); Room D1 (1); Room E2 (1)

HEAD OF BONE INTACT: 6 specimens (fig. 62)

With the exception of the awls in this group, those from Site 616 seemed to be derived almost entirely from the bones of deer and pronghorn and primarily from the metapodials of those animals. Within this group, however, there was considerable variation. All were leg bones from several different species. Two (#1166, #1564, fig. 62g) were the distal ends of deer metapodials, a third (#2048) was the proximal end of a deer ulna, two others (#1164, fig. 62f, #2249) were bird bones, the distal end of a femur and the proximal end of a tibia respectively, and the sixth (#1876, fig. 62e) was the metapodial of a hare. The deer ulna was the longest of the group (11 cm), while the hare metapodial was the shortest (3 cm). The other four averaged 8 cm in length.

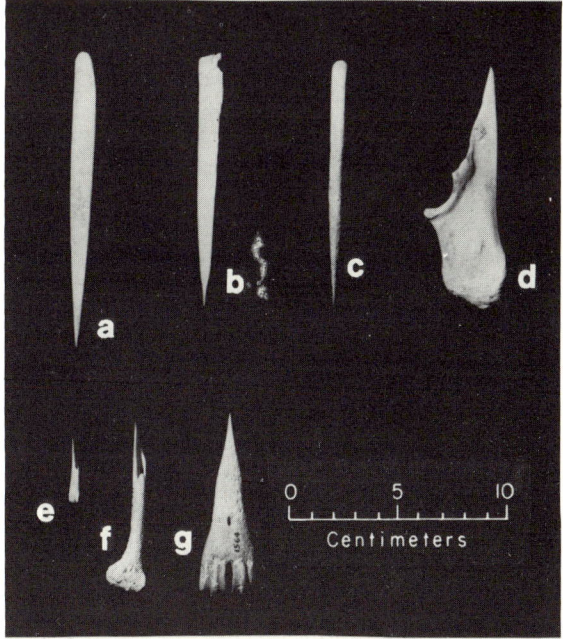

Figure 62. Bone awls from Site 616. Head of bone intact: d. Room C5, floor of mealing bin, #2098 (see also fig. 25); e. Walk-in well, mealing room, fill, #1876; f. Room E1, fill, #1164; g. Room B1, floor, #1564. Head wholly removed: a. Room E2, fill, #1953. Splinter: c. Room B5, embedded in floor plaster, #2173. Eyed: b. Room B1, floor, #1407.

Fill

Room C2 (1); Room C8 (1); Room E1 (1); walk-in well (1)

Floor

Room B1 (1); Room C5 (1)

HEAD WHOLLY REMOVED: 2 specimens (fig. 62a)

In general these two awls showed neither more nor better workmanship than was the general rule, except for the fact that the head was removed. One specimen from the fill of Room E2 (#1953, fig. 62a) was 13.5 cm in length, the second (#1865) 8 cm. Both appeared to be made from deer or pronghorn metapodials.

Fill

Room E2 (2)

SPLINTER AWLS: 2 specimens (fig. 62c)

Both specimens were 11.5 cm in length and seemed to be fragments of deer or pronghorn metapodials. One (#1407) may originally have been an eyed awl that became split longitudinally, and half was reused as a splinter awl, for the remains of a hole could be seen on one side of its broad end. The other (#2173, fig. 62c), embedded in the floor plaster had no eye.

Floor

Room B1 (1); Room B5 (1)

SKEWER AWLS: 13 specimens

These were long slender awls, each with a circular or oval cross section generally constant throughout its length, and with a dull point. Only one specimen (#1324) was complete (length 12 cm), although a fragment of another (#2240) was slightly longer (12.5 cm). The cross sections of different specimens ranged between 0.3 and 0.5 cm. Except for a gradual taper towards the point, the diameter of any one specimen remained fairly constant throughout its length. The shape of the butt was generally flat but in one case (#2247) there was a groove or notch and in another (#1193) a slight concavity. All specimens were completely worked with no original surfaces obviously remaining, and were well polished throughout their lengths.

Kidder seems to include awls somewhat similar to these in his category "Head of bone wholly or almost wholly removed" (Kidder 1932, pp. 211-213, figs. 172, 173, 177). However, the specimens from Site 616 appeared sufficiently distinct and were of sufficient uniformity in manufacture to warrant their separate description. Unlike Kidder's specimens, these characteristically had a dull rather than a sharp point, another factor that set them off from other awl types. It is possible that these implements served some purpose similar to that of the hairpin described below.

Fill

Room A1 (1); Room C1 (1); Room C2 (1); Room C8 (2); Room D5, cist (1); Room E2 (1); walk-in well (2)

Floor

Room B2 (1); Room C2 (2); Room F1 (1)

EYED AWL: 1 specimen (fig. 62b)

This specimen was a broad flat awl-shaped instrument with a large needlelike eye, 0.6 cm in diameter, in the butt end. It was found on the floor of Room C2 and was similar in shape and proportion to an "awl with the head wholly removed." The length of the specimen was 15 cm, the greatest width 1.5 cm (at the point of the drilled hole), and the greatest thickness 0.4 cm. The breadth of the instrument relative to its thickness and length distinguished it from the tools designated by Kidder as needles (Kidder 1932, pp. 222-225, fig. 188).

FRAGMENTS

In addition to the awls described above, 11 unclassifiable fragments were recovered. All appeared to have been made of split deer or pronghorn metapodials but the original condition of the heads could not be ascertained.

Fill

Room B1 (2); Room C7 (1); Room C8 (1); Room E2 (1); kiva (1); walk-in well (3)

Floor

Room D1 (1); Room B5 (1)

GENERAL COMMENT ON AWLS

Except for the initial splitting of the bone and the grinding necessary to obtain the sharp tapering point, none but the skewer awls showed evidence of extensive workmanship. The awls of split deer or pronghorn metapodials with the heads unworked were by far the most common form. Because of their localized occurrence the two awls with the heads worked down and perhaps the splinter awls may be simply variations by two individual artisans. It seems likely that the skewer awls had a different function or were used in a different manner from the other awls, but the nature of this possible difference is unknown.

Scrapers

END SCRAPERS: 3 specimens (fig. 63b, c, d)

All three end scrapers were made from the distal end of the right humerus of the pronghorn. Two were 15 cm long, the third (#1945, fig. 63c) only 13 cm. They appeared to have been manufactured by holding the distal end of the humerus in the hand and grinding the central section of the shaft on an abrader at an angle of approximately 30° to 40°. The remainder of the groove was then formed by abrading the shaft at a lower angle on a convex abrader. The sides and end of the head were smoothed slightly if at all. The shaft of one specimen (#1296, fig. 63d) was decorated with thin incised lines. The design was rectilinear with straight lines and stepped triangles.

Fill

Trench north of Area C (1); Room D3 (1)

Floor

Room D1 (1)

SIDE SCRAPERS: 2 specimens (fig. 63a)

Each of these specimens was formed from the pelvis of a deer by cutting off the projecting portions on either

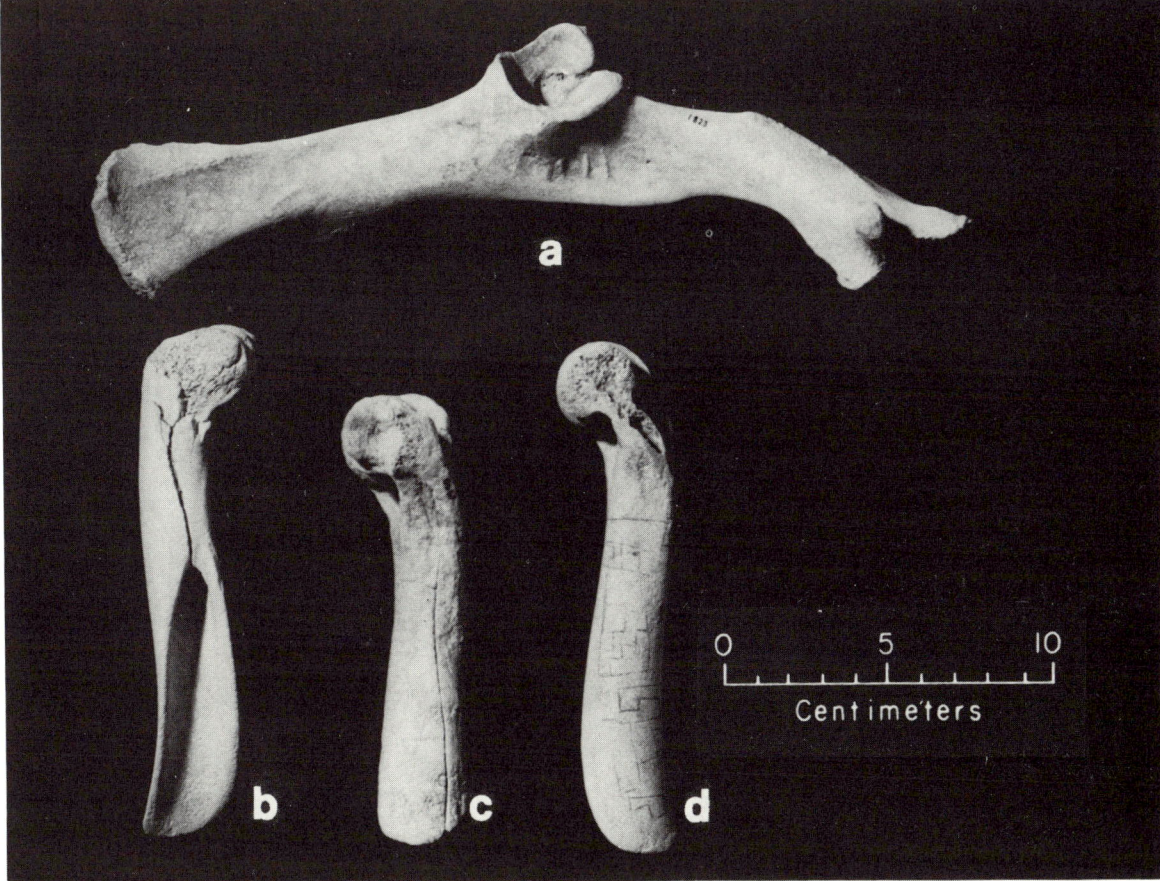

Figure 63. Bone scrapers from Site 616. End: b. Area C, trench, #1065; c. Room D1, floor, #1945; d. Room D3, fill, #1296. Side: a. Room E2, fill, #1823.

end, leaving a long shaft roughly 3 cm in width. The central edge immediately opposite the acetabulum was used for scraping, with the ends apparently serving as handles. It was apparently used in much the same fashion, if not on the same materials, as a modern spokeshave. The two specimens recovered were from the right and left halves of the pelvis respectively, and appeared to be of identical size and proportions. Since both were found in the same level of the fill of Room E2, it is possible that they were made from the pelvis of a single animal.

Rings: 3 specimens (fig. 64c, d, e)

Rings were sections of thin, circular, hollow bone with lengths less than their diameters. All three were well finished and polished, although on the smallest specimen the grooves made when the ring was cut were still evident. They had an average diameter of 2 cm and were 0.7 cm. wide.

The small internal diameter of these rings suggested that they could have been used as finger ornaments solely by children. They may have served some utilitarian purpose such as holding together the cracked but not broken pieces of shaftlike implements.

Fill

Room D5 (1); walk-in well (2)

Tubes: 20 specimens (fig. 64k-o)

Tubes were sections of thin, circular, hollow bone with lengths greater than their diameters. All specimens appeared to have been made from the leg bones of birds and small mammals. In general, they showed a high polish but the ridges and contours natural to the bone had generally not been obliterated, and the ends, while smooth, were not particularly even. In diameter they ranged from 0.7 to 1.3 cm with an average of 1.1 cm; their lengths showed considerable vari-

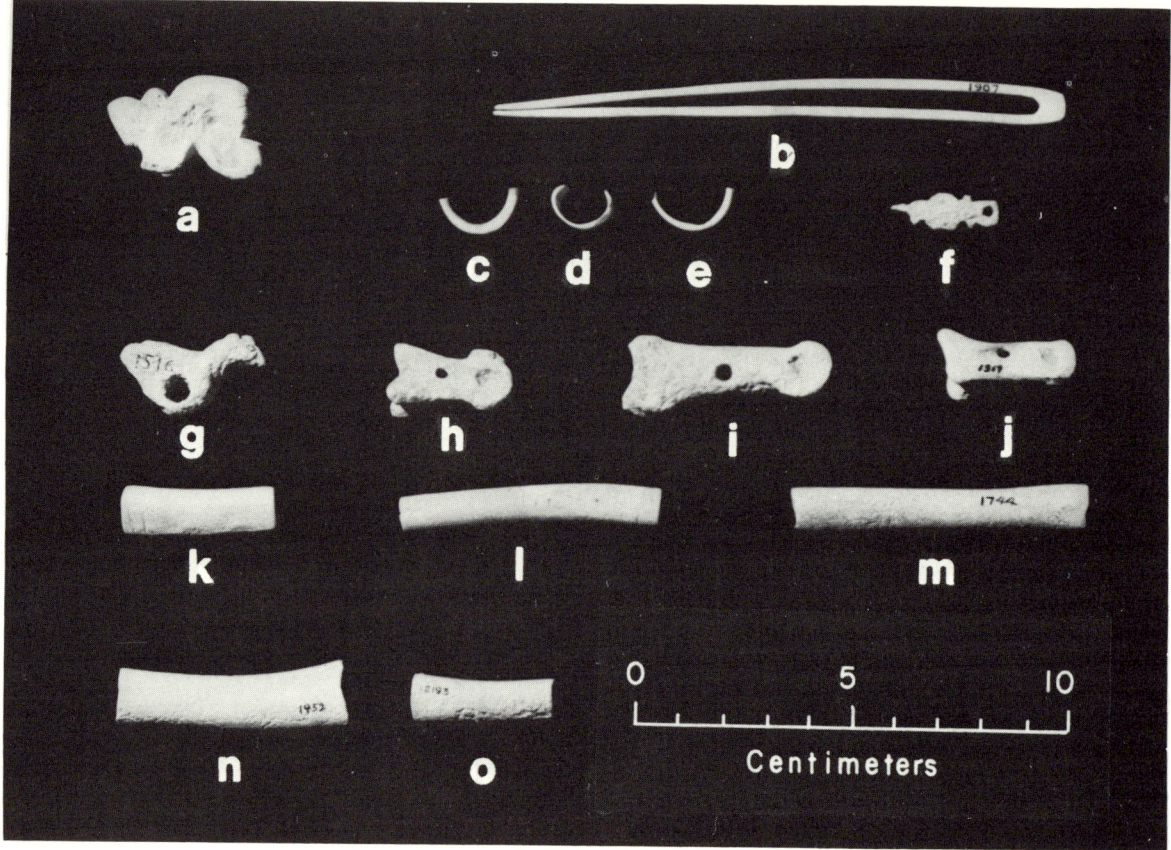

Figure 64. Small bone objects from Site 616. Figurines: a. Room C8, floor, #2229; g. Room C1, fill, #1516. Hairpin: b. Room B5, floor, #1907. Rings (partial): c. Room D5, fill, #1931; d. Walk-in well, fill of mealing room, #2594; e. Walk-in well, fill of mealing room, #2594. Carved pendant: f. Room B1, fill, #1183. Pierced phalanges: h. Room D5, fill of cist; i. Room B5, floor, #2194; j. Walk-in well, fill, #1319. Tubes: k. Room D5, fill, #1932; l. Room B1, floor, #1550; m. Room C2, fill, #1744; n. provenience unrecorded, #1452; o. Room E2, fill, #2193.

ation with a range from 1.4 to 8.5 cm and an average of 4.8 cm. The four tubes from Room C2 all ranged around 7 cm in length; however, the five specimens from Room E2 showed no such consistency, ranging from 3.3 to 8.5 cm in length. Those from Room B1 were fragmentary.

Fill

Room B1 (1); Room B7 (1); Room C2 (1); Room D5 (1); Room E2 (5); walk-in well (3)

Floor

Room B1 (3); Room C2 (4); Room C8 (1)

Pierced Phalanges: 13 specimens (fig. 64h-j)

Twelve of these specimens were the second phalange from a deer or pronghorn, while the thirteenth (from the walk-in well) was a first phalange. On all specimens a central medial-lateral hole had been drilled. In addition, on most specimens the three natural prominences on the proximal end of the second phalange had been smoothed and emphasized. On one or two specimens the natural projections on the distal end had been smoothed or worn away, but in general the distal end and the central section had received little or no attention except for the drilled hole.

Fill

Room B3 (1); Room C2 (1); Room C8 (1); Room E2 (1); Room F1 (1); walk-in well (3)

Floor

Room B1 (3); Room B5 (1); Room D5, cist (1)

Weaving or Matting Tools (?): 3 specimens

These implements were broad, flat, awl-like artifacts with dull, well-polished ends. All were fragmentary.

Two from the kiva had been made from animal rib sections, the other from a splinter of a large leg bone. The sides and rounded edges of all were well smoothed and had a high polish for a distance of about 4 cm above the rounded end of the implement. The largest fragment was 13.5 cm long. The maximum width ranged from 1.7 to 2.6 cm.

Fill

Kiva (2), trench north of Area C (1)

Hairpin (?): 1 specimen (fig. 64b)

This long (13.6 cm), narrow, U-shaped object (each prong was circular in cross section with a diameter of approximately 0.2 cm), found on the floor of Room B5, bore a very close resemblance to the hair ornaments popular in the United States a number of years ago and it has been so designated, though it could have been used in other ways as well. It was carefully finished and well polished on all surfaces.

Pendants: 26 specimens

CARVED PENDANTS: 2 specimens (fig. 64f)

One specimen (#1163) can best be described by reference to the illustration in figure 64f. It was made from a portion of a circular bone shaft and had an overall length of 2.5 cm. It was perhaps meant to portray an animal such as the horned toad. The second specimen was a bone fragment in the form of an animal incisor 3 cm long and 1 cm thick at the base, which was pierced by a small hole, 0.3 cm in diameter.

Fill

Room B1 (1); Room C3 (1)

DEWCLAW PENDANTS: 21 specimens

Another type of pendant was made from the dewclaws of deer. They were unmodified except for one, two, and sometimes three small holes biconically drilled through the thinner sections of the dewclaws. Fourteen came from the fill of Room C10 and seven were found in the firepit in Room C5.

BISON MANDIBLE PENDANT: 1 specimen

This specimen from the fill of Room C9 consisted of the right half of a bison mandible. A hole 0.6 cm in diameter had been drilled in the anterior proximal corner of the ascending ramus, perhaps for suspension. No other modification of the mandible was apparent. When found, the roots of the teeth remained in the jaw but the weathered condition of the specimen prevented determination of whether the remainder of the teeth had been present during the specimen's use.

FIGURINE PENDANTS: 2 specimens (fig. 64a, g)

Both specimens were made by modifying to a greater or lesser extent a deer or pronghorn astragalus. In one specimen, from the floor of Room C8 (#2229, fig. 64a), the result rather closely resembled a two-headed turtle. Conically drilled holes had been started on either side of the body but in both instances only a slight depression had been formed. In the other specimen, from the fill of Room C1 (#1516, fig. 64g), the result more clearly approximated two birds sitting side-by-side with bodies joined at the wings. The lower portions of their joined bodies had been pierced.

Fragments of Worked Bone

In addition to the bone artifacts discussed above, portions of bone artifacts too fragmentary to identify were found in the following rooms: Room A2 (1); Room B1 (1); Room B7 (2); Room C2 (1); Room C8 (1); Room C9 (1); Room E1 (1); Room E2 (4); Room F2 (1); walk-in well (7); Trench north of Area C (1). The fragments from Room B1 and Room F2 were on the floor.

ANTLER ARTIFACTS

The paucity of artifacts made of antler was somewhat surprising in view of the predominance of deer and pronghorn bone at the site. Only three specimens of worked antler were found, but a few fragments of antler were in the fill of Rooms B1, D1, and E1.

Flaker (?): 1 specimen

This specimen, found in the fill of the walk-in well, while having the general contours of a flaker, had the tip missing and could as easily have been used in connection with some other process. Its overall length was 11.5 cm.

Rubbing Tools: 2 specimens

One antler butt (Room E1, fill) was 15 cm long. The end was smoothed and small facets about 1 by 1 cm had developed as a result of rubbing and grinding. The second specimen (Room B1, fill) was the end of a similar tool.

SHELL ARTIFACTS

Bracelets: 9 specimens (fig. 65i)

One complete specimen and 8 fragments representing at least 6 bracelets were found. All were of *Gly-*

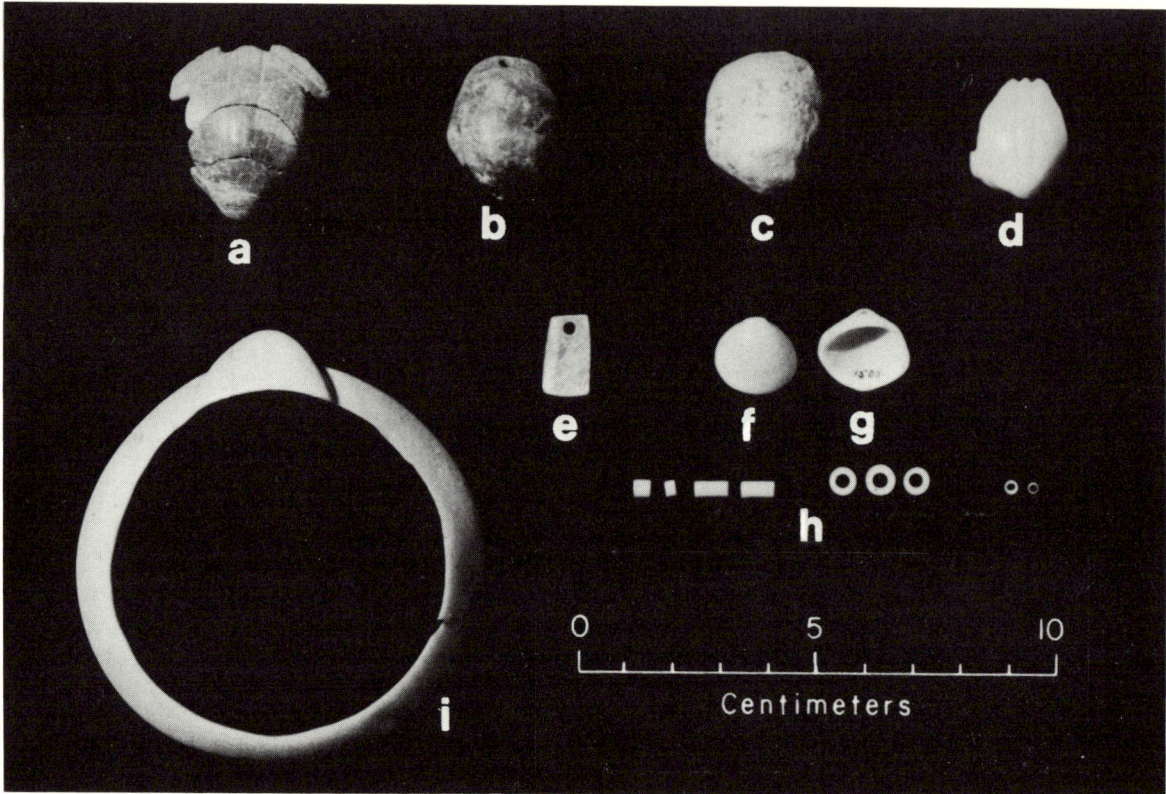

Figure 65. Objects of shell from Site 616. Frog figurines: a. Room C10, fill of firepit, #2813; d. Room A2, floor, #2084. Bat (?) figurines: b. Room D1, fill, #1598; c. Room D2, fill, #1151. Cut shell pendant: e. Room C3, fill, #1576. Pendants of whole shell: f. Room C2, floor, #1505; g. Room C2, floor, #1505. Beads: h. various rooms. Bracelet: i. Room C9, fill, #2238.

cymeris maculatus. The fragmentary specimens were all from bracelets that had been ground down until the shell was approximately 0.4 to 0.6 cm thick. The minimum internal diameter of these bracelets ranged between 4 and 6 cm, and the umbo or peak had been drilled on the two fragments containing this portion of the shell. The only complete specimen, from the fill of Room C9 (#2238, fig. 65i), was of a somewhat different design, and had been worked down apparently by a rasping process until there remained a circle of shell from 1 to 2 cm wide, the internal diameter of which was 7 cm. The natural raised portion of the umbo had been smoothed and modified slightly, so that a raised triangular section remained. It had not been drilled. Three holes had been drilled in the body of this bracelet, apparently in an attempt to repair a crack. One fragment (Room D2, fill) had been similarly drilled.

Fill

Room C9 (1); Room D2 (2)

Floor

Room C3 (5); Room C10 (1)

Pendants: 23 specimens

CUT SHELL: 6 specimens (fig. 65e)

Five of the pendants were from the inner iridescent portion of *Haliotis rufescens*, the exterior surface of which had been ground off. On three of these the remaining portion had been ground to a rectangular shape (approximately 1.5 by 1 cm) and a hole had been drilled near the center of one of the short sides (#1576, fig. 65e). The other two (from Rooms C2 and C5) were similar except that their shape was irregular rather than rectangular. Another pendant from Room C2 was of an unidentified shell and was rectangular but slightly smaller than the other from Room C2.

Fill

Room C1 (1); Room C2 (2); Room C3 (1); Room C5 (1)

Floor

Room A2 (1)

WHOLE SHELL: 15 specimens (fig. 65f, g)

These small (1.5 cm in diameter) shells of *Glycymeris*

maculatus were found together on the floor of Room C2 (#1505 [2], fig. 65f, g). They were unmodified except for a slight smoothing of the edges and a small hole drilled through the umbo.

TINKLER PENDANTS (?): 2 specimens

A fragment of a *Conus princeps* and one of *Conus regularis* were found, the first in Room C7 and the second in Room C1. Both had been polished and the wide end had been ground on a plane surface. Whether or not they were designed for suspension is unknown because of their fragmentary condition.

Disc Beads: 1,748 specimens (fig. 65h)

All but one of the shell beads were made from unidentified white or cream-colored shells. The single exception, (Room C4, fill) was from the reddish portion of the *Haliotis rufescens*. In general the beads were quite uniform in size and thickness. Among them 175 had a diameter ranging from 0.4 cm to 1 cm with an average of 0.6 cm. All of the remainder had a diameter ranging between 0.2 cm and 0.4 cm. All but 66 were from 0.1 to 0.2 cm in thickness, the exceptions ranging from 0.2 cm to 0.7 cm. All but three of the unusually thick specimens also had unusually large diameters and all but one of those having any unusual dimension came from Room C5. The diameter of the hole itself was generally about 0.2 cm, but whereas the holes of the stone beads (except for the unusually large specimens) were generally only slightly tapered, the drilling of the shell beads apparently had been more often accomplished with an instrument with a much broader point, for the diameters of the beginnings of the holes were sometimes as much as twice their minimum diameters. The outside edges of the beads were nearly always well finished and polished.

It is interesting to note that only four beads of shell and very few beads of any material were found outside Area C. Further, very little shell of any nature came from any other area.

Fill

    Room B3 (1); Room C1 (103); Room C3 (110); Room C5 (574); Room C7 (132); Room C9 (200)

Floor

    Room B1 (3); Room C5 (185); Room C8 (100); kiva (2)

Skeleton 2

    Room C2 (27)

Firepit

    Room C10 (300)

Figurines: 4 specimens

FROGS: 2 specimens (fig. 65a, d)

Both frogs were of Glycymeris shell (#2813, #2084, fig. 65a, d), measuring from head to tail 4 cm and 2.5 cm respectively. The umbo of the shell formed the head, and a hole had been drilled through this section in a manner similar to that in pendants of whole shell, perhaps for suspension, though it also served to represent the mouth of the animal. On the smaller specimen (#2084, fig. 65d), from Room A2, two dots had been engraved for eyes, but the other (#2813, fig. 65a), from the firepit of Room C10, was less realistic. Each specimen had two parallel engraved lines running from the center of the head down the back to the tail. The edge of the shells had been carved in the outline of the frog's body and appropriate lines had been engraved to represent the legs. The rear legs of the smaller specimen had been broken but the broken surface appeared worn and it may have continued in use in this condition.

These specimens bore an extremely close resemblance to some found in the Hohokam area (e.g., see Haury 1945, p. 307).

BATS (?): 2 specimens (fig. 65b, c)

Both specimens were made from fossil shell, the species of which could not be identified, though it appears to have been a somewhat circular bivalve. Again, what may have been the umbo section was utilized as the head. Only one of the specimens (#1598, fig. 65b) had been completely carved; on it the wings had been outlined and three holes had been drilled, one through each wing and one in the center of the tail. The eyes had been formed by drilling holes partway through the head. The second specimen (#1151, fig. 65c) resembled the first in general contour but was unworked except for the edges, which had been ground smooth on a plane surface. It is included here on the supposition that it represented an unfinished bat.

Fill

    Room D1 (1); Room D2 (1)

Conical and Cylindrical Objects: 5 specimens (fig. 60g, h)

Conical objects of an unidentified type of shell were quite similar to the conical objects of stone described above (p. 157). In one dimension these specimens had an approximately round cross section, while one end was flat. Four of them tapered gradually from the flat end to a well-rounded point. The fifth specimen (#2094, fig. 60g) resembled a basal section that had been cut off 1.4 cm above the base, with both ends flat and parallel. The base had a diameter of 1 cm and the top a diameter of 0.8 cm. The length and largest diameter respectively of the three specimens from the floor of Room C8 were: 1.4 by 1 cm (the truncated specimen); 3 by 0.8 cm (#2094, fig. 60h); and 3.8 by 0.6 cm. The other two were found just above the floor of Room C3 in immediate association with a conical object of malachite, some limonite, and a piece of unidentified fibrous material. The dimensions of these specimens were 5 by 1 cm, and 2.7 by 0.8 cm respectively. All surfaces were very smooth and even. The nature of the material was such that there were fine black bands encircling the specimens throughout their length.

Worked Fragments

Various fragments of *Haliotis rufescens* that showed some evidence of having been worked were found in the fill of Rooms C4 and C9 and on the floor of Rooms C4 and C10. Four fragments had been drilled, while the edges of five others had been ground down, generally into an arc. None was sufficiently complete for the original form to be recognized. On the floor of Room C8 a polished midsection of a *Turritella* ([?sp] probably *goniostoma*) shell was found. The broken edges were smooth and it could have been strung as a bead through the natural central hole.

Unworked Fragments

Fragments of *Haliotis rufescens* showing no evidence of having been worked were found in the fill of Rooms A1, C1, C5, C6, C9, and D2. In the fill of Room D1 was a fragment of fossil shell.

OTHER ORGANIC ARTIFACTS

Basketry: 3 specimens

The charred and fragmented remains of three baskets were found, all in Area C. One was on the floor of Room C5, and two on the floor of Room C3. All three were coiled but there were slight technical differences among them. The basket from Room C5 (#1902) was of two-rod-and-bundle construction with the two rods placed side by side. The wrapping material was quite fine (about 0.1 cm wide), and there were eight wrappings per centimeter. The rods were approximately 0.3 cm in diameter and the bundle (apparently of juniper bark) slightly smaller. The coils averaged 0.5 cm in thickness. One of the baskets from the floor of Room C3 (#2054) was also of two-rod-and-bundle construction, and the wrapping material, which was about 0.2 cm wide, was sewed through the bundle. There were only four wrappings per centimeter. In some cases the fibers of the bundle had been given a slight S-twist. The rods were approximately the same size (0.3 cm in diameter) as the bundles. The diameter of the coils averaged 0.5 cm in diameter. The third basket had a two-rod-and-splint foundation, the two rods being placed one above the other, so that the individual coils were oval (0.6 by 0.4 cm) with the smaller dimension being the thickness of the basket. The rods were again about 0.3 cm thick and the splints appeared to be simply split sections of the same material as the rods. One fragment had three rods but this probably was from an area where a new rod was being introduced as the end of an old one was approached.

Also in the fill of Room C3 were found fragments of one or perhaps several sticks 1 cm in diameter, wrapped in a manner similar to basketry coils. There was no bundle and no evidence of interlocked wrapping. The technique was so similar that these fragments may have had some connection with the baskets, but this is by no means certain.

Mat Impression: 1 specimen

In the fill of Room C5 there was an adobe fragment showing the impression of a mat. This mat appeared to have been made of coarse grass or slightly flattened reeds, and was of over-two-under-two twill construction. The individual elements ranged between 0.4 and 0.6 cm in width and there were ten elements within 5 cm.

Cotton Cloth

A number of fragments of cotton cloth were found in the fill of Room C3. Despite the small sample, several techniques were represented. The largest group of fragments consisted of simple over-one-under-one plain weave construction. In every case in this group the warp and weft were of single-strand Z-twist threads, but there was slight variation in other details. In one set of fragments the warp and weft were of the same size but there were approximately 12 threads per cm in one direction and 15 threads per cm in the other (it was not possible to distinguish warp from weft); in another group, the warp and weft were of the same size and there were 10 threads per cm in each direction. In a third group the weft threads were about 0.1 cm in diameter with 10 threads per cm; the warp threads had a smaller diameter and there were only eight threads per cm, so that while the weft threads touched one another there were spaces between the warp threads. The remainder of the cloth found was of under-two-over-four twill construction with the threads still consisting of a single-strand Z-twist thread. In one instance the warp and weft were of approximately the same size, and the pattern of successive weft threads shifted over one warp thread each time. The remaining fragments of this group were of tapestry weave, the warp threads completely hidden by the weft threads. In this case, while still of under-two-over-four construction, the weft threads shifted two warp threads each time, so that every other weft thread was identical. In this latter group additional weft threads were introduced in certain areas. These threads progressed for a certain distance, then looped over the adjacent main warp thread and returned in the opposite direction, following an over-one-under-one pattern in most instances; but on some fragments this pattern was extremely irregular, with the threads on occasion passing under (or over) as many as six warp threads. Presumably these additional weft threads were once colored.

Fur Cloth (?)

In Area C, in the fill of Rooms C3 and C9 and on the floor of Room C10, fragments of what may have been fur cloth were encountered. Both the warp and the weft elements consisted of two-strand Z-twist cordage made of yucca fiber. The individual strands comprised about 50 fibers not twisted on themselves, but simply lying parallel. The cord diameters were approximately 0.2 through 0.3 cm. The weft elements were so spaced that the weft cords were 0.5 cm apart. They appeared to have been wrapped with a fine hairy material. The warp elements were more widely spaced with at least 2 cm between adjacent elements. A twine construction technique was used.

Netting

In the fill of Room C3 there also occurred fragments of what appeared to be a net bag. The weaving technique closely resembled that of the fur cloth, but in this case there was no indication that the weft elements were wrapped. Also, while the weft elements continued to be two-strand Z-twist cordage of yucca fiber, the warp elements were of two-strand Z-twist cotton cord. The weft elements were 0.6 to 0.8 cm apart, while the warp elements were 2 cm apart. Twine construction was used. While this net-constructed object did not appear to have been wrapped, a great many fibers were found in direct association with it. These long fibers generally ran parallel to one another and were in the same plane as the warp and weft fibers. Perhaps this net bag had been used to store cotton fibers that had been carded but not yet made into thread.

Wooden Ceremonial (?) Stick: 1 specimen

On the floor of Room C3, in association with a large collection of grass, was a wooden object with a shape suggesting that it may have been the handle of a ceremonial stick. At any rate, it was nearly identical in shape to objects identified as Ceremonial Stick Type 1 by Pepper at Pueblo Bonito (Pepper 1920, pp. 143-145, figs. 53, 54). The fragment was 13.6 cm long and somewhat oval in cross section, 1.5 cm thick and 3.2 cm wide. The unbroken end was 2.6 cm in one dimension and 3.2 cm in the other.

Painted Wood Fragment: 1 specimen

A fragmented wooden base (Room C9, fill) on which paint occurred did not appear to have been more than 0.5 cm thick at any point, and the end and edges of some fragments of this thin base appeared to have been coated with a resinlike substance to which the paint was applied. On other fragments the paint was applied directly to the wood. On a few fragments where both original surfaces were present, blue was used on one side and red (10R 5/8 on Munsell scale) on the other, but on some fragments these two colors occurred on the same side. The pieces were far too small to permit recognition of any pattern.

RAW MATERIALS

The following discussion does not attempt a detailed consideration of the raw materials employed by the occupants of Site 616. It is rather a listing and brief description of such materials found on the floors or in the fill of the living units. It includes materials or objects that are thought to have been brought to the site by individuals for the purpose of subsequent utilization, but which in their present form are unmodified from the materials as found in nature except for their aberrant spatial position. Any human modification observed on this material evidently resulted from its use as a raw material rather than from any predesigned attempt to modify the material itself, for example, the occurrence of flat abraded facets on natural lumps of hematite.

Hematite: 3 lbs, 15 oz

The hematite ranged from irregular lumps as large as 7 cm in diameter down to a fine powder. About half of the lumps exhibited flat facets presumably resulting from their having been rubbed on paint palettes or other surfaces to powder the material prior to use.

Fill

    Room C3 (5 1/2 oz); Room C5 (3/4 oz); Room D5 (5 oz)

Floor

    Room B1 (1 lb, 10 oz); Room B2 (2 1/2 oz); Room C4 (1 lb, 7 oz)

Limonite: 1 lb, 13 oz

The limonite present ranged from an ocherous powder to hard platy fragments of varying sizes up to approximately 7 cm. Although it was found more frequently and in a greater number of living units than hematite, the total quantity recovered was less. Flat, abraded facets occurred on just less than half of the larger fragments.

Fill

    Room B1 (1 oz); Room C1 (1 1/4 oz); Room C2 (7 oz); Room C3 (8 1/4 oz); Room C5 (1 oz); Room D1 (1/4 oz); Room D5 (1/4 oz); Room E2 (3 oz); Room F2 (1/2 oz); walk-in well (1/2 oz)

Floor

    Room B2 (5 oz); Room C4 (1 oz)

Malachite and Azurite: 1 lb, 15 oz

Fragments of malachite were found far more often than were those of azurite. Only two small lumps of azurite — one from Room D3 (3 oz) and the other from the kiva (1/2 oz), neither of which showed any signs of having been worked — were the sole pieces recovered. The azurite was hard but the malachite was generally soft, even powdery, though occasional hard pieces were found. The hard fragments frequently showed signs of abrasion, and although the softer pieces did not, any such marks would have readily disappeared long before their excavation.

Fill

    Room C1 (14 3/4 oz); Room C5 (1/2 oz); Room C8 (5 oz); Room C9 (1/2 oz); Room D2 (1/4 oz); Room D3 (3 oz); Room E2 (1/2 oz); Room F2 (1 3/4 oz); walk-in well (1/4 oz); trenches (1/2 oz)

Floor

    Room B1 (3 1/4 oz); Room C1 (1/4 oz); Room D1 (1/4 oz); kiva (1/2 oz)

Clay

VESSEL CLAY: 10 lbs, 4 oz

The material discussed here as vessel clay, that is, the basic material from which pottery was made, was of two varieties. The first, consisting of a gray, almost pure clay, was found on the floor of Rooms B1 and B2, and in the fill of Rooms C1 and C8. The other variety contained impurities and, while almost of the same gray color, it was less dense. This clay was found in Room B5, and in the fill of the walk-in well. On visual examination this second variety appeared to resemble closely the sample obtained from the clay deposit in the walk-in well.

Fill

    Room B1 (11 oz); Room C1 (5 oz); Room C8 (13 oz); walk-in well (1 lb)

Floor

    Room B1 (1 lb); Room B2 (1 lb, 7 oz); Room B5 (5 lbs)

SLIP CLAY (?): 4 oz

A ball of what seemed to be white kaolin weighing 2 ounces was recovered from the fill of the kiva, and another fragment of about the same size came from the floor of Room B1. No chemical analysis was made of it.

Turquoise: 5 specimens

The turquoise from Site 616 was pale green and of rather poor quality, that is, the pieces were small and far from perfect. Only five small fragments of unworked turquoise, all very thin, were found. Four were less than a centimeter in any dimension, while the fifth (#2399) was 2.1 by 1.4 by 0.6 cm.

Fill (all fragments)

    Room B2; Room C9; Room E2

Iron Pyrite: 1 specimen

A small rectangular crystal (0.8 by 0.8 by 0.5 cm) of iron pyrite was recovered from the floor of Room C5. No modification was apparent.

Calcitic Limestone: 1/4 oz

Approximately one-quarter ounce of finely powdered calcitic limestone came from the fill of the large mealing room associated with the walk-in well.

Diatomaceous Earth: 1/2 oz

Two small lumps of diatomaceous earth (fuller's earth), together weighing just less than one-half ounce, were recovered from the floor of Room B1.

Pine Resin (?)

A small piece of what appeared to be pine resin or lac was found in the fill of Room C9. It may have formed a portion of an artifact rather than raw material as such, but the piece was too small for this to be determined with accuracy. A similar substance was found adhering to the underside of a turquoise fragment, which was inlaid in a large rectangular jet button (#1928) found in Room C5, as well as on the surface of the button, and on the underside of two fragments of turquoise found 1 m from the button and perhaps belonging to it. Apparently this material served as an adhesive or glue (p. 156).

HUMAN SKELETAL REMAINS FROM SITE 616

Skeleton 1 (fig. 6f)

Age: Child (four to six years), based on tooth eruption

Sex: Possibly female

Provenience: Walk-in well, niche

Observations: Medium occipital deformation. This child was buried in a niche excavated into the wall of the ramp leading to the walk-in well. The body had been tightly flexed and placed on its left side facing the rear of the niche, and the head was to the west. The grave had been disturbed by erosion, and the bones were slightly scattered and were not all present. No artifacts were found in association but perhaps these too had been washed away.

Skeleton 2 (fig. 6b, c)

Age: Adolescent. The epiphysial cap on the distal end of the humerus had not united with the shaft; the third molars had begun to form but had not erupted. Despite the fact that none of the epiphysial caps had united, the sagittal suture was almost obliterated.

Sex: Probably female

Provenience: Room C2, probably on roof

Observations: Medium medial occipital deformation. In almost the center of the right parietal there was a rounded rectangular hole with dimensions of 4 by 1.5 cm. In cross section the hole closely resembled that of a slender axe. Very likely the infliction of this injury brought about death. The right arm had been broken off 9 cm below the shoulder, and was not recovered. The severance must have occurred shortly before death, for there was no sign of any healing in the bone. At the time of her death the girl had been wearing a necklace of small, black, stone beads, interspersed with a few beads of shell and turquoise; and it was still in place, suggesting that robbery was not the motive for the killing.

Skeleton 3

Age: Infant (approximately one year), based on tooth eruption

Sex: Unknown

Provenience: Walk-in well, niche in ramp

Observations: Like Skeleton 1 the body of this child had been buried in a niche in the wall of the ramp leading into the walk-in well, about 150 cm up the ramp from Skeleton 1. The body had been tightly flexed and lay on its right side, facing the back of the niche, with its head to the southwest. Some of the bones had been slightly displaced. A small fragment of a worked stone slab (13 by 17 cm) lay at the top of the skull and a mano, #1352 (1231), was at the feet.

Skeleton 4 (fig. 6g)

Age: Young adult, based on tooth eruption, epiphysial union, and cranial suture closure

Sex: Male

Provenience: Room E1, floor

Observations: Medium occipital flattening; an inca bone and several other islands in the sagittal suture to either side of bregma. Skeleton fully articulated and complete. Height measured *in situ*: 1.73 m. The right portion of the occiput appeared to be slightly shattered, although the rest of the cranium was in good condition. This skeleton was found lying face down, the head to the west and facing south (the individual's left). The right arm paralleled the body and the right palm was down. The upper left arm paralleled the body but the lower portion of the arm crossed under the pelvis with the palm up. Both legs were flexed to the individual's right, and one ankle directly overlay the other. This position is not readily or comfortably assumed; nor is it likely for a formal burial arrangement. A sandstone slab rested upon the lower section of the right side of the body, while a second slab lay upon the lower legs. These could have fallen from the roof. A small projectile point lay between the tibia and fibula of the right leg midway between knee and ankle. The evidence for this individual's having died a violent death is not so conclusive as that for Skeleton 2. Nonetheless, the circumstances surrounding his demise certainly are open to this interpretation and his subsequent treatment, or lack of it, appears to have been somewhat out of the ordinary.

Skeleton 5 (fig. 6h)

Age: Young adolescent. The distal epiphysial cap of the humerus was not attached; the conjunction of the ischium with the pubis and ilium was not completed; the permanent second molars had erupted but the third molars, though partially formed, had not erupted.

Sex: Possibly male

Provenience: In niche in east wall of mealing room associated with walk-in well

Observations: Medium flattening of the left half of the occiput; an inca bone present; considerable complexity of the sagittal suture, resulting in several other islands; the skull mesocephalic. The body was tightly flexed and placed on its right side facing the front of the niche, the head to the north. A large Tularosa Black-on-white jar sherd was placed over the face. Two fragments of worked bone, a polishing stone, and an unretouched flake were in the niche.

Skeleton 6

Age: Fetal, based on bone size, e.g., length of tibia shaft: 4 cm
Sex: Unknown
Provenience: Room D5, fill
Observations: This skeleton was found immediately overlying a mano fragment (descriptive type 1931) about 25 cm above the room floor. A number of artifacts were in the immediate area but there was no way to establish positive association. (See discussion of Room D5, pp. 88-91.)

Incomplete Skeletal Remains

Almost half of the rooms excavated contained some human skeletal material and, including the six nearly complete skeletons, at least 20 individuals were represented. Unless otherwise indicated the bones appeared to be those of fully grown individuals.

Room A2, fill: Humerus, left
Room A2, fill: Second cervical vertebra; first thoracic vertebra
Room B1, fill: Parietal, right
Room B1, floor: Premolar; third phalange
Room B2, fill: Ischium, left; calcaneum, left; fibula, left; rib
Room B3, fill: Clavicle, right
Room C2, fill: Femur, right; fibula, right; scapula, right
Room C5, fill: Calcaneum, right; tibia, left; patella, left
Room D1, fill: Humerus, right; ulna, right; radius, right; ulna, left; 3 ribs; sacrum fragment; clavicle, left; patella, left; 2 incisors; femur, left (young child)
Room D2, fill: 5 thoracic vertebrae
Room D3, fill: Incisor; first molar; 2 tali, left; ulna, left
Room E2, fill: Radius, left; scapula, left; pelvis (child)
Trench south of Room C2: Radius, right
Trench north of Room C3: Radius, left

Site 143

Site 143 was situated on the gently rising northeast slope of a low ridge independent from and just west of the north point of Mariana Mesa. An ephemeral stream originating on the western slopes of Mariana Mesa flows near the site along the northern edge of the ridge, and joins the general drainage system flowing west from the north end of Mariana Mesa. At present this stream has cut an arroyo some 4 to 5 m in depth. The ridge itself is covered with a growth of piñon and juniper. On the skirts of the ridge, where the site was located, the trees thin out and the ridge merges almost imperceptibly with the surrounding flat, treeless, grass-covered plain.

The site consisted of five independent architectural units ranging in size from a dozen rooms to 50 or more rooms each. All appeared to have been constructed of sandstone masonry. The larger units may have been the last occupied, for their walls were the only ones of sufficient height to show above ground. The units were arranged in a rough circle in the center of which was a large depression some 20 m in diameter. In addition, there were three smaller depressions, possibly indicative of kivas, located adjacent to the units.

The larger circular depression was the only unit excavated. Work was initiated there primarily because the large circular feature of Site 616 had proved to be basically utilitarian rather than ceremonial in nature, whereas the depression at Site 143 was one of the most prominent and most conveniently located features, suggestive of a large cermonial structure, in the immediate vicinity of Mariana Mesa (fig. 66).

The plan of this pueblo was such that the large circular structure formed the focal point of the entire village, for all the living units were located around its periphery. This central location and the considerable work involved in its construction indicated that it was the result of group endeavor, probably by a representative proportion of the entire pueblo. It would follow from this that the activities associated with the feature formed an important part of the social and probably religious life of the inhabitants. Though in certain respects it may have functioned as a kiva, its very openness and its central plazalike location suggested that it was primarily designed as the focal point for the public performance of religious activities. There seemed to have been other more normal-sized subterranean kivas in the village, which doubtless fulfilled a position as centers for the more secret, esoteric religious practices. The application of the term "great kiva" for certain structures in the Southwest, some of which somewhat resemble the one at Site 143, is inappropriate here, for it implies that the structure had or should have had all of the appurtenances and implications of a full-fledged kiva, differing only in size. It is unlikely that this ever was the case with structures apparently public and communal in nature as this one may have been. As a cultural item for comparative studies, these formalized public areas (for the display of activities that probably were basically religious in content) are significant and deserve recognition; but they should not be confused with kivas as such, nor should they be designated by a term indicating that these were simply enlarged versions of the standard kiva.

The immediate area of Site 143 had apparently been occupied for a considerable period of time. A small lava-cobble masonry unit with pottery of a general Pueblo II style was located 200 m to the south, while 500 m to the south a second unit was littered with pottery fragments of a style usually associated with Late Pueblo I. Some 18 m to the southwest of this latter unit, eroding from a small arm of the arroyo passing north of Site 143, a single burial was observed and excavated. The body had been placed in a prepared pit about 1 m on a side and nearly that deep. The floor of the pit was completely covered with ash and minute fragments of charcoal. The body was in a flexed position with the legs at a 90° angle to the body and the hands under the chin. It had been placed on its right side with the head to the north. The height of the skeleton measured *in situ* was approximately 144 cm. Several pieces of charcoal and several small animal bones

172 • Mariana Mesa

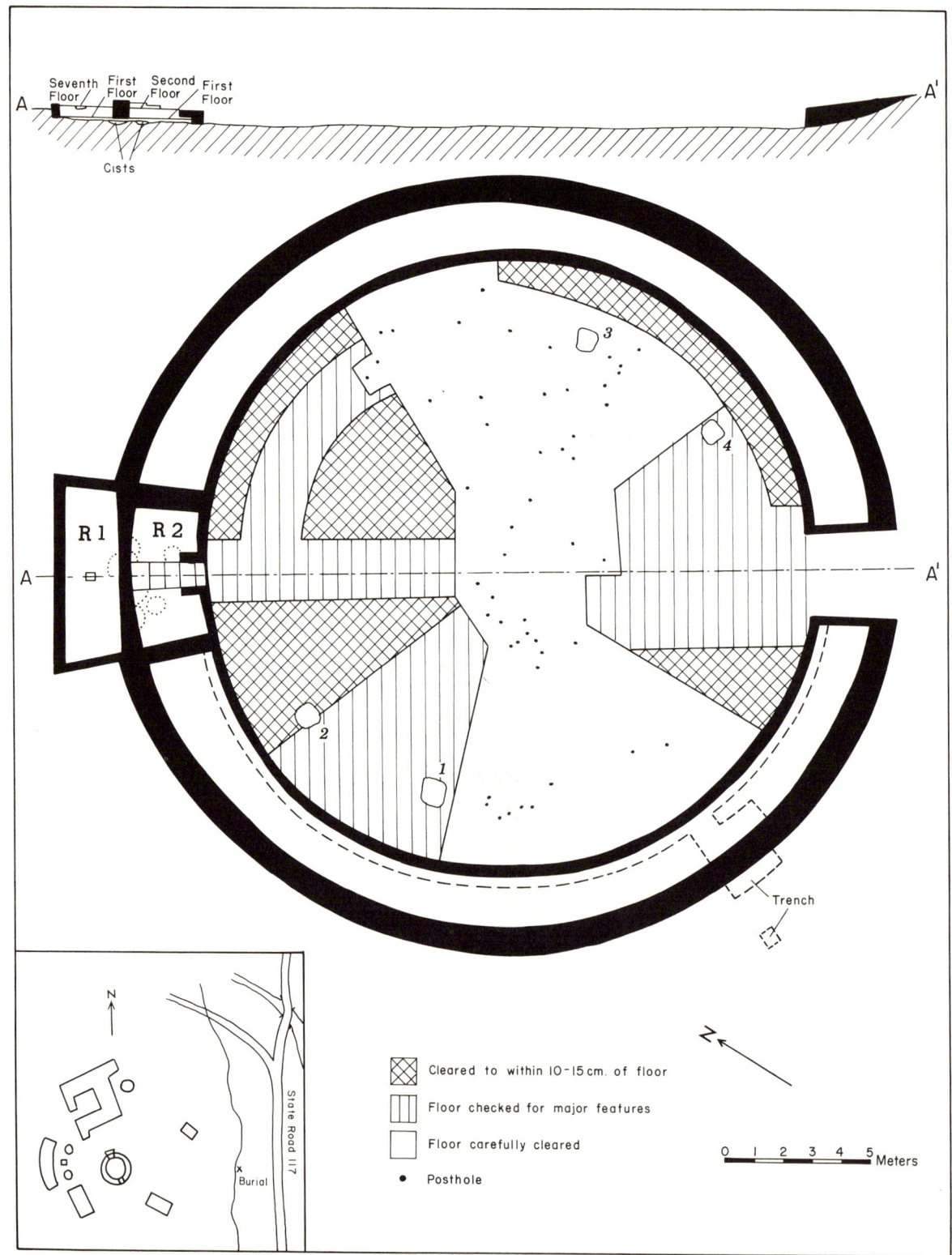

Figure 66. Plan of Site 143.

were located just south of the legs. Three vessels were placed in a north-south line just west of the body. These included a plain gray-paste globular, necked jar, a bowl of Red Mesa Black-on-white, and a brown-paste, neck-banded, open-mouthed jar (fig. 6e). Several animal bones were inside the overturned bowl.

A few pieces of pottery decorated in this earlier tradition were in immediate association with the large ceremonial feature at Site 143 but they probably represented an accidental association or, at best, the utilization of an early design style, since most of the pottery associated with this feature was of a later style. It was generally similar to that found at Site 616 but the paucity of glaze paint on either white- or red-slipped pottery and the lack of experimentation with color on the red-slipped pottery suggested that Site 143, although in large part contemporary with Site 616, was not occupied quite so late. Perhaps the inhabitants of Site 143 contributed to the influx of people postulated at Site 616 during the final period of the occupation of the latter site.

DATING CONSIDERATIONS

No datable tree-ring specimens were recovered from Site 143, but the architecture and the ceramic complex indicated a late Pueblo III occupation. About 67 percent of the pottery consisted of Tularosa Black-on-white and St. Johns Polychrome combined, with a very small trace of Red Mesa Black-on-white. Tularosa Black-on-white has been dated by Breternitz (1966, p. 99) at about A.D. 1100-1250, and St. Johns Polychrome by Breternitz (1966, p. 93) at A.D. 1200-1300, and by Carlson (1970, p. 39) at about A.D. 1175-1300. Thus a period of occupation of the site somewhere during the 1200s appears reasonable. The very small component of Red Mesa Black-on-white may be explained as the remnant of some brief earlier occupation, traces of which were not discovered by the excavation.

ARCHITECTURE

Ceremonial Feature

This unusual feature consisted basically of a large, subsurface, circular floor with a ramp entrance to the south-southeast side and, directly opposite this ramp, two rooms or walled areas entered by means of a stairway leading up from the floor of the central area. The central floor was surrounded by two parallel circular walls, one at normal ground level, the other bordering the central floor. The two rooms were contained between these two walls and the ramp extended from the inner to the outer wall.

CENTRAL AREA

The central area was formed by excavating an area about 20 m in diameter to a level as much as 50 to 100 cm below the general ground surface. In the northeast section little excavation was required, for the normal surface level was that of the central area. However, the soil removed from the central area elsewhere was piled around the border of this northeast section, so that everywhere the central floor had an upsloping border. The sides of the circular excavation were perpendicular and were faced with a single wall of sandstone and lava blocks (at a ratio of approximately eight sandstone blocks to every one of lava). The exposed faces of the blocks, which ranged in size from 22 by 10 cm to 38 by 9 cm, had been pecked to shape and had been placed to present a smooth surface to the interior of the circle. The wall was built in fairly regular courses and chinked with sandstone spalls and occasional sherds. Irregularities between the back of this wall and face of the natural soil behind it were filled with soil removed from the central area. This wall was 40 to 60 cm high and its top was quite level around its entire circumference (more nearly level than the floor, generally reaching a point just below the top of the soil).

The soil removed from the central area was piled just beyond the excavation, probably on all sides. On the naturally lower north and east sides of the central area, this material apparently was used to add greater height to the sides of the excavation and make them more nearly uniform. A low outer wall paralleling the inner one and about 2 m from it was built in a trench dug into the top of this pile of material. The base of the outer wall was slightly higher than the top of the inner one. The outer wall was approximately 80 cm thick, faced on both sides with sandstone blocks laid in rough courses and chinked with irregular sandstone spalls. In the two lower of the three surviving courses, the exposed surfaces of the blocks ranged in size from 30 by 8 cm to 40 by 12 cm, while the blocks in the upper course were quite regular in size (approximately 22 by 10 cm). From the quantity of sandstone in the fill it appeared that the outer wall was never more than one or two courses higher than this. The sandstone blocks on each face of the wall were approximately 25 cm thick and the central core between the facing stones was filled with hard-packed, reddish earth (again probably derived from the central excavation) mixed with frequent, small lava and sandstone cobbles.

The surface of the area between these two walls sloped up gradually from the top of the inner wall to just above the base of the outer wall. We excavated along the outer surface of the inner wall extending from the west wall of Room 2 to the western edge of the ramp. No cross walls were found. This sloping area

Figure 67. Site 143. Traxcavator excavating circular depression (left to right: C. R. McGimsey III, A. H. Rohn, operator, and H. Eberhardt).

between the two walls may have served as a "grandstand" for spectators but no floorlike surface upon it could be determined.

The floor of the central area appeared relatively flat to the eye, although more precise measurement revealed gradual variations of up to 25 cm. All of the floor area was cleared to within 10 to 15 cm of the floor by a Traxcavator and most of it was further cleared by hand to the level of the floor. While a large section of this cleared portion was worked over fairly carefully, the remainder of the clearing work was exploratory in nature, serving primarily to check the presence or absence of major structural features. The only features located were four cists and, in the area carefully cleared, 50 small postholes (?).

These holes were scattered over the floor area in no discernible pattern. They ranged in diameter from 7 to 15 cm and were 5 to 10 cm deep. Most were filled with a reddish sandy soil not unlike the general fill, but five were filled with dark soil and charcoal and six contained ash and charcoal. Even segregating these three groups revealed no pattern in their location or any clue to their use. Perhaps they served as the bases for poles supporting temporary ramadalike structures. If so, these structures had no standard location but at one time or another were located in all areas of the plaza.

The four cists had a more definite though no more readily interpreted arrangement. Each was centered approximately 2 m into the plaza from the inside wall. Cist 1 was 5 m from Cist 2 and Cist 2 was 5 m from a point 2 m into the plaza from the end of the stairway.

Similarly, Cist 3 was 5 m from Cist 4 and Cist 4 was 5 m from a point 2 m in from the center point of the lower end of the ramp. Cist 1 was diametrically opposite Cist 3, and Cist 2 was opposite Cist 4. The cists were straight-walled, unlined excavations into the native soil. Cists 3 and 4 were rounded squares 100 cm on a side and 20 cm deep with flat floors. Cist 2 was similar except that it was 50 cm deep with a slightly concave floor. In the area of Cist 1 the floor was in poor condition and rather irregular but there was a depression (designated Cist 1) approximately 100 cm square and 10 cm deep. Had the other cists not been found, it is likely that this would have been considered to be no more than an irregularity in the floor. As it was, it appeared certain that this depression represented the remains of a shallow cist similar to the others. It was first thought that there would be other cists regularly placed around the edge of the plaza but extensive exploration failed to reveal any others.

RAMP

A ramp, about 3 m wide, penetrated the wall in the southeast segment, rising from the floor to ground surface. A straight line, connecting the midpoint of the ramp with the midpoint of a stairway in the northwest segment of the wall and passing through the center of the central area, had a direction of 150°/330° on an azimuth oriented to true north. This orientation was approximately that for the room walls at most of the sites excavated, and from surface indications it was also true for most of the rooms at Site 143 as well. The floor of the ramp sloped up from the floor of the central area to the natural surface of the ground outside, the angle of slope increasing slightly toward the upper end. The sides of the ramp were faced with single walls of coursed sandstone blocks. These walls conformed to the slope of the ramp both through the successive discontinuation of the lowermost courses and by a slight slope of the courses themselves. Only the uppermost course extended the entire length of the ramp, joining the outer and inner walls of the central area.

STAIRWAY

Directly opposite the ramp was a second break in the inside wall of the central area. From this break a stairway led through the center of Room 2 to the south wall of Room 1 (fig. 68). At the base of the stairway a floor-level niche was set into the wall. It was lined with one large and several small sandstone slabs set in adobe. Beyond this nichelike element there were four steps. The niche was 65 cm wide but the steps gradually became wider, so that the top step, adjacent to the wall of Room 1, was 100 cm wide. The niche was only 38 cm deep but all of the steps were 50 cm deep. The first three risers were 20 cm high, while the last one was only 10 cm high. Both the treads and the risers were faced with sandstone blocks set into adobe. The stairway itself, of coursed sandstone blocks, was built up from the floor of Room 2. The two lower steps were bordered by a continuation of the inner wall of the central area. However, the tread of the third step was level with the top of this wall (which was only 40 cm high at this point) and the two upper steps had no border.

Room 1

The level of the natural soil underlying the general area of the two northern rooms was only a few centimeters higher than the level to which the central area had been excavated. A lenticular pile of fill from the central area was dumped here and the section was leveled off at a height approximately 15 cm above that of the central area. The walls of both rooms were built on this level and it apparently served for some time as a floor in both rooms.

Room 1 was about 6 m long by about 1.8 m wide. Its south wall formed an arc of the outer wall circling the central area. In the construction of Room 1 this arc was modified or else constructed in a different manner from the rest of the outer wall. It was only 53 cm thick and, unlike the major portion of the outer wall, did not have a central rubble core. It consisted of three rows of sandstone blocks in regular courses and set on top of an adobe foundation. The outside rows were smoothly faced on north and south respectively; the north side of the central row also presented a smooth face. The south end of the east wall abutted the central row of the south wall, while the south end of the west wall abutted the north face of the outer wall of the plaza which, since it was thicker, was not continuous with the south wall of Room 1. The lower two courses of the west wall tied into this outer wall. The west, north, and east walls of the room were double, set on an adobe foundation, and built as a single continuous unit. This rather varied abutment pattern and the fact that the construction itself varied somewhat despite the walls' forming a continuous unit (e.g., the east half of the inner face of the north wall alternated layers of sandstone and lava blocks, while the west half used sandstone blocks exclusively) suggests either that the wall was repaired a number of times or else that groups of somewhat independent-minded artisans cooperated in the construction of the room, each building their own section according to their own ideas.

The lenticular stratum of reddish soil removed from the central area was leveled off in the area of Rooms 1 and 2 both by excavation and by the addition of other

Figure 68. Site 143. Stairs leading from central area, across Room 2 to Room 1.

material. The adobe bases of the walls were built on this level, or first floor. The six floors above the level of the original floor in Room 1 were each 2 to 8 cm above the preceding one. Associated with the sixth and/or the fifth floor there was a centrally located firepit, 24 cm square, scooped out of the adobe floor. This was the only floor feature encountered in Room 1, although only the central third and the northeast quarter of the room were excavated completely.

There was considerable rock in the fill of Room 1 and adjacent to it. The walls of Room 1 alone of those associated with the ceremonial feature may have been carried to full height.

Room 2

The stairway divided Room 2 in half and perhaps the two halves should be considered as separate rooms, though in fact it is doubtful that either was a room in the sense of being a completely walled-in enclosure. The entire area of both portions was about 4.5 m long by about 2.2 m wide. The east and west walls of Room 2, like those of Room 1, were built on adobe bases, but unlike those of Room 1, they were approximately 65 cm thick with a rubble core. The original floor of this room may have been used briefly, for it showed good cleavage at least in the west half of the room. However, it was very poor in the east half, and this, plus the fact that the south wall (which was the inner wall of the central area) was not finished with a smooth face on the Room 2 side, would indicate that at an early date

Room 2 had been filled to a level even with the tread on the middle step of the stairway. This second floor was at nearly the same level as the final (seventh) floor in Room 1.

Unlike Room 1, there was not much fallen wall material associated with Room 2 and in all likelihood this area was not a walled room. The south wall extended only a few centimeters above the second floor level and there was no indication that the east and west walls were very high. This area resembled more than anything else a viewing stand but it was not possible to determine its exact function.

CISTS BELOW ROOMS 1 AND 2

In the sterile soil below Rooms 1 and 2 were six roughly hemispherical cists. These ranged from 30 to 95 cm in diameter and from 10 to 30 cm in depth. All had plastered surfaces and the largest had been replastered, with the second floor being 6 cm above the original floor. These cists had all been filled with soil and the tops plastered over before the material removed from the central area was piled over them.

SUBSISTENCE MATERIALS

Sixty of the unworked animal bones recovered could not be identified as to species. They were about equally divided between large and small animals. Those that could be identified included one bison *(Bison bison)* astragalus; a pronghorn *(Antilocapra americana)* femur, tibia, and scapula; a mule deer *(Odocoileus hemionus hemionus)* femur and sacrum; five rabbit or hare bones; and one bone from a turkey or other large bird. These bones came from the fill of the central area and in the fill and beneath the upper floor of Room 2.

The only vegetal materials found were a few yucca seeds in the fill of Room 2.

POTTERY

No attempt was made to abstract modes and descriptive types from the limited pottery sample obtained at Site 143. The primary purpose of the excavations conducted at this site was determining the nature and temporal placement of the large ceremonial feature. For this reason the pottery was simply identified with respect to the regional time-space types represented. Only the sherd material found within the walls of the two rooms is presented, for much of the material found in the low central section probably had been washed there from a considerable area and thus was not reliably associated with the ceremonial feature. Local pottery norms, insofar as these could be determined from the proportionately small and areally restricted sample, are discussed briefly below and summarized in table 10.

Except for the three vessels associated with the single grave excavated at the site (p. 180) no whole vessels were recovered from Site 143.

White-slipped Pottery

With respect to basic constituents and construction techniques, the white-slipped pottery appeared to be very similar to that from Site 616. A flat-white slip was utilized almost exclusively and all exposed surfaces of the vessels were slipped. Glazelike black paint was rarely used. The principal decorative mode employed closely resembled motif I at Site 616, that is, parallel bands of fine lines alternating with broader stripes. In general, these tended to be closely spaced and well executed. The other common decorative modes consisted of bands of diagonal fine-line hatching enclosed within borders of the same width, and, slightly less frequently, lines of opposed solid and hatched sawteeth, opposed solid and hatched scrolls, and opposed solid stepped triangles. The most characteristic feature of the black-on-white pottery decoration was the extremely fine, well-executed lines utilized in the bands and for hatching. The lines were less than a millimeter wide, often closely spaced with 7 to 10 per cm. This feature was less common on those sherds typed as Reserve Black-on-white. Sherds of the Reserve type also contained the few samples of glazelike paint, an association also observed at Site 616. The jar form was predominant but a number of ladles and several bowls were represented. There was a variety of ladle handles; the majority were square or round closed tubes with one or two slight nubbins or ears on the end, but two had figurine heads and a third consisted of two parallel, untouching, circular fillets of clay. Two or three of the bowls had small, horizontally oriented loop handles just below the rim.

Red-slipped Pottery

The red-slipped pottery exhibited considerable variation in appearance, as did that from Site 616. However, the decoration did not have the diverse combinations of black and white paint found at Site 616. At Site 143 black decorations were on bowl interiors and white on exteriors. Only a single sherd had both black and white paint on the interior. Only 20 to 30 sherds had been painted with a black glaze paint. The bowl form was used almost exclusively, and, as was the case at Site 616, bowl rims were markedly incurving. Two jar sherds were recovered, and from the central fill came one red-slipped ladle handle (a closed circular tube).

Plain and Corrugated Pottery

The plain and corrugated pottery was not studied in detail, but limited observation showed that the corru-

Ceramic Types	Room 1						Room 2			
Black-on-white Sherds	Fill	Floor 1-3	Floor 3-4	Floor 4-6	Floor 6-7	Subfloor	Fill	Floor 1-2	Subfloor	Totals
Tularosa Black-on-white jars	235	1	2	2	2		20	37	50	358
Tularosa Black-on-white ladles or bowls	40	1								41
Reserve Black-on-white jars	18	1	8	6	14	5	14	5	62	133
Socorro Black-on-white bowls	7									7
Puerco Black-on-white jars	3								4	7
Red Mesa Black-on-white bowls	1	1						1		3
Bases	48	25	4	8	15	1	11	12	58	182
Totals	352	38	14	16	31	6	45	55	174	731
Black-on-red and Polychrome Sherds										
St. Johns Polychrome jars							2			2
St. Johns Polychrome bowls	218	14	10	13	16	7	86			364
Houck Polychrome bowls	3			1						4
Querino Polychrome bowls		1	2							3
Wingate Black-on-red bowls	19		1	4	4		4			32
Totals	240	15	13	18	20	7	92	0	0	405

Table 10. Distribution by descriptive types of all pottery sherds from Site 143.

gated pottery was very similar to that encountered at Site 616 with respect to materials and techniques employed, shapes, and so on. All corrugated bowls had smudged interiors. Plainware was rare but consistently present in all areas, and was generally in the form of small bowls, a few of which had smudged interiors.

OTHER OBJECTS OF CLAY

Figurines: 2 specimens (fig. 115b, d)

A bird figurine modeled in solid clay was found in the fill below the first floor of Room 2, east of the stairway (#2460, fig. 115b). The figure was unpolished and unpainted, and no details of the body were delineated, but the wings, which were against the body, and the tail were readily apparent. The neck consisted of a short cylinder extending straight forward from the body, which was 3.5 cm long, 2.6 cm wide and 2 cm thick. Two conical holes at the approximate location of the legs penetrated 0.4 cm into the body, and were probably sockets for small sticks. A second figurine of solid clay came from the fill of Room 1 (#2543, fig 115d). It consisted of a barrellike body slightly oval in cross section. The legs, head, and tail were all broken off and missing; but the legs appeared to have extended to the sides rather than down, so the figure may have represented a lizard or similar animal. The body was 4.6 cm long, 2.2 cm wide, and 1.8 cm thick. Similar figurines were found at Site 481 (p. 217), two from the fill of Pithouse 2 (#2561, fig. 115a, c).

Sherd Discs: 9 specimens

The only other objects of clay were nine sherds that had been chipped and ground into discs. All but one were of white-slipped ware. The exception was from an indented-corrugated vessel. Five were circular and the others subrectangular. Only two were well finished with a constant diameter and evenly ground edges. The others were roughly shaped and showed only slight grinding. They ranged in diameter from 1.5

to 18 cm. The largest, a nicely finished fragment, had two closely placed biconically drilled holes near the edge as if for suspension. Four discs came from the fill of Room 1, three from the cists under Room 2, and two from the trenches.

STONE ARTIFACTS

Manos: 12 specimens

Seven manos were of sandstone, five of vesicular basalt. All of the basalt specimens were rectangular in cross section and all but one of these had been used on both broad faces. The exception had been used on only one face. The manos of sandstone showed greater variation. One was rectangular in cross section with one used face, one semiwedge-shaped with the two adjacent faces used, one a truncated pyramid with three adjacent faces used, two triangular with two adjacent faces used, and one triangular with all faces used.

All but one of the specimens were fragmentary. The dimensions of the one complete specimen (sandstone, triangular, two used faces) were 33.7 by 12.8 by 2.8 cm. The width of the others ranged from 7.9 to 12.8 cm, and their thickness from 1.8 to 6.4 cm.

Most of the manos were found in or near the two rooms but may have washed into them from the area of the living units. All had been used on slab metates, and none had finger grips.

Shaftsmoothers: 3 specimens

Only one of these specimens bore a close resemblance to the shaftsmoothers from Site 616. This fragmentary specimen (#2450) of a fine-grained volcanic rock had a single semicircular groove 3.5 cm long, 0.6 cm wide, and 0.4 cm deep. A second specimen (#2541) had a similar central goove but this groove was flanked by a pair of grooves somewhat different in nature. One was nearly as long and wide as the central groove but was angular so that in cross section it was triangular rather than semicircular. The second flanking groove was semicircular but shorter, narrower (0.2 cm), and shallower (0.2 cm) than either of the others. The stones were naturally smooth and polished. Other than the grooves, no modification was apparent. This second specimen was in close association with some of the human bones in the central section. The third shaftsmoother (#2287), if such it was, was of sandstone and comparatively large (29 by 10.8 by 13 cm). Across the short dimension of one end there was a deep (2.5 cm) groove 1.8 cm wide. This object would have served admirably as an abrader for shaftlike objects.

Chipped Shaftscraper: 1 specimen

This volcanic flake (5.4 by 2.4 by 0.6 cm) from below the first floor of Room 2, had two grooves chipped into one end of one of the long edges. These grooves were semicircular in outline, each approximately 0.5 cm deep by 0.8 cm and 0.6 cm wide respectively. This tool could have served to scrape down rather than smooth a shaft or similar object.

Polishing Stones: 2 specimens

Two fairly large quartzite pebbles (approximately 6 by 3 by 2 cm) came from the surface and the fill of the central area. One had one large facet, the other two smaller facets, and all showed striations.

Pecking Stones: 13 specimens

These stones were natural cobbles unshaped except by use. Seven were of quartzite, the others of fine-grained basalt and petrified wood. They ranged in size from 9.1 by 7.8 by 7.7 cm to 4.8 by 4.8 by 2.8 cm with most tending toward the larger end of the range. All showed extensive battering, usually along the more pointed areas or edges. A number of large flakes had been broken from a few specimens either prior to or during use. Their relative abundance was in contrast to the situation encountered at Site 616.

Points and Knives: 5 specimens

All five points were of chalcedony and all had secondary chipping on all major surfaces. There was considerable variation in shape and size (fig. 113i–l).

Gravers: 2 specimens

These two flakes differed considerably in size (5.4 by 4.5 by 2.2 cm and 2.9 by 2.3 by 1.4 cm) but both had been deliberately chipped, so that a short, sharp, triangular point projected out from one straight side approximately 0.5 cm. The smaller graver came from below the first floor of Room 2, while the larger was in immediate association with a shaftsmoother (#2541) and some human bones in the central area.

Side Scrapers: 6 specimens

These large flakes of petrified wood, rhyolite, and chalcedony showed some evidence of casual modification, and small irregular use-chips had been detached from one of their long sharp sides or edges. They ranged in size from 0.6 by 1.7 by 1.4 cm to 5.8 by 5.8 by 2.5 cm. Two were found in the fill of Room 2 and two were on the surface of the remodeled floor. The remaining two came from a trench and the central area.

Unretouched Flakes: 8 specimens

All but one of these flakes were of petrified wood, the eighth of chalcedony. All were small with no dimension exceeding 3 cm, and were somewhat irregular in shape. One naturally sharp edge on each flake exhibited small use-chips. Five came from the fill of Room 1, while the other two were from a trench and the central area.

Chips: 98 specimens

The vast majority of chips were of petrified wood, with a few of rhyolite and andesite. They were small and irregular in shape, generally ranging up to 4 by 4 by 2.5 cm with no dimension on any of them exceeding 6 cm. They were found in all areas but most came from Room 2, both above and below the level of the first floor. Their relative abundance stands in some contrast to that at Site 616.

Core: 1 specimen

A cobble-sized piece of petrified wood, from which a great many chips and flakes appeared to have been removed, was found in the fill of the central area. It had no prepared striking platforms.

Choppers: 6 specimens

The choppers were large, oval cobbles 8 to 12 cm in maximum length. Large flakes had been detached from both sides of one end, leaving a rather sinuous cutting edge. These edges were sharp but often showed abrasion. On one chopper both ends had been so treated. It should be noted that these choppers differed from the artifacts given this designation at Site 616. The use and function of both groups probably were the same but at Site 143 the tools were deliberately fashioned from selected cobbles, whereas at Site 616 the inhabitants evidently simply availed themselves of the ready-made supply in the adjacent dike, with no further preparation being necessary. These tools came from the central area of Site 143.

Flat Stone: 1 specimen

Both surfaces of this flat oval stone (7.1 by 6.5 by 1.8 cm) were very smooth and the edges exhibited slight abrasion. No striations were evident to the unaided eye. The stone came from the fill of the central area.

BONE ARTIFACTS

Awls

SPLINTER AWLS: 3 specimens

All specimens of awls were fragmentary, so total lengths are not known. Two tapered very gradually to a sharp point. The third and largest (13 cm) was 2 cm wide at one end, tapering gradually along its well-smoothed length until the final centimeter; it then tapered rapidly from a width of 1 cm to a sharp point. This specimen and one of the others came from the fill of Room 2; the third came from a trench.

End Scrapers: 2 specimens

The only complete end scraper consisted of a 10-cm length of the proximal end and part of the shaft of a deer tibia. The proximal end was unmodified but the shaft had been cut through at an angle so that an efficient scraping edge was formed. The second scraper was represented by only a small fragment but it appeared to have been similar. One came from the fill of Room 1, the other from that of Room 2.

Rings and Tubes: 3 specimens

Two rings, 1.8 cm and 1.5 cm in diameter and each 0.9 cm wide, were encountered in the fill of Room 1. A fragment of a tube 1.3 cm in diameter but at least 2.4 cm long came from below the first floor of Room 2. The surface of the bone showed little modification but the cut edges were smooth.

Worked Fragments: 5 specimens

Five pieces of bone were found, obviously fashioned into implements of some kind but too fragmentary to identify. One, which came from the floor of the cist below Rooms 1 and 2, was a deer astragalus carved to an unrecognizable shape. Two of the others came from the fill of Room 1, one from Room 2, and the other from the central area.

ANTLER ARTIFACT

The smoothed tip of an antler that may have served as a flaker was found on the floor of the cist below Rooms 1 and 2.

SHELL ARTIFACTS

Only three fragments of shell were recovered, all from beneath the first floor of Room 2. One was a flat solid semicircular disc pendant (2.3 by 1.4 by 0.1 cm) of *Hali-*

otus rufescens with a conically drilled hole near the center of the arc. The second was a solid circular disc (4.5 cm in diameter and 0.5 cm thick) roughly chipped into shape and resembling chiefly the rough discs made from sherds. The third was a bead that might have been made from a small *Olivella* shell.

RAW MATERIALS

Six ounces of limonite were found in the fill of Room 2, while 3 ounces were recovered from the fill of Room 1.

HUMAN SKELETAL REMAINS

In the fill of the central area was found a set of fully articulated lower legs of an adult, including the right and left tibiae and fibulae and both feet. No other portion of the body was recovered, nor was it likely that the Traxcavator that excavated a large part of the central area destroyed any of the skeleton. A shaft-smoother (#2541) and a graver were found in immediate association with these bones.

A few other human bones were found as follows:

Ramp, fill: Occiput; infant

Central area: Femur, right; first cervical vertebra; adult

Trench: Patella, right; femur, right; mandible; adult

Just to the south of Site 143, and between it and the state road, an adult burial was excavated, as described on page 171 (fig. 6e). It probably was associated with an early portion of Site 143 or a small Pueblo II site just to the west.

Site 481

Site 481 was located near the end of a long, low ridge extending north from the north point of Mariana Mesa for a distance of about two miles. Throughout most of its extent the ridge rises approximately 60 m above the valley floor to an average elevation of 2,150 m. The top and sides of the ridge are presently covered with a growth of piñon and juniper. Site 481 was located in a small treeless area at the top of the eastern slope of the ridge, overlooking the valley of the main drainage system passing north of Mariana Mesa. A small ephemeral stream that has recently cut an arroyo about 3 m deep flows from Mariana Mesa along the eastern border of the ridge and joins the main drainage system near the end of the ridge.

Site 481 in its final form consisted of a triple row of rooms formed in a rough L-shape, one leg of the L running approximately north-south, the other approximately east-west. There is some evidence that a wing wall extended east from the southern point of the north-south wing, so that a rectangular plaza may have been enclosed. Erosion has destroyed much of this area and the evidence is not conclusive. A kiva lay within the area embraced by the wings of the L. Walls of the surface rooms stood (at the time of excavation) 30 to 100 cm above the room floors. There was no indication that the original structure was more than one story in height at any point. The kiva and all 34 surface rooms were excavated in whole or in part. Much of the site was built over trash deposits and there were indications of subsurface dwellings. One of these, a rectangular shallow pithouse, was excavated entirely while another subsurface room was trenched. These two units and a cist that had been floored over were the only subsurface features positively identified. The existence of a second shallow pithouse was suggested by test pits. More extensive clearing of the trash underlying the surface rooms might have revealed other subsurface units.

HISTORY

As was the custom, the first settlers of Site 481 selected for their house location the edge of a low rise overlooking valley land. The one excavated sample of these first houses was a shallow rectangular pithouse (Pithouse 1, figs. 69, 70) with main roof supports set into the long walls, a centrally located firepit and ashpit, a sloping ventilator and/or entrance in the middle of the south wall, and in the northeast corner of this room a very large, deep circular cist to which access was gained by means of a single-pole ladder. At least one other evidently similar subsurface room was present (below surface Rooms 17, 22, and 19), but was not excavated. The site may then have been deserted for a brief period between the abandonment of Pithouse 1 and the construction of the first surface room. However, the close alignment of Room 2 (the first surface room) with the north wall of Pithouse 1 and the presence within the pithouse of trash from the first surface rooms suggest that the hiatus was not great. For that matter the possibility cannot be ruled out, on the present evidence, that the same group was involved but that they had simply changed their architectural standards.

It was possible, from a study of the masonry, to determine the sequence in which the surface rooms of the pueblo were constructed (fig. 71). Construction of Room 2 was followed by that of Rooms 1 and 9. Pithouse 2, which probably served as a kiva, was built at this time, or at the time the independent eastern unit was begun. The area later to be occupied by Room 6 was used as a plaza, and a number of outdoor firepits (similar to the one at Site 486) were constructed there. The area that was to contain the eastern unit of Rooms 7, 8, 16, and 17 apparently was used as a dump at this time, for a low mound of trash underlay these rooms. Rooms 7, North 6, and South 6 were built by a second but probably closely related group and the area between the two units continued to be used as a plaza and dump. Subsequently Rooms 10 and 11 were added.

Next, Rooms 3 and 4 were added to the western unit (with Room 11 being remodeled at this time), Room 8 was added to the eastern unit, and Pithouse 2 (a kiva) was abandoned. Probably a kiva in the location of the later kiva was built at this time, though if so, to judge

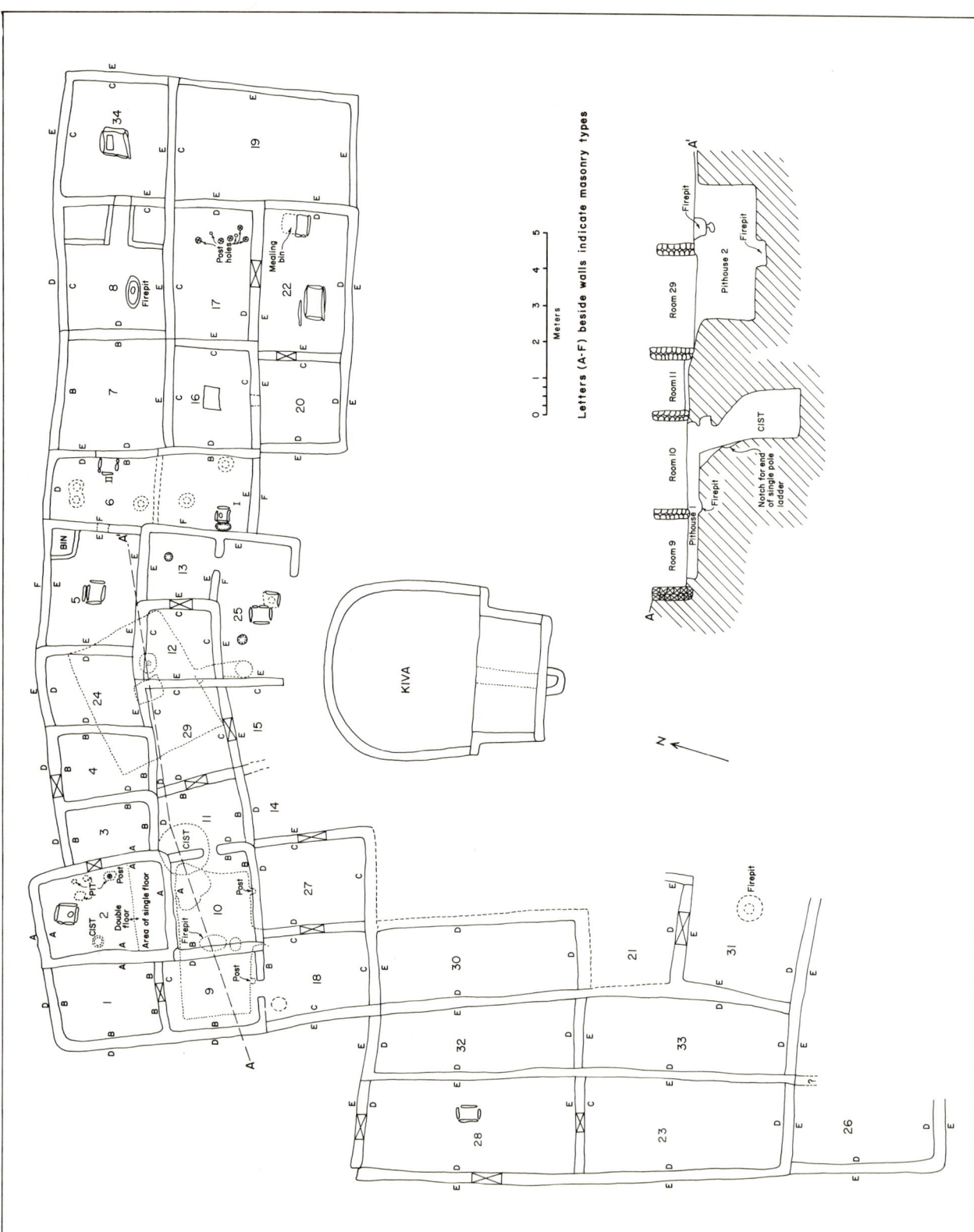

Figure 69. Site 481. Plan of the pueblo.

Figure 70. Site 481. View looking north before excavation. Individual farthest left is standing in area of Room 1; individual farthest right is in area of Room 34. The kiva is in the center of the picture.

from the wall type present when excavated, it was remodeled at a later date. The firepit that underlay both Pithouse 2 and the north wall of Room 12 was probably in use at this time.

It seems that sometime after this a major new group joined the pueblo, for sandstone masonry appeared for the first time, simultaneously with the appearance of a distinctive black-on-white pottery (Intrasite Distribution Type C). These people built Rooms 16 and 17, Rooms 29 and 12, Rooms 18 and 27, and probably Rooms 14 and 15. At the time Rooms 16 and 17 were built, the original occupants of Rooms 7 and 8 evidently worked with them, for Rooms 7 and 8 were remodeled at this time, using the masonry style of the newcomers for the remodeling. The principal reason for thinking that the newcomers did not simply take over Rooms 7 and 8 is that a black-on-white pottery style (Distribution Type B) associated with the earlier inhabitants continued to be associated with these rooms. Before long, Room 34 was added by the new group (if the hypotheses concerning masonry and pottery styles put forward here are valid).

The rather consistent early pairing of rooms in construction (subsequent to Room 2) certainly suggests that a social unit needing separate quarters normally required two rooms rather than simply one. Room 34 was one of the rare identifiable exceptions to this, as, initially, was Room 7. Simultaneous with the possible arrival of a somewhat different group, single rooms for each family unit may have come into vogue, for the pairing of rooms in construction and in remodeling was not apparent thereafter.

New architectural styles appear to have been adopted by all. This is in distinct contrast to the ceramic conservatism of the original group, who evidently declined to utlize the new paste of Intrasite Distribution Type C and experimented only briefly with the new thick creamy slip.

If we accept the ceramic distribution types as indicating separate social units within the pueblo, with type B being associated with the original occupants and type C with a second group, it is certain that the next development was another influx of persons closely related to the second arrivals. This event saw the construction of Rooms 20 and 22, and the construction of the entire west wing, Rooms 23, 32, 30, 28,

184 • Mariana Mesa

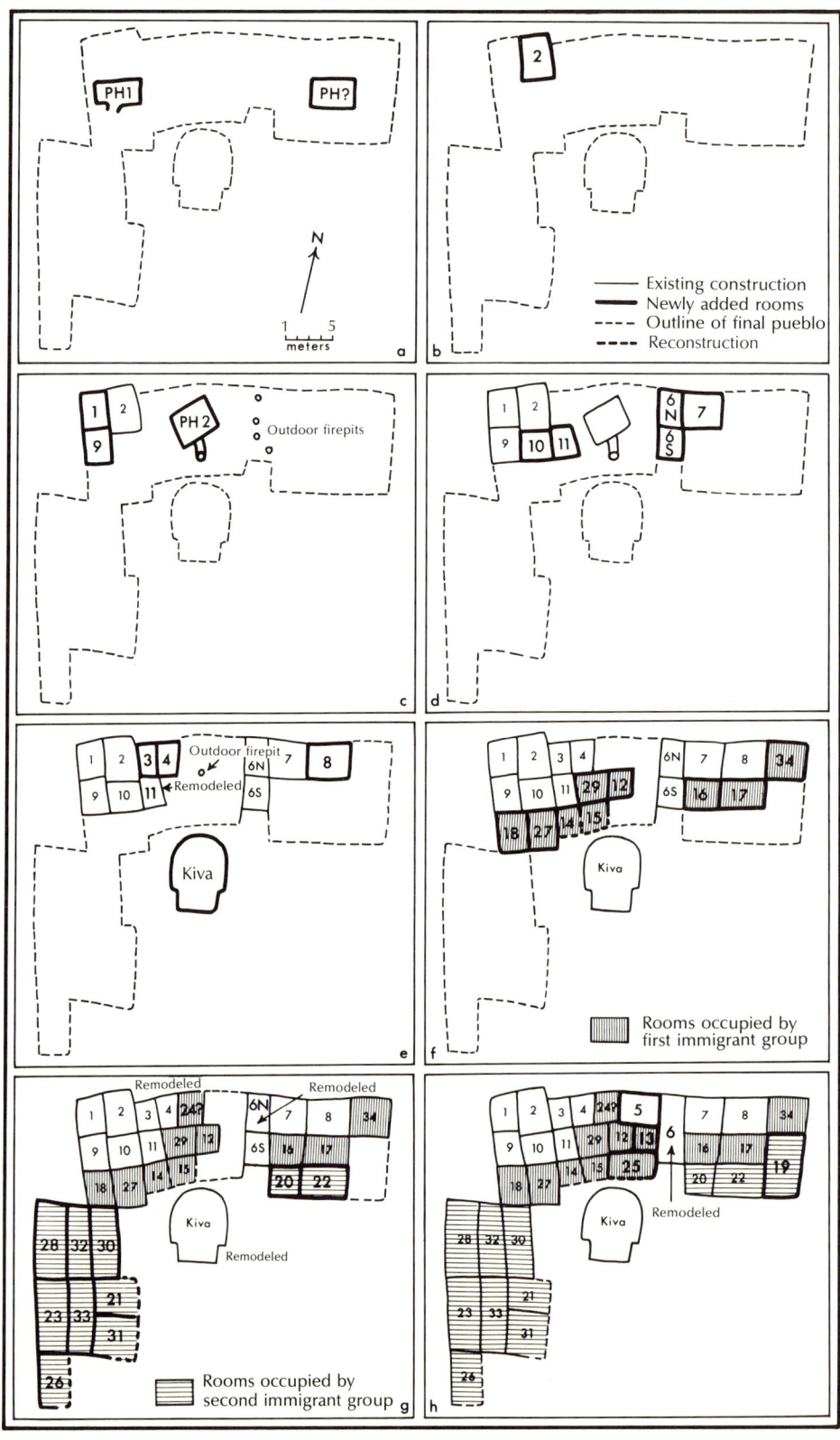

33, 21, 31, and 26. Probably all of this wing was built almost simultaneously. At nearly this same time, the northern half of Room 6 was remodeled by the original occupants using the then popular masonry style. The first group of new arrivals may have been responsible for the addition of Room 24 at this time also. The kiva masonry closely conformed to types newly popular, suggesting that the kiva may have been extensively remodeled then.

Almost the last construction activity at the pueblo served finally to unite the eastern and western units. The early new arrivals probably built Rooms 13 and 25, while the original occupants remodeled the southern half of Room 6 and perhaps made it into a long room at this time, conforming to the new style of longer rooms exhibited in the south wing rather than the nearly square rooms popular earlier; or this may have been accomplished when the north half of Room 6 was remodeled at the time of the west wing construction. The original inhabitants now also built Room 5, rebuilding at this time the west wall of the northern half of Room 6. It would seem the poor housewife in Room 6 had hardly a day when masons and plasterers were not underfoot.

Probably the last room built was another long room by the latest arrivals — Room 19, the only room of the pueblo built with a single wall rather than double walls. Could this indicate less intended permanency and be a prelude to abandonment? It is possible that a wing-wall joining the southwest corner and southeast corner was once present, enclosing the kiva and a plaza. Such a wall started in an easterly direction from

Figure 71. Site 481. Sketches illustrating sequence of room construction from earliest (a) to latest (h).
- a. A group of settlers occupied the ridge and constructed one (and probably two) rectangular semisubterranean pithouses.
- b. A second occupation of the ridge occurred when another family built a nearly square surface room (2). The alignment of this room with the earlier pithouse, and the trash related to the early surface rooms that was present in the pithouse, as well as the dendro and ceramic dating, suggest that though there was a period of nonoccupancy, it was not of long duration.
- c. Two rooms (1 and 9) were soon added, and probably at this time Pithouse 2 was constructed as a kiva, following the model of Site 494. The area east of the kiva served as a plaza with a number of outdoor firepits.
- d. To judge by the similarity of much of the pottery (Intrasite Distribution Type B), a closely related group began the east unit (Rooms 6N, 6S, and 7), while Rooms 10 and 11 were added to the west unit. (Although testing was minimal, the depth of the floor and the rectangular shape of the eastern subterranean structure, southeast of Rooms 6N, 6S, and 7, indicated that it correlated temporally with Pithouse 1 rather than being a second kiva, associated with the eastern room cluster.) In short, the two room clusters evidently were contemporaneous and shared a kiva, in contrast to the situation at Site 494.
- e. Room 11 was remodeled and Rooms 3 and 4 were added to the western cluster and Room 8 to the eastern cluster, again by individuals closely allied (ceramically and architecturally) with those already present. Obviously the kiva associated with the first surface rooms had by now been abandoned and filled, and an outdoor firepit (and Room 4) had been constructed over it. This fact, the assumption that another kiva must have replaced it, and the absence of any trace of a kiva other than the final one, is the only real evidence suggesting initial construction of the final kiva at this time. Because of the extensive kiva remodeling in phase g, there is no hard evidence for the shape of the kiva at this time either. Rather, it is assumed that the new "D" shape might have been at least one reason for the construction of a new kiva.
- f. Both ceramic (Instrasite Distribution Type C) and architectural changes were associated with this phase of construction. This fact, plus the number of rooms constructed, leads to the hypothesis that a new group of individuals, less closely related to the original settlers, was responsible for their construction. It is interesting that two separate architectural clusters were maintained and that there was construction at both by this "new" group. Perhaps a closely related village with a similar social division (clans ?) chose to amalgamate itself with the occupants of Site 481 at this time.
- g. The last major building phase saw the simultaneous or nearly simultaneous construction of the entire southwest wing and the addition of two rooms to the eastern cluster, presumably by new immigrants. Architecturally this group was distinct though ceramically (Intrasite Distribution Type C) closely allied with those responsible for the construction during phase f. Possibly this was yet another related group from a previously separate village, which now chose to join the residents of Site 481. The fact that there were no additions by the original occupants between phases e and h nor by the first new arrivals between phases f and h, except perhaps Room 24, suggests that a very short span of time separated the end of phase e and the beginning of phase h. The kiva evidently underwent considerable remodeling at this time.
- h. The final additions to the pueblo consisted of Rooms 5, 13, 19, 25, and perhaps 24. There was some architectural evidence that construction of Room 24 occurred first and was more nearly contemporaneous with phase g. There were several interesting elements in this final construction. All three of the hypothesized social units now in residence constructed one or more rooms, and the east and west units, so long separate, were now amalgamated. Room 19 may have been the last room built, probably by persons associated with the last group to arrive, and it was the only room with only a single rather than a double masonry wall, which suggests that permanency was not an important consideration at the time it was built, and that abandonment of the site was already under consideration.

Room 26 in the southwest corner, but there was no evidence of a wall extending southerly or westerly from Room 19. This entire section of the site was badly eroded, however, and such a wall, if it had ever existed, may have disappeared.

The surface pueblo thus reached its final form as a result of gradual accretion, over a long period, followed by a major spurt of rapid growth just before its end. Pithouse 1 was apparently the earliest structure at the site, and might have been built as early as about A.D. 950. If it was occupied up to A.D. 1010 or slightly later, as suggested on pages 213 and 214, the surface pueblo construction was probably begun with the construction of Room 2 some time close to A.D. 1020, and continued to expand until around A.D. 1275 or so. Hypothetically it is possible that some of the rooms were abandoned prior to the exodus from the entire pueblo, but this was impossible to determine. None of the surface rooms was conspicuously filled with trash or contained material of an earlier style than that associated with the fill of the other rooms. Trough metates were restricted to the fill of Rooms 2 and 3, two of the earliest rooms in the pueblo, but any suggestion that Room 2 had been abandoned at an earlier time is countered by the presence of a remodeled floor containing a slab-lined firepit. In general, the presence of an interior firepit appeared to be a late feature.

The abandonment of the pueblo as a whole appeared to have been carefully and deliberately effected. All rooms were methodically stripped of usable artifacts, a result possibly achieved with the aid of subsequent passersby. Very few whole artifacts were recovered and almost no material was found on the floors of the rooms. The contrast, in this respect, between Site 481 and Site 616 was indeed striking. The regional time-space pottery types present, the absence of glaze paint, and the limited range of color variations on the red-slipped pottery make it appear that Site 481 was abandoned at some time before Site 616, though perhaps for related reasons. It is even possible that the population of Site 481 moved to Site 616, for a number of features distinctive of Site 481 (sandstone-block masonry, long rooms, firepits with auxiliary holes, double walls with interior faces of smaller cobbles) first appeared at Site 616 at the time of a great population influx. This occurred at that site some time prior to its final abandonment and quite likely at approximately the time that Site 481 was abandoned.

DATING CONSIDERATIONS

This site was clearly occupied (perhaps at different periods) over a comparatively long time. Nine dated tree-ring specimens were recovered from three different rooms of the pueblo, with outer-ring dates varying between A.D. 1213 and 1271, one of them being a bark date at A.D. 1248, as shown below.

TREE-RING DATES

Provenience*	Dates (Bannister, Hannah, and Robinson 1970, p. 14)
Room 27	A.D. 1180 p - 1248 c**
Room 27	1179 - 1271 c
Room 31	1193 - 1248 r B
Kiva	1172 p - 1248 c
Kiva	1186 p - 1248 c
Kiva	1192 p - 1248 c
Kiva	1183 - 1268 vv
Kiva	1151 p - 1213 vv
Kiva	1156 - 1229 vv

*The dating of Pithouse 1 is considered below (p. 213).
**See symbol code, appendix B (p. 294).

Bannister, Hannah, and Robinson (1970, p. 14) express the opinion that a period of major construction occurred around A.D. 1248, with some subsequent repairs before abandonment, perhaps only a few years later.

The ceramic complex was dominated by Reserve Black-on-white and Tularosa Black-on-white, with smaller components of Red Mesa Black-on-white, Gallup Black-on-white, and St. Johns Polychrome, as shown at the top of page 187.

The early Red Mesa Black-on-white at Site 481 may have derived from the pithouses, but from the evidence of both tree-ring and ceramic dates, the surface pueblo clearly fits a late Pueblo II to middle Pueblo III period, which is also consistent with the architecture.

Experimentally, all occurrences of Red Mesa Black-on-white were compiled according to their provenience, using descriptive-type designations that have been ascribed herein to Red Mesa Black-on-white (p. 211). The results are shown on page 187, with the rooms in chronological order as inferred from architectural factors.

The results are peculiar, in that Red Mesa Black-on-white seems to occur everywhere in the site, and in fact shows a higher proportion in some of the very latest rooms than anywhere else: What this means is not clear — perhaps some sherds identified as Red Mesa Black-on-white should be assigned to another type, or perhaps remnants of the early occupation were so broadly scattered about that they became mixed into all contexts.

Some further insights may be had on this situation by reference to the intrasite distribution types (p. 213). These types can be used for a finer under-

CERAMIC COMPLEX

Type	Quantity	Dates Breternitz	Carlson
Red Mesa Black-on-white	307	A.D. 850+–1125	
Reserve Black-on-white	1173	940 –1100+	
Gallup Black-on-white	434	1000 –1125	
Wingate-Puerco Black-on-red*	803	1050 –1200	1100–1200
Tularosa Black-on-white	1604	1150 –1300	
St. Johns Polychrome	473	1175 –1300	1175–1300

*Puerco Black-on-red and Wingate Black-on-red were combined at the Second Southwestern Ceramic Conference in 1959, with Puerco Black-on-red being regarded as a late variant of Wingate Black-on-red.

OCCURRENCES OF RED MESA BLACK-ON-WHITE AT SITE 481
(Rooms arranged in probable chronological order)

Room	Number of Red Mesa Sherds	Percent of Red Mesa to All Painted Sherds	Room	Number of Red Mesa Sherds	Percent of Red Mesa to All Painted Sherds
PH 1	1	1	R 29	7	7
PH 2	13	3	R 8	15	6
R 1	3	12	R 16	9	7
R 2	47	25*	R 17	4	1
R 9	9	5	R 22	25	44*
R 10	3	1	R 31	5	6
R 6	15	10	R 13	8	13
R 3	5	6	R 25	16	33*
R 4	12	20*	R 5	27	20*
R 11	4	5	R 19	2	10
R 12	3	4	R 26	2	28*
R 18	11	12	R 23	6	7
R 27	8	4	Kiva	32	4
R 28	5	4			

*Indicates comparatively high percentages, four of which occur among the very latest rooms.

standing of the history of the ceramic changes at Site 481, but they were developed independently from the above analysis of regional time-space types.

When descriptive types assigned to Red Mesa Black-on-white are reviewed in the light of the general distribution of pottery of Red Mesa style throughout Site 481, it is evident that a subdivision within Red Mesa is possible. In short, all Red Mesa sherds with a thin watery slip (Material Type 4) are affiliated with Intrasite Distribution Type A and that type in turn was associated with the two earliest surface rooms (1 and 2), with Pithouse 2 (all three of which, as suggested below [p. 214], may have had a clan or other ceremonial function) and with the kiva itself. Red Mesa sherds with a thin white slip were associated only with other surface rooms. Of these sherds, those made of the dense gray paste with few inclusions (Material Type 6 and Intrasite Distribution Type B) were associated with the earlier rooms at the site and those adjacent to them (Rooms 3–11). Red Mesa sherds with a thin white slip but made with the gray paste of Material Type 2 (and affiliated with Intrasite Distribution Type C) were associated with the later construction period of the pueblo (and perhaps with a group of late immigrants).

Given this breakdown, made possible by the utilization of descriptive types, the widespread distribution of Red Mesa Black-on-white at Site 481 can perhaps be better understood.

It suggests, in its simplest form, that there was a chronological sequence within Red Mesa pottery from thin watery slip to thin white slip, but that Red Mesa vessels with the thin watery slip continued to be associated with areas occupied later than those with ceremonial connotations. It further suggests that the final major room construction was carried out by a group whose potters used a paste for their Red Mesa style pottery slightly different from that of the first occupants of the site.

Of course either approach to the evidence suggests

that Red Mesa continued in use throughout the occupation of the site.

It is interesting to note that available data support the rather surprising statement by Breternitz (1966, p. 90) that tree-ring associations indicate its indigenous occurrence as late as A.D. 1231, although his own opinion is that it lasted only until A.D. 1125. He says, further, that it has been found in "trade" contexts as late as A.D. 1285. If this is really so, the type is not of much value as a dating fossil, unless chronological modal differences can be recognized within it, substantiating Breternitz's subdivision into Early and Late variants.

ARCHITECTURE

In determining the constructional history of the surface rooms, wall joints and abutment patterns were of primary assistance, for the builders rarely bonded corners. On occasion, when a wall was built around two or more sides of a room they did make the construction continuous. However, a number of other patterns emerged that proved to be of considerable assistance in determining the sequence of room construction. With the exception of those of Room 19, all the walls of Site 481 were double, and the builders tended to use larger stones for the construction of exterior surfaces than for interior surfaces. This pattern proved to be extremely consistent throughout the site. Another factor that helped to determine the construction sequence was the relative height of the room floors. The floor area of new rooms was not excavated, and as trash accumulated outside of rooms the floors of rooms added to earlier ones tended to be slightly higher, for they were built on a greater accumulation of trash. Generally a slight trench was excavated to receive the base of the walls and here, as at Site 494, there was a strong tendency for the basal row of stones of even the sandstone-block walls to be of large basalt boulders.

Masonry Types (fig. 72)

During the construction history of the site a number of different masonry types evolved. Over time, masonry types tended to "move" from the outer to the inner face of a wall. That is, a masonry type would first appear on the outer face of a double wall. In the construction of a subsequent room this type would appear on the inner face, and a new type would, in turn, be employed on the outer face. The inner masonry type of the earlier walls would be dropped altogether, and so on.

The masonry types recognized are described below, as illustrated in figure 72. They are presented in their approximate order of appearance at the site.

Type A: Double wall. Both faces of lava cobbles, unshaped, and varying greatly in size; a few so large as to extend completely through the wall. The cobbles used on the interior face tended to be smaller than those on the exterior. The cobbles were placed irregularly with no definite courses apparent.

Type B: Small unshaped lava cobbles, fairly uniform in size, not laid in any discernible courses; found on interior faces only.

Type C: Medium-sized unshaped lava cobbles laid in fair to good courses; found on interior faces only.

Type D: Medium, with occasional small, slightly shaped sandstone blocks and slabs and some lava cobbles laid in fair to good courses. Employed at first on exterior and subsequently on interior faces.

Type E: Shaped sandstone slabs and blocks laid in generally even courses; pottery or sandstone spall chinking occasionally present. Employed first on exterior and later on interior faces.

Type F: Shaped sandstone blocks laid in excellent courses, with sherd or spall chinking. Employed on exterior faces only.

These masonry types were combined into a number of wall forms for the construction of rooms. The combinations and the rooms in which they were used for construction are outlined briefly below from early to late.

Type A on interior and exterior: Room 2.

Type B on interior, Type D on exterior: Rooms 1, 3, 4, 7, 9, 10, 11, and the southeast section of the east wall of final Room 6, representing an earlier version of this room.

Types C and D: Dividing wall between Rooms 18 and 27, and wing wall extending east from Room 7.

Type C on interior, Type E on exterior: Rooms 8, 12, 14, 15, 16, 18, 27, 29, 34, wall dividing Rooms 20 and 22, wall dividing Rooms 23 and 28.

Type D on interior, Type E on exterior: Rooms 17, 20, 21, 22, 23, 24, 26, 28, 30, 31, 32, 33, and the north and east walls of the final Room 6, representing the first modification of this room.

Type E on interior, Type F on exterior: Rooms 5, 13, 25, and the south wall of Room 6, bringing this room to its final form.

Type E (single wall): Room 19.

LIVING AND EXCAVATION UNITS

For convenience the dimensions and areas of all excavated rooms at Site 481 are consolidated in table 11. Walls are designated as if they were in exact north–south, east–west orientation, so that, for example, what is actually a north–northwest wall has been designated a north wall throughout, and, in the same manner, the kiva bench is described as bordering the south side of the kiva and the ventilator tunnel is described as running in a north–south direction under

Figure 72. Site 481. Masonry types in various rooms (intervals between chalk lines equal 1 m): a. Type A, exterior of south wall, Room 2; b. Type B, interior of south wall, Room 10; c. Type C, interior of north half of east wall, Room 27; d. Type D, exterior of east wall, Room 18; e. Type E, interior of south wall, Room 17 (interior of south wall, Type C, Room 22, in background); f. Type F, exterior of south wall, Room 5.

Room 1

This room was added to the west side of Room 2 at the same time that Room 9 was built. At one time a door connected Room 1 with Room 9. No clear floor level was discernible. There appeared to be irregular piles of adobe in the room and perhaps Room 1 served as a storage area for this material.

Room	Dimensions in meters		Area in square meters
	N-S	E-W	
1	2.8	2.0	5.6
2	3.4	2.2	7.5
3	2.25	1.3	3.0
4	2.4	1.45	3.5
5	2.2	3.1	6.8
6 (NW area)	2.8	1.75	3.9
6 (SE area)	2.6	2.0	5.2
7	2.8	3.0	8.4
8	2.7	3.4	9.2
9	2.6	1.9	4.9
10	2.2	2.5	5.5
11	2.4	1.6	3.8
12	1.8	1.8	3.2
13	1.75	1.6	2.8
14	Not excavated		
15	Not excavated		
16	2.0	2.6	5.2
17	2.1	3.4	7.1
18	3.0	2.1	6.3
19	4.8	2.8	13.4
20	2.2	2.2	4.8
21	2.3	2.9	6.7
22	2.25	3.7	8.3
23	6.1	2.4	14.6
24	2.4	1.8	4.3
25	1.9	3.8	7.2
26	3.8	2.0	7.6
27	3.0	2.3	6.9
28	5.6	2.4	13.4
29	2.0	2.4	4.8
30	5.6	1.9	10.6
31	2.2	?	?
32	5.4	1.6	8.6
33	5.8	1.8	10.4
34	2.8	3.0	8.4
Kiva Floor	4.1	4.5	15.0 (ap
Kiva Bench	1.7	3.1	5.3

Table 11. Dimensions of rooms in Site 481.

ARTIFACTS

Fill

Stone: 3 manos
Pottery: Fragment of Tularosa Black-on-white jar (fig. 84c)

Room 2

This was the first surface room constructed but it seems to have been in use until, or nearly until, the site was abandoned. Two floor levels were present. The original floor was very uneven and difficult to define but quite hard. A rectangular unlined pit 15 cm deep was located in the northeast corner of this earlier floor and may have served as the firepit, though no ash was present at the time of excavation. Several other unlined pits were in the same floor. Two shallow circular pits were against the east wall near the rectangular pit described above, and just south of these was an irregular pit containing the remains of a juniper post 12 cm in diameter. Against the center of the west wall was a shallow bell-shaped cist with a mouth diameter of 25 cm, a maximum diameter of 35 cm, and a depth of 17 cm. This feature, while associated with the early floor, had been plastered over some time prior to the construction of the second and higher floor. There was some indication that the original floor continued under the north wall. This fact plus the presence of juniper posts suggests that the builders of the masonry room made use of the floor of an earlier non-masonry structure in their building. Even so, the room walls were built over a deposit of trash.

At some time subsequent to the original construction of the room a second floor was added to the northern three-quarters of its area. A rectangular sandstone slab-lined firepit in the north-central section was associated with this floor. This firepit had a central bell-shaped cist in its floor. Both the firepit and the subsidiary cist were filled with white ash. There was a sealed doorway in the center of the east wall.

ARTIFACTS

Fill

Stone: Axe (#418, fig. 111e); chip; 5 manos; 3 metates, trough; pecking stone; pendant; point (#333, fig. 113g); 2 polishing pebbles; 2 rubbing stones; scoria cylinder; unretouched flake
Bone: Awls, head of bone intact, 2 fragments; weaving or matting tool
Antler: Flaker
Shell: Bracelet; pendant

Fill between Floors 1 and 2

Stone: 3 pecking stones; worked object; unretouched flake

Bone: Awl, head unworked except by original splitting

Floor 1
Stone: Mano
Bone: 2 weaving or matting tools

Below Floor 1
Stone: Mortar (#562, fig. 110d)

Room 3

Rooms 3 and 4 may originally have been a single room, for the door in the north wall was centrally located for such a room. If so, the modification resulting in the double rooms must have occurred shortly after construction, since the same masonry type was employed. Perhaps at this time the floor area of Room 3 was cleared, for while Rooms 2 and 4 rested on thin trash deposits, the floor of Room 3 was on undisturbed soil.

ARTIFACTS

Fill
Stone: Mano; 3 metates (#15, trough, fig. 109k); 2 rubbing stones

Room 4

The west wall of Room 4 appeared to have been modified several times. The southern quarter of this wall was of much later style of construction than the other parts of it. The floor, which was built over a thin trash deposit, was primarily marked by a color change and a black streak.

ARTIFACTS

Fill
Stone: 6 manos; pecking stone; point (fig. 113h); rubbing stone; unretouched flake
Bone: Tube (#272, fig. 114h)

Floor
Stone: Mano

Room 5

Rocks varying in size were found scattered throughout the fill of this and most of the other rooms. In the 40 cm of fill above the floor in Room 5 there was a considerable quantity of ash, charcoal, and charred beam fragments, and a few centimeters above the floor were eight to ten flat sandstone slabs. These were located primarily in the vicinity of the walls and varied in size from about 10 cm square to (one with) dimensions of 48 by 41 cm. In the northeast corner four slabs were found just above the floor. Immediately under them was approximately one-half of a brown-paste, corrugated, open-mouthed jar. Other pieces of this vessel were found at the same depth at various points along the east wall.

In the center of the south half of the east wall there was an opening at floor level 40 cm square that extended into Room 6. This may have been a pass-through similar to those found at Site 616.

The floor was of hard-packed earth with some admixture of clay. The texture was harder and the color lighter than the fill. The surface was relatively even, though it sloped up toward the edges and corners.

A firepit was located in the approximate center of the room. It was walled on each side by a single flat slab that extended from the floor of the firepit to slightly above the room floor. The north slab was of basalt, while the other three were of sandstone. The firepit was floored with small sandstone slabs and filled with ashes. Three cm to the east of the east wall of the firepit was a similar and parallel sandstone slab, evidently part of an earlier firepit. The area between the two slabs had been floored over.

In the northeast corner of the room there was a shallow basinlike depression in the floor. The east side of this depression was the wall itself but the other three sides consisted of low (5 cm above floor), narrow (15 cm), flat, adobe ridges, on top of which flat stones were inset. One of the stones on the south side was a lava mano. The dimensions of the depression itself were 37 cm east–west, and 47 cm north–south, and it may have served as a mealing bin. If so, it was one of only two possible such bins found at Site 481. No metate was in association.

ARTIFACTS

Fill
Stone: 2 chips; 2 manos; pecking stone; polishing pebble; rubbing stone
Bone: Awl, fragment; tube (#288, fig. 114i)
Shell: Bracelet
Whole vessel: Brownware, clapboard-corrugated bowl

Structural
Stone: Mano

Room 6

The constructional history of this room was more complex than that of any other room at the site. The area underlying it had served for a considerable period of time prior to the room's construction as a work and refuse area, and a number of outdoor firepits were built during this time.

Figure 73. Site 481. Remodeled firepit in plaza east of Pithouse 2, subsequently plastered over before or at the time of construction of Room 6. Note center ash holes. Slab covering left hole is propped open with trowel.

A total of five firepits were found in the 30 to 40 cm of trash that underlay Room 6. All were nearly circular in plan with sandstone-slab floors, sandstone-and-burned-earth walls, and a subsidiary bell-shaped cist in the center of the floor. The floors of the two middle firepits were on undisturbed soil but, except for the floor slabs and the central cist, these two firepits had been destroyed. The floors of the other three subsurface firepits were in the trash levels; and their slab sides, largely still in place, projected in several instances slightly through the floor of the room.

Originally Room 6 included only the south half of the area that ultimately formed the room, and its floor covered the existing outdoor firepits in that area. Later the north half of the room was added, covering the ourdoor firepits there, and the wall dividing the two sections was knocked down, though a low adobe ridge survived to mark its location. Subsequently, the west wall was replaced by the walls that were built to form Rooms 5, 13, and 25. The south wall appeared to have been rebuilt at this time.

Two firepits were associated with the floor of Room 6. One was in the center of the south half of the room against the west wall, while the other was in the center of the north half of the room against the east wall. The southern firepit was rectangular, both floored and lined with sandstone slabs, and a centrally located subsidiary hole was in its floor. Both hole and firepit were filled with ashes. Similar ash-filled holes were found in Rooms 2 and 25 of Site 481 (p. 195), at the Zuni pueblo of Hawikuh (Smith, Woodbury, and Woodbury 1966, p. 56), in Rooms C5 and C10 at Site 616 (pp. 78, 83), and at Sandstone Hill Pueblo (Barnett 1974,

p. 11). Between the firepit and the west wall was a shallow unlined pit that may have served as an ash depository. The northern firepit was square, directly against the east wall, and slab-lined. Its floor was of fired earth and contained no central hole.

ARTIFACTS

Fill

Stone: Axe; 15 manos; 2 pecking stones; turquoise fragment

Floor

Stone: Metate, slab

Below floor

Stone: Mano; 3 pecking stones

Room 7

This was one of the first rooms built in the eastern section of the pueblo. The floor was rather irregular and bare of features.

ARTIFACTS

Fill

Stone: 4 chips; core; hammer, elongated, flat-ended (#73, fig. 112b); 4 manos; ornament; pendant; point (#342, fig. 113d); 7 polishing pebbles; rubbing stone
Bone: Awl, head wholly removed
Clay: Pendant (#292, fig. 115j)
Other: Hematite (4½ oz); kaolin (½ oz); limonite (1½ oz)
Whole vessel: Brownware, indented-corrugated jar

Room 8

In the west end of the south half of this room there was a firepit of rather curious design. It was oval in top view (35 cm north–south, 83 cm east–west) and the edge of this oval was excavated to a depth of 5 cm below the floor. A second oval area, 7 cm in from the edges of the first oval, was excavated to a total depth of 21 cm. In the center of this second oval excavation there was an oval bell-shaped cist with a mouth diameter of 10 by 18 cm, a maximum diameter of 18 by 23 cm, and a depth of 14 cm. The entire firepit was simply excavated into the native soil with no stones in association.

In the center of the east wall of the room, an open door led into Room 34. In the northeast and the southeast corners of Room 8, flanking either side of this door, were two enclosures set off by adobe ridges, 20 cm high, 15 cm wide. The floors of the enclosures were at the same level as the floor of the room.

ARTIFACTS

Fill

Stone: 2 manos; pecking stone; polishing pebble; rubbing stone
Bone: Awl, head of bone intact; ring (#286, fig. 114j)
Other: Figurine, clay

Room 9

This room was added at the same time as Room 1. The southwest corner of Room 2 appeared to have been modified at the same time also.

ARTIFACTS

Fill

Stone: 4 chips; mano; mortar; rubbing stone
Bone: 2 awls, head wholly removed
Whole vessel: Tularosa Black-on-white miniature jar (#541, fig. 84g), some sherds of which were also found in Room 18; Puerco Black-on-red ladle (#481, fig. 84e), some sherds of which were also found in Room 18

Room 10

Room 10 and Room 9 immediately overlay Pithouse 1. The floor of Room 10 was of hard-packed adobe but somewhat irregular.

ARTIFACTS

Fill

Stone: 4 manos; pecking stone; polishing stone; rubbing stone (#678, fig. 109o); whetstone
Bone: Awls, splinter, 3 fragments

Floor

Bone: Awl, fragment
Other: Sherd pendant (#68, fig. 115f); turquoise fragment

Room 11

An open door with the threshold at floor level connected this room with Room 10, and a door had originally connected it to Room 29 but this second door had been sealed. The floor was of hard-packed adobe, smooth but somewhat uneven. Except for some miscellaneous sherds no artifacts were found in this room.

Figure 74. Site 481. View of Room 13, looking northwest.

Room 12

The north wall of this room was built directly over a well-constructed, circular, slab-lined firepit.

ARTIFACTS

Fill

Stone: 2 chips
Bone: Awl, fragment

Room 13

An open door with an adobe sill at floor level connected this room with Room 25. The door in the west wall may have been sealed when Room 13 was built. This room was probably one of the last built at the site. The floor was hard but quite bumpy. An unlined hole 16 cm in diameter and 45 cm deep was located in the center of the north half of the floor.

ARTIFACTS

Fill

Stone: 2 chips; end scraper; unretouched flake
Whole vessels: 2 brownware, clapboard-corrugated jars

Rooms 14 and 15

These rooms were almost entirely destroyed, perhaps by the building of the kiva, and were not investigated.

Room 16

The floor was hard, fairly even, and nearly level. In the southeast corner there was a triangular area slightly higher than the main floor, which may be indicative of a partial reflooring; but since the main floor could not be traced below this area, it probably was just a slightly higher section of the main floor.

The firepit was rectangular with slightly rounded corners, located nearly in the center of the room. The sides were vertical, and while not slab-lined at the time of excavation, they probably had been. The bottom of the pit was irregular and 15 to 20 cm below the room floor. Three basalt cobbles protruded from the bottom of the pit. Diagonally across the east part of the pit, another pit went down 15 to 20 cm below the upper one. This lower pit was lined with basalt cobbles and one corner extended beyond the limits of the present firepit. It may represent an earlier version of the firepit.

In the center of the south wall at floor level was a square passthrough or ventilating tunnel.

ARTIFACTS

Fill

Various fragments of colored sandy soil

Floor

Bone: Figurine (#651, fig. 114e)

Room 17

Sherds from a number of restorable vessels came from the fill of this room just above the floor. One large Tularosa Black-on-white jar had been crushed by a large sandstone slab (54 by 42 cm).

The floor was extremely uneven, sloping generally down to the west but with a marked hump just west of the center line. There were a number of postholes extending roughly in a north – south line across the west end of the room, with no apparent purpose unless it was to support a sagging roof. A sealed doorway with a sill 12 cm above the floor was in the center of the south wall.

Excavation below the floor in this room revealed the outline of what may have been a shallow pithouse similar to Pithouse 1, but lack of time prevented more complete excavation.

ARTIFACTS

Fill

Stone: Chip; 2 manos; points (#647, fig. 113c)
Bone: Pierced phalange (#648, fig. 114d)
Whole vessels: Wingate Black-on-red seed jar (#673, fig. 84a); Wingate Black-on-red jar; 2 St. Johns Polychrome bowls; Tularosa Black-on-white jar

Floor

Bone: Pierced phalange (#649, fig. 114c)

Below floor

Stone: 2 chips; pecking stone

Structural

Stone: Mortar, built into west wall

Room 18

The floor was hard, fairly even, but not perfectly level, sloping upward noticeably toward the north end. Near the northwest corner there was an irregular basin-shaped depression 40 cm in diameter and 18 cm deep in the center.

In the north wall was an open doorway, very well constructed, with sandstone slabs lining its edges. A doorway in the center of the east wall had been sealed. The sills of both doorways were approximately 10 cm above the floor.

ARTIFACTS

Fill

Stone: 5 chips; 2 cores; 7 manos; pecking stone; 2 polishing pebbles; 2 rubbing stones; quartz crystal; 2 shaped objects; disc bead
Bone: Awl, head wholly removed; awl, skewer; 2 tubes
Other: Turquoise fragment; malachite (1 oz)
Whole vessels: Tularosa Black-on-white miniature jar (#541, fig. 84g), some sherds of which were also found in Room 9; Puerco Black-on-red ladle (#481, fig. 84e), some sherds of which were also found in Room 9; toy vessel

Room 19

The east and south walls of this room, which had been built to form the room in the exterior angle adjacent to Rooms 17, 22, and 34, were the only walls in the pueblo that were not double. It was one of the last rooms, if not the last one, to be constructed before the site was abandoned, and the floor, which was quite irregular, had received little use. The insubstantial masonry style may reflect a realization on the part of the builders that the room was not destined to be used for a very long period, rather than represent any basic change in standard construction techniques.

ARTIFACTS

Fill

Stone: Mortar
Other: Limonite (¾ oz)

Room 20

The floor of this room consisted of a layer of caliche 6 cm deep, covered with 2 cm of adobe. The surface was fairly uneven and sloped down to the northeast. There was a sealed doorway in the north half of the east wall.

ARTIFACT

Fill

Stone: Polishing pebble

Room 21

Only limited test trenches were excavated in this room. No artifacts were recovered.

Room 22

An unusually large rectangular firepit, 85 by 65 cm, was situated in the southwest quarter of the floor, its northeast corner very close to the center of the room. Its sides were of sandstone slabs, parallel to the walls of the room, the longer dimension running east – west, and it had a baked earth floor. A sandstone slab from an earlier version of the pit projected through the floor adjacent to the present north wall slab. The bottom of the firepit was 20 cm below the floor of the room.

The only other floor feature was a rectangular paved area in the center of the eastern edge of the floor. This area was 49 cm east – west by 34 cm north – south and was 10 cm below floor level. An upright sandstone slab lined the south edge of the area and there was a low adobe lip on the north edge. This probably was a remnant of a mealing bin. The metate itself may not have been permanently fixed but may have been balanced on rocks to the north of the paved area. This would permit the use of metates of varying degrees of coarseness in the same place.

ARTIFACTS

Fill

Stone: Scoria cylinder; 3 manos; mortar (#650, fig. 110a)
Bone: Awl, splinter

Floor

Stone: 5 manos
Bone: Bead
Other: Figurine, clay

Room 23

A trench was excavated completely outlining the walls of this room and another was excavated along the east

Figure 75. Site 481. Remodeled late-style rectangular firepits built within Room 25, with no central ash hole. Firepit to the right had been plastered over while room was still in use, but wall slabs still showed through the plastered floor.

– west center line of the room. No floor features were encountered.

ARTIFACTS

Fill

Stone: 2 chips; 4 manos; metate, slab; scoria cylinder; unretouched flake

Below floor

Bone: Awl, splinter

Room 24

A sandstone slab chipped to shape, 40 by 50 cm, was found in the northeast corner of this room 50 cm above the floor. The floor was extremely level with a hard surface, and presented a strong contrast to the fill. It consisted of a layer of orange clay with a large admixture of sand approximately 3 cm thick.

ARTIFACTS

Fill

Stone: Mano; rubbing stone; sandstone slab

Floor

Whole vessel: Tularosa Black-on-white miniature seed jar (#558, fig. 84f)

Room 25

A considerable portion of the south wall of this room was missing, and had probably fallen into the kiva depression. The floor was well packed but somewhat uneven. In some places it had been curved upward against the walls.

In approximately the center of the room there was a rectangular firepit walled with sandstone slabs. The pit had a baked clay bottom, 20 cm below the room floor. Bordering the southeast corner of this firepit the tops of the sandstone slabs of a second firepit could be seen projecting through the floor. This abandoned firepit, also rectangular, was both walled and floored with sandstone slabs, and had a bell-shaped hole in the center of its floor. This hole was 10 to 13 cm in diameter and 34 cm deep. Similar ash-filled holes were found in Rooms 2 and 6 at Site 481 (p. 192), at the Zuni pueblo of Hawikuh (Smith, Woodbury, and Woodbury 1966, p. 56), in Rooms C5 and C10 at Site 616 (pp. 78, 83), and in Sandstone Hill Pueblo (Barnett 1974, p. 11).

Just northeast of the firepit was an almost circular unlined hole in the floor of the room 25 cm in diameter and 20 cm deep.

ARTIFACTS
Fill

    Stone: 4 chips; hammer, three-quarter-grooved, flat-ended (#162, fig. 112c); polishing pebble
    Bone: Tube (#285, fig. 114g)
    Whole vessel: Brownware, clapboard-corrugated jar

Room 26

It is possible that this was not a room but simply an area of the plaza, for this section of the pueblo had been badly eroded. A wall extended south in prolongation of the west wall of Room 23, then swung east and may have continued across the entire south edge of the pueblo. There was some indication that the east wall of Room 23 also continued south to form a room in this extreme southwest corner. The area was only trenched, but no definite floor could be discerned.

ARTIFACT
Trench

    Stone: Pestle (#350, fig. 110e)

Room 27

The floor of this room was of hard adobe, rather uneven, and bare of features. There was a sealed doorway in the center of both east and west walls, with sills respectively 15 to 30 cm above the floor.

ARTIFACTS
Fill

    Stone: Mano; rubbing stone

    Bone: 5 awls, 1 with head of bone intact, 1 splinter, 1 skewer, 2 fragments

Room 28

The floor of this room was not in good condition, and sloped down toward the south. There were three doorways, all sealed. One, in the center of the west wall, had a sill 14 cm above the floor, while the sills of the doorways in the north and south walls were almost at floor level.

The centrally located firepit was nearly square and was lined with sandstone slabs. The bottom was of clay, 23 cm below the floor of the room.

ARTIFACTS
Fill

    Stone: 8 manos; polishing pebble; rubbing stone
    Shell: Pendant

Floor

    Pottery: Sherd disc; toy vessel

Room 29

The floor of this room was hard, rather irregular, and bare of features. Doors in the south and west walls, with sills 25 cm above floor, had been sealed.

ARTIFACTS
Fill

    Stone: 9 manos; 2 polishing stones; rubbing stone
    Other: Kaolin (2½ oz)

Floor

    Stone: Mano; hammer
    Bone: Tube (#664, fig. 114b)

Below floor

    Stone: Metate, slab

Room 30

This room was not completely cleared but no features were located adjacent to the walls or in the center of the room.

ARTIFACTS
Fill

    Stone: 6 chips; mano; metate, basin

Floor

    Bone: Awl, head of bone intact

Room 31

This room was not completely cleared but there appeared to be no floor features. Below the floor in the east central section of the room was a circular, slab-lined, and floored cist with a central bell-shaped hole in the bottom. The cist was very similar to that below the north wall of Room 12 and those below the floor of Room 6.

ARTIFACTS

Fill

Stone: 4 manos; mortar (#802, fig. 109m); unretouched flake

Firepit

Stone: Bowl (#738, fig. 109n)

Below floor

Stone: Polishing pebble
Other: Sherd disc; colored sandy soil

Room 32

This room was trenched only. No floor features were found adjacent to the walls or in the center of the room.

ARTIFACTS

Fill

Stone: 5 chips; 2 cores; 2 manos; side scraper

Room 33

This room was trenched only. No floor features were found adjacent to the walls or in the center of the room.

ARTIFACTS

Fill

Stone: Rubbing stone
Shell: Unworked fragment

Room 34

The floor of this room was hard, but uneven, and sloped down to the east. There were indications of subfloor features but lack of time prevented further investigation.

A firepit, almost centrally located, was approximately square, with sandstone slabs lining the walls. The bottom was 20 cm below the floor of the room. A single slab covered the north half of the bottom but the remainder was of clay.

ARTIFACTS

Fill

Stone: Axe (#428, fig. 111b); 4 manos
Other: Limonite (¾ oz)

Kiva

A subterranean kiva was situated only slightly more than a meter southeast of Rooms 15 and 25, in the area embraced by the two arms of the pueblo. Its main floor area was of a general D-shape, with the straight side of the D forming the south or rear boundary of the main floor area. Along this boundary was a masonry wall 4.2 m in length. The sides of the kiva expanded slightly from the rear corners for a distance of about 2 m from the rear, where the kiva reached its widest extent of 4.5 m, and then converged in a continuous curve of almost constant radius across the front of the area, the center point being 4.1 m in front of the straight or rear side.

Extending backward from the rear boundary was an almost rectangular bench, 1.7 m in depth, and varying in width from about 3.2 m at its face to about 3 m at the rear. The floor of the bench was 85 cm above the main floor.

Stones, broken pottery, and occasional artifacts were scattered through the fill. Resting directly on the floor and the bench and concentrated in a layer 30 cm above these levels was a large quantity of charcoal and frequent large fragments of charred beams. There is little question that the roof of the kiva had burned and collapsed to the floor when the kiva was abandoned or shortly after. Perhaps it was intentionally destroyed by the inhabitants at the time of departure. It was the only room at Site 481 with extensive evidence of having been destroyed by fire.

The walls were well constructed of sandstone-slab masonry (Type E). The faces of individual stones averaged 7 cm in height by 18 cm in length. The stones had an average depth of 14 cm, and were set in regular courses and plastered over. There was little indication of extensive replastering, even though the plaster in the lower levels was in a good state of preservation as a result of having been fired at the time the roof burned. The walls extended, in general, 16 cm below the floor.

The surfaces of both bench and floor apparently were entirely paved with sandstone slabs, averaging 2.5 cm in thickness, during one period of the kiva's use. At the time of excavation remnants of the paving of the bench were restricted to the edges of its west, south, and east surfaces and over the ventilator trench that underlay the bench. On the floor, stone paving was found around the floor edges and in some cases projecting a short distance out from the walls. The

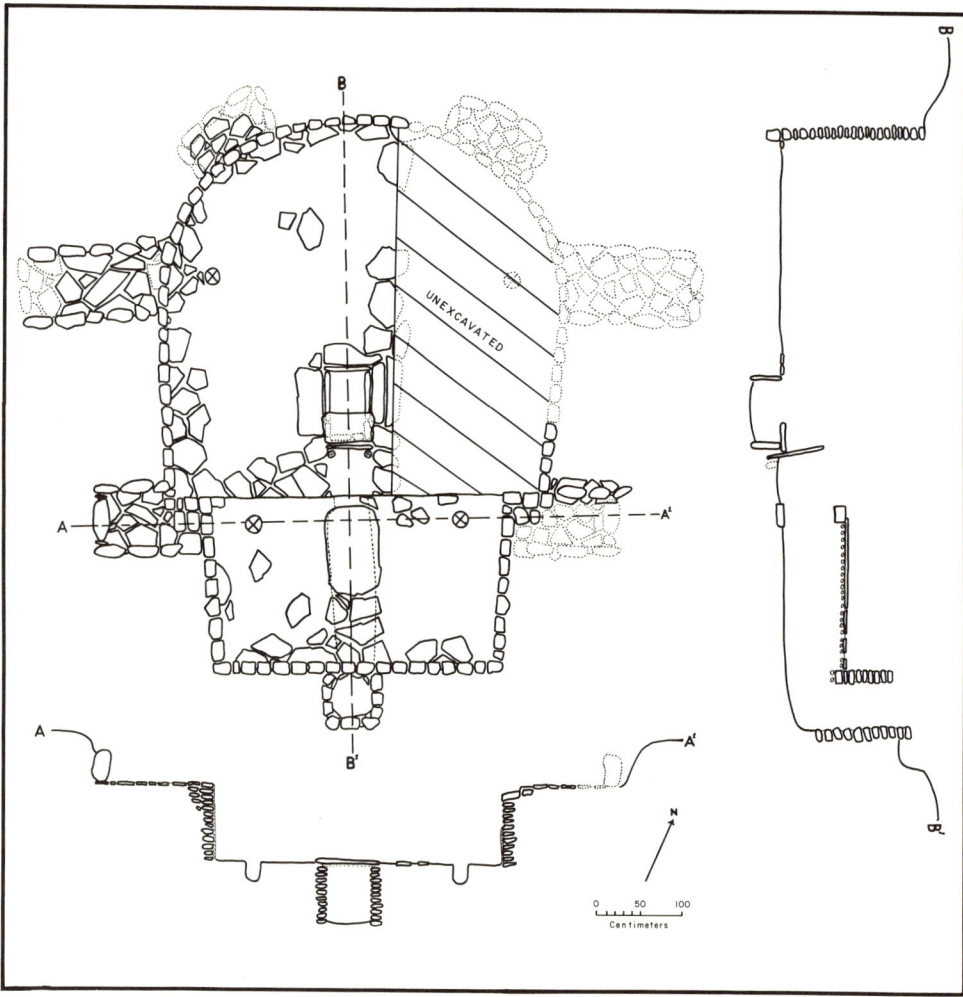

Figure 76. Site 481. Plan of kiva.

firepit area was also bounded by stone slabs on three sides. Along the fourth side, adjacent to the deflector, was a depressed area of hard-packed clay. The areas not paved were of hard-packed clay on a level with the bases of the sandstone slabs. Slight angular depressions were still visible where slabs had been removed (to Site 616?). It appeared that the floor had received at least slight use in this condition, indicating that the kiva might have continued in use, at least for a short time, after the slabs were removed; but more likely this "wear" simply represented traffic during the removal of the slabs. Most of the remaining slabs were small.

FIREPIT

The firepit was comparatively large, 71 by 44 cm. It was walled with sandstone slabs averaging 5.5 cm in thickness, much larger than those found in firepits in the surface rooms. The bottom of the pit was of hard-packed fired clay 30 cm below the kiva floor. A large thick sandstone slab, 50 by 25 cm, had been laid across the tops of the wall slabs, completely covering the rear (south) end of the firepit. The firepit was filled with ash.

DEFLECTOR

A thick sandstone slab, 55 cm wide and 65 cm high, had been set 16 cm into the floor of the kiva immediately to the rear of the firepit, separating it from the ventilator opening. The slab was set at an angle leaning toward the center of the kiva and was in contact with the slab that covered the rear of the firepit.

VENTILATOR

A trench had been dug in a north-south line through the center of the bench meeting a vertical shaft dug into the soil adjacent to the rear or southern wall of the kiva. The vertical shaft was then walled on all sides

Figure 77. Site 481. View of south half of kiva, showing recessed rear bench, firepit, deflector, and ventilator.

with sandstone masonry, the main south wall of the kiva forming the north wall of the shaft. The walls of the horizontal trench were also lined with masonry but the floor was not, except for a sandstone-slab sill set into the floor at the point where the trench opened into the kiva. The horizontal trench was roofed with sandstone slabs supported by small wooden beams averaging 3.5 cm in thickness and 86 cm in length, and placed about 5 cm apart. The sandstone lintel above the aperture at the deflector end of the trench was not supported by beams but was of sufficient size and thickness to have readily borne the weight of a man using it as a step in ascending or descending the ladder, which stood in front of it.

LADDER

The legs of a double-pole ladder were set into depressions 8 cm in diameter in the kiva floor 2 cm to the rear of the deflector and 36 cm apart. The support holes sloped toward the center of the kiva at the same angle as the deflector. A hatchway apparently had been directly over the firepit. A ladder with poles whose basal section was no thicker than 8 cm probably would not have supported the weight of a man on the upper portion of the ladder. Perhaps the section set into the floor had been worked down from a larger diameter or perhaps the poles were inverted from their normal growing position, so that the poles got slightly larger toward the top.

ROOF

The roof was supported by four major posts 20 cm in diameter. Two were set into the floor of the kiva and two into the bench. All four posts were located 50 cm out from the kiva walls. Charred roof beams found in the fill varied in thickness between 11 and 13 cm. The exact method of roof construction was not apparent.

NICHES

Six large wall niches were located approximately 2 m above the kiva floor. The four excavated were paved with sandstone slabs, while the sides and backs were lined with basalt cobbles, the only instance of basalt masonry in association with the kiva. One niche was directly opposite each of the major support posts. These four were each 50 cm wide; the two southern

Figure 78. Site 481. Detailed view of kiva firepit, deflector, and mouth of ventilator. Slab covers rear of firepit. Trowel does not point north.

Figure 79. Site 481. View of northwest corner of kiva, showing height of burned wall plaster and the northwest wall niche.

ones were 100 cm deep, and the two northern ones 150 cm deep. Around the arc of the north end of the kiva were two other niches constructed in a similar manner but of a different shape. These two were approximately 90 cm wide but only 50 cm deep.

Probably the beams placed across the tops of the major support posts extended into these niches but it is unlikely that these beams rested directly on the floor of the niches. That is, the support posts, not the niches, bore the weight of the roof. Had the niches borne the weight, the posts would have been superfluous and the smooth floor of the niches, being wider than the beams, would not have provided a very stable foundation. More likely, the niches served as depositories for objects and the beams extended into the niches at a level above that of the niche floors. Such use of the niches would account for the care taken in their construction.

ARTIFACTS
Fill

    Stone: 38 chips; 2 cores; 14 manos; pecking stone; 2 polishing pebbles; 2 side scrapers; unretouched flake

    Shell: Unworked fragment
    Other: Clay elbow pipe; hematite (3½ oz)

Floor

    Other: Concretion
    Whole vessel: St. Johns Polychrome bowl (#539, fig. 84b)

Pithouse 1

Of all rooms excavated at Site 481, Pithouse 1 was undoubtedly the earliest. It was a rectangular, very shallow pithouse located just below surface Rooms 9 and 10.

The floor of the pithouse was 30 to 35 cm below the floor of the overlying rooms. It consisted of hard-packed adobelike soil and was not very even. The low earthen sides of the room were perpendicular to the floor. A pair of major roof-support posts had been set into the south wall approximately 70 cm in from the east and west walls. To erect these posts an irregular vertical shaft was dug into the face of the wall extending into the earth below it; the post was placed in the center of the hole, and the hole was then packed with stones and earth. The south wall was then plastered over, so that the post was not visible below the original ground level. The southwest post was in an excellent state of preservation. It was of juniper, 12 cm in diameter. On the bottom of the post the marks of a stone axe were still clearly apparent. No other roof-support posts or wall posts were found but an extensive area around the pithouse was not cleared. Probably there were two major support posts beyond the north wall. Perhaps the walls consisted of a jacal arrangement, with the wall posts leaning inward from ground level outside the edge of the pithouse to the beams placed across the four roof posts.

In the center of the floor area was a shallow egg-shaped firepit. It was 70 cm long, north–south, 50 cm wide and 12 cm deep. The sides sloped gradually down to the center. Just to the south of this feature was a second shallow basinlike depression. This was rectangular, 25 cm long, north–south, and 40 cm wide. It may have served as an ash depository for the firepit.

In the center of the south wall, just south of the features described above, was an opening from which a sloping trench or passageway 50 cm wide extended from the level of the floor up to the ground surface. This passageway was approximately 60 cm long. At the ground-level end it was paved with several sandstone and basalt slabs. It may have served as an entrance, a ventilator, or both.

The floor in the entire northeast corner of the room sloped down sharply toward the corner, giving entrance to a tremendous cist. The main body of this cist was 135 cm in diameter and the cist floor was 3 m below the floor of Pithouse 1. Entance and exit was gained by means of a single-pole ladder, the upper end of which rested in a slit or notch in the southeast wall of the cist. The cist was filled with rather loose soil containing some ash, charcoal, and artifacts. Some of these appeared to have been slightly compacted by water standing in the cist. A number of large lava cobbles were also present.

It is doubtful that this pithouse was still in use at the time Room 2, the first surface room, was constructed. It probably had fallen into disrepair and the excavation had become filled partly by natural and then, to a greater extent, by human agencies.

ARTIFACTS

Fill

Stone: Axe (#778, fig. 112a); 2 chips; hammer; mano

Cist

Stone: Point (#3078, fig. 113e); 7 chips; pecking stone
Bone: Weaving or matting tools

Figure 80. Site 481. View of Pithouse 1, looking northeast, with firepit in lower left corner and mouth of large floor cist in upper right.

Shell: Bracelet
Other: Colored sandy substance

Floor

Stone: Point (#2689, fig. 113a); 2 manos

Pithouse 2

This pithouse was not completely excavated. A trench was put through the center, while two arms of this trench followed the south wall for a short distance on either side of the ventilating shaft. More extensive investigation would have necessitated removing the walls of the overlying rooms, a task not feasible in the time available. Although it was known that Rooms 4, 24, 5, 29, and 12 rested on a trash deposit, the existence of an underlying structure was first suggested by the discovery of a shaft, about 50 cm in diameter, leading down from the northwest corner of Room 25. Preliminary investigation of this shaft, made in 1949, showed that it went straight down for a distance of 100 cm and then continued at a right angle to the north. In 1951 work was resumed and the shaft was followed until it opened into a masonry-walled subsurface room, which appeared to be similar in all major respects to the subsurface rooms excavated at Site 494 and identified there as kivas.

The horizontal section of the ventilator (for such the shaft proved to be) was 150 cm long and sloped down slightly until at its entrance into the pithouse it was 170 cm below the overlying rooms.

The portion of the south wall of the room east of the ventilator shaft was faced with a single wall of medium-sized sandstone blocks and lava cobbles laid in fairly regular courses (Masonry Type D). When found, this wall was nine courses high. It did not continue to the west of the ventilator shaft, at least in the meter that was cleared. Nor did the short section of the north wall that was excavated have any masonry facing, but was of smooth adobe. No investigation was made of the east and west walls.

The floor, of a white claylike material, was quite hard and level. In the center of the room was a rectangular firepit filled with ash. It was unlined and had been excavated out of the native soil, with straight sides and a flat bottom.

A considerable quantity of charcoal lay immediately above the floor. Above this, the strata observed in the fill sloped down gradually from each side toward the center of the kiva as if after abandonment it had become a saucer-shaped depression that gradually filled with an accumulation of refuse.

ARTIFACTS
Fill

Stone: 9 chips; 2 cores; 10 manos; metate, slab (#696, fig. 109c); 5 pecking stones; 2 points (#2564, #2559, fig. 113bf); polishing pebble; unretouched flake

Bone: 3 awls, 1 with head unworked except for original splitting; skewer; fragment; serrated tool (#2826, fig. 114a)

Other: 2 figurines of clay (#2561, fig. 115a, c); 2 pendants

SUBSISTENCE MATERIALS

Approximately two-thirds of the 716 unworked animal bones recovered from Site 481 were rabbit, hare, turkey, or other small animals. The other bones included 12 mule deer *(Odocoileus hemionus hemionus)*, 12 pronghorn *(Antilocapra americana)*, 1 bison *(Bison bison)* calcaneum, 1 prairie dog *(Cynomis* sp.) skull, and 2 bobcat *(Lynx rufus)* paws. There were 2 skulls, 1 complete skeleton, and 2 other bones of the dog. These are *Canis familiaris*, short-snouted, although one skull seemed to be of the long-snouted variety. The remaining 250 bones were from unidentified large animals.

The dog skeleton and the two skulls were found in the fill of the kiva just above the floor. The other bones were scattered throughout the site without apparent distributional significance. With the exception of 1 pronghorn and 2 mule deer skulls, a scapula, and 2 vertebrae, all of the deer and pronghorn bones were from the legs of the animals.

The only vegetal materials recovered were some charred corn cobs and kernels from the fill of Room 2, the fill of Pithouse 2, and the fill of the large cists in Pithouse 1.

POTTERY — DESCRIPTIVE TYPOLOGY

Following is a summary of descriptive-type definitions applied to the pottery from Site 481. The distribution of the types within the site is shown in tables 12, 13, 14.

White-slipped Pottery (fig. 81)

MATERIAL: ROW A

1: Gray paste — mode key (A)
   White slip, thickly applied — modes (b) and (g)
   Black mineral paint — mode (a)
2: Gray paste — mode key (A)
   White slip, thinly applied — modes (b) and (h)
   Black mineral paint — mode (a)
3: Gray paste — mode key (A)
   Cream-colored slip, thickly applied — modes (c) and (g)
   Black mineral paint — mode (a)
4: Gray paste — mode key (A)
   Thin and/or watery white slip — modes (b) and (i)
   Black mineral paint — mode (a)
5: Gray paste — mode key (A)
   White slip, thinly applied — modes (b) and (h)
   Black glaze paint — mode (b)
6: Dense gray paste with few inclusions — mode key (C)
   White slip, thinly applied — modes (b) and (h)
   Black mineral paint — mode (a)
7: Brown paste with sand inclusions — mode key (H)
   White slip, thinly applied — modes (b) and (h)
   Black mineral paint — mode (a)
8: Gray paste — mode key (A)
   No slip — mode (a)
   Black mineral paint — mode (a)

VESSEL SHAPES AND AREAS SLIPPED AND PAINTED: ROW B

1: Pitcher — mode (g)
   No slip — mode (a)
   Painted on exterior — mode (d)
2: Bowl — mode (a).
   Interior and exterior slipped, interior painted — modes (a), (b), and (c).
3: Ladle — mode (h)
   Interior and exterior slipped, interior painted — modes (a), (b), and (c)

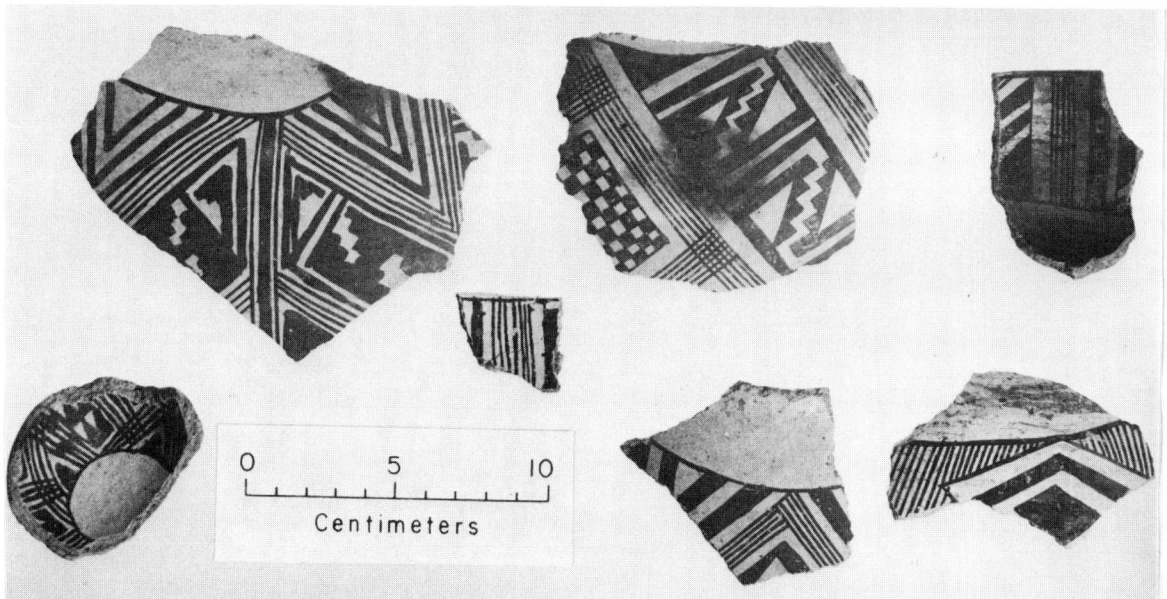

Figure 81. Typical black-on-white sherds from Site 481.

4: Bowl — mode (a)
   Interior slipped and painted — modes (a) and (c)
5: Ladle — mode (h)
   No slip — mode (a)
   Interior painted — mode (c)
6: Jar with narrow neck — mode (d)
   Exterior slipped and painted — modes (b) and (d)

SURFACE FINISH: ROW C

1: Slipped surfaces slightly undulating, smooth to the touch, entire surface reflects light, polishing marks occasionally evident, polished before application of paint — modes (a), (e), (g), and (i)
2: Slipped surfaces even, smooth, or slick to the touch, otherwise similar to type 1 — modes (b), (e), (g), and (i)
3: Similar to type 1 except that only the high points are lustrous — modes (a), (e), (g), and (j)
4: Similar to type 2 except that the surface is matte — modes (b), (e), (g), and (k)
5: Slipped surface slightly undulating, gritty to the touch, matte surface — modes (c) and (k)

DECORATION: ROW D

1: Rectilinear layout of bands of parallel fine and broad lines, fairly closely spaced. Execution ranges from excellent to poorly done with spacing irregular, lines crossing at corners, and of varying thickness. Central elements frequently consist of combinations of solid triangles.
2: Rectilinear layout with bands of diagonal hatching and solid lines. Bordering lines same size as hatching. Execution ranges from excellent to poor with spacing less regular, lines crossing, and narrower (less than 1 cm) bands of hatching. Central elements consist frequently of interlocking opposed hatched and solid stepped triangles.
3: Curvilinear layout, otherwise quite similar to type 2. An emphasis on solid and hatched scrolls and stepped triangles both interlocking and individual. Considerable range of execution.
4: Basically similar to type 2 insofar as elements are concerned but elements much more widely spaced. Hatching lines widely spaced (i.e., a minimum of twice as much space as the thickness of the lines and often as much as 1 cm between lines). Emphasis on opposed solid and hatched pendent triangles and sawteeth, hatched bands, and hatched bands with flags. Lines generally at least 1 mm thick. Obviously no hard and fast division exists between types 2, 3, and 4 but the effect presented by typical examples of the three types is quite different.
5: Checkerboard design. Frequently used as a filler for large triangular elements, which are often pendent from rims of bowls and ladles.
6: Very widely spaced fine parallel lines, generally straight but occasionally wavy; very little design per unit of area. Also pendent dots and solid triangles.

Figure 82. Typical black-on-red sherds from Site 481.

7: Lines of opposed solid sawteeth forming negative lightning or parallelogram designs.
8: Designs with solid interlocking stepped triangles as the dominant motif.

Red-slipped Pottery (fig. 82)

MATERIAL: ROW A

1: Gray to tan to orange paste with angular opaque inclusions — mode key (F)
   Orange slip — mode (d)
   Black mineral paint — mode (a)
2: Gray to tan to orange paste with angular opaque inclusions — mode key (F)
   Orange slip — mode (d)
   Glaze paint — mode (b)
3: Gray to tan to orange paste with angular opaque inclusions — mode key (F)
   Brick-red slip — mode (e)
   Black mineral paint — mode (a)
4: Gray to tan to orange paste with angular opaque inclusions — mode key (F)
   Orange slip — mode (d)
   Black mineral paint with white kaolin — modes (a) and (d)
5: Gray to tan to orange paste with angular opaque inclusions — mode key (F)
   Orange slip — mode (d)
   Black glaze paint and white kaolin — modes (b) and (d)
6: Gray to tan to orange paste with angular opaque inclusions — mode key (F)
   Brick-red slip — mode (e)
   Black mineral paint and white kaolin — modes (a) and (d)

VESSEL SHAPES AND AREAS SLIPPED AND PAINTED: ROW B

1: Bowl — mode (a)
   Interior black-on-red — mode (e)
2: Bowl — mode (a)
   Interior black-on-red, exterior white-on-red —modes (e) and (h)
3: Bowl — mode (a)
   Interior black-on-red, exterior black-on-red, or black-and-white-on-red — modes (e) and (i)
4: Bowl — mode (a)
   Interior black-on-red, exterior black-on-white-on-red or black-on-white-on-red and white-on-red — modes (e) and (k)
5: Bowl — mode (a)
   Interior black-on-white-on-red or black-and-white-on-red, exterior white-on-red — modes (g) and (h)
6: Jar with narrow neck — mode (d)
   Exterior black-on-red — mode (l)

7: Jar with narrow neck — mode (d)
Exterior black-and-white-on-red or black-and-white-on-red and black-on-red — modes (i) and (k)
8: Ladle — mode (h)
Interior black-on-red — mode (e)
9: Neckless (seed) jar — mode (b)
Exterior black-on-red — mode (l)

SURFACE FINISH: ROW C

1: Slipped surface undulating, smooth to the touch, polishing marks occasionally evident, entire surface reflects light, slip polished before application of paint — modes (a), (e), (g), and (i)
2: Similar to type 1 except that slip was polished after application of paint — modes (a), (e), (h), and (i)

DECORATION: ROW D

1: Opposed interlocking and hatched scrolls
2: Lines of solid and hatched sawteeth
3: Rectilinear, thin, and medium stripes with bands and areas of close parallel fine lines
4: All other motifs and elements

Plain and Corrugated Pottery

MATERIAL: ROW A

1: Brown paste with sand inclusions — mode key (H)
2: Dense gray paste with angular opaque inclusions — mode key (I)
3: Cream-colored paste with sand inclusions — mode key (J)

VESSEL SHAPES: ROW B

1: Bowl — mode (a)
2: Bowl with smudged interior — mode (a)
3: Open-mouthed jar — mode (e)
4: Shape of vessel unknown
5: Neckless (seed) jar — mode (b)

CONSTRUCTION AND SURFACE FINISH: ROW C

1: Coiled counterclockwise, indented with left thumb pointing up — mode (a)
Interiors smooth and even, coils unobliterated on exterior — mode (a)
2: Coiled clockwise, indented with left thumb pointing down — mode (b)
Interior smooth and even, coils unobliterated on exterior — mode (a)
3: Presumably coiled, direction unknown mode (d)
Interior surfaces smooth, even, and lustrous, exterior matte and gritty — modes (b) and (c)
4: Presumably coiled, direction unknown — mode (d)
Exposed surfaces even, smooth, and lustrous — mode (b)
5: Presumably coiled, direction unknown — mode (d)
Exposed surfaces even, but matte and gritty — mode (c)
6: Presumably coiled, direction unknown — mode (d)
Exposed surfaces even, but matte and gritty with small striations because of protruding temper — mode (e)
7: Coiled counterclockwise, indented with left thumb pointing down — mode (b)
Interior surfaces smooth and even, coils unobliterated on exterior — mode (a)
8: Presumably coiled, direction unknown — mode (d)
Exposed surfaces undulating, gritty, and matte except for lustrous high points — mode (d)

DECORATIVE EFFECT: ROW D

1: Absence of any decoration — mode (a)
2: Clapboard-corrugated — mode (b)
3: Indented-corrugated — mode (c)
4: Clapboard-corrugated exterior, black-on-white interior — mode (d)
5: Plain and corrugated on same vessel — mode (e)
6: Clapboard-corrugated and punctation on same vessel — modes (b) and (h)
7: Clapboard-corrugated and incision on same vessel — mode (f)

POTTERY — PROBLEM TYPES

Regional Time-Space Types

WHITE-SLIPPED POTTERY

Reserve Black-on-white (fig. 84f, g)
Descriptive types: 2211, 2212, 2213, 2217, 2218, 2243, 2311, 2312, 2314, 2317, 2412, 2442, 2611, 2613, 2615, 2617, 2618, 2643, 2647, 2657, 4213, 4313, 4332, 4341, 4611, 4632, 8511, 8531
Total: 1,173 sherds

Reserve Black-on-white: Variant A
Descriptive types: 5414, 5644
Total: 5 sherds
These were the only black-on-white sherds with a glazelike paint. As was the case at Site 616 this feature occurred in pottery otherwise resembling Reserve Black-on-white.

Table 12. Distribution by descriptive types of black-on-white sherds from Site 481.

Descriptive Types A B C D / Provenience	Totals	1 2 1 1	1 2 1 2	1 2 1 8	1 2 3 1	1 1 3 1 3	1 1 3 1 5	1 1 3 1 7	1 1 4 4 8	1 1 4 4 8	1 1 6 1 1	1 1 6 1 2	1 1 6 1 3	1 1 6 1 4	1 1 6 1 7	1 1 6 1 8	1 1 6 4 6	1 2 6 1 1	2 2 1 2 3	2 2 1 1 4	2 2 1 7	2 2 1 8	2 2 3 6	2 2 4 3	2 2 4 4	2 2 4 5 4	2 2 4 4 2 6	2 6 1 1	2 6 1 2	2 6 1 3	2 6 1 4	2 6 1 5	2 6 1 7	2 6 1 8	2 6 4 3	2 3 1 1	2 3 1 2	2 3 1 4	2 3 1 7	2 3 4 1 2	2 2 4 2	2 4 4 6
Totals	4911	17	14	15	12	52	2	1	6	13	1	1058	208	116	13	4	43	24	3	25	25	40	2	9	1	4	17	29	5	2	1	3	1	344	448	113	113	1	20	10	12	29	5
Rm. 1 Fill	94					2					1	10	4																							23					4		
Rm. 2 Fill	413					11				1		43	29	94	1		19	19															1						1				
Rm. 2 Flr. 1-2	39												1	3				5																									
Rm. 3 Fill	86					1						13																															
Rm. 4 Fill	61																																										
Rm. 5 Fill	118																			3									3							6	6						
Rm. 6 Fill	148											66	7	5						3							4								4	21	16						
Rm. 7 Fill	233	7										14								22			2				3							2	20	37	3			11			
Rm. 8 Fill	254											85	15			4																			60	23	35	21		6				
Rm. 9 Fill	160											37	9																1							15		8		7			6	
Rm. 10 Fill	305																																			36								
Rm. 11 Fill	83	1										3	1																							32							7	
Rm. 12 Fill	72		1	7								30																5								15	8						4	
Rm. 13 Fill	64		7						6																											28							2	
Rm. 16 Fill	119		7				2			12						2						4				2										25	2							
Rm. 17 Fill	297									1		275	1															4								10								4
Rm. 18 Fill	177											107																															
Rm. 19 Fill	19																																		10	2		3		2				
Rm. 20 Fill	146													1																					146									
Rm. 21 Fill	13											11																															
Rm. 22 Fill	58					7						17																															
Rm. 23 Fill	84					3						8		5		2						2						2							16	8	5		2	3		6	
Rm. 24 Fill	36					5						9																								9				5				
Rm. 25 Fill	48											2																								8				2				
Rm. 26 Fill	10				2																															3								
Rm. 27 Fill	191											92	5				19												2	2					2		8						2	
Rm. 28 Fill	103					6						61										1							2	2					38		14		6				
Rm. 29 Floor	95															5						2							7						3	3	2						
Rm. 30 Fill	4																																										
Rm. 31 Fill	21					1						24		12			15					1			1					1						7	4						
Rm. 32 Fill	73					5						17			2																					9							
Rm. 33 Fill	34					1						7																	3							1		3					
Rm. 34 Fill	8					8						39		3	12						21																						
Kiva Fill	82	9																				21																					
Pithse 1 Fill	749		7	10								81	142									1				8									7	48	9	54	1		6		17	
Pithse 1 Floor	150											2																								10	3							
Pithse 2 Fill	207											5												9	1			4						12	23	12	1	19	1	3			5	1
Below floors	39																																		15	13			6				1	

206 • Mariana Mesa

Table 12. Distribution by descriptive types of black-on-white sherds from Site 481.

Provenience	2644 6	2647 7	2654	2657	2711	3211 8	3311 8	3311	3612	3614 4	4213 9	4236 7	4313 5	4332 1	4336 6	4341 1	4613 1	4613 2	4632	4636 6	5414 1	5644 4	6214 4	6216 7	6241 1	6244 6	6247	6311 4	6314 6	6344 4	6346 6	6413 2	6414 6	6441 4	6644 6	6624 1	7214 4	8511 1	8531 8	8154 4	Bases	Totals
Totals	73	23	10	2	1	8	1	3	6	36	9	7	5	1	26	1	9	12	47	20	1	4	2	7	1	26	1	4	4	14	5	2	117	8	7	51	5	1	4	5	1405	
Rm. 1 Fill				2								5		1	3		12		15	15		4																			24	
Rm. 2 Fill, Flr. 1-2			10								9				20					5																					159	
Rm. 3 Fill															3																										27	
Rm. 4 Fill	12						8	1	6																			4	4					8		5					22	
Rm. 5 Fill	2	11				8	1																													8					4	
Rm. 6 Fill	11	12			1					23														7		13				4						14					32	
Rm. 7 Fill	2						1			13																10									7					1	45	
Rm. 8 Fill																						2														15					90	
Rm. 9 Fill	4																															1				2					122	
Rm. 10 Fill																								7		3															31	
Rm. 11 Fill	4																																			4					135	
Rm. 12 Fill																																				3					15	
Rm. 13 Fill	3																																								27	
Rm. 16 Fill	5																																								7	
Rm. 17 Fill	2																								1																41	
Rm. 18 Fill	7																																									
Rm. 19 Fill	2																																								42	
Rm. 20 Fill																																										
Rm. 21 Fill	6																																								12	
Rm. 22 Fill	4																																								40	
Rm. 23 Fill																																									4	
Rm. 24 Fill	3																																								5	
Rm. 25 Fill	16																																								3	
Rm. 26 Fill	2																																								55	
Rm. 27 Fill	6																																								16	
Rm. 28 Fill	3																																								30	
Rm. 29 Floor							2														1																				1	
Rm. 30 Fill																																									8	
Rm. 31 Fill	2																																								32	
Rm. 32 Fill																																									6	
Rm. 33 Fill																																										
Rm. 34 Fill																																									25	
Kiva Fill	15															32																									251	
Pithse 1 Fill/Floor																													4	3			85								34	
Pithse 2 Fill													4			1	9												3				15		1					4	53	
Below floors	19										3																			3			12							5	7	

Table 13. Distribution by descriptive types of black-on-red sherds from Site 481.

Table 14. Distribution by descriptive types of plain and corrugated sherds from Site 481.

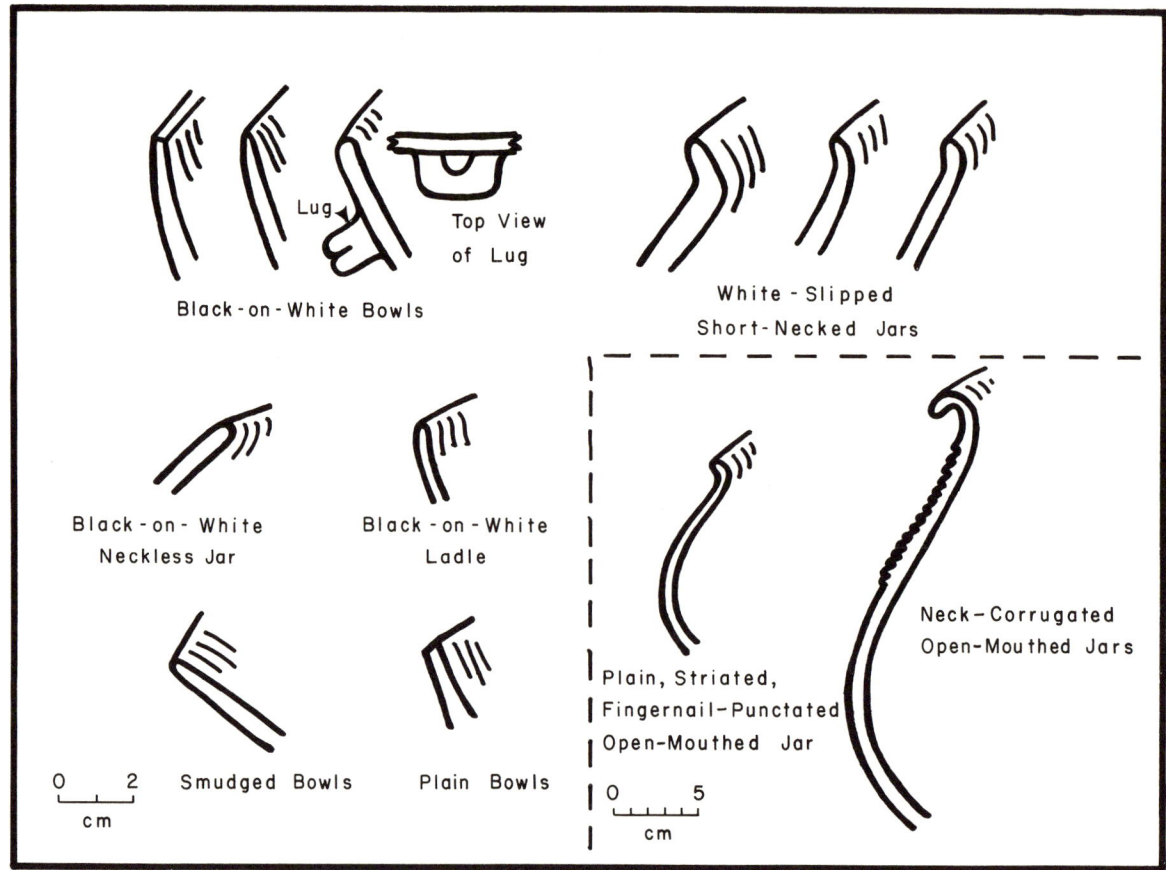

Figure 83. Pottery rim and vessel forms from Site 481.

Tularosa Black-on-white (fig. 84c, d)

Descriptive types: 3211, 3311, 3318, 3611, 3612, 3614
Total: 55 sherds

The thick creamy slip and curvilinear interlocked solid-and-hatched scroll typical of Tularosa Black-on-white were rare at Site 481.

Tularosa Black-on-white: Variant A

Descriptive types: 1211, 1212, 1217, 1218, 1311, 1313, 1315, 1317, 1418, 1611, 1612, 1613, 1617
Total: 1,549 sherds and 3 vessels

It was often extremely difficult to sort between Tularosa Black-on-white and Reserve Black-on-white at Site 481, a situation that has been noted by most investigators who have dealt with these two types elsewhere. On the whole, the decoration on typical Reserve Black-on-white pieces was not as closely spaced or as well executed. There appeared to be extensive design overlap. The division finally effected was based as much on slip as on decoration. Tularosa Black-on-white was restricted to the thick, creamy slip of slip mode (c), while the thin, flat-white slip of slip mode (b) was considered to be typical of Reserve Black-on-white. This left a large group of pottery that was, in a very real sense, transitional between the two. The slip on these vessels was thickly applied, though without the creamy appearance of typical Tularosa Black-on-white. In design also, this group of pottery approached the norms typical of Tularosa Black-on-white and it has been designated Tularosa Black-on-white: Variant A. A second sorting by another investigator, or perhaps even the same analyst, probably would result in a slightly different division of the material, but we feel that the transitional nature of the pottery rather than the particular divisions effected is the point of greater interest. As with the other black-on-white pottery, jars were the most numerous form.

Gallup Black-on-white

Descriptive types: 1414, 1614, 2214, 2244, 2254, 2314, 2614, 2644, 2654, 6214, 6241, 6247, 6311, 6414, 6613, 6614, 6621, 6644
Total: 434 sherds

This group of pottery should perhaps be labeled

"Chaco-like" in decoration rather than identified as any one particular type. It differed from typical Gallup Black-on-white in being generally better finished. The group showed considerable internal variation that might warrant subdivision when further study indicates the causes and significance of the variations. Approximately one-third of this pottery was made of the dense paste of material mode key (C), as was the portion of the pottery decorated in the style of Red Mesa Black-on-white. A number of sherds were quite smooth and had a matte finish. Most, but not all, bowls were slipped on both interior and exterior. The bowl form itself was rare and ladles were represented by only 16 sherds.

Red Mesa Black-on-white

Descriptive types: 1646, 2236, 2246, 2446, 2646, 4236, 4336, 4636, 6216, 6246, 6346, 6446, 6646, 8154
Total: 306 sherds

This pottery was allocated to this type primarily on the basis of decorative similarity to published descriptions. The resultant group showed considerable variation with respect to other features. Some of the sherds, like some of those designated Gallup Black-on-white, were of material mode key (C). The surface finish varied from undulating and gritty through polished and lustrous to smooth and matte.

Mimbres Bold Face Black-on-white

Descriptive type: 7214
Total: 5 sherds

These five sherds appear to have been made of paste normally employed in the Mariana Mesa region for plain and corrugated pottery.

RED-SLIPPED POTTERY

The red-slipped pottery at Site 481, like that of Site 616, was restricted almost entirely to bowls, though a few necked jars, seed jars, and ladles were used. The pottery from Site 481 showed less diversity of decorative color combinations than that from Site 616. That red-slipped pottery was gradually becoming more popular in the area of Mariana Mesa can be seen in the proportionate increase of redware vessels at Sites 494, 481, and 616.

Wingate Black-on-red (fig. 84a)

Descriptive types: 3113, 3114, 3121, 3124, 3614, 3623, 3624, 3924
Total: 272 sherds and 2 vessels

Wingate Polychrome

Descriptive type: 6224
Total: 14 sherds

Puerco Black-on-red (fig. 84e)

Descriptive types: 1111, 1112, 1113, 1114, 1121, 1122, 1123, 1124, 1611, 1614, 1624, 1814, 1824, 1924
Total: 531 sherds and 1 vessel

St. Johns Polychrome (fig. 84b)

Descriptive types: 4211, 4212, 4213, 4214, 4221, 4223, 4224, 4311, 4314, 4411, 4412, 4413, 4414, 4514, 4523
Total: 473 sherds

Heshotauthla Polychrome

Descriptive types: 2111, 2113, 2114, 2614, 5211, 5212, 5213, 5214, 5314
Total: 182 sherds

Artisan Types

As at Site 616, it was hypothesized that a single potter or close-knit group of artisans would favor certain ceramic attributes and that the attribute clusters characteristic of these artisan groups might be recognizable. Subsequent analysis of the distribution of these possible artisan types could also be interesting when viewing such problems as the distribution of social groups and intrasite trade networks.

At Site 481 such an analysis was seriously attempted only with the white-slipped pottery.

WHITE-SLIPPED POTTERY

Artisan Type A

Descriptive types: 6214, 6216, 6241, 6246, 6247, 6311, 6346, 6414, 6446, 6613, 6614, 6621, 6644, 6646
Total: 249 sherds

Diagnostic attributes: Paste type 6, dense gray paste (mode key [C]), white slip, thinly applied (modes [b] and [c]), and black mineral paint (mode [a])

Gray paste (mode key [A]) was used almost but not quite to the exclusion of every other paste at Site 481. However, during the early half of the occupation of the surface pueblo, paste mode key (C) was a minor element. This paste was unique to Site 481. At Site 494 and Site 616 paste mode key (A) was the only paste mode present, while neither mode key (A) nor (C) was present at the earlier sites. Paste mode key (C) appeared macroscopically to represent a different clay and certainly a different pattern of manufacture (e.g., no visible tempering materials and a more compacted clay). Its distribution was restricted to the early surface rooms (Rooms 3 to 11) and the fill of the pithouses. The matte surfaces of finish type 4 were strongly associated with this paste type (and with these early rooms generally). In these early rooms (3 through 12), decorative type 6, while restricted to paste type 6, was associated with a range of surface finishes in contrast to Artisan Type B discussed below.

Figure 84. Pottery vessels from Site 481: a. Room 17, fill, Wingate Black-on-red seed jar, #673 (1914); b. Kiva ventilator, St. Johns Polychrome bowl, #539 (4214); c. Room 1, fill, Tularosa Black-on-white jar fragment, #113 (3119); d. Room 18, fill, Tularosa Black-on-white jar fragment, #540 (3114); e. Rooms 9 and 18, fill, Puerco Black-on-red ladle, #481 (1811); f. Room 24, fill, Tularosa Black-on-white miniature seed jar, #558 (4111); g. Rooms 9 and 18, fill, Reserve Black-on-white miniature jar, #541 (4111).

The only other occurrence of decorative type 6 was on paste mode key 4, which was found only in Rooms 1 and 2.

It may well be that while most potters at Site 481 were following the same tradition of black-on-white pottery making with regard both to source of the material and basic manufacturing techniques, as did all potters at Sites 494 and 616, there were among the founders of the surface pueblo at Site 481 a potter or group of potters with different ideas with respect to materials, techniques of manufacture, and decoration. If so, decorative type 6 may have been produced almost entirely by them, though they also used on occasion decorative types 3 and 4. Strangely, or perhaps not so strangely, since these potters obviously had different ideas about pottery making, they did not use decorative types 1 and 2, which were far and away the most popular motifs with the other potters at the pueblo. Only five sherds of paste mode key 6 were decorated with motif 1 and one of these was on one of the very few sherds of paste mode key 6 associated with a later room.

Artisan Type B

Descriptive types: 1646, 2246, 2446, 2626
Total: 155 sherds

Diagnostic attributes: Matte surface finish (type 4) in association with decorative type 6

In surface Rooms 14 through 34 decorative type 6 is always associated with a matte finish (type 4) and vice versa. One can hypothesize that by the time the last half of the pueblo was built (Rooms 14 through 34) the potters of Artisan Type A had died. They could simply have adopted the prevailing style, but we may surmise that this type of conversion of basic techniques was rare among craftsmen. The only indications of an Artisan Type A potter or group of potters or their influence in association with the later rooms was on those vessels of Artisan Type B which were made in the standard way with standard materials, yet were finished and decorated in the style of this unique earlier group.

We obviously can only speculate about what happened. Assuming that women were the potters, perhaps the only daughter(s) were so young when the mother died that they learned the art of pottery making from a relative who knew or practiced the standard pottery-making techniques; yet the daughter(s) could have grown up with vessels remaining from the mother's pottery making, many of which had a matte finish and decorative type 6, and if so, they may have imitated these.

The rather wide distribution of the vessels of this artisan type in Rooms 13 through 28 and Room 31 suggests (if the hypothesis is correct that these were the work of a single potter or small group of potters and not just a statistical remnant of an earlier style) that every woman was not a potter and that, instead, wares from a few potters were traded throughout the pueblo. This is suspected, on perhaps stronger evidence, at Site 616 as well.

Artisan Type C

Descriptive types: 3211, 3311, 3318, 3611, 3612, 3614
Total: 55 sherds
Diagnostic attributes: A cream-colored slip, thickly applied (slip modes [c] and [g])

Whether the preference for a thickly applied creamy slip found on this small group of sherds was the entire output of a single potter or simply a temporary experiment by one or more potters is impossible to prove; we may hypothesize one or the other of these situations. This same combination of traits appeared on a few sherds at Area B of Site 494 concentrated almost entirely in the last rooms built at that site. At Site 481 they were found (except for 2 sherds in Room 29) only in Rooms 4, 7, 9, and 10. These rooms were all built at about the same time and probably were occupied contemporaneously, though doubtless by separate families — in fact, perhaps by as many as three or four family units. The presence of a fairly wide range of decorative types suggests more than one potter, but unfortunately the sherds themselves were no longer available (in 1970) to enable a visual judgment as to whether they might have been the work of one or several individuals.

It is possible that the occupation of those rooms at Site 481 was contemporaneous with that of the last room built at Area B of Site 494 and that these sherds represented the first appearance at Mariana Mesa of an idea (thickly applied creamy slip) that gained widespread acceptance both here and elsewhere later on. All black-on-white pottery at Site 616 was thickly slipped and most was of the creamy variety. At Site 481, however, the idea was introduced and then dropped, for no sherds of this type were associated with any of the later rooms. It is not impossible that at both Area B of Site 494 and Site 481 they represented a brief flurry of trade with some unknown site where this style of slipping already was dominant.

Intrasite Distribution Types

WHITE-SLIPPED POTTERY

Inspection of the table of descriptive types (table 12) suggested that same distributional variation might be present. Clustering of the descriptive types and further analysis reveal a startlingly consistent breakdown among room groups.

Certain attributes or particular combinations of these attributes appear to have been widespread throughout the site. These include material types 1 and 2 in combination with decorative types 1, 2, and 3 (1201, 1211, 1311, 1313, 1611, 1612, 1613, 2211, 2212, 2213, 2243, 2311, 2312, 2412, 2442, 2611, 2612, 2613, 2643). Sherds of material type 1 were but rarely encountered in association with the fill of pithouses or below floors, implying that the idea of a thickly applied slip was introduced slightly after the site was first occupied.

In contrast, a few other attributes were found only under the floors or in the fill of the pithouses and thus provide the only clue (other than the architecture of the pithouse itself) to the cultural identity of the occupants of Pithouse 1. These attributes include the only brown-paste sherds (7214 — identified as Mimbres Bold Face Black-on-white) and the only unslipped sherds (8154, 8511, and 8531). In addition, the two sherds with decorative type 5 (1315 in the fill of Room 1 and 2615 from the fill of Pithouse 2) appear to be early types associated with the first trash deposits.

Actually the pithouse itself was quite barren of cultural associations, and the few sherds found on its floor were of types associated with the surface pueblo. If we use the regional time-space types found on the floor to place the occupation of the pithouse within the same temporal frame of reference as the surface rooms, we can do so only on the assumption that the sherds were deposited by the pithouse occupants themselves — an unlikely inference, inasmuch as the surface rooms physically overlay the filled and abandoned pithouse.

The fact that the pithouse seemed to have been filled primarily, if not entirely, with trash from the earliest surface rooms (thus providing a logical explanation for the association of a few later sherds with the pithouse floor) as well as the close alignment of Rooms 9 and 10 with the pithouse outline, suggests, as noted earlier, that the pithouse structure was known to the first surface-room occupants and might even have been partially standing when they arrived. Certainly it does indicate that no great period of time intervened between the abandonment of the pithouse and the beginnings of the surface pueblo.

A remnant of the main roof-support post of the pithouse (p. 201) was recovered and submitted to the Laboratory of Tree-Ring Research at the University of Arizona, which provided a probable cutting date of somewhat after A.D. 1010,* indicating fairly convinc-

---

*The specimen involved bears the Laboratory catalog number of HAR 3090. It was of piñon with an undetermined number of rings missing from its inner and outer portions. The earliest surviving ring (not the pith ring) was dated at A.D.

ingly that no great span of time separated the two structures. If there was no gap at all but continuity from Pithouse 1 to Room 2, it would indicate a rather abrupt architectural change from pithouse to surface pueblo, a change not consistent with the more gradual shift suggested by Sites 188 and 601. In all, a slight time lapse between the two occupations seems reasonable.

To get back to the intrasite distributional types — if we eliminate those assumed to be associated with the pithouse and not with the surface pueblo, and also eliminate those descriptive types found throughout nearly all surface rooms, we are left with a group of pottery that can be sorted into three types based on certain attribute clusters that are largely discrete for each block of rooms. Surprisingly few sherds deviated from this pattern of association.

Intrasite Distribution Type A

Descriptive types: 4213, 4236, 4313, 4332, 4336, 4341, 4611, 4613, 4632, 4636, 5414, 5644

Total: 142 sherds

Diagnostic attributes: Material types 4 and 5 (gray paste, thin and/or watery white slip, black mineral paint); decorative type 6 in association with surface finish type 3 also appears to be strongly associated. (The only sherd of decorative type 6 and surface finish type 3 not on material type 4 — 2236 — is from the fill of Pithouse 1 so also would appear to be a style associated with early surface rooms.)

This intrasite distribution type was associated primarily with some of the first rooms constructed (Rooms 1 and 2 and, to a lesser extent, Room 3) plus the sub-floor deposits that could have served as the trash dump of those rooms, and the kiva.

When decorative type 6 was not associated with these rooms or areas it was most often found on sherds with the matte surface finish of type 4, whereas that combination never occurred in Intrasite Distribution Type A.

The five sherds of material type 5 (5414, 5644) may not belong in Intrasite Distribution Type A but the contrast of a new technique (glaze paint) in association with more conservative attributes in consistent with the architectural mixture in Room 2 where, as discussed below, a new architectural feature is associated with the earliest surface room.

The principal unifying characteristic of this type was the presence of a thin watery slip, though decoration was largely restricted to types 2, 3, and 6. These attributes were ones that regionally had an earlier temporal range than did most of the other ceramic traits at Site 481. Approximately half of the pottery of Intrasite Distribution Type A came from Rooms 1 and 2, which were among the first to be built. This was a perfectly logical association. But is that all there is to the story?

Of the decorated sherds found in the fill of Rooms 1 and 2 these early varieties constitute less than 25 percent. Of the remainder approximately 11 percent were of Intrasite Distribution Type C, which was otherwise associated solely with the late rooms constructed at the site.

Curiously, Intrasite Distribution Type B, which was associated only with early rooms, was represented in Rooms 1 and 2 by only two sherds. It could be argued that this was an accident or personal preference, and the mixture of Intrasite Distribution Types A and C in the fill of Rooms 1 and 2 would thus be the result of casual mixture after the rooms fell into disuse. However, sherds of Intrasite Distribution Type C were found between the two floors of Room 2. In short, if these distribution types had temporal significance, as certainly seems likely, Rooms 2 and perhaps 1 were used until or nearly until the end of the occupation of Site 481. Possibly these rooms were among the few of the earlier ones that continued to be used.

There are other clues to late and long usage of Room 2. The very fact that the floor was repaired is one, and, more important, the second floor had a slab-lined firepit — a very late feature at Site 481. If a room was in constant use throughout the occupancy of Site 481 or even if it was cleaned out, repaired, and reused toward the end of that occupancy, the association of early pottery attributes in the fill of the room could not be meaningfully related to the fact that Room 2 was built earlier.

Room 2 was, in fact, the first surface room constructed. For this or some other reason, could Room 2 have had some special significance to the occupants? Perhaps as a clan room? Intrasite Distribution Type A provided the first clue that this might have been the case. Rooms 1 and 2 were initially set apart as a distributional unit because of both the absence of Intrasite Distribution Type B and the frequent presence of Intrasite Distribution Type A. However, the distribution of Type A was not restricted to Rooms 1 and 2. It was also associated with Pithouse 2 (which essentially was a Site 494-style kiva) and with the kiva itself. In short, if we hypothesize that Rooms 1 and 2 had some special significance, then these older ceramic attributes of Intrasite Distribution Type A were restricted in their distribution to special rooms (except for 20 sherds in the fill of Room 3, which was immediately adjacent to Room 2). If so, Intrasite Distribution Type

---

673 and the outermost surviving ring at A.D. 1010, with the estimate of the cutting date given as A.D. 1010++vv. This record has not heretofore been published, but was reported in a letter from Bryant Bannister to Charles R. McGimsey III, dated June 12, 1970.

A logically would represent either heirloom vessels or vessels made in an older style because of their association with ceremonies. This would account for their being clustered in the fill of two and only two surface rooms.

There is, of course, a strong element of circular reasoning if we argue that Room 2 was special because it contained old-style pottery of Intrasite Distribution Type A and that these specimens were heirlooms because of their association with special rooms. However, the association of the diagnostic attributes of Intrasite Distribution Type A with older-style pottery is derived from a wide regional base, and there are other indications of the special nature of Room 2, though taken individually none are very strong.

The fact that Room 2, almost alone of the early rooms, had strong evidence of continued use, in conjunction with its interior features (lacking in Rooms 24, 29, and, for that matter, in Room 1), and the care taken to refinish the floor provide the strongest independent arguments. That it was the first surface room built and that it may have been associated with an even earlier room (the juniper post found in the first floor and the possibility that the first floor continued under the wall suggest this) might also be a factor. The only sherds at Site 481 painted with black glaze paint were in Room 2 as well, for whatever that may imply. Perhaps of greater importance, the only trough metates (an early style) found at Site 481 were in the fill of Rooms 2 and 3.

In any event, the two hypotheses that Room 2 and perhaps adjacent Room 1 were of special, or clan, significance, and that Intrasite Distribution Type A represented heirloom or heirloomlike pottery associated with ceremonial usage would account for the facts as known.

Intrasite Distribution Type B

Descriptive types: 2217, 2236, 2244, 2254, 2317, 2617, 2644, 2647, 2654, 2657, 3211, 3311, 3318, 3611, 3612, 3614, 6214, 6216, 6241, 6246, 6247, 6311, 6346, 6414, 6446, 6613, 6614, 6621, 6644, 6646

Total: 442 sherds

Diagnostic attributes: Material type 3 or 6; material type 2 with decorative type 7; material type 2, with finish type 4 or 5 and decorative type 4

In contrast to the time-space types with which we are accustomed to work this set of intrasite distribution types does not possess even a single element of internal consistency. While it is thought that it does possess temporal and cultural unity it is not the unity of a single set of artisans or recognizable even as a united artistic tradition. Rather it is thought to reflect the black-on-white pottery made by different potters within a culturally coherent but not necessarily a totally ceramically consistent unit. That is, it is hypothesized that it represents a recognizably unique portion of the ceramics of a particular socially integrated group of inhabitants of the site's surface rooms, their new affiliates, and descendants who continued to occupy Site 481 and construct adjoining architectural units.

The first architectural cluster initially consisted of Rooms 1, 2, and 9; then 10, 11, and a separate cluster consisting of 6N, 6S, and 7 were added. Later, Rooms 3, 4, and 8 and finally Room 5 and the ultimately remodeled Room 6 were built by this group. It would appear that early in this evolution, the initial rooms (1 and 2) became associated with some different, perhaps ceremonial, use which is reflected by the distribution of Intrasite Distribution Type A.

At least two different styles of slipping and finishing seem to have been utilized by this group: (1) a thinly applied or watery white slip with a surface finish which ranged from matte to lustrous (finish types 1, 4, and 5, but never the slick lustrous finish of finish type 2), with a strong tendency toward decorative type 4, 6, and 7; and (2) a thickly applied creamy slip with the consistently lustrous finish of finish type 1 (but again no finish type 2), and with an orientation toward decorative types 1, 2, and 4. No distributional association of these two variations within this unit of rooms could be detected.

Intrasite Distribution Type B was restricted almost entirely to surface Rooms 3 through 11 and to subfloor deposits that could readily enough represent the trash from those nine rooms. A few of the descriptive types included were found only in subfloor deposits but were included here because of their basic conformity to the type description, so that logically they fit here rather than being thought of as associated with Pithouse 1. Only 15 sherds conforming to the diagnostic attributes listed above were found outside of the nine rooms or related subfloor deposits.

As noted above, Intrasite Distribution Type B was associated with a unit of two-room clusters, each containing the earliest surface rooms constructed (except for Rooms 1 and 2). The first cluster was attached to Rooms 1 and 2 and consisted of Room 9 (which perhaps by now was closed off from Room 1) and Rooms 10 and 11. The curious thing here was that Room 9, though evidently built by this first surface group, and thus logically associated with Intrasite Distribution Type B, when found had an open door to Room 18, a later room and one associated with the hypothesized first immigrant group. With the construction of the door, Room 9 must have been associated with Room 18, which was associated with Intrasite Distribution Type C; ergo, why was not the pottery from Room 9 similarly associated regardless of when and by whom the room was built? It would seem that it should be and actually the room does contain a mixture. There may have been some unknown extenuating circumstances in Rooms 9 and 18. Perhaps 100 percent correlation is too much to expect.

The second cluster of rooms with Intrasite Distribution Type B was that of the first eastern group to be built, including Room 7, and subsequently Room 8 and the variously remodeled Room 6. The last room of this second cluster was Room 5, adjacent to Room 6 and one of the last rooms built at the pueblo.

If Intrasite Distribution Type B did identify a social unit larger than a single household it was a group that settled as two separate living units shortly after the surface pueblo was established and continued to occupy the same spaces, with considerable architectural remodeling, until abandonment of the pueblo. Only one room, Room 9, evidently was given over to the newcomers.

Intrasite Distribution Type C

Descriptive types: 1217, 1218, 1317, 1414, 1418, 1614, 1617, 1618, 1646, 2214, 2218, 2246, 2314, 2446, 2614, 2618, 2646

Total: 446 sherds

Diagnostic attributes: Material type 1 (gray paste, thickly applied white slip and black mineral paint) in association with decorative types 4, 7, or 8; material type 2 (gray paste with thinly applied white slip and black mineral paint) in association with decorative types 4 or 8; either material type 1 or 2 in association with decorative type 6 when finished with the even smoothly matte finish of finish 4. Except when decorated with decorative type 6 the sherds of this intrasite distribution type were finished with the lustrous, slightly undulating finish of finish type 1.

As in the case of Intrasite Distribution Type B there is considerable internal variation but the distribution of the type is both consistent and logical when compared with the architectural history and other evidence.

There is one possible major distributional difference between Intrasite Distribution Type B and Intrasite Distribution Type C. Each is associated with separate sets of rooms with separate architectural histories (Rooms 3 through 11 for Intrasite Distribution Type B and Rooms 12 through 34 for Intrasite Distribution Type C) but while Intrasite Distribution Type B has almost no association with ceremonial structures, Intrasite Distribution Type C, like Intrasite Distribution Type A, has many examples (approximately half of the total) from the fill of the kiva and Pithouse 1 (also probably a kiva) and with Room 2. In large part, and perhaps totally, this can be explained by the simple process of erosion for the first units built by the immigrants associated with Intrasite Distribution Type C were in immediate proximity to the recently abandoned Pithouse 1 and the rooms associated with this type almost entirely surrounded the kiva and it filled naturally with debris from these adjacent rooms subsequent to the abandonment of the site. Only the 24 sherds of Intrasite Distribution Type C in Room 2 cannot readily be accounted for in this manner, but the juxtaposition of early and late traits in Room 2 has already been noted.

There was a total of 1,030 sherds of Intrasite Distribution Types A, B, and C and together they comprised essentially all of the sherds with attributes which apparently were not distributed more or less throughout all major architectural units of the site. Of this total, only 52 sherds were inappropriately associated with respect to a hypothesis of their correlation with separate social groups within the pueblo: 20 sherds of Intrasite Distribution Type A were not so associated (but all came from the perhaps associated Room 3), 15 sherds of Intrasite Distribution Type B were not associated with Rooms 3 to 11, and 17 sherds of Intrasite Distribution Type C were not associated with Rooms 12 through 34 (but, of these, 10 were found in the somewhat enigmatic Room 9).

It seems unlikely that such a consistent association was accidental. Some outside "proof" lies in the fact that these attribute clusters did occur in adjacent rooms that could logically be interpreted as belonging to unified social groups on architectural grounds, and in the fact that Intrasite Distribution Type C appeared on the scene for the first time just as a considerable expansion of the pueblo occurred and at the same time that a new style of architecture was introduced — one adopted by both groups.

Whole and Restorable Vessels

Fourteen whole or restorable vessels were recovered from Site 481, as listed on page 217.

OTHER OBJECTS OF CLAY

Sherd Discs: 4 specimens recorded

The four specimens recorded were typical of the somewhat larger sample encountered at the site. Two were chipped into a rough circular shape, 3.1 and 4.4 cm in diameter, with the edges not smoothed; one was rectangular, and one was irregular in outline with both flat surfaces ground smooth. Three were from black-on-white sherds, while the fourth was black-on-red. Most of the worked discs recovered were circular, roughly finished, and from black-on-white vessels.

VESSELS

Specimen	Provenience	Figure
Brownware clapboard-corrugated bowl	Room 5, fill	---
Brownware indented-corrugated jar	Room 7, fill	---
2 brownware clapboard-corrugated jars	Room 13, fill	---
Brownware clapboard-corrugated jar	Room 25, fill	---
Wingate Black-on-red seed jar	Room 17, fill	84a
Wingate Black-on-red jar	Room 17, fill	---
2 St. Johns Polychrome bowls	Room 17, fill	84b
St. Johns Polychrome bowl	Kiva, floor	---
Puerco Black-on-red ladle	Rooms 9 & 18, fill	84e
Tularosa Black-on-white seed jar	Room 24, floor	84f
Tularosa Black-on-white jar	Rooms 9 & 18, fill	84g
Tularosa Black-on-white jar	Room 17 fill	---

Sherd Pendants: 4 specimens (fig. 115f, j)

Four worked sherds had been drilled near one edge so that they may have served as pendants. Three were circular and the fourth was rectangular. Except for the drilled hole they were identical to the sherd discs. All were of black-on-white pottery. Two were from the fill of Pithouse 2, while the others were from the fill of Room 7 (#292, fig. 115j) and the floor of Room 10 (#68, fig. 115f).

Pipe: 1 specimen

A fragment of a clay elbow pipe was found in the fill of the kiva. The clay portion of the stem was 2.6 cm long but apparently an additional section of the stem had been made of a more perishable material. The outside dimensions of the bowl sections were 1 cm in diameter and 3 cm in height. The walls of the bowl were quite thin but the interior was only 1.8 cm deep.

Toy Vessels: 2 specimens

Two miniature bowls had been formed by pressing a finger into a small ball of clay. Both had been fired but were roughly finished. One, from the floor of Room 28, was 1.8 cm in diameter and 1 cm high; the second, from the fill of Room 18, was 1.5 cm in both diameter and height.

Figurines: 5 specimens (fig. 115a, c)

Two of the figurines were of animals with barrellike bodies, 1.5 cm and 2 cm in diameter respectively. Short nubbins without features had been added to each to represent the four legs and the head. Both were broken and no species identification was possible. One came from the floor of Room 22, the other from a trench south of Room 20.

Two of the other three specimens were ducklike birds modeled in solid clay. The wings were clearly delineated in the round, while the head and neck were formed by fillets of clay projecting upward from the body and then curving forward. In each specimen holes had been drilled a short distance into the body in the correct location for legs but the legs and feet were otherwise unrepresented. Perhaps sticks had originally been inserted in the holes. One, from the fill of Pithouse 2, was 4.8 cm long (fig. 115c); the other, from the fill of Room 8, was 2.6 cm long. Each one closely resembled a bird figurine found at Site 143 (#2460, fig. 115b). The other bird figurine found in the fill of Pithouse 2, was formed from a fillet of clay in a basic U-shape. The tail section of the U had been thinned to a point and the head section was bent forward. This figurine had a length of 4.2 cm (fig. 115a).

STONE ARTIFACTS

Manos: 132 specimens (table 15)

Because of the close similarity of the general characteristics of the manos of Sites 481 and 616 the same modal key has been employed at both sites. Only 23 of the manos found at Site 481 were completed.

MATERIAL: ROW A

Mode 1: Sandstone: 98 specimens

Approximately 75 percent of the manos present were of sandstone, a proportion that held true for Site 616 also. No gradations of coarseness were recognized.

Mode 2: Vesicular basalt: 34 specimens

The three manos with finger grips were of basalt. All basalt manos were rectangular in cross section (shape modes 1 and 2) and, except for two with finger grips, all apparently were made in conformance with the short size type recognized at Site 616 (p. 133).

There was some variation in the coarseness of the

Provenience		Totals	A:1 B:1 C:2 D:1	1/1/2/2	1/2/2/1	1/3/2/1	1/3/2/2	1/4/2/1	1/7/2/1	1/7/2/2	1/8/2/1	1/8/2/2	1/9/2/1	2/1/2/1	2/1/2/2	2/2/1/1	2/2/1/2	2/2/2/1	2/2/2/2
		132	24	3	25	14	2	1	22	1	4	1	1	14	6	2	1	10	1
Room 1	Fill	3	1						1									1	
Room 2	Fill	5	3		1	1													
	Floor 1	1																1	
Room 3	Fill	1							1										
Room 4	Fill	6	1		1				1					2				1	
	Floor	1			1														
Room 5	Fill	2			1				1										
	Structure	1																1	
Room 6	Fill	15	4		1	2			4			1		1	1			1	
	Subfloor	1																1	
Room 7	Fill	4	1	1	1													1	
Room 8	Fill	2							1									1	
Room 9	Fill	1	1																
Room 10	Fill	9	3			2			2					1	1				
Room 17	Fill	2			1													1	
Room 18	Fill	7	1		4	1			1										
Room 22	Fill	3	1						1					1					
	Floor	5	1		1				1	1				1					
Room 23	Fill	4			1									2	1				
Room 24	Fill	1												1					
Room 27	Fill	1							1										
Room 28	Fill	8	4		2				2										
Room 29	Fill	9	1		4				1	1				1				1	
	Floor	1				1													
Room 30	Fill	1			1														
Room 31	Fill	4			1	1			1	1									
Room 32	Fill	2			1											1			
Room 34	Fill	4			2	1			1										
Kiva	Fill	14	1	2	1				1					4	4	1			
Pithouse 1	Fill	1						1											
	Floor	2				1					1								
Pithouse 2	Fill	10			2	3	1	1	1		1								1
Surface		1	1																

Table 15. Distribution by descriptive types of manos from Site 481.

basalt manos but most were of a medium grade of coarseness. No distributional clustering of basalt manos as a whole or with respect to degree of coarseness was observed.

SHAPE: ROW B

Mode 1: Rectangular in cross section, one face used: 47 specimens

Twenty of these manos were of basalt, which accounts for more than half of all basalt manos recovered. All but six of the manos employed on trough metates were of this form. On the majority the utilized face was convex in both dimensions.

Mode 2: Rectangular in cross section, two faces used: 39 specimens

Fourteen, including the three with finger grips, were of basalt, while 25 were of sandstone. On all specimens the two used faces were basically parallel, but over half were markedly convex in the short dimension. The rocker motion that caused convex rather than flat wear of the grinding face was much more prevalent at this site than at Site 616. It apparently represented a slightly different motor pattern.

Mode 3: Semiwedge-shape in cross section, one or two faces used: 16 specimens

Mode 3 is the first of the modes indicating use of the

mano at an angle to, rather than flat upon, the metate. Eight of these manos had received use only at an angle; seven (one each from the fill of Rooms 2, 10, 17, 31, 34, and two from Pithouse 2) had been used at an angle but the same face had also (first?) been used flat (i.e., parallel to the opposite unused face and perpendicular to the sides). On one mano (from the fill of Room 6), one face had been used flat, while the opposite face had been used at an angle to such an extent that the used face extended over nearly the entire area, resulting in an almost wedgelike cross section.

Two manos (from the floor of Pithouse 1 and the fill of Pithouse 2) had been used on trough metates.

Mode 4: Semiwedge-shape in cross section, three faces used: 1 specimen

On this mano both faces had been used flat (in the manner of mode 2) and one edge of one of these faces had also received (subsequent?) use at an angle. The absence or near absence of shape modes 4, 5, 6, and 8 and the fact that 8 of the 15 manos of mode 3 had received use only at an angle suggest a greater dichotomy between manos used at an angle and those used flat than was the case at Site 616. The angled form was proportionately more popular at Site 481 as well. The purpose of these different methods of use or the significance of this slight tendency for individual manos at Site 481 not to be used for both is not known.

Mode 5: Truncated pyramid in cross section, three faces used: none present at Site 481

Mode 6: Truncated pyramid in cross section, four faces used: none present at Site 481

Mode 7: Triangular in cross section, two faces used: 22 specimens

The two used faces, both used at an angle, meet, forming the apex of the triangle. In one instance (Room 10, fill) the two faces did not quite join, leaving a flat but unused area dividing them. In cross section this specimen resembled shape mode 3. These specimens were too fragmentary to give any clear indication of the presence of any angle to the line separating the two used faces.

Mode 8: Triangular in cross section, three faces used: 4 specimens

These manos had been used flat as well as at an angle.

Mode 9: Diamond-shape in cross section, four faces used: 1 specimen

This specimen appeared to have been used only at an angle.

FINGER GRIPS: ROW C

Mode 1: Presence of finger grips: 3 specimens

These manos were equipped with two opposed finger grips centrally located in each of the two long sides. The identified grip areas were short and shallow. All three manos were of basalt, rectangular in cross section with one face used, and were long and thick. Only one had been used on a trough metate.

Mode 2 and Mode 3: Absence of finger grips: 129 specimens

Most of the manos recovered at Site 481 were fragments, and largely because of this, rather than the extent of their use, it was often impossible to determine that finger grips definitely had been absent. Nonetheless, it is probably safe to assume that while finger grips were known to the inhabitants of Site 481, they were used only rarely.

ASSOCIATED METATE TYPE: ROW D

Mode 1: Slab: 117 specimens

The overwhelming majority of the manos were used on slab metates. However, on a considerable number of manos the grinding face was convex in the long dimension as well as occasionally in the short dimension. This certainly implies that some of the slab metates were not absolutely flat but were shaped in such a manner that they had a slight basin or shallow, rounded trough. Apparently the transition from deep straight-sided trough metates to flat-slab metates was not abrupt. In the area of Mariana Mesa the completely flat metate did not come into its own until the advent of the mealing bin.

Mode 2: Trough: 15 specimens

Eight of the convex manos were of vesicular basalt. The seven of sandstone included the only ones not rectangular in cross section: one was semiwedge-shaped in cross section with one face used at an angle, one was semiwedge-shaped in cross section with one face used at an angle and an adjoining face slightly used flat, one was triangular in cross section with two faces used, and one was triangular in cross section with three faces used. The others of sandstone were rectangular in cross section with one face used, as were all but two of the basalt manos. The other two of basalt were rectangular in cross section with two faces used, but in each case one face was used on a trough metate, while the second face was used on a slab metate. At Site 481 only one major face of manos was customarily used in connection with grinding on a trough metate. The used faces of trough manos were nearly always flat in the long dimension rather than slightly convex in the manner of some of the slab manos discussed above.

SIZE

The occupants of Site 481 seem to have conceptualized mano size types that were very similar to those employed at Site 616. The size types present are listed below. The determination of length was based on 13 specimens for type A and 10 for type B.

MANO SIZE TYPES, SITE 481

	Size Type A	Size Type B
Length: Average	27.5 cm	20.4 cm
Length: Range	23.5–36.0	17.4–23.0
Width: Average	11.2	11.4
Width: Range	9.0–14.0	11.0–12.0
Height: Average	2.9	2.8
Height: Range	1.2– 6.4	1.8–5.0

All trough manos (basalt and sandstone) appeared to have been of the short type, as did all manos of basalt except for the two slab manos with finger grips.

Metates: 13 specimens

TROUGH METATES: 6 specimens (fig. 109k)

All trough metates were of vesicular basalt, and none was complete, though one was nearly so. The trough seemed to have been open at both ends, and was slightly concave in both directions. The sides of the trough rose abruptly at a sharp angle from the base of the trough. The length of the trough on the one almost complete specimen was 38 cm. The width of the trough was approximately 20 cm on the two specimens on which this could be measured. The trough extended nearly the entire width of the irregularly shaped cobble. These metates must have been propped up and partially supported by small rocks, for several were not flat-bottomed and would not have been stable supports. All trough metates came from two rooms and all were fragmentary (#125, fig. 109k).

Floor

Room 2 (3); Room 3 (3)

SLAB METATES: 5 specimens (fig. 109c)

The three sandstone metates (Pithouse 2, fill, #696, fig. 109c; Room 6, floor; Room 24, fill) averaged approximately 46 cm long by 33 cm wide. The remaining two (Room 23, fill; Room 29, below floor) were of vesicular basalt and fragmentary. The grinding face of each extended over the entire upper surface and exhibited very little convexity.

Fill

Room 23 (1); Room 24 (1); Pithouse 2 (1)

Floor

Room 6 (1)

Below floor

Room 29 (1)

BASIN METATE: 1 specimen

A fragment of a basin metate of vesicular basalt came from the fill of Room 30. The worn basin area extended to the edges of one surface of the irregular cobble. The width of the basin was about 22 cm and its maximum depth was at least 9 cm.

Mortars: 6 specimens

Three mortars were made from quartzite cobbles, two of vesicular basalt, and one of sandstone. Only one had been shaped on any area other than the grinding surface. This exceptional specimen was almost circular in top outline, with the top and bottom surfaces flat. Shallow grinding faces occupied nearly all of both surfaces. On the others a nearly circular, well-smoothed grinding face had been formed on one surface of an otherwise unworked cobble. One had a thick integument of red ochre, with occasional streaks of yellow ochre over the grinding face.

CHARACTERISTICS AND PROVENIENCES OF MORTARS

Cat. No.	Dimensions	Concavity	Provenience	Illustration
382	12.0 × 9.5 × 4.0 cm	5.0 × 5.0 × 0.5 cm	Room 9, fill	---
562	16.0 × 13.0 × 7.0	7.0 × 7.0 × 1.0	Room 2, below floor	110d
650	8.4 × 8.0 × 3.8	6.6 × 6.6 × 1.7 5.5 × 5.5 × 0.4	Room 22, fill	110a
739	25.2 × 18.8 × 12.0	17.5 × 11.5 × 9.5	Room 19, fill	---
802	32.5 × 32.2 × 21.2	27.0 × 24.5 × 10.7	Room 31, fill	109m
824	26.0 × 22.0 × 14.0	15.0 × 11.0 × 6.5	Room 17, east wall	---

Pestle: 1 specimen (fig. 110e)

This specimen was a long cylindrical object of fine-grained basalt with rounded and slightly battered ends. It was 26.5 cm long by 4 cm in diameter, and was found in a trench in the area of Room 26.

Bowl: 1 specimen (fig. 109n)

This specimen was very similar to the larger mortars described above. However, in this case, the walls were relatively thin and of nearly constant thickness. It was of vesicular basalt and was found in the firepit of Room 31. It was 20 cm in diameter and 10.8 cm high; the concavity was 14 cm in diameter and 9 cm deep. The widest part of the concavity was midway between the rim and the base of the concavity. The rim diameter of the concavity was only 13 cm.

Polishing Pebbles: 23 specimens

Fourteen pebbles were of quartzite, three of quartz, three of diorite, and one each of petrified wood, felsite, and siltstone. They ranged in size from 6.5 by 5.7 by 4.6 cm to 2.6 by 2.5 by 1.3 cm. All but four had only one polishing facet, one had two facets, and three had three facets. They varied considerably in shape, some being nearly circular, others triangular and still others quite irregular. Three of the larger ones had received secondary use as small pecking stones.

Fill

Room 2 (2); Room 5 (1); Room 7 (7); Room 8 (1); Room 10 (1); Room 18 (2); Room 20 (1); Room 25 (1); Room 28 (1); Room 29 (2); kiva (2); Pithouse 2 (1)

Below floor

Room 31 (1)

Rubbing Stones: 17 specimens

These artifacts were, in a sense, intermediate between polishing pebbles and manos. They were large enough to be one-hand manos but, like the polishing stones, they were unshaped except for the irregularly placed grinding facets. These facets ranged in size from 4 by 4 cm to 12 by 7 cm. One stone had three facets, four had two facets, while the remainder had only one. All were naturally smooth, waterworn cobbles of quartzite (9), sandstone (5), and basalt (3). They ranged in size from 19.5 by 15 by 10 cm to 9 by 3.5 by 2.5 cm.

Fill

Room 2 (2); Room 3 (2); Room 4 (1); Room 5 (1); Room 7 (1); Room 8 (1); Room 9 (1); Room 10 (1) (#678, fig. 109o); Room 18 (2); Room 24 (1); Room 27 (1); Room 28 (1); Room 29 (1); Room 33 (1)

Pecking Stones: 23 specimens

These irregularly shaped, fist-sized cobbles were of a variety of materials: quartzite, basalt, felsite, sandstone, and petrified wood, in that order of frequency. All were unshaped except through use. In most cases a single limited area on each tool had been used for pecking, but there were two exceptions, one of which had two definite pecking areas, while the other exhibited evidence of pecking over much of its surface.

Surface

(1)

Fill

Room 2 (1); Room 4 (1); Room 5 (1); Room 6 (2); Room 8 (1); Room 10 (1); Room 18 (1); kiva (1); Pithouse 1 (1); Pithouse 2 (5)

Below floor

Room 2, between Floors 1 and 2 (3); Room 6 (3); Room 17 (1)

Axes: 3 specimens

Two axes were complete, but on one the bit end only survived. All were of fine-grained basalt polished all over. They were three-quarter-grooved, rectangular in horizontal cross section, and the poll was flat. The dimensions of the two complete specimens were 6.3 by 3 by 9.5 cm and 6 by 3.5 by 11.5 cm. The ratio of poll height to overall height, which proved so reliable at Site 616 (p. 143-144), was not so readily applicable at Site 481. On the larger specimen the groove was only 2.5 cm below the top of the poll (which made the axe too long by 1 cm for the location of the groove even in its present condition, if the Site 616 action type is applied). On the smaller axe the groove was 3.5 cm below the top of the poll, which, applying the Site 616 formula, would place its mint-condition measurements within the limits found at that site.

Fill

Room 2 (1) (#418, fig. 111e); Room 6 (1) (#263, fig. 111d); Room 34 (1) (#428, fig. 111b); Pithouse 1 (1)

Whetstone: 1 specimen

This rectanguloid sandstone block (27.3 by 19 by 10 cm) from the fill of Room 10 had a groove 5.2 cm wide,

20 cm long, and 0.5 cm deep worn in its top surface. It appeared to have served as an axe polisher and sharpener.

Hammers: 4 specimens (fig. 112a, b, c)

Two hammers were of fine-grained basalt, one of quartzite, and one of volcanic scoria. The specimen of scoria (Pithouse 1, fill, #778, fig. 112a) was like the irregular flat-ended hammers from Site 616 except that it was full-grooved. All three dimensions ranged between 9 and 10 cm. One elongated flat-ended basalt hammer (Room 7, fill, #73, fig. 112b) was rectangular in cross section (7.5 by 5 cm, with a height of 6.5 cm) and had a three-quarter groove approximately 2 cm down from the top. The groove sloped so that it was 0.5 cm nearer the top at the grooved end than at the ungrooved end. Only the bottom surface, which was quite smooth, showed evidence of use. The second elongated flat-ended basalt hammer (Room 25, fill, #162, fig. 112c) had an oval cross section in top view and was a rounded rectangle in end view (8.6 by 7.5 cm, with a height of 10.2 cm). Both top and bottom surfaces had been used for battering. The groove, which was full, was centrally located. The quartzite specimen (Room 29, floor) had the general contours of the bit end of a very dull axe (6.6 by 4.9 cm, with a height of 8 cm), though this seems to have been the natural shape of the cobble. A shallow three-quarter groove had been pecked around the cobble at a point 2.5 cm from the top. Only the bottom had been used for battering.

Fill

Room 7 (1) (#73, fig. 112b); Room 25 (1) (#162, fig. 112c); Pithouse 1 (1) (#778, fig. 112a)

Floor

Room 29 (1)

Points: 9 specimens (fig. 113c, e, f)

Six points were small and triangular with almost straight bases and side notches. Three of these six had a double notch on one side. Three were of petrified wood, and the other three were of obsidian. A seventh point (Room 17, fill, #647, fig. 113c) was also small and triangular but had a concave base and no notches. It was of obsidian. Of the remaining two, both of chalcedony, and larger than the others, one (Pithouse 2, fill, #2559, fig. 113f) was basically triangular with a deeply concave base and highly placed side notches, while the other (Pithouse 1, cist, #3078, fig. 113e) was leaf-shaped.

Fill

Trench along south wall (1); Room 2 (1) (#333, fig. 113g); Room 4 (1) (fig. 113h); Room 7 (1) (#342, fig. 113d); Room 17 (1) (#647, fig. 113c); Pithouse 1 (1) (#3078, fig. 113e); Pithouse 2 (2) (#2559, #2564, fig. 113f, b)

Floor

Pithouse 1 (1) (#2689, fig. 113a)

Side Scrapers: 4 specimens

Irregular thin flakes ranging in size from 6 by 4 cm to 3.5 by 2 cm, one side of which had been chipped to form an effective edge, had been used as side scrapers. Three were of petrified wood and the other was of obsidian.

Surface

(1)

Fill

Room 32 (1); kiva (2)

End Scraper: 1 specimen

A flake of fine-grained quartzite, egg-shaped in outline (5.2 by 3.8 cm), had been chipped across the narrow end, forming an effective scraping edge 2 cm long. It came from the fill of Room 13.

Unretouched Flakes: 15 specimens

Nine flakes were of petrified wood, two of obsidian, two of chert, one of basalt, and one of quartzite. They ranged in size from 5.8 by 5.1 cm to 2.4 by 1.6 cm. None had been deliberately shaped, but all exhibited small use chips along one or more edges.

Fill

Room 2 (1); Room 2, between Floors 1 and 2 (1); Room 4 (1); Room 13 (1); Room 23 (1); kiva (1); Pithouse 2 (8)

Chips: 96 specimens

More than 90 percent of the chips were of petrified wood. The remainder were of obsidian, fine-grained basalt, quartzite, and chert. The size range was approximately the same as that of the unretouched flakes.

The dominance of chips of petrified wood both here and at other sites around Mariana Mesa suggests that perhaps other chipped stone artifacts were, in considerable proportion, traded in, while tools of petrified wood were made locally.

Fill

   Room 2 (1); Room 5 (2); Room 7 (4); Room 9 (4); Room 12 (2); Room 13 (2); Room 17 (1); Room 18 (5); Room 23 (2); Room 25 (4); Room 30 (6); Room 32 (5); kiva (38); Pithouse 1 (9); Pithouse 2 (9)

Below floor

   Room 17 (2)

Cores: 9 specimens

Eight cores were of petrified wood, one of felsite. They were irregularly shaped cobbles from which flakes had been detached, apparently by blows upon any convenient surface; no striking platform was prepared.

Fill

   Room 7 (1); Room 8 (2); Room 32 (2); kiva (2); Pithouse 2 (2)

Scoria Cylinders: 3 specimens

All three had a roughly circular cross section with diameters ranging between 2.5 and 3 cm. The two complete specimens were 7 cm long. One had a slight gradual taper toward one end.

Fill

   Room 2 (1); Room 22 (1); Room 23 (1)

Disc Bead: 1 specimen

Only one bead, a flat discoidal specimen of red stone, was found. It was drilled with a circular hole in the center that showed no bevel on either side. The bead was 4.5 cm in diameter, 2 cm thick, with a central hole 2 cm in diameter. It came from the surface.

Pendants: 2 specimens

One pendant was a flat, triangular piece of petrified wood perforated near the truncated apex of the triangle by a small biconically drilled hole. The base of the triangle was 4.5 cm, its height 3 cm, and its thickness 0.3 cm. It came from the fill of Room 2. The second specimen, from the fill of Room 7, was a thin flat piece of red stone of unusual shape with a small perforation near one corner.

Fill

   Room 2 (1); Room 7 (1)

Ornament (?): 1 specimen

A fragment of a small, very smooth carved stone came from the fill of Room 7. It was too small for the nature of the carving to be recognized but the workmanship was excellent.

Disc: 1 specimen

An oval disc (6 by 4.5 by 0.6 cm) of sandstone was found in the fill of Room 18. It may have served as a palette. No abrasion was evident but it had what appeared to be a yellow pigment stain over one flat surface.

Grooved Objects: 3 specimens (fig. 110c)

Three unidentified objects came from unshaped fist-sized cobbles, two of quartzite and the third of sandstone. They were similar in that one or two V-shaped notches had been cut and/or worn in them. These grooves were straight, 3 to 5 cm long, approximately 0.7 cm wide in their widest part and up to 0.5 cm deep. The sides tapered inward but the grooves were flat-bottomed and extended to the edges of the stone in both directions. Perhaps they served as sharpeners of some sort. Two came from the fill of Room 18 (#484, fig. 110c), and the third was between Floor 1 and Floor 2 in Room 2. A similar groove was found on a shaft-smoother from Site 143 (p. 178).

Quartz Crystal: 1 specimen

A small fragment of a quartz crystal was found in the fill of Room 18.

Concretion: 1 specimen

A small (2.5 by 1.2 cm) concretion with a faint resemblance to a human head and neck was found on the floor of the kiva.

BONE ARTIFACTS

Awls: 30 specimens

HEAD OF BONE INTACT: 4 specimens

All four specimens were leg bones, three from birds or small mammals and one from a deer. The deer bone was 16 cm long, two of the others were 10 cm long, and the fourth was only 5.1 cm long. There was a gradual taper toward the point on all specimens.

Fill

   Room 2 (1); Room 8 (1); Room 27 (1)

Floor

Room 30 (1)

HEAD OF BONE UNWORKED EXCEPT BY ORIGINAL SPLITTING: 2 specimens

Both specimens seemed to be from the proximal portion of deer metapodials. They tapered gradually to a sharp point. One, from the pit in Floor 2 of Room 2, was 11.1 cm long; the other, from the fill of Pithouse 2, was 9.5 cm long.

Fill

Pithouse 2 (1)

Floor

Room 2, floor pit (1)

HEAD WHOLLY REMOVED: 4 specimens

All specimens appeared to be from deer or pronghorn metapodials. In cross section two were triangular, while the others were flat and rectangular. One tapered gradually to a point but the other three had a rather sharp taper. The opposite end in all cases was flat. They ranged in length from 6.5 to 12 cm.

Fill

Room 7 (1); Room 9 (1); Room 18 (1)

SPLINTER AWLS: 4 specimens

Casual splinters of long bones of large animals seemed to have been used as awls, one naturally pointed end of which was further ground and polished to a sharp point. Except for the points, no effort was expended on the artifacts and the bodies remained rough and irregular. They ranged in length from 8.7 to 14.3 cm. There was a very gradual taper to the point on all four specimens.

Fill

Room 10 (1); Room 22 (1); Room 27 (1)

Below floor

Room 23 (1)

SKEWER AWLS: 4 specimens

Skewers were thin (3 to 5 mm in diameter) straight awls, polished overall, so that no trace of the original contours of the bone remained, and they tapered to a very sharp point. The two complete specimens were 10.7 and 6.5 cm in length. The shorter one had a shallow notch in the flat end.

Surface

(1)

Fill

Room 18 (1); Room 27 (1); Pithouse 2 (1)

AWLS OF UNIDENTIFIED FORM: 12 specimens

In addition to the awls listed above, there were 12 pieces of awls too fragmentary to identify. Most were apparently from deer or pronghorn metapodials, though at least two were from smaller animals. The tips tapered gradually to the point in those specimens on which that feature could be observed.

Fill

Room 2 (2); Room 5 (1); Room 10 (3); Room 12 (1); Room 27 (2); Pithouse 2 (2)

Floor

Room 10 (1)

Weaving or Matting Tools (?): 4 specimens

All four of these specimens were fragmentary but they appeared to have been long, thin, flat, spatulalike objects with rather sharp parallel sides and a convex end. They were well polished. The two nearly complete specimens were both 10 cm long, 1.3 cm wide, and 1 cm thick in the thickest central portion.

Fill

Room 2 (1); Pithouse 1 (1)

Floor

Room 2, Floor 1 (2)

Ring: 1 specimen (fig. 114j)

A segment of the shaft of a long bone with the cut edges ground smooth had been used as a ring. Its diameter was 2 cm, and its width 1.1 cm (#286, fig. 114j). It came from the fill of Room 8.

Tubes: 7 specimens

Tubes were portions of the naturally tubular shafts of long bones. They varied in diameter between 1 and 2 cm and the two complete specimens varied considerably in length, 10 cm and 1.6 cm respectively. They were well polished but otherwise little modified. The longer specimen had a single hole drilled through one side 2 cm from one end.

Fill

Room 4 (1) (#272, fig. 114h); Room 5 (1) (#288, fig. 114i); Room 7 (1); Room 18 (2); Room 25 (1) (#285, fig. 114g)

Floor
  Room 29 (1) (#664, fig. 114b)

Pierced Phalanges: 2 specimens (fig. 114c, d)

Two deer or pronghorn phalanges (from the fill and the floor of Room 17) had been pierced by a centrally located hole extending from one to the other side (medially–laterally) of the bone (#648, #649, fig. 114c, d).

Figurine: 1 specimen (fig. 114e)

A figurine had been carved from a deer or pronghorn astragalus, perhaps to resemble two birds sitting side by side with adjoining wings. The "neck" area between the two "birds" had been perforated (#651, fig. 114e). It was found on the floor of Room 16.

Disc Bead: 1 specimen

The only bone bead recovered came from the floor of Room 22. It had a diameter of 0.3 cm, a thickness of 0.2 cm, and a hole diameter of 0.1 cm.

Serrated Tool: 1 specimen (fig. 114a)

This tool fragment seemed to derive from an implement not unlike the weaving tools in appearance except that one edge had been nicked, so that it looked serrated (#2826, fig. 114a). It came from the fill of Pithouse 2.

ANTLER FLAKER: 1 specimen

The smoothed tip of an antler that bore a few scratches suggesting use as a flaker came from the fill of Room 2.

SHELL ARTIFACTS

Bracelets: 3 specimens

Three fragments of shell (probably representing three bracelets) were from *Glycymeris maculatus*. All had been ground down so that the cross section of the bracelet was rectangular, approximately 0.4 cm wide and 0.3 cm thick. All were too fragmentary for the diameter of the bracelet to be estimated. The one surviving umbo section had been drilled.

These fragments differed from those found at Site 616 in the marked angularity of their cross section. The specimens from Site 616 were more nearly oval in cross section.

Fill
  Room 2 (1); Room 5 (1); Pithouse 1 (1)

Pendants of Whole Shells: 2 specimens

Two complete shells were of small *Glycymeris maculatus*, 15 cm in diameter. They were unworked except for limited smoothing of the edges and a hole drilled through the umbo section.

Fill
  Room 2 (1); Room 28 (1)

Unworked Fragments

There were two fragments of unidentified shell showing no evidence of having been worked, one in the fill of the kiva, the second in the fill of Room 33.

RAW MATERIALS

Hematite: 8 oz

Over half of the hematite came from the fill of Room 7, the remainder from the fill of the kiva ventilator. A few of the pieces exhibited abraded facets. Some of the hematite from Room 7 was quite soft and claylike.

Limonite: 3 oz

Small fragments of powdery or platy limonite were found, half from the fill of Room 7, the remainder from the fill of Rooms 19 and 34.

Malachite: 1 oz

Two small fragments of malachite came from the fill of Room 18.

Kaolin: 3 oz

What appeared to be four irregular pieces of kaolin were found in the fill of Room 29. A single fragment was found in the fill of Room 7.

Turquoise: 3 fragments

Of three thin small fragments of turquoise (under 1 cm in any dimension) only one had been smoothed (Room 6, fill). The other two had been roughly shaped but were unsmoothed or polished (fill of Room 18, floor of Room 10).

Other

A number of pieces of a sandy substance colored white, pink, or yellow came from the fill of Room 16 and Pithouse 1 and from below the floor of Room 31.

HUMAN SKELETAL REMAINS

No skeletons and very few human remains were encountered at Site 481 despite the rather extensive excavations. This was in marked contrast to Site 616. A fragment of an occiput was in the fill of Room 9; an incisor in the fill of Room 13; and the greater trochanter of a left femur and the epiphysial cap of the proximal end of a right humerus were in the fill of Pithouse 2.

SITE 494

DESCRIPTION AND HISTORY

Site 494 was located on the southern edge of a low ridge or mound of gravel, perhaps a remnant of a former stream terrace, which rises 18 to 20 m above the valley floor and forms the northern border of the main drainage system passing north of Mariana Mesa. The surface of this ridge is covered with piñon and juniper and the site is situated within this tree zone. The site comprised two units, each composed of a double row of masonry rooms with a roughly rectangular subterranean structure just to the southeast of each unit. The more northerly unit, Area A, consisted of four surface rooms and an adjacent subterranean pithouse or kiva. The southern unit, Area B, consisted of eight rooms and an adjoining pithouse or kiva. These 12 surface rooms and the two pithouses or kivas were excavated in their entirety (figs. 85–92).

In all probability very little time separated the establishment and occupation of the two units at Site 494 but there are indications that they were not, or at least not always, occupied simultaneously. The masonry construction of both units involved the use of double walls and almost exclusive use of lava cobbles. In Area A, construction was comparatively neat and precise with a layer of larger basalt cobbles alternating with one or two layers of smaller cobbles, and the result was quite striking. In this architectural feature, Area A differed from Area B and from any other of the sites excavated. In Area B the predominant masonry style was of medium to small lava cobbles laid in irregular or fairly regular courses with (in all but the two earliest rooms) a basal layer of large lava boulders. At Site 494 there was first observed the tendency in the area for the inner face of a double wall to be of smaller stones than the outer face, a feature that was prominent throughout the constructional history of Site 481.

Masonry joints and other keys to constructional history were not readily available on the generally low walls surviving but it seemed that in Area A, Rooms A1, A2, and A3 were built in rapid order with Room A4 being added somewhat later.

In Area B, Room B2 was the first built. The floor of this room was excavated approximately 35 cm into sterile soil. This was a characteristic feature of earlier sites and is the primary reason for suspecting that Room B2 and perhaps Room B5 were built prior to the construction of any of the rooms in Area A.

When Room B5 was added, its floor was excavated to nearly the same level. However, the builders of Room B2 had carried the walls down to the floor level, whereas when Room B5 was built, the walls were based on ground level and the floor area within these walls was excavated. Perhaps the wall dividing the two rooms was destroyed at this time to form a single large room, or perhaps this was done later.

The next room to be added was Room B4. Its walls were based on sterile soil and the floor was excavated slightly. A wing wall extending north from Room B4 (the east wall of what was later to become Room B6) may have been built at this time, for it also was based on sterile soil, whereas all subsequent walls were constructed on top of trash deposits. It was in the construction of the walls of Room B4 that the idea of a basal layer of large lava boulders first appeared. This room may have housed a separate family group, and, as had been the case with the occupants of Room B2, more space soon became a necessity and Room B6 was added. The north and west walls of Room B6 were built on trash but the floor area was cleared to sterile soil. No wall was found separating Room B4 from Room B6 and although the floor of the latter room was 16 cm higher, the two may have been joined to form a single large unit when Room B6 was built.

Room B3 was constructed in a manner similar to Room B6, and at that time the north wall of Room B5 seems to have been extensively remodeled. A doorway between Rooms B6 and B3 had been sealed and carefully finished on the Room B3 side.

Room B1, the next room added, possibly housed a

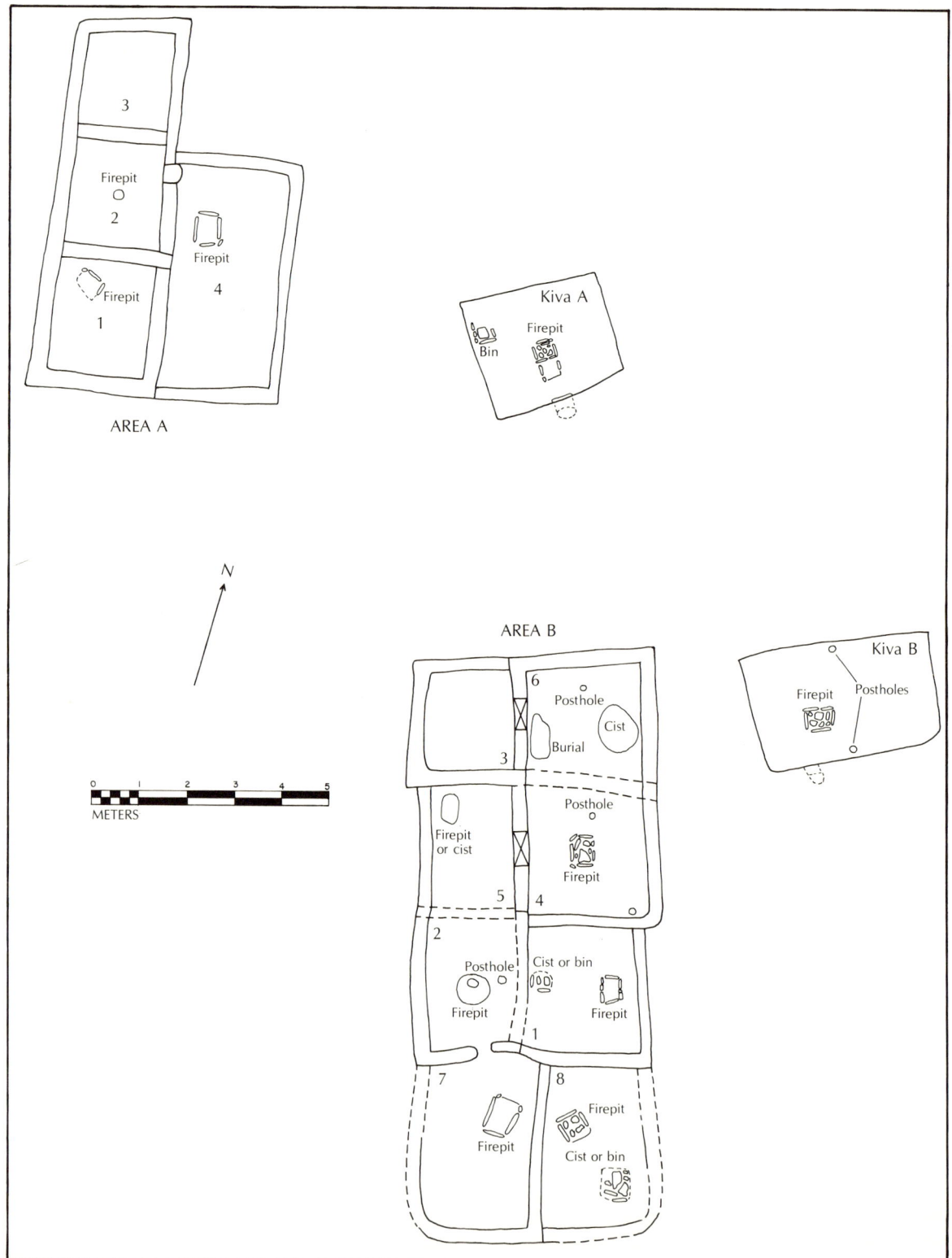

Figure 85. Plan of Site 494.

third family unit. This room had a firepit and a cist or mealing area and thus combined in a single room the features found in the combination of Rooms B2 and B5 and that of B4 and B6. The so-called cist area looked very much like a floor section of the mealing bins at Site 616, though there did not appear to be any provision for a permanently placed metate. Perhaps the metate was propped on rocks during use and placed against the wall when idle.

The first inhabitants of Area B later may have felt a need for even more space and Room B7 was constructed with an open doorway between it and Room B2. The walls of this room were built on trash and not even the floor area was excavated to sterile soil. As a consequence the floor of Room B7 was 40 to 50 cm higher than that in Room B2. The sill of the connecting doorway was at the level of the floor of Room B7.

The last room to be built was Room B8. Like Room B1, it contained a firepit and what may have been a mealing bin area.

Both Areas A and B had a subterranean room or kiva in immediate association with their living rooms.

The great majority of the black-on-white, and to a lesser extent the corrugated, pottery was quite uniform in techniques of construction and decoration. Very little red-slipped pottery was present and, as in later times, was restricted primarily to bowls. Corrugated bowls were more popular at this time than later, but the emphasis on the jar form in black-on-white pottery and on the open-mouthed jars in corrugated pottery was already clearly established. Typical black-on-white sherds are illustrated in figure 93a and b, and whole and restorable vessels in figure 95a–n.

Both slab and trough metates were in use, but for the first time the slab metate was more popular than its more ancient associate.

Firepits were nearly always slab-lined, and there appeared the first suggestion of a permanent mealing bin arrangement.

DATING CONSIDERATIONS

On the basis of masonry styles, Site 494 was probably built at about the same time as the first section of the surface rooms at Site 481. The time-space pottery types associated with Site 494 provide the most accurate indication of its final period of occupancy, and they suggest that Site 494 was abandoned earlier than Site 481. Correlating the site with the others in the Mariana Mesa area and using the same rough time scale, Site 494 appeared to have been occupied by around A.D. 1120, and may have been inhabited for some 20 to 30 years.

A single estimated date of shortly after A.D. 1191 (Bannister, Hannah, and Robinson 1970, p. 15) from the fill of Kiva B was the only tree-ring date recovered from Site 494. It indicates, however, an end of occupation of the site perhaps in the early years of the 1200s.

On architectural evidence the site qualifies as a late Pueblo II structure, perhaps developed in the course of about 30 years. This is consistent with the ceramic complex. Significant components of the several recognized types occurred, as listed in the table below, which also shows the dates ascribed to each type by Breternitz 1966, pp. 76, 90, 98–99, 102–103.

A date of abandonment as late as A.D. 1150 would be consistent with the ceramics but not with the single tree-ring date of 1191+. If that date is accepted, and if the site was occupied for only about 30 years, as seems plausible, it would have been built sometime around A.D. 1150 to 1160. A termination date after 1191 seems too late for most of the pottery, which was predominantly Reserve Black-on-white, ending soon after A.D. 1100. On the other hand, Reserve Black-on-white may indeed have endured for a considerable time after its assigned date of 1100+. Such an inference would be supported by the later dates ascribed to the other types found at the site.

Perhaps for some reason, however, the tree-ring

CERAMIC COMPLEX

Type	Quantity	Dates (Breternitz)
Reserve Black-on-white	556	A.D. 940–1100+
Tularosa Black-on-white	13	1100–1250
Puerco Black-on-white	27	1010–1125
Gallup Black-on-white	6	1000–1125
Wingate-Puerco Black-on-red*	81	1050–1200

*Puerco Black-on-red was combined with Wingate Black-on-red (as a variant perhaps as late as A.D. 1250) at the Second Southwestern Ceramic Conference in 1959. Carlson (1970, pp. 7–17), however, continued to regard Puerco Black-on-red as a "valid" type, dating from about A.D. 1000 to 1200.

Room	Dimensions in meters		Area in square meters
	N-S	E-W	
A1	2.25	2.00	4.50
A2	2.10	1.85	3.85
A3	1.95	1.80	3.50
A4	4.40	2.30	10.15
B1	2.60	2.20	5.70
B2	2.50	1.80	4.50
B3	2.00	1.80	3.60
B4	2.45	2.40	5.90
B5	2.45	1.60	3.90
B6	2.15	2.30	4.90
B7	3.40	2.20	7.50
B8	3.20	2.10	6.70
	SE-NW Front-Rear	SW-NE Width	
Kiva A	2.40	2.80	6.75
Kiva B	2.40	3.80	9.10

Table 16. Dimensions of rooms in Site 494.

date is misleading. A wholly satisfactory adjustment does not readily appear, but a safe compromise might be somewhere between A.D. 1100 and 1150. This would be consistent with the inference that the earliest architecture at Site 616 was similar to that at Site 494.

LIVING AND EXCAVATION UNITS

Dimensions of the rooms and kivas in the two separate units of Site 494 are given in meters and square meters in table 16.

Room A1 (figs. 85, 86, 87)

In the northwest corner of this room a firepit had been excavated into the floor at a slight angle to the walls of the room. It was rectangular in outline (the south corner was rounded) with roughly perpendicular sides and a flat bottom. The sides and bottom were unfinished except for the east corner, where two small sandstone slabs lined the walls. The pit was filled with ash.

ARTIFACTS

Fill and floor

  Stone: Mano (1821); 2 chips; rubbing stone; shaped object; hematite cylinder; kaolin (1 oz)
  Bone: 2 tubes
  Pottery: Worked sherds; black-on-white ladle handle

Room A2 (figs. 85, 86, 87)

An open doorway connected this room with Room A4. Approximately in the center of the room a small pit, 25 cm in diameter, had been dug to a depth of 15 cm. The sides and bottom were roughly finished. It was filled with ashes and, though unusual in size and shape, had apparently served as a firepit.

ARTIFACTS

Fill and floor

  Stone: Mano (1121); 2 polishing pebbles
  Bone: Awl

Room A3 (figs. 85, 86, 87)

No floor could be clearly determined in this room. Most of the sherds were concentrated on a level equal to the base of the north, east, and west walls, and test pits below this level indicated that it probably marked the original floor. In the southeast corner of the room, an open-necked corrugated jar apparently had been set into the floor several centimeters, presumably to stabilize it in an upright position. This room may have served as a storeroom.

ARTIFACTS

Fill and floor

  Stone: 2 chips; polishing pebble
  Pottery: Worked sherd
  Vessels: Indented-corrugated jar, fragment (fig. 95b); redware bowl (fig. 95f)

Room A4 (figs. 85, 86)

Room A4 was the largest of the rooms in this area and probably the last built. At the north end of the west wall an open doorway connected it with Room A2. A rectangular firepit had been excavated into the floor to a depth of 60 cm, and a single sandstone slab projecting 20 cm above the floor of the room lined each wall. A small slab had been placed at an angle in one corner where the main slabs did not join. The floor of the firepit was of natural earth. The six manos found on the room floor came from a small area near the north end of the east wall.

ARTIFACTS

Fill

  Stone: 3 manos (2221, 2222 [2]); polishing pebble; unretouched flake

Floor

  Stone: 6 manos (1121, 1221 [2], 1321 [2], 1822)

Figure 86. Site 494, Area A. General view, looking south.

Below floor
    Stone: 2 manos (1321, 2221)
    Vessel: Reserve Black-on-white bird figurine (fig. 95a)

Kiva A (figs. 85, 88)

This subterranean room was roughly rectangular in outline and had been excavated to a depth of 200 cm below the present ground surface. It was located 3.5 m east of Area A and appeared to have been associated with it, presumably functioning as a kiva.

The northeast, southeast, and southwest walls of the kiva were faced with a single wall of medium-sized lava cobbles to a height of 40 to 60 cm above the floor. This masonry facing petered out to the northwest. The northwest wall and adjacent sections of the two adjoining walls were of natural soil, covered, as was the masonry, with a heavy coat of plaster.

The floor was hard, plastered, and rather uneven. The firepit was centrally located and nearly square. It

Figure 87. Site 494, Area A. View looking north over Rooms 1 and 3.

Figure 88. Site 494, Area A. View of kiva, looking south.

Figure 89. Site 494, Area B. Rooms 4 and 6, looking northwest.

was walled and floored with thick sandstone slabs. At both Sites 481 and 494, the slabs lining the firepits in the kivas were much thicker than those used to line the firepits of the surface rooms. To the southeast of the firepit, and with a common wall, was another pit of nearly the same size, lined with slabs on two sides. This pit, which had a gravel bottom, may have served as an ash depository. In the center of the southeast wall a tunnel had been cut to meet an oval shaft dug down from the surface, to serve as a ventilator. The shaft was unlined. The tunnel began at floor level, and above 40 cm it had been walled over (the masonry wall was double at this point) flush with the wall of the kiva. The sides of the basal opening were bordered with small cobbles and the opening had a sandstone lintel. In the ventilator was a Tularosa Black-on-white pitcher (fig. 95n). A well-finished sandstone slab just larger than the opening was leaning against the wall in front of the ventilator. It apparently served to seal the opening and to act as a portable deflector.

In the west corner of the kiva was a paved area just lower than the general floor level and bordered by sandstone slabs on all but the northwest side. This feature, like those in Rooms B1 and B8, may have been part of a mealing bin. On the floor were three indented-corrugated bowls with smudged interiors (fig. 95k), as well as a miniature indented fillet-rim bowl (fig. 95e) and a fragment of an indented-corrugated bowl that may have been used as a *puki* (fig. 95c).

ARTIFACTS

Fill

Stone: 3 manos (1121, 1122, 2222); 4 polishing stones; rubbing stone; scoria cylinder; 2 unretouched flakes
Bone: Awl

Floor

Stone: 3 manos (1121, 1221, 2222); hammer; axe; 2 pecking stones; 2 polishing pebbles
Bone: Tube
Antler: Flaker (fig. 114f)
Vessels: 3 indented-corrugated bowls, with smudged interiors (fig. 95k); indented fillet-rim bowl, miniature (fig. 95e); indented-corrugated jar fragment used as a *puki*? (fig. 95c)

Ventilator

Vessel: Tularosa Black-on-white pitcher (fig. 95n)

Room B1

The floor was very hard but rather uneven with as much as 20 cm of relief. The firepit was in the center of the eastern half of the room. It was rectangular with sandstone-slab walls and a baked earth bottom, which was 20 cm below the room floor. Directly opposite, near the west wall, were the remnants of a rectangular slab-floored cist with a bottom only 10 cm below the room floor. The south and west edges of this cist were walled with sandstone slabs that projected 15 cm above the room floor. It is possible that this cist was actually the floor section of a semipermanent mealing area.

ARTIFACTS

Fill

Stone: 2 manos (1121, 1821); trough metate; hammer; 2 rubbing stones; 3 scoria cylinders; unretouched flake; hematite (2½ oz)
Bone: Awl; pierced phalange

Floor

Stone: 2 manos (1121, 1221); kaolin (1½ oz)

Figure 90. Site 494, Area B. View looking east over Rooms 3 and 6.

Room B2 (fig. 85)

This appeared to have been the first room built in Area B. The floor was excavated slightly into sterile soil, so that the floor of this room was lower than those of the surrounding rooms, most of which were built on top of trash. A roughly circular firepit occupied the center of the room. Its sides sloped inward and were unlined; against its northern edge a circular hole had been dug 10 cm deeper than the rest of the pit, which was itself approximately 20 cm below the room floor.

ARTIFACTS

Fill

   Stone: Mano (1421); gypsum crystal; hematite (2 oz)
   Shell: Pendant

Room B3 (figs. 85, 90)

Room B3 had a very good, hard, gray floor and was the only room in Area B without floor features of some kind, nor were any artifacts found in the fill. A doorway in the center of the east wall had been sealed, apparently from the side opening into Room B3. The sill of this doorway consisted of a sandstone slab, 10 cm above the floor in Room B3.

Room B4 (figs. 85, 89)

The floor of this room was rather uneven. A firepit was centrally located and was both floored and walled with sandstone slabs. Its bottom was 20 cm below the floor of the room. A doorway in the center of the west wall had been sealed. Its sill was 15 cm above the floor.

ARTIFACTS

Fill and floor

   Stone: 2 manos (1121 [2]); whetstone; mortar; rubbing stone; 7 pecking stones

Room B5 (fig. 85)

No wall was found separating this room from Room B2. However, there was a break in the floor level, with the floor of Room B5 being 10 cm higher than that of Room B2. A break in the side walls was discernible at

Figure 91. Site 494, Area B. View looking northwest over Rooms 4 and 6, showing different floor levels.

this same point. The wall structure was much the same but the walls of Room B2 were based on sterile soil, while those of Room B5 were built on trash. An unlined rectangular pit in the northwest corner of the room was filled with ash and may have served as a firepit. Its sides sloped inward slightly and it was 20 cm deep in the center. The sill of a sealed doorway in the center of the east wall was 15 cm above floor level.

ARTIFACTS

Floor

    Stone: 3 manos (1121 [2], 1721)
    Vessel: Indented-corrugated bowl, miniature (fig. 95j)

Room B6 (figs. 85, 89, 90, 91)

No wall separating this room from Room B4 was found but, as was the case with Room B5, there was a break in floor level and, to a lesser extent, a change in masonry between the two rooms. The floor of Room B6 was 16 cm higher than that of Room B5. The intervening wall may have been torn down while the two rooms were still in use. In the center of the east half of the room was a large circular unlined cist, the walls of which had been lightly plastered. They sloped inward slightly to the flat base, 40 cm below the floor of the room. Seven sandstone slabs and a fragment of a clay figurine were found in the fill of this cist. Against the west wall, a rectangular pit 20 cm deep had been excavated into the floor. The body of a young child (aged four to six) had been placed in this pit on its right side in a flexed position with the head to the northwest (fig. 6d). The pit did not appear to have been sealed and, when found, the body seemed to be lying partially out of the pit. There were no artifacts in association. Perhaps the presence of this burial was the cause for sealing off Rooms B4 and B6.

ARTIFACTS

Fill

    Stone: Mano (1321)
    Pottery: Clay figurine

Floor

    Stone: Mano (1221); metate; slab; pecking stone; projectile point; polishing pebble; whetstone
    Pottery: Indented-corrugated bowl, fragment, perhaps used as a *puki*

Room B7 (fig. 85)

The floor of Room B7, like that of Room B1, was 40 to 50 cm higher than the floor of Room B2. The sandstone sill of the open doorway connecting Room B7 with Room B2 was at the level of the floor of the former room. The floor of Room B7 was not well marked and seemed to have been subjected to little use; this perhaps is related to the fact that Room B7 was one of the last built in Area B. The firepit was rectangular and lined with sandstone slabs on three sides. The fourth side and the bottom, which was 15 cm below floor level, was of baked clay.

ARTIFACTS

Fill and floor

    Stone: 3 manos (1121, 2221 [2])
    Shell: Worked fragment
    Vessels: Indented-corrugated bowl, fragment (fig. 95i); indented-corrugated jar (fig. 95g); Tularosa Black-on-white ladle (fig. 95m); Wingate Black-on-red bowl (fig. 95l)

Room B8 (fig. 85)

This was the last room built in Area B. The floor was not well marked, and was on a level with that of Room B7. Near the center of the western half of the room was a rectangular firepit with sandstone slabs on three sides and the bottom, which was 20 cm below the room floor. The southeast wall was without a slab but originally may have had one. In the southeast corner of the room was a rectangular paved area set approximately 10 cm below the room floor. The south wall of this area was lined with an upright sandstone slab, which rose some 20 cm above the room floor. This, like the paved area in Room B1, may have been a remnant of a cist or the floor area of a mealing bin.

Figure 92. Site 494, Area B. View of kiva, looking southwest.

ARTIFACTS

Floor

    Stone: Polishing pebble
    Bone: Awls (2)

Kiva B (figs. 85, 92)

This subterranean room was located just east of the north end of Area B and in all probability was associated with it.

Scattered over a small area, in the fill of the west corner just above the floor, were portions of the skeleton of an adolescent male (fig. 6a), including the skull, vertebrae, ribs, and clavicles. None of the bones were articulated when found; nor was the remainder of the skeleton encountered.

The floor was spotty but good where identifiable. Two postholes, 15 cm in diameter, were present in the kiva floor midway along the two long sides and 20 cm out from the walls.

The southwest wall and adjacent portions of the southeast and northwest walls were finished with single-masonry facings of medium-sized lava cobbles in irregular courses to a height between 40 and 80 cm above the floor. The southeast wall to the east of the ventilator shaft, the northeast wall, and the section of the northwest wall immediately adjacent were without masonry. Here plaster had been applied directly to the native soil.

The firepit was located in the south-center of the western half of the kiva. It was lined and floored with thick sandstone slabs. Immediately adjoining the firepit to the south was an unlined depression that may have served as an ash receptacle.

The ventilator was in the southeast wall nearly opposite the firepit. The tunnel and shaft were simply cut from the hard sterile soil and had no masonry walls or lintel. The tunnel curved slightly to the east before it sloped up gently to join the vertical shaft. The mouth of the tunnel was approximately 40 cm square. A thick sandstone slab just larger than the tunnel mouth was leaning against the wall nearby.

ARTIFACTS

Fill

    Stone: 2 manos (1121, 2221); scoria cylinder

Floor

    Stone: 4 manos (1121 [3], 1721); 2 projectile points; scoria cylinder; unretouched flake; turquoise fragment

    Vessels: Indented-corrugated bowl fragment, perhaps used as a *puki*; Reserve Black-on-white pitcher; Reserve Black-on-white ladle (fig. 95d)

Ventilator

    Vessel: Indented-corrugated bowl (fig. 95h)

SUBSISTENCE MATERIALS

A total of 237 unworked animal bones were recovered from Site 494. Of these, 175 could not be identified. The identified specimens were as follows: pronghorn (*Antilocapra americana*), 3; mule deer (*Odocoileus hemionus hemionus*), 2; spotted skunk (*Spilogale* sp.), 1; prairie dog (*Cynomys* sp.), 1; turkey or other large bird, 1; rabbit or hare, 54.

Approximately half (115) of these bones came from the fill and 14 were from the floor of Kiva B. The remainder were evenly distributed over the site. Sixty-eight of the bones were found on the floors of the various rooms.

No vegetal material was recovered.

POTTERY — DESCRIPTIVE TYPOLOGY

The descriptive categories recognized were basically similar to those at Site 616, and the same numeration is employed.

White-slipped Pottery

MATERIAL: ROW A

1: Gray paste — mode key (A)
    Thin and/or watery white slip — modes (b) and (i)
    Black mineral paint — mode (a)
2: Gray paste — mode key (A)
    White slip, thinly applied — modes (b) and (h)
    Black mineral paint — mode (a)
3: Gray paste — mode key (A)
    Creamy slip, thickly applied — modes (c) and (g)
    Black mineral paint — mode (a)
4: Gray paste — mode key (A)
    No slip apparent — mode (a)
    Black mineral paint — mode (a)

VESSEL SHAPES AND AREAS SLIPPED AND PAINTED: ROW B

1: Bowl — mode (a)
    Interior and exterior slipped, interior painted — modes (a), (b), and (c)
2: Bowl — mode (a)
    No slip, painted on interior — mode (c)
3: Necked jar — mode (d)
    Exterior slipped and painted — modes (b) and (d)
4: Pitcher — mode (g)
    Exterior slipped and painted — modes (b) and (d)
5: Ladle — mode (h)
    Interior and exterior slipped, interior painted — modes (a), (b), and (c)

SURFACE FINISH: ROW C

1: Surfaces undulating but smooth to the touch, high points of slipped surfaces lustrous; polishing marks generally evident; slip polished before application of paint — modes (a), (f), (g), and (i).

DECORATION: ROW D

1: Contrasted solid and hatched broad lines and bands, sawteeth, and scrolls the dominant motifs. Diagonal hatching, solid triangles, broad and fine lines, dots, and hooked elements frequent. Ticked rims common. Patterns generally rectilinear and either allover or banded. Hatching elements widely spaced. Usually less than 50 percent of vessel surface decorated. Execution often rather poor. Pitchers and jars decorated with a band of solid elements around the neck and a wide band of contrasted solid and hatched elements around the body of the vessel, occasionally with an open star pattern on the base formed by the lower outline of the decorated area. On bowls a wide interior band from the rim, or just below it, with an undecorated central area below.

2. Large triangles frequently filled with checked patterns, solid opposed stepped keys, panels of vertical and horizontal lines. Often panels of vertical parallel lines alternating with solid elements. Placement usually within bands, but frequently in independent units, pendent from the rim. Execution generally poor.

3: Interlocking opposed solid and hatched scrolls and stepped figures, including angular, curvilinear, or interlocked scrolls; single, narrow-lined scrolls; small close-set key figures; fine-line herringbone; and fine-line hatching closely spaced (this element almost always present). Neck frets of solid elements, chevron nests, or balanced solid and hatched elements, but never panels of vertical lines. Jars decorated with bands on neck and body with the latter often ending in an open star or polygonal base. Bowls decorated with interior bands. Execution excellent.

4: Triangles in successions of steps, solid and hatched; hatched bands; fine lines; straight or

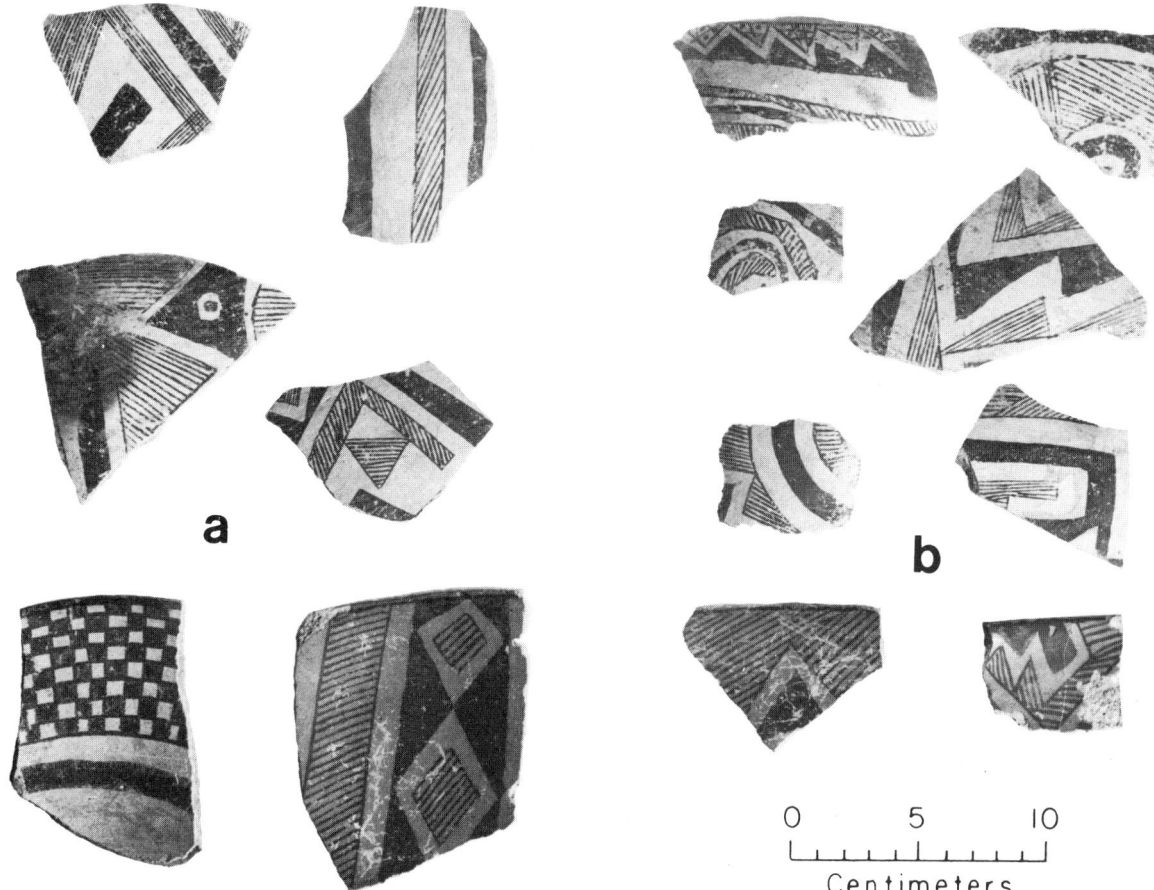

Figure 93. Typical black-on-white sherds from Site 494: a. Area A; b. Area B.

wavy hatching (bordering lines thicker); scrolls single or occasionally interlocked. Band layout on jars and bowls, at or just below the rim. Painted stripe often along rim.

Red-slipped Pottery

MATERIAL: ROW A

1: Gray to tan to orange paste — mode key (F)
   Orange slip — mode (d)
   Black mineral paint — mode (a)
3: Gray to tan to orange paste — mode key (F)
   Brick-red powdery slip — mode (e)
   Black mineral paint — mode (a)

VESSEL SHAPES, AREAS PAINTED, AND COLORS COMBINED: ROW B

1: Bowl — mode (a)
   Interiors black-on-red — mode (a)
6: Globular small-necked jar — mode (c)
   Exteriors black-on-red — mode (h)

SURFACE FINISH: ROW C

1: Slipped surfaces smooth and only slightly undulating; lustrous over entire surface though streaks of a hard polishing tool occasionally apparent; slip polished before application of the paint — modes (a), (e), (g), and (i)

DECORATION: ROW D

1: Opposed interlocking solid and hatched scrolls

Plain and Corrugated Pottery

MATERIAL: ROW A

1: Brown paste with sand inclusions — mode key (H)
2: Gray paste with angular opaque inclusions — mode key (I)
3: Gray paste with coarse sand inclusions — mode key (J)

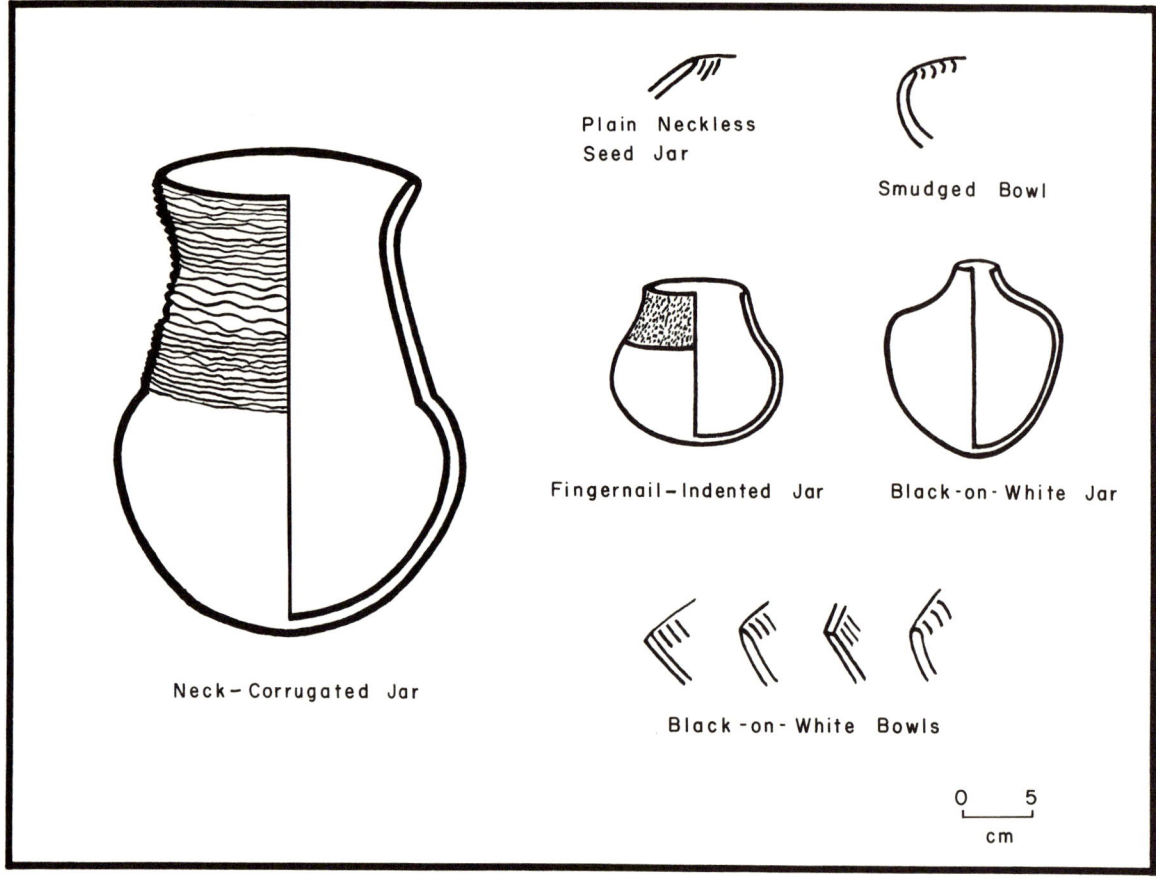

Figure 94. Pottery-rim and vessel forms from Site 494, Areas A and B.

VESSEL SHAPES: ROW B

1: Bowl — mode (a)
2: Globular neckless (seed) jar — mode (b)
3: Open-mouthed jar — mode (e)
4: Basal sherds from bowls or jars — modes (a) and (e)

CONSTRUCTION AND SURFACE FINISH: ROW C

1: Coiled counterclockwise, indented with left thumb pointing up — mode (a)
  Interior surfaces smooth and even, coils unobliterated on exterior — mode (a)
2: Coiled clockwise, indented with right thumb pointing up — mode (c)
  Interior surfaces smooth and even, coils unobliterated on exterior — mode (a)
3: Presumably coiled, direction unknown — mode (d)
  Surfaces even but matte, small striations, gritty to the touch — mode (e)
4: Presumably coiled, direction unknown — mode (d)
  Exposed surfaces even, smooth, and lustrous — mode (b)
5: Presumably coiled, direction unknown — mode (d)
  Exposed surfaces even, gritty, and matte — mode (c)

DECORATIVE EFFECT: ROW D

0: Plain surface without corrugations or other decorative effects — mode (a)
1: Narrow clapboard corrugation — mode (b)
2: Indented corrugation — mode (c)
3: Pattern-indented corrugation — mode (d)
4: Plain and corrugated combined — mode (e)

The major portion of the corrugated pottery was similar to that from Site 616. In contrast to Site 616, however, there was a much higher proportion of clapboard corrugation, and indentations, when present, tended to be smaller and made at an angle more nearly perpendicular to the base of the coil. A few indentations even had a slight backslant and there were almost no indentations with a marked forward slant, a characteristic common at Site 616. Though there were only 17 sherds from vessels indented with the right thumb, these sherds represented at least six vessels, a much more frequent occurrence of this technique than was found at Site 616. Corrugated bowls were also more frequent at Site 616.

POTTERY — PROBLEM TYPES

Regional Time-Space Types

WHITE-SLIPPED POTTERY

Reserve Black-on-white (fig. 95a, d)

Descriptive types: 1312, 2111, 2211, 2311, 2411, 2511, 4211
Total: 555 sherds and 3 vessels

In design and execution this pottery was very similar to examples of Reserve Black-on-white from other sites in the Mariana Mesa region, and like them it differed from the published descriptions in several respects, particularly in the slipping of bowls on the exterior as well as on the interior, and in the rarity of vessels with a thin or watery slip.

Puerco Black-on-white

Descriptive types: 2112, 2312, 2512
Total: 27 sherds

Typed as Puerco Black-on-white primarily on the basis of decoration, but differing from the published descriptions in being better polished, a variation consistent with normal Mariana Mesa practice.

Gallup Black-on-white

Descriptive types: 2314, 3314
Total: 7 sherds

Designs were similar to those on standard Gallup Black-on-white, but slip and surface finish on all but one sherd was like Tularosa Black-on-white.

Tularosa Black-on-white (fig. 95m, n)

Descriptive types: 3211, 3313, 3411
Total: 13 sherds and 2 vessels

Similar to other Tularosa Black-on-white in the Mariana Mesa area. There was considerable design overlap with Reserve Black-on-white, but the elements were more closely placed on Tularosa Black-on-white.

RED-SLIPPED POTTERY

Wingate Black-on-red (fig. 95l)

Descriptive types: 3111, 3611
Total: 76 sherds and 3 vessels

Similar in all major respects to the published descriptions.

Puerco Black-on-red

Descriptive type: 1111
Total: 6 sherds

This pottery differed from Wingate Black-on-red primarily in the slip employed.

Whole and Partially Restorable Vessels

Twenty whole and partially restorable vessels were recovered from Areas A and B of Site 494, as listed below (all corrugated and fillet-rim vessels were of the brown-paste mode key [H]).

VESSELS

Specimen	Provenience	Figure
Indented-corrugated bowl	Kiva B, ventilator	95h
Indented-corrugated bowl, miniature	Room B5, floor	95j
Indented-corrugated bowl, fragment	Kiva A, floor	95c
Indented-corrugated bowl, fragment	Room B6, floor	---
Indented-corrugated bowl, fragment	Kiva B, floor	---
Indented-corrugated bowl, fragment	Room B7, fill	95i
3 indented-corrugated bowls, smudged interior	Kiva A, floor	95k
Indented-corrugated jar	Room A3, floor	---
Indented-corrugated jar	Room B7, floor	95g
Indented-corrugated jar, fragment	Room A3, floor	95b
Indented fillet-rim bowl, miniature	Kiva A, floor	95e
Redware bowl, plain	Room A3, fill	95f
Wingate Black-on-red bowl	Room B7, floor	95l
Reserve Black-on-white ladle	Room B7, floor	95m
Reserve Black-on-white pitcher	Kiva B, floor	---
Reserve Black-on-white bird figurine	Room A4, below floor	95a
Tularosa Black-on-white ladle	Kiva B, floor	95d
Tularosa Black-on-white pitcher	Kiva A, ventilator	95n

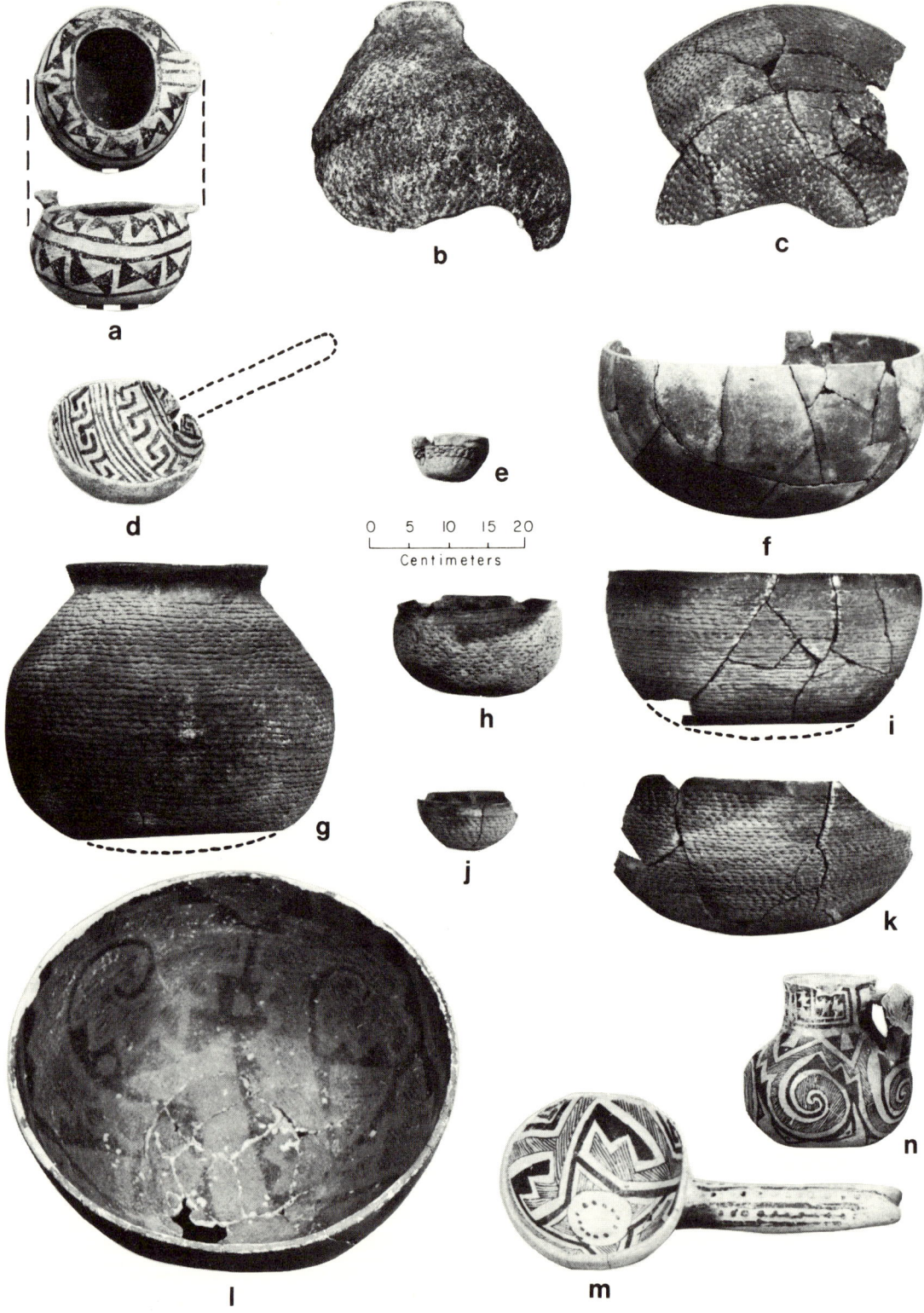

Intrasite Distribution Types

WHITE-SLIPPED POTTERY

Intrasite Distribution Type A

Descriptive types: 1312, 4211
Total: 6 sherds
Diagnostic attributes: Thin, watery slip (slip mode [i]) in association with decorative types 1 and 2.
Characteristic of Area A only, see comments below.

Intrasite Distribution Type B

Descriptive types: 2112, 2312, 2512
Total: 27 sherds
Diagnostic attributes: Thin white slip (modes [b] and [h]) in association with decorative type 2.
Characteristic of Area A, though the 2 sherds of 2512 were found in Room B2 which, interestingly, was evidently the first room built in Area B; see comment below.

Intrasite Distribution Type C

Descriptive types: 2314, 3211, 3313, 3314, 3411
Total: 20 sherds
Diagnostic attributes: A thickly applied creamy slip (modes [c] and [g]) and/or decoratives modes 3 or 4.
Characteristic of Area B only; see comments below.

Comment

Even though the entire site was excavated, the ceramic sample was too small to permit recognition of artisan types or even site types (that is, any clusters of attributes that might have been meaningful to or characteristic of potters at Site 494). On the other hand the intrasite distribution types abstracted above does suggest a cultural or temporal nonconformity between Area A and Area B.

There were slight but probably culturally or temporally significant differences between the ceramic samples from the two units. The only thin, watery-slipped sherds (slip mode [i]) and the only unslipped sherd came from Area A, while the only sherds with a thick creamy slip (slip modes [c] and [h]) were found in Area B. Decorative type 2 was associated with Area A and the earliest room in Area B, while decorative types 3 and 4 were associated only with Area B.

A close look at the attributes present and their proportional distribution in all three major classes of pottery (black-on-white, redware, and utility ware) strongly suggests that Areas A and B were, ceramically speaking, not closely integrated. Either the two groups were at least in part contemporaneous, with the people of unit B being more "progressive" in their pottery ideas, or (and, to my mind, more likely) Area B represented basically a slightly later reoccupation of the site. This interpretation is based upon several points. It is true that every paste attribute was identical for all of the black-on-white pottery found in both units. Moreover, the paste attributes were identical to those found at Site 616 (which also was uniform in its black-on-white paste attributes) and to most of the black-on-white paste found at Site 481. This certainly suggests not only similar sources of raw material but also a closely patterned continuity of preparation and firing techniques for both units of Site 494 and for the generally somewhat later sites, 481 and 616.

Similarly, though the decoration of the vast majority of the sherds was the same (decorative mode 1), the variations from the norm tended to cluster. Decorative mode 2 was almost entirely restricted to Area A, while decorative modes 3 and 4 were restricted to Area B, and, with one exception, to sherds with the thickly applied creamy slip. It should be noted, too, that the emphasis on finer execution, more closely spaced hatching, and interlocking scrolls of decorative modes 3 and 4 were usually later attributes than the more open, sloppier execution of decorative mode 2.

When I classified these sherds in terms of time-space types, I allowed the slip mode to outweigh the decorative mode and placed the thinly slipped sherds in Reserve Black-on-white even though one descriptive type (1312) was decorated with a mode otherwise placed in Puerco Black-on-white. Similarly, the two sherds with a thick creamy slip but decorated with a "Reverse mode" (3211, 3411) were placed in Tularosa Black-on-white.

This example serves to point up advantages of the descriptive type approach, however, for it can be argued that I was wrong in placing greater weight on the slip mode and that I should have allocated sherds

Figure 95. Pottery vessels from Site 494, Areas A and B: a. Area A, Room 4, below floor, Reserve Black-on-white bird-figurine vessel, #666 (2411); b. Area A, Room 3, floor, indented-corrugated jar fragment, #110 (1112); c. Area A, kiva, floor, indented-corrugated bowl fragment, #324 (1317) (may have served as a *puki*); d. Area B, kiva, floor, Reserve Black-on-white ladle, #316; e. Area A, kiva, floor, indented fillet-rim miniature bowl, #204; f. Area A, Room 3, fill, plain redware bowl, #206; g. Area B, Room 7, floor, indented-corrugated jar, #581 (1112); h. Area B, kiva, ventilator, indented-corrugated bowl, #543 (1316); i. Area B, Room 7, fill, indented-corrugated bowl, #654 (1316); j. Area B, Room 5, floor, indented-corrugated miniature bowl, #612 (1112); k. Area A, kiva, floor, indented-corrugated bowl, #510 (1316); l. Area B, Room 7, floor, Wingate Black-on-red bowl, #582 (1124); m. Area B, Room 7, floor, Tularosa Black-on-white ladle, #580; n. Area A, kiva, ventilator, Tularosa Black-on-white pitcher, #542 (3414).

White-slipped Pottery

Descriptive Types / Provenience	A B C D	1 3 1 2	2 1 1 1	2 1 1 2	2 2 1 1	2 3 1 1	2 3 1 2	2 3 1 4	2 4 1 1	2 5 1 1	2 5 1 2	3 2 1 1	3 3 1 3	3 3 1 4	3 4 1 1	4 2 1 1	Bases
Totals	639	5	21	3	6	458	22	1	21	16	2	1	11	6	1	1	64
Rm. A1 Fill	7		1			3											3
Rm. A2 Fill	11	5		1		4											1
Rm. A3 Fill	128					115	2									1	10
Rm. A4 Fill	20					8	12										
Rm. A4 Floor	8					8											
Kiva A Fill	24	1	1			11	6										5
Kiva A Floor	18		11			5	2										
Rm. B1 Fill	62					60											2
Rm. B1 Floor	4					4											
Rm. B2 Fill	91					61		8		1				6			15
Rm. B2 Floor	39					26		12		1							
Rm. B3 Fill	14					9											5
Rm. B4 Fill	13	1				10			2								
Rm. B4 Floor	11	8				2		1									
Rm. B5 Fill	20					15			1								4
Rm. B6 Fill	14					6											8
Rm. B6 Floor	10					10											
Rm. B7 Fill	40			1		22							11				6
Rm. B7 Floor	17			3		2			12								
Rm. B8 Fill	16			1		14						1					
Rm. B8 Floor	15			1		13			1								
Kiva B Fill	41					34	1								1		5
Kiva B Floor	16					16											

Red-slipped Pottery

Descriptive Types / Provenience	A B C D	1 1 1 1	3 1 1 1	3 6 1 1
Totals	81	6	73	2
Rm. A1 Fill				
Rm. A2 Fill				
Rm. A3 Fill	3		1	2
Rm. A4 Fill	1		1	
Rm. A4 Floor				
Kiva A Fill	15		15	
Kiva A Floor				
Rm. B1 Fill	8	6	2	
Rm. B1 Floor				
Rm. B2 Fill	2		2	
Rm. B2 Floor				
Rm. B3 Fill				
Rm. B4 Fill	1		1	
Rm. B4 Floor				
Rm. B5 Fill				
Rm. B6 Fill	1		1	
Rm. B6 Floor				
Rm. B7 Fill	1		1	
Rm. B7 Floor				
Rm. B8 Fill	4		4	
Rm. B8 Floor				
Kiva B Fill	45		45	
Kiva B Floor				

Plain and Corrugated Pottery

Descriptive Types / Provenience	A B C D	1 1 1 3	1 1 1 4	1 1 2 3	1 1 4 0	1 1 5 0	1 2 1 1	1 2 1 2	1 2 2 3	1 2 2 2	1 2 4 3	1 2 4 0	1 3 1 1	1 3 1 2	1 3 1 3	1 3 2 2	1 3 4 0	1 3 5 1	1 4 1 0	1 4 3 0	1 4 5 1	2 3 1 2	2 3 2 2	2 3 2 2	2 3 5 0	2 4 5 0	3 3 1 1	3 3 1 2	3 3 2 2	3 4 3 0
Totals	1019	3	1	1	2	8	8	173	9	4	2	10	229	494	22	6	6	4	1	4	2	10	2	1	2	2	9	3	1
Rm. A1 Fill	8													8															
Rm. A1 Floor	22					2	7						10			1	2												
Rm. A2 Fill	13				2						4	1	2			1	1			2									
Rm. A3 Fill	25												16	6							1						1	1	
Rm. A3 Floor	1													1															
Rm. A4 Fill	16					1		2	2		1	1		7														2	
Rm. A4 Floor	18			1				5	1			1		9				1											
Kiva A Fill	72							10		1			35	21								3	2						
Kiva A Floor	48							4	1	3	1		31	7											1				
Rm. B1 Fill	70				1	1		30					12	23		1						1			1				
Rm. B1 Floor	73	1						20					1	50	1														
Rm. B2 Fill	103							44	1			1	38	14	2	1						1			1				
Rm. B2 Floor	35								1				22	11											1				
Rm. B3 Fill	24					1	2	1			1		1	10	6		1						1						
Rm. B4 Fill	4								1				1	1					1										
Rm. B4 Floor	17												5	12															
Rm. B5 Fill	18					2	3						5	4	2		2												
Rm. B5 Floor	3						1														1								
Rm. B6 Fill	79			1	1		7						1	67	1			1											
Rm. B6 Floor	33				3	1							4	24	1														
Rm. B7 Fill	49	3					14	1					11	15		5													
Rm. B7 Floor	17		1		1	8								2												5			
Rm. B8 Fill	10					1							7	1							1								
Rm. B8 Floor	13				1								2	9							1								
Kiva B Fill	182					9					2		24	133	7					3		1		2			1		
Kiva B Floor	65					4							2	57	1												1		
Ventilator	1							1																					

Table 17. Distribution by descriptive types of all pottery sherds from Site 494, Areas A and B.

of descriptive type 1312 to Puerco Black-on-white and those of descriptive types 3211 and 3411 to Reserve Black-on-white. With a standard method of presenting sherd counts the reader would not have known of my "erroneous" decision nor of its basis. By a listing of the descriptive-type designations after each typological category a reader who might feel that decoration should be primarily emphasized is made aware of my (to him, false) placement and, equally important, is also free to place sherds of particular descriptive types into another problem type for his own analysis; for he will know exactly where the sherds came from, their context, and what other internal attributes are associated with them.

I freely admit that in this case I am straining at a gnat to illustrate an advantage of the descriptive type approach. Since so few sherds are involved, no interpretations are likely to be affected by these typological shifts. However, the principle would be the same if the sherd count were of significant size. If descriptive typology is employed each analyst is free to apply his own criteria and everyone will be aware of precisely which artifacts his various problem types are based upon.

The small redware sample also can offer little definitive evidence, but it can be noted that the only orange-slipped sherds (again, an earlier attribute) and the only sherds from the small-necked jar form came from Area A.

The corrugated pottery is more informative because the sample was larger. With this pottery, though there was almost total overlap in attributes, their respective percentages of occurrence provided further evidence that Area B potters were marching to the tune of a slightly later drum. At Area A the sherds with narrow clapboard (decorative-effect mode [b]) and indented corrugation (decorative-effect mode [c]) were nearly equal in number and each comprised almost 48 percent of the sample from the area. At Area B a shift occurred, with indented corrugation making up 75 percent of the sample and narrow clapboard sherds just under 20 percent -- a ratio of the two types that rather closely approached the one found at Site 616.

There is no way to prove that the occupants of Area B were not simply a more "progressive" group. Given the probable mobility (though perhaps within a limited area) of small groups such as this, it would seem more likely that the variations seen in the pottery and other characteristics reflect an actual time difference, with two separate occupations of the site, though probably by closely allied groups or even by the same group. If this interpretation is correct, the attribute clusters noted above should more properly be considered site types rather than intrasite types, with most if not all of the diagnostic attributes of the types having temporal significance.

OTHER OBJECTS OF CLAY

Figurine: 1 specimen

A fired clay image of an unidentifiable quadruped came from a pit in the floor of Room B6. Only the head and body remained. The body was somewhat cylindrical as were the head and neck. The ears projected from the top of the head, while slits had been made to represent the eyes and mouth. The complete figurine probably was about 6 cm long.

Worked Sherds: 4 specimens

Two sherd discs of black-on-white pottery, 3 and 3.8 cm in diameter respectively, were recovered. The first, from the floor of Room A1, was well finished, and the other, from the fill of Room A3, was only roughed out. A corrugated sherd from the floor of Room A1 was well finished, 4 cm in diameter, and had a centrally drilled hole 0.5 cm in diameter. A hollow cylinder-style black-on-white ladle handle came from the floor of Room A1. It had two perforations in the body of the handle and one in the "closed" end. The slightly flaring bowl end had been smoothed, giving the object the appearance of a miniature clarinet.

STONE ARTIFACTS

Manos: 48 specimens (fig. 108c, p, q, s)

The modes employed for the description of manos from Sites 616 and 481 also applied to Site 494. Though the original dimensions on 32 of the 48 specimens could be determined, many were broken or chipped (table 18).

MATERIAL: ROW A

Mode 1: Sandstone: 35 specimens

Only three of the sandstone manos had been used extensively on trough metates but all of the manos used at an angle were of sandstone. The proportion of sandstone to basalt manos was approximately the same as at Sites 616 and 481.

Mode 2: Vesicular basalt: 13 specimens

The basalt manos were all rectangular in cross section, although there was some variation in their sizes. One was the shortest (12.6 cm) mano found, while another was unusually large (26.7 cm).

Mariana Mesa

Provenience		Material: A Shape: B Grips: C Type: D	1 1 2 1	1 1 2 2	1 2 2 1	1 2 2 2	1 3 2 1	1 4 2 1	1 7 2 1	1 8 2 1	1 8 2 2	2 1 1 1	2 1 2 1	2 1 2 2	2 2 2 1	2 2 2 2
		Totals	48	16	1	4	1	4	1	3	4	1	1	1	1	5	5
Room A1	Floor		1							1							
Room A2	Floor		1	1													
	Fill		3													1	2
Room A4	Floor		6	1		2		2			1						
	Subfloor		2					1							1		
Room B1	Fill		2	1						1							
	Floor		2	1		1											
Room B2	Fill		1					1									
Room B4	Fill		1	1													
	Floor		1	1													
Room B5	Floor		3	2						1							
Room B6	Fill		1					1									
	Floor		1										1				
Room B7	Fill		2	1												1	
	Floor		1										1				
Kiva A	Fill		3	1	1												1
	Floor		3	1			1										1
Kiva B	Fill		2	1												1	
	Floor		4	3						1							
Trenches	Area A		4			1					2					1	
	Area B		4	1					1				1				1

Table 18. Distribution by descriptive types of manos from Site 494, Areas A and B.

SHAPE: ROW B

Mode 1: Rectangular in cross section, one face used: 20 specimens

Mode 2: Rectangular in cross section, two faces used: 15 specimens

Modes 1 and 2 together account for the major portion of the manos (and all of the basalt manos).

Mode 3: Semiwedge-shape in cross section, one or two faces used: 4 specimens

Three of these had adjacent surfaces that had been used flat and at an angle, respectively. The fourth (Room A4, below floor) had been used only at an angle.

Mode 4: Semiwedge-shape in cross section, three faces used: 1 specimen

Mode 5: Truncated pyramid in cross section, three faces used: None present

Mode 6: Truncated pyramid in cross section, four faces used: None present

Mode 7: Triangular in cross section, two faces used: 3 specimens

The line dividing the two used faces on these manos and those of shape mode 8 was approximately parallel to the edges of the mano. No angle was apparent as was often the case at Site 616.

Mode 8: Triangular in cross section, three faces used: 5 specimens

Mode 9: Diamond-shape in cross section, four faces used: None present

FINGER GRIPS: ROW C

Mode 1: Presence of finger grips: 1 specimen

The one specimen with finger grips was of vesicular basalt. One shallow groove 5 cm long was present in what probably was the center of one edge. The specimen was broken and it was impossible to determine if a second groove had been opposite the first. This specimen was no wider than normal but was slightly thicker (3.8 cm).

Mode 2: Absence of finger grips: 47 specimens

ASSOCIATED METATE TYPE: ROW D

Mode 1: Slab: 39 specimens

Some of the manos may have seen slight service on trough metates but not sufficiently for the ends to become extensively abraded. The used faces on a number of them were convex in both dimensions, particularly the short dimension. These features occurred occasionally on the trough manos also, but on the whole these features were not as frequent here as at Site 481.

Mode 2: Trough: 9 specimens

There was a certain amount of variation in the trough manos. Three were of sandstone; two of these were unusually long (26.7 and 28 cm), and one was triangular in cross section with three faces used. Five of the remainder were rectangular in cross section with two faces used, while the sixth had only one face used. This tendency to use two or even three faces on a single mano for grinding on a trough metate differentiated the specimens at Site 494 from those at Site 481. At the latter site, nearly all the trough manos had been used on only one face; when a second face was used it generally was on a slab metate.

SIZE

With rare exceptions the manos at Site 494 were constructed with dimensions similar to those of the short type from Sites 616 and 481. The average length was 20.3 cm and all but four manos were within the range of 16.7 to 23.3 cm (with rather even distribution within this range). One vesicular basalt mano was only 12.6 cm long and one was 26.7 cm long. Two sandstone manos were unusually long (25.5 and 28 cm). The average width was 11.5 cm with a range of 8.8 cm to 14.4 cm. The average height was 2.5 cm with a range of 1.1 cm to 5 cm. The manos of vesicular basalt tended to be thicker than those of sandstone. The trough manos were thicker in general than the slab manos.

Metates: 2 specimens

The two metate fragments were of vesicular basalt, both from Area B. One fragment was from a trough metate with a trough 6.5 cm deep. It came from the fill of Room B1. The other was a fragment of a slab metate from the floor of Room B6.

Mortar: 1 specimen

In one surface of a flat quartzite slab, rectangular in cross section and nearly square in top view, a centrally located small circular depression had been pecked. The slab measured 5.8 by 5.6 by 2.3 cm, while the depression, which was 3.5 cm in diameter, gradually sloped to a maximum depth of 0.3 cm. The slab was only roughly finished but the depression was very regular and quite smooth. It came from the floor of Room B4.

Polishing Pebbles: 12 specimens

Nearly all polishing pebbles were of quartz or quartzite, one perhaps of diorite. Each bore only a single polishing facet, usually as large as permitted by the size and shape of the pebble. The pebbles were very smooth overall but irregular in shape. They ranged in size from 7 by 5.7 by 1.9 cm to 3 by 2.5 by 1.5 cm.

Rubbing Stones: 5 specimens

Two unshaped cobbles of sandstone and three of quartzite bearing one or more grinding facets were identified as rubbing stones. The facets were generally slightly convex following the natural contours of the rock. None showed extensive wear. Two bore only a single facet, two had two facets, and the fifth had several facets over most of the surface of the cobble. They ranged in size from 15.5 by 11 by 5.5 cm to 7 by 6.5 by 7.5 cm.

Pecking Stones: 10 specimens

These pecking stones — irregular, unshaped, fist-sized cobbles exhibiting battering at one or more points — were of petrified wood (6), quartzite (3), and basalt (1). On six, only one end had been used for pecking, on the others the two opposite ends had been so used. The average size was about 7 by 6 by 3 cm.

Axes: 4 specimens

One specimen seemed to be the bit end of a chipped axe, probably similar to the notched axe found at Site 616. The length of the bit was 5.4 cm with the length of the blade itself slightly less. It was only 1.3 cm thick at the break, which was 4 cm above the blade. This axe was found on the surface of Area A. (See p. 145, fig. 55c).

The other three axes were all grooved. They were not well finished. It would appear that a stone was selected as close to the proper size and proportions as possible and a minimum amount of modification effected. They were oval in top view. One (#264, fig. 111a), from the floor of Kiva A, was of quartzite and full-grooved. Another (#381), from the trench outside Area A, was of basalt and full-grooved, and a third (#349, fig. 111c), from the fill of Room B1, also of basalt, was three-quarter-grooved. Their dimensions in the above order were as follows: 11.5 by 8 by 4.5 cm, 11.2 by 4.5 by 3.8 cm, and 10 by 6 by 3.5 cm. On the first and last specimens the groove was located 4 cm below the top of the poll, while on the second it was 3.5 cm below. On the three-quarter-grooved axe, the groove sloped up from the grooved edge rather than being parallel to the blade.

Hammers: 2 specimens

Both were of basalt, full-grooved, oval in top view, and rectanguloid in side view. On the one from the floor of Kiva A (#265, fig. 112d) the groove was centrally located. It measured 7 by 4 cm with a height of 8.9 cm. On the one from the floor of Room B1, the groove was 3.5 cm below one end. This latter specimen, with dimensions of 7 by 4 cm with a height of 9 cm, may have been a reworked axe.

Whetstones: 2 specimens

One was a quartzite cobble (8.8 by 6.9 by 3 cm) with one rectangular (7 by 4.5 cm) concave grinding face. This artifact may have served to sharpen axes or other tools. It came from the floor of Room B6.

The second whetstone was a reused mano (1121) from Room B4, fill. A sharpening groove 6 cm wide was worn across one end of the short diameter of the used face of the mano.

Points: 3 specimens

All were of petrified wood. Two, from the floor of Kiva A, were small and triangular with a slightly concave base. Both were 1.6 cm long with a basal width of 1.1 cm. The third (Room B6, floor) was triangular, 4.2 cm long and 1.5 cm wide at the base. It was side-notched with a suggestion of a second notch on one side.

Unretouched Flakes: 6 specimens

All but one were of petrified wood, the exception being of chalcedony. All exhibited use with chips along one edge or, in the case of one bladelike specimen, along two edges. They were irregular in shape, less than 1 cm in thickness, and ranged in size from 4.6 by 3.3 cm to 3.6 by 1.4 cm.

Chips: 4 specimens

Two were of petrified wood, one of obsidian. All were small (less than 3 cm in any dimension).

Core: 1 specimen

A fist-sized cobble of felsite from which a number of flakes had been detached was found on the floor of Kiva B.

Scoria Cylinders: 6 specimens

These were fairly smooth, approximately circular or slightly oval cylinders. They ranged in diameter from 2.5 to 3 cm and in length from 6 to 9 cm. The ends were rounded in most instances, though on one they were only slightly convex.

Hematite Cylinder: 1 specimen

This cylinder, with slight longitudinal facets and flat ends, was 0.5 cm in diameter and 2.9 cm long. It was found on the floor of Room A1.

Shaped Stone Object: 1 specimen

This keg-shaped object of gypsum had one end flat and the other slightly convex. It was well smoothed on all surfaces, 0.9 cm in diameter and 1.6 cm high, and was found on the floor of Room A1.

BONE ARTIFACTS

Awls: 5 specimens

One awl, of a small light bone, was of the type described as "head of bone intact." It was 10.4 cm long and tapered gradually to the point. It came from below the floor of Room B8.

The other four specimens were splinter awls. They tapered gradually to a point and exhibited very little workmanship other than grinding and polishing in the immediate area of the point. The two complete specimens were 10.4 cm and 8.7 cm in length, and appeared to be from the long bones of a large mammal. They were found in Kiva A, Rooms A2, B1, and B8.

Tubes: 3 specimens

These three tubes had been polished and the cut ends smoothed. Their respective dimensions were as follows: 8 by 0.4 cm, 1.7 by 0.6 cm, and 1 by 0.9 cm. The two short ones were on the floor of Room A1, the other on the floor of Kiva A.

Pierced Phalange: 1 specimen

The proximal end of a deer or pronghorn phalange had been cut off and the phalange perforated near this end. The cut surface had not been smoothed. It was found in the fill of Room B1.

ANTLER FLAKER: 1 specimen

An antler tip, 11.7 cm long, which may have been used to chip stone, came from the floor of Kiva A.

SHELL ARTIFACTS

Only two fragments of shell were encountered. One, from the floor of Room 7, was an unworked fragment of *Haliotis rufescens*. The second, from the pit in the floor of Room 2, was a fragment of a *Conus* sp., the wide end of which had been ground flat and a hole drilled near this edge. It may originally have been a tinkler pendant that broke, and this fragment was drilled for further use as a pendant.

RAW MATERIALS

The raw materials found are listed below.

RAW MATERIALS

Material	Quantity	Provenience
Kaolin (?)	1 oz	Room A1, floor
Kaolin (?)	1½ oz	Room B1, floor
Hematite	2½ oz	Room B1, fill
Hematite	2 oz	Room B2, fill
Gypsum	1 crystal	Room B2, fill
Turquoise	1 fragment	Kiva B, floor

HUMAN SKELETAL REMAINS

Skeleton 1 (fig. 6a)

Age: Adolescent
Sex: Probably male

Medium occipital deformation. No central inca bone but a number of islands between the occipital and parietal bones. Upper and lower third molars had not yet erupted, and there was no room in the mandible for the later. The upper third molars, also cramped for space, had begun to develop, but could be seen only where the bone had been broken away. An additional cause of potential dental discomfort doubtless occurred in the upper left incisors. The upper left lateral incisor had grown medially at a sharp angle, taking up the space of both incisors, so that the upper left medial incisor, in paralleling this, had grown directly against the central portion of the root of the upper right medial incisor.

The recovered portions of this skeleton came from the fill of Kiva B just above the floor. Most of the bones were within a fairly limited area but none were articulated. Only the cranium, the clavicles, a fragment of a humerus, and a number of ribs and vertebrae were found, and probably did not represent a formal burial, since no artifacts were demonstrably in association.

Skeleton 2 (fig. 6d)

Age: Child, four to six, based on tooth eruption; all milk teeth but no permanent teeth were present; general bone size argues against a younger estimate.
Sex: Unknown but possibly female.
Medium occipital flattening.
This body had been placed in a shallow pit in the floor of Room B6 against the west wall. The pit did not appear to have been sealed; in fact, the top of the skull was at a level slightly higher than the room floor. The body was flexed, on its right side, with the head to the northwest. This room had been sealed off, apparently from the Room B3 side, perhaps as a result of this burial. Despite the fact that it seemed to have been a deliberate burial, no artifacts were in association.

Incomplete Skeletal Remains

In addition to the skeletons in Kiva B and Room B6, occasional human bones were found in the fill of four rooms and Kiva A. All appeared to be from fully grown individuals.

Room A2, fill: Scapula, left; distal end of femur, left.
Room A3, fill: Metatarsal.
Room B1, fill: Lumbar vertebra.
Room B3, fill: Ulna, right; radius, right.
Kiva A, fill: Femurs, left and right; tibia, right; fibula, right; talus, right; calcaneum, right; several ribs. All of the foregoing seemed to be from one individual. A second individual was represented by a right and a left talus.

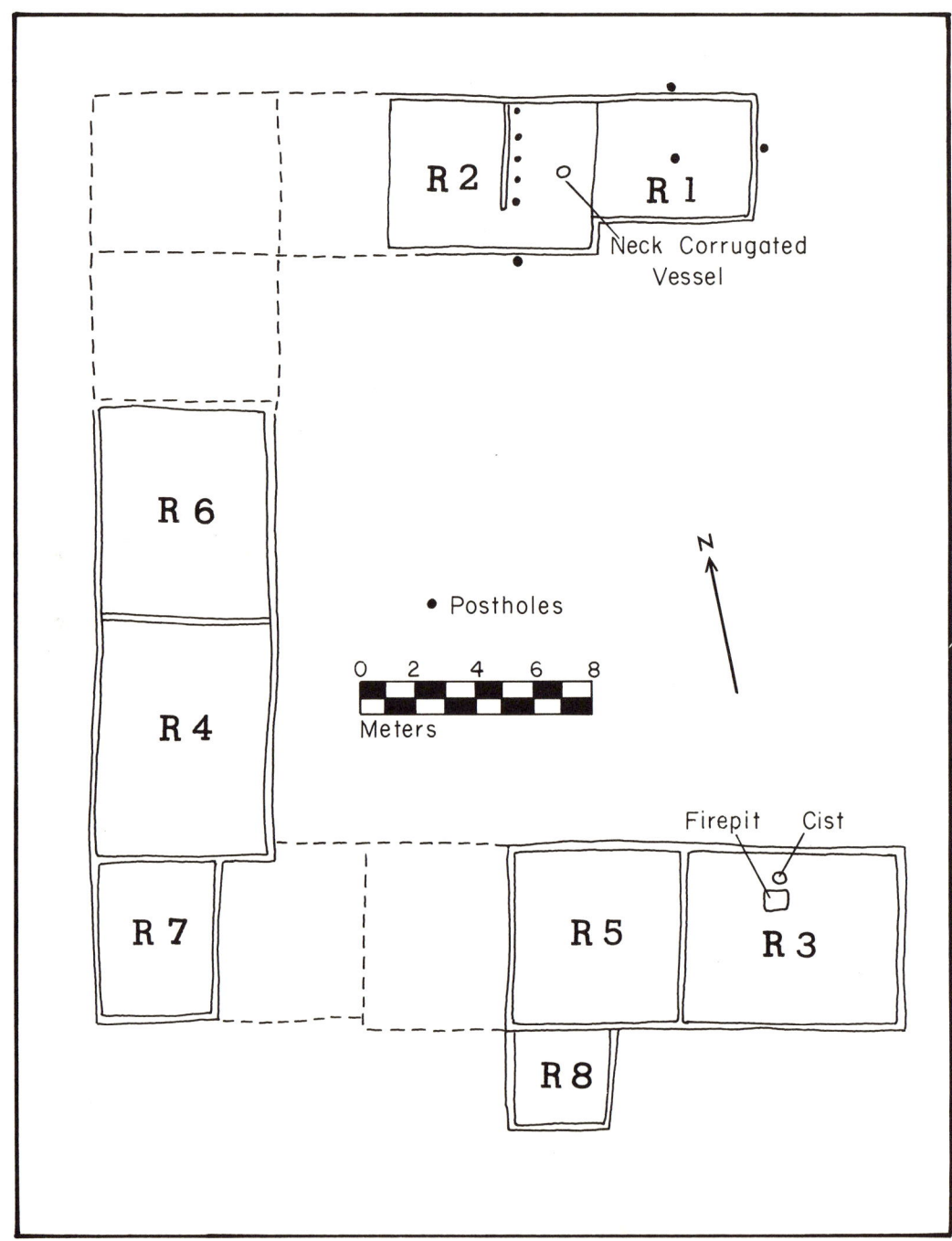

Figure 96. Plan of Site 601.

Site 601

The northeast slope of Mariana Mesa is striped with numerous small valleys that open onto a larger valley, lying between Mariana Mesa and Trechado Peak. The largest of these valleys, the main portion of which is over two miles long and just under one quarter of a mile wide, contains two of the sites excavated. Site 601 was located some 6 m above the valley floor atop a gravel terrace bordering the west side of the valley. The tops of the terraces have a steady stand of juniper, and the valley floor is covered with a heavy growth of grass. No deep arroyo has developed in the valley floor.

The site was a U-shaped unit of a single row of rooms with the open portion of the U to the east. The end room of each wing (Rooms 1 and 3) was completely cleared. Two other rooms (Rooms 2 and 4) were partially excavated while four other rooms were outlined or trenched. No kiva depression was evident within the wings of the U as was the case at Site 481. A large circular depression, 21 m northeast of Room 1, was observed and tested with indefinite results.

Site 601 was the earliest excavated example of the multiple, contiguous-roomed surface units in the Mariana Mesa area. As the size of the community grew, rooms were added, resulting finally in a U-shaped structure. Double rows of contiguous rooms were apparently a feature of a later period. As was the case with the two other early sites, no kiva was definitely in association. All rooms except Rooms 1 and 2 seem to have been constructed of rough lava-cobble masonry, though possibly this masonry did not extend to the full height of the wall. The walls of Rooms 1 and 2 were of jacal and adobe outlined with lava cobbles or perhaps with a low cobble-masonry base. Room 1 was serving as a storeroom or granary at the time the site was abandoned. If these two rooms were the first built (a hypothesis postulated solely because of the general similarity in their construction to the slightly earlier structures at Site 188), then they may also have served at an earlier time as living quarters. It is possible, however, that the selection of jacal construction reflected a desire on the part of the builders for a simple, rapid construction technique to provide storage space or perhaps to shelter the produce of a harvest.

Insofar as could be determined by the limited excavation that was done, the earliest rooms were those of the north wing with the site gradually growing southward. One or two rooms were added at a time. Room 3, on the extreme east end of the south wing, appeared to have been built as an independent unit with rooms subsequently added to the west; and in one instance to the south, until a junction with the main unit was effected. The size and growth of the site suggested a larger, more stable community than had previously existed in the area.

Along with the adoption of surface masonry, this site provided the first indication of the changeover from the basin-and-trough metate to the slab metate for grinding. The manos, however, were still short and used on only one face.

Nearly all the pottery vessels were jars of one form or another. The only jar form exemplified for the white-slipped vessels was a short globular-necked style with no sharp juncture between the neck and the body of the vessel. Nearly all the brown-paste vessels were open-mouthed, neck-corrugated jars, though the existence of a few wiped-finish plain jars was suggested from sherds. Bowls of any type were extremely rare (only 25 sherds). The white-slipped bowls apparently had slightly outsloping walls, while the walls of the brown-paste bowls were more nearly straight. All of the latter had smudged interiors, a characteristic that appeared considerably earlier in this region than to the north of Mariana Mesa.

DATING CONSIDERATIONS

Although no tree-ring dates were recovered from Site 601, its occupation can be estimated approximately by inference from the ceramics found there. Red Mesa Black-on-white and Escavada Black-on-white were the principal painted types, and they have been dated by Breternitz (1966, pp. 74, 90) respectively at about A.D. 850 + − 1125 and at A.D. 925+ − 1125.

Architecture, tool types, and ceramic decoration, taken together, suggest the temporal placement of this site relative to the others excavated. It seems to have been occupied slightly later than Site 188 but earlier than Site 494. Thus it might have been occupied as late as A.D. 1125, a date consistent with the architecture, which is of late Pueblo II – early Pueblo III style. This would be the very latest possible date, however, and probably slightly earlier — around A.D. 1000 – 1100 would be a reliable estimate of its occupation.

LIVING AND EXCAVATION UNITS

Room 1

Rooms 1 and 2, on the basis of architecture, appeared to have been the earliest built, for both were of jacal construction. The footings of the walls consisted of irregular lava cobbles set in liberal quantities of adobe. The walls themselves were of upright poles 3 to 4 cm in diameter (set into the adobe of the wall base) to which smaller poles were lashed horizontally. Adobe several centimeters thick was plastered over this framework. Room 1 burned and a considerable quantity of adobe bearing the impression of the poles and lashings was found in and around the room. Major support posts (8 to 10 cm in diameter) were placed at the center point of each wall (none was found at the south wall), set 10 cm into the ground just outside the line of adobe and stone. Another pole was placed in the center of the room. No satisfactory explanation of the exact technique of supporting the roof, based on this evidence, has suggested itself.

The floor of Room 1 was of packed clay, and was only 10 to 15 cm below the present ground surface. There were no floor features other than the center post. Charred kernels and corncobs were found scattered over the floor in all parts of the room. Charred beans *(Phaseolus vulgaris)* were strewn over the floor in the southeast corner of the room.

ARTIFACTS

Fill and floor

   Mano; hematite (2 oz)

Room 2

Room 2 was similar in construction to Room 1 though slightly larger. The east post (which apparently served Rooms 1 and 2) and the north post were within the walls of the room; but the south post was outside. Only the eastern half of the room was cleared. An adobe ridge and a series of four small postholes 2 to 3 cm in diameter and 5 to 10 cm deep, set into the floor of the room in a line between the north, center, and south main support posts, indicated that this room had been divided in half by a north – south jacal wall. The apparent absence of posts in the southern quarter of this wall suggested that the doorway was located in this area. No lava cobbles were present at the base of this wall. Such cobbles may have been used only for outside walls. The floor, like that of Room 1, was of hard-packed clay. There were no floor features.

ARTIFACTS

Fill and floor

   2 manos; metate fragment; neck-corrugated jar (fig. 98)

Room 3

Unlike Rooms 1 and 2, the fill of Room 3 contained abundant lava cobbles presumably deriving from the exterior walls. These walls, which had been set into a trench excavated 5 to 10 cm below the room floor, were constructed of irregular lava cobbles set in adobe. Little or no attempt was made to have any smooth side of the rocks facing the room. None of the walls was more than three courses high when excavated.

The floor was of a slightly darker material than the fill and was located just above a dark red clay, which seemed to be the native soil of the terrace. The surface of the floor was spongy and very crumbly. A rectangular adobe-lined and plastered firepit, containing ashes, was located in the center of the north half of the room. Fifteen centimeters north of the firepit, there was an unlined hole in the floor 10 cm in diameter and 10 cm deep, which contained a small amount of charcoal.

ARTIFACTS

Fill and floor

   Mano; 2 fragments; metate fragment; pecking stone; stone bead; worked stone; 6 stone chips; hematite (3 oz)

Room 4

Room 4 was only partially excavated. The contents of the fill closely resembled those of Room 3.

ARTIFACTS

Fill

Metate fragment; point (#2818, fig. 113n); neck-corrugated jar

Other Rooms

Four other rooms were briefly tested. They appeared to be similar to Room 3. No floor features were encountered, but there probably had been some.

ARTIFACTS

Fill

Metate fragment; 3 stone chips; fragment of point

Circular Depression

A slight depression 12 m in diameter was observed 21 m northeast of the northeast corner of Room 1. Nine test holes were made by auger and a small test trench was dug into this depression in an attempt to determine if it was a cultural feature, specifically a kiva. The test holes extended in a line from just outside one edge of the depression to the opposite edge. The first two holes encountered rock almost immediately. Through the center portion of the depression, rock generally was encountered between 100 and 140 cm, though in two cases it was found at 50 to 60 cm. A thin layer of an unidentified chalky white substance found just below the surface outside of the depression ended abruptly at its edge. Charcoal was brought up from a depth of 130 cm in one hole. The trench was 3 m long, 75 cm deep, and extended from within the depression to beyond it. There was no indication of any wall.

The depression itself, the abrupt end of the chalky substance, and the charcoal suggested that this may have been a cultural feature; but the absence of any discernible wall and the occurrence of rock at 50 cm near the center of the depression (which could be individual loose boulders) made any identification extremely tenuous.

Compare the hypothetical "dance plaza" at Site 636, about 16 miles southwest of Site 601 (Smith 1973, pp. 9, 10).

POTTERY — DESCRIPTIVE TYPOLOGY

White-slipped Pottery

MATERIAL: ROW A

1. Dense gray paste with opaque angular material and rare sand inclusions — mode key (D)
   Slip flat-white, thinly applied — modes (b) and (h)
   Mineral paint — mode (a)
2. Gray friable paste with sand and rare opaque angular inclusions — mode key (E)
   Slip flat-white, thinly applied — modes (b) and (h)
   Mineral paint — mode (a)
3. Gray friable paste with sand and rare opaque angular inclusions — mode key (E)
   Slip flat-white, applied thinly with paste visible in patches — modes (b) and (i)
   Mineral paint — mode (a)
4. Dense cream-colored paste with sand inclusions — mode key (J)
   No slip — mode (a)
   Mineral paint — mode (a)

The dense and the friable gray pastes were about equally popular and exhibited a similar range of decorative elements. The vessels of dense gray paste were better finished than those of the friable gray paste. Similarly it was only on the friable gray paste that the poorly or thinly applied slip was used. These two paste types may represent local production, perhaps the output of two artisans or groups of potters. The hypothesis that the vessels of material type 4 (dense cream-colored paste with sand) were imported rests primarily on their scarcity at the site.

VESSEL SHAPES AND AREAS SLIPPED AND PAINTED: ROW B

1: Bowl — mode (a)
   Interior and exterior slipped, interior painted — modes (a), (b), and (c)
2: Bowl — mode (a)
   Interior slipped and painted — modes (a) and (c)
3: Narrow-necked jar — mode (d)
   Exterior slipped and painted — modes (b) and (d)
4: Ladle — mode (h)
   Interior and exterior slipped, interior painted — modes (a), (b), and (c)

Jars were the most popular form. Bowls and ladles of any type were sufficiently rare to suggest that some nonceramic objects served in their place.

SURFACE FINISH: ROW C

1: Slipped surfaces slightly undulating, smooth to the touch, entire surface reflecting light, polishing marks occasionally evident, polished before application of paint — modes (a), (e), (g), and (i)
2: Slipped surfaces even, smooth, or slick to the

touch, otherwise similar to type 1 — modes (b), (e), (g), and (i)

3: Similar to type 1 except that only the high points were lustrous — modes (a), (e), (g), and (j)

4: Similar to type 2 except with matte surfaces — modes (b), (e), (g), and (k)

5: Slipped surface slightly undulating, gritty to the touch, matte — modes (c) and (k)

6: Slipped surface even but gritty because of protruding sand inclusions, matte — modes (d) and (k)

Types 5 and 6 appeared not to have been polished with a hard polishing tool.

DECORATION: ROW D

1: Bands of straight-line diagonal hatching in both rectilinear and curvilinear patterns (generally not on a single vessel). Hatching lines same thickness as bordering lines, and widely spaced, with approximately three lines per centimeter.

2: Widely spaced thin (approximately 2 mm) parallel lines, in rectilinear patterns. Lines occasionally cross at the corners, forming patterns with solid triangles with pendent dots. Occasionally, interlocking-line scrolls extending from the ends of the triangles. Broad (approximately 1 cm) lines sometimes utilized. Closely similar to type 1 at Site 486 and type 1 at Site 188.

3: Solid triangles pendent from rectilinear lines, often interlocking to form a negative zigzag pattern.

4: Solid squares connected with fine lines and interspersed with rectilinear squiggly lines.

5: Bands approximately 1 cm wide filled with widely spaced diagonal squiggly lines. Lines fine, occasionally crossing at the corners.

6: Checkerboard design with fine (approximately 1 mm) bordering and framing lines.

The rims of descriptive types 1122 and 1241 were black.

Plain and Corrugated Pottery

MATERIAL: ROW A

1: Brown paste with sand inclusions — mode key (H)

2: Gray paste with coarse sand inclusions — mode key (J)

VESSEL SHAPE: ROW B

1: Bowl — mode (a)
2: Eccentric — mode (i)
3: Open-mouthed jar — mode (e)

The plainware bowls had sides more nearly perpendicular than was the case with the white-slipped bowls; all plainware bowls had smudged interiors.

The jar was the dominant form. All or nearly all were open-mouthed, neck-corrugated vessels. No rim sherds of descriptive type 1330 were found and sherds of this type may represent portions of the base of neck-corrugated jars; but basal sherds, from this and other sites, identifiable as portions of neck-corrugated vessels, had the smooth finish of descriptive type 1340, whereas at other sites, some plain vessels did have a rough or wiped appearance similar to the sherds of descriptive type 1330 from Site 601. For this reason these sherds were believed to represent plain jars. The neck-corrugated jars of both material types were similar in form.

Sherds of descriptive types 1311, 1312, and 1340 could and probably did come from different portions of the same or similar jars, with 1340 representing portions of the base, 1312 the confluence of base and corrugated neck, and 1311 the neck-corrugated portion of the vessel. A similar relationship existed between descriptive types 2321, 2322, and 2323.

A vessel that may be similar to the so-called eccentric vessel from Site 601 (fig. 99) is illustrated by Gladwin (1945, pl. 22g, h), but that vessel had a vertical loop handle.

CONSTRUCTION AND SURFACE FINISH: ROW C

1: Coiled counterclockwise, indented with left thumb pointing up — mode (a)
  Interiors smooth and even, coils unobliterated on the exterior — mode (a)
2: Coiled clockwise, indented with the right thumb pointing up — mode (c)
  Interiors smooth and even, coils unobliterated on the exterior — mode (a)
3: Presumably coiled, direction of coiling unknown — mode (d)
  Surfaces even but matte with small striations, gritty to the touch because of protruding temper — mode (e)
4: Presumably coiled, direction unknown — mode (d).
  Exposed surfaces even, smooth to the touch, occasionally with polishing streaks — mode (b)
5: Coiled counterclockwise, indented with the left thumb pointing down — mode (b)
  Interiors smooth and even, coils unobliterated on the exterior — mode (a)
6: Presumably coiled, direction unknown — mode (d)
  Exposed surfaces even but matte and gritty to the touch, occasional small pits in surface — mode (c)

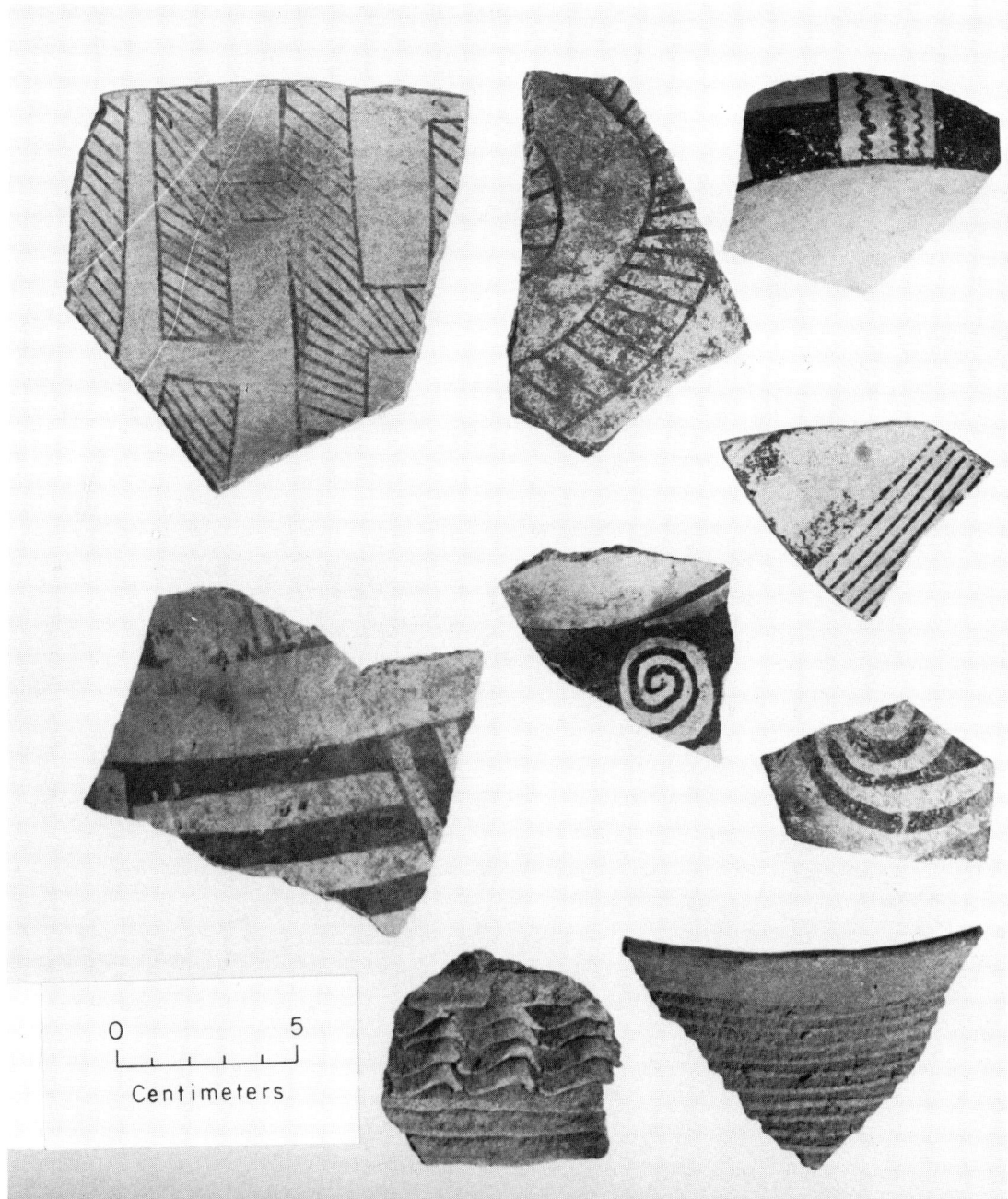

Figure 97. Typical sherds from Site 601.

Noncorrugated surfaces tended to be slightly undulating with the low portions indicating the area of jointure between coils. On this basis the coil size is estimated to be about 1.5 to 2 by 0.5 cm. A new coil usually abutted the end of the preceding coil rather than overlapped it.

Interiors of jars were unusually well smoothed. As a consequence, some sherds from plain bowls may have been counted as jar bases but all bowl rims were from smudged vessels.

The evidence is not completely satisfactory but the indications are that the vessels of material type 1 were

White-slipped Pottery

Provenience		Totals	\multicolumn{17}{c}{Descriptive Types}	Bases
			A	1	1	1	1	1	1	1	1	1	1	2	2	2	2	3	4	
			B	1	2	2	3	3	3	3	3	3	4	4	1	3	3	4	1	1
			C	2	1	4	1	1	1	1	2	4	1	2	1	3	5	2	2	6
			D	2	2	1	1	2	3	4	1	1	5	2	6	2	2	?	1	?
	Totals	511		1	2	1	5	35	45	8	60	1	2	6	3	190	8	1	26	5	112
Room 2	Fill	295			2	1		33	45	8	60			5			7		24		110
Room 2	Floor	7						1						1			1		2		2
Room 3	Fill	113										1	2			110*					
Room 3	Floor	78		1												77*					
Room 4	Fill	11												3	3					5	
Room 5	Fill	6					5	1													
Room 6	Fill	1																	1		

* Nearly all from a single vessel.

Plain and Corrugated Pottery

Provenience		Totals	\multicolumn{15}{c}{Descriptive Types}
			A	1	1	1	1	1	1	1	1	1	2	2	2	2	2
			B	1	2	3	3	3	3	3	3	3	3	3	3	3	3
			C	4	1	1	1	1	3	4	4	5	1	2	2	2	6
			D	5	4	1	2	7	8	0	0	7	6	1	1	2	3	0
	Totals	805		21	1	121	28	1	3	9	512	1	1	2	41	3	7	54
Room 1	Fill	26		10							14	1		1				
Room 2	Fill	533				89	23				317				41	3	7	53
Room 2	Floor	107				22			3		80		1*					1
Room 3	Fill	59		4		6	4				45							
Room 3	Floor	61		5		4	1				50			1				
Room 4	Fill	4		2	1*						1							
Room 5	Fill	6							1		5							
Room 6	Fill	9								9								

* Restorable vessel

Table 19. Distribution by descriptive types of all pottery sherds from Site 601.

coiled counterclockwise, whereas those of material type 2 were coiled clockwise.

DECORATIVE EFFECT: ROW D

0: Absence of any decoration — mode (a).
1: Narrow clapboard corrugation — mode (b). There were 2 to 3 coils per cm. An exception was the vessel of descriptive type 1212; here the three neck coils were each 2 cm wide.
2: Plain and clapboard corrugation — mode (e). On all but three sherds of this type the first (lowest) clapboard coil bore some form of decoration. Most of these (representing about ten vessels) had been incised with a chevron design (on half the vessels the chevrons pointed to the right, on the other to the left). On one vessel the lower coil had been decorated with vertical incisions (made with the left thumbnail), and on another with parallel diagonal incisions. On approximately three vessels, the lower coil had been indented. These indentations were large (one per cm), giving a wavy effect. The coils on this vessel were slightly larger than on most.
3: Pattern-indented corrugated — mode (d). At this site, this designation refers to neck-corrugated vessels the central four or five coils of which were

indented with large wavy indentations with the right thumb pointing up. The one or two vessels of this type appeared to be, in shape and decorative effect, identical to a restorable vessel from Site 188 (fig. 94), but at Site 601 the vessels were all of material mode key (J), whereas at Site 188 they were of material mode key (H) and the indentations were made with the left thumb.

4: Interior of vessel smudged — mode (g). Bowls only.

5: Plain and indented-corrugated — mode (e). The only vessel of this type was the one found on the floor of Room 2 (fig. 98), descriptive type 1355. All four neck coils had broad wavy indentations made with the left thumb pointing down.

POTTERY - PROBLEM TYPES

Regional Time-Space Types

WHITE-SLIPPED POTTERY

The black-on-white pottery of Site 601 appeared to be late Red Mesa or late Escavada Black-on-white. The finish was better than usually attributed to either of these types and bowls were generally slipped on the exterior, but these traits are consistent with the pottery-making practices of earlier and later sites in the Mariana Mesa area. The thin, watery slip, usually characteristic of late Red Mesa and Gallup Black-on-white, was more common at this site than at any other excavated near Mariana Mesa, but still constituted less than 10 percent of the white-slipped pottery.

RED-SLIPPED POTTERY

None present.

Figure 98. Site 601. Neck-corrugated vessel from the floor of Room 2.

PLAIN AND CORRUGATED POTTERY

The plainware bowls may be similar to Reserve Smudged but no type sherds were available for comparison. The neck-corrugated jars without a section of indented corrugation were classified as Mimbres Neck-corrugated, though the presence of basal coil decoration on vessels of this type should be noted. This feature did not occur on such vessels at Sites 188 and 486.

There were no vessels with overall indented corrugation.

OTHER OBJECTS OF CLAY

Figurine: 1 specimen (fig. 115e)

A solid clay figure apparently representing a quadruped was recovered. The head section just forward of the front legs was missing as were three of the legs. The barrellike body was 1.5 cm in diameter and the section remaining was 4 cm long. The tail was represented by a nubbin of clay 1 cm long pointing upward. The front legs were directed straight down but the rear legs were directed at a 45° angle backward and were slightly spraddled. The legs consisted of circular nubbins of clay, more elongated (1.5 cm) than the tail but similarly bare of any detail.

Sherd Discs: 2 specimens

Both were roughly chipped from white-slipped sherds to diameters of 4.5 and 6 cm. The edges were not ground smooth.

STONE ARTIFACTS

Manos: 7 specimens

All manos were rectangular in cross section with one face used. Four were of sandstone, the other three of vesicular basalt. On four of the manos the ends of the used faces sloped up, indicating that they were used on trough metates. The used face was flat or only slightly convex in the long dimension, so that use on a basin metate is unlikely. The other manos had received so little use that the shape of the associated metates could not be judged. One sandstone mano (Room 1, fill) exhibited considerable wear and had apparently been associated with a slab metate. This mano and the single sandstone slab metate from Room 4 are the first appearance of the slab-style metate in the area. The lengths of the manos ranged from 19.1 to 24.2 cm with an average of 22.6 cm; the widths ranged from 10.5 to 13 cm with an average of 11.6 cm; three of the sandstone manos were between

2.8 and 3.5 cm thick, and the fourth was 6.8 cm thick; the three basalt manos were 6.4, 6.6, and 8.5 cm thick. Two of the basalt manos had finger grips centrally located on each of their long sides. The one basalt mano without finger grips (Room 2, floor) was also the largest (24 by 13 by 8.5 cm) and may have been designed for a somewhat different purpose than the others.

Metates: 4 specimens

Two metates (from the trench and Room 2, fill) each had a small (approximately 12 by 14 cm) oval working surface, pecked into the natural surface of a basalt boulder. The third specimen (Room 3, fill) was a fragment of a closed-trough metate of sandstone. The trough was about 22 cm wide and 2 cm deep. The closed end was rounded. The final specimen (Room 4, fill) was a coarse-grained slab metate of vesicular basalt. Its dimensions were 25.8 by 22.6 by 4.2 cm. The bottom and sides had been roughly shaped.

Polishing Pebble: 1 specimen

A single polishing pebble (3.5 by 2.5 by 2.4 cm) came from one of the trenches. It was of fine-grained volcanic material, very smooth, with five facets.

Pecking Stone: 1 specimen

This cobble, from the fill of Room 3 (9 by 8.4 by 5.3 cm), had a flattened oval cross section and all surfaces exhibited pecking. Whether this pecking resulted from use or from preparation for use is not known. If the latter, this tool would more nearly resemble the so-called rubbing stones.

Hammer: 1 specimen

The cross section of this basalt hammer in top view was roughly egg-shaped, while in the other two dimensions the cross section was a rounded rectangle. All surfaces were shaped by pecking and somewhat rough; the ends were flat. The groove was centrally located and approximately 1 cm deep. It was three-quarter-grooved but only 1 cm separated the ends of the groove. The height was 10.6 cm, the length 8.3 cm, and the width 6.8 cm. It came from the fill of Room 3.

Points and Knives: 3 specimens

The specimens were of obsidian, petrified wood, and chalcedony. Only the one of obsidian was complete. It was triangular, 2.4 cm long, with a straight base and side notches and, on one side, a second side notch. The chalcedony point was the largest (approximately 5 cm). It also had side notches but the base was slightly convex. Only the central portion of the third specimen was recovered. It apparently was basically triangular in shape and came from the fill of Room 4. The other two were found on the surface.

Flake and Chips: 25 specimens

One flake (6 by 3.6 cm) exhibited use chips along its naturally sharp convex side (Room 3, fill). Eighteen chips were found in the trenches and six came from the fill of Room 3. All were of petrified wood with dimensions that generally ranged between 2 and 4 cm.

Scoria Object: 1 specimen

An irregularly shaped object of volcanic scoria suggestive of a mano came from one of the trenches. Its dimensions were 7.4 by 4.8 by 1.8 cm. A somewhat similar object was found at Site 616. With its flat surfaces and spongelike appearance, it would have made an excellent abrader for use on soft materials such as animal skins.

Bead: 1 specimen

A single bead of red beadstone was found on the floor of Room 3. It was 0.6 cm in diameter and 0.2 cm thick with a biconically drilled central hole.

RAW MATERIALS

An irregular piece of hematite came from the floor of Room 1 and a similar piece from the floor of Room 3. No abraded surfaces were visible on either specimen.

SUBSISTENCE MATERIALS

The floor of Room 1 was littered with corn, both kernels and cobs, and in the southeast corner of this room was a considerable quantity of common red beans (*Phaseolus vulgaris*). No other vegetal materials and no identifiable animal bones were recovered.

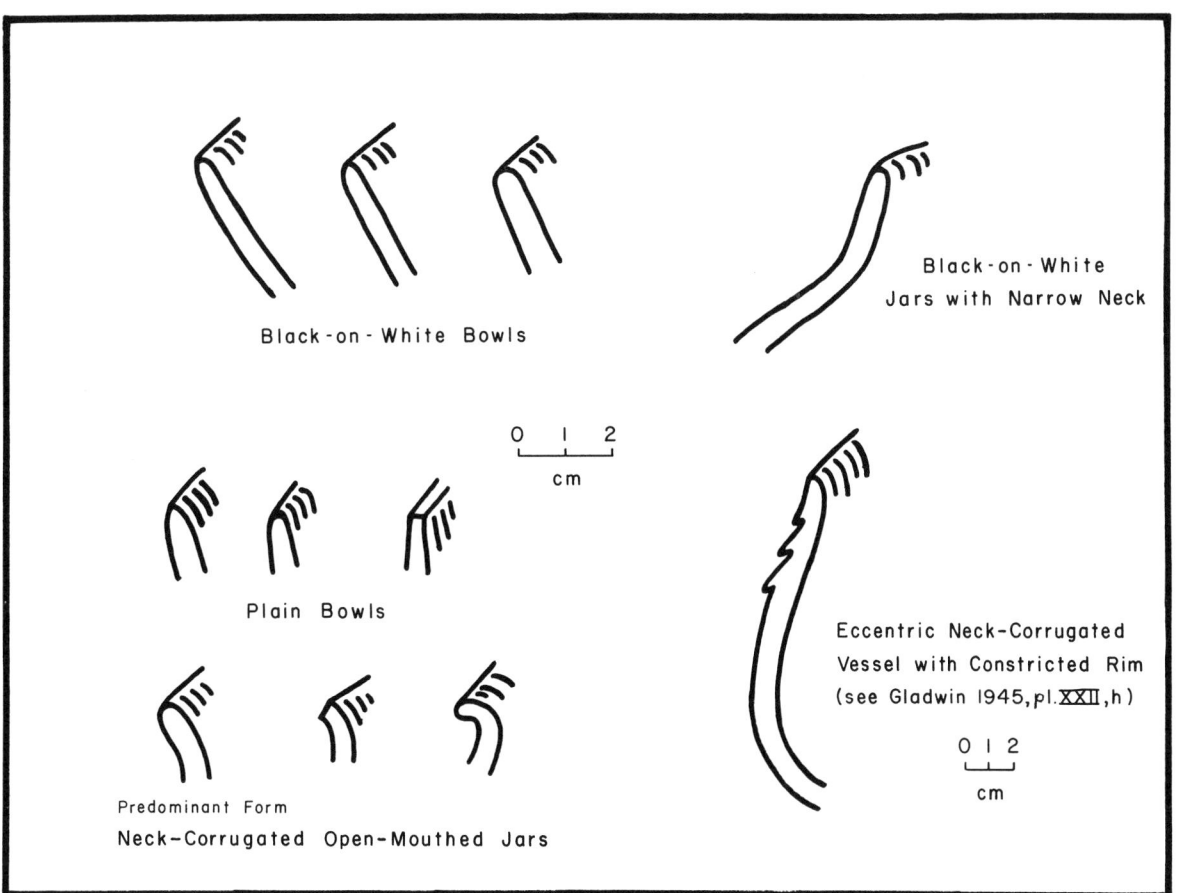

Figure 99. Pottery-rim and vessel forms from Site 601.

258 • Mariana Mesa

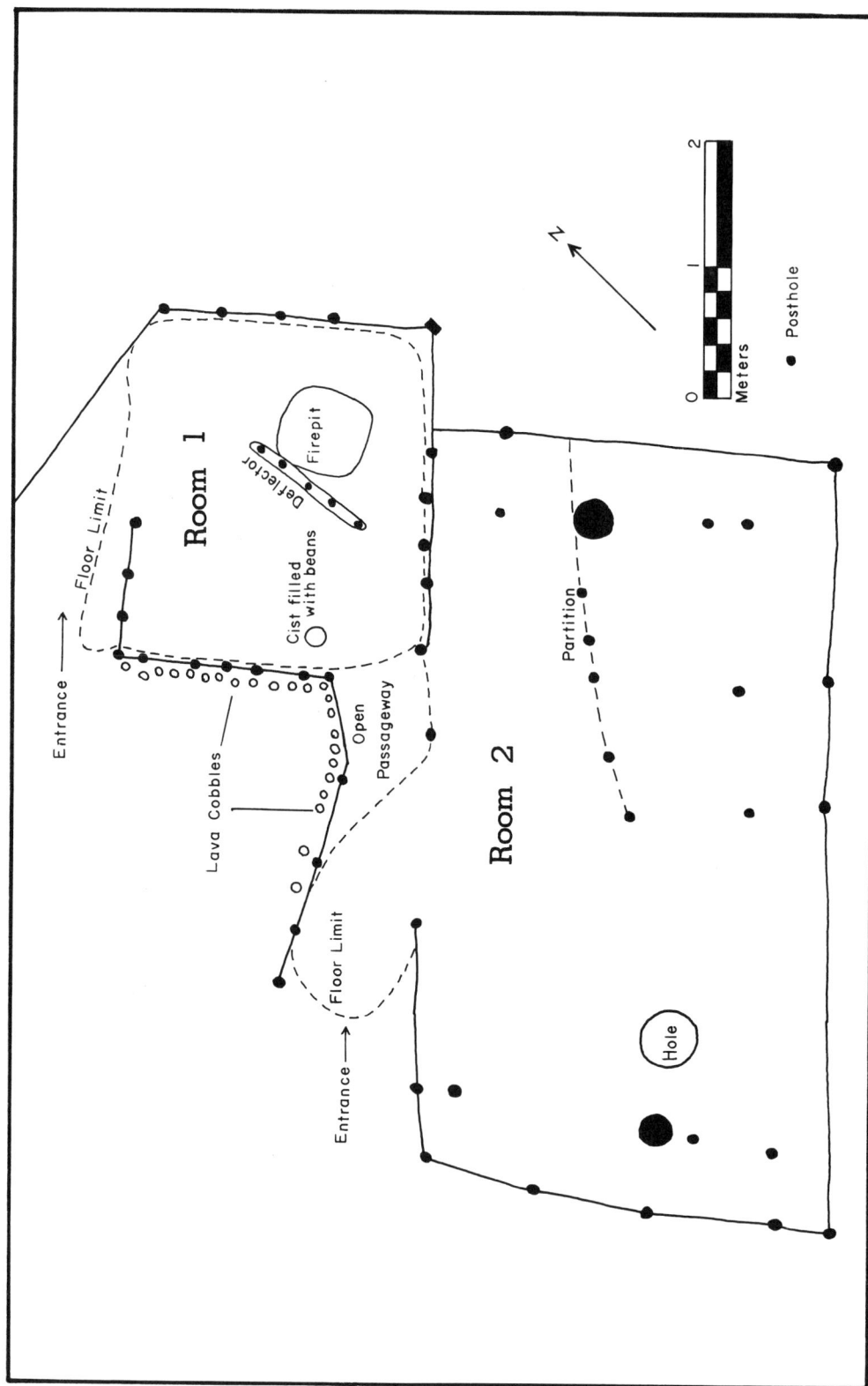

Figure 100. Plan of Site 188.

Site 188

Site 188 was located to the east and directly across the valley from Site 601. It was situated on the north end of a low gravel terrace that borders the east side of the valley. At the point where the site was located, the terrace rises no more than 3 m above the general valley floor. A few piñon and juniper trees grow along this section of the ridge but do not occur in profusion until somewhat higher up the ridge.

The only surface indication of Site 188 was the occurrence of numerous sherds. Extensive trenching during the 1950 season finally revealed a small rectangular jacal structure. While backfilling this site at the close of the season, we noticed indications of a second unit, which was excavated the following year (fig. 100).

A number of two-meter squares were excavated during the search for occupation levels or living units. The upper 40 cm in these pits consisted of light-brown sandy soil with occasional flecks of charcoal and small ash deposits. Sherds and other artifacts were generally present in small numbers. One deposit of ash, 50 by 30 cm in diameter and 10 cm thick, was located 20 cm below the present surface at a point approximately 3 m south of what was later designated as Room 2. No prepared pit was discernible nor were any stones in association, but this may have been an outdoor hearth. Below 40 cm the soil became a hard, dense caliche, barren of cultural materials.

THE HOUSE

The house consisted of two partially adjoining surface rooms, the floors of which were 20 to 35 cm below the present surface of the ground. During construction, the builders probably excavated no deeper than was necessary to clear away the softer topsoil and reach the hard underlying caliche. This dense soil formed the floor of the rooms. For this reason the floors were often difficult to trace. The floors of both rooms were fairly level, if somewhat uneven, and that of Room 2 was 15 cm lower than that of Room 1.

In all probability, these two rooms formed the dwelling of a single family. This family may have been the sole occupants of the low ridge on which their house was located and they may have had the entire small valley to themselves, for there were no indications of a large population in the area of Mariana Mesa at that date. On the other hand, present-day surface indications of sites of this period consist almost entirely of sherds. Houses are difficult to locate and it is not impossible that several other house units may have been present in the immediate vicinity of the one excavated.

Room 2 may have served the family as sleeping quarters and for general activities not carried on outdoors. Room 1, with its firepit, small storage pit, and small floor area, could have been a workroom connected principally with cooking and food preparation. This was the first known occurrence in the area of a unit of contiguous rooms.

DATING CONSIDERATIONS

The single tree-ring specimen from Site 188 provided a cutting date of A.D. 1071 (Bannister, Hannah, and Robinson 1970, p. 13), which would seem to fix the end of occupation at a time somewhat later than that. The ceramic complex was characterized by Red Mesa Black-on-white, which has been dated at about A.D. 850+ – 1125 (Breternitz 1966, p. 90). Thus, an end date of around A.D. 1075 would be consistent with both sources of evidence, although the beginning cannot be satisfactorily estimated. On this hypothesis the occupation Site 188 would have been between that of Site 601 and that of Site 486.

LIVING AND EXCAVATION UNITS

Room 1

Room 1 had an area of about 6.55 sq m, measuring 2.55 m southeast-northwest, by 2.60 m southwest-north-east. In its construction a line of upright posts 20 to 40 cm apart was set into the ground outlining the main floor area and, presumably, a light stringer was placed across the tops of these poles to support the roof. These wall posts were 7 to 10 cm in diameter and had been set into the floor to a depth of 20 to 30 cm. The base of one of these posts found *in situ* was badly charred, suggesting that fire was at least one of the means employed in the cutting and dressing of these timbers. A second post, in the north corner, had flat sides as if the original log had been dressed by splitting. A quantity of burned adobe bearing impressions of smaller sticks and a reedlike grass (*Gramineae sporabolus* or *sacaton*?) was found in and around this room. The wall construction seemed to have been a jacallike arrangement with sticks and reeds tied to and/or woven between the upright posts and then covered with a rather thick layer of adobe.

The floor features of Room 1 included a firepit, a deflector, and a small storage cist. The firepit was a rounded rectangle, 50 by 55 cm, excavated into the floor to a depth of 15 cm. The sides sloped slightly inward and the bottom was irregular. The deflector, set at an angle to the firepit, consisted of a thin wall of adobe supported by five small upright stakes. Perhaps twigs were woven between these stakes for additional strength. The floor cist was a round-bottomed hole with a mouth diameter of 14 cm and a depth of 12 cm. It contained a quantity of charred common red beans *(Phaseolus vulgaris)*. A portion of a red beadstone pendant and a small quantity of hematite were also found on the floor.

Room 2

Room 2 was larger than Room 1, with an area of 18.80 sq m — the southeast-northwest dimension being 3.20 m, and the southwest-northeast 5.90 m — and had been constructed somewhat differently. Here upright posts similar to those used in Room 1 were set into the floor in a line some 50 cm inside the extreme edge of the floor area, but they were more widely spaced than were those in Room 1. More or less in the center of each of the two short sides, there was a single large post (20 and 27 cm in diameter respectively). These probably supported a center ridgepole, which bore the main burden of the roof. The walls seemed to have been constructed by leaning poles at a slight angle from the ground at the edge of the floor area to stringers lying across the tops of the inner row of poles. These outer poles were smaller in diameter and were not set as deeply in the ground. They formed a framework to which other poles, brush, reeds, and grass were lashed. This material may have been the only wall covering, for very little adobe was associated with this room.

The entrance to Room 2 was in the center of the western wall, but the south end of this wall angled out to form a short entranceway, so that initial entry was gained in the southwest corner. The entrance to Room 1 probably was similar in design, for, although no posts were found outlining such an entrance, it is significant that this southwest corner was the only area where a floor could be traced beyond the limits of the upright wall posts. There may have been an open passage between the south corner of Room 1 and the entrance of Room 2. If so, traffic was not sufficiently heavy for the floor in this area to have been preserved. Perhaps, if an opening was present, it simply served as a passthrough for materials. The rather odd angle of the deflector in Room 1 may reflect an attempt to compromise in protecting the firepit from both the draft caused by the doorway and that caused by such a passageway.

There was a large circular hole in the floor of Room 2. The sides of this hole were straight and the bottom flat but it was not smoothly finished. It had a diameter of 36 cm and a depth of 20 cm. No ash or other material was found in association providing any clue to the purpose of this feature. A small quantity of hematite was on the floor. The northern half of the room appeared to have been divided by a partition extending south from the north wall to the middle of the room.

SUBSISTENCE MATERIALS

Some two dozen fragments of animal bones were recovered. Two seemed to be rabbit or hare bones, and one was from a large bird. The others could not be identified but were from animals of various sizes up to that of a deer. These bones were found in the trenches and in the fill of both rooms, and one was on the floor of Room 1 adjacent to the floor cist.

In and immediately around the floor cist in Room 1 there was a quantity of common red beans *(Phaseolus vulgaris)* and some charred corncobs and kernels. A small amount of charred corn was also found in one of the trenches.

POTTERY — DESCRIPTIVE TYPOLOGY

White-slipped Pottery

The white-slipped pottery consisted of bowls and narrow-necked jars with widely spaced decorations in black paint. The bowls were all of the same material and all were well finished. The jars exhibited greater variation in materials and in finishing techniques. Nearly all of the unslipped pottery was in the form of open-mouthed jars with clapboard-corrugated necks. The jars of gray paste differed slightly from those made of brown paste in that on the former the unobliterated coils were flatter and broader, and the coarse sand temper tended to protrude. There were four sherds from small, plain, straight-sided, smudged bowls and two from a globular, plain, neckless jar. No red-slipped pottery was present. The entire pottery sample was too small for any reliable conclusions to be drawn but the diversity displayed in materials, techniques, and their combination suggested that these vessels were not all the work of a single artisan. This is particularly interesting in view of the small number of people occupying the site. Were several potters active within this small social unit? Was this a temporary residence of a group that at other times resided in closer contact with other similar semi-independent groups, perhaps obtaining some of their pottery from these occasional neighbors? Or did they regularly trade for pottery with groups residing elsewhere and with whom they had only transitory contact?

In general, the white-slipped pottery at Site 188 appeared to represent a slightly later period in the development of the regional black-on-white tradition than the pottery at Site 486; but, while the pottery and general features of house construction at Site 188 seemed to place its occupation intermediate in time between Sites 601 and 486, it is unlikely that any long period separated the three sites. I suggest that Site 188 was occupied around A.D. 1000–1075.

MATERIAL: ROW A

1: Dense gray paste with opaque angular fragments and quartz sand inclusions — mode key (D)
   No slip — mode (a)
   Mineral paint — mode (a)
2: Dense gray paste with opaque angular fragments and quartz sand inclusions — mode key (D)
   Slip dull white of same material as the paste, thinly applied — modes (e) and (h)
   Mineral paint — mode (a)
3: Dense gray paste with opaque angular fragments and quartz sand inclusions — mode key (D)
   Slip flat-white, thinly applied — modes (b) and (h)
   Mineral paint — mode (a)
4: Dense cream-colored paste with coarse sand inclusions — mode key (J)
   Slip flat-white, thinly applied — modes (b) and (h)
   Mineral paint — mode (a)

Some sherds, particularly bowl sherds, of mode key (D) contained a considerable quantity of sand inclusions, though in no case was it as coarse or frequent as in the sherds of mode key (J).

The eight unslipped sherds seemed to be all from a single vessel. This jar and the jar slipped with paste clay were the only exceptions to the use of the thin white slip, which apparently was standard on all other specimens.

VESSEL SHAPES AND AREAS SLIPPED AND PAINTED: ROW B

1: Bowl — mode (a)
   Interior and exterior slipped, interior painted — modes (a), (b), and (c)
2: Bowl — mode (a)
   Interior slipped and painted — modes (a) and (c)
3: Jar with narrow neck — mode (d)
   Exterior slipped and painted — modes (b) and (d)

The bowls, unlike those from later sites, had outsloping sides and rims. All of the bowls were painted only on the interior but most were slipped on all surfaces. Three sherds were from bowls slipped only on the interior.

The jars were smaller and had contours (in particular a marked high shoulder) that differed from the later globular straight-necked jars. They were slipped and painted only on the exterior. The jars appeared to have been built up by coiling as far as the shoulder, after which the vessel was allowed to dry before the upper portion was added, for a distinct break at the shoulder could be seen on the interior surface of the restorable vessel and on several of the sherds.

SURFACE FINISH: ROW C

1: Slipped surface undulating, smooth to the touch, slip polished before application of paint, high points only reflecting light, polishing marks readily apparent — modes (a), (f), (g), and (j)
2: Slipped surface even, smooth or slick to the touch, polishing marks readily apparent, slip polished before application of paint, entire surface reflecting light — modes (b), (f), (g), and (i)
3: Slipped surface slightly undulating, gritty to the touch, polishing marks readily apparent, slip polished before application of paint, matte surface — modes (c), (f), (g), and (k)
4: Slipped surface even but gritty because of protruding coarse sand temper, polishing marks readily apparent, slip polished before application of paint, entire surface reflecting light — modes (d), (f), (g), and (i)

All of these vessels seemed to have been lightly polished with a polishing pebble. The unslipped surface

Figure 101. Typical sherds from Site 188.

of types 1, 2, and 4 were slightly undulating and gritty. No attempt was made to polish these surfaces with a polishing pebble but they were occasionally marked with fine striations as if they had been wiped smooth with the fingers, grass, or a piece of cloth. The interiors of the jars of type 3 were irregular and rough.

DECORATION: ROW D

1: Solid triangles often bordered with pendent dots; pendent triangles connected by and bordered with fine lines crossing slightly at the corners; rarely, dots superimposed on fine lines. This type was quite similar to black-on-white type 1 at Site 486 and type 2 at Site 601.
2: Zigzag bands (1 to 2 cm wide) filled with diagonal hatching, the zigs ending in pendent triangles similarly treated and generally in sets of two; tips of the triangles often solid black; bordering lines of the bands same width as the hatching lines.
3: Independent parallel wavy lines widely spaced; occasionally occurring as widely spaced hatching in broad (2 to 3 cm) bands.
4: Checkerboard.

5: Bands composed of short lines with opposed solid pendent triangles.

These designs were all widely spaced with more space between lines than in the width of the lines, and the design elements occupied less than half of the surface area. The placement was generally in the form of bands 2 to 3 cm wide running parallel to the rim of the vessel and, on bowls, placed below the rim on the interior. No bowls were decorated in broad bands extending from just below the rim nearly to the center of the vessel, in the manner typical for black-on-white bowls at Site 616. In the surface collection were several sherds with a fine-line design similar to decoration type 4 at Site 486.

Plain and Corrugated Pottery

MATERIAL: ROW A

1: Brown paste with sand inclusions — mode key (H)
2: Gray paste with angular opaque inclusions — mode key (I)
3: Gray paste with coarse sand inclusions — mode key (J)

VESSEL SHAPE: ROW B

1: Bowl — mode (a)
2: Neckless seed jar — mode (b)
3: Open-mouthed jar — mode (e)

All bowls had straight outflaring sides. Insofar as could be determined from sherds, there was little difference in vessel shape between open-mouthed jars of material mode key (H) and those of material mode keys (I) and (J) except for a tendency for those of material mode key (I) to have a slightly less flaring lip.

The open-mouthed jar was the overwhelmingly predominant vessel shape in the corrugated pottery. The finding of a single handle in one of the test pits dug while attempting to locate Room 1 suggests that at least some of the neck-corrugated, open-mouthed jars were equipped with vertical handles. The handle recovered was of four spirally coiled clay fillets set in a "split pea pod" type of handle. It appeared to be identical to those described by the Cosgroves (1932, pp. 85–86, pl. 98).

Vessel wall thickness ranged from 6 to 8 mm, with an average of 7 mm. Paste hardness was 4 to 5 on Mohs' scale.

CONSTRUCTION AND SURFACE FINISH: ROW C

1: Coiled counterclockwise, indented with left thumb pointing up — mode (a).
   Interior surfaces smooth and even, coils unobliterated — mode (a).

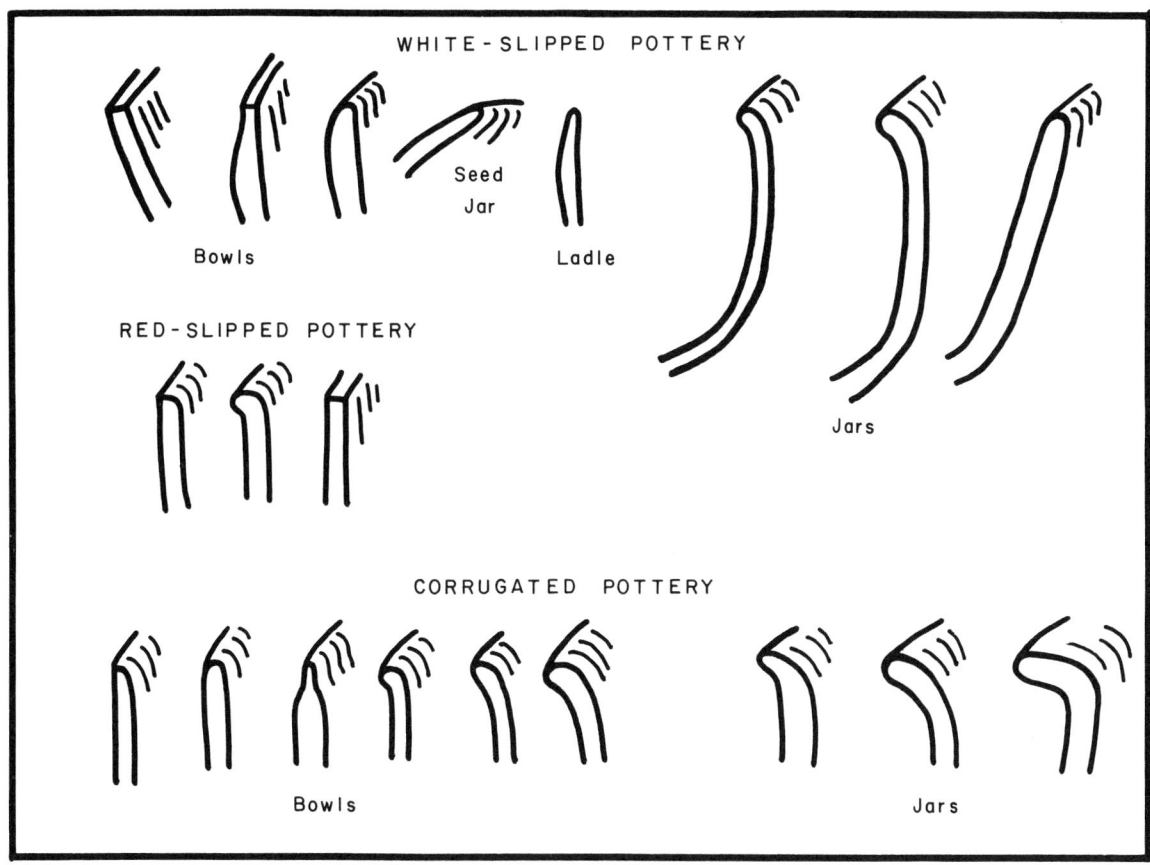

Figure 102. Pottery-rim and vessel forms from Site 188.

2: Presumably coiled, direction unknown — mode (d).
   Exposed surfaces even, smooth, and lustrous — mode (b).
3: Presumably coiled, direction unknown — mode (d).
   Exposed surfaces even but matte, small striations, gritty to the touch because of protruding temper — mode (e).

DECORATIVE EFFECT: ROW D

0: Plainware without decoration — mode (a).
1: Narrow-band clapboard corrugation — mode (b). The number of coils per 2 cm consistently ranged between 4 and 5. This decorative mode occurred only on vessels of material mode (H).
2: Indented corrugation — mode (c). This treatment was found only on vessels of material modes (I) and (J). There were between 2 and 4 coils per 2 cm and from ½ to 3 indentations per 2 cm. Both the widest coil and the most broadly spaced indentations occurred on a single sherd of material mode (J).
3: Wide-band clapboard corrugation — mode (b). Vessels of decorative type 3 consistently had 2 to 2½ coils per 2 cm. This decorative type seemed to have been distinct from type 1 above, and the two types did not intergrade. In addition to the width of the visible coil, the coils on vessels of decorative type 3 were flatter (there was less cross-sectional relief in the corrugation) than was the case with the narrow-band clapboard-corrugated vessels.
4: Plain surface and clapboard corrugation — mode (e). This mode covers those sherds of neck-banded vessels that contained portions of the plain basal section as well as portions of the upper corrugated section. This mode was originally sorted separately from modes (a) and (b), because sherds of these latter modes could have come from vessels of other forms.
5: Clapboard corrugation and incision — mode (f). Incision occurred only over the narrow-band corrugations found on material mode key (H). On two sherds this incision consisted of short (0.5 cm or less) perpendicular incisions, almost punctations, placed along the lower border of the first (lowest) coil; on two others these short incisions were placed at intervals along the lower border of

White-slipped Pottery

Provenience \ Descriptive Types								
A	1	2	3	3	3	3	3	4
B	3	3	1	1	1	2	3	3
C	3	1	2	2	2	2	1	4
D	5	2	1	3	4	1	3	?
Totals: 79	*8	43	9	1	2	3	10	3
Room 1**: 50	6	22	6		2	1	10	3
Room 2: 29	2	21	3	1		2		

Plain and Corrugated Pottery

Provenience \ Descriptive Types													
A	1	1	1	1	1	1	1	1	2	2	2	3	3
B	1	2	3	3	3	3	3	3	3	3	3	3	3
C	2	2	1	1	1	2	2	3	1	1	2	1	1
D	7	0	1	4	5	0	6	0	2	3	0	2	3
Totals: 121	4	2	14	4	6	32	3	3	6	9	32	1	5
Room 1**: 77	4		5	3	5	23	2	3		2	24	1	5
Room 2: 44		2	9	1	1	9	1			6	7	8	

* Sherds of each descriptive type were apparently from a single vessel.

** Two restorable neck-corrugated jars were also found in Room 1. Descriptive types of their included sherds were: 1311, 1314, 1320.

Table 20. Distribution by descriptive types of all pottery sherds from Site 188.

every coil. Moreover, two other sherds had widely spaced (2 cm apart) diagonal, straight-line, round-bottomed incisions extending over the corrugated area in a crosshatch pattern.

6: Fingernail punctation — mode (h). On one vessel diagonal punctations had been made in such a manner that a lenticular depression was left (clay removed under the fingernail?). These were arranged in irregular, closely spaced diagonal spirals on the neck of a small open-mouthed jar. A single sherd from a second jar exhibited a similar decorative technique except that the punctations were arranged in parallel horizontal lines.

7: Smudged interior — mode (g).

None of the corrugated sherds recovered from Site 188 had come from the basal portions of vessels, whereas many plain sherds did. It was therefore assumed that all corrugated sherds came from neck-corrugated vessels. Furthermore, since no plain sherds, other than the single rim sherd of the neckless seed jar, appeared to have come from the upper portion of a jar, the inference was strong that all open-mouthed jars (other than those of decorative type 6) were neck-corrugated specimens regardless of the material used in their manufacture. It is possible that the neckless seed jar bore some decoration but too little of the vessel remained for this to be determined.

POTTERY — PROBLEM TYPES

Regional Time-Space Types

WHITE-SLIPPED POTTERY

The decorative features on the black-on-white pottery from Site 188 closely resembled those of Red Mesa Black-on-white. In contrast to the pottery so designated and described by Gladwin (1945, pp. 56-57, pl. 29a, f), vessels found at Site 188 nearly all had a thin white slip with the paste never visible, and all had been polished. It would appear that the artisans responsible for this pottery, though influenced in their decoration by regional styles, nonetheless conformed more closely to local traditions in the construction and finishing of the vessels. The sherds of a single restorable Red Mesa Black-on-white jar were scattered through the fill of the two rooms.

PLAIN AND CORRUGATED POTTERY

The plain brown-paste pottery conformed to the general standards established for the Alma series with Alma Plain (descriptive type 1220 and perhaps some of 1320, though most of this latter type were probably bases of neck-banded jars), Alma Rough (descriptive type 1330, some of which also may have been bases of neck-banded jars), and Alma Punched (descriptive type 1326). There were six sherds of incised-corrugated (descriptive type 1315). The brown-paste neck-banded jars (descriptive types 1311, 1314, 1315) were Mimbres Neck-corrugated. The similar jars made of material mode keys (I) and (J) did not conform to any regional type designation.

STONE ARTIFACTS

Manos: 3 specimens

A fragment and two complete manos were recovered. All were of sandstone and basically rectangular in cross section with one face used. The used face was slightly convex in both dimensions and the abraded area sloped up sharply to the two short ends as if the manos had been used on a shallow trough or deep basin metate. The dimensions of the two complete specimens were: 21.3 by 13.5 by 5.5 cm and 18.5 by 12.4 by 2.8 cm. One of these was found on the floor of Room 1, the other and the fragment in the fill of the same room.

Metates: 2 specimens

One metate, from the fill of Room 2, was made from a natural boulder of coarse sandstone (28 by 21 by 9.9 cm). The grinding face was smooth and slightly basin-shaped. The second metate, a fragment from one of the trenches, was a vesicular basalt boulder basically unshaped except for a shallow trough on the upper surface. The trough was 0.8 cm deep, and its bottom very slightly concave; the sides sloped up sharply, being nearly perpendicular. It is not known whether the trough was open or closed at the ends.

Pecking Stones: 3 specimens

Three fist-sized (6 to 8 cm in diameter) natural cobbles, two of basalt and the other of quartzite, came from the fill of Room 1. One end of two had been used for battering, while both ends of the third specimen had been so used.

Point: 1 specimen (fig. 113m)

An elongated triangular point of chalcedony, from the fill of Room 1, had a maximum width of 1.9 cm and an estimated total length of 3.5 cm.

Scrapers and Unretouched Flakes: 9 specimens

All the utilized flakes came from the fill of the two rooms. One was quite large (9.5 by 9.2 by 3.7 cm) but most were 2 to 3 cm on a side and 0.5 to 1 cm thick. Nearly all were of petrified wood, though a few were of quartzite and one of basalt. The large flake and one other had some secondary chipping along the used edge. One specimen could be termed a scraper plane. It was an irregular cobble (7.6 by 7.1 by 5.6 cm) with one flat side and one nearly straight edge that evidently had been used for scraping.

Chips: 24 specimens

These unmodified and, so far as could be determined, unused chips were found principally in the trenches, though two were from the fill of Room 2 and one from the fill of Room 1. Half were of petrified wood, while the others were of chalcedony and quartzite. The average size was 3.5 by 3 by 0.5 cm.

Pendant: 1 specimen (fig. 115k)

This pendant, from the floor of Room 1, was of the fine-grained, red beadstone described at Site 616. It was broken but apparently had originally been a thin (1 mm) flat triangle with rounded corners. A small hole, probably for suspension, had been drilled in one corner and a much larger hole was drilled in the center of the remaining area. The original dimensions were approximately 1 by 1.5 cm.

Flat Sandstone Slabs: 4 specimens

The large flat surfaces of these pieces of tabular sandstone were unmodified. All were approximately 2 cm thick. One was nearly circular (12 cm in diameter) with the edges ground smooth and nearly perpendicular to the flat faces. The other three were rectangular, the edges roughly shaped by chipping, and approximately 20 by 30 cm. All were found in or near Room 1.

BONE ARTIFACTS

Awls: 2 specimens

Both awls appear to be from the proximal end of deer metapodials. The head of the bone was unworked except by the original splitting. The shaft tapered only gradually to within 2 cm of the point; it then tapered abruptly to a rather sharp point. One was 11.8 cm long, the other 7.7 cm. Both came from the fill of Room 1.

SHELL ARTIFACTS

Two specimens of shell were recovered. The first, from Room 2, was a nearly complete fragment of a bracelet of *Glycymeris* with only the umbo section missing. Its external diameter was 5 cm and the shell in cross section was a parallelogram, 0.4 by 0.6 cm.

The second specimen appeared to be a remnant of a *Glycymeris* bracelet that had been reused. It was a thin (0.4 cm in diameter) curved fragment. The curve covered approximately one-quarter of the arc of a circle and the distance between the two ends was 4.8 cm. A small hole had been biconically drilled through each end. It was found in the fill of Room 1.

ORGANIC ARTIFACTS AND RAW MATERIALS

Matting (?)

What appeared to be the impression of a fragment of a checkerwork mat woven of reeds was observed on one of the pieces of burned adobe from Room 1.

Hematite: 7 oz

Small pieces of hematite were found on the floor of both rooms.

266 • Mariana Mesa

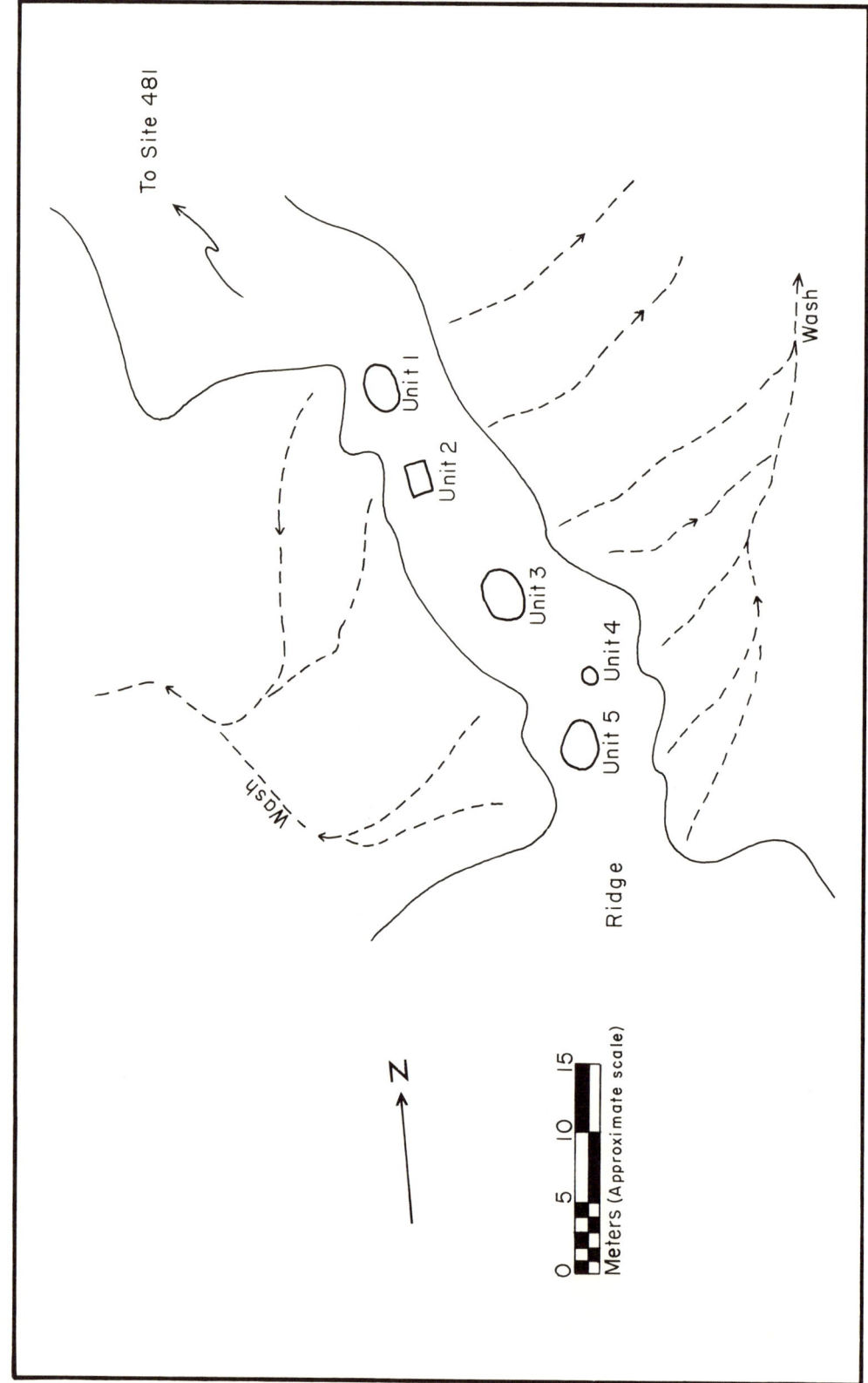

Figure 103. Plan of Site 486.

specimens were: 21.3 by 13.5 by 5.5 cm and 18.5 by 12.4 by 2.8 cm. One of these was found on the floor of Room 1, the other and the fragment in the fill of the same room.

Metates: 2 specimens

One metate, from the fill of Room 2, was made from a natural boulder of coarse sandstone (28 by 21 by 9.9 cm). The grinding face was smooth and slightly basin-shaped. The second metate, a fragment from one of the trenches, was a vesicular basalt boulder basically unshaped except for a shallow trough on the upper surface. The trough was 0.8 cm deep, and its bottom very slightly concave; the sides sloped up sharply, being nearly perpendicular. It is not known whether the trough was open or closed at the ends.

Pecking Stones: 3 specimens

Three fist-sized (6 to 8 cm in diameter) natural cobbles, two of basalt and the other of quartzite, came from the fill of Room 1. One end of two had been used for battering, while both ends of the third specimen had been so used.

Point: 1 specimen (fig. 113m)

An elongated triangular point of chalcedony, from the fill of Room 1, had a maximum width of 1.9 cm and an estimated total length of 3.5 cm.

Scrapers and Unretouched Flakes: 9 specimens

All the utilized flakes came from the fill of the two rooms. One was quite large (9.5 by 9.2 by 3.7 cm) but most were 2 to 3 cm on a side and 0.5 to 1 cm thick. Nearly all were of petrified wood, though a few were of quartzite and one of basalt. The large flake and one other had some secondary chipping along the used edge. One specimen could be termed a scraper plane. It was an irregular cobble (7.6 by 7.1 by 5.6 cm) with one flat side and one nearly straight edge that evidently had been used for scraping.

Chips: 24 specimens

These unmodified and, so far as could be determined, unused chips were found principally in the trenches, though two were from the fill of Room 2 and one from the fill of Room 1. Half were of petrified wood, while the others were of chalcedony and quartzite. The average size was 3.5 by 3 by 0.5 cm.

Pendant: 1 specimen (fig. 115k)

This pendant, from the floor of Room 1, was of the fine-grained, red beadstone described at Site 616. It was broken but apparently had originally been a thin (1 mm) flat triangle with rounded corners. A small hole, probably for suspension, had been drilled in one corner and a much larger hole was drilled in the center of the remaining area. The original dimensions were approximately 1 by 1.5 cm.

Flat Sandstone Slabs: 4 specimens

The large flat surfaces of these pieces of tabular sandstone were unmodified. All were approximately 2 cm thick. One was nearly circular (12 cm in diameter) with the edges ground smooth and nearly perpendicular to the flat faces. The other three were rectangular, the edges roughly shaped by chipping, and approximately 20 by 30 cm. All were found in or near Room 1.

BONE ARTIFACTS

Awls: 2 specimens

Both awls appear to be from the proximal end of deer metapodials. The head of the bone was unworked except by the original splitting. The shaft tapered only gradually to within 2 cm of the point; it then tapered abruptly to a rather sharp point. One was 11.8 cm long, the other 7.7 cm. Both came from the fill of Room 1.

SHELL ARTIFACTS

Two specimens of shell were recovered. The first, from Room 2, was a nearly complete fragment of a bracelet of *Glycymeris* with only the umbo section missing. Its external diameter was 5 cm and the shell in cross section was a parallelogram, 0.4 by 0.6 cm.

The second specimen appeared to be a remnant of a *Glycymeris* bracelet that had been reused. It was a thin (0.4 cm in diameter) curved fragment. The curve covered approximately one-quarter of the arc of a circle and the distance between the two ends was 4.8 cm. A small hole had been biconically drilled through each end. It was found in the fill of Room 1.

ORGANIC ARTIFACTS AND RAW MATERIALS

Matting (?)

What appeared to be the impression of a fragment of a checkerwork mat woven of reeds was observed on one of the pieces of burned adobe from Room 1.

Hematite: 7 oz

Small pieces of hematite were found on the floor of both rooms.

266 • Mariana Mesa

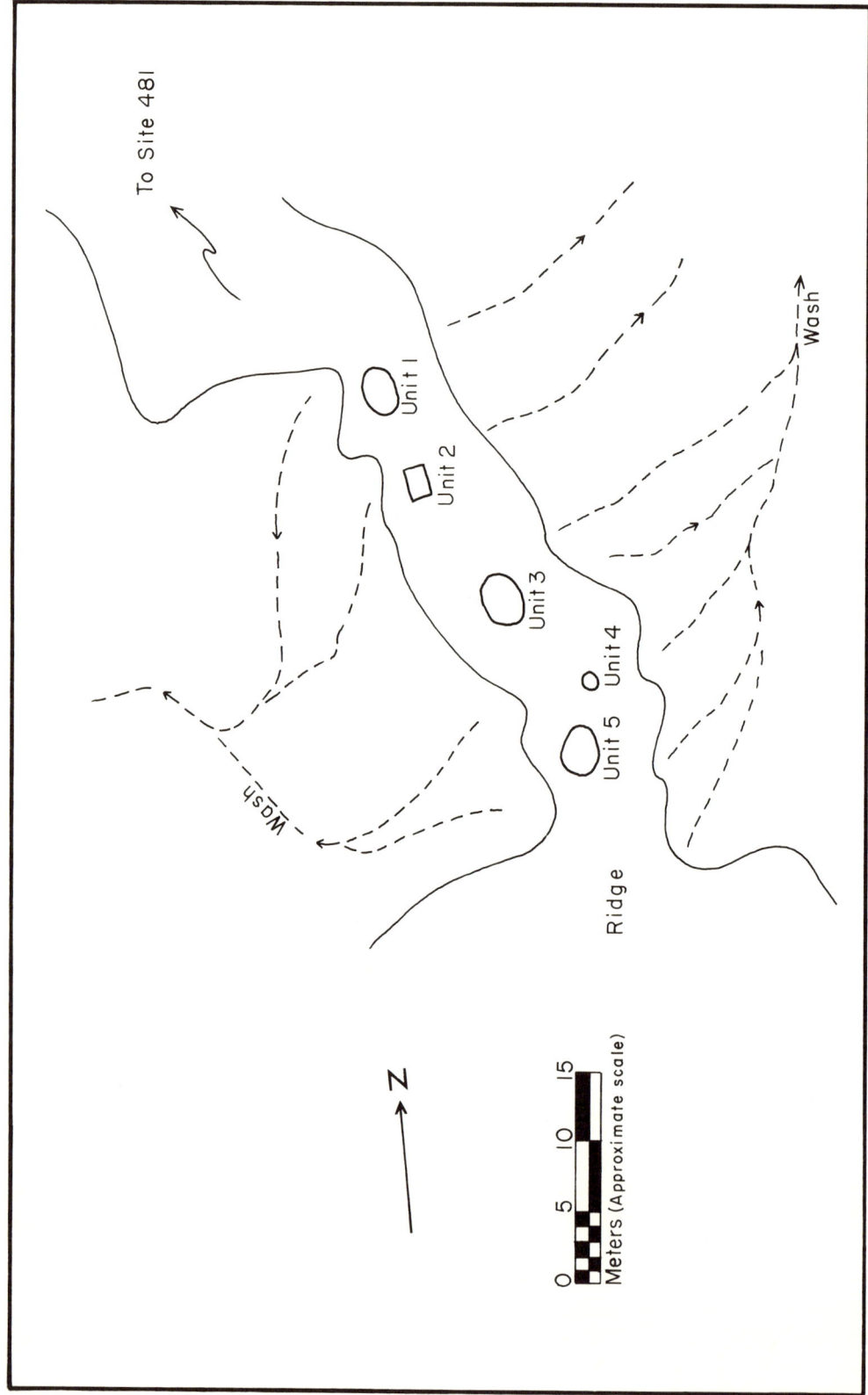

Figure 103. Plan of Site 486.

Site 486

Site 486 was situated on top of a long, narrow, precipitous ridge extending generally westward from the northerly point of Mariana Mesa. It was about one-half mile southeast of Site 481 (Danson 1957, pp. 70–74, table 14) and about 150 m higher.

Material from the site was scattered over approximately 100 m along the top of the ridge, which at this point is barely 25 m wide. The site looks down through a heavy growth of piñon and juniper to level land suitable for farming in both the southeast and northwest. These sandy slopes are now badly eroded and the destruction has extended over most of the site area. Excavation established that Site 486 had been almost completely washed away. Trash and fill had become scattered over the sides of the ridge and in the nearby washes and arroyos. Although there were five or six areas of concentrated lava cobbles apparent on the surface, excavation revealed that the original structures had been eroded to such an extent that, with the exception of the remnant of wall found in Unit 2, only a few stones maintained any semblance of their original alignment. Very few artifacts or sherds were recovered in the course of excavation, but a large surface collection of stone and pottery fragments was made. In all, four areas were excavated or trenched. One of these, described below as Unit 4, consisted simply of a stone-lined cist. Only one of the three trenches through the areas of concentrated lava cobbles revealed the outlines of a room (Unit 2). No alignments suggestive of walls were encountered in the other two trenches, nor could any floor levels be discerned. After three days excavation at the site was discontinued.

The small amount of material recovered and the condition of the site prevented any extensive reconstruction of the material and nonmaterial culture of the site's inhabitants beyond more or less obvious generalizations. The resident group was small, probably fewer than a half dozen families, if the individual room-size structures can be taken as indicative of single-family shelters. There is no direct evidence that the people were agriculturists but agriculture has been definitely associated with similarly equipped groups throughout the Southwest, making it reasonable to infer that the inhabitants of Site 486 knew the techniques of crop cultivation, whether or not they practiced it during their stay at this site. Certainly potential fields were readily available, so that this may have been a farming community temporarily occupied during a number of seasons, if perhaps not continuously.

A very small percentage of the artifacts recovered came from the excavations; the majority were found on the surface, and there was thus a somewhat greater than normal chance that some of them were not actually left behind by the inhabitants of the site — a possibility enhanced by the fact that heavy erosion of the entire area had taken place since abandonment. On the other hand, the pottery (which was the only part of the collection with anything approaching significant sample size) from the excavations and on the surface formed, with rare exceptions, a consistent unit, so that any extensive occupation foreign to the living units excavated seemed relatively unlikely. As a result, all the material found has been treated herein as if it were contemporary with the main occupation of the site.

Considering the relative abundance of manos (11), the complete absence of metates (unless the single grinding slab is so identified) is rather surprising. The only large jars, which presumably were for storage, were of the plain and neck-banded types. The smaller closed-mouth jars and most of the bowls were painted.

Only two groups of sherds were sufficiently aberrant to suggest intergroup trade. Of course a large portion of the remainder of the pottery could have been imported, but without a detailed technological analysis and greater knowledge of the geology of the region this becomes difficult to determine. The number of polishing pebbles recovered at least suggested that the group made some of its own pottery, although pebbles of this nature were doubtless used for purposes other than polishing pottery. The aberrant sherd types, Wingate Black-on-red and Mimbres Bold Face Black-on-white, had centers of distribution in opposite directions. The remainder of the pottery, even if locally made, showed a similar tendency in its derivation. Both the paste and the shape of the plain and corrugated vessels were similar to those of contemporary and earlier sites to the south, while the black-on-white wares fell within the bounds of a decorative tradition found in a region to the north, centering, on the basis of present knowledge, around the White Mound Valley and the Puerco River of the West.

DATING CONSIDERATIONS

Since no datable tree-ring specimens were recovered from Site 486, its chronological placement is almost wholly dependent upon a comparison of the black-on-white pottery, although certain stone forms, particularly the manos, offered some general corroboration. Unfortunately, the precise typological placement of the bulk of the black-on-white material from Site 486 into regional time-space types was difficult. The combination of Red Mesa and Kiatuthlanna diagnostics, with a decided emphasis on the former, suggested that the material from this site was made perhaps during the early part of the Red Mesa phase — as this is defined by Gladwin (1945, pp. 49–63) — after the Kiatuthlanna elements had lost their cohesion but before they disappeared altogether as individual elements. An alternative hypothesis might be that the material from Site 486 was representative of an early "purer" location of the Red Mesa tradition, into which elements of a more northerly Kiatuthlanna tradition had diffused by synchronic rather than diachronic communication. At any rate, if Gladwin's dates for the Kiatuthlanna (A.D. 800 to 870) and Red Mesa (A.D. 870 to 930) phases (Gladwin 1945, pp. 45, 63) are accepted and if the variation represented by this transition proceeded concurrently in the Mariana Mesa area, it seems reasonable to place Site 486 somewhere between A.D. 850 and 900. This is consistent with dates assigned by Breternitz (1966, pp. 80, 90) to these same types. Obviously any such estimate of the date of occupation can be viewed only as extremely tentative.

The Wingate and Mimbres Bold Face types reached their peak of popularity somewhat later than this period but both were in existence during at least part of it. The absence of any red-slipped pottery from Sites 601 and 188 suggested that the recovery of three such sherds from Site 486 may have resulted from accidental association, since all three sherds were found on the surface.

LIVING AND EXCAVATION UNITS

Unit 1

A low mound containing numerous lava cobbles. A trench revealed no architectural features.

ARTIFACTS

Pecking stone; rubbing stone; chips

Unit 2 (fig. 104)

Apparently a rectangular excavation had been made to a depth of approximately 25 cm below present ground level, but presumably the original ground level was slightly higher than at present. The sides of this excavation were faced with irregularly coursed unshaped lava cobbles averaging 5 to 15 cm in diameter. Three courses were present in the south wall but fewer remained in the others. There was nothing to indicate the nature of the wall construction above ground level but the paucity of cobbles in the fill would suggest that the entire wall was not of masonry. No definite floor area could be recognized nor were there any floor features.

ARTIFACT

A single chip of petrified wood from the fill

Unit 3

A low mound with many lava cobbles. No features were encountered.

ARTIFACTS

Chip; malachite

Unit 4 (fig. 105)

The use of this area as a hearth was indicated by the presence of an almost circular hole walled with upright sandstone slabs and floored with irregular basalt cobbles. Small rocks served to fill chinks between the sandstone slabs. The basal diameter of the hole averaged 56 cm, while the diameter at the mouth ranged between 79 and 86 cm. That this hole had been a firepit was shown by the fill of ash and charcoal, the charcoal being concentrated in the upper 10 cm. No trace of a room floor could be discovered in the general area surrounding the firepit nor were any walls in evidence; however, tree roots had badly disturbed the area, making the search difficult.

Figure 104. Site 486. View of Unit 2, looking south.

The lack of association of any discernible house features and the overall size of the unit relative to that of the single house encountered (Unit 2) made it appear likely that the firepit was constructed outside of any house, as were several found at Site 481 dating from the early part of the occupation of that site.

The floor of the firepit was 40 cm below the present ground surface, and some of the sandstone slabs forming the side walls extended several centimeters above the surface. There were no artifacts in direct association.

Unit 5

A low mound containing numerous lava cobbles. No excavations were made.

SUBSISTENCE MATERIALS

Vegetal: No vegetal remains were found.
Animal: A total of 32 fragments of animal bone were recovered, representing deer, fox, and hare. It would take no more than two deer and a single fox and hare to account for the entire collection, all of which came from Unit 1 except for a few deer fragments from Unit 3. Only scapulae and pelvic and long-bone fragments were included.

POTTERY — DESCRIPTIVE TYPOLOGY

White-slipped Pottery

MATERIAL: ROW A

1: Gray crumbling paste with sand and opaque angular inclusions — mode key (E)
   Slip flat-white, thinly applied — modes (b) and (h)
   Mineral paint — mode (a)
2: Gray crumbling paste with sand and opaque angular inclusions — mode key (E)
   Slip flat-white and watery, paste visible in patches — modes (b) and (i)
3: Brown paste with sand inclusions — mode key (H)

Figure 105. Site 486. Exterior firepit in Unit 4. Note resemblance to exterior firepits at Site 481 (fig. 73), although this one had no central ashpit.

Slip creamy white in color, thickly applied — modes (c) and (g)
Mineral paint — mode (a)

The paste of type 3, although slipped with a thick white slip, appeared macroscopically to be identical to that of mode key (H), a type generally associated with plain and corrugated pottery.

The flat-white slip of type 1 occasionally rubbed off.

VESSEL SHAPES AND AREAS SLIPPED AND PAINTED: ROW B

1: Bowl — mode (a)
   Interior and exterior slipped, interior painted — modes (a), (b), and (c)
2: Ladle — mode (h)
   Interior and exterior slipped, interior painted — modes (a), (b), and (c)
3: Short-necked jar — mode (c)
   Exterior slipped and painted — modes (b) and (d)
4: Neckless (seed) jar — mode (b)
   Exterior slipped and painted — modes (b) and (d)
5: Short-necked jar — mode (c)
   Exterior slipped — mode (b)
6: Bowl — mode (a)
   Interior slipped and painted — modes (a) and (c)

The jars ranged in height from 12 to 15 cm and had a maximum diameter of 10 to 12 cm. The bowls had a height of 8 to 10 cm and a maximum diameter of 15 to 20 cm. No whole or restorable vessels were present.

The rim sherds of the short-necked jars suggested vessels with slightly insloping walls and occasional out-turned rims. All of the bowls had rather straight-outsloping sides. One bowl had two opposed exterior lugs, each formed of two parallel coils of clay placed 2 cm below the rim.

The estimated numbers of vessels of each shape were: short-necked jars — 15 to 20; neckless (seed) jars — 1; bowls — 23 to 28; ladles — 2.

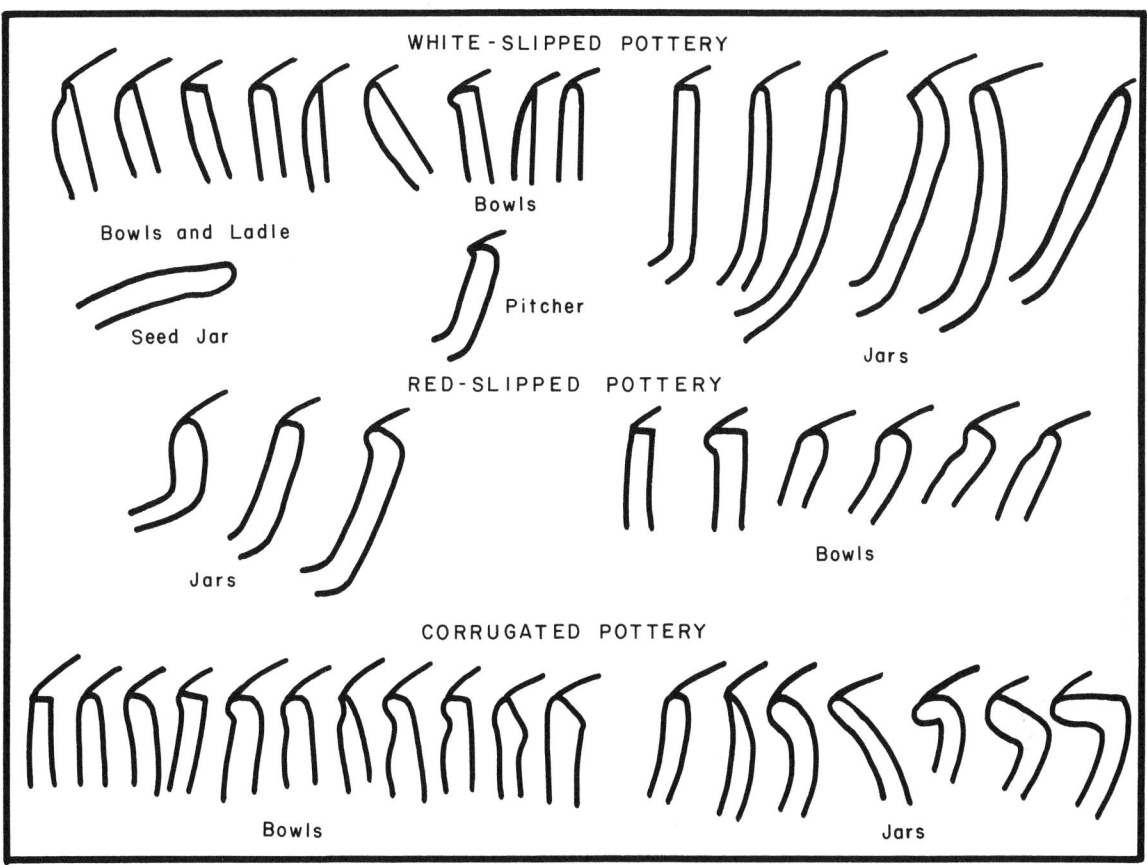

Figure 106. Pottery-rim and vessel forms from Site 486.

SURFACE FINISH: ROW C

1: Slipped surface undulating but smooth to the touch, high points reflecting light, polishing marks apparent, slip polished before application of paint — modes (a), (f), (g), and (j)
2: Similar to type 1 except that the slip was polished after the application of paint — modes (a), (f), (h), and (j)
3: Slipped surface even, smooth to the touch, nearly entire surface reflecting light, polishing marks and dull streaks occasionally apparent, slip polished before application of paint — modes (b), (e), (g), and (i)

Type 3 occurred only on bowls. The exterior surfaces of these vessels were not as even as the interiors and the slip was less uniformly applied and polished. On the three sherds of material mode key (H) there was no slip.
The interiors of the jars bore shallow fine-line striations in horizontal bands about 0.8 cm wide.

DECORATION: ROW D

1: Solid triangles with occasional pendent dots bounded by fine lines crossing at the corners; to these lines were frequently added superimposed dots or pendent dots on alternative sides of the line; cross-hatching and scrolls rare; rims black. Not unlike black-on-white type 1 at Site 188 and type 2 at Site 601.
2: Thin parallel lines. This decorative mode occurred on only one sherd. It was segregated because it was the only example of thin lines and appeared on the only sherd of surface finish mode 2.
3: Solid triangles, straight fine lines, bands with wavy fine-line hatching, parallel horizontal wavy lines (bowls only); rims black.
4: A horizontal band 4 cm wide containing opposed pendent solid triangles with interlocking scroll hooks; occasionally pendent dots attached to the triangles; band placed approximately 1 cm below the rim on the interior of bowls; rims black.
5: Bands of fine parallel diagonal hatching with

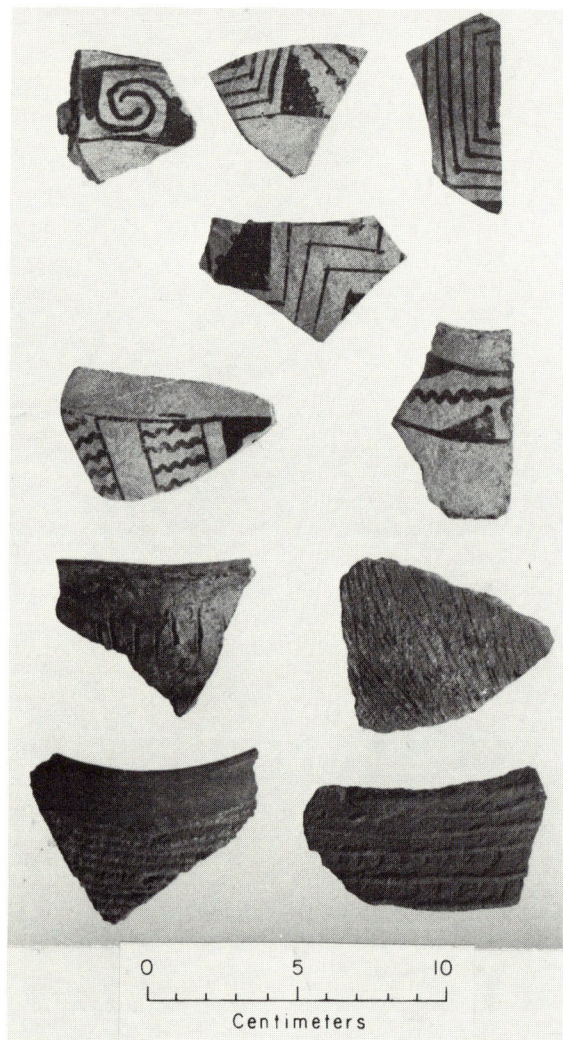

Figure 107. Typical sherds from Site 486.

banding lines of same size; curvilinear scrolls; rims black.

Decoration on jars was predominantly of fine parallel lines and fine straight and wavy-line hatching in bands, solid triangles, occasional pendent dots, and rare scrolls. Bowl and ladle decoration consisted of generally horizontal, fine straight and wavy lines and bands connecting and/or separating solid triangles in a rather free arrangement — that is, not confined within bordering lines. There were occasional pendent dots and rare scrolls and cross-hatching. The decoration was never pendent from the rim nor did it cover the center of the bowl. One small group of sherds representing at least three bowls (descriptive type 1114) were decorated with a single horizontal band 4 cm wide running around the interior of the bowl about 3 cm below the rim. The bands contained opposed pendent solid triangles with interlocking scroll hooks and occasional pendent dots.

Red-slipped Pottery

The three red-slipped sherds recovered conformed to the definition of Wingate Black-on-red (Colton and Hargrave 1937, pp. 118–119; Carlson 1970, pp. 11–17).

Plain and Corrugated Pottery

MATERIAL: ROW A
1: Brown paste with sand inclusions — mode key (H)
2: Gray paste with coarse sand inclusions — mode key (J)

VESSEL SHAPE: ROW B
1: Bowl — mode (a)
2: Open-mouthed jar — mode (e)

No whole or restorable vessels were present. Nearly 75 percent of the corrugated sherds were from jars. Though only 23 sherds (10 percent) definitely came from bowls, 34 equivocal sherds had been treated equally on both surfaces and, in general, had an even, gritty texture. Since the interiors of jars were often treated like their exteriors, it was impossible to distinguish bowl sherds from jar sherds in this group. (This uncertainty is indicated by a question mark in Row B of table 21.)

A short open-mouthed jar with a fairly constricted neck was the only plain jar form suggested by the sherds. This type and the plain, striated, and fingernail-punctated jar forms were all small.

There were two jar forms, similar in general outline but differing in size, decoration, and degree of constriction of the neck. The plain, striated, and fingernail-punctated vessels were short open-mouthed jars with a fairly constricted neck. Probably all such vessels were made from the brown friable paste of material mode key (H). The plain sherds of material mode key (J) appeared to be bases of neck-banded vessels. There was greater variation in the neck-banded vessels and both material types were employed with about equal frequency. The neck-corrugated jars were larger (but probably less than 25 cm in total height) and had less constricted necks. One sherd of a neck-banded jar with only a slightly constricted neck had a globular thumb-sized lug just below the rim.

The plain bowls had straight, slightly outsloping walls and were without decoration. The bowls with smudged interiors had sharply outsloping walls.

White-slipped Pottery

Descriptive Types / Provenience																					Bases
A					1	1	1	1	1	1	1	1	2	2	2	2	2	2	3		
B			1	1	1	1	1	3	3	3	4	1	1	1	1	2	3	3	5		
C			1	1	1	3	3	1	1	2	1	1	1	3	3	1	1	1	3		
D			1	3	4	1	3	1	3	2	1	1	3	1	3	3	1	3	5		
Totals	122	28	1	7	4	1	33	1	1	1	14	2	3	6	1	14	1	3			1
Unit 1	11	2					8														1
Unit 2	3	1														1					1
Unit 3	10	3					5													1	1
Surface	98	22	1	7	4	1	20	1	1	1	14	2	3	6	1	13	1				

Red-slipped Pottery

Surface	3 sherds Wingate Black-on-red (accidental association?)

Plain and Corrugated Pottery

Descriptive Types / Provenience																							
A					1	1	1	1	1	1	1	1	1	1	1	1	1	1	1	2	2	2	2
B			1	1	1	1	1	1	2	2	2	2	2	2	2	2	?	?	?	2	2	2	2
C		2	2	3	5	6	6	1	1	2	4	5	5	5	7	2	4	5	1	1	4	5	
D		0	5	0	5	0	5	1	2	0	0	0	3	4	1	0	0	0	1	2	0	0	
Totals	223	10	6	3	2	1	1	29	2	34	29	2	1	1	1	2	4	28	30	1	10	26	
Unit 1	38	6						7	1								4	17	2	1			
Unit 2	38			1				2		30						2		2	1				
Unit 3	47	10		1	1	1		6		4	7							9				8	
Surface	100		3					14	1		22	2	1	1	1			27			10	18	

Table 21. Distribution by descriptive types of all pottery sherds from Site 486.

CONSTRUCTION AND SURFACE FINISH: ROW C

1: Coiled counterclockwise, coils annealed with left thumb point up — mode (a).
   Interior surfaces smooth and even, coils unobliterated on exterior — mode (a).

2: Presumably coiled, direction unknown — mode (d).
   Exposed surfaces even, smooth, and lustrous — mode (b).

3: Similar to type 2 except that the exteriors of bowls were gritty and matte — construction mode (d); surface finish modes (b) and (c).

4: Presumably coiled, direction unknown — mode (d).
   Exposed surfaces undulating and gritty with only the high points slightly lustrous — mode (d).

5: Presumably coiled, direction unknown — mode (d).
   Exposed surfaces even, gritty, and matte — mode (c).

6: Presumably coiled, direction unknown — mode (d).
   Exposed surfaces even but matte, small striations; gritty to the touch because of protruding temper — mode (e).

7: Coiled counterclockwise, coils annealed with left thumb pointing down — mode (b). This technique often left the lower edge of the clapboard coil below the indentations as a raised ridge.

Interior surfaces smooth and even, coils unobliterated on exterior — mode (a).

Insofar as could be determined, the primary and perhaps the only construction technique was coiling. Whether the basal sections of any vessels were first molded could not be determined; however, on a number of plain vessels, slight ridges suggesting coils that had not been completely smoothed extended to the base of the vessel.

The craftsmanship was adequate, the walls of a constant thickness, and the surfaces generally even; yet no great care seems to have been lavished on the construction of these vessels. The extent and nature of the surface finish had no discernible patterning with other features and showed such variability that we could only assume that any culturally defined standards in this regard were not rigidly adhered to.

DECORATIVE EFFECT: ROW D

0: Plainware without decoration (the presence, absence, and extent of polishing is considered under construction) — mode (a)

1: Clapboard corrugation — mode (b)

2: Plain and clapboard corrugation on individual sherds — mode (e)

Basal portions of vessels plain with corrugations extending over upper (neck) section

3: Overall irregularly parallel vertical striations — mode (i)

Individual striations round-bottomed, approximately 1 mm in diameter, and several centimeters long

4: Vertical fingernail punctations in a rough semblance of horizontal rows — mode (h)

Punctations irregularly spaced and approximately 2 centimeters apart

5: Interior of vessel smudged — mode (g)

COMMENT

It is evident that sherds categorized in decorative types 0, 1, and 2 might derive from a single vessel. In fact, at Site 486 no basal sherds with clapboard corrugations were encountered, so it is likely that all type 1 and 2 sherds did derive from the same vessels. On the other hand, plain sherds could be portions of plainware vessels or the bases of neck-banded vessels. No indented-corrugated sherds were found nor any indications of vessels with overall corrugation. Jar decoration appeared to have consisted primarily of the neck-banded variety — narrow clapboard corrugations that extended from the rim or from several coils below the rim for a distance approximately two-fifths of the way down the vessel. There was a single jar decorated with fingernail punctation and another with vertical striations. These, as well as several plain jars, were smaller than the neck-banded jars. Except for the interiors of nine bowl sherds that were slightly smudged the bowls were completely without decoration.

POTTERY — PROBLEM TYPES

Regional Time-Space Types

WHITE-SLIPPED POTTERY

If the Kiatuthlanna-Red Mesa types were looked upon primarily as representative of steps in the evolution of a tradition of pottery decoration, then obviously the pottery under consideration can be included within this general tradition. That these two types do represent little more than segments of the same decorative tradition is suggested by the almost complete overlap of descriptive criteria — e.g., all design elements listed by Gladwin as typical of Red Mesa are illustrated on his Kiatuthlanna sherd board (Gladwin 1945, p. 41, pl. 23). As nearly as can be determined from the written descriptions and the typological collections at hand (including 43 sherds from the pithouse at Wingate 11:24 selected by Gladwin), the principal developmental trends consisted of a decreasing number of vessels whose slipped portions were well polished and, associated with this, the application of an increasingly diluted and/or a decreased quantity of slip. If Hawley's Escavada type (Hawley 1936, p. 32) is considered equivalent to Red Mesa (as Gladwin 1945, p. 56 suggests, though Kluckhohn and Reiter 1939, p. 155, would place it later), then there was also a contemporary, perhaps regionalized, extension of the portion of the vessel to which the slip was applied, since Hawley notes that often an inch or more of the exterior of Escavada bowls was slipped. Accompanying these trends was a porportional change in the design element utilized, the most noticeable of which, according to Gladwin, was the sharp decrease in the use of wavy-line hatching.

Though it is evident that nearly all of the black-on-white pottery from Site 486 could be included under the definitions of these two types, the sherds did not conform precisely to either of the two defined segments of this developmental sequence. There was, in addition, a distinctive local variation from this tradition in the application of a white slip over the entire exterior of all bowls.

Rather than attempt a somewhat arbitrary segregation of the materials into one or the other of these two types, it seemed better simply to describe the type and quantity of features present (table 21). Any categorization of most of the sherds as Red Mesa or Kiatuthlanna would have had to ignore the mixture of diagnostic features on single sherds and, furthermore, require the reader to assume that the material from Site 486 was characterized by the entire range of design elements and constructional techniques listed in the published descriptions of these two types. Such conclusions would do violence to the facts and inhibit the effective application of the material to any future detailed investigation of areal and temporal variation or the determination of the cultural affiliations of the group occupying the site.

In general, it can be said that the "Kiatuthlanna element" was in the minority, if that category is defined by the occurrence of a well-polished white slip and the use of wavy-line hatching. These features, at least to the north of Mariana Mesa, reached their greatest popularity previous to most of the other ceramic elements present. However, at Site 486 these "early" features did not all occur on the same vessels with any significant regularity.

Three sherds (descriptive type 3635) that differed in most characteristics from the remainder of the black-on-white pottery present were identified as Mimbres Bold Face Black-on-white.

PLAIN AND CORRUGATED POTTERY

Descriptive types 1211 and 1212 were Mimbres Neck-corrugated, while descriptive type 1120 was Alma Plain. The sherds of descriptive type 1220 could derive from Alma Plain jars or from the bases of Mimbres Neck-corrugated vessels. Sherds of Alma Punched (descriptive type 1254) and Reserve Smudged (descriptive type 1125) were also present. The remainder of the brown-paste sherds, including several smudged sherds, differed from recognized regional time-space types primarily in not being so well finished, though the product was not so rough and uneven as the material generally identified as Alma Rough. Descriptive type 1271 was unusual in that the coils had been annealed with the left thumb pointing down.

STONE ARTIFACTS

Manos: 11 specimens

CONVEX SURFACE (for use with basin or trough metates): 9 specimens

Shape: Rectangular to rounded-rectangular; no finger grips

Transverse Cross Section: Considerable variation: (1) rounded-rectangular, fairly uniform, upper surface and grinding faces slightly convex (#3, #5, #6, #8); (2) lenticular, greater convexity of upper surface and grinding faces, the two faces meeting along an edge on those specimens of less than 3-cm thickness; (3) those with a greater thickness, sublenticular in shape (#2, #7, #36, #37); (4) wedge-shaped, slightly convex grinding face (#38).

Longitudinal Cross Section: Lenticular and half-lenticular, the variation depending on whether the unshaped upper surface was naturally flat or convex.

Grinding Face: Fore-and-aft convexity approximately 0.5 cm (distance measured from a plane tangent to the center of the surface to the outer end of the grinding face); side-to-side convexity 1.5 cm with two-thirds of the difference coming in the outboard 2 cm.

ONE-HAND MANOS: 2 specimens

Both of these specimens conformed to Woodbury's definition of this type. There was sufficient convexity on the end of the grinding face to suggest use on a trough metate or perhaps a grinding slab such as that described below, where the trough was incipient rather than developed. The end of one of the two specimens (#24) had also been used for hammering.

Shape: Round
Cross Section: Ovoid

CONVEX SURFACE MANOS

Cat. No.	Length	Width	Thickness	Material	Provenience
2	16.1 cm	10.5 cm	2.3 cm	Basalt	Surface
3	18.0	12.2	4.6	Sandstone	Surface
5	(11.4)	11.2	4.2	Basalt	Surface
6	(14.5)	10.3	3.6	Basalt	Surface
7	(12.5)	10.3	3.1	Basalt	Surface
8	(10.0)	9.0	2.3	Basalt	Surface
36	(11.9)	11.2	3.6	Basalt	Surface
37	(12.5)	11.4	2.6	Vesicular basalt	Surface
38	8.0	9.9	1.9	Fine-grained basalt	Surface

Grinding Face: A single grinding face whose contours conformed with the ovoid cross section, with only a slight flattening of the grinding face itself.

ONE-HAND MANOS

Cat. No.	Diameter	Thickness	Material	Provenience
24	6.5 cm	4.6 cm	Sandstone	Surface
44	6.5	2.5	Fine-grained basalt	Unit 1

Grinding Slab: 1 specimen

This specimen (#42) was found on the surface, and had been made from an unshaped basalt cobble, its only modification resulting from use. Either the motor habits of the users were somewhat erratic, causing the slightly uneven wear, or else the specimen was in the process of being shaped through use rather than through previously pecking the grinding face to shape. Originally, it was probably rectangular, though the fragment when found was almost square with a triangular cross section. The upper (grinding) face that formed the "base" of the triangle apparently was naturally flat.

The single grinding face covered most of the large flat area but did not extend to any original edge. The face was convex and slightly undulating rather than flat or basin-shaped. Very little wear was apparent.

Rubbing Stones: 5 specimens

These were unshaped, naturally smooth, globular, rectangular, and ovoid cobbles; one (#10) was irregularly angular but the flat surfaces were naturally smooth.

The working faces were more or less uniformly convex in all dimensions but did not extend over a large portion of a curve; that is, in no case was the edge of the working face more than 1 cm lower than a plane tangent to the center of the face. The working faces showed little evidence of extensive wear and their curvature depended upon the natural curvature of the stone. The maximum length of the working faces ranged from 4 to 10 cm with a mean of 8 cm. On the ovoid cobbles (#1, #4) there were two opposing faces. The angular cobble (#10) had three contiguous faces; the globular cobble (#11) had three noncontiguous irregularly placed faces; the four long sides of the rectangular cobble (#16) were working faces.

The difference in use between rubbing stones and manos may often have been slight but, because of the uniform convexity, it is unlikely — none was returned to the Museum for microscopic examination — that the rubbing motion was consistently fore-and-aft. In contradistinction to the manos, rubbing stones were thicker relative to their width and on occasion were even globular; they also tended to have more working faces. Rubbing stones were distinguished from polishing pebbles primarily by their larger size and lesser degree of smoothness. Although the material was often the same, the small polishing pebbles generally had a higher degree of smoothness and often a sheen.

Polishing Pebbles: 6 specimens

These were irregularly shaped (but not angular) globular pebbles. None were elongated and two (#15, #18) were somewhat flattened spheres. The rubbing facets were irregularly placed, though generally taking advantage of any naturally less convex areas, and were oval to subrectangular in outline and convex in all directions with little flattening apparent. Maximum length of rubbing facets ranged from 1.5 to 5 cm with a mean of 3 cm.

POLISHING PEBBLES

Cat. No.	Maximum Diameter	Minimum Diameter	Material	Provenience
14	3.7 cm	2.1 cm	Quartz	Surface
15	3.2	1.5	Quartzite	Surface
17	5.5	2.6	Quartzite	Surface
18	6.0	3.3	Quartz	Surface
19	3.7	2.3	Quartzite	Surface
30	4.0	2.4	Fine-grained quartzite	Surface

(See Rubbing Stones for basis of differentiating these two categories.) No microscopic examination was made to determine directions of striations.

Pecking Stones: 5 specimens

All but #45 were of petrified wood with a globular ovoid shape. The exception was of sandstone and had the shape of a steep-sided truncated pyramid. None were intentionally shaped. All showed battering on one end, except #12, which was more nearly spherical

RUBBING STONES

Cat. No.	Maximum Diameter	Minimum Diameter	Material	Provenience
1	10.9 cm	4.2 cm	Quartzite	Surface
4	10.0	4.7	Quartzite	Surface
10	6.9	4.3	Quartzite	Surface
11	8.2	4.7	Quartzite	Surface
16	8.3	3.8	Quartzite	Surface

than the others, with battering evident over most of its surface. All but the sandstone specimen, which came from Unit 1, were found on the surface. Mean maximum diameter: 6.5 cm; mean minimum diameter: 5.5 cm.

Points and Knives: 13 specimens

SECONDARY CHIPPING ON ALL MAJOR FACES: 5 specimens (fig. 113q-s)

All five specimens in this category came from the surface and all except #23, which was of obsidian, were made of petrified wood. Three were comparatively small (2.1–3.1 cm). Though two of these (#20, #22, fig. 113q, r) were triangular with side notches, #23 was almost equilateral with convex edges and a slightly concave base. The others were broken but had been probably 6 to 8 cm in length. One (#21, fig. 113s), which was nearly complete, had straight edges, corner notches, and a slightly expanding stem with a straight base. All were from the surface.

Only #21 appeared to be large enough (it was broken but originally was probably about 8 cm long) to have served effectively as a knife. The others were thin and relatively delicate, those of petrified wood being almost translucent.

SECONDARY CHIPPING ON MAJOR EDGES ONLY: 8 specimens

Flakes and blades were of petrified wood (one was of felsite), modified only by secondary chipping on both faces of their two long edges. They originally had probably ranged in length from 5 to 10 cm and in width from 2 to 3 cm. All came from the surface.

The use of the implements in this category doubtless overlapped that of those in the category above. It seems more likely, however, that most of these served as knives or possibly even as scrapers. No apparent effort was made to facilitate hafting and these implements may have been used without hafts.

Flakes: 10 specimens

Ten irregular flakes of petrified wood exhibited use chips along one or, rarely, more edges. All came from the surface.

Cores and Unidentified Fragments

Some 40 fragments of petrified wood, in addition to those already mentioned, were recovered from the site. They varied in size from approximately 11 by 8 by 5 cm (two specimens from the surface) to small chips only a centimeter or so in length. Most fragments of sufficient size showed evidence of having been used as cores.

The provenience of these specimens was: Surface (30); Unit 1 (8); Units 2 and 3 (1 each).

Chopper: 1 specimen

A corelike block of petrified wood, found on the surface, 6.7 by 5.6 by 3.5 cm in size, with an irregular surface. No intentional shaping was apparent. One long naturally(?) sharp edge had been used for chopping, with the result that irregular chips had been dislodged from both faces.

Chipped Slab: 1 specimen

A naturally (?) flat slab of fine-grained basalt, 8.5 by 6.1 by 0.9 cm, rectangular in outline except for one short side, which was convex; the convex edge was roughly chipped on both faces.

Minerals: 2 specimens

A small fragment of malachite, less than a centimeter in diameter, came from Unit 3; and a calcite crystal, 1 cm in greatest diameter, from the surface.

ANTLER FLAKER (?): 1 specimen

An antler tine, with the tip slightly blunted and polished, had an uncertain function. Its weathered condition did not permit the recognition of the minute scratches that would be expected on a flaker. Possibly the implement was used for polishing or for working with softer materials.

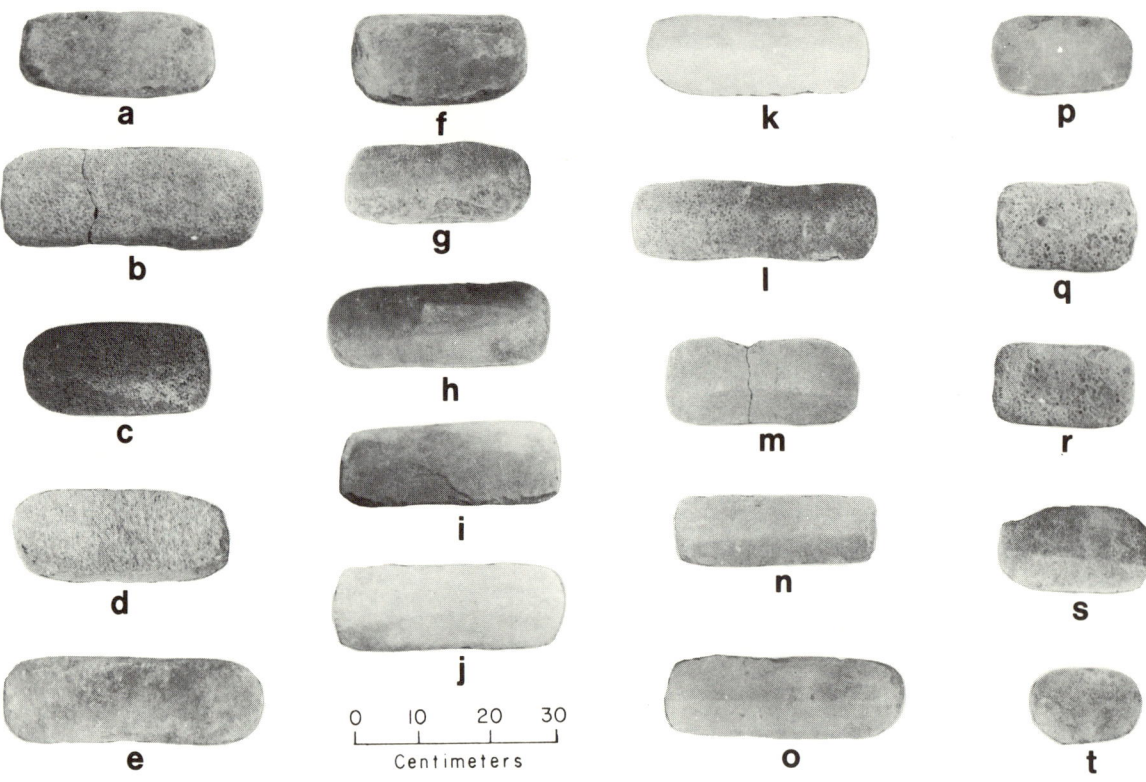

Figure 108. Manos from various sites: a. Site 481, Room 29, fill, #447 (1121); b. Site 481, Room 23, fill, #465 (1221); c. Site 494, Area A, kiva, inside ventilator, #267 (2222); d. Site 616, Room C2, fill, #1278 (1221); e. Site 616, Room B1, floor, #1350 (1021); f. Site 616, Room C9, fill, #2000 (1221); g. Site 481, Pithouse 2, fill, #685 (1321); h. Site 616, Room C3, floor, #1856 (1421); i. Site 481, Pithouse 2, fill, #676 (1721); j. Site 616, Room D2, fill, #1120 (1731); k. Site 616, Room C4, fill, #1473 (1731); l. Site 616, Room C2, floor, #1465 (2831); m. Site 616, Room C9, fill, #2016 (3821); n. Site 616, Room C1, fill, #2001 (3921); o. Site 616, Room D2, fill, #1118 (1931); p. Site 494, Area A, Room 4, floor, #279 (1122); q. Site 494, Area A, Room 4, below floor, #281 (2122); r. Site 616, Room C5, floor, #1999 (2221); s. Site 494, Area A, Room 4, floor, #380 (1822); t. Site 486, surface, #2 (2122).

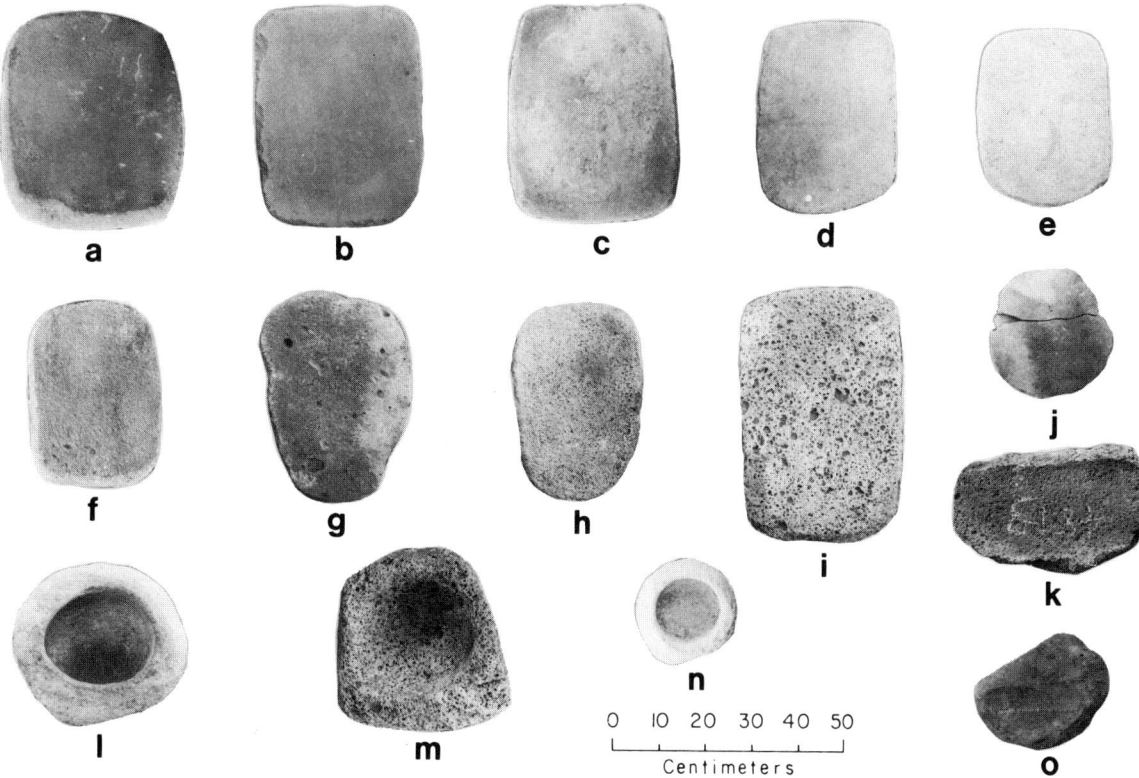

Figure 109. Metates, bowls, mortars, rubbing stone from various sites. Slab metates: a. Site 616, Room D3, fill, fine sandstone, #1218; b. Site 616, Room D2, set in mealing bin, fine sandstone, #2262; c. Site 481, Pithouse 2, fill, fine sandstone, #696; d. Site 616, Room B1, fill, fine calcareous tuff, #1207; e. Site 616, Room D2, floor, medium-fine calcareous tuff, #1213; f. Site 616, Room C5, set in mealing bin, medium calcareous tuff, #2049; g. Site 616, Room B1, floor, medium vesicular basalt, #1362; h. Site 616, Room C8, fill, medium-coarse vesicular basalt, #1843; i. Site 616, Room C7, fill, coarse vesicular basalt, #1458; j. Site 616, Room D2, set in mealing bin, fine sandstone, #2361. Trough metate: k. Site 481, Room 3, fill, #125. Stone bowls: l. Site 616, Room C7, fill, #1459; n. Site 481, Room 31, firepit, #738. Mortar: m. Site 481, Room 31, fill, #802. Rubbing stone: o. Site 481, Room 10, fill, #678.

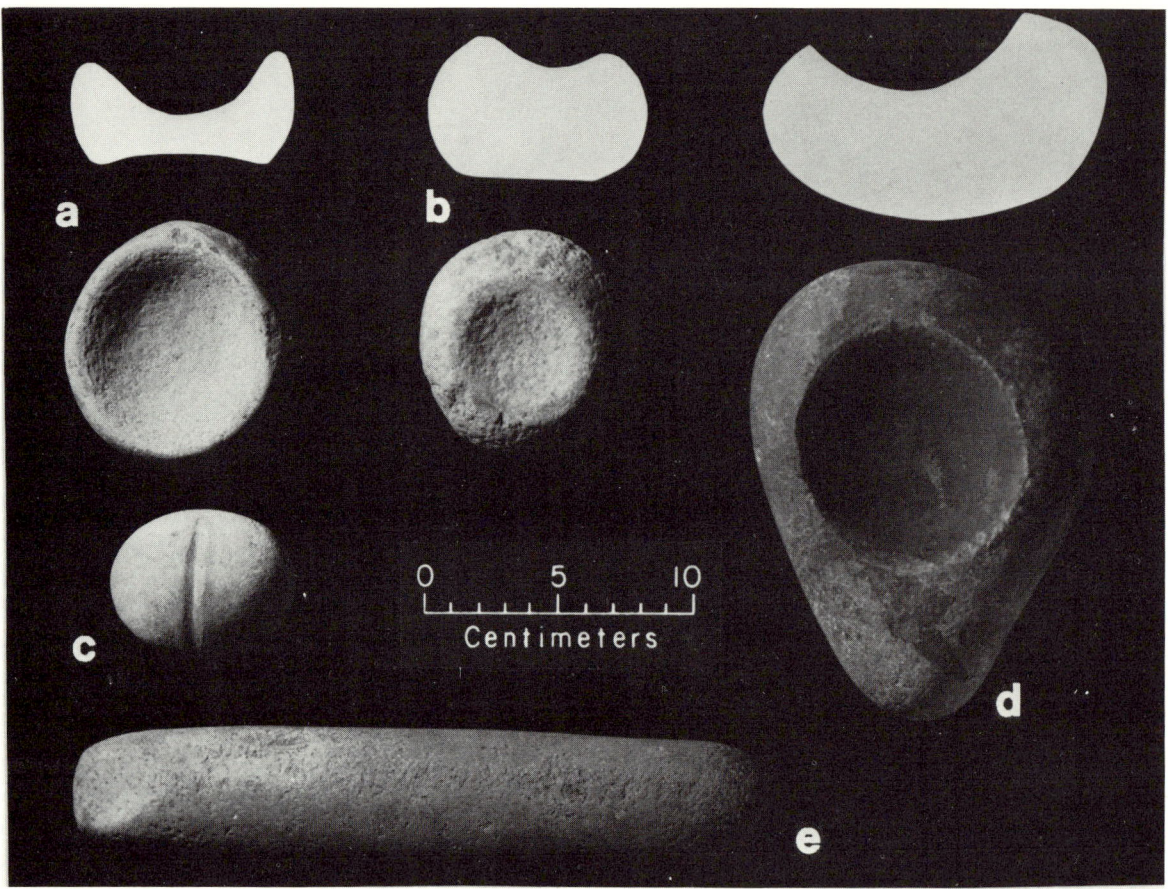

Figure 110. Mortars, grooved tool, and pestle from various sites. Mortars: a. Site 481, Room 22, fill, #650; b. Site 616, walk-in well, fill of mealing room, roughly shaped, #1811; d. Site 481, Room 2, below floor, #562. Grooved tool (shaftsmoother): c. Site 481, Room 10, fill, #484. Pestle: e. Site 481, trench in area of Room 26, #350.

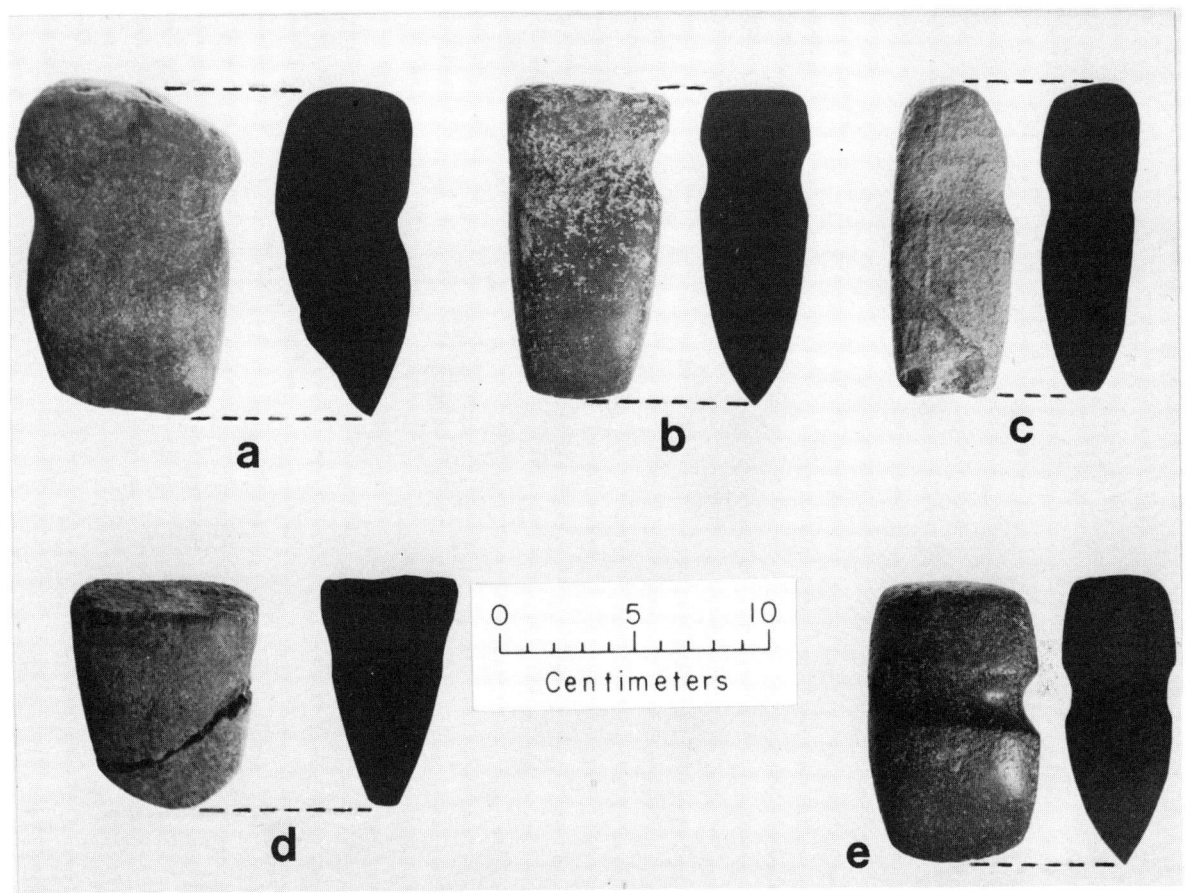

Figure 111. Axes from various sites. Full-groove: a. Site 494, Area A, kiva, floor, #264. Three-quarter-groove: b. Site 481, Room 34, fill, #428; c. Site 494, Area B, Room 1, fill, #349; d. Site 481, Room 6, fill, bit end, #263; e. Site 481, Room 2, fill, #418.

Figure 112. Hammers from various sites. Full-groove: a. Site 481, Pithouse 1, fill, #778; b. Site 481, Room 7, fill, #73; d. Site 494, Area A, kiva, floor, #265. Three-quarter-groove: c. Site 481, Room 25, fill, #162.

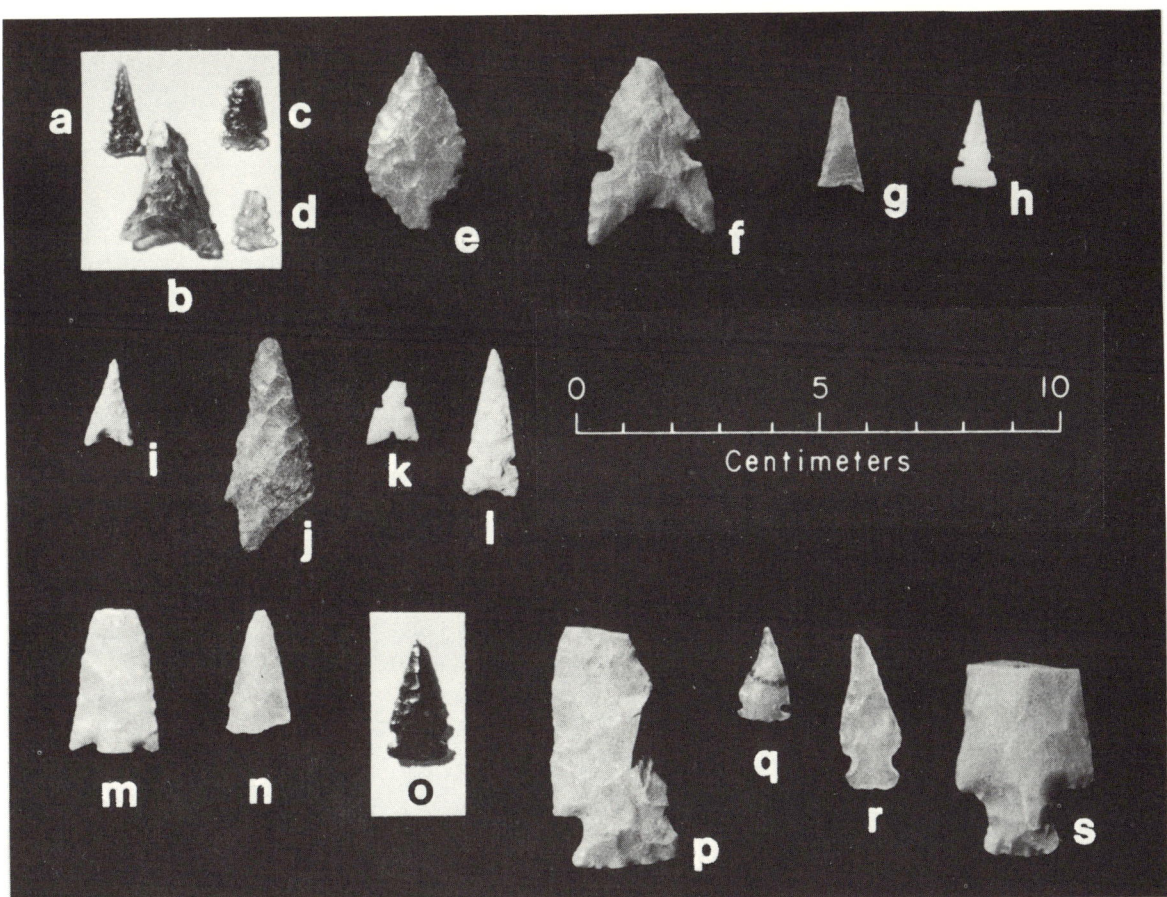

Figure 113. Points from various sites: a. Site 481, Pithouse 1, floor, #2689; b. Site 481, Pithouse 2, fill, #2564; c. Site 481, Room 17, fill, #647; d. Site 481, Room 7, fill, #342; e. Site 481, Pithouse 1, cist, #3078; f. Site 481, Pithouse 2, fill, #2559; g. Site 481, Room 2, fill, #333; h. Site 481, Room 4, fill; i. Site 143, surface, #729; j. Site 143, Room 1, on floor 2, #2546; k. Site 143, Room 1, fill, #2539; l. Site 143, Room 1, fill, #2531; m. Site 188, Room 1, fill, #208; n. Site 601, Room 4, fill, #2818; o. Site 601, surface, #2725; p. Site 601, trench along north wall, #2201; q. Site 486, surface, #20; r. Site 486, surface, #22; s. Site 486, surface, #21.

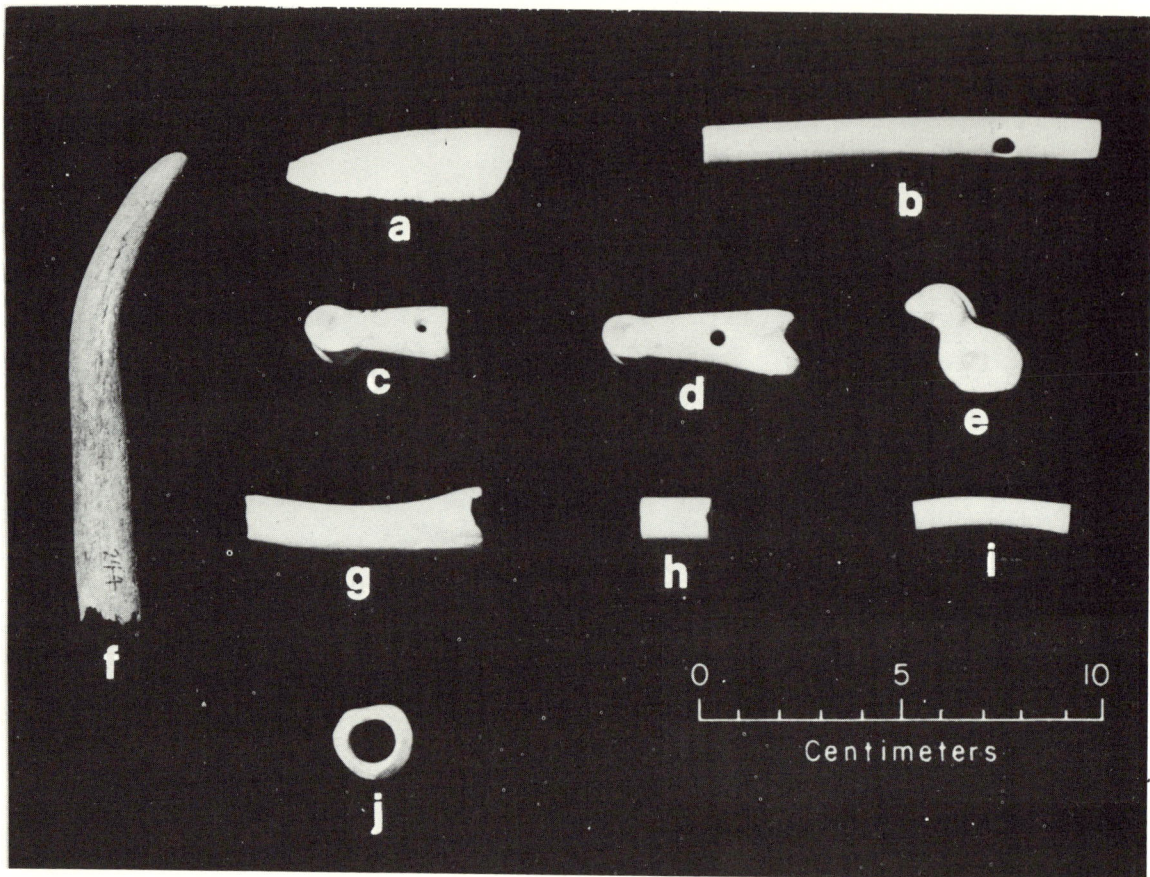

Figure 114. Bone and antler objects from various sites. Serrated tool: a. Site 481, Pithouse 2, fill, #2826. Tubes: b. Site 481, Room 29, floor, #664; g. Site 481, Room 25, fill, #285; h. Site 481, Room 4, fill, #272; i. Site 481, Room 5, fill, #288. Pierced phalanges: c. Site 481, Room 17, floor, #649; d. Site 481, Room 17, fill, #648. Figurine: e. Site 481, Room 16, floor, #651. Antler flaker: f. Site 494, Area A, kiva, floor, #244. Ring: j. Site 481, Room 8, fill, #286.

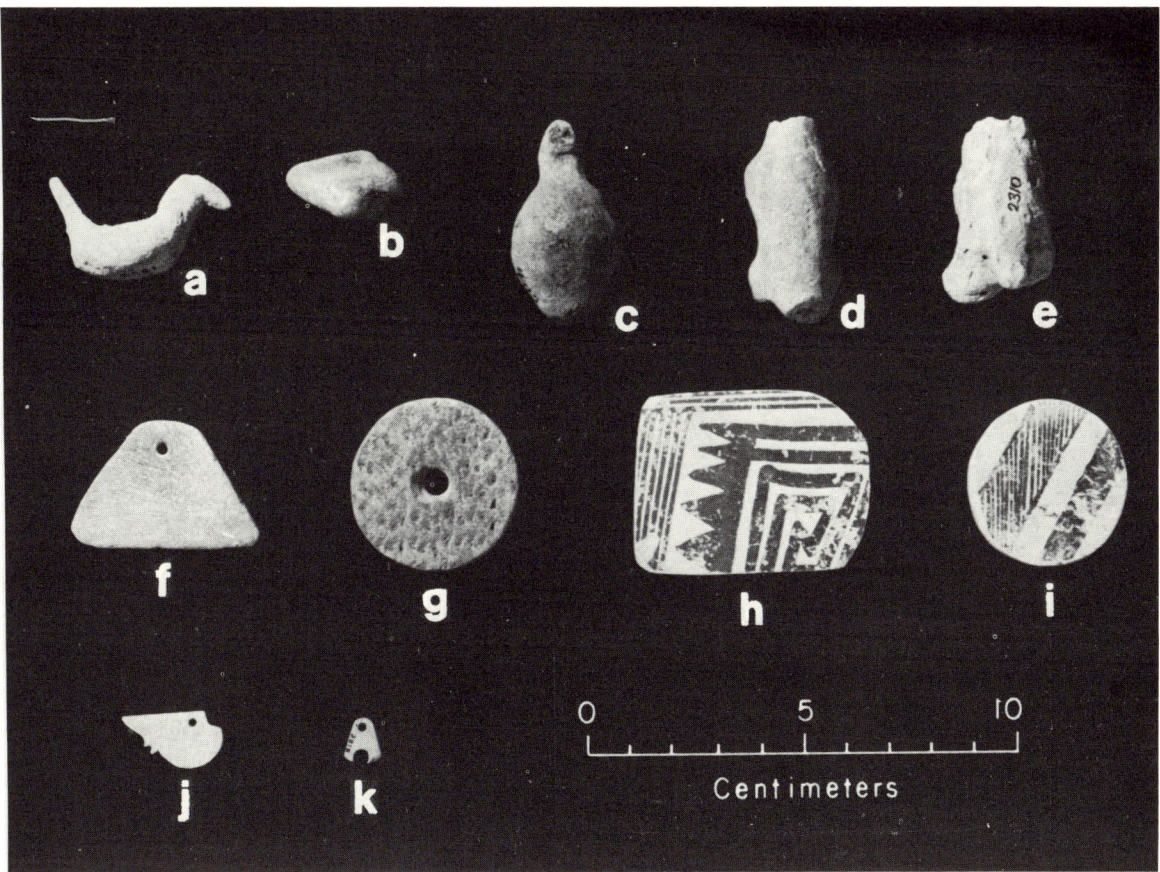

Figure 115. Clay objects from various sites. Figurines of birds: a. Site 481, Pithouse 2, fill, #2561; b. Site 143, Room 2, below floor 1, #2460; c. Site 481, Pithouse 2, fill, #2561. Figurines: d. Site 143, Room 1, fill, #2543; e. Site 601, trench, #2310. Pendants: f. Site 481, Room 10, fill, #68; j. Site 481, Room 7, fill, #292; k. Site 188, Room 1, floor, #2212. Sherd discs: g. Site 494, Area A, Room 1, floor, #217; h. Site 616; i. Site 616.

Sandstone Hill Pueblo

The only systematic excavation in the Mariana Mesa area subsequent to the work reported in this volume was carried out in 1971 at an 18-room pueblo known as Sandstone Hill, located about 13.5 miles north of Quemado, about 3.25 miles northwest of Site 143, and about 4.5 miles almost due west of Site 616. For complete data on the site see the published report (Barnett 1974), where the date of occupancy is estimated at about A.D. 1115–1300 (pp. 30–31), a little later than that of Site 481.

Barnett reports further that abandonment seemed to have been deliberate, and he suggests a possible migration to Site 616 (Barnett 1974, p. 33).

The report contains excellent and useful photographs of more than 200 whole vessels, now in private collections, from the Quemado area, but mostly without precise recorded provenience (ibid., pp. 35–56).

Appendix A

POTTERY DESCRIPTION FOR ALL SITES

Paste

Since detailed information on the geology of the immediate region was lacking and the pottery was not subjected to detailed technological analysis, the discussion of the raw materials utilized and firing techniques employed in the construction of Mariana Mesa pottery must be limited in scope. Although identifications were based upon rather extensive observations with an eleven-power binocular microscope, the author's limited experience in recognizing materials precluded any attempt at precise mineralogical identifications. Such identifications and a more precise knowledge of the characteristics of the clay would doubtless add greatly to the interpretative value of the ceramic material.

Detailed technological analysis of every sherd recovered from sites in regions like the Southwest will never be possible. Such analysis must be conducted on a sample of sherds from a previously established typological group. This necessitates the assumption that the selected sample is actually representative of a particular type. It must further be assumed, *a priori*, that the readily observable features by which particular types were established (design, vessel shape, surface color, generalized temper and/or paste characteristics, and so on) correlate significantly with variations in material and technique discoverable only by more precise technological analysis. If 60 sherds out of a total sample of 600 sherds of type A (established on the basis of similarity evident in surface color, tempering materials, and other characteristics observed macroscopically) prove to have identical mineralogical inclusions and clay characteristics, then it can reasonably be assumed that the other 540 sherds do so as well, and thus the type can be applied to the analysis of problems requiring identity of basic materials. If, however, 20 of the sherds analyzed are found to have different mineralogical inclusions, this discovery, to have greatest general applicability, must be correlated with some readily observable characteristic so that the entire collection may be separated on this basis without necessitating the almost impossible task of analyzing every sherd microscopically. The questions that arise in the field-worker's mind naturally center around what observable characteristics or combinations thereof are most likely to yield typological groups basically similar in temper and paste constituents.

In this report it is assumed that if sherds were "identical" with respect to the observable features discussed below (e.g., surface treatment, decoration, and so on), the mineralogical and technological properties of the clay and inclusions were also identical. Until this assumption is tested, the material modes discussed should be used with appropriate caution. In practice, an average of about one in every 100 sherds was observed through the binocular microscope but this proportion varied widely with particular circumstances. Sherds from every restored vessel were observed microscopically.

In the formation of the material modes several features were considered. Shepard (Kidder and Shepard 1936, pp. 406–411) has demonstrated that microscopic observations of these features are not dependably indicative of either the material used or the firing technique employed, but the gross variations or modal tendencies that can be recognized in the excavated sample, reflect in a general, even if in a somewhat unreliable way, these two aspects, and their observation has in the past proved to be of value in the analysis of certain problems, despite the lack of a high degree of precision. In differentiating modes, greatest weight was placed upon variations in paste consistency, extreme variations in color (or else consistent occurrence of a limited range of color), the nature and amount of inclusions, and any observed clustering of particular traits.

In the pottery descriptions the following characteristics were observed:

Color: Standard and range of variation.

Core: Presence, absence, location, and frequency of carbon streak.

Clay texture: Denseness or friability of the paste.

Fracture: Crumbling or shattering; this is simply another expression of the same characteristics reflected in "appearance" and "texture" with the addition of the factors of quantity and type of inclusions.

Appearance in cross section: The appearance of the paste in cross section in relation to two characteristics — angularity of the surface, and tendency to reflect light.

Inclusions: The phrase "angular opaque" is used generally to refer to sherd inclusions but certain other materials such as tuff may well be included. The use of the term "sherd temper" indicates that recognizable fragments of crushed pottery were definitely identified. "Sand" refers to predominantly quartzlike materials. Frequency and size are expressed in terms of Shepard's scale (Kidder and Shepard 1936, pp. 409-410).

Let me emphasize again that if a particular sherd differed in any recognizable degree as to any one of these observed characteristics, it was assigned to a separate descriptive type.

Construction

Except for the corrugated vessels, which were constructed entirely of concentric coils, the basic features of construction can only be hypothesized, not observed. Coil fracture occasionally could be seen even on basal sherds but in general the coils were sufficiently well amalgamated to prevent its frequent occurrence. With the exception of miniature vessels, there was no evidence that large basal sections were molded and upper sections coiled, but limited use of this technique cannot be conclusively denied. Similarly, it was impossible to determine whether spiral or closed-ring (banded) coiling was more popular or whether, as with the corrugated vessels, spiral coils were employed. The evidence on coil size for corrugated vessels and the scanty evidence in the other groups indicated the consistent use of a coil of rather small diameter, ranging between one and two centimeters. Because of this slight evidence for uniformity and the inability to recognize variation, these basic techniques generally did not enter into the definition of construction modes, which were delineated primarily on the basis of variations in the technique and character of surface treatment.

The corrugated vessels were an exception to this procedure. Since construction coils remained clearly evident on corrugated vessels, it was possible to recognize a number of variant basic techniques, and an attempt was made to observe or estimate the following features: direction of coiling, hand and finger used for indentation, and position of hand during indentation. It was hoped that by so doing patterns might be recognized that would prove to be typical of groups of potters at different sites or perhaps even within a particular site.

When the basal pat was present the direction of coiling could be directly observed, the direction being expressed from the point of view of a person looking down upon an upright vessel. With sherd material, this, as well as the hand used and the position of the hand, had to be interpreted by observing the patterns of fingerprints and direction of the indentations. Here my interpretations differ in certain respects from those of Shepard (Kidder and Shepard 1936, pp. 554-561). In indenting the body of the pot (disregarding for the moment the technique of indenting the basal portion) it is, as Shepard notes, most likely that the potters worked on the side of the pot nearest to them. Indentation of the far side would involve working blindly and would seem to be awkward and physically uncomfortable. However, the awkwardness at least could be overcome by using the thumb side of the first finger. In indenting the near side of the vessel it appears to be most practical (i.e., easy and rapid) to use the thumb in one of three positions: (1) pointing up with the outboard side (side away from the fingers) used against the clay, (2) pointing down with the outboard side against the clay, and (3) pointing down with the inboard side against the clay. The thumb may be straight up and down or at an angle, ranging between 90° and 45°, and directed toward the center of the potter's body (right thumbs point left and vice versa). Either hand may be used, of course, but with exertion of backward pressure it was found most comfortable to use the left hand on counterclockwise coils and the right on clockwise coils. Backward pressure by the right thumb on a counterclockwise coil tends to pull the fingernail away from the finger, with a similar tendency for the left thumb on a clockwise coil. Aside from comfort, the correlation of left hand with counterclockwise coil seems to afford greatest facility (at least the author, to an inexperienced potter).

As Shepard indicates, the outboard edge of the thumb when held obliquely and down tends to leave an impression of horizontal fingerprints, while a vertical pattern results when the thumb is held obliquely and up. Unfortunately for this neat correlation, a vertical pattern also occurs when the thumb is held obliquely and down and the inboard edge is pressed to the clay (a position I at least found more convenient and practical than with the outboard edge in this position). Unless there has been sufficient backward pressure to permit determining the direction of indentation, it would seem difficult to distinguish between indentations made with the inboard side of the right thumb pointing down and the outboard side of the left thumb pointing up, since both the angle of the indentation and the angle of the fingerprint are the same in both cases. However, when backward pressure is exerted, the sharper drop-off or slope of the raised ridges will tend to be on the side of the thumb used and the fingerprints will tend to appear on the opposite slope, i.e., if the left slope drops sharply and/or fingerprints appear on the right slope, the left thumb pointing upward was used. The correlation of the slope of the indentation and the fingerprint provides a reasonably dependable and (once the general principles are understood) rapid means of recognizing and sorting sherds in relation to this aspect of construction technique. These correlations are diagrammed in the accompanying chart. The arrow indicates the direction of the thumb and angle of the indentation, the second line the angle of the fingerprint.

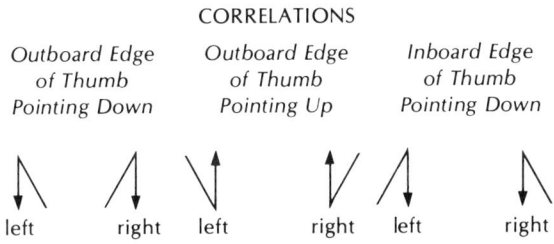

CORRELATIONS

Outboard Edge of Thumb Pointing Down	Outboard Edge of Thumb Pointing Up	Inboard Edge of Thumb Pointing Down
left right	left right	left right

When the base as well as the body of the vessel is indented it is not necessary that the hand be reversed, as Shepard suggests, in order to keep the same angle of indentation throughout. Whereas it is awkward at best to work on the far side of a vessel of any considerable size it is possible to work with almost equal facility on either side of the basal pat. Thus it is quite easy to begin with a clockwise coil, indenting the far side with the outboard edge of the left thumb pointing obliquely down, and then, when the basal section is completed, to turn the vessel over, continuing with the left thumb in an oblique position, although now the thumb points upward and the coiling has become counterclockwise. It would be equally possible to begin on the near side with the thumb changing to the left, as above, when the vessel position is reversed. The fingerprints and indentation patterns resulting from these two alternatives are so nearly identical that it is unlikely that they can be consistently and reliably distinguished.

In an attempt to recognize patterns of construction that might prove to be significant, the details of surface appearance and treatment were observed fairly closely in the plain and slipped pottery groups as follows:

Surface Texture: On a scale of slick, smooth, and gritty.

Surface Appearance: On a scale of even, undulating, and irregular.

Surface Irregularities: Marked striations, anvil marks, and protruding temper noted.

Surface Luster: Dull, lustrous, and highly lustrous as defined by the reflection of light; location and extent of lustrous areas noted.

Defects: In material — spalling, crazing, peeling; in workmanship — fireclouds with area and size noted.

Decoration

It has been frequently pointed out that decoration is perhaps the most important aspect of pottery to the archaeologist. Consequently, the colors used, the amount, placement, and execution of design, and special features of technique were all observed in some detail. The design elements were described whenever possible in terms of the outline published by the Clearing House for Southwestern Museums (Douglas 1941, pp. 120–124). Motifs and elements dominant at each site were abstracted, and other elements considered by other authors to be diagnostic of regional time-space types were observed. (However, for a much more detailed analysis of the decoration of pottery vessels from Site 616 the reader is referred to Washburn 1977.)

Vessel Shapes and Sizes

Adequate definition of terms is an essential element of scientific analysis and practical scientific reporting. Without it the analyst is unable to convey information to others with accuracy. On the other hand, restricting the general descriptive terms within narrow problem-oriented limits can inhibit rather than facilitate adequate communication. In the analysis of vessel shape and size, I was primarily concerned with attempting to recognize and convey to the reader the various action types executed by the occupants of the sites under consideration. No predetermined clinical categories or mathematical definitions of what constitutes a "bowl" or a "plate" are likely to further this end. Of course, once action types for particular sites have been delineated through recognizing and demonstrating mathematically (or otherwise) expressed "thresholds," it often becomes feasible, even desirable, to present the limits and central tendencies of these types by means of mathematical formulas. This was not attempted, for, with the possible exception of Site 616, the samples were small and the categories recognized were necessarily broad, so that the impressions conveyed by words and pictures are as accurate a guide as the data permit.

Other Aspects

In addition to modes established with respect to the features discussed above, other features were noted and included in the general discussion, e.g., handles, lugs, drilled holes, grooves, reworked collars, stains, and so forth.

Whole Vessels versus Sherds

During the analysis of the pottery an attempt was made to sort out and group together sherds from individual vessels. Whenever sufficient sherds of a single vessel permitted observation of all features generally noted on a complete vessel, that aggregate of sherds was designated as a whole vessel.

Recognizing and sorting out these whole vessels was not as difficult as had been anticipated. The possible range of variation and details of execution on the slipped and painted vessels was so great that little difficulty was experienced in identifiying sherds of a single vessel. Also, we were usually working with material derived from a single room or small group of rooms. When refuse deposits are being studied, this kind of analysis is rarely possible. Needless to say, the plain and corrugated vessels were more difficult than the painted vessels. While it is felt that the plain and corrugated vessel descriptions as presented are in fact descriptions of original entire vessels, less confidence can be placed on the exactness of the sherd count than is the case with the painted vessels. That is, it is not only probable that some sherds from each vessel were missed, but it is also likely that at least in some instances some of the sherds ascribed to each vessel did not derive from that vessel. It is felt, however, that the vessel itself is the important thing. Minor errors in sherd count are of significance only in the comparison of the two techniques of counting the material. Of greater importance is the likelihood that not all possible corrugated vessels were recognized and sorted out. If the major portion of a vessel was present, it is likely that it was recognized, but unless a vessel represented by only a few sherds (albeit enough for complete description had they all been recognized) had some distinctive feature, it was doubtless overlooked.

While this is unfortunate, it is unavoidable. The result is that the total count of whole plain and corrugated vessels probably is a slightly lower percentage of the entire sample than is the case with the painted groups.

It was originally hoped that it would be possible to make an estimate of the minimal and probable number of vessels represented by the sherds in each excavation or living unit. However, this did not always prove practical. It is interesting that nearly all of the sherds found on the floors of rooms at Site 616 could be assigned to individual vessels.

Pottery Modes and Attributes for All Sites

PASTE: ALL POTTERY
Mode Key A*

Color: average: dull white; range: buff to dark gray. Carbon streak: rare in all forms, most often present on the inner half of jar sherds. Clay texture: generally friable but occasionally dense. Fracture: crumbling or shattering (this seems to vary more with the amount of firing than with the amount of inclusions). Appearance in cross section: irregular and dull (occasional sherds were more angular and had a slight lustrous or vitreous appearance). Inclusions: gray, opaque, angular material with rare rounded and angular, generally clear, sand; fine to medium in size with rare coarse fragments; moderate in frequency.

Mode Key B

Color: average: gray; range: light to dark gray. Carbon streak: rare. Clay texture: friable but occasionally dense. Fracture: crumbling or shattering (varying with amount of inclusions). Appearance in cross section: irregular, dull, and powdery, though occasionally almost angular. Inclusions: dark to light gray, angular opaque material and occasionally clear or cloudy rounded quartz grains, fine to medium in size, sparse.

The larger amount of sand proportionally and the general sparseness of the temper helps to distinguish sherds of mode key B from mode key A.

Mode Key C

Color: average: gray; range: light to dark gray. Carbon streak: rare. Clay texture: dense and very compact. Fracture: shattering. Appearance in cross section: angular and slightly vitreous. Inclusions: except for rare fine patches of lighter or darker gray, no inclusions evident.

*If *any* sherd differed beyond the defined and observable limits with respect to *any* of the included attributes (e.g., color, carbon streak, and so on) it was *not* included in this mode, but was placed in another mode, or, if necessary, a new mode was established to accommodate it.

This material has a decided "ring" to it, though its hardness is less than 5 on the Mohs' scale. It is generally lightly slipped and very smooth and even.

Mode Key D

Color: average: gray; range: buff to dark gray. Carbon streak: rare, but occasionally present on inner half of jars. Clay texture: dense. Fracture: shattering. Appearance in cross section: straight, dull, and powdery. Inclusions: light gray, angular, opaque material with rare, round, cloudy quartz, fine to medium in size, moderate in frequency.

Generally similar to mode key B, except for denseness and shattering quality.

Mode Key E

Color: average: gray; range: light gray to brown. Carbon streak: rare but occasionally present on interiors of jars. Clay texture: friable. Fracture: crumbling to shattering. Appearance in cross section: irregular and dull. Inclusions: clear and cloudy rounded quartz with some gray angular opaque fragments, medium in size, moderate in frequency.

Mode Key F

Color: gray to tan to light orange. Carbon streak: great variation, color ranging from tan to black, thickness ranging from absence to four-fifths of the thickness of the sherd. Clay texture: friable. Fracture: crumbling though occasionally tending to shatter. Appearance in cross section: irregular and dull though sometimes almost vitreous. Inclusions: gray to tan to orange angular opaque material, medium to coarse in size, moderate in frequency.

This paste type is associated with red-slipped pottery.

Mode Key G

Color: light buff to gray. Carbon streak: occasionally present. Clay texture: friable. Fracture: crumbling. Appearance in cross section: irregular, dull and powdery. Inclusions: buff or gray or cream angular opaque material, medium to coarse in size and moderate in frequency, with rare coarse quartz, and occasional fine red or black fragments.

This paste type is associated with red-slipped pottery.

Mode Key H

Color: average: dull brown; range: carbon black through tan and buff to brick red. Carbon streak: rare though occasionally present on inner half of jars. Clay texture: friable. Fracture: generally crumbling but occasionally almost shattering. Appearance in cross section: irregular, dull, and powdery to slightly lustrous. Inclusions: clear and cloudy rounded and/or angular quartz, occasional rose or cream-colored sand, white or black specks, and clear or golden mica; fine to coarse in size (this size range can occur in a single vessel, though some vessels tend to be uniformly one or the other); heavy frequency.

This paste type is associated primarily with corrugated pottery.

Mode Key I

Color: average: cream gray; range: light cream through slate gray to brown to carbon black. Carbon streak: rare though occasionally with a brown area on inner half. Clay texture: dense. Fracture: shattering (crumbling when poorly fired). Appearance in cross section: angular, dull, and powdery to slightly vitreous. Inclusions: white to gray or buff angular opaque material, rare black specks and clear or cloudy, generally coarse, angular sand; medium to coarse in size with occasional fine fragments (size fairly constant within any one vessel); moderate frequency.

Mode Key J

Color: average: cream; range: gray to dark brown. Carbon streak: absent. Clay texture: dense. Fracture: shattering (frequently crumbling as a result of large quantities of tempering materials). Appearance in cross section: angular, dull, and powdery. Inclusions: clear with occasional cloudy, round and angular quartz with occasional fine black specks and white or gray angular opaque material, coarse in size, moderate to heavy in frequency.

SLIP: WHITE- AND RED-SLIPPED POTTERY

Mode a: No slip.
Mode b: Slip flat-white in color.
Mode c: Slip creamy white in color.
Mode d: Slip orange in color; range: brown to red; slip tends to crackle.
Mode e: Slip brick-red or maroon in color; slip often has a powdery appearance and tends to wear away fairly readily; it never exhibits crackling.
Mode f: Slip of same material as the paste, dull white in color.
Mode g: Slip thickly applied, and visible in cross section with the naked eye.
Mode h: Slip thinly applied, and visible in cross section only with the aid of a magnifying glass (14x used); slip is not translucent and the paste cannot be seen through it.
Mode i: Watery slip, applied so thinly and/or in such a dilute solution that paste can be seen in patches.

PAINT: WHITE- AND RED-SLIPPED POTTERY

Mode a: Black mineral paint
Mode b: Black semiglaze or glaze paint
Mode c: Black carbon paint
Mode d: White (kaolin?) paint

VESSEL SHAPES: ALL POTTERY

The following modes delineate general form types. There are variations and subtypes within all of them. Usually these variations correlate with different sites, and also with different construction and finishing techniques. The nature and extent of this variation is considered herein during the discussion of the pottery from each site.

Mode a: Bowl
Mode b: Neckless (seed) jar
Mode c: Short-necked jar
Mode d: Jar with narrow neck
Mode e: Open-mouthed jar
Mode f: Jar with upper half insloping from central inset ridge
Mode g: Pitcher
Mode h: Ladle
Mode i: Eccentrics and miniatures

AREAS SLIPPED AND PAINTED: WHITE POTTERY

Mode a: Interiors slipped
Mode b: Exteriors slipped
Mode c: Interiors painted
Mode d: Exteriors painted

AREAS SLIPPED AND PAINTED: RED POTTERY

Mode e: Interiors black-on-red
Mode f: Interiors black- and white-on-red
Mode g: Interiors black-on-white-on-red and white-on-red
Mode h: Exteriors white-on-red
Mode i: Exteriors black- and white-on-red
Mode j: Exteriors black-on-white-on-red
Mode k: Exteriors black-on-white-on-red and white-on-red
Mode l: Exteriors black-on-red

SURFACE FINISH: WHITE- AND RED-SLIPPED POTTERY*

Mode a: Slipped surfaces slightly undulating, smooth to the touch
Mode b: Slipped surface even, smooth or slick to the touch
Mode c: Slipped surface slightly undulating, gritty to the touch
Mode d: Slipped surface even but gritty because of protruding sand temper

*When these modes are used with reference to the rare sherds or vessels totally unslipped, the description applies to the unslipped surface.

Mode e: Polishing marks occasionally evident
Mode f: Polishing marks readily apparent
Mode g: Slip polished before application of paint
Mode h: Slip polished after application of paint
Mode i: Entire surface reflecting light
Mode j: High points only reflecting light
Mode k: Matte surface
Mode l: Slipped surface unpolished

DECORATION: WHITE- AND RED-SLIPPED POTTERY

Decorative motifs, elements and modes abstracted are presented and discussed in connection with the individual sites.

CONSTRUCTION: PLAIN AND CORRUGATED POTTERY

Mode a: Coiled counterclockwise, coil indented and/or annealed by pressure from the outside edge of the left thumb pointing upward. It is impossible to determine if the basal section was made by working on the near side of the vessel with the right thumb pointing up or working on the far side of the vessel with the left thumb pointing down.
Mode b: Coiled counterclockwise, coils indented and/or annealed by pressure from the inside edge of the left thumb pointing down. This technique often leaves the lower edge of a clapboard coil as a raised ridge — not possible if either thumb had been used pointing upward.
Mode c: Coiled clockwise, coils indented and/or annealed by pressure from the outside edge of the right thumb pointing upward.
Mode d: Presumably coiled, direction of coiling and method of annealing unknown.
Mode e: Vessel molded (miniature or toy vessels only).

SURFACE FINISH: PLAIN AND CORRUGATED POTTERY

Mode a: Interior surfaces even, smooth, matte: coils and indentations unobliterated on the exterior surface although occasionally a polishing tool was rubbed lightly over the vessel, smoothing the outermost edges of the coils.
Mode b: Surface even, smooth to the touch, and lustrous, with streaks of a hard polishing tool evident.
Mode c: Surface even but gritty to the touch with occasional small pits in the surface; matte.
Mode d: Surface undulating and gritty to the touch with occasional pits; matte except

for the high points, which are lustrous. This mode found on miniature or toy vessels only.

Mode e: Surface even but with small striations, gritty to the touch because of protruding temper; matte.

DECORATIVE EFFECT: PLAIN AND CORRUGATED POTTERY

Mode a: Absence of decoration.
Mode b: Clapboard corrugation.
Mode c: Indented corrugation.
Mode d: Pattern-indented corrugation — both clapboard and indented on a single sherd or vessel.
Mode e: Plain and corrugated (indented and/or clapboard) areas on single sherds or vessels. As with sherds of mode d, these sherds represent specific portions of vessels, the majority of whose sherds were doubtless allocated to other modes. On jars, this mode has reference to basal corrugation and plain neck of vessels of shape mode d; on bowls, this mode has reference to those of the so-called fillet rim variety, where several coils just below the rim were left unsmoothed and indented, the rest of the bowl being plain.
Mode f: Clapboard corrugation and incision.
Mode g: Interior of vessel smudged.
Mode h: Fingernail punctation.
Mode i: Overall irregularly parallel vertical striations.

COMMENT

The modes listed above present the general categories abstracted. The execution and utilization of these modes varied at the different sites. These variations are brought out in connection with the discussions of pottery from the individual Sites.

Appendix B

TREE-RING SPECIMENS

In this appendix are compiled all dates derived from wood or charcoal specimens recovered from the sites discussed in this volume. The number of such specimens is disappointingly small, but collectively they do provide some evidence, when considered together with the ceramic materials, for at least approximate dating of the sites involved. All dates were determined by the Laboratory of Tree-Ring Research at the University of Arizona, and have (except for HAR-3090) been reported in Bannister, Hannah, and Robinson 1970, pp. 13–16, as listed below.

TREE-RING DATES

Specimen No.	Provenience	Dates (Bannister, Hannah, and Robinson 1970)
HAR— 2605	Site 188, Room 1	A.D. 1006 p–1071 r
HAR— 481 —31	Site 481, Room 27	A.D. 1180 p–1248 c
30	Room 27	1179 –1271 c
34	Room 31	1193 –1248 r B
6	Kiva	1172 p–1248 c
3	Kiva	1186 p–1248 c
25	Kiva	1192 p–1248 c
1	Kiva	1183 –1268 vv
7	Kiva	1151 p–1213 vv
35	Kiva	1156 –1229 vv
HAR— 3090	Pithouse 1	673 –1010 ++vv
HAR— 494B—33	Site 494, Kiva B	A.D. 1088 p–1191 v
HAR— 1860— 1	Site 616, Room C3	A.D. 1203 p–1247 v
1861— 1	Room C3	1195 p–1282 v
1860— 2	Room C3	1231 p–1285 v
2063	Room C5	1190 p–1286 vv
2315	Kiva	1166 p–1236 c
2644	Kiva	1142 p–1243 c
0000	Kiva	1159 p–1243 r
2642	Kiva	1189 p–1263 c

No specimens were recovered from Sites 143, 486, and 601.

Symbols used above are defined by the Laboratory of Tree-Ring Research as follows:

year only — no pith ring present.

p — pith ring present.
B — bark present.
r — less than a full section is present, but the outermost ring is present around the available circumference.
c — the outermost ring is continuous around the full circumference.

v — a subjective judgment that, although there is no direct evidence of the true outside on the specimen, the date is within a very few years of the cutting date.
vv — there is no way of estimating how far the last ring is from the true outside.
++ — a ring count is necessary because of the fact that beyond a certain point the specimen could not be dated.

Appendix C

CORN

A small quantity of corn was recovered, primarily from Site 616, Area C. The other sites yielding samples were Sites 188, 481, and 601.

The material was largely fragmentary and only in a few instances was it possible to obtain dimensions of an entire ear. The data on these whole specimens follow:

One cob from the firepit of Room C5, Site 616: 7.2 cm long with a diameter of 2.6 cm. On this specimen the upper glumes were about as long as the lower, and there were long hairs on the upper glumes. The glumes indicated a weak pod corn, nontripsacoid. Typical kernels were 8.4 by 8.9 by 4.5 mm, 7.8 by 7.2 by 5.1 mm, and 7.5 by 7.5 by 5.2 mm.

One cob from the fill of Room 2, Site 481: length 4.7 cm, diameter 12 by 8 mm. The spikelets were widely spaced, lower glumes thicker than the upper, and the cupules shallow.

A second cob from the fill of Room 2, Site 481: length 2.5 cm, diameter 1.3 by 1 cm. This tripsacoid specimen was nine-rowed including one row of single spikelets. The lower glume was thicker than the upper.

One cob from the fill of Pithouse 2, Site 481: length 3.4 cm, diameter 1 cm, ten-rowed. The spikelets were widely spaced. The upper and lower glumes were about the same thickness. The cupules were tiny and shallow and the kernels must have been very small.

One cob from the floor of Room 1, Site 601: length 3.5 cm, diameter 1.4 cm, ten-rowed. The spikelets were widely spaced. The upper and lower glumes were about the same thickness.

At Site 616 eight specimens had 8 rows each, one had 10 rows, and two had 12 rows each. At Site 481 two specimens had 8 rows each, four had 10 rows each, and one had 12 rows. At site 601 one specimen had 10 rows and one had 12 rows.

At Site 616 the range of typical kernel size is listed below.

The kernels from Site 481 varied rather widely in size but all were broad, thick, and short. At Sites 601 and 188 the kernels were within the range of the medium kernels at Site 616.

TYPICAL KERNEL SIZE

Length	Width	Thickness	
10.0 mm	8.3 mm	6.1 mm	
8.5	9.9	4.0	Typical large kernels
8.3	9.7	5.1	Flint or flour corn
7.3	8.8	3.4	
8.8	9.0	4.3	
9.0	8.9	4.2	Typical medium kernels
7.9	9.0	4.2	Flint or flour corn
9.1	8.8	4.6	
6.9	6.6	4.8	
6.4	5.8	3.2	
8.1	5.9	3.9	Typical small kernels
6.0	5.9	3.4	Popcorn like Mexican race chapalore
6.5	5.3	5.9	

References

Bailey, Florence M.
   1928   *Birds of New Mexico.* New Mexico Department of Game and Fish, Sante Fe, New Mexico.

Bailey, Vernon
   1913   *Life Zones and Crop Zones of New Mexico.* North American Fauna, no. 35, Bureau of Biological Survey, United States Department of Agriculture, Washington, D.C.
   1931   *Mammals of New Mexico.* North American Fauna, no. 53, Bureau of Biological Survey, United States Department of Agriculture, Washington, D.C.

Bannister, B., J. W. Hannah, and W. J. Robinson
   1970   *Tree-Ring Dates from New Mexico M-N, S, Z, Southwestern New Mexico Area.* Laboratory of Tree-Ring Research, University of Arizona, Tucson, Arizona.

Barnett, Franklin
   1974   *Sandstone Hill Pueblo Ruin: Cibola Culture in Catron County, New Mexico.* Albuquerque Archaeological Society, Albuquerque, New Mexico.

Bartlett, Katharine
   1933   *Pueblo Milling Stones of the Flagstaff Region and Their Relation to Others in the Southwest. A Study in Progressive Efficiency.* Museum of Northern Arizona, Bulletin 3, Flagstaff, Arizona.

Breternitz, David A.
   1966   *An Appraisal of Tree-Ring Dated Pottery in the Southwest.* Anthropological Papers of the University of Arizona, no. 10, University of Arizona Press, Tucson, Arizona.

Brew, John O.
   1946   *Archaeology of Alkali Ridge, Southeastern Utah.* Papers of the Peabody Museum of Archaeology and Ethnology, Harvard University, vol. 21, Cambridge, Massachusetts.

Bryan, Kirk
   1929   "Flood-water Farming," *The Geographical Review,* vol. 19, no. 3, pp. 444-456.
   1941   "Pre-Columbian Agriculture in the Southwest, as Conditioned by Periods of Alluviation," *Annals of the Association of American Geographers,* vol. 31, no. 4, pp. 219-242.

Bullard, William R.
   1962   *The Cerro Colorado Site and Pithouse Architecture in the Southwestern United States prior to A.D. 900.* Papers of the Peabody Museum of Archaeology and Ethnology, Harvard University, vol. 44, no. 2, Cambridge, Massachusetts.

Bunzel, Ruth L.
   1929   *The Pueblo Potter: A Study of Creative Imagination in Primitive Art.* Columbia University Press, New York, New York. Republished, 1973, AMS Press, New York, New York.

Carlson, Roy L.
   1970   *White Mountain Redware: A Pottery Tradition of East-Central Arizona and Western New Mexico.* Anthropological Papers of the University of Arizona, no. 19, University of Arizona Press, Tucson, Arizona.

Colton, Harold S.
   1953   *Potsherds. An Introduction to the Study of Prehistoric Southwestern Ceramics and Their Use in Historic Reconstruction.* Museum of Northern Arizona, Bulletin 25, Flagstaff, Arizona.
   1962-   *Pottery Types of the Southwest.* Museum of Northern Arizona, Ceramic Series, Flagstaff, Arizona.
   1965

Colton, H. S., and L. L. Hargrave
   1937   *Handbook of Northern Arizona Pottery Wares.* Museum of Northern Arizona, Bulletin 12, Flagstaff, Arizona.

Cory, Harry T.
   1935   *Inventory of the Water Resources of the Colorado River Drainage Area.* Second edition. Abstract of a Report to the Water Resources Section, U.S. National Resources Board, Washington, D.C.

Cosgrove, H. S., and C. B. Cosgrove
   1932   *The Swartz Ruin: A Typical Mimbres Site in Southwestern New Mexico.* Papers of the Peabody Museum of Archaeology and Ethnology, Harvard University, vol. 15, no. 1, Cambridge, Massachusetts.

Dane, C. H., and G. O. Bachman
   1965   *Geologic Map of New Mexico.* U.S. Geological Survey, Department of the Interior, Washington, D.C.

Danson, Edward B.
   1950   "Preliminary Report of the Peabody Museum Upper Gila Expedition, Reconnaissance Division, 1949," *El Palacio,* vol. 57, no. 12, pp. 383-390, Sante Fe, New Mexico.
   1957   *An Archaeological Survey of West Central New Mexico and East Central Arizona.* Papers of the Peabody Museum of Archaeology and Ethnology, Harvard University, vol. 44, no. 1, Cambridge, Massachusetts.

Danson, E. B., and H. E. Malde
   1950   "Casa Malpais, a Fortified Pueblo Site at Springerville, Arizona," *Plateau,* vol. 22, no. 4, pp. 61-67, Flagstaff, Arizona.

Dean, Jeffrey S.
- 1969 *Chronological Analysis of Tsegi Phase Sites in Northeastern Arizona.* Papers of the Laboratory of Tree-Ring Research, University of Arizona, no. 3, Tucson, Arizona.

Dick, Herbert W.
- 1965 *Bat Cave.* The School of American Research, Monographs, no. 27, Santa Fe, New Mexico.

DiPeso, Charles C.
- 1951 *The Babocomari Village Site on the Babocomari River, Southeastern Arizona.* The Amerind Foundation, no. 5, Dragoon, Arizona.
- 1953 *The Sobaipuri Indians of the Upper San Pedro River Valley, Southeastern Arizona.* The Amerind Foundation, no. 6, Dragoon, Arizona.

Douglas, F. H.
- 1941 "Final Report on Design Questionnaires," *Clearing House for Southwestern Museums, Newsletter*, no. 35, pp. 120-124, Denver, Colorado.

Fenneman, Nevin M.
- 1931 *Physiography of Western United States.* McGraw Hill Book Company, New York, New York.

Ford, James A.
- 1954 "Comment on A. C. Spaulding, 'Statistical Techniques for the Discovery of Artifact Types'," *American Antiquity*, vol. 19, no. 4, pp. 390-391.

Gladwin, Harold S.
- 1945 *The Chaco Branch. Excavations at White Mound and in the Red Mesa Valley.* Medallion Papers, no. 33, Gila Pueblo, Globe, Arizona.

Hack, John T.
- 1942 *The Changing Physical Environment of the Hopi Indians of Arizona.* Papers of the Peabody Museum of Archaeology and Ethnology, Harvard University, vol. 35, no. 1, Reports of the Awatovi Expedition, no. 1, Cambridge, Massachusetts. Reprinted, 1974, Kraus Reprint Company, Millwood, New York.

Hargrave, Lyndon L.
- 1974 "The Determinants in Southwestern Ceramics and Some of Their Implications," *Plateau*, vol. 46, no. 3, pp. 76-95, Flagstaff, Arizona.

Haury, Emil W.
- 1945 *The Excavation of Los Muertos and Neighboring Ruins in the Salt River Valley, Southern Arizona.* Papers of the Peabody Museum of Archaeology and Ethnology, Harvard University, vol. 24, no. 1, Cambridge, Massachusetts.

Hawley, Florence M.
- 1936 *Field Manual of Prehistoric Southwestern Pottery Types.* University of New Mexico, Bulletin, no. 291, Anthropological Series, vol. 1, no. 4, Albuquerque, New Mexico. Revised November 1, 1950.

Judd, Neil M.
- 1916 "The Use of Adobe in Prehistoric Dwellings in the Southwest," *Holmes Anniversary Volume*, pp. 241-252, privately printed, Washington, D.C.

Kidder, Alfred V.
- 1932 *The Artifacts of Pecos.* Papers of the Southwestern Expedition, Phillips Academy, no. 6, Andover, Massachusetts.

Kidder, A. V., and A. O. Shepard
- 1936 *The Pottery of Pecos*, vol. 2. Papers of the Southwestern Expedition, Phillips Academy, no. 7, Andover, Massachusetts.

Kluckhohn, C., and P. Reiter, editors
- 1939 *Preliminary Report on the 1937 Excavations, Bc 50-51, Chaco Canyon New Mexico.* University of New Mexico, Bulletin, no. 345, Anthropological Series, vol. 3, no. 2, Albuquerque, New Mexico.

Krieger, Alex D.
- 1944 "The Typological Concept," *American Antiquity*, vol. 9, no. 3, pp. 271-288.
- 1949 "Remarks on Typology," in *Proceedings of the Fifth Plains Conference for Archeology*, Note Book no. 1, pp. 70-73, Laboratory of Anthropology, University of Nebraska, Lincoln, Nebraska.

Kroeber, Alfred L.
- 1949 "The Concept of Culture in Science," *Journal of General Education*, vol. 3, no. 3, pp. 182-196.

Martin, P. S., and J. B. Rinaldo
- 1950 *Sites of the Reserve Phase, Pine Lawn Valley, Western New Mexico.* Fieldiana: Anthropology, vol. 38, no. 3, Chicago Natural History Museum, Chicago, Illinois.

McGimsey, Charles R., III
- 1972 *Public Archeology.* Seminar Press, New York, New York.

Morris, Earl H.
- 1939 *Archaeological Studies in the La Plata District, Southwestern Colorado and Northwestern New Mexico.* Carnegie Institution of Washington, Publication no. 519, Washington, D.C.

Pepper, George H.
- 1920 *Pueblo Bonito.* Anthropological Papers of the American Museum of Natural History, vol. 27, New York, New York.

Phillips, P., J. A. Ford, and J. B. Griffin
- 1951 *Archaeological Survey in the Lower Mississippi Alluvial Valley 1940-1947.* Papers of the Peabody Museum of Archaeology and Ethnology, Harvard University, vol. 25, Cambridge, Massachusetts.

Rinaldo, J. B., and E. A. Bluhm
- 1956 *Late Mogollon Pottery Types of the Reserve Area.* Fieldiana: Anthropology, vol. 36, no. 1, Chicago Natural History Museum, Chicago, Illinois.

Rouse, Irving
- 1939 *Prehistory in Haiti: A Study in Method.* Yale University Publications in Anthropology, no. 21, Yale University Press, New Haven, Connecticut.

Ruppé, Reynold J., Jr.
- 1957 *The Acoma Culture Province: An Archaeological Concept.* Unpublished Ph.D. dissertation, Department of Anthropology, Harvard University, Cambridge, Massachusetts.

Shepard, Anna O.
- 1956 *Ceramics for the Archaeologist.* Carnegie Institution of Washington, Publication, no. 609, Washington, D.C.

Smith, Watson
- 1950 "Preliminary Report of the Peabody Museum Upper Gila Expedition, Pueblo Division, 1949," *El Palacio*, vol. 57, no. 12, pp. 392–399, Santa Fe, New Mexico.
- 1952 *Kiva Mural Decorations at Awatovi and Kawaika-a, with a Survey of Other Wall Paintings in the Pueblo Southwest.* Papers of the Peabody Museum of Archaeology and Ethnology, Harvard University, vol. 37, Reports of the Awatovi Expedition, no. 5, Cambridge, Massachusetts.
- 1962 "Schools, Pots, and Potters," *American Anthropologist*, vol. 64, no. 6, pp. 1165–1178.
- 1971 *Painted Ceramics of the Western Mound at Awatovi.* Papers of the Peabody Museum of Archaeology and Ethnology, Harvard University, vol. 38, Reports of the Awatovi Expedition, no. 8, Cambridge, Massachusetts.
- 1973 *The Williams Site, a Frontier Mogollon Village in West-Central New Mexico.* Papers of the Peabody Museum of Archaeology and Ethnology, Harvard University, vol. 39, no. 2, Cambridge, Massachusetts.

Smith, W., R. B. Woodbury, and N. F. S. Woodbury
- 1966 *The Excavation of Hawikuh by Frederick Webb Hodge. Report of the Hendricks-Hodge Expedition, 1917–1923.* Museum of the American Indian, Heye Foundation, Contributions, vol. 20, New York, New York.

Spaulding, Albert C.
- 1953 "Statistical Techniques for the Discovery of Artifact Types," *American Antiquity*, vol. 18, no. 4, pp. 305–313.
- 1954 "Reply to Ford," *American Antiquity*, vol. 19, no. 4, pp. 391–393.

Steward, Julian H.
- 1954 "Types of Types," *American Anthropologist*, vol. 56, no. 1, pp. 54–57.

Taylor, Walter W.
- 1948 *A Study of Archeology, American Anthropologist*, vol. 50, no. 3, pt. 2, Memoir no. 69. Republished, 1964, 1967, Southern Illinois University Press, Carbondale, Illinois.

Washburn, Dorothy K.
- 1977 *A Symmetry Analysis of Upper Gila Area Ceramic Design.* Papers of the Peabody Museum of Archaeology and Ethnology, Harvard University, vol. 68, Cambridge, Massachusetts.

Wheat, J. B., J. C. Gifford, and W. W. Wasley
- 1958 "Ceramic Variety, Type Cluster, and Ceramic System in Southwestern Pottery Analysis," *American Antiquity*, vol. 24, no. 1, pp. 34–47.

Whitehead, Alfred North
- 1925 *Science and the Modern World.* The Macmillan Company, New York, New York.

Woodbury, Richard B.
- 1954 *Prehistoric Stone Implements of Northeastern Arizona.* Papers of the Peabody Museum of Archaeology and Ethnology, Harvard University, vol. 34, Reports of the Awatovi Expedition, no. 6, Cambridge, Massachusetts.